T0191645

Communications
in Computer and Information Science　　1307

More information about this series at http://www.springer.com/series/7899

Germania Rodriguez Morales ·
Efraín R. Fonseca C. · Juan Pablo Salgado ·
Pablo Pérez-Gosende · Marcos Orellana Cordero ·
Santiago Berrezueta (Eds.)

Information and Communication Technologies

8th Conference, TICEC 2020
Guayaquil, Ecuador, November 25–27, 2020
Proceedings

 Springer

Editors
Germania Rodriguez Morales ⓘ
Universidad Técnica Particular de Loja
Loja, Ecuador

Efraín R. Fonseca C. ⓘ
Universidad de las Fuerzas Armadas ESPE
Quito, Ecuador

Juan Pablo Salgado ⓘ
Universidad Politécnica Salesiana
Cuenca, Ecuador

Pablo Pérez-Gosende ⓘ
Universidad Politécnica Salesiana
Guayaquil, Ecuador

Marcos Orellana Cordero ⓘ
Universidad del Azuay
Cuenca, Ecuador

Santiago Berrezueta ⓘ
CEDIA
Cuenca, Ecuador

ISSN 1865-0929   ISSN 1865-0937 (electronic)
Communications in Computer and Information Science
ISBN 978-3-030-62832-1   ISBN 978-3-030-62833-8 (eBook)
https://doi.org/10.1007/978-3-030-62833-8

This Springer imprint is published by the registered company Springer Nature Switzerland AG
The registered company address is: Gewerbestrasse 11, 6330 Cham, Switzerland

Preface

The 8th edition of the Information and Communication Technologies Conference of Ecuador (TICEC 2020) took place in Guayaquil, Ecuador, during November 25–27, 2020, in virtual mode, at the Universidad Politécnica Salesiana (UPS) headquarters. TICEC is one of the most important conferences in Ecuador since it brings together researchers, educators, professionals, and students from different parts of the world for the dissemination of results and research activities regarding the development, problems, and forecasts of the use of information and communications technologies (ICT) in multiple fields of application. The UPS and the Corporación Ecuatoriana para el Desarrollo de la Investigación y la Academia (CEDIA) jointly organized the event.

According to the research area, the conference included more than 40 presentations distributed in the event's sessions.

The content of this volume has been divided into the following areas:

- Biomedical Sensors and Wearables Systems
- Data Science
- ICT's Applications
- Industry 4.0
- Smart Cities
- Software Development
- Technology and Environment

The 8th edition of TICEC received 117 manuscripts from 355 authors from 15 countries. Only 85 articles passed the control of the maximum percentage of similarity with previous works, which were reviewed by peers by the TICEC 2020 Program Committee, which consisted of 96 highly experienced researchers from 29 countries. To ensure a high-quality and careful review process, we assigned at least three reviewers to each article. Based on the peer-review results, 36 full articles and 7 short articles were accepted, representing an acceptance rate of 37.6%.

November 2020   Efraín R. Fonseca C.

Organization

Honorary Committee

Nicolay Samaniego Erazo	CEDIA, Ecuador
Juan Cárdenas Tapia	Universidad Politécnica Salesiana, Ecuador
Juan Pablo Carvallo Vega	CEDIA, Ecuador

General Chair

Germania Rodriguez Morales	Universidad Técnica Particular de Loja, Ecuador

Program Committee Chairs

Efraín R. Fonseca C.	Universidad de las Fuerzas Armadas, Ecuador
Pablo Pérez-Gosende	Universidad Politécnica Salesiana, Ecuador
Juan Pablo Salgado	Universidad Politécnica Salesiana, Ecuador
Marcos Orellana Cordero	Universidad del Azuay, Ecuador

Organizing Committee

María Isabel Carpio	Universidad Politécnica Salesiana, Ecuador
César Andrade Martínez	Universidad Politécnica Salesiana, Ecuador
David Mora Bocca	Universidad Politécnica Salesiana, Ecuador
Wendy Luna Ramos	Universidad Politécnica Salesiana, Ecuador
Galia Rivas Toral	CEDIA, Ecuador
Ana Isabel Ordoñez	CEDIA, Ecuador
Paul Arevalo	CEDIA, Ecuador
Santiago Ruilova	CEDIA, Ecuador
Francisco Toral	CEDIA, Ecuador
Santiago Morales	CEDIA, Ecuador
Karina Abad	CEDIA, Ecuador
Santiago Berrezueta	CEDIA, Ecuador

Program Committee

Adam Wojciechowski	Lodz University of Technology, Poland
Agustin L. Herrera-May	Universidad Veracruzana, Mexico
Agustín Yagüe	Universidad Politécnica de Madrid, Spain
Alex F. Buitrago-Hurtado	Universidad Externado de Colombia, Colombia
Alvaro Llaria	University of Bordeaux, France

John Castro	Universidad de Atacama, Chile
José Martinez-Carranza	Instituto Nacional de Astrofísica, Óptica y Electrónica, Mexico
José Olivas-Varela	Universidad de Castilla-La Mancha, Spain
José-J. De-Moura-Ramos	University of A Coruña, Spain
José-Juan Pazos-Arias	Universidad de Vigo, Spain
Kamanashis Biswas	Australian Catholic University, Australia
Katarzyna Harezlak	Silesian University of Technology, Poland
Khalid Saeed	Bialystok University of Technology, Poland
Laura Tarantino	Università degli Studi dell'Aquila, Italy
Luis Martin-Pomares	Qatar Environment and Energy Research Institute, Qatar
Luis Urquiza	Universitat Politècnica de Catalunya, Spain
Marcin Bernaś	University of Bielsko-Biała, Poland
Marcin Ciecholewski	University of Gdańsk, Poland
María-Luisa Martín-Ruíz	Universidad Politécnica de Madrid, Spain
Mariusz Giergiel	University of Science and Technology, Poland
Mariusz Kostrzewski	Warsaw University of Technology, Poland
Martín López-Nores	Universidad de Vigo, Spain
Massimo Merenda	Università Mediterranea di Reggio Calabria, Italy
Mikhail Basarab	Bauman Moscow State University, Russia
Mohammad Shojafar	Ryerson University, Canada
Mohammad A. Al-Mashhadani	Al-Maarif University College, Iraq
Noman Naseer	Pusan University, South Korea
Noor Zaman	Taylor's University, Malaysia
Panagiota Yota-Katsikouli	Technical University of Denmark, Denmark
Patricio Galdames	Universidad del Bio-Bio, Chile
Paulo-J. Sequeira-Gonçalves	Instituto Politécnico de Castelo Branco, Portugal
Piotr Dziurdzia	AGH University of Science and Technology, Poland
Prasanta Ghosh	ICEEM, India
Przemysław Mazurek	West Pomeranian University of Technology, Poland
Robert-Alexandru Dobre	Politehnica University of Bucharest, Romania
Roberto Murphy	INAOE, Mexico
Rosaria Rucco	University of Naples Parthenope, Italy
Ruoyu Su	Memorial University of Newfoundland, Canada
Saleh Mobayen	University of Zanjan, Iran
Sara Paiva	Oviedo University, Spain
Shernon Osepa	Internet Society, The Netherlands
Sunday-Cookeyn Ekpo	Manchester Metropolitan University, UK
Tomasz Bieniek	Institute of Electron Technology, Poland
Tuan Nguyen-Gia	University of Turku, Finland
Vahid Masrour	Wikipedia, France
Valerio Baiocchi	Sapienza University of Rome, Italy
Vera Ferreira	Federal University of Pampa, Brazil
Vinayak Elangovan	Penn State Abington, USA

Yanhua Luo   University of New South Wales, Australia
Yudong Zhang   University of Leicester, UK
Yves Rybarczyk   Universidade NOVA de Lisboa, Portugal

CORPORACIÓN ECUATORIANA
PARA EL DESARROLLO DE LA
INVESTIGACIÓN Y LA ACADEMIA

UNIVERSIDAD POLITÉCNICA
SALESIANA
—— ECUADOR

EIGHTH CONFERENCE ON INFORMATION AND
COMMUNICATION TECHNOLOGIES OF ECUADOR

Contents

Data Science

ICT's Applications

Industry 4.0

Smart Cities

Software Development

Technology and Environment

Biomedical Sensors and Wearables Systems

Design of a Glove Controlled by Electromyographic Signals for the Rehabilitation of Patients with Rheumatoid Arthritis

E. D. Aguiar Salazar[1] ⓘ, A. S. Alcivar Carmigniani[1] ⓘ, B. P. Aldaz Luna[1] ⓘ,
D. F. Clavijo Calderón[1] ⓘ, P. P. Echeverría Ortíz[1] ⓘ, M. A. Madrid Pérez[2] ⓘ,
G. F. Villalba-Meneses[1,3(✉)] ⓘ, and D. Almeida-Galárraga[1] ⓘ

[1] School of Biological Sciences and Engineering,
Universidad Yachay Tech, Urcuquí 100119, Ecuador
gvillalba@yachaytech.edu.ec
[2] Universidad Autónoma de Chihuahua, Chihuahua 60022916, México
mmadrid@uach.mx
[3] Aragón Institute of Engineering Research (I3A), Universidad de
Zaragoza, Zaragoza 50018, Spain
762301@unizar.es

Abstract. Among the various systemic disorders that hands can suffer, rheumatoid arthritis is one of the most common. This disease affects the synovial tissue of the joints, making extension and flexion movements difficult. Currently, there are drugs on the market to treat it, but they produce dangerous side effects affecting the quality of life of the patient. In this context, physical rehabilitation plays an important role as a complement to the work of conventional medications. The present work describes the hand rehabilitation device that can be used to improve the mobility of people with rheumatoid arthritis. This glove shaped device can move all five fingers, using the measurement of the action potential of other healthy muscles. The data collection is done through a muscle sensor which processes the signal and sends the order to the glove, allowing contraction or relaxation of the hand. The glove was designed in 3D using the Fusion 360 software. In this case, this device captures the movements of patterns generated in a muscle and reproduces them in the fingers of the hand to increase the level of movement and prevent muscle atrophy in patients with this disease.

Keywords: Electromyogram · Muscle sensor · Rheumatoid arthritis · 3D glove · Action potential · Rehabilitation

1 Introduction

The hands can be affected by numerous disorders or problems caused by external factors including carpal tunnel syndrome, trigger finger, De Quervain's syndrome, ganglion cysts, Dupuytren's disease, and rheumatoid arthritis [1, 2]. The last one is the best-known

© Springer Nature Switzerland AG 2020
G. Rodriguez Morales et al. (Eds.): TICEC 2020, CCIS 1307, pp. 3–11, 2020.
https://doi.org/10.1007/978-3-030-62833-8_1

complication due to the large number of people affected by this condition, being 1.3 million in the United States and 1% of the world population [3]. Rheumatoid Arthritis (RA) can be defined as a chronic systemic autoimmune disease that causes damage mediated by cytokines, chemokines and metalloproteinases, mainly affecting synovial joint tissues [3–5]. This disease is most often found in the peripheral joints, such as wrists, ankles, joints of the fingers and toes; however, it can also affect other joints [4–6]. The common symptoms of RA are stiff, hot, swollen, and painful joints, exhaustion, weakness, and rheumatoid nodules [3, 5, 6]. The cause of this condition is unknown, but some researchers argue it may be caused by genetics, bacteria that cause autoimmune reactions, hormonal or lifestyle factors such as smoking [6]. RA as an autoimmune disease has not cure, but can be treated with physical therapy, occupational therapy, surgery, or medications such as corticosteroids, non-steroidal anti-inflammatory drugs, disease-modifying antirheumatic drugs, and biological response modifiers [3, 5–7]. Additionally, rehabilitation is an option for those people whom long-term RA has not been well managed. The rehabilitation aims to better treat the disease in daily life, allow patients to return to work again, and reduce the possibility of long-term problems [6, 8]. In spite of the importance of RA's rehabilitation for patients, there are only commercial assistive devices that function as protection but not joint rehabilitation [9].

One technology that can be applied in rehabilitation is the use of Electromyography (EMG) which is the procedure used to measure the electrical activity of individual muscles [10, 11]. This electrical activity appears as a response of the muscle to the stimulation of a nerve, and evaluates the health of the motor and muscle neurons [11, 12]. There are two types of EMG: intramuscular and surface. Intramuscular (EMG) can be used with a range of recording electrodes and different types. For example, a fine wire inserted into a muscle with a reference surface electrode. On the other hand, surface EMG can be recorded through a pair of electrodes or through a more complex multi-electrode array. This type of EMG can only provide an evaluation of the superficial muscles [12]. However, in therapy robots, using signals of EMG surface provides the ability to aid in early successful recovery because it can measure surface EMG in severely affected patients with little or no activity in fingers and hands during voluntary contractions [12].

This research presents a glove for the rehabilitation of patients affected by RA. The glove will allow patients to rehabilitate the fingers through a series of movements resulting from the EMG signal from the surface of other healthy muscles. In addition, each finger can be independently regulated, allowing for different movement patterns.

2 State of the Art

Nowadays, there are many treatments or strategies that use medications to treat RA. However, if an early diagnosis of the disease is not made, the patient will not be able to achieve remission. Despite early diagnosis, the use of the conventional medications can trigger unwanted side effects. Some of these effects are caused by medications such as antirheumatic disease modifiers (DMARDs), non-steroidal anti-inflammatory drugs and corticosteroids. The side effects include fatigue, nausea, damage to the central nervous system, diabetes, enhanced RA and therefore liver damage [13–17].

Conventional medications used for the treatment of RA can be considered a double-edged sword since they help the patient to treat the disease, but at the same time causing damage to other systems. In the case of corticosteroids, the misuse would potentiate the disease. Moreover, it is important to mention that patients depend on these medications as they have gone through difficult and painful situations during the treatment. Some patients lose all their progress because the medication did not work as expected and this may lower their compliance, leading to depression, which will negatively affect future treatment.

Currently, there are treatment options using the concepts of biomechanics, rehabilitation, and computer-aided designs to develop new technologies in the field of biomedical devices, as Beyermann [18] demonstrated the potential use and efficiency of pneumatic orthopedic devices in correcting finger malformations caused by Dupuytren's contracture. In 2016, Heng et al. introduced a new rehabilitation device for computer-assisted diagnosis and finger realignment in RA patients. In the experimental part, the authors used the hand of a mannequin that simulated the hand of a patient with lateral deformities caused by RA. In addition, they simulated deformations in the index finger with 60° in the Distal Interphalangeal Joint (DIP), Proximal Interphalangeal Joint (PIP) and Metacarpophalangeal Joint (MCP). The results after applying their device were: 25° for DIP, 18° PIP, and 15° for MCP. Using this device, realignment of the laterally bent finger was achieved demonstrating the potential use of a computer-assisted mechanism for rehabilitation [18, 19].

3   Methodology

3.1   Design of the Electronic Part

A MyoWare™ muscle sensor (AT-04-001) was used to minimize hardware design as it provides an amplified, rectified and integrated signal. Also, a NEMA17 stepper motor was required which is capable of loading with 3.2 kg/cm (44 oz-in). This motor needed an A4988 controller circuit, to limit the current, preventing overheating and ensuring correct operation. An Arduino board was also required to program. Additionally, two buttons were needed to control manually the movement of the glove. A simulation was performed in the program Fritzing to verify the operation of the circuit, and design a copper plate (6 × 7 cm approx.), to make the device compact and comfortable for the patient when performing the therapy.

3.2   3D Design of the Prosthetic Glove

For the design, it was necessary to take the influence of the variables of geometry, dynamics, structure and brain-computer interaction to control the hand correctly [20]. The glove design was obtained from the Thingiverse platform and modified using Autodesk Fusion 360 [21]. The glove exercises flexion and extension movements of the patients to regain grip and fingering functions. The design was made with the condition that the measurements can be modified for the patient, this will ensure correct adaptation of the fingers and avoid discomfort during rehabilitation (see Fig. 1).

The most suitable material for printing is Nylon, it offers good stability, rigidity, and resistance to shocks [22, 23]. Also, it has the standards for the printing of final products, including prostheses [24]. It has a high biocompatibility, making it the most suitable for being in contact with the skin without causing inconvenience to the patient [25].

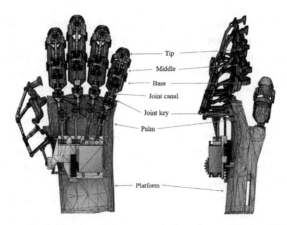

Fig. 1. Geometric distribution of the anatomical sections of the hand in 3D design.

4   Results

4.1   Kinematic Analyses of the Fingers

According to the kinematics of the wrist and fingers, a hand consists of rotary-type joints in the phalanges and saddle joints in the MCP and the wrist [22]. As it was indicated above, in the glove only the fingers move and the wrist is static. Therefore, the MCP, IP, PIP and DIP joints were considered of the rotary type [23, 24]. The glove was developed according to the anthropometric measurements of an Ecuadorian male student who is 23 years old, weighs 69 kg and is 1.79 m tall. Table 1 shows the data on the measurements of the structures of the hands in mm and the angles generated when performing flexion and extension movements [25, 26].

Table 1. Data of measurements of phalanges and angles of Flexion Extension of hand joints

Finger	Measurements in cm			Joints			
	Proximal	Half	Distal	Dip	PIP	MCP	IP
Thumb	4.3	–	2.8	–	–	50°	85°
Index finger	4.6	2.6	1.9	60°	100°	90°	–
Middle finger	5.0	3.1	2.3				–
Ring finger	4.5	3.0	2.3				–
Pinky	3.8	2.1	1.9				–

The biomechanical analyses of the fingers were realized considering each finger is made up of the proximal phalanx, the intermediate phalanx and the distal phalanx. AB,

BC and CD segments represented these phalanges. MCP denoted by "A" point will not be activated because it is taken as a reference point to generate movement. Conforming to the PIP and DIP joint, represented by points "B" and "C" respectively, they are designed to rotate by any linear actuator, based on active dynamics. Therefore, the thumb has one degree of freedom, and the other four fingers have two degrees of freedom (see Fig. 2).

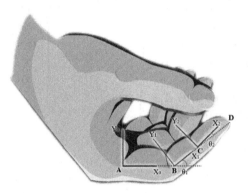

Fig. 2. Geometric representation of link frame assignment of the linkage finger mechanism.

Denavit-Hartenberg (DH) Analyses. Direct kinematic analyses have been carried out using the DH parameter approach [26]. DH parameters are four: a_i is the distance between z_{i-1} and z_i, d_i is the distance between x_{i-1} and x_i, α_i is the angle between z_{i-1} and z_i measured along x_i, and θ_i is the angle between x_{i-1} and x_i, measured along z_i. According to the described approach (see Fig. 2), the DH parameters are shown in Table 2.

Table 2. Denavit-Hartenberg link parameters

Link no.	DH parameter			
	$\alpha(i-1)$ degrees	$a(i-1)$ mm	d_i mm	θ_i degrees
0	0	0	0	0
one	0	AB	0	$\theta 1$
two	0	BC	0	$\theta 2$

Having the necessary data in Table 2, it could be replaced in the results shown in Table 2, and thus obtain the DH parameters for the five fingers. The homogeneous transformation matrices (T-Matrix) for each joint were calculated in MATLAB software. These matrices allow the correct position and identification for each element

(finger) in the Cartesian plane, points X, Y, Z. These points are in position T14, T24 and
T34. The following matrices were obtained:

$$
T_{Thumb} \equiv \begin{bmatrix} -0.98 & -0.18 & 0 & -4.2 \\ 0.18 & -0.98 & 0 & -0.76 \\ 0 & 0 & 1 & 0 \\ 0 & 0 & 0 & 1 \end{bmatrix}
\qquad
T_{Ring} \equiv \begin{bmatrix} -0.98 & -0.22 & 0 & 0.95 \\ 0.22 & -0.98 & 0 & -1.6 \\ 0 & 0 & 1 & 0 \\ 0 & 0 & 0 & 1 \end{bmatrix}
$$

$$
T_{Index} \equiv \begin{bmatrix} -0.98 & -0.22 & 0 & 1.4 \\ 0.22 & -0.98 & 0 & -1.8 \\ 0 & 0 & 1 & 0 \\ 0 & 0 & 0 & 1 \end{bmatrix}
\qquad
T_{Pinky} \equiv \begin{bmatrix} -0.98 & -0.22 & 0 & 1.2 \\ 0.22 & -0.98 & 0 & -1.5 \\ 0 & 0 & 1 & 0 \\ 0 & 0 & 0 & 1 \end{bmatrix}
$$

$$
T_{Middle} \equiv \begin{bmatrix} -0.98 & -0.22 & 0 & 1.3 \\ 0.22 & -0.98 & 0 & -1.9 \\ 0 & 0 & 1 & 0 \\ 0 & 0 & 0 & 1 \end{bmatrix}
$$

4.2 Design

The design contains 75 different pieces with three basic elements: an immobilized forearm, a control unit and five-finger mechanisms (the total mass is 310 g) [20]. The glove
was designed according to the measurements in Table 2 (see Fig. 3). The different colors
represent the part in contact with the patient's skin in yellow and the part where the
electronic components are located in pink. Those simple distinctions can mean a change
in print materials. The mechanism works with servo motors connected to the Arduino
board that will move the entire assembly from the top of the hand using cables. It should
be noted that the index finger is the smallest, and it is the most complex due to the grip
functions it performs (see Fig. 4).

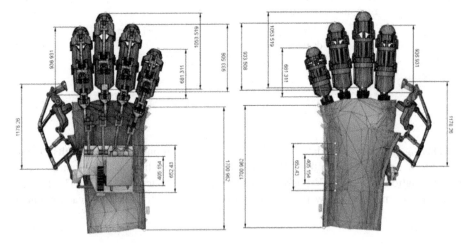

Fig. 3. Glove design dimensions.

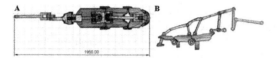

Fig. 4. Detail of the index finger design. A) Side view. B) Top view

5 Discussion of Results

These types of non-invasive rehabilitation devices are very useful for patients who have suffered brain damage, accidents or who have degenerative diseases to the point that they can be used as permanent prosthesis. Many studies demonstrated the positive effects of these devices [16]. Compared to conventional therapy, the use of biomedical devices has not brought consequences or damage to other body systems. In fact, due to the weakness of muscles near joints affected by RA, it is necessary to propose a prototype using the action potential of muscles that are not affected by RA to promote movement of damaged joints. Therefore, generating muscle growth and recovery. There are many devices aimed for rehabilitation. However, the principle of this device helps patients to recover on their own, unlike other devices that need assistance.

6 Conclusion

Treatments with myoelectric devices have been proven for many years since their use is easy for therapists and patients. However, the most considerable difficulty is the cost of the equipment, and implementation requires highly qualified personnel. However, new open source technology developments and open 3D design databases have reduced the cost of manufacturing, these devices opened up the possibility of easier deployment anywhere it is needed. The development and refinement of these systems also benefit from the increasing number of people using them. Therefore, they have collected much more information. Regarding the glove presented in this investigation, it is an excellent rehabilitation proposal due to the mechanism and possibilities that this glove can offer to people with RA.

Regarding recommendations, previous analyses should be carried out with flexion sensors to measure the real flexion and extension capacities of the patient who is going to use the glove for rehabilitation. For future prototypes, it is recommended to create and incorporate an EMG sensor to avoid the use of commercial sensors that can affect the cost of the device. It is recommended to investigate the use of the device for therapeutic purposes of different traumatic injuries to the hands that have left consequences in the movement of the joints. Finally, brain signals, such as electroencephalogram (EEG) waves, can be used in combination with EMG signals to enhance the glove's motion control.

References

1. Steinberg, D.: Overview of Hand Disorders - Bone, Joint, and Muscle Disorders - MSD Manual Consumer Version (2020). https://www.msdmanuals.com/home/bone,-joint,-and-muscle-disorders/hand-disorders/overview-of-hand-disorders

2. The British Society for Surgery of the Hand Disorders. https://www.bssh.ac.uk/patients/con
   ditions/hand_disorders. Accessed 25 June 2020
3. Rheumatoid Arthritis by the Numbers: Facts, Statistics, and You. https://www.healthline.com/
   health/rheumatoid-arthritis/facts-statistics-infographic#4
4. Dugowson, C.: Rheumatoid arthritis. In: Women and Health, pp. 674–685. Academic Press,
   Cambridge (2000). https://doi.org/10.1016/B978-012288145-9/50062-0
5. Kontzias, A.: Rheumatoid arthritis (RA) (2020). https://www.msdmanuals.com/professio
   nal/musculoskeletal-and-connective-tissue-disorders/joint-disorders/rheumatoid-arthritis-
   ra?query=RheumatoidArthritis(RA)
6. Institute for Quality and Efficiency in Health Care: Rheumatoid Arthritis: Overview (2006).
   https://www.ncbi.nlm.nih.gov/books/NBK384455/
7. Freeman, J.: RA Facts: What are the Latest Statistics on Rheumatoid Arthritis? (2018). https://
   www.rheumatoidarthritis.org/ra/facts-and-statistics/
8. Księzopolska-Orłowska, K., Sadura-Sieklucka, T., Kasprzak, K., et al.: The beneficial effects
   of rehabilitation on hand function in patients with rheumatoid arthritis. Rheumatology **54**,
   285–290 (2016). https://doi.org/10.5114/reum.2016.64903
9. Krabak, B., Minkoff, E.: Rehabilitation Management for the Rheumatoid Arthritis Patients
   from Johns Hopkins Arthritis. https://www.hopkinsarthritis.org/patient-corner/disease-man
   agement/rehabilitation-management-rheumatoid-arthritis-patients/#orthoses
10. Novak, D.: Biomechatronic applications of brain-computer interfaces. In: Handbook of
    Biomechatronics, pp. 129–175. Elsevier, Amsterdam (2019). https://doi.org/10.1016/B978-
    0-12-812539-7.00008-8
11. Electromyography (EMG) - Mayo Clinic. https://www.mayoclinic.org/tests-procedures/emg/
    about/pac-20393913
12. Lamkin-Kennard, K.A., Popovic, M.B.: Sensors: natural and synthetic sensors. In: Biomecha-
    tronics, pp. 81–107. Elsevier, Amsterdam (2019). https://doi.org/10.1016/b978-0-12-812939-
    5.00004-5
13. Lopez-Olivo, M.A., Siddhanamatha, H.R., Shea, B., et al.: Methotrexate for treating rheuma-
    toid arthritis. Cochrane Database Syst. Rev. (2014). https://doi.org/10.1002/14651858.CD0
    00957.pub2
14. Smolen, J.S., Landewé, R., Bijlsma, J., et al.: EULAR recommendations for the management
    of rheumatoid arthritis with synthetic and biological disease-modifying antirheumatic drugs:
    2016 update. Ann. Rheum. Dis. **76**, 960–977 (2017). https://doi.org/10.1136/annrheumdis-
    2016-210715
15. Fleischmann, R., Mysler, E., Hall, S., et al.: Efficacy and safety of tofacitinib monotherapy,
    tofacitinib with methotrexate, and adalimumab with methotrexate in patients with rheumatoid
    arthritis (ORAL Strategy): a phase 3b/4, double-blind, head-to-head, randomized controlled
    trial. Lancet **390**, 457–468 (2017). https://doi.org/10.1016/S0140-6736(17)31618-5
16. Combe, B.: Progression in early rheumatoid arthritis. Best Pract. Res. Clin. Rheumatol. **23**,
    59–69 (2009). https://doi.org/10.1016/j.berh.2008.11.006
17. Ong, C.K.S., Lirk, P., Tan, C.H., Seymour, R.A.: An evidence-based update on nonsteroidal
    anti-inflammatory drugs. Clin. Med. Res. **5**, 19–34 (2007). https://doi.org/10.3121/cmr.200
    7.698
18. Beyermann, K., Jacobs, C., Prommersberger, K.J., Lanz, U.: Die präoperative intermit-
    tierende pneumatische dehnungsbehandlung bei ausgeprägter Dupuytrenscher kontraktur.
    Handchirurgie Mikrochirurgie Plast Chir **34**, 118–122 (2002). https://doi.org/10.1055/s-2002-
    32305
19. Chua, M.C.H., Hoon, L.J., Yeow, R.C.H.: Design and evaluation of Rheumatoid Arthritis
    rehabilitative Device (RARD) for laterally bent fingers. In: Proceeding of IEEE RAS EMBS
    International Conference on Biomed Robot Biomechatronics, July 2016, pp. 839–843 (2016).
    https://doi.org/10.1109/BIOROB.2016.7523732

20. Abdallah, I., Bouteraa, Y., Rekik, C.: Design and development of 3D printed myoelectric robotic exoskeleton for hand rehabilitation. Int. J. Smart Sens. Intell. Syst. **10**(2), 341–366 (2017). https://doi.org/10.21307/ijssis-2017-215
21. Thingiverse, MakerBot. https://www.thingiverse.com/thing:2799056. Accessed 21 June 2020
22. Geizans, R.: Developing 3D Printed Prosthetic Hand Model Controlled by EMG Signal from Forearm (2018)
23. Kotkar, T., Masure, P., Modake, P., et al.: Modeling and testing of spur gear made of different 3D printed materials, pp. 1389–1394 (2018)
24. Aslanzadeh, S., Saghlatoon, H., Honari, M.M., et al.: Investigation on electrical and mechanical properties of 3D printed Nylon 6 for RF/microwave electronics applications. Addit. Manuf. (2018). https://doi.org/10.1016/j.addma.2018.02.016
25. Ortiz, J., Tonato, G.: Anthropometric evaluation of hands in students of the physical therapy career of the PUCE for the elaboration of a database applied in the redesign of an exoskeleton, 33–41 (2018)
26. Herath, H.M.C.M., Gopura, R.A.R.C., Lalitharatne, T.D.: An underactuated linkage finger mechanism for hand prostheses, 121–139 (2018). https://doi.org/10.4236/mme.2018.82009

Hand Exoskeleton Design for the Rehabilitation of Patients with Rheumatoid Arthritis

Roberto Moya-Jiménez[1]([☒]), Teresa Magal-Royo[2], Diana Ponce[1], Michelle Flores[1], and Mario Caiza[1]

[1] Universidad Central del Ecuador, Ciudadela Av. Universitaria, Quito, Ecuador
rcmoya@uce.edu.ec
[2] Universitat Politècnica de Valencia, Valencia, Spain
tmagal@degi.upv.es

Abstract. Starting in 2015, various exoskeleton designs have been developed to facilitate interventions in the rehabilitation of patients with movement disabilities aimed primarily at flexing and extending the finger joints. This article covers the review and generation of a device for the physical rehabilitation of people diagnosed with rheumatoid arthritis (RA). Among the determining aspects for its manufacture, it has been detected that most have been designed with different technological tools with limited degrees of freedom (GDL) and the application of mechanical systems without studies of interaction with the user. The applied methodological framework for the development of exoskeletons of the hand includes a systematic review of the devices, referring to their mechanical, electronic and functional attributes according to the technological trends of the last five years. The information analyzed in this article allows the generation of an exoskeleton with the use of rapid prototyping techniques within user-centered digital manufacturing processes.

Keywords: Rheumatoid arthritis · Hand · Exoskeleton · Physical rehabilitation · Systematic review

1 Introduction

Knowledge about rheumatoid arthritis, RA, is transforming, as currently there are more problems due to inflammatory diseases within immunological pathogenesis and more frequent nature that affects the joints of patients. These types of complications critically affect quality of life but can be transformed with more frequent treatment [13, 15].

The hand is crucial in carrying out the daily activities necessary. One's functional disability demands the assistance of third parties, thus causing a socio-economic impact due to the limitations of the patient's productive capacity, therefore causing family income decreases whilst having increased medical expenses [18].

G. Rodriguez Morales et al. (Eds.): TICEC 2020, CCIS 1307, pp. 12–21, 2020.
https://doi.org/10.1007/978-3-030-62833-8_2

Knowledge about rheumatoid arthritis, RA, is transforming, as currently there are more problems due to inflammatory diseases within immunological pathogenesis and more frequent nature that affects the joints of patients. These types of complications critically affect quality of life but can be transformed with more frequent treatment [13, 15].

The hand is crucial in carrying out the daily activities necessary. One's functional disability demands the assistance of third parties, thus causing a socio-economic impact due to the limitations of the patient's productive capacity, therefore causing family income decreases whilst having increased medical expenses [18].

1. Analysis of the current situation of the patient's hand: Physical limitations, postures, movement capacity, strength, power, flexibility, among others;
2. The patient is asked to perform certain finger flexion-extension movements, grasping movements, while the exoskeleton control system analyzes the sensor signals and determines the expected movement;
3. Movement capture [20]: the control system selects a movement pattern and adjusts it to the current position of the patient, thus allowing movement with its own force;
4. After repeating the movement, the system analyzes the situation again, then prepares to anticipate the following movements of the user.

Therefore, the design of a portable hand rehabilitation device [17] with programmable movement functions may be important for the periodic rehabilitation of the patient. The device must be able to assess the state of the motor functions of the hand, such as stiffness of a finger, independence of the finger, articulation angles and/or external force of the hand. In addition, it should help the voluntary movement of the patient for both flexion and extension of the fingers, allowing force to be applied to each finger joint.

In contrast to conventional prosthetics, a hand exoskeleton serves as a multipurpose, medical device because it is designed and constructed based on the anthropometry of the human hand. Furthermore, it adjusts easily to movements while minimizing patient discomfort, in addition to expanding and improving the skills selected by the user.

2   State of Art of Hand Exoskeletons Today

For the development of the device, a review was established in different databases such as Dialnet, IEEE Xplore and RedMed from 2015.

Inclusion and exclusion criteria corresponding to the requirements for the construction of the exoskeleton were applied based on the search results. The inclusion criteria for the existing information in the articles analyzed were as follows.

– The study and/or article presents a prototype or approaches to hand exoskeleton designs.
– The study applies the design of a hand exoskeleton to the rehabilitation of RA patients.
– The study exhibits mechanical, electronic and/or functional attributes of the hand exoskeleton.
– The studio features robotic finger or hand designs, pneumatic finger or hand and/or rehabilitation gloves.

The exclusion criteria were as follows:

- The study has not been published in English or Spanish.
- The device has been used for rehabilitation of patients with cerebral palsy.
- The device does not use functional components.
- The study and/or article presents a prosthetic hand device instead of an exoskeleton.

53 studies/articles on handheld devices applied in physical rehabilitation were analyzed, but in the end 45 were chosen for the study and the systematic review because some designs were used for different purposes.

Additionally, it is highlighted that, despite the similarity of prosthetic hands with hand exoskeletons, the study focused on the physical rehabilitation of RA patients with the assistance of an exoskeleton.

In the last five years, the number of studies that contribute to the development of hand exoskeletons and that are relevant for their review and analysis has increased. Many of these devices have adapted to new technologies and have evolved in the use of materials, thus overcoming the limitations within the traditional design of exoskeletons. This article presents the proposals that meet the following requirements:

- The exoskeleton allows flexion-extension movement of the fingers.
- The exoskeleton uses mechanisms that allow dynamic movement of the patient's hand.
- There is an adaptation of the exoskeleton to the variety of anthropometric hand measurements.
- The patient can control the exoskeleton in relation to degrees of freedom (DOF).

3   Research Contributions

Thirty-six hand exoskeletons were reviewed according to the criteria de-scribed above. The devices were organized in chronological order and classified according to their attributes of mechanism, control and unit of action, described in Table 1.

Table 1. Summary of the mechanical, electrical and functional attributes of robotic hand exoskeletons since 2015 (Source: Own Elaboration, 2020).

Year	Actuation	Force of output (N)	Degrees freedom	Finger movements	Range movement	Weight	Functionality	References
2015	Hybrid tire	1.3	3	Flex	150	–	Rehab	[8–11]
	Hydraulic	8	15	Flex and Ext	250	<500 g	Rehab	[1]
	Pulley cable	680	15	Flex and Ext	–	711 g	Rehab	[5]

(*continued*)

Table 1. (*continued*)

Year	Actuation	Force of output (N)	Degrees freedom	Finger movements	Range movement	Weight	Functionality	References
	Tire	29,5	99	Flex and Ext	112	194 g	Rehab	[17]
	Tire	13	3	Flex	149	–	Rehab	[30]
	Tire	10,35	15	Flex	141,2	200 g	Rehab	[34, 35]
	Tire	9,25	12	Flex	191,2	180 g	Rehab	[36]
	Tire	2 N	3	Flex and Ext	143,5	25 g	Rehab	[19]
	Tire	–	3	Flex	165	–	Rehab	[40]
	Tire	–	–	Flex	99,7	200 g	Rehab	[33]
2016	Linear actuator	3,125 N	1	Flex	–	–	Rehab	[30]
	Tire	–	15	Flex and Ext	–	–	Rehab	[24–26]
	Tire	35 N	15	Flex	105,9	–	Rehab	[41]
	Tire	17 N	3	Flex and Ext	93	–	Rehab	[28]
	Tire	10 N	12	Flex and Ext	–	<100 g	Rehab	[38]
	Tire	5 N	3	Flex	–	–	Rehab	[37]
	Tire	2 N	3	Flex	40	–	Rehab	[4]
	Tire	2,2 N	4	Flex		–	Rehab	[31]
2017	Pulley cable	10 N	2	Flex	–	–	Rehab	[6]
	Pulley cable	16 N	15	Flex	141,2	300 g	Rehab	[22]
	Tire	11 N	14	Flex and Ext	96	85,03 g	Rehab	[32]
	Tire	35 N	44	Flex and Ext	90	–	Rehab	[16]
	Tire	–	15	Flex	–	–	Rehab	[18]
	Pulley cable	–	2	Flex and Ext	120	90 g	Rehab	[2]
	Tire	5 N		Flex and Ext	110	285 g	Rehab	[27]
2018	Tire	4 N	3	Flex and Ext	171	–	Rehab	[39]

(*continued*)

Table 1. (*continued*)

Year	Actuation	Force of output (N)	Degrees freedom	Finger movements	Range movement	Weight	Functionality	References
	Tire	–	–	Flex and Ext	–	<150 g	Rehab	[23]
	Tire	>10 N	6	Flex and Ext	–	–	Rehab	[12]
2019	Tire	4 N	–	Flex	–	75 g	Rehab	[7]
	Neumatic	–	4	Flex and Ext	106	156 g	Rehab	[14]

4   Design of the Hand Exoskeleton System

The development of the rehabilitation device consists of two parts. The first focuses on development through rapid prototyping and digitization of the hands of study subjects for the establishment of necessary measures and GDL; on the other hand, the mechanical design is established by means of actuators and resistance bands.

4.1   Control of the Exoskeleton in Relation to DOF

Control of hand strength and position is an important aspect that allows the exoskeleton to provide the patient with repetitive and precise movements [30]. Therefore, there are devices that have addressed the use of specialized sensors to obtain force and position. Among the most relevant works is [18] a glove used to measure the flexion angle of the finger using curvature sensors based on a three-layer back propagation neural network (BP). This project highlights that the most important part in the design of the mechanical system is the connection between the actuator and the glove.

Another exoskeleton analyzed was that of a robotic orthosis that becomes a functional prototype of the Exoskeleton System (HES) where the mechanism leads to the use of simple actuation systems and control algorithms, but is characterized by being able to adapt to the movement of each Finger powered with 2 DOF linear electric actuators that ensures independent movement of each finger phalanx. The novelty of these HES is the incorporation of the 1 DOF mechanism never used in this field of design and that is capable of providing precise movements of the phalanges [6].

4.2   Preliminary Study

Preliminary study starts from the verification of the GDL necessary for a correct rehabilitation considering the analysis of force, loads, and resistances according to the material; in this case the development is a printed prototype in three dimensions.

Rehabilitation is carried out through therapeutic exercises. According to the APTA, American Physical Therapy Association, therapeutic exercises are defined as the planned systematic application of physical movements, postures, or activities designed to 1) remedy or prevent impairment, 2) improve function, and 3) improve physical condition.

The development of the device will be verified in a patient in the initial state of RA, where he does not yet have symptoms of constant pain, significant deformation, or motor disability (Fig. 1).

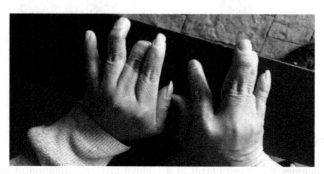

Fig. 1. Patient with rheumatoid arthritis initial stage (Source: Own Elaboration, 2020).

4.3   Final Prototype

The prototype consists of a glove-like structure that covers the hand with 3D printed actuators located at the junction of each phalanx to generate the flexo-extension action of these guided by a servomotor that exerts a contrary force.

The guides will facilitate the movement of the affected joints. The objective is to generate an organic movement of each of the phalanges, providing functional stability and correct support for the patient's hand; the pain factors net of the disease was taken into account, therefore the range of movement of the device will be predetermined by a test carried out on the patient and analyzed by photogrammetry and thus not exceed unnecessary pain limits, facilitating good performance and movement progression (Fig. 2).

In rehabilitation therapies for the hand, it must comply with international regulations, which is why the device must comply with the APTA regulations mentioned above. A maximum of 58° of range of motion will be achieved at the MCP (metacarpophalangeal) joints and at an approximate angle of 60° at PIP (proximal interphalangeal).

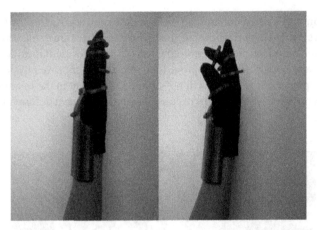

Fig. 2. Exoskeleton prototype (Source: Own Elaboration, 2020).

5   Conclusions

This article includes the development of a comparative investigation of the development of exoskeletons for rehabilitation, to take guidelines and requirements around RA, resulting in the design of a device that adjusts to the research base and real needs. from a patient; This will allow evaluating both the factors related to the device-patient interaction and the control adjustment of the programmed effort system for each patient that allows detecting the improvement of mobility through a therapeutically controlled rehabilitation.

References

1. Al-Fahaam, H., Davis, S., Nefti-Meziani, S.: Power assistive and rehabilitation wearable robot based on pneumatic soft actuators. In: Proceedings of the 2016 21st International Conference on Methods and Models in Automation and Robotics (MMAR), Miedzyzdroje, Poland, 29 August–1 September 2016, pp. 472–477 (2016). https://doi.org/10.1109/mmar.2016.7575181
2. Ben Abdallah, I., Bouteraa, Y., Rekik, C.: Design and development of 3D printed myoelectric robotic exoskeleton for hand rehabilitation. Int. J. Smart Sens. Intell. Syst. **10**, 341–366 (2017). https://doi.org/10.21307/ijssis-2017-215
3. Chua, M.C.H., Lim, J.H., Yeow, R.C.H.: Design and characterization of a soft robotic therapeutic glove for rheumatoid arthritis. Assis. Technol. 1–9 (2017). https://doi.org/10.1080/10400435.2017.1346000
4. Chua, M.C., Hoon, L.J., Yeow, R.C.: Design and evaluation of rheumatoid arthritis rehabilitative device (RARD) for laterally bent fingers. In: Proceedings of the 2016 6th IEEE International Conference on Biomedical Robotics and Biomechatronics (BioRob), Singapore, 26–29 June 2016, pp. 839–843 (2016). https://doi.org/10.1109/biorob.2016.7523732
5. Diftler, M.A., et al.: RoboGlove—a grasp assist device for earth and space. In: Proceedings of the 45th International Conference on Environmental Systems, Bellevue, WA, USA, 12–16 July 2015
6. Florence University: A Novel Kinematic Architecture for Portable Hands Exoskeletons. Departament of Industrial Engineering, vol. 3, p. 50139 (2016)

7. Gómez, J., Moreno, J., Gil, G.V., Orozco, C.: Rehabilitación de la mano con órtesis robóticas. Asociación Colombiana de Medicina Física y Rehabilitación, pp. 174–179 (2018). https://doi.org/10.28957/rcmfr
8. Haghshenas-Jaryani, M., Carrigan, W., Nothnagle, C., Wijesundara, M.B.: Sensorized soft robotic glove for continuous passive motion therapy. In: Proceedings of the 2016 6th IEEE International Conference on Biomedical Robotics and Biomechatronics (BioRob), Singapore, 26–29 June 2016, pp. 815–820 (2018). https://doi.org/10.1109/biorob.2016.7523728
9. Haghshenas-Jaryani, M., Carrigan, W., Wijesundara, M.B.: Design and development of a novel soft-and-rigid hybrid actuator system for robotic applications. In: Proceedings of the ASME 2015 International Design Engineering Technical Conferences and Computers and Information in Engineering Conference, Boston, MA, USA, 2–5 August 2015, pp. 1–6. American Society of Mechanical Engineers, New York (2018)
10. Haghshenas-Jaryani, M., et al.: Kinematic study of a soft-and-rigid robotic digit for rehabilitation and assistive applications. In: Proceedings of the ASME 2016 International Design Engineering Technical Conferences and Computers and Information in Engineering Conference, Charlotte, NC, USA, 21–24 August 2016, pp. 1–7. American Society of Mechanical Engineers, New York (2018). https://doi.org/10.1115/DETC2017-68291
11. Haghshenas-Jaryani, M., Nothnagle, C., Patterson, R.M., Bugnariu, N., Wijesundara, M.B.: Soft robotic rehabilitation exoskeleton (REHAB glove) for hand therapy. In: Proceedings of the ASME 2017 International Design Engineering Technical Conferences and Computers and Information in Engineering Conference, Cleveland, OH, USA, 6–9 August 2017, pp. 1–10. American Society of Mechanical Engineers, New York (2018). https://doi.org/10.1115/DETC2017-68291
12. Hansen, C., Gosselin, F., Mansour, K.B., Devos, P., Marin, F.: Design-Validation of a Hand Exoskeleton Using Musculoskeletal Modeling. Centro de investigación Royallieu. Sorbonne Universités, Universidad de Tecnología de Compiègne, Compiègne, Francia (2018)
13. Holguera, M.R., Turrión Nieves, A., Pérez Gómez, A., Álvareez de Mon-Sot, M.: Artritis reumatoide. Departamento de Medicina. Universidad de Alcalá de Henares. Alcalá de Henares, Madrid, España (2017)
14. Jo, I., Park, Y., Lee, J., Bae, J.: A portable and spring-guided hand exoskeleton for exercising flexion/tension of the fingers. Department of Mechanical Engineering, UNIST, Ulsan, Korea (2019). https://doi.org/10.1016/j.mechmachtheory.2019.02.004
15. Kevin, D., Deane, M., Holers, M.: The Natural History of Rheumatoid Arthritis. Division of Rheumatology, University of Colorado Denver Anschutz Medical Campus, Aurora, Colorado, USA (2016)
16. Lee, H., Kang, B.B., In, H., Cho, K.-J.: Design improvement of a polymer-based tendon-driven wearable robotic hand (exo-glove poly). In: Gonzalez-Vargas, J., Ibáñez, J., Contreras-Vidal, J.L., van der Kooij, H., Pons, J.L. (eds.) Wearable Robotics: Challenges and Trends. BB, vol. 16, pp. 95–99. Springer, Cham (2017). https://doi.org/10.1007/978-3-319-46532-6_16
17. Lee, J., Park, W., Kim, S., Bae, J.: Design of a wearable hand rehabilitation system for quantitative evaluation of the stroke hand. Departamento de Ingeniería Mecánica. UNIST, Ulsan, Korea (2016). https://doi.org/10.1109/iccas.2016.7832354
18. Li, H., Cheng, L.: Preliminary study on the design and control of a pneumatically actuated hand rehabilitation device. In: 2017 32nd Youth Academic Annual Conference of Chinese Association of Automation (YAC), pp. 860–865. IEEE (2017). https://doi.org/10.1109/yac.2017.7967530
19. Low, J.H., Ang, M.H., Yeow, C.H.: Customizable soft pneumatic finger actuators for hand orthotic and prosthetic applications. In: Proceedings of the 2015 IEEE International Conference on Rehabilitation Robotics (ICORR), Singapore, 11–14 August 2015, pp. 380–385 (2015). https://doi.org/10.1109/icorr.2015.7281229

20. Lu, Z., Tong, K., Shin, H., Li, S., Zhou, P.: Advanced myoelectric control for robotic hand-assisted training: outcome from a stroke patient. Departamento de Medicina Física y Rehabilitación, Centro de Ciencias de la Salud de la Universidad de Texas en Houston, TX, USA (2017)

21. Moya, R., Magal-Royo, T.: Diseño y prototipado de un dispositivo de rehabilitación para la artritis reumatoide de mano. Tsantsa. Revista De Investigaciones Artísticas, vol. 7, pp. 233–240 (2019). ISBN 1390-8448

22. Popov, D., Gaponov, I., Ryu, J.H.: Guante portátil de exoesqueleto con estructura suave para asistencia manual en actividades de la vida diaria. Transacciones IEEE/ASME en Mecatrónica **22**(2), 865–875 (2016)

23. Portnova, A.A., Mukherjee, G., Peters, K.M., Yamane, A., Steele, K.M.: Design of a 3D-printed, open-source wrist-driven orthosis for individuals with spinal cord injury. PLoS ONE **13**(2), e0193106 (2018). https://doi.org/10.1371/journal.pone.0193106

24. Radder, B., et al.: Preliminary findings of feasibility of a wearable soft-robotic glove supporting impaired hand function in daily life. In: Proceedings of the 2nd International Conference on Information and Communication Technologies for Ageing Well and e-Health (ICT4AWE), Rome, Italy, 21–22 April 2016. SciTePress, Belfast (2018)

25. Radder, B., et al.: A wearable soft-robotic glove enables hand support in ADL and rehabilitation: a feasibility study on the assistive functionality. J. Rehabil. Assist. Technol. Eng. **3**, 2055668316670553 (2016)

26. Radder, B., et al.: Preliminary evaluation of a wearable soft-robotic glove supporting grip strength in ADL. In: Ibáñez, J., González-Vargas, J., Azorín, J.M., Akay, M., Pons, J.L. (eds.) Converging Clinical and Engineering Research on Neurorehabilitation II. BB, vol. 15, pp. 1245–1250. Springer, Cham (2017). https://doi.org/10.1007/978-3-319-46669-9_203

27. Randazzo, L., Iturrate, I., Perdikis, S., Millán, J.D.: mano: A wearable hand exoskeleton for activities of daily living and neurorehabilitation. IEEE Robot. Autom. Lett. **3**, 500–507 (2018). https://doi.org/10.1109/lra.2017.2771329

28. Reymundo, A.A., Muñoz, E.M., Navarro, M., Vela, E., Krebs, H.I.: Hand rehabilitation using soft-robotics. In: Proceedings of the 2016 6th IEEE International Conference on Biomedical Robotics and Biomechatronics (BioRob), Singapore, 26–29 June 2016 (2016)

29. Smolen, J.S., et al.: EULAR recommendations for the management of rheumatoid arthritis with syn- thetic and biological disease-modifying antirheumatic drugs: 2016 update. Ann. Rheum. Dis. **76**(6), 960–977 (2017). https://doi.org/10.1136/annrheumdis-2016-210715

30. Tarvainen, T.V., Yu, W.: Preliminary results on multi-pocket pneumatic elastomer actuators for human-robot interface in hand rehabilitation. In: Proceedings of the 2015 IEEE International Conference on Robotics and Biomimetics (ROBIO), Zhuhai, China, 6–9 December 2015, pp. 2635–2639 (2015). https://doi.org/10.1109/robio.2015.7419737

31. Yang, J., Xie, H., Shi, J.: A novel motion-coupling design for a jointless tendon-driven finger exoskeleton for rehabilitation. Mech. Mach. Theory **99**, 83–102 (2016)

32. Yao, Z., Linnenberg, C., Argubi-Wollesen, A., Weidner, R., Wulfsberg, J.P.: Diseño biomimético de un guante de músculo blando ultracompacto y ligero. Ingeniería de Producción **11**(6), 731–743 (2017)

33. Yap, H.K., Lim, J.H., Nasrallah, F., Goh, J.C., Yeow, R.C.: A soft exoskeleton for hand assistive and rehabilitation application using pneumatic actuators with variable stiffness (2015)

34. Yap, H.K., Ang, B.W., Lim, J.H., Goh, J.C., Yeow, C.H.: A fabric-regulated soft robotic glove with user intent detection using EMG and RFID for hand assistive application. In: Proceedings of the 2016 IEEE International Conference on Robotics and Automation (ICRA), Stockholm, Sweden, 16–21 May 2016, pp. 3537–3542 (2015)

35. Yap, H.K., Lim, J.H., Nasrallah, F., Goh, J.C., Yeow, R.C.: A soft exoskeleton for hand assistive and rehabilitation application using pneumatic actuators with variable stiffness. In:

Proceedings of the 2015 IEEE International Conference on Robotics and Automation (ICRA), Seattle, WA, USA, 26–30 May 2015, pp. 4967–4972 (2015)

36. Yap, H.K., et al.: MRC-Glove: a fMRI compatible soft robotic glove for hand rehabilitation application. In: Proceedings of the 2015 IEEE International Conference on Rehabilitation Robotics (ICORR), Singapore, 11–14 August 2015, pp. 735–740 (2015)

37. Yeo, J.C., Yap, H.K., Xi, W., Wang, Z., Yeow, C.H., Lim, C.T.: Flexible and stretchable strain sensing actuator for wearable soft robotic applications. Adv. Mater. Technol. **1**, 1600018 (2016)

38. Yi, J., Shen, Z.; Song, C., Wang, Z.: A soft robotic glove for hand motion assistance. In: Proceedings of the 2016 IEEE International Conference on Real-Time Computing and Robotics (RCAR), Angkor Wat, Cambodia, 6–10 June 2016, pp. 111–116 (2016)

39. Zaid, A.M., Chean, T.C., Sukor, J.A., Hanafi, D.: Development of hand exoskeleton for rehabilitation of post-stroke patient. AIP Conf. Proc. **1891**, 020103 (2017)

40. Zhang, J., Wang, H., Tang, J., Guo, H., Hong, J.: Modeling and design of a soft pneumatic finger for hand rehabilitation. In: Proceedings of the 2015 IEEE International Conference on Information and Automation, Lijiang, China, 8–10 August 2015, pp. 2460–2465 (2015)

41. Zhao, H., et al.: A helping hand: soft orthosis with integrated optical strain sensors and EMG control. IEEE Robot. Autom. Mag. **23**, 55–64 (2016)

Development of a Home Accompaniment System Providing Homework Assistance for Children with ADHD

Laura López-Pérez[1]([✉]) [ID], Jonnathan Berrezueta-Guzman[1,2] [ID], and María-Luisa Martín-Ruiz[1] [ID]

[1] Universidad Politécnica de Madrid, 28031 Madrid, Spain
{laura.lopezp,s.berrezueta}@alumnos.upm.es,
marialuisa.martinr@upm.es
[2] CEDIA, Cuenca 010203, Ecuador
santiago.berrezueta@cedia.org.ec

Abstract. This manuscript presents a system for homework assistance for children with Attention Deficit Hyperactivity Disorder - ADHD. This system consists of a robot and a set of smart objects constantly monitoring the child's activities during the performance of his tasks. The design of this system is focused on creating a robot-child relationship. It is possible for the child with this type of disorder to acquire the different capacities that allow him to carry out his tasks independently and effectively through short instructions and different methodologies (such as short physical exercise). Besides, it is a support tool for parents and therapists to better comprehend the behavior of their children and patients, respectively. This system allows a better understanding of the patient's clinical characteristics, his evolution, and the therapeutic options that may have a greater effect on him. This project is focused on the implementation of an information processing software and a User Interface UI for the Atent@ robot. Thanks to the software the robot is provided with many functionalities for inter-acting with the child. This system is based on IoT architecture. Both the robot and the smart objects are connected to a Realtime Database so that the data can be processed and shared with parents and therapists in real-time through a mobile application. This work shows the entire design and implementation of this software as well as the functional tests and their results.

Keywords: ADHD · Software development · Human-machine interaction · Robotic assistance · UIX

1 Introduction

Attention Deficit Hyperactivity Disorder (ADHD) is a conduct disorder with a growing number of detected cases over the last years. Generally, its diagnosis and therapy require human involvement in most cases. The symptoms of this behavioral disorder are inattention, hyperactivity, and impulsiveness, all of which seriously interfere with the

© Springer Nature Switzerland AG 2020
G. Rodriguez Morales et al. (Eds.): TICEC 2020, CCIS 1307, pp. 22–35, 2020.
https://doi.org/10.1007/978-3-030-62833-8_3

child's learning. This in turn leads to lower school performance than the average. Due to recent cataloging, this disorder was not included in the American Academy of Psychiatry Manual of Classification and Diagnosis of Mental Disorders (DSM-V) until 2000. ADHD is a disorder that raises great social attention as it mostly occurs in children. It commonly leads to the overdiagnosis of this disorder and, consequently, to the abuse of psychotropic treatments [1].

The treatment is carried out exclusively in a therapeutic center. This treatment consists of teaching the child guidelines that help him carry out daily activities such as cleaning up the room, doing homework, eating, etc. The fact that the child has to move for regular follow-ups makes the treatment not as effective as it could be since it is not practiced in the child's natural environment. The environment plays a truly important and strategic role, especially if we consider that the evaluation of ADHD symptoms, according to the DSM-V, must be carried out, in different settings and contexts to obtain an accurate diagnosis. This project seeks to transfer the therapy environment to the patient's home where he can put into practice the guidelines recommended by his therapist in carrying out daily tasks. In this project, the day-to-day task that becomes relevant is performing homework.

On the other hand, Robotics has experienced greater importance in its application in the therapeutic and educational field. The therapy robot for children with autism spectrum disorders called Aisoy is a clear example of this [2]. As ADHD is a much more recent disorder than Autism Spectrum Disorder, it has been less immersed in research and the advancement in assistant robots helping therapy for children with this type of disorder has not been developed yet. Therefore, this work focuses especially on children with ADHD.

It is very important that the child feels comfortable and enjoys interacting with the robot. For this reason, this project implements the software and the design of an easy, friendly, and fun graphic interface that encourages the child to interact with it. The user interface increases participation and helps the child to associate the robot as a necessary element when performing his homework. Through this adaption, the information collected is much more in line with reality. All this information is accessible from a mobile application. The parents and therapists can monitor and evaluate the interaction with the robot, the information collected and processed during homework sessions, and the autonomy advances that the child develops throughout the therapy with the system.

2   Attention Deficit and Hyperactivity Disorder - ADHD

ADHD is a neurobiological behavior disorder with a genetic component caused by the existence of an imbalance between two brain neurotransmitters: norepinephrine and dopamine [3]. These substances do not work adequately in the prefrontal cortex of the brain, directly affecting self-control and avoiding inappropriate behavior. This leads to a lack of control in functions such as attention, hyperactivity, and impulsivity [4].

2.1 ADHD Statistics

ADHD is one of the most frequent psychiatric disorders in the world, ranking above schizophrenia or bipolar disorder. Furthermore, it constitutes the most frequent neuropsychiatric diagnosis of childhood [5]. ADHD affects between 3 and 12% of children and adolescents, having a worldwide prevalence of 5.3% according to the World Health Organization (WHO) [6]. Although ADHD is a disorder that predominates in childhood, it has been shown that between 4 and 5% continue to show symptoms in adulthood [7].

Today, diagnosing this type of disorder continues to be very difficult due to the great comorbidity that exists with other disorders. In a study carried out in Sweden by the Gillberg group, it was shown that 87% of children who met all the criteria for ADHD had at least one comorbid diagnosis and that 67% met the criteria for at least two comorbid disorders [8].

2.2 ADHD Types

The core symptoms of ADHD are independent of each other and therefore occur in different combinations, at different levels, and with different types of associated problems. However, most people with this type of disorder show symptoms of both, inattention and hyperactivity-impulsivity. According to the Manual of Classification and DSM-V [9], there are three presentations or subtypes of ADHD:

1. ADHD with a predominance of attention deficit
2. ADHD with predominantly hyperactive-impulsive
3. ADHD combined type

2.3 Treatments

The treatment which has proven to be most effective, both in children and in adults with ADHD, is a multisystem treatment which is a pharmacological and psychosocial treatment. Pharmacological treatment helps to compensate for the irregular production of the neurotransmitters involved in this disorder; dopamine and norepinephrine. In people with ADHD, stimulants calm them and tranquilizers make them more nervous, as stimulants raise and balance the level of neurotransmitters [10]. The most widely used drug in these treatments is methylphenidate, but it can have side effects [10]. Effective non-pharmacological treatments are essential, especially in those patients who are resistant to the use of medications to treat ADHD.

Psychosocial treatment includes psycho-pedagogical, neuropsychological, cognitive, behavioral, and family therapies that help decrease the symptoms of this disorder [10]. Specific behavioral approaches are important to focus on areas such as social relationships and organizational skills [11].

Another approach includes intensive computerized training of attention, inhibition, working memory, and neurofeedback. Computerized training approaches operate on the principle that underlying deficits in brain networks and associated cognitive processes can be remedied by structured exposure to repeated cognitive tasks, in which task's difficulty is continually raised to challenge but not to overwhelm the child's abilities [11].

2.4   Robotic Therapeutic Assistance

One of the fastest-growing technological areas today is robotics. Although robotics has been more widely used in general industrial sectors due to its ability to perform repetitive tasks, which need to be very precise and sometimes contain dangers, a special interest has been awakened by the contributions of robotics in educational processes since the 1970s, generating a new area of study: educational robotics [12].

Educational robotics or pedagogical robotics is a discipline that creates and operates robotic prototypes as well as specialized programs for pedagogical purposes. Pierre Nonnon and Jean Pierre Theil affirm that the use of robotic tools favors the teaching and learning process since they allow easy integration of the theoretical with the practical [13]. Educational robotics is strongly linked to the theories of constructivism. Jean Piaget's constructivist theory ensures that learning is not the result of a transfer of knowledge, but rather an active process of constructing learning based on experiences. Constructivism maintains that learning manifests as the student interacts with his reality and performs activities on it. From constructivist theory, the use of technological tools provides an alternative way of learning and creates experiences for students to build knowledge [13].

The development of therapies carried out with robots allows the reduction of prevalent disorders in society intuitively and pedagogically [14]. This allows us to provide a feasible solution to combat prevalent disorders such as ADHD. They also help to maintain greater attention in the performance of their tasks thanks to the manipulation, experimentation, and interaction with this type of tool, acquiring capabilities and methodologies that help them to carry out the different procedures. The robot becomes the therapist and at the same time a therapeutic tool.

Currently, there is a wide variety of techniques and resources that are used as technological support to promote academic learning [12]. A current example is PAT, a robotic assistant that supports children in the initial age on the prevention of traumatic accidents [15]. This project has had very promising results, overcoming traditional prevention teaching methodologies inside pre-scholar schools.

3   Methodology

3.1   Scenario

The setting of this project is based on the need to make an exhaustive observation of children with ADHD in their natural environment which is of great importance for further treatment by therapists and specialists. Currently, this is not done as children with ADHD must go to a therapeutic consultation for diagnosis and treatment. This, in particular, restricts the correct care of the patient, and the extrapolation of the results is influenced by an environment with which the child is unfamiliar.

The proposed scenario for the implementation of the system is shown below (Fig. 1).

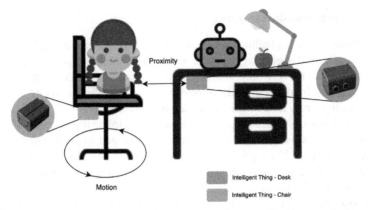

Fig. 1. Scheme of the project scenario. The system implemented in this scenario is made up of the Atent@ robot and the two smart objects, one under the desk and the other under the chair.

3.2 Atent@ Robot

The Atent@ robot is an intelligent device whose main function is to serve as a support tool to help children with ADHD to carry out their school tasks. This element is the basis of the project [16]. It carries the intelligence of the homework process and is in charge of carrying out all the necessary interactions with the child. Being an essential element placed in the workspace, its dimensions are small and are made for being portable while at the same time it does not represent a distraction when the child gets to work. The robot has a touch screen so that the child can enter the different activities he wants to do, such as starting the homework, going to the bathroom, asking for help, etc.

The robot allows him to apply organizational and planning techniques that reinforce the therapy sessions carried out by his therapist, at home. Also, it allows the parents and therapists to carry out constant monitoring of the child's behavior during the performance of his duties, which can help gain more detailed information about the case, observe the progress, and reroute his therapy if necessary [16].

3.3 Intelligent Things

Intelligent Things are two devices connected to the internet just like Atent@, which have been placed under both the desk and the chair. Their main function is collecting data while the child performs his tasks. They are not perceived by the child, therefore not causing any distraction during the tasks. The devices are continuously measuring the parameters and sending all the information for further processing into the cloud [16]. The intelligent thing installed in the chair allows detecting movements. This object has an integrated accelerometer sensor, which obtains the acceleration values and the orientation of the object, thus being able to determine if the child is moving with the chair or not.

The intelligent thing installed in the desk detects the distance between the child and the desk, by using an ultrasonic proximity sensor (hc-sr04). This sensor obtains the distance between the child and the desk, allowing the observation to detect whether the child is in his working position or if he has moved away from the desk.

The information obtained from both intelligent objects allows us to know: Whether the child is concentrated on doing his homework, has been distracted, or left his workplace. Besides, it allows the collection of very important information for the therapists. Since they are quantifiable it can be verified whether the therapy is effective, or if, on the contrary, improvements have to be made since no progress can be seen in the child.

3.4 Proposed System

An intelligent software system is designed and developed, which implements all the functionalities required for assistance in carrying out school tasks in children with ADHD between the ages of 6 and 9 years. This system is not only designed to teach but is also a source of information for both parents and therapists. Parents are informed of the progress of their children, while therapists will be able to continuously monitor the child in more realistic ways and environments.

To achieve this child-parent-therapist communication, a mobile application is designed and developed allowing to consult, in real-time, the data from the session with the robot. Besides, the stored local data from previous sessions can be consulted later, making the monitoring by the therapy much more effective.

The following figure shows which are the interactions that take place in the system (Fig. 2).

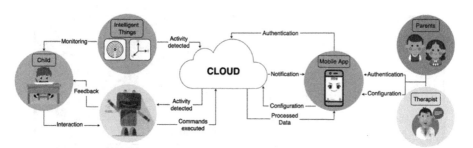

Fig. 2. Scheme of the system and the main interactions between its elements.

3.5 System Architecture

The global architecture of the system takes the IoT layer model as a reference. This architecture is subdivided into three main layers:

The first, called the acquisition layer, is responsible for collecting all the information from the robot, through the instructions indicated by the child, and collected thanks to the touch screen, as well as through the sensors inside the smart objects. This data is sent to the knowledge layer through the internet connection.

The second, knowledge layer, encompasses the processing of the data collected by the sensors as well as storing this information to obtain knowledge. It is proposed to perform Edge Computing, locating the main computation in the robot. Thus, it will be avoided that the behavior of the robot depends on a connection to the network, ensuring that in the event this connection does not exist, the robot can still perform all its tasks correctly. Besides, a massive upload of data will be avoided, sending only the data which is considered to be of interest to the cloud.

The third layer, of services, is in charge of providing the necessary information through different types of interaction to different users. In the case of the robot, these interactions can be sound or audiovisual type.

The following figure shows the architecture of the system discussed previously (Fig. 3).

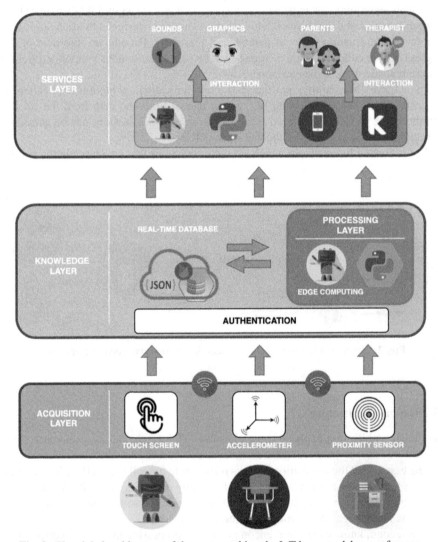

Fig. 3. The global architecture of the system taking the IoT layer model as a reference.

3.6 UIX

The user interface offers the child with ADHD a unique experience because as Atent@ can perform gestures while reproducing feedback sounds. In this way, the child associates Atent@ as an important member when doing homework.

These are the designs created to represent Atent@ (Fig. 4).

Fig. 4. Screenshots of some of the gestures that Atent@ can perform while interacting with children.

The user interface has several screens and options that give the child a more complete user interface experience. The child can indicate to the robot his state of mind before starting any activity. Additionally, the child can indicate whether to do homework, a relaxation activity, or consult his parents for help during any activity. If the child selects the task activity, a menu will be displayed to start new homework, continue with another one, or check pending tasks. Finally, the child can display a menu at any time to indicate if he needs help from his parents, drinks water, or use the bathroom.

Below are the graphical interfaces of the designs designed (Fig. 5).

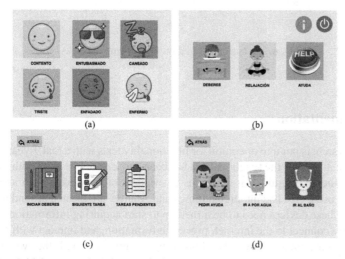

Fig. 5. UI. a. Initial screen when the mood of the children is chosen. b. Screen for asking which activity the child wants to do. c. Screen with the homework menu. d. Screen menu with options between tasks.

In the homework scenario, Atent@ first prepares the child before starting any task. First, it reminds the child to check his schedule (Fig. 6 a) for pending tasks. In this way, the child will be able to mark on the next screen in which subjects he has pending tasks (Fig. 6 b). The next instruction recommends that the child prepares things to start (Fig. 6 c). Finally, Atent@ asks him if there is a need to go to the bathroom before starting the work session (Fig. 6 d). After this preparation, the child is ready to start (Fig. 6 e).

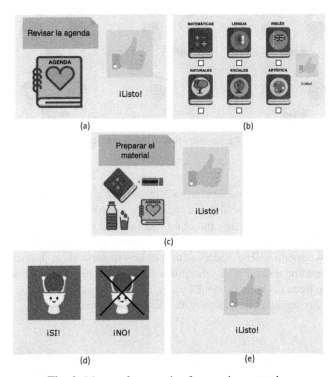

Fig. 6. Menus of preparation for carrying out tasks.

4 Implementation

The entire system is put into operation for functionality tests with a real 9-year-old child. Due to the health crisis, the functional test has been carried out in a child without ADHD but as he is the age required, it allows us to evaluate other aspects such as usability, the language used, etc. The intelligent things and Atent@ are located around the child's workspace. These devices need to be turned on to start acquiring information, then they automatically connect to the internet, process information, and interact with the child.

The following image shows the child using Atent@ and with the two intelligent things connected (Fig. 7).

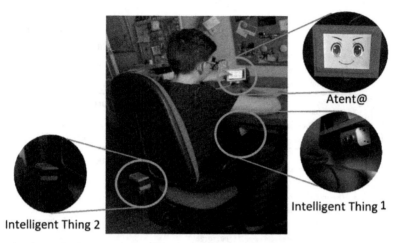

Fig. 7. Implementation of Atent@ and intelligent things in the child's workspace.

In the functional test, the child carried out a full cycle of homework with a total number of 2 tasks. The child was able to develop perfectly with the robot, he did not encounter usability problems and he found in Atent@ a clear and concise language with a pleasant voice. His final impression was that Atent@ had helped him to prepare well to carry out his duties and had guided him correctly. The parents and the therapist followed closely the steps that the child was taking while the performance of homework and verified the values collected by the system when the child performed his duties in an everyday place for him.

4.1 Monitoring Process

Intelligent Things are responsible for capturing information related to the child's movement. Thanks to this information and through Edge Computing in the Atent@ robot, we will obtain knowledge that allows us to determine different events. These events occur asynchronously in the program execution so that, if either is accomplished during homework, the normal program execution will be interrupted to provide the child with the necessary feedback. The following table of possible scenarios depending on the behavior performed by the child has been defined with the occupational therapist (Table 1).

All these events are gathered by the Realtime Database in Firebase. Following the flow of events, this information is updated constantly, allowing the robot to use this knowledge to provide feedback to the child during the homework sessions.

The following figure is a screenshot of the Realtime Database in Firebase (Fig. 8).

The Firebase Realtime Database is structured in four blocks:

– Activities: Shows the data of interest corresponding to the three main activities. Homework, going to the bathroom, and going to drink water.
– Intelligent Objects: Shows the data collected from the sensors under the chair and the desk.

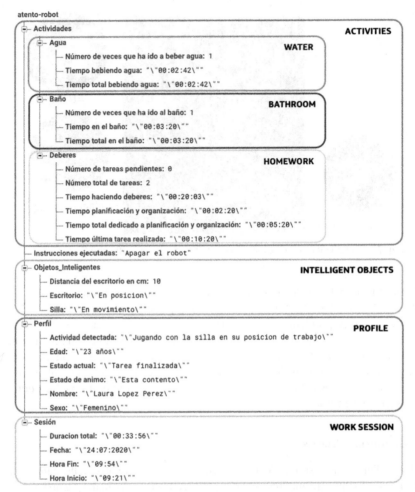

Fig. 8. Screenshot of the Realtime Database with all the information acquired by Atent@ and the Intelligent Things.

Table 1. Identification of events through Intelligent Things.

	Desk	Chair	Time	Knowledge
Events	In position	Without movement	<20 min	Doing the tasks
	In position	Without movement	>20 min	Need a break
	In position	With movement	<30 s	Getting into place
	In position	With movement	>30 s	Playing with the chair
	Move away	Without movement	>30 s	Gone away from the desk
	Move away	With movement	>30 s	Playing

– Child's profile: All the data related to the child's profile, name, age, mood, etc. are shown.
– Work session: Shows the information related to the session, start time, duration, etc.

The collected data is relevant to check the child's evolution and it is stored locally at the end of the work session in Excel. In this way, we managed to obtain a database that would serve for subsequent studies on the evolution of the child. The data corresponding to the work session is stored, as well as other data of interest, such as mood, duration times of the activities, etc. The local database's summary is shown below (Fig. 9).

Session					Activities						
Date	Start time	End time	Total time	Mood	Total number of tasks	Time planning and organization	Time doing homework	Number of times bathroom	Total time bathroom	Number of times water	Total time water

Fig. 9. Collected data organization to store the information of each homework session.

4.2 Mobile App

The developed mobile application allows access to the Firebase Realtime Database to observe the behavior of the child during the work session. Additionally, and only previously starting a new session, it is possible to consult the information collected in the previous sessions.

Below are the screens from each of the submenus of the mobile application (Fig. 10).

Fig. 10. The user interface of the developed mobile app for monitoring children with ADHD during a task session.

5 Results

This chapter summarizes the resulting system and systematically mentions the most significant tests that the system has been subjected to as well as showing the observed results. Firstly, a system has been designed and implemented for the Atent@ robot that accomplish the objectives set out in this project which helps children with ADHD to carry out their duties effectively. Besides, the data from the sensors have been collected to obtain knowledge: Whether the child is doing homework or, on the contrary, is being restless and distracted.

Secondly, a database has been created for the local storage of the data of interest collected by the sensors as well as a mobile application, which has been designed and implemented to display the data from the Firebase Realtime Database. This application was created for parents and therapists to track and monitor the child and his activities in real-time.

Regarding the tests carried out on the system, numerous performance tests have been carried out with different assumptions to verify that the system responds as expected. It has been verified that the developed system is a robust system that reacts correctly while being confronted with different scenarios.

As an example, the tests performed on the to-do button are presented:

– Assumption 1. Include the pending matters before starting the homework: The system stores the corresponding matters, showing them as pending matters by the time the homework has started. The assignment of the subjects by priority is done correctly (the trunks first).
– Assumption 2. Add pending matters after starting the homework. The system updates the number of pending tasks and the total number of tasks to be performed correctly. When changing tasks (Next task), the system takes into account the new subjects added and prioritizes the trunks correctly.
– Assumption 3. Add pending subjects after completion of homework: The behavior is the same as expected in assumption 1.

Regarding the performance and acceptance tests carried out, a test of the correct operation of the system has been carried out with a 9-year-old child.

6 Conclusions and Future Work Lines

The main objective of this project is to help children with ADHD with tools that allow them to organize themselves and plan correctly to carry out their duties. Also, provide parents and therapists with the information necessary to contribute to the treatment of children with ADHD.

The development of the intuitive and user-friendly interface with audiovisual variables has generated a unique user experience for the child where it shares the experience of performing homework efficiently with Atent@.

The mobile application serves as a source of information for parents and therapists, allowing them to see the information coming from the robot in real-time through their mobile phones. All the information from different sessions stored locally will serve as a study tool for proposals for updates on therapies with children with ADHD.

As future work lines are proposed:

– Optimizing the application to improve its efficiency as well as including new functionalities.
– Including Bluetooth technology in intelligent things.
– Developing an intelligent thing to interpret movement and gestures' meaning.
– Developing push notifications in the mobile application.

References

1. De Burgos, R., Barrios, M., Engo, R., García, A., Gay, E., Guijarro, T., et al.: Trastorno por déficit de atención con hiperactividad. Editorial Glosa, SL, Guía para padres y educadores Barcelona (2011)
2. Hoyo Sánchez, Á.: Robótica social: Estudio y aplicación a la dependencia con el robot Aisoy (2016)
3. Feaadah, F.: Federación Española de Asociaciones de Ayuda al Déficit de Atención e Hiperactividad (2002). Recuperado de: http://www.feaadah.org/es/. (Consulta el 20 de mayo de 2017)
4. De Burgos, M.R., Barrios, A.M., Engo, P.R., García, C.A., Gay, P.E., Guijarro, G.T.: Trastorno por déficit de atención con hiperactividad. Guía para padres y educadores Unidad de Salud Mental Infanto-Juvenil del Hospital Universitario Reina Sofía Ed Glosa SL (2009)
5. Acosta, M.: Aspectos genéticos y moleculares en el trastorno por déficit de atención/hiperactividad: búsqueda de los genes implicados en el diagnóstico clínico. Revista de neurología **44**(2), 37–41 (2007)
6. Loro-López, M., et al.: Actualización en el tratamiento del trastorno por déficit de atención/hiperactividad. Rev. Neurol. **49**(5), 257–264 (2009)
7. Hidalgo-López, C., Gómez-Álzate, A.M., García-Valencia, J., Palacio-Ortiz, J.D.: Riesgo de trastorno por déficit de atención e hiperactividad y otros trastornos psiquiátricos de los hermanos de pacientes con TDAH. Revista colombiana de psiquiatría **48**(1), 44–49 (2019)
8. Artigas-Pallarés, J.: Comorbilidad en el trastorno por déficit de atención/hiperactividad. Rev. Neurol. **36**(Suppl. 1), S68–S78 (2003)
9. American Psychiatric Association: Guía de consulta de los criterios diagnósticos del DSM-5®: Spanish Edition of the Desk Reference to the Diagnostic Criteria From DSM-5®. American Psychiatric Pub (2014)
10. Pascual-Castroviejo, I.: Trastornos por déficit de atención e hiperactividad (TDAH). Asociación Española de Pediatría y Sociedad Española de Neurología Pediátrica Protocolos de Neurología **12**, 140–150 (2008)
11. Thapar, A., Pine, D., Leckman, J., Scott, S., Snowling, M., Taylor, E.: Rutter's child and adolescent psychiatry (2015). https://doi.org/10.1002/9781118381953
12. Gomez, R.G., Arroyo-Sagasta, A., Llorente, P.A., Vitoria-Gasteiz, H., Abajo, J.M.: Experiencia Bee-bot con alumnado universitario: pensamiento computacional como reto para mejorar las habilidades colaborativas
13. Bravo Sánchez, F.Á., Forero Guzmán, A.: La robótica como un recurso para facilitar el aprendizaje y desarrollo de competencias generales (2012)
14. Cabrera, F.R., Rodríguez, C.F., Zabala, M.A., Santacruz, F.J.: Implementación de técnicas de visión artificial para el beneficio de niños con déficit de atención e hiperactividad a través de un ejercicio psicomotriz utilizando el robot NAO
15. Berrezueta-Guzman, J., Serpa-Andrade, L., Robles-Bykbaev, V., Montalvo, M.: Robotic assistant for the teaching in trauma accidents prevention in children of initial age. In: 2020 IEEE International Conference on Consumer Electronics (ICCE), pp. 1–6. IEEE (2020)
16. Berrezueta-Guzman, J., Pau, I., Martín-Ruiz, M.-L., Máximo-Bocanegra, N.: Smart-home environment to support homework activities for children. IEEE Access (2020)

Creation of an Intelligent System to Support the Therapy Process in Children with ADHD

María Dolón-Poza[1]([☒]) [iD], Jonnathan Berrezueta-Guzman[1,2] [iD],
and María-Luisa Martín-Ruiz[1] [iD]

[1] Universidad Politécnica de Madrid, 28031 Madrid, Spain
{maria.dolonp,s.berrezueta}@alumnos.upm.es,
marialuisa.martinr@upm.es
[2] CEDIA, Cuenca 010203, Ecuador
santiago.berrezueta@cedia.org.ec

Abstract. This article is a proposal for an intelligent system that facilitates the therapy process for children with Attention Deficit Hyperactivity Disorder - ADHD. This project focuses on the analysis, design, and implementation of an intelligent architecture, which uses machine learning techniques for a therapeutic robot to help develop new tests and other resources to support the treatment of ADHD. Its general purpose is to identify common patterns in the behavior of children with ADHD, between 6 and 9 years old during the performance of homework to help the therapist diagnose and predict the future behavior of children in this area. A system has been proposed whose development and implementation is carried out by a cloud computing platform, taking advantage of all its benefits such as low latency, unlimited storage, functionalities to deploy a project based on artificial intelligence and data security. Therefore, using these functionalities from the platform, a machine learning model has been deployed. This model is a binary classification since it groups the results according to the diagnosis (ADHD or not ADHD). However, what this model provides are the rules that compare the data obtained from the robot's sensors to the set of results expected to be obtained (ADHD or not ADHD). To obtain these rules, an algorithm already developed by this platform and a set of data will be used. This first part is known as model training, in which the model has been built. Once the rules are obtained, another set of data will be used for testing. In this second part, the model will be able to identify whether the new data entered matches the criteria of a child with ADHD or with a typical development. The data processing is carried out from the cloud platform, offering data availability and accessibility at all times. The results of the correlation between the obtained data and the predicted diagnosis showed remarkable results.

Keywords: Machine learning · Automatic learning · Artificial intelligence · Cloud computing · IoT · ADHD

1 Introduction

One of the most common disorders which are diagnosed today in children and adults is attention deficit hyperactivity disorder (ADHD). As its name indicates, the symptoms

© Springer Nature Switzerland AG 2020
G. Rodriguez Morales et al. (Eds.): TICEC 2020, CCIS 1307, pp. 36–50, 2020.
https://doi.org/10.1007/978-3-030-62833-8_4

that characterize this disorder are attentional difficulty, impulsiveness and motor agitation, as well as hyperactivity. This disorder affects more than 5% of children in the world and 6% of children in Spain, between 6 and 17 years of age [1]. Some of the symptoms usually appear before the age of 12 and have a significant impact on the person, causing them to progressively deteriorate their performance [2].

Children with ADHD tend to underperform academically and also interfere in the family and social environment [3]. Sometimes they present difficulties in understanding instructions from their parents or teachers and stand out for being impulsive in the organization: they are not able to properly control time, they do not know how to organize tasks and they tend to live in a disorderly environment [4]. This in turn leads to a low mood, which can cause anxiety, stress, and frustration in most cases.

However, early diagnosis and adequate treatment for each case have shown a positive evolution of the disorder, which is the main motivation behind this project. Detection and diagnosis consist of carrying out a series of normative tests following the criteria set out in the Diagnostic and Statistical Manual Of Mental Disorders (DSM-V) [2]. Usually, the treatments are done in a therapeutic center which the child must visit regularly. Here the child learns to adequately carry out activities of daily life: eating, sleeping, doing her homework, etc. In this way, the therapist monitors the evolution of improving the performance of these activities.

The fact that the child has to go to a medical center for regular follow-up means that the treatment is not completely effective as it is not being implemented in the child's natural environment. Moving the therapy to their home would detach the treatment from a specific place and time. The environment in which the treatment is carried out must be strategic and plays a very important role in the therapy. Another additional benefit of performing therapy at home is being able to involve the family in it.

An alarming problem is the lack of knowledge of the average citizen about this disorder. In addition to that, there are not yet complete and entirely effective therapies which help to improve different cases and differentiate them from other disorders. A misdiagnosis makes the child responsible for its behavior which in turn seriously affects its consciousness by e.g. creating negative situations, which can even further harm the stability of children, making even every day or ordinary situations stressful.

2   Background

With the digital transformation and the evolution of information and communication technologies (ICT), which our society is experiencing, new techniques and technologies are being incorporated, which provide optimization and automation of the different processes that surround us. Robots that help with different treatments have been developed and incorporated in the academic and therapeutic sectors. Some examples we have based our research on are:

– A robot for therapy of children with autism spectrum disorder called Aisoy, which provides a breakthrough in therapy and can be used both at home and at school. It allows autistic children to relate differently: The robot, who can behave like the child, interacts with the child, recognizes it, communicates with the child, and helps to develop the children's intellectual abilities [5].

- An Expert system is based on signal processing techniques and deep learning that allows the detection of ADHD from the data of day and night activity of school-age patients. This project uses artificial intelligence techniques to identify and classify the data corresponding to ADHD patients [6].
- A lego robot developed to carry out neuropsychological evaluations that allow the detection and diagnosis of neurological and motor diseases in children between 6 and 12 years old. During its development, the robot was put into practice with boys and girls with ADHD. This project seeks the child's planning capacity through interactive playing scenarios [7].
- A web application that allows the monitoring of behavior in boys and girls with ADHD so that parents and therapists can better understand them [8].

Therefore, in the case of assistant robots that assist in the therapy of children with ADHD, there is very little research. Robots for diagnosis and treatment of children with autism spectrum disorder predominate. Therefore, to complement and improve the robots that are already developed, it has been decided to develop a proposal for an intelligent system for a robot assistant called Atent@ which helps children with ADHD to carry out their school tasks at home [9] (Fig. 1).

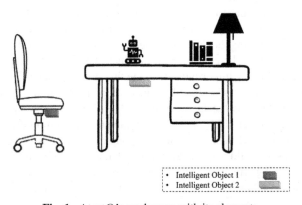

Fig. 1. Atent@'s workspace with its elements.

For this project, the data and information of the child will be collected, which we will use to develop the architecture to be deployed in the environment in which the assistant robot is to be used. Among its parts is the development of a system that, using Knowledge Engineering and Artificial Intelligence techniques, can provide intelligence to the robot which is based on the information collected. To carry out the entire deployment, a cloud computing platform is used to the resources and capacity necessary for the development. This platform will store the data and carry out the tests and steps necessary to deploy a first model based on which the system will be developed. This model is created from an algorithm based on machine learning. For the preparation and visualization of the data, the help of an occupational therapist has been required, who has pointed out the main characteristics of the database, as well as their visualization model. This data is used to make a therapeutic evaluation.

3 Methodology

In this project, an intelligent system is designed which performs all the functionalities related to data storage, treatment, and processing from a cloud platform, using artificial intelligence techniques (machine learning). Therefore, this project must meet the following specifications:

- The environment and the data that have been evaluated and analyzed for the development of this project is for children aged between 6 and 9 years.
- The data and results in the final report must be presented according to the needs of the occupational therapist or the child's guardians. Besides, the report is subject to modification at the request of users.
- The information displayed must be optimized and synthesized to clearly show the behavior of children.
- When selecting the cloud platform, we must consider the different restrictions that each one poses, taking into account the times of latency, the storage capacity, and its architecture. It is also important to consider the different functionalities that exist in each one and the compatibility with the rest of the applications and software used for the development of the project.
- Almost all platforms allow pay-per-use and many of them offer a trial period, making it easy to check whether they are suitable for the specific project.
- Code development platforms are freely distributed.
- When having multiple data sources (the robot and the smart objects), a combination of these should be made to consider all the possible options for information collection.
- The data, both input and output must be gathered.
- The algorithm developed must consider the processing of the data to solve possible writing errors that may exist.
- Security mechanisms must be applied to guarantee the confidentiality of the data.
- The evaluation of all these restrictions is recommended to guarantee the proper development and implementation of the project.

3.1 Proposed System

The objective of this project is to provide Atent@ with the necessary functionalities for the processing, integration, and representation of the data obtained by the sensors and the rest of the hardware that comprise it. The processed data will create relevant knowledge for the treatment and diagnosis of ADHD. Therefore, the main objective is to develop a model based on automatic learning that allows us to identify the behavior patterns that a child with ADHD presents when carrying out her school tasks. First, a set of data is obtained from the robot that will be analyzed and describe the behavior the child has had at the time of performing the duties. This data will be stored in a cloud platform for subsequent analysis.

Using machine learning (ML) techniques, the data is being processed (in case there are possible failures in the previous extraction of these). Second, the data will be used to create a first predictive model and, with another set of data extracted, an evaluation will be made. This evaluation provides information about which patterns are presented by children with ADHD and which ones are typically developed by children when doing homework (Fig. 2).

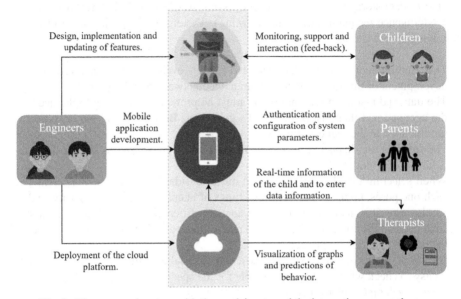

Fig. 2. The proposed system with the participants and the interaction among them.

The diagnosis of children with ADHD consists of objective observation of the behavior to determine what symptoms occur and how often. Our use case is to develop a system that identifies if the child has ADHD. The data correspond to children between 6 and 9 years old with a diagnosis of ADHD and without ADHD. Comparison and diagnosis with other treatments are outside the scope of this project and therefore not furtherly considered. To define our use case, the intervention of an occupational therapist was necessary to contrast our proposal and define the user's requirements.

To carry out this project, its development has been divided into five phases. These phases coincide with those necessary to create a machine learning model, in which it is necessary to: (1) explore and prepare the data, (2) training and model execution, (3) model evaluation, (4) obtaining predictions, and (5) visualizing the results.

3.2 Exploration and Data Treatment

Many ADHD diagnoses apply a protocol for observing impulsivity, attention, and mobility, which is based on the frequency register of Barkley (1990). This measures the frequency of behaviors considered relevant to the diagnosis during 15 min and at 15-s intervals [4]. For this reason, we have estimated times of no more than 15 min between tasks. This will not pose any problem since the objective will be to obtain an algorithm that, by employing and using the children's data, either theoretical or experimental, is capable of making predictions and inferences. The data that will be used to achieve our model is divided into data for training, validation, and testing. All these data sets are structured in the same number of characteristics, except for the "ADHD Diagnosis" characteristic that only appears in the training data set. Each data set shows different values from the rest of the sets. The training methods are used to obtain the parameters of the learning model. The data values will have to be modified until an adequate learning model is achieved. Once achieved, the evaluation is performed with the validation data set. Finally, test data is used when the algorithm and model are fully accomplished. Therefore, the first step is to create the database.

Table 1. Acquired information by the algorithm to process new knowledge.

Information	Value or range
Identifier	Unique for each child
Date of the session	Between May to June 2020
Sex	Woman (M) and Male (H)
Age	Between 6 and 8 years old
Academic course	2019/2020
Language subject score	Between 0 to 10 score
Math subject score	Between 0 to 10 score
English subject score	Between 0 to 10 score
Mood	Sick, Unmotivated, Tired, Happy, Excited
Total session time (sum of start time and total time to perform homework)	Between 20 and 93 min
Start time (introduction and adaptation to the robot)	Between 5 and 10 min
Total time to perform homework (is the sum of total task time, total organization time, rest time, the time it takes to go to the bathroom before starting, water time, distracted time)	Between 15 and 83 min
Total task time (sum of task 1 and task 2 times)	Between 10 and 50 min
Total organization time (sum of task 1 and task 2 organizational times)	Between 5 and 15 min
Time to perform task 1 (considering bathroom distractions 1)	Between 5 and 25 min
Time to do only task 1 (without distractions)	Between 5 and 20 min
Time to organize task 1	Between 4 and 10 min
Time to perform task 2 (considering bathroom distractions 2)	Between 5 and 25 min

(continued)

Table 1. (*continued*)

Time to do only task 2 (without distractions)	Between 5 and 20 min
Time to organize task 2	Between 1 and 5 min
Rest	Between 0 and 5 min
Total bath time throughout the session	Between 0 and 15 min
Total bath time before starting tasks	Between 0 and 5 min
Bath time during the first task	Between 0 and 5 min
Bath time during the second task	Between 0 and 5 min
Time to go for water	Between 0 and 3 min
Total distracted time (sum of time distracted, time to go for water, bath time 1 and bath time 2)	Between 0 and 15 min
Distracted time	Between 0 and 5 min
Strong movements detected	True or False
Number of times that the child got up from the chair	Between 0 and 10 times
Number of clicks of the help button	Between 0 and 3 times.
ADHD diagnosis	True or False

All these features are subject to those that have been established in the Firebase application. In these characteristics, the values detected by the application are stored, as well as the ones detected by the sensors from the robot and intelligent objects. From Firebase only the characteristics that are most useful to predict the ML model are being selected, followed by defining the most important characteristics. As shown in Table 1, a child can take between 20 and 93 min to carry out the session with the robot assistant. This time depends on factors such as mood and whether it has been diagnosed with ADHD or not. Starting with this basis, a database with a dimension of 32 characteristics is created, of which some will be more decisive than others when making the diagnosis prediction. Table 2 shows the characteristics that are going to be most important as well as how they are being weighted. The established value has been agreed upon in knowledge acquisition meetings held with an occupational therapist. This database analysis process is called Characteristics Engineering. The characteristics that will be decisive in observing if the child exhibits a behavior similar to that which it would have if it had ADHD are, above all, the number of times it would rise from the chair and if sudden movements were detected during the session.

A theoretical database has been created, where information has been selected for 526 boys and girls with ADHD and 520 boys and girls with typical development.

Another set of data has also been made in which four cases are compared:

– Evolution of a girl with ADHD using the robot for two weeks.
– Evolution of a girl without ADHD using the robot for two weeks.

Table 2. Information weighting.

Data	Weighting	Order of importance
Number of times that he has got up from the chair	17%	1
Strong movements detected	16%	1
Total organization time	15%	2
Time while being distracted time	15%	2
Total bath time throughout the session	10%	3
Time to go for water	10%	3
Number of clicks of the help button	10%	3
Rest time	7%	4

– Evolution of a boy with ADHD using the robot for two weeks.
– Evolution of a boy without ADHD using the robot for two weeks.

The training is carried out in a first step with the first set of data, which is a total of 1046 boys and girls who carry out the session for one day. This first step will serve to classify the values between children with ADHD or children with typical development. In this first database, the "ADHD Diagnosis" feature is present. This data is stored in the Google Cloud Platform (GCP) BigQuery. From here the data exploration is carried out. This test is done with synthetic data. In a second phase, it will be using the data from the Firebase real-time database, using the information collected by the Atent@ project in real-time.

In Fig. 3, we see these differences. Figure 3a shows children diagnosed with ADHD rise more times from the seat during the session, with an average of approximately 8 times. In contrast, children with typical development get up an average of 3.2 times. Figure 3b shows information about the time it takes to organize both the desktop and the tasks during the session. Times are measured in minutes. ADHD children take an average of 12.6 min while normally developed children take approximately 6.9 min. In Fig. 3c, we see the relationship between the time spent distracted during the session and the number of sudden movements that have been detected. As expected, the more movements detected, the greater the distraction time.

Furthermore, Fig. 3d shows that children with ADHD are more likely to spend more time distracted, with an average of approximately 12.1 min. On the other hand, children with typical development are distracted an average of 5 min during the session. Therefore, we see that the more time a child spends distracted, the more likely it is that they have ADHD. It can be seen that the more time distracted is spent, the more likely it is to observe sudden movements, indicating it is more likely to have ADHD.

This theoretical data has been modified to obtain a curve that shows the possible improvement in the total time to carry out the session, which these children can have while using the assistant robot. In Fig. 4, the images corresponding to identifiers a and c refer to a boy with ADHD and a girl with ADHD, respectively. In contrast, b and d refer to a boy and a girl with typical development, respectively. All four children are the same

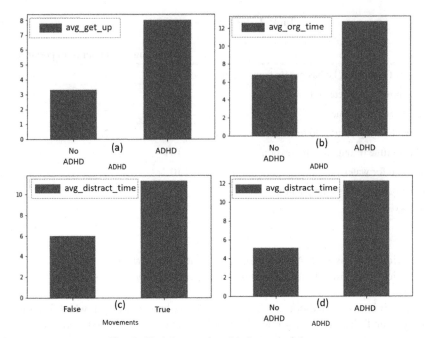

Fig. 3. Training results with theoretical data.

age, and all graphs collect data from sessions conducted over 10 business days. As we can see, children who have a typical development, Fig. 4b and d, present an evolution curve with more abrupt decreases and whose maximum does not exceed 66 min, which refers to the total time that the session lasted. This indicates that the longer they are working with the robot, the better their results will be, and the better (shorter) the duration of homework.

In contrast, children with ADHD, Figs. 4a and c, show graphs whose time difference between days is not relevant. In the case of the child with ADHD, Fig. 4a, the total time difference is not very high and varies between 60 and 72 min, maintaining an almost constant line during the last five sessions. In the case of the girl with ADHD, Fig. 4c, the times vary between 56 and 70 min, with the shortest times occurring on the last days of working with the robot. All these times may depend on other factors such as the child's mood.

3.3 Data Exploration with AutoML

From the new AutoML Tables tool offered by GCP, a complete machine learning model can be prepared in which future predictions are obtained from past data. AutoML requires that there be at least 1,000 rows in the dataset and that each class has at least 100 rows. In our case it is a binary classification problem, the prediction will have to classify a set of values in a given category. As previously indicated, there will be 526 data rows from one class (ADHD) and 520 data rows from the other (not ADHD). For this project, 32

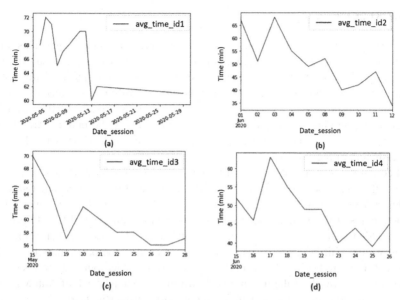

Fig. 4. Predictions about the evolution of the treatment.

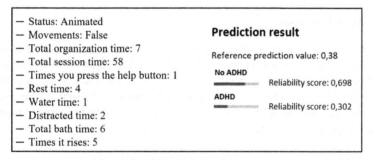

— Status: Animated
— Movements: False
— Total organization time: 7
— Total session time: 58
— Times you press the help button: 1
— Rest time: 4
— Water time: 1
— Distracted time: 2
— Total bath time: 6
— Times it rises: 5

Prediction result

Reference prediction value: 0,38

No ADHD
Reliability score: 0,698

ADHD
Reliability score: 0,302

Fig. 5. The first prediction of the reliability of ADHD according to the entered data.

attributes have been considered. Therefore, enough rows are generated to guarantee a good implementation of the model.

To carry out feature engineering, the data is classified according to its typology: numerical, categorical, or timestamp. Also, the data is purged, indicating whether null values are supported. On the other hand, is a binary classification model. The column "ADHD" has been selected as the objective column so that AutoML assigns the training data with the prediction that is sought. After feature engineering is done, AutoML will segment the dataset into three partitions: a training dataset (80% of the total), a validation set (10%), and another test set (10%).

3.4 ML Model Training

When starting the training, the application asks us to enter a training budget. This refers to the number of hours it takes for training. In this project, as there are less than 100,000 rows in the database, the budget is a value between 1 and 3 h. Another piece of information to indicate is the metric with which we want the ML algorithm to optimize the model. In the case of this project, the optimization objective can be achieved with the parameter receiver operating characteristic (ROC) curve, which is why the option "Area below the receiver operating characteristic curve" has been selected, which will allow the distinguishment of the classes.

All columns except those that can filter target information have been selected. The attributes that have been considered coincide with the attributes that are related to the relevant characteristics. Those attributes are movements, total_time_organization, help_button, rest, time_water, time_distracted, total_time_ban, times_lift. Additionally, we have added status and total_session_time attributes. However, in each training, a different weight will be given to each attribute. After all these parameters have been established, training begins. The training that we have carried out did not take more than an hour. The result of the training is shown in the "Models" tab of AutoML. The first model created with the theoretical dataset, imported from BigQuery, gives a perfect result, which will be analyzed in detail in the Results chapter.

3.5 ML Model Analysis

The post-training step is evaluation. AutoML also provides functionalities to achieve this. For the evaluation, the data segment that has been created with 10% of the total base will be used. With this segment, comparing it with the training data segment, the evaluation is performed. The process will be done automatically so that when we enter the tab "Evaluate" we will see the results. The evaluation will be in charge of measuring the precision, performance, and quality of the created model [10].

- The area below the ROC curve. It is a value between 0 and 1.
- The area below the Precision-Recall (PR) curve. It is a value between 0 and 1.
- Accuracy. It measures the total number of correct predictions that have been made.
- Logarithmic loss. This refers to the entropy that has been entered into the model. It is a value between zero and infinity. The lower, the better the performance.
- True positive rate. Refers to the number of correct predictions.
- False-positive rate. This refers to the number of predictions that have been classified into a class but do not belong to it.

Other metrics offered by AutoML for model evaluation are the confusion matrix and the graph with the attributes ordered from highest to lowest importance. The more impact the attribute has on prediction, the greater is the importance. This weight changes with each workout.

3.6 Predictions

On the other hand, the AutoML tool offers the necessary functionalities to test and analyze a model. For this, it is necessary to implement the model and thus be able to perform the online prediction functionality. These online predictions consist of entering a data line with the attributes that we specify manually, obtaining the expected diagnostic result for that child with the corresponding data. Deploying a model also consumes node time and can take up to half an hour. It is important that when the appropriate predictions with the model finish, the deployment is being stopped as well to not invoice more time than used.

In the case of Fig. 6, several values have been entered for which the model has given a probability of 0.722 that the child does not have ADHD, as well as a probability of 0.278 that it has ADHD. Furthermore, for the analysis of the prediction, a percentage of importance has been generated for each characteristic. What should be attempted is that these percentages match the theoretical importance that we have established. In the Results chapter, we will evaluate and analyze the different models that we have trained and developed.

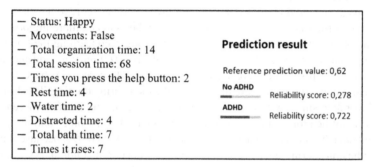

Fig. 6. A second prediction of the reliability of ADHD according to the entered data.

4 Results

This chapter describes the results obtained in the different training tests that have been carried out until obtaining the most suitable model. Based on the Google Cloud Platform, a machine learning model has been developed to detect which pattern children with ADHD meet. The results that have been obtained in the training sessions have always been in perfect alignment with the correct answers and the diagnostic correspondence to the data. This is because the database used corresponds to synthetic data. This data was obtained based on studies and averages of duration times, being agreed on by a therapist. The algorithm associates the values to a certain pattern, always showing a 100% success. When real data is available, we will only have to feed our algorithm with this data and run the model to observe the behavior obtained. The first model has been created with the ROC curve precision assessment tool. The result of the area below the curve is 1, which implies that the precision is 100%, without errors, with a perfect assignment of values by the model. The training we have carried out has a preparation cost of no more than 0.98 node hours.

The more attributes we introduce to train a model, the higher will be the precision and the greater the probability of success will be made by the prediction. We could consider this as a favorable and even perfect result. However, when we have real results, many of them will likely introduce errors because they are null or incorrect, causing the prediction probability to decrease. To make predictions online, this model is displayed and the data we want to carry out the tests with is entered. The following data has been entered:

With this data (Fig. 5), it is expected that the result obtained will classify the child as a child with typical development since the times are low and no sudden movements have been detected. The prediction that is obtained is the expected one. With a probability of 0.698, the child will be classified without ADHD, and with a probability of 0.302, it will be classified with ADHD. If we make another prediction, but with higher time data and without sudden movements, we should expect a result that classifies it as ADHD, since high organization and distraction times should be associated with the diagnosis of ADHD. The data that has been entered is:

With this data, a prediction is obtained that gives a higher score to the classification with ADHD. Furthermore, each of the attributes can be assigned more important when making the prediction. In this case, the important changes concerning the training and greater importance are given to the value of total organization time and the number of times the child rose. The weights refer to the loss of scores who have lost those characteristics concerning the score that was established during training. This last model is more favorable, since, with fewer characteristics to evaluate, it offers more realistic diagnostic identification results. It is always important that the other option, in which the entered data, has not been classified as a score greater than 0.099, because if not, we would not be considering the possible exceptions that occur in children. For example, a child who makes sudden movements but takes a short time to get organized does not have ADHD. The model must take this into account, even if higher scores are still associated with ADHD.

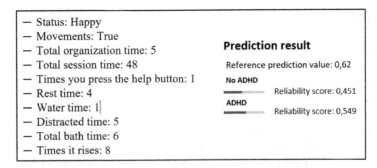

Fig. 7. Third prediction of the reliability of ADHD according to the entered data

The value with the highest weight has been the number of times it is raised, (0.158). The weighting for the attributes of detected movements and organization time was − 0.001 and −0.167, respectively (Fig. 7).

5 Conclusions

The development of this project shows us an algorithm to identify characteristic patterns that children diagnosed with ADHD present at the time of carrying out their school activities. The information generated will serve the therapist as an additional normative test. The information provided indicates how the child reacts and influences the child at the same time to behave in a certain way. Also, it offers the advantage of motivating the child when studying. This way long-term positive results are being assumed since the child will acquire an order and an affinity to do homework.

To achieve this, it is necessary to deploy an intelligent architecture in the robot, allowing the therapist and the parents to observe and receive reports about the child's behavior. From GCP any model can be deployed, without limitations in storage or capacity. The machine learning mechanism has been selected using a binary classification to display the model. Therefore, from the platform, a model has been created, developed, and trained from an algorithm that is already implemented in the platform itself. It is only necessary to include the data and the weight indications of the attributes of the database. The rest oversees the platform.

The results that have been obtained differ from reality. Having used data based on theoretical studies and not on practical tests of the robot with a child, the results obtained are almost perfect, differing only in logistical loss.

However, by using fewer attributes in training and its subsequent prediction, it has been proven that results are more consistent with reality since they can consider more cases. This results from percentages of probabilities greater than 10% (0.1) to each of the classes that have been associated. Despite the results, the system meets the stated objectives.

For the development of the evolution curves of the different children, it would be advisable to use the robot for a month (20 business days), to obtain more random data and to predict behavior. Therefore, it has been verified that more amounts of data would be needed, and, above all, it must be data obtained from children while using the robot (Atent@), real-time data. Also, this project will help conduct future research in the diagnosis of ADHD.

In general, the IoT is gaining more presence in many areas of our lives. However, as the IoT evolves, it is necessary to simultaneously improve and implement security in the different devices that make up this technology. This project manages large amounts of data, which must be protected with the different existing mechanisms to avoid possible cyberattacks. Whenever the amount of data that a device manages is increased, we will increase the vulnerability to suffering a cyber-attack. The vulnerability is present before exporting data to the cloud platform.

That is why one of the future jobs, and which is essential for this robot, would be the implementation of a security system that encrypts the data and manages it securely before entering it on the cloud platform. It may also be interesting to create a visual web interface that shows and collects all the information from all the sessions, with graphs of the evolution of the diagnosis. This interface must be interactive and comprehensive for the therapist.

References

1. Polanczyk, G., De Lima, M.S., Horta, B.L., Biederman, J., Rohde, L.A.: The worldwide prevalence of ADHD: a systematic review and metaregression analysis. Am. J. Psychiatry **164**(6), 942–948 (2007)
2. Guha, M.: Diagnostic and statistical manual of mental disorders: DSM-5. Reference Reviews (2014)
3. Pujol, B.M., Amador, J.A.: Guía práctica para educadores: el alumno con TDAH: Trastorno por Déficit de Atención con o sin Hiperactividad. Mayo (2006)
4. Puig, C., Gómez, C.B.: Estrategias Para Entender Y Ayudar a Ninos Con Trastorno Por Deficit De Atencion Con O Sin Hiperactividad/Strategies to Understand and Help Children with ADD and Hyperactivity. Grupo Planeta (GBS) (2006)
5. Camarero, J.M.: Aisoy Robotics: Robots con cabeza… y corazón. Inversión: el semanario líder de bolsa, economía y gestión de patrimonios **2013**(915), 66 (2013)
6. Amado, C.P.: Ayuda al diagnóstico de TDAH en la infancia mediante técnicas de procesado de señal y aprendizaje (2019)
7. Sanchez, R.E.A., Pinzón, L.D.J., Luna, J.A.G.: Búsqueda de la ruta óptima mediante los algoritmos: genético y dijkstra utilizando mapas de visibilidad. Scientia et technica. **2**(51), 107–112 (2012)
8. Spachos, D., Chifari, A., Chiazzese, G., Merlo, G., Doherty, G., Bamidis, P.: WHAAM: a mobile application for ubiquitous monitoring of ADHD behaviors. In: 2014 International Conference on Interactive Mobile Communication Technologies and Learning (IMCL2014), pp. 305–309. IEEE (2014)
9. Berrezueta-Guzman, J., Pau, I., Martín-Ruiz, M.-L., Máximo-Bocanegra, N.: Smart-home environment to support homework activities for children. IEEE Access (2020)
10. Lee, D.J.L., Macke, S., Xin, D., Lee, A., Huang, S., Parameswaran, A.G.: A human-in-the-loop perspective on AutoML: milestones and the road ahead. IEEE Data Eng. Bull. **42**(2), 59–70 (2019)

An Expert System to Design Intervention Strategies for Children with Disabilities in Multi-Sensory Stimulation Environments

J. Llanes-Coronel[1], K. Pucha-Ortíz[1], V. Robles-Bykbaev[1(✉)] [ID],
P. Carrera-Hidalgo[2], and E. O. Zhimnay-Valverde[3]

[1] GI-IATa, Cátedra UNESCO Tecnologías de apoyo para la Inclusión Educativa,
Universidad Politécnica Salesiana, Cuenca, Ecuador
{kpucha,jllanes}@est.ups.edu.ec, vrobles@ups.edu.ec
[2] Ecosistema de Investigación, Innovación y Emprendimiento, Universidad
Politécnica Salesiana, Cuenca, Ecuador
pcarrera@ups.edu.ec
[3] Fundación HOPE, Cuenca, Ecuador
oswy9912@outlook.com

Abstract. The Multi-Sensory Environments (MSEs) have the objective of improving the development of thought, intelligence, and social skills of children with and without disabilities. However, in developing countries, due to the lack of personnel and resources, the process of designing intervention plans for children with disabilities in MSEs is carried out from an empirical perspective. For these reasons, in this paper, we present a system that relies on a multi-sensory environment consisting of 7 rehabilitation modules and an expert system to automatically determine which rehabilitation activities are appropriate for children with disabilities. To this aim, the expert system uses a model based on decision trees regressors with multi-outputs and suggests a therapy plan selecting pairs activity-module (from a total of 7 modules). We tested the system with a group of experts using three criteria: completeness of the plan, coherence (activities versus child's profile), and applicability (relation between activities and each module). Currently, the system can suggest plans for children with different disabilities such as Infantile Cerebral Palsy (ICP), autism, hypogenesis of the corpus callosum, intellectual disability, epilepsy, and hydranencephaly.

Keywords: Multi-Sensory Environments · Multi-output decision tree regressor · Children with disabilities

1 Introduction

According to the World Report on Disability carried out by the World Health Organization (WHO) and the World Bank (WB) [1] more than a billion people

© Springer Nature Switzerland AG 2020
G. Rodriguez Morales et al. (Eds.): TICEC 2020, CCIS 1307, pp. 51–63, 2020.
https://doi.org/10.1007/978-3-030-62833-8_5

live worldwide with some form of disability and almost 200 million experience considerable difficulties in their operation. The assessment raise concern as the numbers are increasing showing that there is an adequate lack of programs for rehabilitation, care and therapy. In Ecuador, the National Council for Equality of Disabilities (CONADIS, Spanish acronym) points out that 485,325 people registered, suffer physical, hearing, intellectual, psychological, visual and/or language disabilities [4]. Within this group there is a significant population of children and young people who suffer from problems related to communication and language.

In developing countries, it is common for a therapist or expert in special education to be in charge of several activities more than providing rehabilitation services for children with disabilities or special educational needs. In this line, this professional must prepare reports, design therapy plans, schedule appointments for diagnosis/intervention sessions, among many others. Several studies have provided evidence that a decision-support system is useful for decreasing the time required by therapists during the diagnosis, planning, and intervention stages on patients with disabilities [10–12].

In the same line, the review of the state of the art allowed verifying that several Assistive Technologies (AT) that seek to help in the rehabilitation, inclusion and educational support for these people have been developed. However, not all the tools developed have an intelligent scheme that provides an efficient support and recommendations to therapists and special education professionals. For this reason, this article presents an expert system to design intervention strategies for children with disabilities in MSEs for the HOPE foundation (Original Children Special Parents), in the city of Cuenca, Ecuador. The proposal presents on one hand, an approach that promotes the use of independent modules controlled by a central module for therapy activities, on the other hand, a system capable of providing support, automatically proposing new exercises and recording the activities carried out by users of the room in the following areas:

- Stimulation of sense perceptions.
- Speech stimulation.
- Playful learning and art.

In order to carry out activities and tasks mentioned above, a rule-based approach is used to organize the therapy sessions according to the areas to be stimulated. In this means, given a specific profile of the patient, the rule estimates the percentage of time that each of the modules of the system must be worked on, in the three areas sense perceptions, stimulation of speech and playful learning and art.

To this aim, we designed and built a MSE consisting of the following modules and functionalities:

- A big dice that changes the light's color of the MSE according to each face.
- A pictogram panel to work in semantic fields.
- A lighted piano to stimulate the children's auditory system.
- Two colored tubes to play games similar to "Simon says", and perform visual perception activities.

- A customized version of a Standard Volume Indicator (VU Meter) to stimulate voice and speech exercises for children.
- A central control module to store children's activities and therapy results.

The rest of the paper is organized as follows. In Sect. 2, we present some relevant proposals related to special education. The system's general architecture as well as the expert system, are described in Sect. 3. In Sect. 4, we show the results and analyze them. Conclusion and future work are described in Sect. 5.

2 Related Work

The multi-sensory stimulation environments or Snoezelen rooms have a wide range of applications in the rehabilitation are of patients with special educational needs or health problems. Some researches have successfully used this type of tool to promote the improvement of an emotional state caused by strokes, such as the case presented in [6]. The authors describe the effects of performing therapies on snoezelen on the emotional state of people; the research was conducted on veterans of the Vietnam war who had brain injury problems caused by exposure to defoliants, in this case, snoezelen therapies had a positive impact on the emotional stability of the person.

On the other hand, in [3] the authors describe an exploratory study where the MSE a tool for delivering playful content for children with disabilities. This research aims to document the use of multisensory stimulation environments with the use of games and playful activities from a professional perspective. It proposes therapeutic activities for children with disabilities; open interviews were carried out with 12 professionals who work in multisensory stimulation environments. The data suggests that multisensory stimulation environments are used as versatile spaces, considered and explored by professionals interviewed for their playful potential. This result brings attention to the interest in multisensory environments, particularly for the play area in Occupational Therapy, in which the use of the computer-mediated play experience is a recognized possibility [3].

In the older adults area, [7] presents a study to determine the effect of MSEs on cognitive disorders and the quality of life of patients with Alzheimer's disease. This study is aimed to determine the effect of multisensory stimulation on cognitive state and quality of life of patients with Alzheimer's disease. In this quasi-experimental research plan, the samples were divided into experimental and control groups; both were tested three times: before, during, and after the intervention. Ninety patients with Alzheimer's disease were recruited using the available sampling technique, and the groups were established using the random allocation method. Data was collected using a demographic questionnaire, a geriatric quality of life questionnaire, and a mini-mental state examination (MMSE). As a result, it was found that multisensory stimulation can be a good method in stabilizing the signs and symptoms of patients with Alzheimer's dementia, therefore improving their quality of life [7]. In a similar research field, the authors explore in [8] the multisensory systems for virtual therapy of people with Alzheimer's. This project develops a prototype of a multisensory virtual therapy system aimed at the treatment and evaluation of a person with Alzheimer's Disease (AD) in its initial phase, this disease being a type of dementia that affects a part of the population of older adults aged between 65 and over, the main diagnosis is memory loss in both the short and long term, causing the person to be unable to communicate or to be excluded from their daily activities. For this reason, this project is intended for the treatment and evaluation of the different abilities that AD affects in a person, as a result of which the use of multisensory therapy with virtual reality glasses for patients with AD helps to improve the concentration of a person when playing the games since being immersed avoids unnecessary distractions from the environment, giving the patient more peace of mind when choosing what to do within each application [8].

In the field of Autism treatment, a group of students developed the application "SensoryPaint". It is an interactive surface that manages to generate visual and auditory feedback of their body movements since children with Autism have sensory disorders that limit their ability in their movements. Because of their disease they experience atypical movements used by them as compensatory movements. The objective was to explore how tangible computation can help children in their body awareness that they need in their sensory therapies. To assess the impact of using SensoryPaint on sensory therapies for children with autism, the system was integrated into typical sensory therapies for 4 children with autism. The results showed that an interaction model that takes into account body movements and interactive surfaces increases the child's attention on their body movements, allowing children to focus on their body, improving sensory skills and promoting socialization, in comparison with traditional body awareness therapies [14].

Finally, a research related to the transition to adult life with the support of MSEs is described by [2]. The authors describe how this tool works in a special education center, noting its importance, the elements it contains and how it can be worked on with students from Early Childhood Education, Compulsory Basic Education (EBO) and Transition to Adult Life between the ages of 3 and 21 years and with associated multiple deficiencies [2]. The results show great improvements in communication, expression, and physical and emotional well-being are generated since the objective of the rooms is to be able to potentiate the aforementioned activities.

3   General System Architecture

As can be seen in Fig. 1., our system is organized into 4 layers and several modules. With this approach, we can change the functionality of any module without affecting other modules or layers. The main elements of the system are described below:

The MSE consists of six modules aimed at providing rehabilitation activities to develop and stimulate the visuomotor coordination and the visual perception, to improve the learning of semantic fields and sequencing, and improve the control of voice volume. Below we describe the main characteristics of each module.

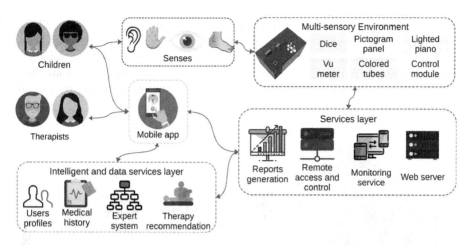

Fig. 1. The main layers and modules that are part of the developed system.

The **pictogram panel** allows children to learn associations of idea/concept-image pairs. At the same time, during the therapy, they must select a pictogram (pressing an illuminated button that contains the image) according to the requested concept. To achieve this objective, each child must determine the position of the pictogram and coordinate how to press it to reach the goal. Through the mobile application (control module), the therapists can establish which pictograms show and which belong to the requested command.

The **dice** is a module that was built with two objectives. The first one is to stimulate children's gross motor skills. When a child throws the dice, the illumination of the MSE will change according to the color represented in the die's face. The second objective is to teach children how to associate two colors (environment and dice's color).

The **lighted piano** allows therapists to provide children with exercises to stimulate the auditory, visual, and gross motor skills. The control module can be used during therapies to change the colors of each piano key. Similarly, the **colored tubes** can be used to work in sequencing and colors' perception. Each tube will be illuminated with different colors (using RGB LEDs) using different sequences. For example, the module lights on the tubes in this order 1st, 1st, 2nd, and 3rd. The child must repeat the sequence pushing a button associated with each tube.

The **VU Meter** is a module that provides a visual response to the patient's volume of his/her voice. For each volume level, the VU Meter will activate a colored cell. In the same way, the **control module** has a function to adjust the colors of each cell of this module. Another functionality of the control module is providing games and exercises to be performed with or without the modules of the MSE.

As can be seen in Fig. 2, there are presented four pictures of some modules of the MSE built. The top-left image is a 3D diagram that shows the modules' disposition in the physical space of the HOPE Foundation. The top-right photo depicts the lighted piano and how therapists added pictograms to each of its keys. The bottom-left image shows a child using the VU Meter to perform rehabilitation exercises to improve the control of the voice volume. In the bottom-right picture, we can see how a therapist introduces the pictogram panel to a child that will be using it for the first time.

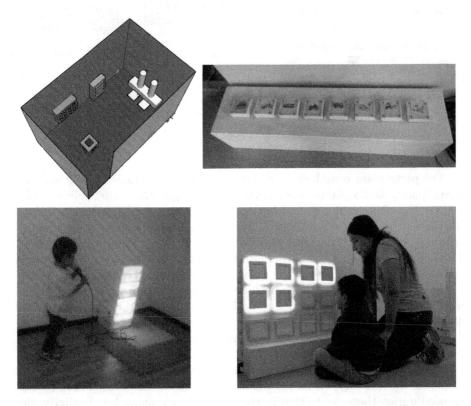

Fig. 2. Some of the elements of the MSE. The 3D model of the general disposition of the MSE's modules (top-left diagram), the lighted piano built (top-right picture), a child using the VU Meter module (bottom-left image), and how a therapist works with a patient in the pictogram panel (bottom-right pic).

The **services layer** provides several functionalities to facilitate the work of therapists. Some examples of these services are the following: a) a module to generate reports, allowing summarizing the results of therapies, the interaction patient-module, and his/her progress in the different areas; b) an interface to remotely configure any module according to patients needs (colors, exercise difficulty level, et.); c) a monitoring interface that shows the interaction process online; d) a web server that stores all information related with the intervention process.

3.1 The Expert System Module

The expert system helps therapists and practitioners choosing which exercises could be carried out in specific modules of the MSE. Similarly, this module is useful to train students and interns of occupational therapy, special education, and other related careers. In this section, we describe the first development stage of the system that can handle children's profiles with one or more of the diagnoses depicted in Table 1. The diagnosis indicated with * refers to a condition where the expert system analyzes two concomitant disabilities. For each disability, we provide the International Classification of Diseases, 11th Revision codes (to avoid ambiguities in diagnosis) [13].

Table 1. Disabilities that the expert system can handle to provide intervention strategies.

Disability	ICD-11 Code	Disability	ICD-11 Code
Autism spectrum disorder	6A02	Mental, behavioural or neurodevelopmental disorders, unspecified	6E8Z
Paralytic symptoms & Disorders of intellectual development*	——	Disorders of intellectual development	6A00
Epilepsy due to structural or metabolic conditions or diseases	8A60	Other specified epilepsy or seizures	8A6Y
Dissociative neurological symptom disorder, with paresis or weakness	6B60.6	Hydranencephaly	LA05.62
Corpus callosum agenesis	LA05.3	Cerebral Palsy	——
Lennox-Gastaut syndrome	8A62.1	Diseases of the visual system	09

On the other hand, the experts of the HOPE Foundation defined 32 activities that can be carried out using the different modules of the MSE. Table 2 shows the activities that the therapists must work with children according to their profiles.

On this base, our expert system relies on a model based on two granularity levels. In the first one, the system determines in general terms which activities are appropriate for each patient according to the presence of specific disabilities. To this aim, the reasoning module uses an approach to deal with Multi-Output Dependence Learning (MODL) problems has is detailed in [5,9]. The Eq. 1 describes the first granularity level given the following

Table 2. The 32 rehabilitation that are activities related to the different modules of the MSE.

ID	Activity	ID	Activity
ES1	Motor sensory integration techniques	ES2	Identification and color recognition
ES3	Fruits, animals recognition	ES4	Psychomotor precision exercises
ES5	Sequences with pictograms for AVD	ES6	Sensory integration in the dark room
ES7	Application of various sensory stimuli	ES8	Active mobilization
ES9	Body massage, aromatherapy, music Therapy	ES10	Desensitization exercises to body contact
ES11	Track simple rhythmic patterns	ES12	Perception of light, textures, temperatures stimuli
ES13	Application of various sensory stimuli in the dark room	ES14	Body massages
ES15	aromatherapy	ES16	Music therapy
ES17	Active body mobilization	ES18	Stretching exercises
ES19	Application of various sensory stimuli	ES20	Body self-awareness
ES21	Search and follow different sounds	ES22	Multisensory discrimination
ES23	Identification and recognition of colors and geometric figures	ES24	Recognition of fruits, animals, means of transport, body parts
ES25	Pictogram identification	ES26	Attention-concentration exercises
ES27	Sphincter control techniques	ES28	Perception of various visual stimuli
ES29	Discrimination of sounds	ES30	Tactile scanning, fingerprint painting
ES31	Body contact desensitization exercises	ES32	Multisensory discrimination

sets: a) patient's profile (p), b) activities $\mathcal{A}$ (Table 2), c) the MSE's modules $(\mathcal{M} = \{0 = \text{No-module}, 1 = \text{pictogram panel}, 2 = \text{dice - lights}, 3 = \text{VU Meter}, 4 = \text{colored tubes}, 5 = \text{lighted piano}, 6 = \text{control module/sounds}\})$, and d) the disabilities $\mathcal{D}$ (Table 1):

$$\mathcal{R} = \bigcup_{i=1}^{T} \left\{ (C(p), m_i, a_i) \,\middle|\, a_i \subset \mathcal{A} \wedge k \in [1,3] \wedge m_i \in \mathcal{M} \wedge C(p) \in \binom{\mathcal{D}}{k} \right\} \quad (1)$$

where:

- $\binom{\mathcal{D}}{k}$ represents the combinations (comorbidities) of the disabilities depicted in Table 1, according to the child's profile (p), and subject to:

$$C_p \ is \begin{cases} \text{accepted,} & \text{if } C_p \in \text{Medical History} \vee constraint(C_p) == TRUE \\ \text{rejected,} & \text{otherwise} \end{cases}$$

$$(2)$$

- The rule verifies if comorbidity $C(p)$ is in the Medical History (described above). However, if this does not occur, the expert system determines if the comorbidity has a sense from the medical viewpoint through the function $constraint(C(p))$. This function relies on several rules; for example, only 7% of children with Cerebral Palsy (CP) present autism.
- T represents the total of educational activities $\mathcal{A}$ (Table 2). It is important to note that each activity can be performed only in one module, therefore, the module (m_i) and the activity (a_i) share the index i.

The second level of granularity (currently under development), uses the general activities and modules of the MSE selected in the previous stage to determine more specific variables according to patient's profile:

- The therapy time and exercises difficulty level in accordance with the children's intellectual development.
- The number of weekly repetitions required to get better results in both learning and rehabilitation processes.
- A set of reinforcement activities that must be done at home with parents' support and supervision.

4   Experiments and Preliminary Validation

To determine the real feasibility of the system, we have worked during two months period with four experts of the HOPE Foundation. They have conducted several therapy sessions in the MSE with children with disabilities described in Table 1.

The experts have between 4 and 8 years (SD = 1.89) of experience working in the following areas: early education, early intervention, and physical therapy. The volunteers have ages between 25 and 40 years (SD = 6.48) and work in the HOPE Foundation, attending 14 children with percentages of disabilities between 40% and 90%.

To train the expert system, we worked with the profiles of the 30 children attending the HOPE Foundation. After that, we asked the system to generate new 14 intervention plans for the children in charge of the four volunteers described above. The system generated two different plans (using two levels of depth for the tree: 15 and 30, respectively). We used the following criteria to evaluate each plan:

- **Completeness:** This criterion is used to determine if a plan considers an appropriate number of modules of the MSE to be used during the therapy session, considering the patient's profile.

- **Applicability:** This criterion allows determining if a plan contains appropriate guidelines of which modules can be used by a child during therapy. For example, a patient with cerebral palsy with 90% of disability can't use some modules that required visuomotor coordination.
- **Coherence:** This criterion is used to evaluate if a module selected for therapy by the expert system, has an adequate difficulty level for a patient with a specific disability. For example, a patient with 70% of intellectual disability could not understand complex exercises to be carried out in the pictogram panel but can use the VU Meter module without problems.

As can be seen in Fig. 3, the expert system has reached excellent results for autism and cerebral palsy. The first test was performed using the 15 tree depth, whereas the second test used 30, for this last one was possible to improve the applicability and coherence criteria for these disabilities.

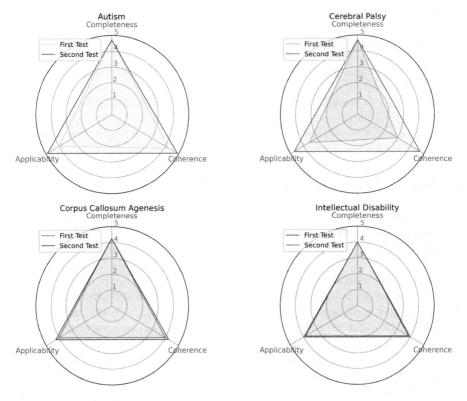

Fig. 3. Results obtained by the expert system according to the evaluation criteria of the HOPE Foundation's experts for the following disabilities: autism, cerebral palsy, corpus callosum agenesis, and intellectual disability.

However, in the case of corpus callosum agenesis and intellectual disability, the results obtained in the two tests were very similar. This situation is produced due to the complexity of these two disabilities (especially when they are present with other pathologies).

Figure 4 shows the results achieved by the expert system for the other three disabilities. For epilepsy due to structural or metabolic conditions or diseases and hydranencephaly, the results are similar to the two different depth levels used in the trees. For the disability other epilepsy or seizures, the system reaches a significant improvement (gaining 1 point in applicability and coherence criteria).

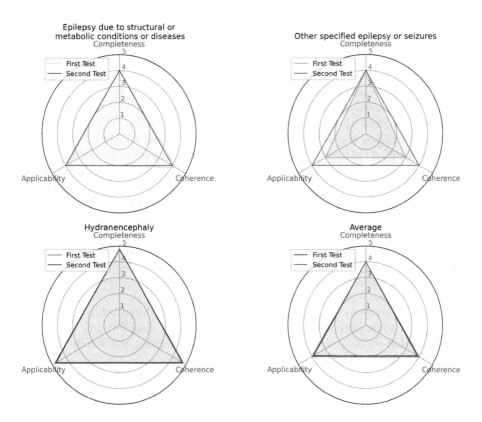

Fig. 4. Results obtained by the expert system according to the evaluation criteria of the HOPE Foundation's experts for the following disabilities: epilepsy due to structural or metabolic conditions or diseases, other specified epilepsy seizures, and hydranencephaly. The last plot shows the average precision of the system.

The importance of the parameters used to train and test the multi-output regressor tree is coherent with the feedback and suggestions provided by the experts. How it can be seen below, three disabilities have no relevance when the decision tree makes the inference:

- Autism (0.518), mental, behavioral or neurodevelopmental disorders, unspecified (0.0755), paralytic symptoms & disorders of intellectual development

(0), disorders of intellectual development (0.0037), epilepsy due to structural or metabolic conditions or diseases (0.0644), other specified epilepsy or seizures (0.0429), dissociative neurological symptom disorder, with paresis or weaknesses (0), hydranencephaly (0.0152), corpus callosum agenesis (0.135), cerebral palsy (0.135), Lennox-Gastaut syndrome (0), diseases of the visual system (0).

5 Conclusions

Undoubtedly, design and develop tools for children with disabilities is an interdisciplinary work that requires the involvement of professionals from various fields such as special education, health, psychology, speech therapy, medicine, computer science, and electronics.

As can be shown in this paper, the outcome of the expert system is encouraging as they show the improvement in patient scores. Also, the result shows that best therapies are given with durations of 15, 30 and 45 min.

It was verified that the recommender system can suggest to the therapist the possible therapies and its duration, so it can be a positive supporting decision making tool to choose the therapy that better suits the patient with disability.

The results obtained with this study show that is possible to automate several activities related to MSEs, with the aim to provide a better service to patients with several kinds of disabilities. In the same way, the use of expert systems allows reducing significatively the time needed to conduct several activities related to therapy planning, assessment, and report generation.

As lines of future work, we propose the following ones:

- To have a communication structure able to monitor children behavior (despite their age, some patients with autism or intellectual disability are not aware of how dangerous are some actions, for example, crossing the streets without paying attention, talking with strange people, etc.).
- To automatically adapt educational contents to each patient using virtual or robotic intermediaries for improving the interaction flow in teaching-learning process.

Acknowledgments. The authors express their gratitude to the UNESCO Chair on Support technologies for Educational Inclusion, to the Research Group on Artificial Intelligence and Assistive Technologies (GI-IATa) and to the Universidad Politécnica Salesiana for the support and financing given to the project "Sistemas Inteligentes de Soporte a la Educación Especial (SINSAE v5)".

References

1. Bickenbach, J.: The world report on disability. Disabil. Soc. **26**(5), 655–658 (2011)
2. Carbajo Vélez, M.d.C.: La sala de estimulación multisensorial. Tabanque: Revista pedagógica (27), 155–172 (2014)

3. Castelhano, N., Silva, F., Rezende, M., Roque, L., Magalhães, L.: Ludic content in multisensory stimulation environments: an exploratory study about practice in portugal. Occup. Ther. Int. **20**(3), 134–143 (2013)
4. Consejo Nacional para la Igualdad de Discapacidades (CONADIS): Estadística de personas con discapacidad (2020). https://www.consejodiscapacidades.gob.ec/estadisticas-de-discapacidad/. Accessed 1 July 2020
5. Jog, A., Carass, A., Pham, D.L., Prince, J.L.: Multi-output decision trees for lesion segmentation in multiple sclerosis. In: Medical Imaging 2015: Image Processing, vol. 9413, p. 94131C. International Society for Optics and Photonics (2015)
6. Lee, S.K., Lee, S.Y., Kim, M.K.: Snoezelen to promote improved emotional status in stroke caused by defoliat exposure in the Vietnam war: case study (2013)
7. Mahboubinia, M., Dalvandi, A., Nourozi, K., Mahmoudi, N., Sadat Safavi, S., Hosseinzadeh, S.: The effect of multi sensory stimulation (MSS) on cognitive disturbances and quality of life of male patients with Alzheimer's disease. Iran. Rehabil. J. **10**(1), 50–55 (2012)
8. Medina, J., Encalada, P.: Sistema multisensorial para terapia virtual de personas con alzheimer (2018). http://192.188.46.193/. Accessed 1 July 2020
9. Morris, R.G., Martinez, T., Smith, M.R.: A hierarchical multi-output nearest neighbor model for multi-output dependence learning. arXiv preprint arXiv:1410.4777 (2014)
10. Robles-Bykbaev, V., López-Nores, M., García-Duque, J., Pazos-Arias, J.J., Arévalo-Lucero, D.: Evaluation of an expert system for the generation of speech and language therapy plans. JMIR Med. Inform. **4**(3), e23 (2016)
11. Robles-Bykbaev, V.E., López-Nores, M., Pazos-Arias, J.J., Arévalo-Lucero, D.: SPELTA: an expert system to generate therapy plans for speech and language disorders. Expert Syst. Appl. **42**(21), 7641–7651 (2015)
12. Timbi-Sisalima, C., Robles-Bykbaev, V., Guiñansaca-Zhagüi, E., Capón-Albarracín, M., Ochoa-Arévalo, G.: ADACOF: una aproximación educativa basada en tic para el aprendizaje digital de la articulación del código fonético en niños con discapacidad. Perfiles educativos **37**(149), 187–202 (2015)
13. World Health Organization: The International classification of diseases: 11th revision (ICD-11). WHO Press (2020)
14. Zalapa Cardiel, C.: Cómputo tangible en apoyo en las terapias sensoriales para niños con autismo. Master's Thesis, Centro de Investigación Científica y de Educación Superior de Ensenada, Baja California, Ensenada, Baja California, México (2014)

IoT as an Alternative Way to Improve the Telemedicine Methods Against COVID-19 in Vulnerable Zones

Leslie Pozo-Guzman[1](✉) and Jonnathan Berrezueta-Guzman[2,3]

[1] Universidad Católica de Cuenca, Cuenca 010107, Ecuador
lcpozog74@est.ucacue.edu.ec
[2] Universidad Politécnica de Madrid, 28031 Madrid, Spain
s.berrezueta@alumnos.upm.es
[3] CEDIA, Cuenca 010203, Ecuador
santiago.berrezueta@cedia.org.ec

Abstract. This article presents the design, construction, and implementation of an IoT system as an alternative proposal to improve the telemedicine and telediagnosis processes of isolated COVID-19 patients in remote areas or vulnerable zones of Ecuador. This project has been developed to provide the aforementioned patients with more personalized care, enabling doctors to receive the real-time health status of the patient and allow an application of the necessary emergency protocols on time. At a technical level, this proposal combines the acquisition of biomedical data (Heart rate, body temperature, and oxygen saturation) through the implantation of non-invasive sensors into a bracelet, pre-data processing stage (Edge Computing) to optimize the network traffic, the creation of a LoRAWAN link to send the processed information and the development of a web and mobile application to illustrate information in real-time. The following sections show the design, construction, and implementation process of this system step by step. Additionally, the conducted experiments as well as the obtained results are shown, including a proposal for future usage.

Keywords: COVID-19 · IoT · Telemedicine · LoRaWAN · Cyberphysical systems · App development

1 Introduction

COVID-19 has caused serious problems such as the collapse of sanitary systems. The coronavirus pandemic has triggered economic, political, and social problems [1]. According to the latest statistics, Latin America has been drawing more general attention as the number of deaths registered by COVID-19 compared to the number of inhabitants has been noticed as being exceptional [2, 3]. Ecuador is a clear example of the strength of this virus against a poor health system or without sufficient resources to provide the necessary care to its population [4]. The relationship between the number of deaths concerning the number of inhabitants surpassed some European countries and even China.

© Springer Nature Switzerland AG 2020
G. Rodriguez Morales et al. (Eds.): TICEC 2020, CCIS 1307, pp. 64–76, 2020.
https://doi.org/10.1007/978-3-030-62833-8_6

COVID-19 has caught this South American country off guard, bringing a wave of deaths and contagion that grew fast and continues to grow [4]. The WHO fears for the social and economic well-being of Latin America and warns that the worst is yet to come [5].

During the pandemic, Ecuador was the focus of international media regarding several aspects. Most of which were related to considered mismanagement of the pandemic. This is because the health centers were unable to provide care to all those infected people who were waiting to be treated [4, 6, 7]. Among the number of infected people who increased day by day in the country, there is a group of infected patients who needed to remain isolated in their homes, but many of them were people belonging to towns far away from the bigger cities and therefore far from health centers. Ecuador is a multicultural country with concentrations of people in isolated places from the capital cities [8]. Access to health care is limited by the location of these towns. It is important to have a way of applying some telemedicine techniques to attend to an emergency presented by an isolated COVID-19 patient at their place of residence. But many of these places have the closest point of access to the internet or telephone tens of kilometers away.

In this context, the monitoring of isolated COVID-19 patients was designed. This proposed system does not depend 100% on the internet connection as it is based on the cyber-physical system developing that can read the temperature, oxygen saturation and heart rate status of the isolated patient using biomedical sensors, microcontrollers with a long-range transmitter, and show the results in near real-time through a mobile or web application.

2   Covid-19

SARS-CoV-2 is a beta-type coronavirus with a positive RNA strand causing Covid-19 disease. The virus encodes structural and accessory proteins such as S glycoproteins (essential for entry into the host cell), proteins small E-envelopes (function as ion channels), M-membrane proteins (responsible for shaping the virus membrane), and nucleocapsid N proteins (bind to the virus RNA genome) [9].

Through glycoprotein S, the virus binds to the angiotensin-converting enzyme (ACE2). It is in the epithelial cells of various tissues. This enzyme converts angiotensin I and II. Additionally, it helps the formation of secondary polypeptides with several effects such as vasoconstrictor, proinflammatory, and retention of sodium. These effects cause multisystem damage which can be observed in this disease [10].

Symptoms of infected patients are generally fever, fatigue, cough, and respiratory distress. There is evidence of the spread of the virus to the lungs, neurological system, and heart due to the high expression of ACE2 in these organs [11].

One of the recurring symptoms of Covid-19 is the presence of fever caused by SARS-Cov-2 activity because it causes the cascade of inflammation by activating pathogenic T cells. These cells initiate the release of inflammatory cytokines, IL-1, IL-6, and IFN. Besides, it activates CD14, CD16 cells, and monocytes. This cellular activation increases the production of IL-6 cytosines causing fever and cellular damage to the organs due to the great immune response. Furthermore, SARS-CoV-2 attacks T lymphocytes by infiltrating epithelial cells of the respiratory mucosa. This additionally causes negative changes as well as inflammatory response and is related to acute respiratory distress syndrome (ARDS) and septic shock [10].

Respiratory distress syndrome is the most frequent manifestation, due to the affinity of SARS-CoV-2 for ACE2 receptors. This bond is prepared by serine protease 2 (TMPRSS2). Both the ACE2 receptor and TMPRSS2 are expressed at the level of lung tissue cells, bronchial cells, and mostly in transient bronchial secretory cells. These effects massively generate the cascade of inflammation and cause cellular damage [12]. Neuronal damage caused by SARS-CoV-2 may be another cause of respiratory failure as the virus invades the brainstem that controls heart function, blood pressure, and respiration [10].

Patients also have cardiovascular manifestations due to multi-organ inflammation. Another common symptom is an acute myocardial injury caused by the acute respiratory disease that corrupts the relationship between oxygen supply and myocardial demand. Myocardial injury can lead to heart failure, and increased metabolic demand can offset the patient's pre-existing heart failure [13]. Heart failure caused by Covid-19 appears mostly in patients with cardiovascular disease due to the high expression of ACE2 in cardiomyocytes. These cells are important for the spontaneous and individual contraction of the cardiac muscle representing the contractile unit of the myocardium [14].

3   Ecuador as an Example of COVID-19 Effect Over Latin America Countries - Statistics

Ecuador has a population of around 17.08 million inhabitants throughout its territory. The health system in this South American country consists of 4165 health care establishments while taking into account public and private establishments. Which means that each

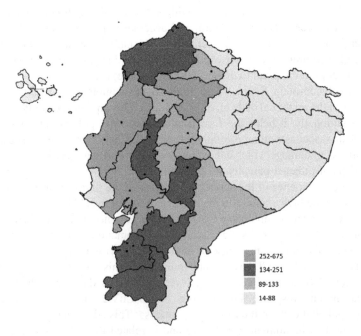

Fig. 1. Health care centers distribution.

center should serve around 4200 patients. The distribution of these centers is connected to the number of inhabitants in each province [15] (Fig. 1).

The first case registered in Ecuador was on February 29, 2020. On March 19, 2020, 260 confirmed cases and 4 deaths from Covid-19 were registered. On April 1, 2020, 2,758 cases of Covid-19 and 174 total deaths were confirmed. On May 1, 2020, 26,336 cases of Covid-19 were registered, with 2,669 total deaths. On July 9, 2020 (the last date that data was taken for this paper), there were 65,018 cases of Covid-19 and a total of 8,221 deaths [16, 17] (Figs. 2 and 3).

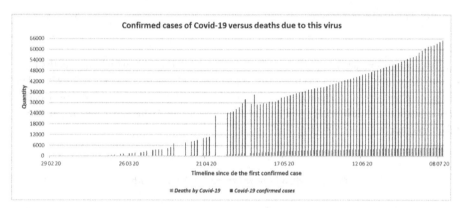

Fig. 2. Evolution of the number of confirmed cases of COVID-19 and the number of deaths caused by it.

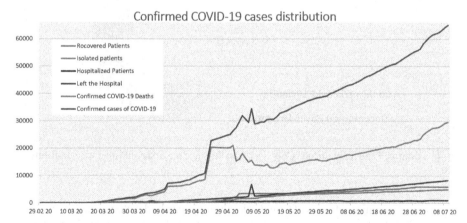

Fig. 3. Confirmed COVID-19 cases distribution since the first confirmed case.

Table 1. Statistics of the distribution of the COVID-19 cases along the time [16, 17].

Cases	February 29	March 19	April 1	May 1	July 9
Confirmed	1	260	2,758	26,336	65,018
Deaths	0	4	98	1,063	4,939
Recovered patients	0	3	301	1,913	5,900
Patients in home isolation	0	236	2,301	20,988	29,545
Hospitalized patients	0	17	301	486	957
Patients with hospital discharge	0	0	58	1,886	8,263

Two subgroups are registered in the number of total deaths, which are deaths from Covid-19, which represent 60.08% and probable deaths from Covid-19, 39.92%. The last percentage was due to the lack of resources to assist these patients in the overloaded public hospitals. Additionally, the lack of resources to apply the test to these patients is taken into account [16, 17] (Fig. 4).

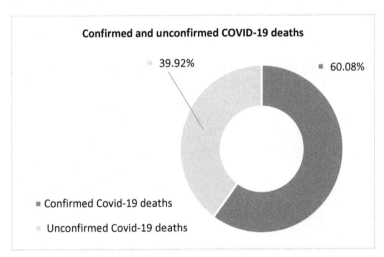

Fig. 4. Confirmed and unconfirmed COVID-19 deaths since the first confirmed case until July 9, 2020.

Among the confirmed cases of Covid-19, subgroups can be developed such as patients with hospital discharge representing 15.6%, hospitalized patients representing 1.8%, patients in home isolation representing 55.7%, and total deaths representing the 15.5% [16, 17] (Fig. 5).

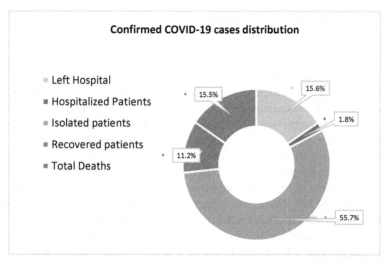

Fig. 5. Confirmed COVID-19 cases Distribution since the first confirmed case until July 9, 2020.

4 The Proposed Solution for Monitoring COVID Patients in Vulnerable Zones

4.1 Vulnerable Zones

As it is shown in section three, Ecuador has become one of the most affected zones in Latin-American. Data about deaths over the population show that the health system was/is not enough to assist diagnosed COVID patients. Seeing the previous problem, it is necessary to add that people located in isolated zones (such as mountains, amazon jungle, little towns, etc.) have no opportunity to receive assistance in a hospital because there are no ones near. Ecuador is a pluricultural country with many settlements in difficult places to access for a healthcare entity [18].

People are required to travel to big cities to get the required assistance from a doctor. There were/are cases that show no presence of symptoms which would lead to a recommendation of artificial respiration. These people just needed to be monitored to see the evolution of the virus and how it affects their health [18].

4.2 Problem Contextualization

Many people panicked from the first confirmed case in Ecuador, hospitals wanted to prioritize older adults and children. Those who were infected with very serious symptoms and others who were infected by attending the hospital for fear of having the virus. There were people who, despite presenting the virus, only needed to be monitored as a point of transmission while there was no need to be hospitalized. Which in turn lead to them being asked for home isolation. The question is: What about people who had to return home but lived/live in vulnerable areas? A way was/is needed for doctors to monitor these people while having the common problem that in vulnerable areas there is no telephone service and even less Internet service.

4.3   Oxygen, Heart Rate, and Temperature

As presented in Chapter Two, the complication caused by SARS-CoV-2 is acute hypoxemic respiratory failure. Its evolution causes various changes in oxygenation. Therefore, the evaluation of oxygen through pulse oximetry is necessary for patient management and respiratory treatment. The oximeter is a non-invasive method used to quantify the Oxygen Saturation (SpO2) circulating in the blood. Use the photoplethysmographic wave. A common oximeter on the one side contains two light-emitting diodes that project two wavelengths of light. On the other side, it has a photodetector [19].

For its assessment, the dissociation curve of hemoglobin related to oxygen saturation (Sat. O2) and Partial Respiratory Failure (PaO2) must be taken into account. If the curve has a projection to the right, hemoglobin gives more oxygen to the tissues On the other hand, if it turns to the left, it gives less oxygen to the tissues. A PaO2-60 mmHg resulting from 90% O2 saturation is considered a respiratory failure [20].

In the SpO2 titration mechanism the 660 nm red light characteristic of oxyhemoglobin and the near 940 nm infrared light characteristic of reduced hemoglobin is projected through the tissues, the unabsorbed light is captured by the photodetector on the opposite side [19].

4.4   Proposal System

It is necessary to monitor the parameters associated with the symptoms of COVID-19 to know if the patient is stable or if there is a need for immediate assistance in a health center. An IoT solution was designed to improve the traditional telemedicine methodology by applying a technological solution that does not require a complete internet connection. In this way, the patient who had to be in isolation at home could be monitored and if any complications occurred, doctors from the closest hospital were able to determine which patient and where to give immediate assistance.

5   Methodology

Once the physical context and the conditions in which the problem develops are analyzed, the solution based on an Internet of Things development is proposed. Followed by the design of a cyber-physical system where COVID patients, doctors on duty, and assisting doctors are involved through a deployment of hardware and software that interacts with each party in real-time. This will allow doctors to know the status of isolated patients without them traveling long distances (Fig. 6).

5.1   System Topology

See Fig. 6.

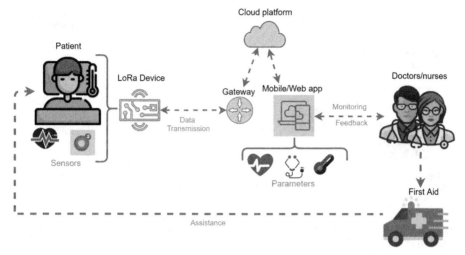

Fig. 6. Implemented Cyber-physical System to offer an IoT solution to the treatment of COVID-19 through Telemedicine.

5.2 LoRaWAN Technology

A Low Power, Wide Area (LPWA) networking protocol was designed to wirelessly connect battery operated 'things' to the internet in regional, national or global networks, and targets key Internet of Things (IoT) requirements such as bi-directional communication, end-to-end security, mobility, and localization services [21].

LoRaWAN network architecture is deployed in a star-of-stars topology in which gateways relay messages between end-devices and a central network server. The gateways are connected to the network server via standard IP connections and act as a transparent bridge, simply converting RF packets to IP packets and vice versa. The wireless communication takes advantage of the long-range characteristics of the LoRa physical layer, allowing a single-hop link between the end-device and one or many gateways [21] (Fig. 7).

Data Acquisition Stage. There are three measurable parameters. Temperature, oxygen saturation in the blood, and the heart rate. These parameters are associated with the determination of the health status of the patient diagnosed with COVID-19, which has been isolated.

To acquire the temperature, an MCP9808 sensor is used, which is connected to the upper part of the patient's wrist. For the acquisition of the oxygen level in the blood and the heart rate, the MAX30100 sensor is used in the lower part of the wrist. These sensors are connected by I2C BUS to the ESP 32 LoRa 32 module [22, 23] (Fig. 8).

The bracelet gathers these parameter levels and stores these values momentarily. The device has a lipo battery that supplies the microcontroller which in turn supplies energy to the sensors. The ESP 32 LoRa LCD screen shows the information provided by the doctor (remainders or advice).

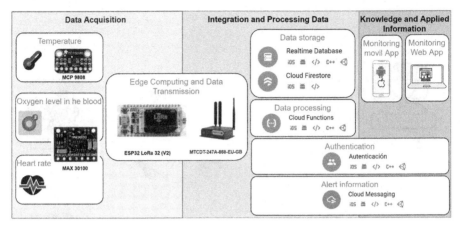

Fig. 7. IoT System Architecture. There are three stages with their elements and the technology applied in all of them.

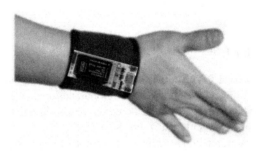

Fig. 8. Implementation of the sensors and ESP 32 LoRa in a bracelet for the monitoring of Heart rate, body temperature, and Oxygen saturation.

Edge Computing and Data Transmission. The measured parameters are pre-processed to be sent only to the gateway when there is a significant change between the new value and the previous value. In this way, the LoRa device saves energy and is saturated with repetitive information in the cloud database. The LoRa device sends information to the cloud platform through a Lora Gateway located close to the near-est internet access point. This gateway uploads the information to the cloud platform. The communication is generally bidirectional. The gateway gathers the information and notifications from the mobile/web application, forwarding them to the patient's device.

Integration and Processing Data. For data integration, a Backend as a Service (BaaS) called Firebase is used. This cloud tool is powered by Google, allowing the collection of information in real-time. Within a realtime database, the information is constantly updated [24]. There is a tool called Cloud Firestore where the information can be saved in collections, being accessible from a mobile/web application [25].

Furthermore, the necessary comparisons are made for decision-making using the Cloud Functions tool. This utility opens the chance to program criteria to make decisions according to the updated information in the real-time database and the cloud firestore.

Cloud functions could create, delete, and update information in the databases inside the firebase [26].

Focussing on the communication part, there is a tool called cloud messaging. This application allows sending alert messages to the final monitoring and control devices (mobile phones or web apps). In this project when some medical parameters become critical, an emergency alert is sent to the doctors. The messaging alert is a link to access the patient information and verify the previous status as well as the status in real-time [27].

Knowledge and Applied Information. All information is presented objectively in a dashboard in the mobile or web application. All this information is protected which allows only the doctors of the nearest hospital to have access. Firebase has a tool called Authentication which allows establishing unique credentials to get access to the patient's information [28]. In this way, we guarantee the security of the medical information of patient 1 and patient 2.

It is possible to access the information by mobile phone, tablet, or web page, its update in real-time, and the historical record of the health status of patient 1 and patient 2. At the same time, the doctor could send a notification, advice, and reminders to the patients by the same interface. The patient will see them through the ESP 32 LoRa LCD screen. These messages must use less than 120 characters (Fig. 9).

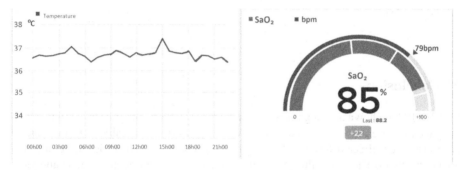

Fig. 9. Dashboard to visualize the temperature, oxygen saturation, and the heart rate of a COVID-19 positive patient.

Additionally, the doctor can send notifications to the patient's bracelet, indicating if any additional medication is needed or if everything is going well according to the treatment.

6 Experiments and Results

Tests with this device have been carried out on two patients who had symptoms of the virus in the same week and who were diagnosed with the virus in the same week. Both patients were recommended for home isolation. Both patients used the device for several days (thirteen days for patient 1 and 19 consecutive days for patient 2). Once diagnosed with the virus, they did not need to attend a health center again because their final (virtual) medical evaluation was that they had overcome the virus. Table 1 shows the results obtained during experimentation (Table 2).

Table 2. Results of the analyzed parameters through the implemented IoT system with two COVID patients.

Analyzed parameters	Patient 1	Patient 2
Gender	Male	Female
Age	42	30
Date of diagnostic	May 23	May 19
The location from the nearest hospital	17 km away	29 km away
Isolation days	13	19
Associated symptoms	Fever and moderate breathing problems	Fever and body ache
Critical day	Day 3–4	Day 6–8
Emergency alerts to doctors	26	14
Medical feedback	20	12

7　Conclusions

COVID-19 has shown a strong impact in the underdeveloped countries because they did not have the necessary health system to face this epidemic. Vulnerable or isolated areas have also been affected because access to medical services turned out to be an even greater problem. Therefore, this proposal for a remote monitoring and remote attention system in isolated areas has proven useful in the tests carried out. The results of this project show that the IoT proposal as a solution-oriented to telemedicine could be very beneficial at the national level if it is scaled and oriented to the care of people who live in areas far from health centers. This solution could help to reduce the number of patients under observation within a hospital and in turn reduce the traffic of people through towns. Most likely it could even help to reduce the risk of contagion in medical centers. This proposed Cyber-physical system could be replied and scaled to provide remote medical attention as well as health monitoring to zones with no or little telecommunications links. We consider this system to help reduce the overload of patients in hospitals, allowing prioritization of critical patients.

We would like to mention that we are planning the integration of machine learning algorithms as a methodology to provide feedback to the patients when some parameters are relevant to decide for and on a patient. In this way, the patient would be monitored any time and he/she could get ideal feedback from an algorithm that is using the previous information to determine alternatives to face the occurring symptoms. This proposal does not intend to move the doctors out of the cyber-physical system. The algorithm will help the doctors to make an objective and well-based decision when a situation requires the analysis of a lot of information provided by a patient and the systems.

References

1. Velavan, T.P., Meyer, C.G.: The COVID-19 epidemic. Tropical Med. Int. Health **25**(3), 278 (2020)
2. Rodríguez-Morales, A.J., et al.: Preparación y control de la enfermedad por coronavirus 2019 (COVID-19) en América Latina. Acta Medica Peruana. **37**(1), 3–7 (2020)
3. Sánchez-Duque, J.A., Arce-Villalobos, L.R., Rodríguez-Morales, A.J.: Enfermedad por coronavirus 2019 (COVID-19) en América Latina: papel de la atención primaria en la preparación y respuesta. Atención Primaria. **52**(6), 369 (2020)
4. Navarro, J.-C., Arrivillaga-Henríquez, J., Salazar-Loor, J., Rodriguez-Morales, A.J.: COVID-19 and dengue, co-epidemics in Ecuador and other countries in Latin America: pushing strained health care systems over the edge. Travel Medicine and Infectious Disease (2020)
5. Cucinotta, D., Vanelli, M.: WHO declares COVID-19 a pandemic. Acta bio-medica: Atenei Parmensis. **91**(1), 157–160 (2020)
6. Ogonaga, S., Chiriboga, S.: COVID-19 en Ecuador: análisis descriptivo de las provincias y ciudades más afectadas. GICOS: Revista del Grupo de Investigaciones en Comunidad y Salud, **5**(2), 67–82 (2020)
7. Ruiz, G.P.I., León, A.C.I.: Evolución de la enfermedad por coronavirus (COVID-19) en Ecuador. La Ciencia al Servicio de la Salud. **11**(1), 5–15 (2020)
8. De la Torre, C.: Ethnic movements and citizenship in Ecuador. JSTOR (2006)
9. Phan, T.: Genetic diversity and evolution of SARS-CoV-2. Infect. Genet. Evol. **81**, 104260 (2020)
10. Zhang, Y., et al.: New understanding of the damage of SARS-CoV-2 infection outside the respiratory system. Biomed. Pharmacother. **2020**, 110195 (2020)
11. Jin, X., et al.: Epidemiological, clinical and virological characteristics of 74 cases of coronavirus-infected disease 2019 (COVID-19) with gastrointestinal symptoms. Gut **69**(6), 1002–1009 (2020)
12. Lukassen, S., et al.: SARS-CoV-2 receptor ACE 2 and TMPRSS 2 are primarily expressed in bronchial transient secretory cells. EMBO J. **39**(10), e105114 (2020)
13. Bansal, M.: Cardiovascular disease and COVID-19. Diab. Metabol. Syndr. Clin. Res. Rev. (2020)
14. Nicin, L., et al.: Cell type-specific expression of the putative SARS-CoV-2 receptor ACE2 in human hearts. Eur. Heart J. **41**(19), 1804–1806 (2020)
15. en Cifras, E.: Instituto nacional de estadísticas y censos (2017). Recuperado de http://www.ecuadorencifras.gob.ec/documentos/web-inec/Sitios/LIBRObuenvivir/files/assets/downloads/page0032.pdf
16. Emergencias SNdGdRy: Informes de Situación e Infografias – COVID 19 – desde el 29 de Febrero del 2020 (2020)
17. Emergencias SNdGdRy. COE Nacional (2020)
18. Hernández, E.P.: El Estado y la interculturalidad en el Ecuador. Editorial Abya Yala (2005)
19. Nasr, V., DiNardo, J.: Pulse Oximetry. Pediatrics in review. **40**(11), 605 (2019)
20. Tobin, M.J.: Basing respiratory management of COVID-19 on physiological principles. Am. Thorac. Soc. (2020)
21. Alliance, L.: LoRaWAN 101 A technical introduction. LoRa-Alliance org (2017)

22. Martinos, J., Martinos, T.: Data sheet/digital thermometer using ARDUINO and MCP9808 digital temperature sensor (2018)
23. Strogonovs, R.: Implementing pulse oximeter using MAX30100. Morf-Coding and Engineering (2017)
24. Moroney, L.: The firebase realtime database. In: Moroney, L. (ed.) The Definitive Guide to Firebase, pp. 51–71. Springer, Berkeley (2017). https://doi.org/10.1007/978-1-4842-2943-9_3
25. Firestore, C.: Firebase. Google, Mountain View (2018)
26. Moroney, L.: Cloud functions for firebase. In: Moroney, L. (ed.) The Definitive Guide to Firebase, pp. 139–161. Springer, Berkeley (2017). https://doi.org/10.1007/978-1-4842-2943-9_8
27. Moroney, L.: Firebase cloud messaging. In: Moroney, L. (ed.) The Definitive Guide to Firebase, pp. 163–188. Springer, Berkeley (2017). https://doi.org/10.1007/978-1-4842-2943-9_9
28. Moroney, L.: Using authentication in firebase. In: Moroney, L. (ed.) The Definitive Guide to Firebase, pp. 25–50. Springer, Berkeley (2017). https://doi.org/10.1007/978-1-4842-2943-9_2

Clustering of Reading Ability Performance Variables in the English Language Based on TBL Methodology and Behavior in the Left Hemisphere of the Brain

Delio R. Patiño-Alarcón[1], Fernando A. Patiño-Alarcón[1],
Leandro L. Lorente-Leyva[2]([✉]) [iD], and Diego H. Peluffo-Ordóñez[2,3,4] [iD]

[1] Academia del Conocimiento, Ibarra, Ecuador
deliricard@hotmail.com
[2] SDAS Research Group, Ibarra, Ecuador
leandro.lorente@sdas-group.com
[3] Yachay Tech University, Urcuquí, Ecuador
dpeluffo@yachaytech.edu.ec
[4] Coorporación Universitaria Autónoma de Nariño, Pasto, Colombia

Abstract. This research presents an application of the clustering based on Thinking Based - Learning methodology (TBL), which offers guidelines to promote students' reflective thinking. Within this methodology, the Intelligence Execution Theory (IET) tool will be used to encourage this kind of thinking in the classroom. Having in mind that, in any educational process, methodologies and pedagogical tools have a pivotal role as they are one of the bases for optimizing cognitive intelligence. In this case, it was given a priority to the potential development of a specific linguistic skill. This study presented a mixed methodology with an exploratory and descriptive scope. The main objective of this research was the clustering of the variables of functioning of the reading ability in the English language based on the TBL methodology and its behavior in the left hemisphere of the brain, specifically to analyze the improvement of the reading ability in the English language of the participants of this case study. With the expectation of generating sustainability of adequate levels of performance, instruction and learning of the English language of students at all levels.

Keywords: Thinking based-learning · Intelligence execution theory · Cognitive intelligence · Linguistic skill · Clustering

1 Introduction

The society has been involved in several problems as the purchasing power of a good process or course of learning a second language due to its high price, besides, negligence and lack of willingness to overcome personal are one of the first places as a factor affecting the learning of a second language. Traditional methodologies are still used by some teachers in much of formal education in Ecuador for many years. This affects the process

© Springer Nature Switzerland AG 2020
G. Rodriguez Morales et al. (Eds.): TICEC 2020, CCIS 1307, pp. 77–90, 2020.
https://doi.org/10.1007/978-3-030-62833-8_7

of learning and teaching in a foreign language such as frustration and repetitive teaching of grammatical rules, the fundamental component in the instruction. The objective that its pursued is to change the way teachers teach and facilitate foreign language learning. This is one of the factors that affect Ecuador's level of English in the world ranking, placing us at level #81, corresponding to Very Low according to a study [1].

One of the innovative methodologies that positioning itself as one of the most effective methods in this field is Thinking Based Learning. This methodology uses the horizon of anticipating deficiencies that affect the learning and acquisition of the English language. It makes complex types of thinking viable, such as: broadening ideas, improving skills, making decisions, conceptualizing, relevance and precision in all arguments [2].

From the above mentioned, an adequate and intelligent corrective measure is generated, which is used as a forceful, powerful and effective tool to optimize learning skills and enable greater neuronal connections within the left hemisphere of the brain, facilitating future decision making and strategies to be implemented. This has evolved with the help of computer-assisted language learning (CALL), and the flexible learning model of recent times [3].

The new model of intelligence of the human brain far beyond efficiency and experience allows taking advantage of the information effectively to be processed again. Our brain is linked to two different levels of input, known as information redaction [4]. Seeking solutions to a problem when there is no known solution, having only poorly learned sequences of action or those containing new elements, of vital importance are those that are not a habit [5].

Successful learning in university education can be advanced by the competence of students to self-regulate their learning; students often possess insufficient skills to adequately regulate their learning [6]. Demetriadis et al. [7] provide evidence that individual learning can be enhanced in a case-based learning technology environment by implementing appropriate challenge strategies. In 2009 Thomas [8] argues that the development of thinking is the critical element in education related to sustainability and holistic thinking. Other research [9] provides accessible educational practices that teachers can use in standards-based content instruction in any subject or grade level. It also presents a new way to stimulate learning, creativity, and thinking [10] and a web-based simulation learning framework to enhance students' critical thinking skills [11].

Other authors [12] present a social epistemological framework for the teaching of critical thinking in the school curriculum. In 2016, Goodman [13] in his doctoral work researched to improve scientific literacy among Israeli university students. In the same year, Chen and Law [14] conducted a study that offered instructions for designing scaffolding in play-based learning environments. Others identify the challenges of computer-based science learning and state that student modeling has been used in computer-based learning environments to model mastery knowledge [15, 16]. Recent research [17] describes and examines a personalized guidance approach aimed at eliminating performance differences based on a range of student characteristics. Others analyze students' critical thinking skills [18] and develop a study to examine the impact of cooperative learning on the development of students' computational thinking skills [19].

Many studies have also suggested that in the educational area there is only one internal control function, while others can be identified because it seems that there are functions in isolation.

The rest of this manuscript is structured as follows: Sect. 2 describes the behavior of left cerebral hemisphere in learning, delimitation of the population and sample selection. In Sect. 3 are presents the results and discussion. Finally, the conclusions are shown in Sect. 4.

2 Materials and Methods

Left Cerebral Hemisphere and Its Behavior in Learning

Teaching-based executive intelligence generation functions clearly explain the percentage of what each student's left hemisphere captures and retains. As can be seen in Table 1, in the first section the student learns 5% of what he or she hears and so on.

Table 1. Executive functions of the generating intelligence according to its teaching activities and learning actions.

%	The student learns
5	From what you hear
10	From what you read
20	From what he hears and observes
30	From what they show you
50	From what he hears, observes, debates and expresses
75	From what he discusses, expresses and practices
90	What he discusses, expresses, practices, does and teaches others

Self-regulation of Cognitive Learning

Once we have mastered the reality of learning results as an elemental factor for students, we could undertake a reflection on thinking, and we could specify the whole self-regulating process of learning and its cognitive process [20] (Fig. 1).

Relationship systems

- Practical activity (Will, interest, Experiences);
- Assessment activity (Purpose, needs);
- Cognitive activity (Meaning, feelings).

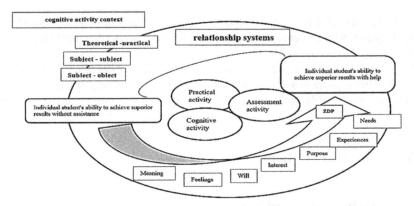

Fig. 1. Context of cognitive activity [20].

Knowing how to order one's own thought is closely linked to the method (Fig. 2), by which we mean, in essence, (Thinking Based Learning), through induction. It is vitally important to emphasize that in every thinking process there are two elements [21, 22]:

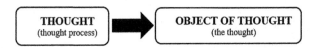

Fig. 2. Infusion and thought processes.

Research Focus (Approach)
The two samples employ careful, methodical and empirical processes in their effort to generate knowledge, these methods use five similar and related strategies:

- They carry out the observation and evaluation of phenomena;
- Establish assumptions or ideas as a result of observation and evaluation;
- They demonstrate the degree to which assumptions or ideas have a basis;
- They review such assumptions or ideas on the basis of evidence or analysis;
- They propose new observations and evaluations to clarify, modify and substantiate assumptions and ideas or even to generate new ones.

Quantitative Sampling
The sampling is limited and, once it is defined, objectives and research questions are derived, the literature is reviewed and a framework or theoretical foundation is built, as shown below in Fig. 3 [23]:

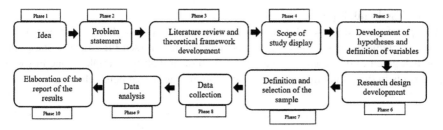

Fig. 3. Quantitative process.

Qualitative Sampling

Often, these activities serve first to discover what the most important research questions are, and then to refine and answer them. Investigative action moves dynamically in both directions: between facts and their interpretation, it is a rather "circular" process in which the sequence is not always the same, as it varies with each study. This process is represented in Fig. 4, as shown below [23]:

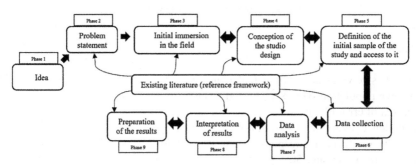

Fig. 4. Qualitative process.

Delimitation of the Population Under Investigation

The characteristics of the population will be very clear and detailed as this specifies where exactly the study will be carried out, as shown in Fig. 5.

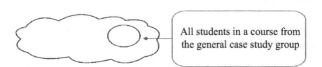

Fig. 5. Delimitation of the population under investigation.

Sample Used and Type

The type of sample chosen for this case study will be probabilistic since any of the sampling elements or students in this case can be chosen (see Fig. 6), this due to the approach given to the research posed. A random or probability sample is one in which all subjects in the population have had the same probability of being chosen.

$$n = \frac{N}{1 + \frac{e^2(N-1)}{z^2 pq}} \tag{1}$$

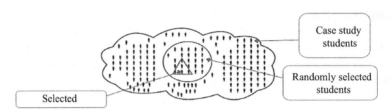

Selected   Case study students   Randomly selected students

Fig. 6. Representation of the sample.

Where:

n = sample size you want to know (calculate);
N = known population size ($\sum_1^5$ selected levels);
e = margin of error (2%);
z = confidence level (98%) – (z: 2,38);
p = positive or affirmative response rate (50% ≈ 0.5);
q = refusal response rate (50% ≈ 0.5).

Characteristics of the Sample Selection

Although it is known that two essential characteristics are observed in a probability sampling such as: sample size and the selection procedure, that in this case the sample elements are always chosen at random to ensure that each element has the same probability of being chosen. The characteristics of the sample selection procedure are detailed below and presented in Fig. 7.

- Select the number of students, the sample obtained previously;
- Select the lower limit (it will always be 1);
- Select the upper limit, the sample size number;
- View and select from the list the students with the numbers obtained;
- Get our final sample.

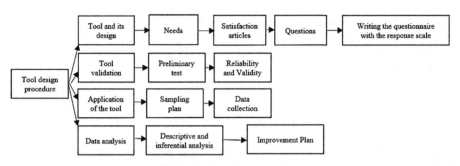

Fig. 7. Tool design procedure.

Sample and Population Surveyed

By means of the contribution generated by the confidential source of the case study, being the agent and main actor of the present investigation, who facilitated the viability and data for the corresponding statistical analysis to know the selected sample (students) to survey of each population (academic level), and the investigator creating an important synergy between both involved in the investigative project. In addition, it is possible to emphasize that the process is validated statistically, generating absolute relevance and validity to the process of information survey and results found (Table 2).

Table 2. Total number of men and women surveyed by each academic level.

	I	II	III	IV	V
Men	8	7	5	5	10
Women	8	10	12	11	5
Total	16	17	17	16	15

Collection and Tabulation of Information

This mixed-method study examined 14 different variables of reading ability in students at all five existing levels at the case study site to increase comprehension and, of course, student motivation (N = 81). The data consisted of information from a known population for each level, pre-survey and a sample to be surveyed. The data will be used quantitatively to mention the results found by gathering information about current reading comprehension through reading ability and its motivational degree for acquiring a new language, thus ensuring after the application of the methodology a significant improvement in the motivation for learning and obviously their skills with the new language, the results will always have dimensions and characteristics to improve, thus practicing continuous improvement, ensuring quality assurance in academic processes in general and learning a new language such as English specifically the ability of reading (Tables 3 and 4).

Variable 1: Conformity with the methodology
Variable 2: Willingness to change methods
Variable 3: Previous knowledge of TBL methodology
Variable 4: Knowledge of the functioning of the brain
Variable 5: Level of professional impact awareness
Variable 6: Level of compliance
Variable 7: Attitudinal perception and predisposition of the teacher
Variable 8: Internal user satisfaction
Variable 9: Frequency of language generation and use in learning in the family environment
Variable 10: Frequency of language generation and use in learning in the social environment
Variable 11: Frequency of language generation and use in learning in the academic environment
Variable 12: Frequency of language generation and use in learning in the work environment
Variable 13: Application of a new methodology
Variable 14: Frequency of language generation and use in learning

Table 3. Tabulation of data resulting from the value judgements made by each question.

Question	Option	Students	Percentages
1	Satisfied	36	44,44%
2	Some agreement	35	43,21%
3	Never	56	69,13%
4	Some	31	38,27%
5	Totally	41	50,61%
6	Some discontent	28	34,66%
7	Very good	35	43,21%
8	Very good	33	40,74%
9	Very good	24	29,63%
10	More often	30	37,04%
11	Always	32	39,50%
12	Always	34	41,97%
13	Very willing	42	51,85%
14	Sometimes	41	50,61%

Table 4. Tabulation of the number of students per academic career from the English levels surveyed.

Question	Option
Industrial engineering	1
Electrical engineering	3
Communication	6
Accounting and auditing	6
Business administration	2
Automotive engineering	1
Graphic design	1
Economy	3
Basic education	9
Plastic arts	5
Psychopedagogy	10
Pedagogy physical activity of sport	3
Gastronomy	1
Pedagogy in arts and humanities	5
Early education	5
Pedagogy of experimental sciences	1
Biotechnology engineering	3
Engineering in Renewable Natural Resources	3
Engineering in tourism	3
Bachelor of science in nursing	2
Agricultural engineering	3
Physical Education	1
Mechatronics Engineering	2
Software engineering	1

Ward Method and Clustering

By compressing all variables and their components with this exploratory data analysis technique, data interpretation and analysis of their ordered and grouped behavior is allowed, also using the tree system by clustering (grouping of hierarchically ordered and classified data) in groups and subgroups of data (dendogram), to subsequently identify through the component graph the proximity and location of each variable within the dimensions that project the left hemisphere of the brain and finally in a two-dimensional plane to project the acquisition weight from the point of origin of the information generation and to be able to observe which level through the collected data has a greater transition of functions in the left hemisphere, specifically with the reading ability.

3   Results and Discussion

Declaration of variables

Once the variables are declared, the processing and interpretation of the data is facilitated to obtain the desired results, then we can see the configuration and introduction of the variables (Tables 5 and 6):

Table 5. Declaration of programmable variables and their label.

Declared variable and questions	Label declared programmable
n1	Conformity with the methodology
n2	Willingness to change methods
n3	Previous knowledge of TBL methodology
n4	Knowledge of the functioning of the brain
n5	Level of professional impact awareness
n6	Level of compliance
n7	Attitudinal perception and predisposition of the teacher
n8	Internal user satisfaction
n9	Frequency of language generation and use in learning in the family environment
n10	Frequency of language generation and use in learning in the social environment
n11	Frequency of language generation and use in learning in the academic environment
n12	Frequency of language generation and use in learning in the work environment
n13	Application of a new methodology
n14	Frequency of language generation and use in learning

Table 6. Weights of each question by case study level.

Level	n1	n2	n3	n4	n5	n6	n7	n8	n9	n10	n11	n12	n13	n14
1	6	4	0	0	12	0	6	6	3	8	1	9	5	0
2	3	10	0	0	11	0	7	6	1	4	10	8	13	0
3	0	8	0	0	6	0	1	6	0	4	7	3	7	2
4	5	6	0	0	5	1	5	4	6	6	6	6	8	2
5	7	1	2	1	7	0	2	4	3	7	8	8	9	2

Dendogram

The results of the analysis are shown in the dendrogram (Fig. 8) where the stages of the melting process and the distances between the melted elements are represented on a standardized 25-point scale. The solution shown offers a structure collected in two clusters. In cluster 1, items 1, 4, and 5 are collected. In cluster 2, items 2 and 3 are collected.

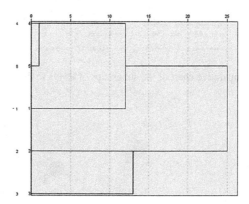

Fig. 8. Representative dendogram of groups and subgroups.

Weights Using the Ward Method

This weighting allows the analysis of independent weights for each variable declared or question at each level of the case study evaluated (See Table 7 and Fig. 9).

Table 7. Weights of each question by case study level.

Level	n1	n2	n3	n4	n5	n6	n7	n8	n9	n10	n11	n12	n13	n14
1	6	4	0	0	12	0	6	6	3	8	1	9	5	0
2	3	10	0	0	11	0	7	6	1	4	10	8	13	0
3	0	8	0	0	6	0	1	6	0	4	7	3	7	2
4	6	3.5	1	0.5	6	0.5	3.5	4	4.5	6.5	7	7	8.5	2

Clustering of Declared Variables

The graphic representation of the variables declared in the left hemisphere specifically in the reading area is generated, both in a 2D and 3D representation, strength of each level from its reading function origin (Fig. 10) and proximity between each of the variables in the presented area (Fig. 11).

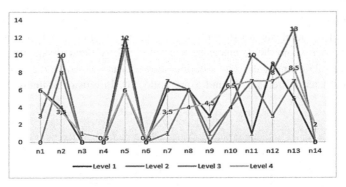

Fig. 9. Comparative chart of the subgroups of levels in the case study.

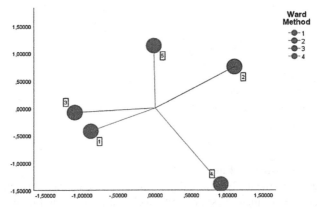

Fig. 10. Two-dimensional representation of the force of each level from its origin of functions.

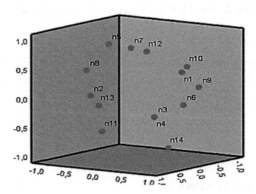

Fig. 11. Three-dimensional representation of the proximity of the case study variables.

4   Conclusions

The collection and clustering of the case study generated a distribution and weighting of each one of the questions or also called declared variables. By developing the plots in two dimensions, it was possible to clearly observe from the beginning the projection of each level of study and at the same time in three dimensions the proximity of each question to another, which refers to how much similarity one has with another.

The statistical inferential model used was a structured and developed random sampling, obtaining an accurate and valid sample for data processing.

Using the Ward method, we were able to visualize the behavior of the data collected through tools such as: dendrogram, component graph and distribution of programmed variable functions from their origin, achieving a clear analysis of the statistical behavior of the data.

Acknowledgment. The authors are greatly grateful by the support given by the SDAS Research Group (https://sdas-group.com/).

References

1. EF EPI (2020). https://www.ef.com.ec/epi/. Accessed 9 Mar 2020
2. Marina, J.A.: Swartz y Costa: el aprendizaje basado en el pensamiento (2015). https://www.joseantoniomarina.net/articulo/swartz-y-costa-el-aprendizaje-basado-en-el-pensamiento/
3. Mogrovejo, A.B., Mamani, G., Tipo, M.L.: Juego y Simulación de Programas Concurso de Televisión como Técnica Didáctica para Mejorar el Aprendizaje del Vocabulario Inglés en Estudiantes de Habla Hispana. Información tecnológica 30(1), 225–236 (2019)
4. Defagó, C.: Tras los rastros del lenguaje: revisión teórica del modelo RR de Karmiloff-Smith. Revista Argentina de Ciencias del Comportamiento 4(1), 44–55 (2012)
5. Shallice, T., Cooper, R.: The Organisation of Mind. Oxford University Press, Oxford (2011)
6. De Backer, L., Van Keer, H., Valcke, M.: Promoting university students' metacognitive regulation through peer learning: the potential of reciprocal peer tutoring. High. Educ. 70(3), 469–486 (2014). https://doi.org/10.1007/s10734-014-9849-3
7. Demetriadis, S.N., Papadopoulos, P.M., Stamelos, I.G., Fischer, F.: The effect of scaffolding students' context-generating cognitive activity in technology-enhanced case-based learning. Comput. Educ. 51(2), 939–954 (2008). https://doi.org/10.1016/j.compedu.2007.09.012
8. Thomas, I.: Critical thinking, transformative learning, sustainable education, and problem-based learning in universities. J. Transform. Educ. 7(3), 245–264 (2009). https://doi.org/10.1177/1541344610385753
9. Swartz, R., Costa, A., Beyer, B., Reagan, R., Kallick, B.: Thinking-Based Learning: Promoting Quality Student Achievement in the 21st Century. Teachers College Press, New York (2010)
10. Pang, K.: Creating stimulating learning and thinking using new models of activity-based learning and metacognitive-based activities. J. Coll. Teach. Learn. (TLC), 7(4) (2010). https://doi.org/10.19030/tlc.v7i4.112
11. Salleh, S.M., Tasir, Z., Shukor, N.A.: Web-based simulation learning framework to enhance students' critical thinking skills. Procedia-Soc. Behav. Sci. 64, 372–381 (2012). https://doi.org/10.1016/j.sbspro.2012.11.044
12. Lim, L.: Critical thinking, social education and the curriculum: foregrounding a social and relational epistemology. Curriculum J. 26(1), 4–23 (2015). https://doi.org/10.1080/09585176.2014.975733

13. Goodman, S.: An investigation into improving scientific literacy in Israeli university students within an academic English reading programme. Doctoral thesis (Ph.D.), University of Sussex (2016)
14. Chen, C.-H., Law, V.: Scaffolding individual and collaborative game-based learning in learning performance and intrinsic motivation. Comput. Hum. Behav. **55**, 1201–1212 (2016). https://doi.org/10.1016/j.chb.2015.03.010
15. Basu, S., et al.: Identifying middle school students' challenges in computational thinking-based science learning. Res. Pract. Technol. Enhanced Learn. **11**(1), 1–35 (2016). https://doi.org/10.1186/s41039-016-0036-2
16. Basu, S., Biswas, G., Kinnebrew, J.S.: Learner modeling for adaptive scaffolding in a computational thinking-based science learning environment. User Model. User-Adap. Inter. **27**(1), 5–53 (2017). https://doi.org/10.1007/s11257-017-9187-0
17. Backhaus, J., Jeske, D., Poinstingl, H., Koenig, S.: Assessing efficiency of prompts based on learner characteristics. Computers **6**(1), 7 (2017). https://doi.org/10.3390/computers6010007
18. Mutakinati, L., Anwari, I., Kumano, Y.: Analysis of students' critical thinking skill of middle school through stem education project-based learning. Jurnal Pendidikan IPA Indonesia, **7**(1), 54–65 (2018). https://doi.org/10.15294/jpii.v7i1.10495
19. Saad, A.: Students' computational thinking skill through cooperative learning based on hands-on, inquiry-based, and student-centric learning approaches. Univ. J. Educ. Res. **8**(1), 290–296 (2020). https://doi.org/10.13189/ujer.2020.080135
20. García, Y., Mompié, A., Ramos, A.: El proceso de evaluación como contextualizador de la autorregulación del aprendizaje (Revisión). Roca: Revista Científico-Educaciones de la provincia de Granma, **15**(1), 186–198 (2019)
21. Farkas, W.A., Jang, B.G.: Designing, implementing, and evaluating a school-based literacy program for adolescent learners with reading difficulties: a mixed-methods study. Read. Writ. Q. **35**(4), 305–321 (2019). https://doi.org/10.1080/10573569.2018.1541770
22. Abdel-Hafez-Pérez, S.: Implantación del Thinking Based Learning (TBL) en el aula de Educación Primaria. Bachelor's thesis (2013)
23. Sampieri, R., Collado, C.: Metodología de la Investigación (6ta Edición ed.). Mc Graw Hill, DF México (2014)

Real-Time Hand Gesture Recognition Using KNN-DTW and Leap Motion Controller

Rubén Nogales$^{(\boxtimes)}$ (ID) and Marco Benalcázar$^{(\boxtimes)}$ (ID)

Escuela Politécnica Nacional, Quito, Ecuador
{ruben.nogales,marco.benalcazar}@epn.edu.ec

Abstract. The advances in artificial intelligence have been boosting the development of applications in different fields. Some of these fields work in real-time and based on development and implementation in machine learning models. The problems presented by these fields of study involve pattern recognition, which consists of selecting a label and specify the instant of time that defines the gesture. In this context, the paper presents a specific model of real-time hand gesture recognition using the leap motion controller and machine learning algorithms. This model recognizes five static gestures. The gestures are open hand, fist, wave in, wave out, and pinch. The modules used to develop the model are data acquisition, pre-processing, feature extraction, classification, and postprocessing. The input signals to the model are the spatial positions and the direction. These signals are pre-processed by a translation and rotation matrix. Also, these are normalized and smoothed by a Butterworth filter. For the feature extraction module, we use the windows division technique. The model was tested with a window of 7 and 10 features. This signal is delivered to the KNN classifier. It tested the model with k = 1, and k = 3, and with DTW as a distance metric. We are varying the signal warping parameter in w = 1, 5, and w = 7. Finally, the model report 92.22% of classification accuracy and 77.64% of recognition accuracy in 287 ms.

Keywords: Hand gesture recognition · K nearest neighbors (KNN) · Dynamic time warping (DTW) · Leap motion controller

1 Introduction

Communication plays an essential role in human interaction. Because it can expresses feelings, actions, emotions, among others. To communicate, people use *verbal* and *nonverbal* elements. These elements are adequately addressed by artificial intelligence. *Verbal* communication has been adequately covered by natural language recognition. At the same time, *nonverbal* communication is related to the execution of gestures that transmit information [1]. In this sense, hand gesture recognition consists of identifying the type of gesture executed and the moment in time when it was executed [2].

In this context, the output of hand gesture recognition can use in many application fields as robotic, medicine, entertainment, human-computer interaction systems, sign language translator, among others. In the scientific literature present any studies with

© Springer Nature Switzerland AG 2020

G. Rodríguez Morales et al. (Eds.): TICEC 2020, CCIS 1307, pp. 91–103, 2020.
https://doi.org/10.1007/978-3-030-62833-8_8

different models, techniques, and technologies that attempt to boost these application fields.

[3] presents the architecture of a generic model of machine learning. It consists of *data acquisition, pre-processing, feature extraction, classified,* and *postprocessing.*

For *data acquisition,* in the scientific literature presents many devices. In [4] presents a comparison of the basic motion techniques capture such as marker-based optical, bend-sensor gloves, markerless optical, and depth cameras. However, in [5] presents a survey in which mention that the Kinect and leap motion controller devices are most used in hand gesture recognition problem using infrared information. Also, electromyographic sensors are used [6]. To develop this work, we will use the leap motion controller (LMC).

The *pre-processing* module smoothes the signal, noise delete, and prepares the signal as the input of the feature extraction module. A brief review of the scientific literature shows techniques such as data standardization [7], the movement of the coordinate axis from the LMC center to the palm [8]. The use of Gaussian filter [9], median filter [10].

Perhaps the *feature extraction* module is one of the most important in the architecture of the machine learning. It consists of obtaining meaningful, non-redundant information, usually in the form of n-dimensional feature vectors. For hand gesture recognition, the most common domains for feature extraction are time, frequency, and the combination of these two. Among the most used techniques reported in the scientific literature are fingers spatial positions [7, 11], statistical measures of central dispersion [12], segmented images [11, 12], the distance between center palm and fingertips [8, 13–17], mathematical operations from spatial positions [18], and convolution.

The *classification* module takes the feature vector as input and returns a label representing the class or gesture executed. The most used classification algorithms are support vector machine (SVM), k neigh neighbors (KNN), recurrent neural networks (RNN), also use algorithms as the feed-forward artificial neural network (ANN), hidden Markov models (HNN), and long short-term memory (LSTM).

In this context, in the scientific literature, various models and techniques are presented. However, these models are not comparable with each other because each one uses different classes, different datasets with different numbers of samples; these datasets can be private or public. Also, the articles presented do not clearly describe the metric of recognition evaluation, and some do not mention it, this makes it difficult to confuse classification with recognition. In this paper, we will provide a specific hand gesture recognition system that uses both spatial positions and finger direction. The commercial LMC sensor acquires the data. In the pre-processing module, we will move the coordinate axis from LMC to the hand palm center, generate a rotation matrix, normalized data, and filtered. For feature extraction, it is using the window division technique. The classification module used KNN with DTW as a distance metric. Finally, it used a refinement of the response delivered by the classifier as postprocessing. Also, in this paper, the evaluation metric for gesture recognition is presented. The gestures are fist, wave in, wave out, pinch, and relax.

The following present the distribution of the paper: In Sect. 1.1 presents the goals that will achieve the investigation, Sect. 2 of the paper presents the proposal description, Sect. 3 describes the empirical evaluation, Sects. 4 and 5 present the discussion and conclusions respectively, and finally, last section presents the acknowledgments.

1.1 Research Objectives

1. To propose an evaluation metric for hand gesture recognition system using machine learning algorithms and infrared information.
2. Build a specific hand gesture recognition system using KNN and DTW with the window division method as feature extraction.

2 Proposal Description

To develop this work, we will define the gestures that the system will recognize. The gestures are fist, wave in, wave out, pinch, and relax. These gestures are selected because they are very used in human-machine interaction or hand rehabilitation system.

Moreover, this study describes the architecture used. It is data acquisition, pre-processing, feature extraction, classifier, and postprocessing.

For the *data acquisition module,* use LMC. This device is small, fast, and very accurate. It specializes in capturing 3D hand movements. Accuracy is guaranteed when the hands are within a field of view of 60 cm. at the top of the device, while to the sides extend between 120 to 150°. The software of this device returns the spatial positions of 27 elements between bones and joints, returns the direction in which the fingertips point and the speed that the hand and fingers move. This device can track hand movement in the dark because it has three infrared sensors and two biconvex cameras [19].

In this context, the dataset was built with 38 volunteer subjects, mostly students of the system's career. For starting the data acquisition, the subjects must be located in front of the sensor, situate the hand 20 cm over the sensor, and execute the gesture. The subject repeats each gesture 30 times, and it will be executed at any instant in time within 5 s. In this way, a dataset of 5700 samples is obtained (5 gestures × 30 repetitions × 38 subjects). The participating subjects are between 19 and 45 years old, who have not suffered injuries to the right hand. The data acquisition and saved are made in real-time using a proprietary interface developed in Matlab. These data are stored in structures that contain the spatial positions and the directions that represent the movement hand.

The *pre-processing module* presents three sub-processes. These are *movement and rotation of the cartesian plane, normalization,* and *filtered.*

For the *movement and rotation,* the reference data of the hand position is extracted, the data are the normal vector and the direction vector. Between these two vectors, the cross product is calculated, obtaining a new vector.

Then, we obtain the unit vectors from the normal vector, of the direction vector, and the new vector generated by the cross product. With these elements, the rotation matrix is generated. Next, the new spatial positions of the fingers are calculated, taking as a reference to the coordinate system with the axis in the center of the hand palm.

Finally, a new vector is obtained by multiplying the new spatial positions of the fingers with the rotation matrix, as shown in Fig. 1.

The *normalization* sub-process is generated because to represent the hand movement, the data of each finger is added. In this sense, the amplitude of the signal is enlarged, and it is necessary to represent it in values between 0 and 1.

Finally, the *filtering* sub-process is generated using a Butterworth filter to smooth the signal. The cut-off frequency for the filter is 19 Hz. The filter is of 5'th order and has

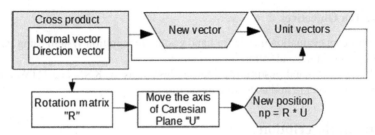

Fig. 1. A systematic process for moving the axis of the Cartesian plane from LMC to the palm center, generating a rotation matrix, and obtains a rotated signal.

a sampling frequency of 140 Hz. These parameters are selected based on experiments. If the cut-off frequency is higher to use, it lets all the frequencies pass, and the signal does not soften, and DTW is very sensitive to sudden changes. In the same sense, if the cut-off frequency is lower to used, the signal tends to flatten, and the classifier tends to get confused. Regarding the order of the filter, if they are of a higher or lower order than the one used, the model reports lower recognition accuracy.

In this paper, the *feature extraction module* aims to split the signal into windows. For this process, a signal is entered from the spatial positions discretized into approximately 70 points; each of the points represents the position of the hand in an instant of time. Also, the direction data formed by three column vectors are entered for each finger discretized in approximately 70 points. The window is probed between 7 or 10 points with a stride of 7 or 10, respectively. Besides, the technique of division by windows helps the recognition process.

For *classification,* uses the KNN algorithm with DTW as the distance metric. The gestures to classify are fist, wave in, wave out, and pinch, shown in Fig. 2.

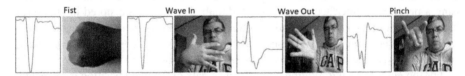

Fig. 2. Gesture to be recognized by the system based on KNN and DTW: fist, wave in, wave out, pinch.

In this work, we use the KNN algorithm due is very fast. It does not have an explicit training process. It consists of stores the labels and their samples. While the prediction is the comparison of a query point with all dataset points, and it returns the label based on a similarity measure with the k nearest neighbors.

For these reasons, the KNN is considered as a lazy or discriminative algorithm [20].

$$D = \left(X^i, f\left(X^i \right) \right) \tag{1}$$

Where X_i is stored training example, and D is the dataset.

In [21], after an exhaustive review of more than 800 articles, they conclude that DTW is the best algorithm for distance measurement. DTW is an algorithm that maps two-time series that have a similar shape but are out of phase. This algorithm consists of building a matrix of Euclidean distances between the two-time series, point to point and point to multipoint. In this matrix, the alignment between the time series is defined by contiguous elements that form a diagonal that starts and finished in the opposite corners. The parameters that defined this algorithm is w, $w_k = P_{(i,j)_k}$. It consists of the number of contiguous elements in the diagonal above described.

$$DTW(ts_1, ts_2) = \min \sqrt{\sum_{k=1}^{k} w_k} \qquad (2)$$

As shown in Fig. 3.

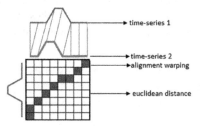

Fig. 3. Elements of DTW algorithm, time-series, the matrix of the euclidean distance, and the alignment warping.

In this context, we propose a specific model per-user that uses KNN and DTW. In terms of processing speed, this model is high-speed, but each time that a person uses the model, it needs to be training. In terms of accuracy, it is better than the general model, as demonstrated in the predecessor paper (in reviewed). Nevertheless, the general model does not need training each time it is used.

In the specific model, the data of each user is split by 60% for training and 40% by testing. The input signals for the KNN classifier are a signal describing hand movement based on spatial positions $D_s = \sum norm(position(x, y, z))$, also, 15 signals describe the direction in $(D_f)_i^{(x,y,z)}$; $i = (1, 2, 3, 4, 5)$ of each finger.

The classifier processes the signals in windows $w = 7\ or\ 10$, and $stride = 7\ or\ 10$, in this sense, it returns a label for each window, finally have labels vector $\hat{L} = \left(\hat{l}_1, \hat{l}_2, \ldots, \hat{l}_n\right)$. But the classifier needs to return only one label, then calculates the most probability label from the labels vector $\hat{y} = P(y|X_i)$.

The postprocessing module is for tuning the set of labels that results from the evaluation of each window, as explained in the classification module. In this sense, the elements of the labels vector probably are not the same.

Then, the labels vector $\hat{L} = \left(\hat{l}_1, \hat{l}_2, \ldots, \hat{l}_n\right)$ is evaluated one to one, and if the label in the evaluated position $\hat{l}_i$ is different from its immediate predecessor $\hat{l}_{i-1}$, but if the label immediately before the evaluated one is the same as the one immediately after the evaluated one $\hat{l}_{i-1} == \hat{l}_{i+1}$, the evaluated label changes the value and takes the value of the previous label $\hat{l}_i := \hat{l}_{i-1}$.

3 Empirical Evaluation

3.1 Evaluation Metric for Hand Gesture Recognition

In [22] proposed a protocol for evaluation of a hand gesture recognition model based on electromyography signals (EMG). In this sense, we use this protocol and adapt it to work with infrared signals retrieved by the LMC.

In this work, to execute the recognition, the labels vector is taken, and this is input to the postprocessing as explained in the previous section. As a result of this process, a vector of zeros and ones is obtained, where the zeros indicate the non-gesture and the ones indicate the presence of the gesture, each one of these values is associated with an instant of time. This instant of time serves to expand the vector, shown in Fig. 4.

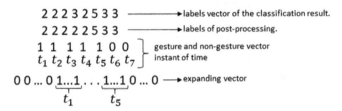

Fig. 4. Process for obtaining the expanded recognition vector.

The continuity of the expanded vector is verified; this step evaluates two scenarios.

1. If the ones vector is continuous the signal is considered accepted for the next evaluation.
2. If the ones vector is not continuous the signal is rejected.

To verify if the recognition of the executed gesture is valid, it is necessary to map the vector of the original signal transformed into zeros and ones with the signal of the expanded vector. To generate the vector of zeros and ones from the original signal, it was manually segmented. In the segmentation process, the initial point is where the user starts the execution of the gesture and the final point where the user ends the execution of the gesture. Then, the vector of zeros and ones is created with ones between the space delimited as the start and end of the gesture as explained in the previous paragraph, and the remaining spaces of the vector with zeros that represent the non-gesture.

The zeros and ones vector of both the original signal A and the classified signal B are then aligned to determine the validity of the recognition.

As shown in Fig. 5.

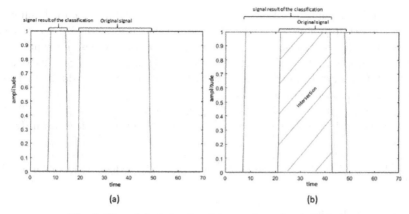

Fig. 5. The original signal and the resultant signal aligned.

The measured intersection value gives gesture recognition between the A and B signals. Figure 5a shows that there is no intersection. Therefore, this signal is not recognized. At the same time, the signal presented in Fig. 5b shows that there is an intersection between signals A and B.

If the value of the intersection is higher than the threshold $\tau = 0.25$, the signal is accepted as recognized $\rho \geq \tau$. The intersection value is given by the following calculation [22]:

$$\rho = 2x\frac{|A \cap B|}{|A| + |B|} \tag{3}$$

3.2 Evaluation Metric of the Specific Recognition Model

In this work, we test the model by changing the value of the window of the feature extraction module. Besides, we change the value of k of KNN and changing the value of w of the distance metric DTW. Furthermore, the model was tested in a laptop with CPU Intel Core i7-7500u of 2.70 GHz, with 2 cores and 4 logical processors, with 16 GB of RAM.

In this sense, the model was tested with the feature extraction window in 7 and 10, the k of the KNN with 1 and 3, finally, the w of the warping of the DTW with 1, 3, and 5.

The protocol used to evaluate the classification accuracy, recognition accuracy, and the model processing time is the average obtained from each user concerning their measured parameters, as shown in Eqs. 4 and 5.

$$C(X)_{user} = \frac{1}{n}\sum_{i=1}^{n} \varphi(x_i) \tag{4}$$

$$C(X)_{general} = \frac{1}{N}\sum_{i=1}^{N} C(X)_{user_i} \tag{5}$$

Where n is the number of test samples for each user, and N is the total number of test users. In (4) $\varphi(x_i)$ represents the classification value, if it returns 1 it is a hit and if it returns zero it is an error. In this sense, the sum of the hits divided for the number of samples of each user returns the accuracy of the model measured in each user, and to obtain the total accuracy of the model the accuracies of each user are added and divided for the total number of users tested (5).

In this context, the first evaluation of the model is made with a window of 7 and a stride of 7. by k = 1, 3. and w = 1, 5, and 7. The values obtained are presented in Table 1.

Table 1. Percentage and time in milliseconds of the first evaluation of the specific recognition model.

Window = 7, stride = 7								
wDTW = 1			wDTW = 5			wDTW = 7		
Class.	Recog.	Time	Class.	Recog.	Time	Class.	Recog.	Time
k = 1	89.58	79.44	408	89.86	78.89	428	89.86	78.89	433
k = 3	90.14	79.58	388	89.86	79.72	311	89.86	79.72	383

Table 1 shows a difference between the classification and recognition values. This difference occurs because classification only designates the correct label, while recognition designates the label and the time in which the gesture was executed.

In Fig. 6, the difference between the accuracy of classification and recognition is better observed.

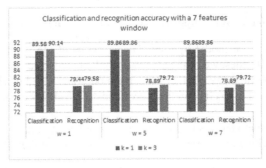

Fig. 6. Percentage values of classification and recognition reported by the recognition model.

In this respect, processing time plays an important role. The time measures the response of the algorithm after the user executes the gesture, and to report that the work is in real-time according to [6] the response must be less than 300 ms.

The figure shows the reported recognition times (Fig. 7).

Also, the model is evaluated for the second time using a window of 10 features, and in the same sense using k = 1, 3, and w = 1, 5, and 7.

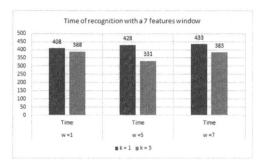

Fig. 7. Recognition time reported by the recognition model.

Table 2. Percentage and time in milliseconds of the second evaluation of the specific recognition model.

Window = 10, stride = 10								
	wDTW = 1			wDTW = 5			wDTW = 7		
	Class.	Recog.	Time	Class.	Recog.	Time	Class.	Recog.	Time
k = 1	90.42	75.56	358	91.39	76.81	324	91.39	76.67	325
k = 3	90.83	75.97	305	92.22	77.64	287	92.08	77.5	298

The values are reported in Table 2.

In the same way as the evaluation with a window of 7 features, with a window of 10 features, the difference between classification and recognition accuracy is observed, shown in Fig. 8.

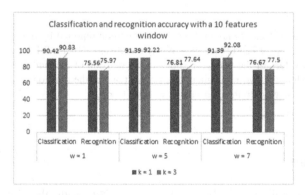

Fig. 8. Percentage values of classification and recognition reported by the recognition model.

However, this evaluation reports times of less than 300 ms. As shows in Fig. 9.

Finally, we present a comparison of the classification and recognition values with the windows of 7 and 10 characteristics.

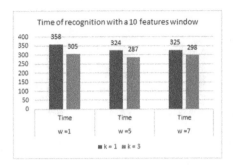

Fig. 9. Percentage values of classification and recognition reported by the recognition model.

As shows in Fig. 10.

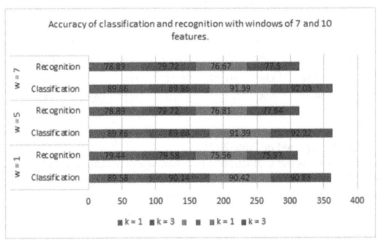

Fig. 10. Percentage values of classification and recognition reported by the recognition model measured with windows of 7 and 10 features. Where w corresponds to the DTW warping parameter, and the first two values of the bars correspond to the division of the signal into windows of 7 characteristics, while the two remaining values correspond to the division of the signal into 10 characteristics evaluated with the respective k = 1 and k = 3.

4 Discussion

In this paper, a specific model of hand gesture recognition using the LMC is presented, as well as the evaluation metric for gesture recognition. To train and evaluate the model, 5 static gestures are used, these are: open hand, fist, wave in, wave out, and pinch. The modules used are data acquisition, pre-processing, feature extraction, classification, and postprocessing. Many reported models do not distinguish between classification and recognition problems. However, there is a difference in accuracy values between classification and recognition models. In this work, with a 10 features window, k = 3, and wDTW = 7, we obtain an accuracy of 92.22%, while for the recognition, it is 77.64%. This difference occurs because the classification problem consists of given a set of features; the system returns a label. While in the recognition, it returns a label that represents the gesture and the instant of time in which the gesture was executed. The time that the system reports is 287 ms, which indicates that it works in real-time. This is necessary because the fields of application that use gesture recognition work in real-time. In the same sense, in the literature, some models do not report the processing time

The highest value of recognition accuracy is obtained with a 7 features window, with k = 3, and wDTW = 5, the value is 79.72%.

This difference may be because with 7 features, the label vector is higher than the label vector with 10 features, and this results in the expanded vector explained in the previous section having more chance of entering the threshold presented in the recognition protocol.

5   Conclusions

The per-user specific model was evaluated by varying the window size in the feature extraction module between 7 and 10 features. Also, the value of the k near-neighbors of the KNN classifier was varied with k = 1 and k = 3. Also, the value of the warping of DTW of the distance metric varied in w = 1, and w = 5. The model recognizes 5 statics gestures open hand, fist, wave in, wave out, and pinch. Also, it uses the modules of data acquisition, pre-processing, feature extraction, classification, and postprocessing. The model is developed with samples of 38 subjects. In addition, it requires 30 repetitions of each gesture by each user to obtain a classification accuracy of 92.22% and 77.64% recognition accuracy, and that works in real-time, reporting an average of 287 ms.

In this context, it is concluded that the window of 10 features is the one that best represents the signal, together with the hyperparameters of k = 3 and wDTW = 5.

For future work, a feature extractor based on statistical data and values in the frequency domain will be presented.

Acknowledgment. The gratitude to the Escuela Politécnica Nacional and its doctoral program in computer science, for having the best human resources for the development of its students. Thanks, are also due to the Universidad Técnica de Ambato, for providing the facilities for continuous improvement. And to the Corporación Ecuatoriana para el Desarrollo de la Investigación y la académia "CEDIA" with the call CEPRA XIII-2019.

References

1. Gong, S., Mao, H., Wang, Y., Xu, A.: Machine learning in human-computer nonverbal communication. In: NeuroManagement and Intelligent Computing Method on Multimodal Interaction. AICMI 2019. https://doi.org/10.1145/3357160.3357670
2. Konar, A., Saha, S.: Gesture Recognition: Principles, Techniques and Applications (2014)

3. Nogales, R. Benalcazar M.: Real-time hand gesture recognition using the leap motion controller and machine learning. In: 2019 IEEE Latin American Conference on Computational Intelligence LA-CCI 2019, pp. 1–7 (2019). https://doi.org/10.1109/LA-CCI47412.2019.903 7037

4. Wheatland, N., Wang, Y., Song, H., Neff, M., Zordan, V., Jörg, S.: State of the art in hand and finger modeling and animation. Comput. Graph. Forum **34**(2), 735–760 (2015). https://doi.org/10.1111/cgf.12595

5. Nogales, R., Benalcázar, M.E.: A survey on hand gesture recognition using machine learning and infrared information. In: Botto-Tobar, M., Zambrano Vizuete, M., Torres-Carrión, P., Montes León, S., Pizarro Vásquez, G., Durakovic, B. (eds.) ICAT 2019. CCIS, vol. 1194, pp. 297–311. Springer, Cham (2020). https://doi.org/10.1007/978-3-030-42520-3_24

6. Benalcázar, M.E. et al.: Real-time hand gesture recognition using the Myo armband and muscle activity detection. In: 2017 IEEE Second Ecuador Technical Chapters Meeting, pp. 1–6 (2017). https://doi.org/10.1109/etcm.2017.8247458

7. Stinghen, I.A., Chen, E.N., Maia, J., Silva, R.: Gesture Recognition Using Leap Motion : A Comparison Between Machine Learning Algorithms (2014)

8. Li, F., Li, Y., Du, B., Xu, H., Xiong, H., Chen, M.: A gesture interaction system based on improved finger feature and WE-KNN. In: ACM's International Conference Proceedings Series, pp. 39–43 (2019). https://doi.org/10.1145/3325730.3325759

9. Marin, G., Dominio, F., Zanuttigh, P.: Hand gesture recognition with jointly calibrated Leap Motion and depth sensor. Multimedia Tools Appl. **75**(22), 14991–15015 (2015). https://doi.org/10.1007/s11042-015-2451-6

10. Jiang, X., Xiao, Z.G., Menon, C.: Virtual grasps recognition using fusion of Leap Motion and force myography. Virtual Reality **22**(4), 297–308 (2018). https://doi.org/10.1007/s10055-018-0339-2

11. Liu, F., Du, B., Wang, Q., Wang, Y., Zeng, W.: Hand Gesture Recognition Using Kinect via Deterministic Learning, pp. 2127–2132 (2017)

12. Ameur, S., Ben Khalifa, A. Bouhlel, M.S.: A comprehensive leap motion database for hand gesture recognition. In: 2016 7th International Conference on Sciences of Electronics, Technologies of Information and Telecommunications SETIT 2016, no. July 2013, pp. 514–519 (2017). https://doi.org/10.1109/setit.2016.7939924

13. Ramos, A.L.A. et al.: Alphabet Hand Gesture Recognition Using Histogram of Oriented Gradients, Support Vector Machine and K – Nearest Neighbor Algorithm. vol. 6, no. 04, pp. 200–205 (2019)

14. Naguri, C.R., Bunescu, R.C.: Recognition of dynamic hand gestures from 3D motion data using LSTM and CNN architectures. In: Proceedings of 16th IEEE International Conference on Machine Learning and Applications ICMLA 2017, vol. 2018, pp. 1130–1133 (2018). https://doi.org/10.1109/icmla.2017.00013

15. Vamsikrishna, K.M., Dogra, D.P., Desarkar, M.S.: Computer-vision-assisted palm rehabilitation with supervised learning. IEEE Trans. Biomed. Eng. **63**(5), 991–1001 (2016). https://doi.org/10.1109/TBME.2015.2480881

16. Almasre, M.A., Al-nuaim, H.: Recognizing Arabic Sign Language Gestures Using Depth Sensors and a KSVM Classifier, pp. 146–151 (2016)

17. Avola, D., Bernardi, M., Cinque, L., Foresti, G.L., Massaroni, C.: Exploiting recurrent neural networks and leap motion controller for the recognition of sign language and semaphoric hand gestures. IEEE Trans. Multimed. **21**(8):1 (2018). https://doi.org/10.1109/tmm.2018.2856094

18. Rossol, N., Cheng, I., Basu, A.: A multisensor technique for gesture recognition through intelligent skeletal pose analysis. IEEE Trans. Human-Mach Syst. **46**(3), 350–359 (2016). https://doi.org/10.1109/THMS.2015.2467212

19. Ultraleap. Leap Motion Controller The world' s leading hand tracking technology. pp. 15–16 (2019)

20. Raschka, S.: STAT 479: Machine Learning Lecture Notes (2018). http://stat.wisc.edu/~sra schka/teaching/stat479-fs2018/
21. Dau, H.A., et al.: Optimizing dynamic time warping's window width for time series data mining applications. Data Min. Knowl. Disc. **32**(4), 1074–1120 (2018). https://doi.org/10. 1007/s10618-018-0565-y
22. Benalc, M.E., Anchundia, C.E., Zambrano, P., Segura, M.: A Model for Real-Time Hand Gesture Recognition Using Electromyography (EMG), Covariances and Feed-Forward Artificial Neural Networks

Design, Simulation, and Construction of a Prototype Transhumeral Bio-mechatronic Prosthesis

John Romero-Bacuilima[1]($\boxtimes$), Ronald Pucha-Ortiz[1]($\boxtimes$), Luis Serpa-Andrade[1,2]($\boxtimes$), John Calle-Siguencia[1]($\boxtimes$), and Daniel Proaño-Guevara[1]($\boxtimes$)

[1] Research Group on Biomedical Engineering, Universidad Politécnica Salesiana, Cuenca, Ecuador
`{jromerob1,rpucha,dproanog}@est.ups.edu.ec,`
`{lserpa,jcalle}@ups.edu.ec`
[2] Research Group on Artificial Intelligence and Assistive Technologies GIIATa, UNESCO Member for Inclusion, Cuenca, Ecuador

Abstract. This document presents the development of a low-cost, right limb transhumeral prosthesis prototype, which incorporates basic movements to recover the performance of some activities of daily living for people who have suffered an amputation of the limb above the elbow. Firstly, the anthropometry of the patient's limb is defined, which will set the prosthesis's dimensioning. Afterward, a mechanism is established that meets the required degrees of freedom, and finally, the prosthesis prototype is designed considering materials, dimensions, and geometry for each part. It is mainly used 3D printing by deposition with ABS material, and conventional manufacturing processes with chip removal. The elements were designed, taking into account the anthropometric measurements of a 45-year-old transhumeral amputation patient with a height of 1.61 m, a 3D scan of the healthy arm, and the stump was performed with the Eva Artec scanner. The results consist of a prototype prosthesis with 4 degrees of freedom: flexion-extension of the elbow with a range of movement of 120°, prone supination with a range of movement of 180°, flexion-extension of the wrist with a range of movement of 60° and in the ulnar-radial deviation with a range of movement of 70°, with a total weight of 1.65 kg. The transhumeral prosthesis adapts to the prototype of the "MAKI 3.0" hand prosthesis, which has only one degree of freedom and a weighs 326 g.

Keywords: Transhumeral prosthesis · MAki 3.0 · Degrees of freedom · Anthropometry · Amputation · Stump

1 Introduction

A person experiencing a loss of their upper limb is limited in developing their activities of daily living. With the advancement of technologies and the development of new materials, the field of prosthetics has evolved rapidly, having prostheses with movements that simulate a limb. However, the price is high, and the vulnerable sectors of society

G. Rodriguez Morales et al. (Eds.): TICEC 2020, CCIS 1307, pp. 104–114, 2020.
https://doi.org/10.1007/978-3-030-62833-8_9

cannot afford these devices. The purpose of prostheses' development is to help people who have suffered the amputation of one of their limbs so that they can fulfill and resume their activities of daily living (ADLs).

Nowadays, prostheses that require a greater complexity of movement depend on a better understanding of the anatomical study of the human upper limb, taking into account the complexity and multiple degrees of freedom (DoF) of the arm joints and the lack of appropriate muscles from which EMG signals can be acquired. With these requirements, there are two types of upper limb prostheses: the body-powered type and the myoelectric type [1–4].

When developing this type of prototypes, it is critical to know the prostheses currently available in the market, how many degrees of freedom they have, what type of actuators they use, and other elements that must be taken into consideration. Carrying out the study of state of the art, in the paper "A Gas-Actuated Anthropomorphic Prosthesis for Transhumeral Amputees", shows that consists of 21 degrees of freedom with pneumatic piston-type actuators, which are powered by gas for which makes it not portable, is subsequently analyzed "Design of a Myoelectric Transhumeral Prosthesis" that consists of 24 degrees of freedom, its actuators are brushless dc motors, its transmission is by gear chains, the power of these motors is by batteries that allows the prosthesis to be portable, "The RIC arm - a small, anthropomorphic transhumeral prosthesis" which consists of 5 degrees of freedom, its actuators are, its transmission is by planetary gears, it is battery-powered, and finally "Diseño y construcción de un mecanismo paralelo para prototipo de prótesis transhumeral", consists of 3 degrees of freedom, uses linear actuators that perform their movements and their source of energy are batteries [4–7].

According to the Consejo Nacional para la Igualdad de Discapacidades (CONADIS), there are 455,829 people with disabilities in Ecuador. Physical disability occupies the highest percentage with a total of 46.68%, which is equivalent to 212766 people. The province of Azuay has a total of 14,571 people with physical disabilities, among which we have that 33.20% (4838) represent the amputation of limbs. Azuay is one of the provinces with the highest rate of people with disabilities in active employment. (CONADIS: 12/02/2018).

In Ecuador, more than 8% of the population has upper or lower limbs incapacity, due to malformations, medical amputations, or accidents [8], research endeavor in this type of devices are necessary for the society, besides in Ecuador there are few centers dedicated to the research and development of this type of prototypes, until 2018, the *Ministerio de Salud Pública* had three orthosis and prosthesis workshops throughout Ecuador: at the Guayaquil hospital the Eugenio Espejo hospital in Quito, and the Isidro Ayora hospital in Loja.

The prosthesis prototype developed in this article considers 4 degrees of freedom, 4 in the arm and forearm, this device initially has an open-loop ON-OFF control but is designed to have feedback and controlled with a closed-loop system that will be considered in future work.

In the section "Methods and materials", the movements and ranges that make up the prosthesis are exposed, such as: flexion - elbow extension, pronation, radial deviation - ulnar and wrist extension flexion, to then give way to the choice of actuators of they will help develop these movements, finally the material chosen for each of the elements that will make up the prosthesis and the different elements are bushings and shafts are exposed. For the "Stress simulation" section there are graphs of torques and speed that the actuators must develop to perform the movement, with this then give way to the "Results and discussion" section, where a comparison of the prosthesis with others on the market is made and with this, to have a perspective of the prosthesis, finally in the "Conclusion" section to expose what has been developed.

2 Methods and Materials

The movements and degrees of freedom (DOF) that constitute the prosthesis, start from a previous study of the environment in which it is to be developed, and then give way to its design. Afterward, the mechanisms and components are designed to satisfy the range of movements established in the research of state of the art.

2.1 Prototype Design

The critical point in the design of a transhumeral prosthesis is to determine its degrees of freedom, and this will determine the optimal equilibrium between the weight and skill of the prosthesis [6]. Based on these criteria, it was decided to develop a prototype prosthesis with 4 degrees of freedom that allow basic limb movements (Fig. 1): 2-DoF at the wrist (Flexo-Extension, radial-ulnar deviation), 1 -DoF in the elbow (Flexo-extension), 1-DoF of the forearm (Prono-supination). This prosthesis will be attached to the "Maki 3.0" prototype (Fig. 2) [9], a right-hand prosthesis that is already developed at the *Universidad Politécnica Salesiana*, Cuenca, Ecuador, which has 1 degree of freedom with seven basic movements

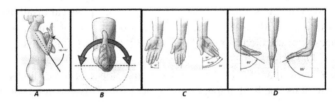

Fig. 1. Proposed movements for the thanshumeral prosthesis [4]. A) Elbow flexo-extension. B) Forearm pronation-supination. C) Abduction-adduction. C) Wrist flexo-extension.

Fig. 2. Final prototype of "Maki 3.0" developed at the *Universidad Politécnica Salesiana* [9–11].

2.1.1 Elbow Flexion-Extension

The total range of action defined of a healthy elbow is usually 0 degrees (fully extended) to approximately 145° (fully flexed), although it is stated that most activities of daily living can be performed with a range of motion between 30 and 130°, i.e., 100° of movement [12].

A range of motion can be set from 0°–120°, and the speed will depend on the actuator to be used, although a speed equal to or greater than 155°/s would be adequate.

2.1.2 Pronation-Supination

The total range of movement defined is between 0° (intermediate position) to approximately 90° (supination) and 85° (pronation), that is, it has a total movement range of 175° [13].

The range of motion is established from 0° to 175°, and a suitable speed for the prosthesis pronation-supination is 150°/s due to higher speeds are oversized to carry out activities of daily living.

2.1.3 Radial-Ulnar Deviation

Radial deviation consists of the abduction of the hand. It ranges from 0 to 25° [13].

The ulnar deviation consists of the abduction of the hand, and it has an amplitude of 0° to 30° [13].

It is established for radial deviation from 0 to 20° and ulnar deviation from 0 to 45°.

2.1.4 Wrist Flexion-Extension

Flexion is the inclination of the palm towards the forearm and goes from 0 to 80° [13].

The extension is observed when the palm moves away from the forearm, and it goes from 0 to 70° [13].

The range of motion in this joint is established from 0° to −30° in flexion and 0° to 30° in extension, 0 being when the hand is parallel to the frontal plane.

2.2 Movement Generation

To generate movements on the prosthesis, the torques must be considered to generate said movements. Reviewing the literature, the flexion-extension of the elbow found that the maximum torque was 5.5 Nm in flexion [14], for pronation-supination it would require approximately 1.4 Nm [4], followed by this the radial-ulnar deviation ranges from 7.9 to 15.3 Nm and the ulnar deviation ranges from 5.9 to 11.9 Nm [14], finally for wrist flexo-extension the torque for flexion ranges from 5.2 to 18.7 Nm and for the extension it ranges from 3.4 to 9.4 Nm [15].

For the necessary torque in the movements, the dynamic analysis was performed considering that the arm will lift a maximum weight of 0.5 kg in the palm, enough weight to carry out activities of daily living, in addition to the "Maki 3.0" it has an approximate weight of 326 g, and the weight of the prosthesis should not exceed 2 kg.

The results can be seen in Fig. 3. Here we observe that for the elbow flexion-extension it was found that the maximum torque was 2800 Nmm approximately 2.8 Nm, for the pronation-supination movement it would require 1745 Nmm approximately 1,745 Nm, in the radial - ulnar deviation a force of 39.5 is obtained because this movement was designed with a linear actuator. Finally, for wrist flexo-extension, a torque of 472 Nmm was obtained approximately 0.48 Nm, taking these torque as a basis we consider a safety factor 1.8 for the choice of the actuators of these movements.

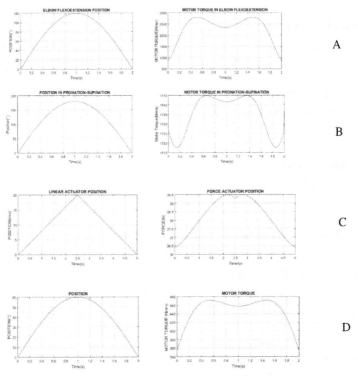

Fig. 3. Dynamic simulations of prosthetic movements. A) Flexo elbow extension. B) Prone supination of the forearm. C) Abduction and Adduction actuator force. C) Flexo wrist extension.

For the flexo elbow extension, the ANNIMOS brand servo motor is chosen, which has a 7.4 v torque of 60 kg * cm approximately 6500 Nmm, also has a speed of 0.15 s/60°, which means that it has a speed of 400°/s, sufficient values to cover what is requested for said movements.

For wrist pronation-supination and flexo-extension, the ANNIMOS brand servo motor is chosen, which has a 7.4 V torque of 35 kg * cm approximately 3500 Nmm, also has a speed of 0.11 s/60° without load which means that it has a speed of 545°/s, sufficient values to cover what is requested for said movements.

For the ulnar radial deviation, a linear actuator of the ACTUONIX PQ12 brand with a 20 mm stroke is chosen, the maximum force that it gives us at 12 V is 50 N, with a maximum stem output speed of 10 mm/s.

The chosen servomotors have an internal circuit that allows the position to be controlled using the pulse width; this consists in generating a PWM (Pulse Width Modulation) wave using specialized hardware, for the control of the servomotor and the actuators, a PIC 16F887 and the input and output of the actuator stem, use is made of an integrated L293D.

At the moment, the controller's programming is ON-OFF type, so the actuators' movement is individual to verify their ranges of movements. With more robust programming, the prosthesis can perform specific routines.

2.3 Material Selection

The chosen material is ABS polymer due to its fluidity, resistance to heat and impact, and ease of processing, considering that the prototype is going to be built in 3D printing Luzbot TAZ 6, it is a suitable choice [15].

For the support system and the joints, the chosen material is aluminum due to its high strength-to-weight ratio, its resistance to corrosion, its appearance and ease of forming and manufacturing, and eases the gear system in the movement of the elbow. Finally, pronation-supination is made using bronze as the base material for these gears.

2.4 Stress Simulation

With the assembly in the Autodesk Inventor software, it goes to the static analysis environment, where the fixing restrictions are placed; also, the loads considering a 0.5 kg are placed in the palm, the materials used are ABS plastic for the aesthetic part, aluminum for the structure and bronze for pins and gears.

According to [16], a 3D printed piece in ABS has a yield stress of 8.77 MPa, and the maximum stress that the material withstands before suffering a fracture is 21.24 MPa. In the simulation, it is observed that the Von Mises stress in the ABS pieces varies from 0 to 4.05 MPa (Fig. 4. Blue color), this value is less than the elastic limit and the maximum stress supported by the material, taking this into account and with the simulation results show that the safety factor varies from a minimum value of 4.7 to a maximum of 14. In summary, this prosthesis will support its weight and loads of 0.5 kg in the palm, without suffering deformation or rupture, It is also observed that the deformation will be 0.12 mm, which is an insignificant value.

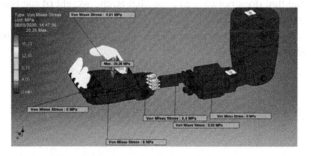

Fig. 4. Prosthesis stress simulation. (Color figure online)

2.5 Transhumeral Prosthesis Prototype Construction

The prosthesis is constructed with the chosen materials and assembled, making the mechanisms work according to the established degrees of freedom, and the ON-OFF control is integrated to verify functionality (Fig. 5)

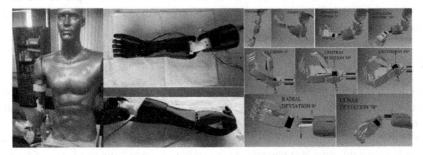

Fig. 5. Transhumeral Prosthesis final prototype.

3 Results and Discussion

The biomechatronic transhumeral prosthesis has four degrees of freedom for movements of flexion-extension of the elbow, pronation-supination, radial-ulnar deviation and flexo-extension of the wrist, the weight of the prosthesis is 1.65 kg which fits perfectly in the weight of a real arm, the actuators were chosen considering the dynamic simulations to lift a weight of 0.5 kg in the palm of the hand, and by means of a safety factor of 1.8, we have the chosen actuators which give us the torques of Table 1, in addition to this we have the torques of the flexo wrist extension which is 3.4 Nm and a linear actuator for the movement of radial-ulnar deviation of 39.5N.

In Table 2 a comparison of the Transhumeral Biomechatronic Prosthesis of the *Universidad Politécnica Salesiana* with other prostheses developed in various studies is shown, here it is observed that the ranges of movement of the other prostheses are less than those achieved in this study; also the latter has the four movements mentioned above that very few prostheses have and also comparing the weight we see that they all have a very close value that does not exceed 2 kg, that is, the weight of the prosthesis in this study remains on average.

Due to the chosen actuators (servomotors), the speeds can be programmed with the maximum values given in Table 1.

Table 1. Torque and speed comparison.

	Elbow flexo-extension			Pronation - Supination		
	Torque [Nm]	Angular speed [deg/s]	Range of motion [°]	Torque [Nm]	Angular speed [deg/s]	Range of motion [°]
Prosthesis						
Prótesis transhumeral Universidad Politécnica Salesiana	*8,8*	*266°/s*	*120°*	*5,15*	*340°/s*	*180°*
A Gas-Actuated Anthropomorphic Prosthesis for Transhumeral Amputees [5]	*30*	*Not specified*	*95*	*4.2*	*Not specified*	*150*
Design of a Myoelectric Transhumeral Prosthesis (2016) [4]	*16*	*250*	*30 ° to 130 ° in flexion*	*1.5*	*150*	*180*
The RIC arm - a small, anthropomorphic transhumeral prosthesis (2017) [6]	*12*	*80*	*Not specified*	*2.5*	*500*	*Not specified*
Diseño y construcción de un mecanismo paralelo para prototipo de prótesis transhumeral (2014) [7]	*Not specified*	*90*	*20°-125°*	*Not specified*	*Not specified*	*180*
LTI Boston Elbow [6].	*12.1*	*113*	*Not specified*	*Not specified*	*Does not apply*	*Does not apply*
Motion control [6] [19].	*Does not apply*	*Does not apply*	*Does not apply*	*0.7*	*216*	*180*
Otto Bock wrist [6].	*Does not apply*	*Does not apply*	*Does not apply*	*Not specified*	*130-160*	*Not specified*
Utah Arm ProWrist Rotator [6].	*Does not apply*	*Does not apply*	*Does not apply*	*1.7*	*300*	*Not specified*

Then comparing the torques and the speeds of the prostheses (Table 2), it can be seen that in the flexion-extension of the elbow, the motor torque is lower than the others. However, it must be taken into account that this prototype prosthesis is made for positioning in space and grasping objects of daily life weighing less than 0.5 kg, the speed in this movement is 266°/s which is appropriate and as we see higher than the speed of the other prostheses.

If we compare the pronation-supination motor torque, we see that the value of 5.15 Nm is higher than the other values, and the speed is at an appropriate value of 340°/s, which is within the speed range of all these devices.

In the stress simulation, it is observed that the Von Mises stress in the ABS pieces varies from 0 to 4.05 MPa (blue color), these values are less than the elastic limit and the maximum limit supported by the material, taking this into account and with the simulation results that show us that the safety factor goes from a minimum value of 4.7 to a maximum of 14, we can conclude that this prosthesis will support its weight and loads of 0.5 kg in the palm without suffering deformation or breakage.

Finally, the construction gives us satisfactory results by having an open-loop control; in future works, it will be possible to integrate the whole control part and the signal socket.

Table 2. Prosthesis comparison.

	Prótesis Transhumeral Universidad Politécnica Salesiana	A Gas-Actuated Anthropomorphic Prosthesis for Transhumeral Amputees [5].	Design of a Myoelectric Transhumeral Prosthesis [4].	The RIC arm - a small, anthropomorphic transhumeral prosthesis [6].	Diseño y construcción de un mecanismo paralelo para prototipo de prótesis transhumeral [7].
Degrees of freedom	4 degrees of freedom, 12 independent actuators	21 degrees of freedom, 9 independent actuators	24 degrees of freedom, 12 independent actuators	5 active DOF: a hand driven by 2-DOF, a 2-DOF wrist and a 1-DOF elbow	3 degrees of freedom:. Humeral rotation, flexion-extension and pronation-supination
Weight	1.65kg	2kg	1.9kg	1,5 Kg	1 Kg
Actuators	Servo motors and linear actuators	Cylinders for mechanical movement of elbow and wrist	DC brushless motor	Motor	Linear actuators
Elbow range of motion	120°	105°	100°	Not specified	20°-125°
Pronation range of motion	180°	95°	180°	180	180°
Wrist flexión-extension range of motion	60°	105°	Does not apply	Not specified	Does not apply
Ulnar-radial range of deviation	70°	40°	Does not apply	Not specified	Does not apply
Energy source	Battery	Gas (Not portable)	Gears	Battery	Battery

4   Conclusion

The prototype of a transhumeral prosthesis is a device that allows a person with amputation of this type to carry out daily tasks, in this project it was possible to build a low-cost device (2300 USD), with various functionalities, aesthetic and personalized.

The construction of the transhumeral prosthesis was carried out with a methodology that guaranteed the achievement of the results; Firstly, an analysis of the anthropometry and ranges of movement of a person, here we obtained, as a result, the 3D scan files, as well as the measurement of the patient, then in the part of the design we tried to give the prototype the same stockings of the patient having a good result that is very close to the real arm and also the manufacturing processes allowed to obtain the designed product.

The dynamic analysis already allows the prototype design to carry out the simulations to determine the forces and torques needed in the actuators to choose the indicated actuator for each movement. The stress analysis ensures that all parts of the prototype support the indicated loads, obtaining very favorable results, and although this prosthesis is developed for positioning rather than lifting loads, it can lift a load of 0.5 kg in the palm.

The construction of the prototype that was carried out by 3D printing and conventional machining in the materials defined in the design guarantees functional and aesthetic parts. The development and integration of the electronic test board for the open-loop control of the device make it possible to demonstrate that all the defined movements were obtained.

Finally, it can be said that it has a device with four degrees of freedom with the movements and ranges established in the process, it weights 1.65 kg similar to the weight of a real arm, they also have a very aesthetic appearance and will finally favor the incorporation of a closed-loop control system for future work.

References

1. Proaño-Guevara, D., Procel-Feijóo, J., Zhingre-Balcazar, J., Serpa-Andrade, L.: Biomimetical arm prosthesis: a new proposal. In: Duffy, V., Lightner, N. (eds.) AHFE 2017. AISC, vol. 590, pp. 549–558. Springer, Cham (2018). https://doi.org/10.1007/978-3-319-60483-1_57
2. Taylor, C.L.: The biomechanics of control in upper-extremity prostheses. Artif. Limbs **2**(3), 4–25 (1955)
3. Gade, J., Hugosdottir, R., Kamavuako, E.N.: Phantom movements from physiologically inappropriate muscles: a case study with a high transhumeral amputee. In: 2015 37th Annual International Conference of the IEEE Engineering in Medicine and Biology Society (EMBC), pp. 3488–3491 (2015)
4. Bennett, D.A., Mitchell, J.E., Truex, D., Goldfarb, M.: Design of a myoelectric transhumeral prosthesis. IEEE/ASME Trans. Mechatron. **21**(4), 1868–1879 (2016)
5. Fite, K.B., Withrow, T.J., Shen, X., Wait, K.W., Mitchell, J.E., Goldfarb, M.: A gas-actuated anthropomorphic prosthesis for transhumeral amputees. IEEE Trans. Robot. **24**(1), 159–169 (2008)
6. Lenzi, T.: The RIC arm - a small, anthropomorphic transhumeral prosthesis. IEEE/ASME Trans. Mechatron. **21**, 1–11 (2016)
7. Vázquez, J.R.M., Uribe, A.Z.E., Cuevas, I.D.R.: Diseño y construcción de un mecanismo paralelo para prototipo de prótesis transhumeral (2014)
8. Ecuador fabrica prótesis externas con orientación social : Variedades : La Hora Noticias de Ecuador, sus provincias y el mundo. https://lahora.com.ec/losrios/noticia/1102296461/ecuador-fabrica-protesis-externas-con-orientacion-social. Accessed 15 May 2020
9. Calle, J., Encalada-Seminario, G., Pinto León, R.A.: Design and kinematic analysis of a biphalange articulated finger mechanism for a biomechatronic hand prosthesis, pp. 1–7 (2018). https://doi.org/10.1109/ropec.2018.8661357
10. Cuzco, J., Quinde, M., Brito, J., Calle, J., Urgilés, F.: Diseño, construcción e implementación de prótesis de mano biomecánica derecha. In: 2014 IEEE ANDESCON, Cochabamba, pp. 1–1 (2014). https://doi.org/10.1109/andescon.2014.7098537
11. Cajamarca, L.F., Matute, J., Calle, J., Yunga, F., Vargas, J., Urgiles, F.: Design, development and implementation of a biomechanical right-hand prosthesis: second stage. In: 2017 IEEE Global Humanitarian Technology Conference (GHTC), San Jose, CA, 2017, pp. 1–6 (2017). https://doi.org/10.1109/ghtc.2017.8239283
12. Neumann, D.: Fundamentos De Rehabilitacion Fisica. Paidotribo, Barcelona (2007)
13. Ibrahim, A., Kapandji, I.A., Torres Lacomba, M.: Fisiología articular: esquemas comentados de mecánica humana. Médica Panamericana (2006)
14. Bennett, D.A., Mitchell, J., Goldfarb, M.: Design and characterization of a powered elbow prosthesis. In: Annual International Conference of the IEEE Engineering in Medicine and Biology Society EMBS, vol. 2015, pp. 2458–2461. Novem (2015)

15. Delp, S.L., Grierson, A.E., Buchanan, T.S.: Maximum isometric moments generated by the wrist muscles in flexion-extension and radial-ulnar deviation. J. Biomech. **29**(10), 1371–1375 (1996)
16. Pacheco, G.: Análisis de tracción de probetas impresas en 3d mediante deposición de hilo fundido de pla, abs y pla/mlo. Universidad Politécnica Salesiana, Cuenca, Ecuador (2019)
17. Pucha-Ortiz, R., Romero-Bacuilima, J., Serpa-Andrade, L.: Structural anatomical study of the upper limb to design a transhumeral prosthesis. In: Kalra, J., Lightner, Nancy J. (eds.) AHFE 2020. AISC, vol. 1205, pp. 152–157. Springer, Cham (2020). https://doi.org/10.1007/978-3-030-50838-8_21
18. Romero Bacuilima, J.M., Pucha Ortiz, R.I., Serpa-Andrade, L.: Mechatronic design of transhumeral prosthesis based on a goniometry and anthropometry study. In: Kalra, J., Lightner, Nancy J. (eds.) AHFE 2020. AISC, vol. 1205, pp. 145–151. Springer, Cham (2020). https://doi.org/10.1007/978-3-030-50838-8_20
19. Motion Control, Inc., is the leading U.S. manufacturer of myoelectric and externally powered prosthetic arm systems. http://www.utaharm.com/. Accessed 03 May 2020

Data Science

Behavior of a Polymer Electrolyte Fuel Cell from a Statistical Point of View Based on Data Analysis

Ester Melo[1]([✉]), Ángel Encalada[2] [ID], and Mayken Espinoza-Andaluz[3] [ID]

[1] Facultad de Ciencias Sociales y Humanísticas, Escuela Superior Politécnica del Litoral, ESPOL, Campus Gustavo Galindo Km. 30.5 Vía Perimetral, P.O. Box 09-01-5863, Guayaquil, Ecuador
emelo@espol.edu.ec

[2] Facultad de Ingeniería en Mecánica y Ciencias de la Producción, Escuela Superior Politécnica del Litoral, ESPOL, Campus Gustavo Galindo Km. 30.5 Vía Perimetral, P.O. Box 09-01-5863, Guayaquil, Ecuador
angaenca@espol.edu.ec

[3] Facultad de Ingeniería En Mecánica y Ciencias de la Producción, Centro de Energías Renovables y Alternativas, Escuela Superior Politécnica del Litoral, ESPOL, Campus Gustavo Galindo Km. 30.5 Vía Perimetral, P.O. Box 09-01-5863, Guayaquil, Ecuador
masespin@espol.edu.ec

Abstract. Alternative energy sources appear as a suitable solution as the energy demand is growing. Fuel cells are one of the promising devices to face the mentioned energy demand in a green manner. Predicting the behavior of a Polymer Electrolyte Fuel Cell (PEFC) in certain conditions is a useful step to enhance its mechanical properties and understand the impact of the diffusion media and the impact of the inlet reactant gases into the cell. This study aims, based on experimental data, to propose empirical correlations that describe and predict the current density in the function of other parameters measured in a Fuel Cell (FC) such as power density, voltage, anode flow and cathode flow. The approach presented in this study is directed to apply a statistical analysis related to Principal Component Analysis (PCA) to reduce the dimensionality of the involved variable. This study shows the feasibility of describing the behavior of a PEFC with simplified variables. For the proposed correlations, after an adequate selection and treatment of the data, the adjusted R^2 is around 0.99 with confidence bounds of 95%.

Keywords: PEFC · PCA · Temperature · Polynomial regression · Statistical analysis

1 Introduction

Currently, technology plays an important role in the development of daily activities. For instance, to set up an alarm to perform a bank transfer, an electronic device is required. In turn, the electronic device requires an energy source for adequate functioning. Considered the mentioned scenario, during the last decades the demand for energy sources

© Springer Nature Switzerland AG 2020
G. Rodriguez Morales et al. (Eds.): TICEC 2020, CCIS 1307, pp. 117–128, 2020.
https://doi.org/10.1007/978-3-030-62833-8_10

for mobile application devices has increased significantly [21]. The high consumption of conventional energy has resulted in negative and irreversible effects on the environment due to the increment of pollution through the excessive emission of carbon dioxide. To face this problematic, international organizations have declared to combat environmental pollution and, in their fight, they urge governments to establish public policies that allow reducing the emission of greenhouse gases in their industrial and production activities [23].

The use of renewable energy is one of the public policies that is promoted to combat environmental pollution, since this type of energy comes from natural and inexhaustible sources from which no reserves are required, as in the case of fossil fuels [22]. For a "clean energy" conversion process, there are various alternatives, including fuel cells (FCs); whose procedure is to transform the chemical energy present in chemical compounds using electrochemical reactions into electrical energy and water as by product [20]. A polymer electrolyte fuel cell (PEFC) is an electrochemical device that produces electrical energy from chemical reactions that occur in two regions called catalytic areas where interaction between fuel flow (H_2) and oxidant flow (O_2) exists.

Nowadays, research is focused on increasing the efficiency of fuel cell (FC) systems and reducing the manufacturing costs [14], looking for new material to build some parts or combining materials to enhance the mechanical properties in general. Specifically, to improve the diffusion transport process several studies have been performed [7, 13, 26], because this a crucial process during the energy conversion process. Water management is one of the most important factors at the time of measure FC efficiency [3, 5, 12, 25]. For example, during the energy conversion process, the water vapor can produce flooding inside the FC stack and in consequence reducing the efficiency of the process. If there is not exist right water management, the FC system can produce dehydration when the system works under high temperatures.

The temperature is another important factor in the energy conversion process because it is intimately related to relative humidity (RH) which defines how the system is working under the generation of water vapor during the conversion. Following this perspective, this paper aims to present correlations based on the measured parameters during an energy conversion process, like temperature, flow cathode, flow anode, power density, current density, etc. To understand or predict a phenomenon, a principal component analysis (PCA) can be an adequate method to reduce the number of variables involved in the study, and therefore, a system simplification is obtained. The data used in this study are provided from experimental tests performed in a renewable energy laboratory.

The rest of the paper is divided as follows: Sect. 2 is devoted to present related work about this problematic, Sect. 3 is mainly dedicated to present the methodology applied in the current study. Results are presented in Sect. 4, and in Sect. 5, results and some conclusions are developed.

2 Related Work

Concerning the study of PEFC from a statistical point of view, there is a lack of information, because the most of studies are related to aspects like maintenance costs, building materials, mathematical modeling and simulation, performance optimization, etc. Really few studies related to the problem addressing in this paper were found (Fig. 1).

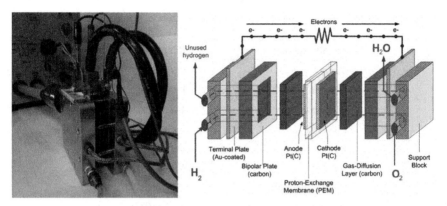

Fig. 1. PEFC equipment used in this study (left), and an explained view of a FC (right). Adapted from [8]

Zhu et al. [27] worked in a mathematical model to analyze performance parameters based on the comparison between experimentation and simulation of the performance in an FC. Through this model, it is possible to predict the performance of an FC in different work conditions. However, there is a limitation in the part of FC control and design.

On the other hand, Espinoza et al. [6] proposed correlations for power and current density as a function of RH. They analyzed the RH as a function of the reactive inlet gas temperature, as well as the power and current density as a function of the reactant gas temperature gradient.

Specifically, for the problem addressed in this study, two works were developed from a statistical analysis. Bahanova et al. [2] worked in a detailed statistical description of the microbial FC performance using PCA as the main base. Likewise, Okorie et al. [17] established an important relationship between FC data analysis and remanufacturing, where it is important for the identification and classification of parameters that generate benefits and damages in FC performance. Also, they presented an appropriate benchmark in the circular economy paradigm through an approach focused on the performance and efficiency of manufacturing systems.

3 Methodology

For the development of this study, a database obtained from experimental tests is used. The database provided the following variables described in Table 1.

As can be seen, there were three types of temperature: cell, hydrogen gas, and oxygen gas. The last two, in turn, reached five different values during the experimentation, $T = 40\ °C$, $50\ °C$, $60\ °C$, $70\ °C$ and $80\ °C$. Since the amount of data per temperature value is different, a random sample of 26 observations was taken for the higher temperatures or equal to $50\ °C$. This number of observations corresponds to the total of data for $T = 40\ °C$. Likewise, each temperature value corresponded to different behaviors.

As we above mentioned, our research aim is introduce the PCA concept into this study to propose a new way to study and understand the behavior of a PEFC. First, we must understand what is and how PCA works. Principal Component Analysis or

Table 1. Description of variables obtained from experimental tests

Variable name	Representation
Time	t (s)
Current	I (A)
Current density	J (mA/cm2)
Power	P (W)
Power density	$\wp$ (mW/cm2)
Voltage	V (V)
Cell temperature	T_{cell} (°C)
Hydrogen gas temperature	T_{anode} (°C)
Oxygen gas temperature	$T_{cathode}$ (°C)
Volumetric flow of hydrogen gas	Q_{anode} (L/min)
Volumetric flow of oxygen gas	$Q_{cathode}$ (L/min)

PCA, is a dimensionality-reduction method that is used to reduce the dimensionality of datasets, either when these are large or when these contain a lot of prediction variables (Fig. 2). When we reduce the dimensionality the accuracy is affected, but the trick in dimensionality reduction is to trade a little accuracy for simplicity, because smaller datasets are easier to explore and visualize and make analyzing data much easier and faster for machine learning algorithms. Thus, the idea of PCA is reduce the number of variables of a dataset, while preserving as much information as possible.

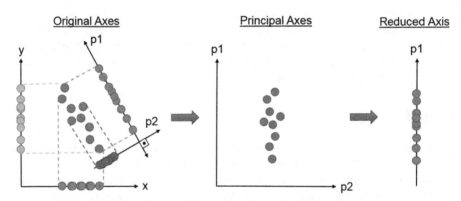

Fig. 2. Explanation of PCA from a graphical point of view

Following the research aim, a polynomial regression model by temperature value is proposed. In this polynomial regression, the independent variables result from a linear combination of certain variables provided by the experimental tests. The mentioned independent variables are the following: power density, voltage, volumetric flow of hydrogen gas, and volumetric flow of oxygen gas. For the regression, the Kaiser-Meyer-Olkin (KMO) index was first used to measure the plausibility of applying PCA [16].

Based on the results of the KMO index by temperature, the data was prepared for the application of PCA. From this analysis, the components to be used as independent variables in the polynomial regression model were obtained. The degree of the polynomial was determined from the trend of each component concerning the current density (dependent variable).

Given the analysis of the results of the regressions, the next step was to propose polynomial multiple regression models that do not include a PCA but instead use the same variables used in the PCA as independent variables of the new models. This is a step performed to contrast the results. Similarly, to determine the best model, the coefficient of determination (R^2), condition number and the variance inflation factor (VIF) were used as indicators, as indicated by Sinha [24].

On one side, the determination coefficient explains the degree to which the independent variables influence the independent variable [24]. While the VIF allows evaluating the multicollinearity of the independent variables in the model, which constitutes a regression principle and influences the relevance in the model [1]. Finally, the condition number fulfills the same function as the VIF [4]. It is recommended that the R^2 be as close to one as the VIF is between 1 and 3, and the condition number is less than 30 [1, 9, 24].

Finally, it should be noted that variables time, current, power, and temperatures were not used in each analysis. Two of them were not used because they are redundant concerning power and current density, respectively, and the rest of them corresponded to categorical variables.

4 Results

Principal Component Analysis (PCA)

Applying the KMO index for each temperature we obtained results, which are shown in Table 2. As observed, for $T = 40$ °C and 50 °C the KMO index was smaller than 0.6, which implied that it was not appropriate to factor the variables corresponding to those temperatures [16]. Therefore, the component analysis was performed for the rest of the temperatures; the results of which are detailed below.

From the results presented in Table 3, it is noted that at $T = 60$ °C, the first component has a strong positive association with the voltage and a strong negative association with the volumetric flow of oxygen and hydrogen. So, this component mainly measures the incidence of volumetric flows and voltage in the operation of the FC. It is also noted that the second component has a significant negative association with the power density; therefore, it mainly measures the incidence of this variable on the behavior of the FC. Furthermore, it is worth mentioning that the first component explains 90.2% of the variance, out of a total of 99.3%.

The results referring to $T = 70$ °C presented in Table 4 show that the first component has a strong negative association with the voltage and a strong positive association with the volumetric flow of oxygen and hydrogen. That is, similar to the first component

Table 2. Summary of KMO index results

Temperature (°C)	KMO index
40	0.584
50	0.540
60	0.694
70	0.659
80	0.701

Table 3. Summary of Principal Component Analysis results for $T = 60\ °C$

Temperature (°C)	PC	Explained variance	Component composition			
			$\wp$ (mW/cm^2)	Voltage (V)	Q_{anode} (L/min)	$Q_{cathode}$ (L/min)
60	1	0.902	−0.447998	0.521361	−0.508663	−0.518403
	2	0.091	−0.867481	−0.074748	0.408937	0.273239
Total		0.993				

at $T = 60\ °C$, it primarily measures the incidence of volumetric flows and voltage on the operation of the FC. While the second component of this temperature has the same function as the second component of $T = 60\ °C$. In the same way, it is observed that the first component explains the greater portion of the variance, being 97.6% of a total of 99.7%.

Table 4. Summary of Principal Component Analysis results for $T = 70\ °C$

Temperature (°C)	PC	Explained variance	Component composition			
			$\wp$ (mW/cm^2)	Voltage (V)	Q_{anode} (L/min)	$Q_{cathode}$ (L/min)
70	1	0.976	0.490083	−0.504315	0.502204	0.503266
	2	0.021	−0.846272	−0.082368	0.398187	0.344219
Total		0.997				

Finally, based on the resulting components for $T = 80\ °C$ in Table 5, it is noted that the first component has a strong positive association with the voltage and a strong negative association with the volumetric flow of oxygen and hydrogen. That is, it fulfills the same role as the first components of the previous temperatures. Likewise, the second component fulfills the same function as the second components of the previous temperatures. In the same way, it is observed that the first component explains the greater portion of the variance, being 96.3% of a total of 99.8%.

Table 5. Summary of Principal Component Analysis results for $T = 80\ °C$

Temperature (°C)	PC	Explained variance	Component composition			
			$\wp$ (mW/cm^2)	Voltage (V)	Q_{anode} (L/min)	$Q_{cathode}$ (L/min)
80	1	0.963	−0.490677	0.506647	−0.498872	−0.503659
	2	0.035	−0.706065	0.238582	0.534866	0.398081
Total		0.998				

4.1 Polynomial Regression

Although the PCA results indicated that it was relevant to consider only the first components in the regression analysis, the second components were not ruled out to determine impact. In this sense, both the first and second components presented quadratic tendencies in the scatter diagram, for which second-degree polynomials were established. The results for each model are summarized in Table 6.

Table 6. Summary of results of polynomial regression using PCA

Temperature (°C)	PC	R^2 adjusted	Regression equation
60	1	0.99	$185.14 \cdot PC_1^2 + 18.85 \cdot PC_1 + 469.41$
	2	0.05	$44.86 \cdot PC_2^2 + 93.86 \cdot PC_2 + 430.69$
70	1	1.00	$254.87 \cdot PC_1^2 + 17.74 \cdot PC_1 + 739.42$
	2	0.29	$627.83 \cdot PC_2^2 + 2346.21 \cdot PC_2 + 478.64$
80	1	0.99	$307.98 \cdot PC_1^2 + 27.43 \cdot PC_1 + 886.09$
	2	0.22	$927.96 \cdot PC_2^2 - 2463.69 \cdot PC_2 + 1403.32$

As can be seen, from the models whose independent variables correspond to the first component, favorable results for R^2, were obtained, all of which were greater than 0.98. Likewise, in each case, the coefficients of the variables were significant, and the regression curve managed to adequately fit the data. These graphics are illustrated in Figs. 3, 4 and 5.

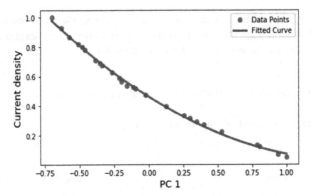

Fig. 3. Second degree polynomial regression for $T = 60\ °C$

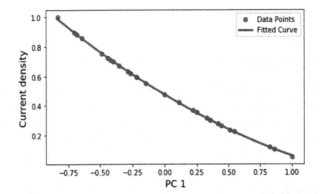

Fig. 4. Second degree polynomial regression for $T = 70\ °C$

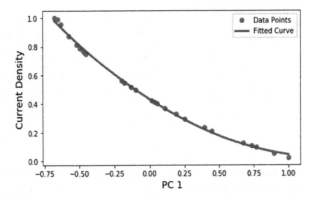

Fig. 5. Second degree polynomial regression for $T = 80\ °C$

On the other hand, the constant and the coefficients of the variables corresponding to the "successful models" (models based on principal component 1) obtained a level of significance of less than 0.05, which implies that they can explain the behavior of the curve and, therefore, are relevant. At the same time, the VIF calculated by each of these was within the acceptable range of inflation, i.e., between 1 to 3. Finally, the inflation tolerance, in each case, was acceptable, given that the values were greater than 0.3. Such results are summarized in Table 7.

Table 7. Variance Inflation Factor (VIF) and its Degree of Tolerance per temperature

	$T = 60\ °C$		$T = 70\ °C$		$T = 80\ °C$	
	VIF	Tolerance	VIF	Tolerance	VIF	Tolerance
Constant	2.4	0.42	2.3	0.43	1.9	0.53
PC_1^2	1.1	0.91	1.1	0.91	1.9	0.53
PC_1	1.1	0.91	1.1	0.91	1.9	0.53

4.2 Multiple Polynomial Regression

As previously mentioned, to contrast the results, polynomial multiple regression models were constructed for $T = 60\ °C$, 70 °C, and 80 °C, considering the variables used in the PCA as independent variables and the current density as the dependent variable. In all cases, R^2 was equal to 1. However, they reported strong cases of multicollinearity, which was observed using the condition number, the value of which must usually be less than 30. These results are summarized in Table 8.

Table 8. Summary of multiple polynomial regression results

Temperature (°C)	R^2 adjusted	Condition number
60	1.00	$2.17 \cdot 10^4$
70	1.00	$2.34 \cdot 10^5$
80	1.00	$3.31 \cdot 10^5$

5 Discussion and Conclusion

The results obtained by the KMO index confirm that other studies have mentioned concerning an FC that: the higher the temperature, the better the energy efficiency of the cell [10]. It can be understood, then, that the combinations of the factors involved in the operation will present trends that could be described through data analysis and, therefore, it is much more plausible to focus the analysis on data from high temperatures.

Though, one of the common problems with FCs is that it is difficult to determine their useful life. The said problem is generally attributed to the voltage [15, 18]. However Heuer et al. [11], through an experimental study, demonstrated that the current density can also provide information on the loss of useful life of an FC. They even propose current density dispersion analysis as an aging verification method, since it is much faster and addresses information that the voltage is not capable of monitoring. In this sense, the present study confirms what these authors have stated and goes much further than analyzing the dispersion, but also describing its behavior based on the other factors that intervene in the FC, as suggested by Prasad [19].

On the other hand, the effectiveness of carrying out a PCA for the application of polynomial regression, in contrast, to directly applying the variables in multivariate polynomial regression, is based on the fact that PCA allows obtaining the variables that they are significant in the behavior of an FC [15]. In this way, aberrant data is omitted and results that are closer to the actual operation are obtained. Another advantage of using PCA is that the results can also be verified through analysis of their visualization. Unlike the multiple polynomial regression, since working with 5 total dimensions, it was not possible to determine the veracity of its high coefficient of determination until a multicollinearity test was performed.

While the proposed analysis can be improved, this study provides a new approach to analyze the operation of an FC. Since, generally, the relationships that have been established have been simple or multiple linear [11, 18], which was also tested and, to a disadvantage, these models did not meet the assumptions proposed by the statistics. Given that, this study also suggests that relationships should be studied from a nonlinear aspect.

Nevertheless, it should be mentioned that the analysis can be improved due to the different limitations presented by this study, such as the amount of data, in-depth analysis of the behavior of each variable concerning current density, in-depth analysis of second-degree polynomial regression degree and multivariate. Therefore, for future work, it is urged to deepen these limitations or improve the study by making use of more experimental data.

Acknowledgment. The authors kindly acknowledge the financial support from FIMCP-CERA-05-2017 project. Computational and physical resources provided by ESPOL are also very grateful.

References

1. Akinwande, O., Dikko, H., Agboola, S.: Variance inflation factor: as a condition for the inclusion of suppressor variable(s) in regression analysis. Open J. Stat. **5**, 754–767 (2014). https://doi.org/10.4236/ojs.2015.57075, http://www.scirp.org/journal/ojs
2. Babanova, S., Bretschger, O., Roy, J., Cheung, A., Artyushkova, K., Atanassov, P.: Innovative statistical interpretation of Shewanella oneidensis microbial fuel cells data. Phys. Chem. Chem. Phys. **16**, 8956–8969 (2014). https://doi.org/10.1039/C4CP00566J

3. Dai, W., et al.: A review on water balance in the membrane electrode assembly of proton exchange membrane fuel cells. Int. J. Hydrogen Energy **34**(23), 9461–9478 (2009). https://doi.org/10.1016/j.ijhydene.2009.09.017
4. Del Valle, J., Guerra, C.: La multicolinealidad en modelos de regresión lineal múltiple, **21**, 80–83 (2012). https://www.redalyc.org/articulo.oa?id=93223755013
5. Dokkar, B., Settou, N.E., Imine, O., Saifi, N., Negrou, B., Nemouchi, Z.: Simulation of species transport and water management in PEM fuel cells. Int. J. Hydrogen Energy **36**(6), 4220–4227 (2011). https://doi.org/10.1016/j.ijhydene.2010.09.060. 3rd International Workshop in Hydrogen Energy
6. Espinoza, M., Sunden, B., Andersson, M.: Impact on diffusion parameters computation in gas diffusion layers, considering the land/channel region, using the lattice Boltzmann method. ECS Trans. **75**(14), 521–530 (2016). https://doi.org/10.1149/07514.0521ecst
7. Espinoza, M., Andersson, M., Sundén, B.: Predicting transport parameters in PEFC gas diffusion layers considering micro-architectural variations using the Lattice Boltzmann method. Int. J. Energy Res. **41**(4), 565–578 (2017). https://doi.org/10.1002/er.3661
8. Fedkin, M.: Zero emission vehicles. Penn State Department of Energy and Mineral Engineering (2020). https://www.e-education.psu.edu/eme807/node/671
9. Gallego, J.: Apuntes de econometría. Iade y le. Technical report, Universidad de Cantabria (2008)
10. Gwak, G., et al.: Performance and efficiency analysis of an HT-PEMFC system with an absorption chiller for tri-generation applications. Energies **12**(905), 1–21 (2019). https://doi.org/10.3390/en12050905
11. Heuer, M., Bernstein, P., Wenske, M., Styczynski, Z.: Results of current density distribution mapping in PEM fuel cells dependent on operation parameters. Energies **6**, 3841–3858 (2013). https://doi.org/10.3390/en6083841
12. Li, H., et al.: A review of water flooding issues in the proton exchange membrane fuel cell. J. Power Sources **178**(1), 103–117 (2008). https://doi.org/10.1016/j.jpowsour.2007.12.068
13. Li, S., Sundén, B.: Effects of gas diffusion layer deformation on the transport phenomena and performance of PEM fuel cells with interdigitated flow fields. Int. J. Hydrogen Energy **43**(33), 16279–16292 (2018). https://doi.org/10.1016/j.ijhydene.2018.07.064
14. Masand, A., Borah, M., Pathak, A.K., Dhakate, S.R.: Effect of filler content on the properties of expanded-graphite-based composite bipolar plates for application in polymer electrolyte membrane fuel cells. Mater. Res. Express **4**(9), 095604 (2017). https://doi.org/10.1088/2053-1591/aa85a5
15. Morán, A., Martínez, A., Rodríguez, J., Posada, R., Sandoval, O.: PEM fuel cell voltage neural control based on hydrogen pressure regulation. Processes **7**(434), 1–15 (2014). https://doi.org/10.3390/pr7070434
16. Nkansah, B.: On the Kaiser-Meyer-Olkin's measure of sampling adequacy. Math. Theory Model. **8**(7), 52–76 (2018). https://iiste.org/Journals/index.php/MTM/article/view/44386/45790
17. Okorie, O., Salonitis, K., Charnley, F., Turner, C.: A systems dynamics enabled real-time efficiency for fuel cell data-driven remanufacturing. J. Manuf. Mater. Process. **2**(4), 77 (2018). https://doi.org/10.3390/jmmp2040077
18. Placca, L., Kouta, R., Candusso, D., Blachot, J., Charon, W.: Analysis of PEM fuel cell experimental data using principal component analysis and multi linear regression. Int. J. Hydrogen Energy **35**, 4582–4591 (2010). https://doi.org/10.1016/j.ijhydene.2010.02.076
19. Prasad, I., Krishna, G., Biswas, M., Das, K.: Performance study of PEM fuel cell under different loading conditions. Energy Proc. **54**, 468–478 (2014). https://doi.org/10.1016/j.egypro.2014.07.289

20. Rincón, E., García, J., Bermúdez, J.: Estado del arte de las celdas de combustible. Revista Colombiana de Tecnologías de Avanzada **1**(33), 37 (2018). https://doi.org/10.24054/169 27257.v33.n33.2019.3320
21. Robles, C., Rodríguez, O.: Un panorama de las energías renovables en el mundo, latinoamérica y colombia. ESPACIOS **39**(34), 10 (2018). https://www.revistaespacios.com/a18v39n34/a18 v39n34p10.pdf
22. Rosero, E., Chiliquinga, B.: Informe final de ecuador (2011). https://www.renenergyobserv atory.org/uploads/media/Ecuador_Producto_1_y_2Esp_02.pdf
23. Samaniego, J., Galindo, L., Mostacedo, S., Ferrer, J., Alatorre, J., Reyes, O.: El cambio climático y el sector de energía en américa latina. Comisión Económica para América Latina y el Caribe, CEPAL (2017). https://www.cepal.org/sites/default/files/news/files/sintesis_pp_ cc_cambio_climatico_y_el_sector_de_energia.pdf
24. Sinha, P.: Multivariate polynomial regression in data mining: methodology, problems and solutions. Int. J. Sci. Eng. Res. **4**(12), 962–965 (2013). https://www.researchgate.net/pub lication/264425037_Multivariate_Polynomial_Regression_in_Data_Mining_Methodology_ Problems_and_Solutions
25. Zhang, J., et al.: PEM fuel cell relative humidity (RH) and its effect on performance at high temperatures. Electrochimica Acta **53**(16), 5315–5321 (2008). https://doi.org/10.1016/j.ele ctacta.2008.02.074
26. Zhao, J., Shahgaldi, S., Alaefour, I., Yang, S., Li, X.: Pore structure and effective diffusion coefficient of catalyzed electrodes in polymer electrolyte membrane fuel cells. Int. J. Hydrogen Energy **43**(7), 3776–3785 (2018). https://doi.org/10.1016/j.ijhydene.2018.01.019
27. Zhu, L., Yu, Q., Huang, Y., Guan, J., Wang, Y., Yan, Y.: Mathematical modelling and operation parameters analysis of proton exchange membrane fuel cell. IOP Conf. Ser.: Earth Environ. Sci. **467**, 012071 (2020). https://doi.org/10.1088/1755-1315/467/1/012071

Pre-processing and Handling Unbalanced Data in CNN for Improving Automated Detection of COVID-19 Cases: Preliminary Results

Hector Mejia[1] , Franz Guzman[1](✉) , Carlos Bustamante-Orellana[4] ,
and Lorena Guachi-Guachi[1,2,3]

[1] Yachay Tech University, Hacienda San José, Urcuquí 100119, Ecuador
`{franz.guzman,lguachi}@yachaytech.edu.ec`
[2] SDAS Research Group, Urcuquí, Ecuador
[3] Department of Mechatronics, Universidad Internacional del Ecuador, Av. Simon Bolivar, 170411 Quito, Ecuador
[4] Arizona State University, Tempe, AZ, USA
`http://www.sdas-group.com`

Abstract. In the context of the COVID-19 pandemic, early diagnosis and treatment are crucial to avoid a drastic increase in the number of new infections. Chest imaging plays an important role in the early detection of the disease since it can be used to identify the initial phase lung infection caused by the SARS-CoV-2 virus. Recently, some researchers have begun to explore Convolutional Neural Networks (CNNs) to detect COVID-19 cases from chest X-ray images. CNN is a category of deep artificial neural networks that has demonstrated great success in computer vision applications, such as video and image analysis. However, this type of network is still affected by abnormal real-world factors such as unbalanced data, presence of noise, blurring, or other quality degradation that can diminish their overall performance when they are not properly handled. This work introduces a methodology to explore and compare the overall accuracy achieved by an Xception-based CNN model when it is combined with benchmark techniques such as unsharp masking, batch balance, and data augmentation aiming at enhancing image details (such as the bone structure and lung) and handling unbalanced datasets. Experiments are done referring to the COVIDx dataset. Preliminary results demonstrate that the proposed methodology leads to higher accuracy when implementing both image enhancement and batch balancing.

Keywords: Chest X-ray classification · Convolutional Neural Networks (CNNs) · Image processing

1 Introduction

The rapid spread of COVID-19 disease over the world is causing the health system of many places to quickly become overwhelmed. Even major health-care

© Springer Nature Switzerland AG 2020
G. Rodriguez Morales et al. (Eds.): TICEC 2020, CCIS 1307, pp. 129–139, 2020.
https://doi.org/10.1007/978-3-030-62833-8_11

centers get over-saturated because lower-level centers are not equipped to evaluate the condition of the patients and the medical personnel starts to become scarce. Recently, some works have begun to explore Convolutional Neural Networks (CNNs) approaches for automatic COVID-19 detection from chest X-ray and CT scan images [1,11,15,16]. CNNs, a category of deep learning approaches, have been extensively adopted for image classification purposes due to its ability to learn key features on their own and its successful precision achieved to general purposes analysis of visual imagery.

Although some works, based on deep learning approaches, presented in the literature have demonstrated high sensitivity for COVID-19 detection, they are still affected by abnormal factors such as unbalance data, presence of noise, blurring, or other quality degradations which may diminish the overall performance of a CNN.

In this sense, to evaluate how pre-processing and handling unbalance data influence on the overall accuracy of CNN-based models, in this work, we propose a methodology to explore and compare the performance achieved by an Xception-based CNN [4]. This CNN was combined with unsharp masking, which is a simple and effective method to enhance edges, batch balancing, and data augmentation. Xception CNN is a deep convolutional neural network organized in blocks that implements a modified separable convolutions procedure, to reduce parameters on the neural network. It was chosen due to its successful results achieved in computer vision applications such as breast cancer diagnosis [8], blood cells classification [9], pneumonia classification [3], among others. As a case study, we used the COVIDx dataset [5] since COVID-19 has become a critical viral disease that might be diagnosed from X-ray images. Images in DCM format, exclusive for medical imaging, were transformed into PNG format for the dataset to be homogeneous, as "COVID-19" images were in the later format; thereby losing detail.

Preliminary results show that pre-processing visually causes a slight reduction in the noise of the images, makes the images more focused and highlights the edges of the bone structure and lungs. Besides, when pre-processing is combined with balance correction, it increases the network's confidences on softmax predictions, as well as precision, recall and accuracy metrics.

The remaining of this paper is organized as follows. Section 2 describes the most relevant related works. The proposed methodology is presented in Sect. 3. The experimental setup is described in Sect. 4. The experimental results obtained on the processed dataset are illustrated and discussed in Sect. 5. Finally, Sect. 6 deals with the concluding remarks and future work.

2   Related Work

Among various CNN standard architectures in COVID-19 context: Darknet, MobileNet, VGG16 or Inception-Resnet-based CNNs have been used as the underlying model structure, aiming at exploring the performance to identify COVID-19 cases from chest X-ray images as binary or multi-class classification problem. The effectiveness of a CNN model to identify COVID-19 cases among two or multiple classes depends mainly on the CNN depth, number of classes, quantity and quality of data. For instance in [11], a framework based on a modified architecture of Darknet [12], with only 17 convolutional layers, formulates COVID-19 detection as a binary classification problem and achieves sensitivity and specificity values of 90.65% and 93.18%, respectively for the COVID-19 class. In order to allow COVID-19 detection on different medical imaging procedures, authors in [1], use 5216 chest X-ray images and 420 Computer Tomography (CT) scans to classify an image as a normal or COVID-19 case using a neural network composed of Inception recurrent residual units. The model reports 84.67% in testing accuracy for X-ray images and 98.78% in CT-images. Aiming at improving the overall performance on a multi-class problem, transfer learning technique has been applied on MobileNet and VGG16 networks [2], from the domain of Imagenet dataset, a large scale set of images of common objects for classification, to chest X-ray images using 1428 samples labeled as Normal, bacterial pneumonia, viral pneumonia or COVID-19 cases. This model reached 98.66%, and 96.46% as sensitivity and specificity metrics, respectively.

In addition, some specialized CNN architectures have been designed to increase sensitivity to COVID-19 cases to limit the number of missed COVID-19 cases as much as possible. For instance, COVID-net [15] achieves precision and recall values of 98% and 91%, respectively, for detecting COVID-19 cases by using projection-expansion-projection-extension design pattern on its deep learning architecture. It also provides enhanced representational capacity while maintaining computational efficiency. This work set the foundations for future models and comparisons, as it was the first successful model built to detect COVID-19 related anomalies in the lungs on a large dataset. On the other hand, a deep neural network called COVID-SegNet is proposed in [16]. This solution is a segmentation-based approach capable of separating the pneumonia-area caused by COVID-19 from lungs in CT images. It follows a sequence of four convolutional encoder layers and three deconvolution-upsampling decoder layers. The work obtained a dice score of 98.7% for lung and 72.6% for COVID-19 segmentation.

3   Proposed Methodology

The proposed methodology consists of three main phases as shown in Fig. 1. Firstly, the X-ray images were collected for training and validation purposes. Then, an Xception-module-based CNN is trained to learn features from COVIDx dataset. Finally, the trained model is tested to determine its ability to correctly classify X-ray images into three classes: Normal, Pneumonia or COVID-19. In order to increase the overall accuracy achieved by the Xception model, two variations are applied over the proposed methodology: a) the X-ray images are pre-processed using benchmark image enhancement techniques to make details more visible, and b) batch balancing is used to cope the unbalance in distribution among class samples.

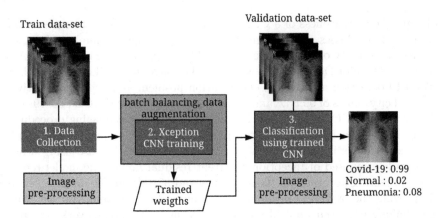

Fig. 1. Proposed methodology using an Xception-based CNN with pre-processing and batch balancing techniques.

1. **Data Collection:** This work uses COVIDx dataset [15]. It is a compilation of chest X-ray images from multiple sources. COVIDx dataset contains a total of 13.8K PNG and RGB images of normal, COVID-19 and pneumonia related cases. Images have different resolutions as 720×1024, 1024×720, 720×720 and 1024×1024. Table 1 shows image samples distribution per cases for training and testing purposes. As it can be seen, COVIDx includes less COVID-19 samples compared to the other ones. This unbalance is due to the novelty of the virus, and the limited amount of chest X-ray images related to this disease that are available.

Table 1. Number of X-ray samples related to Normal, Pneumonia and COVID-19 cases for training and testing purposes [15].

Type	Normal	Pneumonia	COVID-19 Pneumonia	Total
Train	6049	4163	268	10479
Test	2017	1388	90	3495

2. **Xception-block-based CNN:** Xception-module-based CNN [4] illustrated in Fig. 2 is compounded by 14 Xception modules (with linear residual connections between each module, except for the first and last), a global average pooling layer and finally a fully connected layer with softmax activation function for predictions. Xception modules extend the concept of separable convolutions, which reduces the number of parameters by applying a spatial filter per channel, instead of a 3D filter to the whole input.
The difference between original separable convolutions, implemented in networks like Inception [14], is that the point wise convolution is applied to the input first, before applying spatial filters to reduce the number of parameters, while maintaining performance.

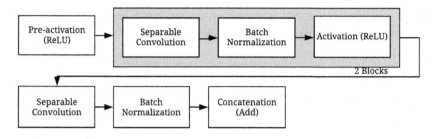

Fig. 2. Core Xception module.

3. **Classification:** This phase uses the trained CNN, where the probability ($p(c_i|x_i)$) achieved by each output allows to classify each X-ray image (x_i) as Normal, Pneumonia or COVID-19 cases (c_i).

3.1 Methodology Variations

1. **Pre-processing based on unsharp masking technique:** Since COVIDx dataset is a compilation of chest X-rays from various sources, image detail, contrast and noise levels can vary. To mitigate this problem, unsharp masking technique is applied. It enhances the visual quality of an image by processing its edges starting with a Gaussian blur with a kernel of k × k and an standard deviation in the direction X of σ_x. This technique separates the edges, amplifies, and sums them back into the image. Then a weighted sum of the images is performed as shown Eq. 1:

$$UM = 1.5 * original - 0.5 * blurred*$$ (1)

2. **Batch balancing and data augmentation:** This step aims to increase the size of a training dataset at each training iteration, generating batches with artificial versions of images. Artificial images are generated by applying horizontal flips, rotations and variations in brightness.

4 Experimental Setup

To evaluate the effectiveness of unsharp masking and batch balancing procedures on the overall accuracy achieved by Xception-module-based CNN, different experiments are conducted. Each one derives from the workflow in 1, where (a) image enhancement or (b) batch balancing procedures can be present or not; resulting in four experiments as follows.

1. RNB: raw images, no balancing correction.
2. RB: raw images with balance correction.
3. EINB: enhanced images, no balance correction.
4. EIB: enhanced images, balance correction.

Xception-module-based CNN receives normalized input images of $224 \times 224 \times 3$, thus, each X-ray image is resized and multiplied by $1/255$ to normalized them.

For experimental purposes, python routines have been implemented using Google Colab with a GPU accelerator. This environment provides 12 GB of RAM and 100 GB ROM. Tensorflow framework with CUDA support was employed for neural network developing, training and testing. OpenCV was used for image pre-processing, meanwhile scikit-learn was used to compute metrics.

Before training, a grid search was performed to select a suitable set of hyper-parameters. The search space is depicted in Table 2:

Table 2. Hyper-parameter values for all experiments.

Hyper-parameter	Value space	Description
batch size	32, 64, 70	Number of samples per training iteration
epochs	10, 15, 20, 25, 30	Number of passes over the whole dataset
input image	(112,112,3), (224,224,3), (448,448,3)	image dimensions, channels included
learning rate	0.01, 0.005, 0.001, 0.0005, 0.0001, exponential decay from 0.005 to 0.001	limits the weight update against gradients
optimizer	Adam, SGD	Optimization algorithm to update weights

For high performance the hyper-parameters that achieve minimal loss were chosen: 64 samples batch size, 20 epochs, exponential decay from 0.005 to 0.0001 for learning rate, (224,224,3) for image shape and Adam as optimizer.

5   Experimental Results

Some of the outputs obtained for the enhanced images of the dataset are depicted in Fig. 3b. It can be observed that the unsharp mask technique leads to a slight improvement on details, such as the bone structure and lungs, which edges are sharper. Also, these images appear more focused as opposed with the images on the Fig. 3a, which have more diffused edges.

Accuracy (A), precision (P) and recall (R) given by Eqs. 2, 3 and 4, respectively, were computed to measure the ability of the proposed methodology to classify X-ray images into the corresponding case, and to determine how the pre-processing and batch balancing techniques influence on the classification performance achieved.

$$A = \frac{T_P + T_N}{F_P + F_N + T_P + T_N} \quad (2)$$

$$P = \frac{T_P}{T_P + F_P} \quad (3)$$

$$R = \frac{T_P}{T_P + F_N} \quad (4)$$

T_P, T_N, F_P, and F_N refer to the total number of true positives, true negatives, false positives and false negatives, respectively, after comparing the predictions of the CNN and the true labels on the test set. In this sense, accuracy quantifies the ratio of correctly classified X-ray images, precision quantifies the ratio of correctly classified positive cases over the total positive samples, and recall describes the proportion of positive cases retrieved by the CNN from the total number of positives samples.

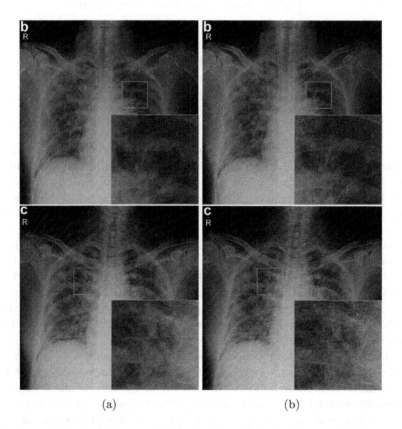

(a)   (b)

Fig. 3. COVID-19 chest X-ray. (a) Samples from COVIDx dataset; (b) Images after enhancement on (a).

To fulfill the experiments and validate that the models' performances are not due to chance, a 5-fold cross validation was performed by partitioning the dataset into five subsets of equal size, then training the model on four of the subsets and testing on the remaining one for five rounds. Each round had a different training and test set where the model was fitted from scratch. Finally, all metrics retrieved from each fold were averaged. Obtained results are exposed in Table 3. It is important to note that performance metrics from COVID-net [15] (a Deep Convolutional Neural Network designed to detect COVID-19 related anomalies on chest X-rays), are included since both studies use the same dataset.

Table 3. Table of results for all experiments and COVID-net as reported in [15].

Class	Metric	Experiment				
		RNB	RB	IENB	IEB 4	COVID-net
Normal	Precision	91.8	**93.8**	93.4	93.4	90.5
	Recall	88.0	**95.4**	91.6	95.2	95.0
Pneumonia	Precision	**95.4**	93.2	89.8	92.0	91.3
	Recall	83.4	90.0	87.8	89.8	**94.0**
COVID-19	Precision	55.4	82.2	75.0	88.0	**98.9**
	Recall	85.6	84.4	76.0	80.0	**91.0**
All	Accuracy	85.2	92.8	89.8	92.8	**93.3**

Table 3 demonstrates that image enhancement and batch balance techniques guarantee higher precision, recall and accuracy on almost all test cases, compared to raw images and no balancing correction. However, the proposed methodology, mainly for COVID-19, reaches (5%) lower overall accuracy with RB and IEB experiments with respect to COVIDNet [15]. This results suggest that more improvements on the data and the CNN model should be explored.

In addition, the receiver operating characteristic (ROC) curve exhibits the performance reached by plotting recall vs false-positive rate at various prediction thresholds [17]. It reveals the capability of a model to distinguish between classes. From Fig. 4, it can be seen that when both variations (image enhancement and batch balance) are present, the model achieves the highest area under the curve from all experiments, demonstrating that the best results in class separability are achieved with the proposed methodology.

It was noticed, when utilizing classic augmentation techniques, as no new patterns are introduced into the training [10] and noise from rotations, translations and brightness changes are added, the benefits of the enhancement applied in this work are reduced. Hence, other augmentation techniques such as neural style transfer and generative adversarial networks [6, 7, 13] should be explored.

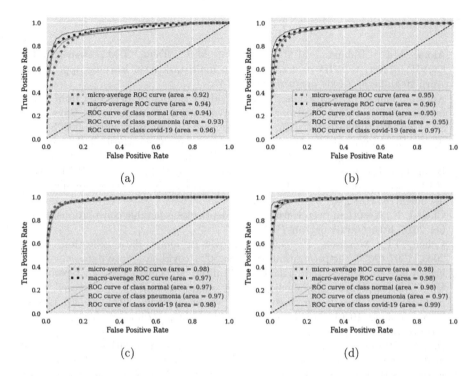

(a)   (b)

(c)   (d)

Fig. 4. ROC curves for (a) Raw and imbalanced image samples on training, (b) Raw, balanced image samples, (c) Enhanced, but imbalanced image samples, (d) Enhanced and balanced image samples.

6   Conclusion

The Xception-based models that implemented batch balancing performed better than those that did not, and although combining this procedure with image enhancement seemed not to improve the metrics on Table 3, the ROC curves showed that the models achieve a higher level of class separability when predicting on this setting. It is important to remark that COVID-Net classifier achieved better performance, but this neural network was specifically designed for the COVIDx dataset, while the model used in this work, Xception, is more general. Besides, this work used a considerably bigger test sets in a 5-fold cross validation, giving more fidelity on its results. As future work, new and improved CNN architectures along with other class imbalance optimizations must be used to further increase precision and recall values for COVID-19 class. Besides, a better approach for data augmentation must be explored. Generative adversarial neural networks, and style transfer have shown promising results creating synthetic images for a specific class [6,7,13].

References

1. Alom, M.Z., Rahman, M.M.S., Nasrin, M.S., Taha, T.M., Asari, V.K.: COVID$_M$TNet: COVID-19 detection with multi-task deep learning approaches, April 2020. http://arxiv.org/abs/2004.03747

2. Apostolopoulos, I.D., Mpesiana, T.A.: Covid-19: automatic detection from X-ray images utilizing transfer learning with convolutional neural networks. Phys. Eng. Sci. Med. **43**(2), 635–640 (2020). https://doi.org/10.1007/s13246-020-00865-4

3. Ayan, E., Unver, H.M.: Diagnosis of pneumonia from chest X-Ray images using deep learning. In: 2019 Scientific Meeting on Electrical-Electronics & Biomedical Engineering and Computer Science (EBBT), pp. 1–5. IEEE, April 2019. https://doi.org/10.1109/EBBT.2019.8741582, https://ieeexplore.ieee.org/document/8741582/

4. Chollet, F.: Xception: deep learning with depthwise separable convolutions, October 2016. http://arxiv.org/abs/1610.02357

5. Cohen, J.P., Morrison, P., Dao, L.: Covid-19 image data collection. arXiv 2003.11597 (2020). https://github.com/ieee8023/covid-chestxray-dataset

6. Frid-Adar, M., Diamant, I., Klang, E., Amitai, M., Goldberger, J., Greenspan, H.: GAN-based synthetic medical image augmentation for in- creased CNN performance in liver lesion classification. Neurocomputing **321**, 321–331 (2018). https://doi.org/10.1016/j.neucom.2018.09.013. https://linkinghub.elsevier.com/retrieve/pii/S0925231218310749

7. Han, C., Murao, K., Satoh, S., Nakayama, H.: Learning more with less: GAN-based medical image augmentation, March 2019. http://arxiv.org/abs/1904.00838

8. Kassani, S.H., Kassani, P.H., Wesolowski, M.J., Schneider, K.A., Deters, R.: Breast cancer diagnosis with transfer learning and global pooling, September 2019. http://arxiv.org/abs/1909.11839

9. Liang, G., Hong, H., Xie, W., Zheng, L.: Combining convolutional neural network with recursive neural network for blood cell image classification. IEEE Access **6**, 36188–36197 (2018). https://doi.org/10.1109/ACCESS.2018.2846685. https://ieeexplore.ieee.org/document/8402091/

10. Mikołajczyk, A., Grochowski, M.: Data augmentation for improving deep learning in image classification problem. In: 2018 International Interdisciplinary PhD Workshop, pp. 117–122, May 2018. https://doi.org/10.1109/IIPHDW.2018.8388338

11. Ozturk, T., Talo, M., Yildirim, E.A., Baloglu, U.B., Yildirim, O., Rajendra Acharya, U.: Automated detection of COVID-19 cases using deep neural networks with X-ray images. Comput. Biol. Med. **121**, 103792 (2020). https://doi.org/10.1016/j.compbiomed.2020.103792. https://linkinghub.elsevier.com/retrieve/pii/S0010482520301621

12. Redmon, J., Farhadi, A.: YOLOv3: an incremental improvement, April 2018. http://arxiv.org/abs/1804.02767

13. Sandfort, V., Yan, K., Pickhardt, P.J., Summers, R.M.: Data augmentation using generative adversarial networks (CycleGAN) to improve generalizability in CT segmentation tasks. Sci. Rep. **9**(1), 16884 (2019). https://doi.org/10.1038/s41598-019-52737-x. http://www.nature.com/articles/s41598-019-52737-x

14. Szegedy, C., Vanhoucke, V., Ioffe, S., Shlens, J., Wojna, Z.: Rethinking the inception architecture for computer vision, December 2016. http://arxiv.org/abs/1512.00567

15. Wang, L., Wong, A.: Covid-net: a tailored deep convolutional neural network design for detection of covid-19 cases from chest radiography images (2020)

16. Yan, Q., et al.: COVID-19 chest CT image segmentation - a deep convolutional neural network solution, April 2020. http://arxiv.org/abs/2004.10987
17. Zou, K.H., O'Malley, A.J., Mauri, L.: Receiver-operating characteristic analysis for evaluating diagnostic tests and predictive models. Circulation **115**(5), 654–657 (2007). https://doi.org/10.1161/CIRCULATIONAHA.105.594929. https://www.ahajournals.org/doi/10.1161/CIRCULATIONAHA.105.594929

Descriptive Analysis for Discovery of Patterns of Interest in Student

Franklin Mayorga$^{(\boxtimes)}$ ⓘ, Cristina Frutos, and Javier Vargas ⓘ

Facultad de Ingeniería en Sistemas Electrónica e Industrial, Universidad Técnica de Ambato, Ambato, Ecuador
{fmayorga,ca.frutos,js.vargas}@uta.edu.ec

Abstract. The student desertion is a social problem that is not alien to any Higher Education Institution at the national level, in Ecuador the universities and techno-logical institutes are in the process of evaluation and accreditation carried out by the Council for Quality Assurance in Higher Education (CACES), With relevance being the Retention Rate Indicator, hence the importance of generating strategies to maximize the rate of students who complete their career. The research on the Retention Rate Analysis and its incidence in the detection of student desertion patterns was carried out at the Technical University of Ambato, the research commitment is to detect the Desertion Patterns in students of each of their careers. This research proposes a solution to the problem with the use of techniques and algorithms of Data Mining for the search and discovery of patterns of interest, applying the methodology of the patterns of desertion shown in the Selection process.

Keywords: Student desertion · Data mining · Desertion patterns

1 Introduction

Advanced education presents high rates of student desertion, especially in the first academic semesters, a fact that leads to financial, academic and social effects for both Higher Education Institutions [1]. Student retention has gained relevance in the educational field, due to the felt need to generate alternatives for the promotion of permanence and graduation of students in the higher education system. A student retention program includes the actions developed by the educational apparatus in an institution to guarantee the accompaniment of the student during his or her academic trajectory, in such a way that it can be successfully completed [2]. Although it is true that the term is used in literature worldwide, currently institutions tend to call these actions as programs to promote permanence and academic success. This name is intended to exalt the idea of empowering the student versus retaining him, which implies a character of lesser will and participation of the student [3].

The evaluation model contains the criteria and standards required to ensure minimum levels of quality and its objective is to generate a culture of excellence [4]. The model is established after discussion days with the institutions to be evaluated. In addition, other technical instruments that support the execution of the processes are defined:

© Springer Nature Switzerland AG 2020
G. Rodriguez Morales et al. (Eds.): TICEC 2020, CCIS 1307, pp. 140–149, 2020.
https://doi.org/10.1007/978-3-030-62833-8_12

manuals, guides, computer systems, etc. In addition, it is the coefficient that expresses the relationship between the students who have remained in the career until completing their academic training and the total of those enrolled in the same cohort [5]. The Technical University of Ambato is in process of Evaluation and Accreditation of each one of its careers, being of vital importance the indicator Rate of Retention, reason why it is required to establish processes that allow the detection of patterns of student desertion.

2 Student Retention Rate Model

The objective of the institutional evaluation of universities and polytechnics is to determine the degree of compliance with the quality standards defined in the current evaluation model. This indicator evaluates the ratio of students in the career who were admitted two years before the assessment period and who are currently enrolled [6]. The evaluation process consists of the following stages: Self-Assessment, Information Loading, Documentary Evaluation, Onsite Visit, Appeals and Final Report. The selection process of the students, is understood by means of blocks determined by the indicators to measure their academic efficiency (see Fig. 1). On the other hand, one of the factors that allow to measure this process is the determination of analysis criteria to evaluate the student's situation. The selection of criteria helps decision-making to determine dropout in a measurable and comparable process.

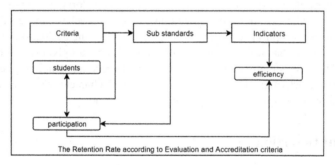

Fig. 1. Selection process for student participation.

The Generic Model for Evaluating Career Quality is a process that consists of evaluating careers, comparing them and contextualizing them within a historical, economic and social framework, which is determined according to the theoretical approach used to define quality, but which is, in essence, a complex process in which multiple factors interact in diverse and unpredictable ways [7]. In this process, by career, the definition used by the CONESUP has been adopted, which indicates that the career represents the basic unit object of the present proposal for the evaluation of the learning environment, and is characterized as: "A curricular organization that prepares students to obtain a Bachelor's degree or a University or Polytechnic Professional Degree, after they have demonstrated that they have reached a formation that allows them to solve problems through the application of scientific knowledge, abilities and skills, procedures and methods, within a determined scientific-technological area".

3 Generic Career Evaluation Model

Based on all these theoretical and methodological considerations and conceptions, a generic career evaluation model has been formulated and is presented in this document. To this end, from the point of view of the Multicriteria Decision Theory [8], five basic criteria have been identified that cover practically all the functions and activities of the careers, such as: the pertinence of the career in the environment, the training offered to future professionals, the quality of its teaching staff, the environment in which academic activities take place, and the relationship and participation of students in these activities [9].

In this way, the criteria corresponding to these activities and functions have been established as: Relevance, Curricular Plan, Academy, Institutional Environment and Students. Based on the above premises, it is necessary to frame the concept of quality with which careers are evaluated and, in addition, the criteria that will be used for such evaluation [10].

This has demanded the adoption by Council for Quality Assurance in Higher Education (CACES) [11] of a conceptualization of quality coming from multiple approaches, such as the tendency to quality, to perfection, to the fulfillment and adjustment of purposes and objectives, to the production of value at a lower cost, or to the transformation of a system [12]. Separately, none of these approaches would exhaust the complexity of university processes, and some might even be incompatible with certain basic postulates that govern the democratization processes of the Ecuadorian university; however, as a whole, and with certain particularizations, these approaches can be satisfactorily approached to a conception according to that desirable for the evaluation of such processes. On the other hand, regarding the selection of criteria to be used in the model, the complexity of the situation has also been taken into account, which implies the evaluation of diverse activities of different nature, in whose characterization elements that demand a more or less qualitative evaluation may intervene.

4 Student Desertion

In order to define student desertion, it is necessary to begin with the meaning of the term desertion, which was found in the article published on the Internet "Definition of School Desertion" is defined as, abandoning obligations and separating oneself from the concurrences that used to be frequented, and that school desertion is used to refer to those students who stop attending classes and remain outside the educational system [13]. In order to define the study of the causes of student desertion, certain influencing factors were determined, such as: Personal Reasons, refers to the causes that influenced in a particular way in each one of the individuals in the decision to abandon their university studies [2]. Academic reasons, are those causes that refer to the level of instruction with which they begin their university studies and the methodology and study techniques that are used for learning. Institutional Reasons, these refer to the characteristics of the educational institution, in the teaching methodology and the educational proposal of the same, which do not meet the expectations of the student.

5 Data Mining (Survey Conducted)

The results shown below are based on the survey of UPE Teachers of each of the careers at the Technical University of Ambato. The survey consists of 7 questions and was applied to 40 UPE Responsible Teachers and 4 DEAC Officials (see Table 1).

Table 1. Question results

Questions	Frequency		Field managers
	No.	%	Interpreting
Does the Institution generate any report on the Student Retention Rate?	YES 40 NO 0	100%	In the Survey carried out to the teachers responsible for the UPE of the Technical University of Ambato, it can be observed that 100% of the teachers affirm that the Student Retention Rate is currently obtained from an information system
Is an analysis of the Student Retention Rate performed?	YES 0 NO 44	100%	The UPE teachers of the careers of the Technical University of Ambato only obtain the Student Retention Rate because it is an indicator of evaluation and accreditation
Are there strategies to maximize the Student Retention rate?	YES 25 NO 15	63% 37%	63% of UPE teachers consider that the functions of the Department of Student Welfare make arrangements that contribute to Student retention, while 37% consider that NO activities are carried out to improve the rate of Student Retention
Is Student Retention important to the institution?	YES 40 NO 0	100%	Clearly it can be observed that Student Retention is an important factor in Educational Institutions
Does the institution allow to obtain the index of Student Desertion?	YES 0 NO 40	100%	The Integrated System of the University does NOT have an Application from which the Student Desertion Index is obtained
Is it important for the institution to identify Student Dropout Patterns?	YES 40 NO 0	100%	The importance of identifying the Student Defection Patterns in the Technical University of Ambato, would contribute in a significant way in the Decision Making

(continued)

Table 1. (*continued*)

Questions	Frequency		Field managers
	No.	%	Interpreting
Will Student Dropout Pattern Detection allow processes to be established to maximize the Student Retention Rate?	SI 40 NO 0	100%	UPE Faculty members indicate that identifying Student Dropout Patterns will establish processes for student welfare and maximize the Student Retention Rate which is an Indicator of Institutional Assessment and Accreditation

For verification, a question was selected to determine the relationship between the two, Analysis of the Retention Rate as variable A and positively the Detection of Student Dropout Patterns as variable B. This process is to determine the calculation of the experimental Chi-Square (X2) summarized from the statistical interpretation of the incidence of student desertion [14] (Table 2).

Table 2. Analysis of the Retention, Chi-Square Test

Alternatives	Calculations				
	Observed frequencies (O)	Expected frequencies (E)		$(O - E)^2$	$(O - E)^2/E$
variable A	SI	0	20	400	20
	NO	40	20	400	20
variable B	SI	40	20	400	20
	NO	0	20	400	20
$X_C^2 =$					80

According to the Chi-Square distribution table and the degrees of freedom the value obtained for is: 3.8415, value of the distribution table Chi - Square and degrees of freedom 1 of the value obtained. Therefore, 80 > 3.8415 determining that it is in the standardized waste acceptance zone, then the analysis of the retention rate SI influences the detection of patterns of student desertion in the Technical University of Ambato.

6   Retention Rate Analysis

In order to show the functioning of the application, the careers of the Faculty of Systems, Electronics and Industrial Engineering will be taken as an example, in order to determine the formula value of the TR, Student Retention Rate. NEMA: It represents the number of students enrolled during the ordinary academic period in which the evaluation of the institution is carried out, who were admitted two years before. NTEA: Represents the total number of students who were admitted to the career two years before the evaluation period. A student retention program comprises the strategies developed by the educational apparatus in an institution to guarantee the accompaniment of the student during his or her academic trajectory, in such a way that it can be successfully completed. Its objective is to provide the necessary tools for the completion of the different cycles and stages in the established times, and additionally to ensure the necessary knowledge and the development of skills and attitudes essential to develop in life. The report obtained (see Fig. 2) of the application of the formula of Student Retention Rate corresponding to the degree in Computer and Information Systems Engineering in the period October 2016–March 2017.

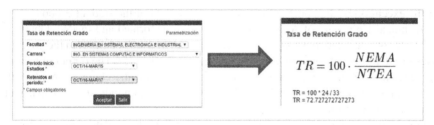

Fig. 2. Systems Retention Rate period October 2016–March 2017.

The report obtained (see Fig. 3) of the application of the formula of Student Retention Rate corresponding to the degree in Electronic Engineering and Communications in the period October 2016–March 2017.

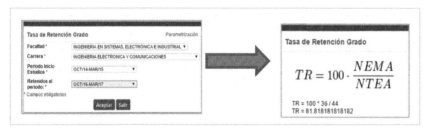

Fig. 3. Electronic Withholding Rate October 2016–March 2017

The report obtained (see Fig. 4) of the application of the student Retention Rate formula corresponding to the Industrial Engineering and Automation Processes degree in the periods October 2016–March 2017.

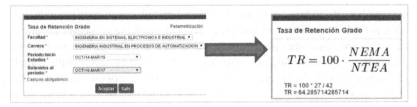

Fig. 4. Industrial Retention Rate period October 2016–March 2017.

7 Descriptive Analysis: Grouping Student Retention Rate

For the execution of the complete project, the clean data of the student dropouts from the Technical University of Ambato are extracted, transformed and loaded. Obtaining all the data is continued to the segmentation of the same, which come from the grouping tables of the Extract, Transform and Load processes (ETL) [15]. The output of the data is processed through queries, to these tables to be subsequently exported in a flat file, which will allow the decision making that will show based on indicators the managers of the student desertion.

For the grouping of the large amount of student data it was determined to use the tool known as Weka (data mining platform) and thanks to the K-medias algorithm to be able to group the observations of the students according to the criteria determined to measure the level of dissertation [16].

FULL DATA the total number of attributes analyzed is 106006.

Subsequently, the indicators are described based on criteria that determine the level of incidence of desertion (CLOUSTER 4) (Fig. 5).

FULL DATA	
Attribute	Full Data (106006.0)
1» ¿EDAD_DESERCION	21.2689
PERIODO	MAR/12-AGO/12
HDASISTENCIA	87.7517
CURSO	3.5061
GENERO	MASCULINO
ETNIA	MESTIZA
DISCAPACIDAD	NINGUNA
ESTADO_CIVIL	SOLTERO
TITULO_CEOLEGIO	CIENCIAS
PROMEDIO_CELEGIO	16.0173
CARRERA	INGENIERIA CIVIL
FACULTAD	INGENIERIA EN SISTEMAS ELECTRONICA E INDUSTRIAL
COLEGIO	INS TEC SUP BOLIVAR
CIUDAD	AMBATO
CANTON	AMBATO
PROVINCIA	TUNGURAHUA
MATERIA	FISICA I

Fig. 5. FULL DATA (Weka).

- Where the average age with the highest incidence of desertion is 21.
- The period that registers greater number of desertions is the academic period March. August
- The percentage of attendance of students who drop out is 87%.
- Mestizo students are the most likely to drop out.
- Students with no type of disability are those with the highest dropout rate.
- Students with single marital status are those who have the greatest impact on desertion.
- Students with a bachelor's degree in science are those who have the greatest incidence of desertion.
- Students who average "16" are those with the highest dropout rate.
- The students of the Civil Engineering degree are the ones with the highest incidence of desertion.
- The faculty with the highest incidence of desertion is the Faculty of Systems, Electronics and Industrial Engineering.
- The students graduated from the Institute Technologic Superior Bolívar College is the one with the highest number of incidences of desertion.
- The students who reside in the city and canton Ambato are those with greater number of incidences in desertion.
- The subject with the highest incidence of desertion is Physics I.

The incidence of desertion per faculty is shown in the desertion index for each of the faculties of the Technical University of Ambato (see Fig. 6).

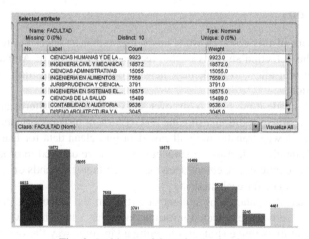

Fig. 6. Incidence of desertion by faculty.

In addition to these data on incidence of desertion by Faculty, it is also possible to determine the level of incidence by demographic data such as: gender, ethnicity (see Fig. 7), disability, etc.

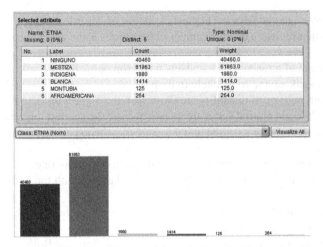

Fig. 7. Incidence of desertion by ethnicity.

As a summary to determine the dropout, we conclude that; Students who do not have any type of disability present a higher dropout rate without considering that a large number of students do not specify whether or not they have a disability. The male gender has a higher dropout rate than the female gender. The career with the highest dropout rate is Civil Engineering.

8   Conclusions

The development of this research work made it possible to select the relevant information from the defection students of the Technical University of Ambato, in a data warehouse that will allow to implement new models for the detection of patterns of Student Defection.

Data mining made it possible to discover student desertion patterns at the Ambato Technical University. In addition, using the ETL (Extraction, Transformation and Loading) process, it allowed transforming all raw data into clean data for Data Mining. In CLOUSTER 4, incidence factors for student desertion are detailed in order, these data allow making academic management decisions. Each factor depends on the evaluation criteria and acceptance for each student.

Once detected the patterns of student desertion in the Technical University it is recommended to spread the detected information to the Authorities, with the purpose of establishing administrative strategies to mitigate in some way the factors that affect directly in the student desertion. On the other hand, to deepen in methods of mining of data to find the most optimal algorithm for the discovery of knowledge of academic data of the institution.

References

1. Alban, M.S., Mauricio, D., Albán, M.: Decision trees for the early identification of university students at risk of desertion. Int. J. Eng. Technol. **7**, 51–54 (2018)

2. Rosa, E., et al.: Academic performance, school desertion and emotional paradigm in university students. Contemp. Issues Educ. Res. (CIER), **3**, 25-36 (2010)
3. Sadler, D.R.: Interpretations of criteria-based assessment and grading in higher education. Assess. Eval. High. Educ. **30**, 175–194 (2005). https://doi.org/10.1080/026029304200026 4262
4. Lane, M., et al.: Dimensions of student success: a framework for defining and evaluating support for learning in higher education. High. Educ. Res. Dev. **38**, 954–968 (2019). https://doi.org/10.1080/07294360.2019.1615418
5. Brown, A.L., Campione, J.C., Day, J.D.: Learning to learn: on training students to learn from texts. Educ. Res. **10**, 14–21 (1981). https://doi.org/10.3102/0013189X010002014
6. Solis, M., Moreira, T., Gonzalez, R., Fernandez, T., Hernandez, M.: Perspectives to predict dropout in university students with machine learning. In: 2018 IEEE International Work Conference on Bioinspired Intelligence, IWOBI 2018 - Proceedings. Institute of Electrical and Electronics Engineers Inc. (2018). https://doi.org/10.1109/IWOBI.2018.8464191
7. Modelos de evaluación para la acreditación de carreras. Análisis de su composición y una propuesta para las carreras de Ecuador. http://www.scielo.org.mx/scielo.php?pid=S1405-666 62016000401249&script=sci_abstract&tlng=es. Accessed 09 Oct 2020
8. Greco, S., Matarazzo, B., Slowinski, R.: Rough sets theory for multicriteria decision analysis. Eur. J. Oper. Res. **129**, 1–47 (2001). https://doi.org/10.1016/S0377-2217(00)00167-3
9. Joekel, R.G.: Student activities and academic eligibility requirements. NASSP Bull. **69**, 3–9 (1985). https://doi.org/10.1177/019263658506948302
10. Álvarez-Silva, L., Gallegos Luna, R.M., Herrera López, P.S.: Estrés académico en estudiantes de tecnología superior (2018). http://www.scielo.senescyt.gob.ec
11. CACES: Modelo genérico de evaluación del entorno de aprendizaje de carreras presenciales y semipresenciales de las universidades., Quito (2015)
12. Jazmany, G., Verdesoto, Z., Guisela, K., Mora, R., Humberto, L., Torres, G.: Análisis de la deserción estudiantil en las universidades del ecuador y américa latina (2018). http://www.revista-academica.utb.edu.ec
13. Castro, D.V., Narváez, M.U.: Estudio sobre la deserción estudiantil en Pontificia Universidad Católica del Ecuador (2011)
14. Lindquist, E.: Design and analysis of experiments in psychology and education (1953)
15. Hounsell, D., McCune, V., Hounsell, J., Litjens, J.: The quality of guidance and feedback to students. High. Educ. Res. Dev. **27**, 55–67 (2008). https://doi.org/10.1080/072943607016 58765
16. Rubiano, S.M.M., García, J.A.D.: Formulation of a predictive model for academic performance based on students' academic and demographic data. In: Proceedings - Frontiers in Education Conference, FIE. Institute of Electrical and Electronics Engineers Inc. (2015). https://doi.org/10.1109/FIE.2015.7344047

Analysis of the Perception of University Students About the Use of Microsoft OneNote as an Electronic Laboratory Notebook in Response to Non-Face-to-Face Education in Pandemic Times

Nicolás Grijalva-Borja[1]([✉]) [ID], Vanessa Espinosa[2] [ID], Stefanny Quinteros[2] [ID], and Anthony Salguero[2] [ID]

[1] Laboratorio de Ciencias de La Vida, Universidad Politécnica Salesiana, Quito, Ecuador
ngrijalva@ups.edu.ec
[2] Universidad Politécnica Salesiana, Carrera de Biotecnología, Quito, Ecuador
{jespinosab2,squinterose,asalguerot1}@est.ups.edu.ec

Abstract. Electronic Laboratory Notebooks (ELN) have been used in scientific laboratories for their flexibility in collecting non-standardized data. Microsoft OneNote emerges as a useful working tool for different educational institutions where technology allows you to optimize your resources. Because of the coronavirus disease (COVID-19) pandemic, over 850 million students in the world have been affected, so that 1 in 4 students has had to adapt to non-classroom learning conditions. In the present study, an analysis of the perception of the use of Microsoft OneNote as an ELN were carried out for students from three engineering degrees at the Universidad Politécnica Salesiana in Quito, in Ecuador during the months of April to June 2020. The results show that students rate the use of this tool as useful (52%) to very useful (36%) compared to a paper notebook. Also, most of the students (>80%) recommend the use of the electronic notebook in the laboratory's development practices, they would recommend its use to other students and teachers. Finally, the general perception was rated as good (37%) and very good (32%). These results allow to conclude that the use of electronic resources is accepted by students, adopting information and communication technologies (ICT) to enhance virtual education in pandemic times.

Keywords: Electronic laboratory notebook · Microsoft OneNote · Pandemic times

1 Introduction

Non-face-to-face education uses digital technologies to transform the learning experience, this is a turning point for online education, the coronavirus pandemic could be a way to foster innovation that could transform online teaching [1]. In response, universities have recommended the use of distance learning programs, applications, and

G. Rodriguez Morales et al. (Eds.): TICEC 2020, CCIS 1307, pp. 150–162, 2020.
https://doi.org/10.1007/978-3-030-62833-8_13

open educational platforms that teachers can use to reach students and limit disruption of education [2]. However, the development of the practical component in the training of university students, in technical careers, has been the most affected since distance measures have made its application impossible.

At the end of March 2020, over 850 million students in the world affected by SARS-CoV-2, 89.4% of the total number of students enrolled in 184 countries that have implemented closures for the pandemic, reason one in four higher education students has had to adapt to it [3]. In higher education, the coronavirus has forced to adopt measures that have not had enough time to be planned [4]. Thus, the answer has been to digitize content, to substitute classroom hours for synchronous class hours with the help of a videoconference tool, besides sending reading material, among other solutions. Using the different tools has had a clear impact on the students and on their educational process [5]. This has turned them into resources with great potential for university education.

Although non-face-to-face education already existed in Ecuador before the pandemic [6], because of this, the virtualization of education at all levels was necessary to meet the need to isolate itself to prevent the spread of the coronavirus. Such is the case of careers of technical origin; Biotechnology, Biomedicine and Industrial Engineering from the Salesian Polytechnic University in Quito, Ecuador, which in search of strategies to optimize the teaching-learning process, implement the use of Microsoft OneNote as a notebook for laboratory subjects.

Microsoft OneNote emerged in 2003 but was not part of Microsoft Office until 2016 [7] is a free program that helps the collection of information, note taking and collaborations with different users, allows you to organize notebooks, attach notes, images, diagrams and different multimedia elements, including audios, videos, recordings, captures. We can use it through tablets, computers, smart phones [8]. In addition, an application that facilitates student development, provides new resources and technologies that go beyond the professional future, even increasing student motivation because its use is very easy, it allows you to interact and build knowledge inside and outside the classroom; it helps to stimulate non-contact work while fostering more cooperative learning; it serves to create a work-learning environment that complements teaching processes [9].

It has also extended its use in scientific laboratories such as ELN for the extensive amount of data that is collected daily. The notebook in Microsoft OneNote allows all these jobs to be done quickly and easily [10]. Other programs have also ELNs, such as Evernote [11] or Google Docs [12]. However, Microsoft OneNote has been chosen as one of the best for its different functionalities, specifically, its greater flexibility when collecting non-standardized data [13, 14].

In the present work, an analysis of the perception of the students of the careers of Biotechnology, Biomedicine and Industrial Engineering of the Salesian Polytechnic University, Quito, on the use of Microsoft OneNote as an ELN for development of the practical component of laboratory, as a response to the health emergency in the country since March 2020.

2 Materials and Methods

In the first place, it was necessary to implement the use of OneNote as an ELN, to analyze the perception of the use of the careers of Biotechnology, Biomedicine, and Industrial Engineering at the "Universidad Politécnica Salesiana" in Quito. In this sense, the procedure carried out in each of these stages is described below.

2.1 Implementation of Microsoft OneNote as an ELN

Microsoft OneNote is a program that makes note taking, information gathering, and multi-user collaboration easy. Its greatest advantage is the ease of rearranging the record or the cumulative recording of information. OneNote has desktop application for computer and on mobile or tablet with the possibility of synchronization on all these devices. For the implementation, we used Microsoft Teams, a remote teamwork software that allows the OneNote application to be inter-articulated, where a team was created for each subgroup of students, Microsoft Teams allows creating class notebooks for each student. Table 1 shows the study group of this work. The work was carried off with 218 undergraduate students corresponding to three majors: Biotechnology, Biomedicine and Industrial Engineering at the Salesian Polytechnic University, Quito, Ecuador who was chosen by a Convenience Sampling [15].

Table 1. Summary of tested students

Degree	Level	Subject	N° of group	N° of students
Biotechnology	Second	Organic Chemistry	1	32
			2	11
	Seventh	Toxicology	1	18
			2	14
Biomedicine	First	General Chemistry	1	38
	Second	Organic Chemistry	2	25
Industrial Engineering	Second	General Chemistry	1	39
			2	37
			3	4
Total				**218**

A laboratory notebook for each student was created; all the students have trained in the use of the notebook trough a template for them to use as a guide. Figure 1 shows the welcome screen of the laboratory notebook in Microsoft Teams and Microsoft OneNote, and the groups created for work in Microsoft Teams.

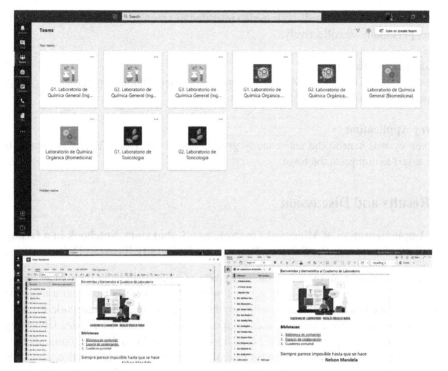

Fig. 1. (Top) Microsoft Teams main screen with the studied subgroups. (Bottom left) Lab notebook screen in Microsoft Teams. (Bottom right) Lab notebook screen in Microsoft OneNote.

2.2 Analysis of the Perception of the Students of the Careers of Biotechnology, Biomedicine, and Industrial Engineering

For the development of this stage, a descriptive quantitative study was carried out where a survey of an instrument was sent to the students of Biotechnology, Biomedicine and Industrial Engineering who had previously used Microsoft OneNote as ELN. The steps carried out are explained below.

Survey Design
14 questions were designed, which were divided into three categories, to get a better perspective on the results. The first category encompasses the general perception of the students regarding the Microsoft OneNote application, which seeks to know the perception of the use of the tool in a general way, with general questions about their experience; Within the second category, the advantages and disadvantages of this were tested compared to the use of a paper notebook, taking into account that the use of Microsoft OneNote has not been commonly used as a laboratory notebook by the students of the study group. Finally, the last category details a general evaluation, by the students, on the use of this tool, in which it is intended to know their final experience, after having

already used the tool as an ELN. It is also intended to know your intention of use in the future, personally or collectively.

Preparation of the Surveys
The surveys were designed in Microsoft Forms, a tool for designing, preparing, receiving, and analyzing the results offered to Microsoft users.

Survey Application
The survey was sent to the entire study group through Microsoft Teams, all students were asked to complete the form.

3   Results and Discussion

3.1   Implementation of Microsoft OneNote as a Laboratory Notebook in a Group of Students from the Salesian Polytechnic University Based in Quito

The students made a summary of the procedure of each practice in their ELN, under the instructions of the laboratory teacher. For this, the work was based on a template designed by the laboratory teacher, with which the students executed the work. Figure 2 shows an example of the procedure development of an Organic Chemistry laboratory practice, second-level, group 1 of the biotechnology degree. With the development of the laboratory notebook, the intention was that students have stored information about the execution of laboratory practices. One advantage of Microsoft OneNote is the articulation in digital devices: tablet, mobile, watches, computer [13]. Another important feature for students is the possibility of including, within the ELN, a lot of information such as spreadsheets with results, videos with procedures, links to articles. In this way, it becomes a comprehensive and non-perishable learning tool, since the intention is that we can use the ELN, as a consultation tool, for subsequent procedures. Finally, it is also intended that, once the face-to-face laboratory practices are resumed, the notebook is an indispensable tool for its development, since the students will already be trained in its development, and will complement their technical learning With what they have previously done, in this way, non-contact education imposed by the pandemic does not result in a waste of time for students, nor for teachers, in the practical sense of university education. Finally, one more advantage is that the teacher creates shared Microsoft OneNote files to support discussion and note-taking during meetings and project-level notebooks to store subproject information in a central repository. In this way, practical development is complemented by learning in the students' classes.

3.2   General Comparisons of Student Perception

The study was aimed at a group of students belonging to the degrees of Biotechnology, Biomedicine, and Industrial Engineering of the "Universidad Politécnica Salesiana"; This group comprised 218 students, from which 163 responses were got, equivalent to 74% of the total of the respondents.

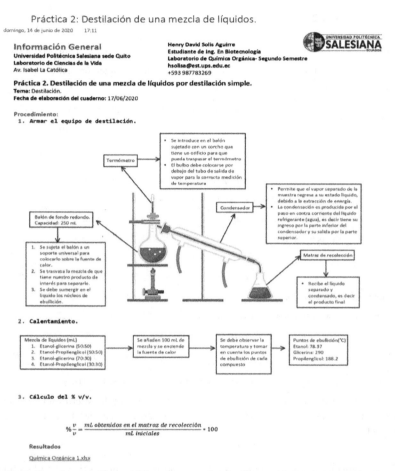

Fig. 2. Example of a page from a laboratory notebook. Corresponds to an organic chemistry practice, group 1 of the biotechnology degree.

General Perception of Students

Within this category, three questions related to accessibility and management offered by this tool to users who were tested, determine the students' assessment of these variables. The questions that were asked are shown in Table 2 (questions 1 and 2) and Fig. 3 (question 3), accompanied by the results obtained. It is mandatory to mention that question 3 comprises a data collection in which eight unique aspects were tested.

The results show that the perception of the students consulted about the use of Microsoft OneNote as an ELN was good with 43.5% and excellent with 27.2%. Andrade [16] points out that, according to the teaching method, technology-mediated learning has gained emphasis and leads to differentiated human interactions, so the use of Microsoft OneNote should be implemented in the following academic cycles. Another important point is to consider whether students have appropriate technological means for tele-education, according to Pérez & Tufiño [17] in Ecuador, there must be a process of

Table 2. Percentage of the results obtained in questions 1 and 2.

Question	Answer	Percentage
Do you have Microsoft OneNote on your computer, cell phone, tablet, or some other electronic means?	Yes	89%
	No	11%
Have you previously used Microsoft OneNote as an electronic lab notebook?	Yes	12%
	No	88%

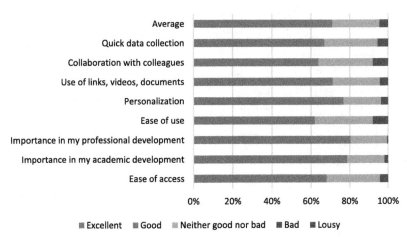

Fig. 3. Results of the general perception of the students in front of the Microsoft OneNote application (question 3). On average, 43.5% of the surveyed students consider the general perception of the tool Good.

analysis and discussion at the state level, for the advancement of science and technology through efficient use of Information and Communication Technologies (ICT), Learning and Knowledge Technologies (LKT) and Technologies for Empowerment and Participation (TEP) and likewise Bonilla [18] mentions that the use of ICT also implies choosing and adapting the material, guiding students in the selection of content, for socially relevant learning. According to the students consulted, 89% has access to a computer, tablet, cell phone or some other electronic device. The reality of students from public universities is definitely different from the reality of students from private universities in Ecuador; Using ICT implies, in the first place, secure access to these tools, therefore, the primary thing is to guarantee access to all students.

Specifically, in life sciences, Guerrero [14] stresses that today scientific laboratories accumulate an extensive amount of data that varies in quality and utility. The search functionality of Microsoft OneNote allows users to retrieve relevant information in stored experiments, therefore, its use as a tool to carry out a review of laboratory practices in a non-face-to-face manner is proposed as useful for students of the scientific-technical careers of the Salesian Polytechnic University.

Advantages and Disadvantages of ELN vs a Paper Notebook

This category tests the advantages and disadvantages that this application provides compared to a paper laboratory notebook. Points to consider allowed analysing whether it is feasible to use Microsoft OneNote as a laboratory notebook.

One variable to consider in determining use and transition to this tool was whether students have ever used a paper notebook as study material for laboratory practices. The results show that 73% of the surveyed students have previously used the paper lab notebook (question 4), while 27% have never used it and 88% have never used Microsoft OneNote as an ELN.

Likewise, the time to prepare their reports was consulted in the two laboratory notebook options: paper and digital. The questions that were asked are detailed in Table 3 (questions 5 and 6) and in Fig. 4 (questions 7 and 8) accompanied by the results got.

Table 3. Percentage of the results obtained in questions 5 and 6 related to the time spent

Question	Answer (time)	Percentage
Time you have spent, on average, doing a practice in a paper laboratory notebook	45–60 min	41%
	15–45 min	31%
	1–2 h	21%
	over 2 h	8%
Time it takes you, on average, to do a practice in the electronic lab notebook	45–60 min	41%
	15–45 min	27%
	1–2 h	25%
	over 2 h	7%

Furthermore, 52% of the students mentioned that the use of Microsoft OneNote as a laboratory notebook seems useful to them and 56% mentioned that the paper notebook is useful, however, 36% mentioned that they find ELN very useful compared to 25% who thinks the same about the paper notebook. According to Otero [19], one advantage of Microsoft OneNote is the ease of reorganizing the information, besides tracking it on all the pages of all the notebooks it has created and finally mentions that Microsoft OneNote has a desktop application for a computer and also on a mobile phone. or tablet, with the possibility of synchronization on all these devices. This is ratified by Guerrero [13, 14] who mention the easy portability of Microsoft OneNote between different digital platforms.

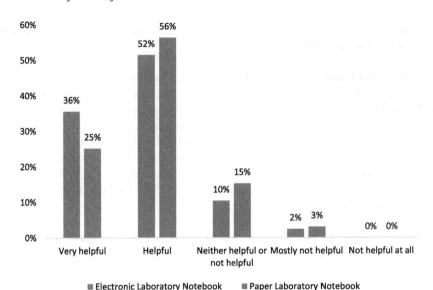

Fig. 4. Results obtained from questions 7 and 8 regarding the perception and comparison of the student between a paper laboratory notebook and an electronic one.

According to Jeschke [20], this technological tool also encourages collaboration, facilitates communication, evaluation and solves the continuous problem of information storage, it is also of valuable importance since it has been taught to students new resources that they can use in their professional future. Microsoft OneNote is a flexible tool that allows users to establish their own design. This could cause significant variations in adoption and quality among members of the laboratory [10, 21].

Electronic laboratory notebooks are also transforming the way we capture the scientific record with a revolutionary transformation from paper notebooks to digital capture of experiments [22]. It is important to emphasize that ELNs eliminate the need for manual transcription, facilitate note management and simplify the inclusion of digital resources [8].

Intent to Use Microsoft OneNote as a Lab Notebook
In this category, users' compliance with the use of this tool is analyzed, to where it is a recommended application for both students and teachers as a first option in times of crisis. The questions that were asked (questions 9, 10, 11, 12 and 13) are detailed in Fig. 5.

The results show that students (76%) would use Microsoft OneNote as ELN voluntarily, without the teacher asking for it, it is also observed that the majority (83%) would recommend its use to a classmate. At least, the students (88%) believe that implementing this tool has been a good option for the development of non-face-to-face laboratory practices and believe that, indeed, the ELN can replace a laboratory paper notebook (73%).

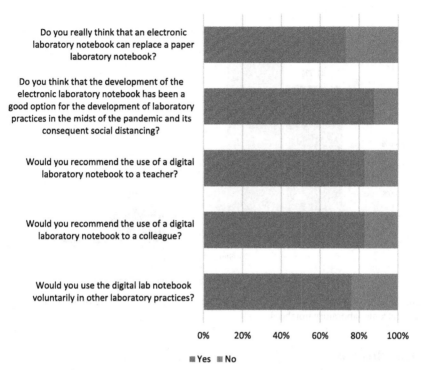

Fig. 5. Results of questions 9, 10, 11, 12 and 13 regarding the intention of using the electronic laboratory notebook. A positive result is observed in all questions.

Finally, with 37% approval by students (Fig. 6), Microsoft OneNote becomes a tool with potential to be applied within laboratory practices; According to Dirnalg [23], all professionals who carry out active research in life sciences must keep a laboratory notebook. However, while science has transformed in recent centuries, laboratory notebooks have remained essentially unchanged since pre-modern science.

According to a study in one of the Cambridge University labs, OneNote has become a personal ELN, recording notes about experiments and analyses daily, and importing supporting materials such as key charts and web resources to produce an account of progress and for discussions with others. As a collaboration tool, the lab notebook pages are shared among research staff to collect feedback, we store both the experiment data and all OneNote files on the laboratory's network servers and all research files are accessible to everyone [24, 25].

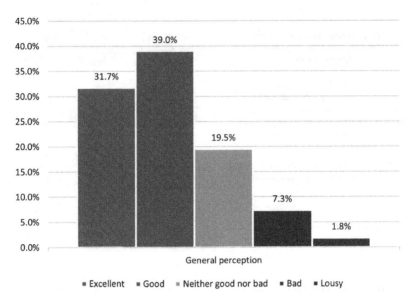

Fig. 6. Results of question 14 regarding the general perception of the use of Microsoft OneNote as an electronic laboratory notebook.

4   Conclusions

The application of ELN has allowed students from the Biotechnology, Biomedicine and Industrial careers of the Salesian Polytechnic University to develop their laboratory practices in person without using Microsoft OneNote as an ELN to review the procedures, including a Results section that will be useful when you can resume face-to-face activities, and to get a valuable consultation tool for your professional development.

Of all the students surveyed, 89% have access to some electronic device, while 87% have never used Microsoft OneNote like a lab notebook. The importance of accessibility to electronic devices is highlighted so we can use this digital tools. The general perception about Microsoft OneNote was, on average, good (44%) and very good (27%), which shows, preliminarily, that the students agree with its use.

Regarding the advantages and disadvantages of the ELN compared to a paper notebook, it was found that most of the students (41%) take 45 to 60 min to complete any of the two notebooks, so time cannot. However, the results show that the perception of the usefulness of the notebook by students is, in the very useful variable, greater (36%) compared to the results of the same variable of the paper notebook (25%). This tool can be turned into a replacement to the use of traditional laboratory notebooks and reduction of the amount of paper becoming something very useful nowadays. Although the ELN preparation time does not show any advantage over the paper notebook, the ELN has become a brilliant tool this year because it has simplified the learning process and made it purely virtual. 73% of the surveyed students believe that it is possible to substitute a paper notebook for an ELN.

The students have responded with approval to the use of the laboratory notebook, so much so, that they would recommend its use to a classmate, or to a teacher (83%), in the same way, they would use it with no teacher asking (76%). We have already used Microsoft OneNote for scientific-technical purposes. This is for its flexibility to collect data from non-standardized experiments because it has tools that facilitate access to various content anywhere and anytime, it can be updated regularly, making work much easier to do. Do it, it is ideal for education.

Finally, the final perception of the students has been positive, since they think implementing this ELN in response to the coronavirus pandemic has been an excellent option and they have rated their experience between good (39%) and very good (32%). In times of pandemic, the correct use of ICTs has allowed the learning process to be innovative, correctly implementing virtual education, which has facilitated adaptation to this new teaching process, and the students who took part in this study, look with approval and optimism its application. We should note if we do not intend the use of this tool to substitute for face-to-face laboratory practices, it is a tool that can be implemented to work as a complement to these.

References

1. García-Peñalvo, F.J., Corell, A., Abella-García, V., Grande, M.: La evaluación online en la educación superior en tiempos de la COVID-19. Educ. Knowl. Soc. **21**, 26 (2020). http://doi.org/10.14201/eks.23086
2. Barret, S.: Coronavirus on campus: college students scramble to solve food insecurity and housing challenges. In: CNBC (2020). https://www.cnbc.com/2020/03/23/coronavirus-on-campus-students-face-food-insecurity-housing-crunch.html
3. Gonzáles, N., Tejada, A., Espinosa, C., Ontiveros, Z.: Impacto psicológico en estudiantes universitarios mexicanos por confinamiento durante la pandemia por Covid-19. **644**, 1–17 (2020). https://doi.org/10.1590/SciELOPreprints.756
4. Sterzer, S.: Impacto del coronavirus en el sistema educativo: ejemplos en el continente asiático. Rev. del Dep Ciencias Soc UNLu **07**, 64–74 (2020)
5. Patchigalla, P.: A Critical Evaluation of The Implementation of Microsoft OneNote Class Notebook at One New Zealand Secondary School (2019)
6. Aldas, M., Blaciom, R., Corral, D., et al.: La educación a distancia y virtual en Ecuador. Una nueva realidad universitaria, Observator. Universidad Técnica Particular de Loja, Loja - Ecuador (2013)
7. Ruiz, A.M., Garza, I.L., Juárez, B., Cotera, E.: Strategies to use mobile tools in the process of accreditation. In: Hacia la transformación de la calidad en programas basados en TIC. Ciudad de México (2016)
8. Kanza, S., Willoughby, C., Gibbins, N., et al.: Electronic lab notebooks: can they replace paper? J. Cheminform. **9**, 1–15 (2017). https://doi.org/10.1186/s13321-017-0221-3
9. Gil, D., Benlloch-Dualde, J.V.: Use of digital ink technologies to facilitate student-teacher interaction in a German course for engineers. @Tic Rev D'Innovació Educ. 66–73 (2015). http://doi.org/10.7203/attic.15.5158
10. Rubacha, M., Rattan, A.K., Hosselet, S.C.: A review of electronic laboratory notebooks available in the market today. JALA J. Assoc. Lab. Autom. **16**, 90–98 (2011). https://doi.org/10.1016/j.jala.2009.01.002
11. Walsh, E., Cho, I.: Using evernote as an electronic lab notebook in a translational science laboratory. J. Lab. Autom. **18**, 229–234 (2013). https://doi.org/10.1177/2211068212471834
12. Bromfield, D.: Implementation and student perceptions on google docs as an electronic laboratory notebook in organic chemistry. J. Chem. Educ. **95**, 1102–1111 (2018). https://doi.org/10.1021/acs.jchemed.7b00518

13. Guerrero, S., López-Cortés, A., García-Cárdenas, J.M., et al.: A quick guide for using microsoft onenote as an electronic laboratory notebook. PLoS Comput. Biol. **15**, 1–9 (2019). https://doi.org/10.1371/journal.pcbi.1006918

14. Guerrero, S., Dujardin, G., Cabrera-Andrade, A., et al.: Analysis and implementation of an electronic laboratory notebook in a biomedical research institute. PLoS ONE **11**, 1–11 (2016). https://doi.org/10.1371/journal.pone.0160428

15. Etikan, I., Abubakar, M., Alkassim, R.S.: Comparison of convenience sampling and purposive sampling. Am. J. Theor. Appl. Stat. **5**, 1–4 (2016). https://doi.org/10.11648/j.ajtas.2016050 1.11

16. de Andrade, L., Rodrigues, W., Franca, G., Nadler, D.: Use of technologies in Brazilian public higher education in times of pandemic COVID-19. J. Chem. Inf. Model. **53**, 1689–1699 (2019). https://doi.org/10.1017/CBO9781107415324.004

17. Pérez, M., Tufiño, A.: Teleeducación y COVID-19. Cienc Am UTI (2020)

18. Bonilla, J.: Las dos caras de la educación en el COVID-19. CienciAmérica **9**, 89 (2020). http://doi.org/10.2307/344831

19. Otero Rodríguez, L., Calvo Díaz, M.I., Llamedo Pandiella, R.: Herramientas digitales para la comunicación, la tele-docencia y la tele-orientación educativa en tiempos de COVID-19. Rev AOSMA N° **Extra 28**, 92–103 (2020). https://dialnet.unirioja.es/servlet/articulo?codigo=738 1639

20. Jeschke, S., Natho, N., Zorn, E.: New media in education and research—a sophomore lecture at TU Berlin. In: 2009 5th IEEE GCC Conference Exhibition, pp. 1–5 (2009). https://doi.org/ 10.1109/IEEEGCC.2009.5734276

21. Hart, E.M., Barmby, P., LeBauer, D., et al.: Ten simple rules for digital data storage. PLoS Comput. Biol. **12**, 1–12 (2016). https://doi.org/10.1371/journal.pcbi.1005097

22. Borman, S.T.U.: Electronic laboratory notebooks may revolutionize research record keeping. Chem. Eng. News Arch. **72**, 10–20 (1994). https://doi.org/10.1021/cen-v072n021.p010

23. Dirnagl, U., Przesdzing, I.: A pocket guide to electronic laboratory notebooks in the academic life sciences. F1000Research, **5**, 1–12 (2016). https://doi.org/10.12688/f1000research.7628.1

24. Natho, N., Knipping, L., Pfeiffer, O., et al.: Collaborative learning in teaching information management. Eur. J. Eng. Educ. **35**, 405–413 (2010). https://doi.org/10.1080/03043797.2010. 483278

25. Oleksik, G., Milic-frayling, N.: Study of an electronic lab notebook design and practices that emerged in a collaborative scientific environment. In: CSCW2014 Proceedings of the 17th ACM Conference on Computer Supported Cooperative Work and Social, pp. 120–133 (2014). https://doi.org/10.1145/2531602.2531709

Brief Review of Functional Data Analysis: A Case Study on Regional Demographic and Economic Data

Adrián Padilla-Segarra$^{(\boxtimes)}$ (ID), Mabel González-Villacorte(ID), Isidro R. Amaro(ID), and Saba Infante(ID)

School of Mathematical and Computational Sciences, Yachay Tech University, Urcuquí, Ecuador
{adrian.padilla,mabel.gonzalez,iamaro,
sinfante}@yachaytech.edu.ec

Abstract. Functional data analysis (FDA) is an important recent field in statistics that enables us to analyze data with dependency over continuous frames and has many applications in various scientific areas. In Ecuador, there is not much use of these methods, and even less in the analysis of demographic and economic variables. In the present study, we firstly describe the general techniques used in FDA and some relevant studies performed with data from Ecuador. Then, we carry out an exploratory analysis with FPCA, functional clustering and PCA on data sets considering fertility, infant mortality, life expectancy, MPI, HDI and GDP growth indexes as variables. Observations for twenty Latin American countries during time frames around 1960–2018 were obtained. We found evidence for homogeneous behavior of variance among life expectancy, MPI and HDI. GDP growth rates reported to have a different functional nature. Haiti, Honduras and Venezuela were determined to have outlying observations for some variables. Our conclusions emphasize the advantages of using FDA techniques in comparison to classical multivariate methods for creating holistic approaches in data analysis.

Keywords: Functional data analysis · Principal component analysis · Cluster analysis · Demographic data

Mathematics Subject Classification (2020): 62R10 · 62H25 · 62H30

1 Introduction and Justification

In general terms, functional data analysis (FDA) is a set of techniques developed in statistics that is used to analyze data presented as functions. This is, rather than working with measurements of discrete amounts, it studies data samples which vary over a continuum like surface area or time. The techniques used in FDA have properties that can be highly useful for researchers studying data of those characteristics [1].

Historically, while the development of the theory of FDA emerged in 1997 with the publication of the book *Functional Data Analysis* by J.O. Ramsay and B. Silverman [2], this area saw its beginning stages with the works of Grenander (1950) [3] and Rao (1958)

© Springer Nature Switzerland AG 2020
G. Rodriguez Morales et al. (Eds.): TICEC 2020, CCIS 1307, pp. 163–176, 2020.
https://doi.org/10.1007/978-3-030-62833-8_14

[4].[1] FDA has had a big impact in applications of data analysis and computer science. Particularly, since 2005, applied FDA techniques have appeared in a large number of publications across various fields of sciences, especially where data is obtained from measurements reported by devices in a time series, such as in biomedical engineering [5]. These techniques expand the mathematical notions for multivariate statistics while harnessing the computational power of data analysis. The intrinsic high dimensionality of functional data brings challenges for the study of both theory and computation. However, the large or infinite dimension structure of the data is a rich source of information offering many possibilities for research and analytics [1]. Even though the benefits of using FDA techniques are clear, a complete assimilation of its advantages is still limited [5].

In our particular case study, we emphasize that socio-economic development in Latin America depends on many factors that range from social indicators to demographic and economic indexes. Studies have shown that in the last three decades, while economic growth in the region has been very slow, the poverty rates have continued to fall significantly and some other demographic indicators have improved [6]. In this sense, some variables appear to have significant relevance in the study of the socio-economic development of the region. In fact, many researchers consider demographic variables as the "final and most important factors" when studying the economics of Latin America [7]. Therefore, we presume that variables such as fertility rate, infant mortality rate, life expectancy and the Human Development Index (HDI) have similar structures of data (in terms of variance, nature and relationships) to socio-economic variables like GDP growth rate and the Multidimensional Poverty Index (MPI).

Therefore, in this work, we present an analysis on demographic and economic data from various countries in Latin America using techniques from FDA. We expect to: (i) make an exploratory analysis in order to find insights in the variables aforementioned; and (ii) compare methods from classical multivariate statistical analysis and FDA (principal components and classification) in their capacity to describe data structures that preserve information and allow dimension reduction. The use of FDA techniques represents an improvement to classical multivariate methods where considering such analysis is not feasible due to the intrinsic characteristics of the data and the problem of high dimensionality.

The remaining sections in this paper are organized as follows. In Sect. 2 of literature overview, we briefly present the theoretical background of FDA and characteristics for its main techniques. Here, we also mention previous works that use FDA techniques for data analysis in Ecuador. In Sect. 3, we specify the methods and notions for techniques used to carry out our case study analysis. In Sect. 4, the data sets used for the analysis and main results are presented with the respective explaining plots. We interpret and discuss the results in Sect. 5 by a descriptive validation process through a comparison among the established methods. Finally, we give our main conclusions and final remarks in Sect. 6 as well as the guidelines we are following for expanding this study.

---

[1] Grenander's article from 1950: *Stochastic processes and statistical inference* and Rao's 1958 publication: *Some statistical methods for comparison of growth curves* are the first references for sampling functional data that emerged.

2   Literature Overview

In general, FDA works with samples of random functions using a variety of methods, some of which are inspired by classical multivariate statistical methods. Among the main techniques used in FDA, there are the following:

Functional Principal Component Analysis (FPCA): This is a highly relevant method that can be used to manage functional data that are sparsely observed. It is often considered the most prevalent tool in FDA [5]. This is due to the dimension reduction which is possible through this technique. It facilitates the conversion of inherently infinite-dimensional functional data to a finite-dimensional vector of random components, denoted as functional principal components (FPC). Also, under mild assumptions, the underlying observed random processes can be expressed as countable sequences of the FPC's, which in many practical applications, are truncated to finite vectors [1]. Then, the methods of classical multivariate data analysis can be readily applied to the resulting random vector, thus, accomplishing the goal of dimension reduction.

Functional Clustering: Hierarchical clustering and other classification methods of functional data are also relevant techniques used in FDA for application in different areas. Classical clustering concepts for vector-valued multivariate data can typically be extended to functional data by making careful considerations like discrete approximations of similarity or dissimilarity measures, and preliminary dimension reduction of the infinite-dimensional functional data objects [8]. Particularly, k-means type algorithms for clustering are widely used to analyze and classify functional data [1]. This is generally the most used technique for classification and has been extended to functional data by using mean functions as the cluster centers [9]. In this method, we can consider two typical approaches: functional clustering via functional basis expansion and via FPCA [2].

Functional Canonical Correlation Analysis (FCCA): Often, when analyzing different sets of data, there is an aim to search for any relationships between the variables in the data sets. However, when the data is continuous and of high dimensionality, the classical statistical techniques from multivariate analysis do not suffice. Hence, in the theory of FDA, we can find different approaches that allows us to identify components of variability in each of the sets of observations which are highly correlated with one another. Some of this approaches are functional canonical correlation analysis and functional correlation measures, which are thoroughly explored in [1, 2, 10].

Functional Linear Models: In several cases, one of the goals in analyzing a data set is to construct a forecasting model that allows the researchers to infer valuable information from the original data set. In this scenario, one can extend the classical notions from multivariate linear regression techniques and use them to construct functional linear models. Using these techniques, it is possible to build models with scalar or functional response depending on the goal of the analysis. Moreover, functional linear regression models can be particularly useful for the analysis of sparse longitudinal data, as explained in [1, 11].

In particular, different techniques from FDA have been implemented in some studies with data from Ecuador. Nevertheless, it is important to note that these are not popular methods in the country for conducting data analysis, much less of demographic variables, in accordance to our search in academic databases.[2] In general, studies that use FDA are more commonly related to applications in fields like biomedicine, ecology, or meteorology [5]. On the other hand, as stated by a CEPAL review [6], most of the works that analyze demographic and economic data from Latin America use multivariate-based techniques such as regression analysis. Hence, to our knowledge, this functional approach has not been implemented for studying this type of data. Following, we will mention some relevant studies from Ecuador that use FDA techniques as their main approach, as a manner of exemplification of the notions used in FDA.

Among the most relevant applications in meteorology in Ecuador, there is the study conducted by Ballari et al. [12]. The authors use data of precipitation in different provinces in order to identify and classify the regions according to their precipitation seasonality. For this purpose, they firstly obtain the functional data by Fourier-basis approximations and built a weighted dissimilarity measure that consider time and spatial dependencies without dimension reduction. These considerations allowed them to obtain homogeneous regions that are spatially delineated and depict similar precipitation seasonality and intensity. The implementation was made on R software using mainly the fda library.

Also, Castillo-Páez et al. in [13] studied financial risk variables from a functional data perspective: late payment index and net profit margin of credit unions. The authors conducted functional exploratory analysis and constructed a model of supervised functional classification in order to determine which institutions in Ecuador are considered to be "in risk" by the guidelines of the regulatory entities.

3 Methods

The main purpose of our work is to make an exploratory analysis of demographic and economic variables with data from Latin-American countries by using FDA and classical data analysis techniques.

In multivariate statistics, we usually consider analytic methods which consist of N independent numerical observations samples of p variables. Nevertheless, functional data is mainly characterized because the samples of observations are defined over a continuum, for instance, time as in our case study. So, in order to find an approximation that allows us to make our data a functional object, we need to express each observation as a function defined by a weighted sum. This function will consist of certain basis elements and coefficients.

There are various basis systems for performing FDA that are used depending on the characteristics of each data set.[3] As from the mathematical standpoint, we consider a basis function system as a set of known functions ϕ_k, linearly independent among each other. Arbitrarily well, any function of the vector space can be approximated by taking

---

[2] We refer mainly to Elsevier's Scopus (https://www.scopus.com/) Ten results were obtained when searching for articles about FDA with Ecuador as affiliation country.

[3] Different basis systems are thoroughly explained in the book by Ramsay and Silverman [2].

a weighted sum or linear combination of a sufficiently large number of these functions [9]. Thus, a function $x(t)$ can be represented as $x(t) = \sum_{j=1}^{K} c_j \phi_j(t)$ where K denotes the total number of basis functions ϕ_j, and c_j represents the coefficients or weights used to achieve the approximation. We can infer, then, that via this approximation we can obtain values for the entire interval where our data is defined, even if we only have data measurements at certain different points [14]. An important property that we search for in functional data is smoothness. This is, when we approximate a function $x(t)$ to discrete data, it must be such that any pair of adjacent data values are unlikely to be too different from each other, as explained in [2].

For this study, we consider basis systems generated by *B-splines* approximations. These are generally explained as differentiable curves defined by polynomials in intervals, which are flexible and numerically stable [14]. We chose this basis since the data we analyzed consists of non-periodic variables measured over time. Also, we followed the next criteria: number of basis functions = order of basis functions + number of knots - 2, as suggested in [10], so that we can achieve the best approximation possible of the data while not losing the smoothness required. Moreover, we considered that the knots of evaluation where equidistant from each other since our data consists of indexes measured yearly.

We use FPCA as the main technique for analyzing each of the variables in the data sets. A number of FPC's that accounts for at least 80% of the variance explained for each variable is chosen, respectively, according to [10]. We work by considering elements in the infinite-dimensional functional space $L^2(\mathcal{T}_j, \mathbb{R})$, where $\mathcal{T}_j$ is the time interval observed domain for each respective variable.

Some of these retained FPC's are plotted for the entire period that corresponds to each variable and interpreted. We present a score plot analysis of each variable by considering the first two principal component (PC) scores in order to complement the FPCA.

Furthermore, we carry out a functional cluster analysis in an exploratory study manner. In this case, we work directly with the functional data rather than previously obtaining dimension reduction by performing a FPCA, as explained in [8]. The approach used by the clustering method is by means of the dissimilarity distance induced by the L^2-norm. Indeed, we consider the variable $x(t)$ on $t \in \mathcal{T}$ in functional form. For observations x_i and x_j (countries observation functions in this case), their dissimilarity distance is given by

$$\|x_i - x_j\|_{L^2} = \left(\int_{\mathcal{T}} |x_i(s) - x_j(s)|^2 ds \right)^{\frac{1}{2}}.$$

Then, once the distance is defined, the hierarchical clustering calculation proceeds in an analogous way as for the multivariate scalar case. For this study, we have decided to carry out a hierarchical cluster analysis with a single linkage method, since the amount of observations N at each variable is small in comparison with the data considered. The dendrograms for each cluster analysis carried out are obtained, as well.

Lastly, we perform a classical principal component analysis (PCA) over the considered variables for all countries observations in the year 2018. Similarly to FPCA, this analysis involves finding scores that can accurately explain the modes of variation as the original data by obtaining new variables which are uncorrelated and in order of importance in terms of variance explanation [2]. In this work, we use this technique with the final goal of contrasting and validating our results from the comparison with the aforementioned FDA methods.

4 Results

4.1 Data Set of Demographic Variables

For the purpose of this analysis we focus on demographic and economic variables with yearly registrations for each country. We note that all variables are functional dependent on time with unit measure in years. Specifically, we consider observations from: Argentina, Bolivia, Brazil, Chile, Colombia, Costa Rica, Cuba, Dominican Republic, Ecuador, El Salvador, Guatemala, Haiti, Honduras, Mexico, Nicaragua, Panama, Paraguay, Peru, Uruguay and Venezuela. Dependencies territories from other countries have not been included. Each considered variable is described in Table 1 with the respective notation and database source. All the explained data analysis techniques have been implemented by aid of R software, version 3.6.0, with packages fda and fda.usc, as described in [15, 16], and base and visualization R libraries.

Table 1. Demographic and economic variables description

Variable	Description	Period	Source[a]
FR: fertility rate	Total births count ratio by total woman population	1960–2018	Population and Estimates Projections, World Bank
IMR: infant mortality rate	Total number of infant deaths count by 1,000 live births	1970–2018[b]	Health Nutrition and Population Statistics, World Bank
MPI: multidimensional poverty index	Index constructed from indicators of poverty level and proportion in population (higher values represent worse poverty situation)	1990–2018	World Environment Situations Database, UNEP
HDI: human development index	Index constructed from education, income and life expectancy values (higher values represent better development level)	1990–2018	World Environment Situations Database, UNEP

(*continued*)

Table 1. (*continued*)

Variable	Description	Period	Source[a]
LE: life expectancy	Life expectancy value in years	1960–2018	Health Nutrition and Population Statistics, World Bank
GDP-GR: GDP growth rate	Gross Domestic Product annual registered growth rate in percentage points	1970–2018[c]	World Political Economy Statistics, WEP Dataverse

[a] All variables data sets have been obtained from https://knoema.com/.
[b] Argentina, Costa Rica and Cuba did not have complete data for the entire period.
[c] Cuba and El Salvador did not have complete data for the entire period.

4.2 Functional Data Analysis Techniques

FPCA was performed with data and methods as described in Sect. 3. In Table 2, we observe the configuration chosen for carrying out the approximation technique in order to obtain the functional variables, as well as the variance explanation resulting from each FPCA. Also, in Fig. 1 we observe some approximations made for the data, where we can notice the functional nature of the variables. In Figs. 2, 3, 4, 5, 6 and 7, the FPC's are plotted as perturbations of the colored mean function while in Figs. 8 and 9 we obtain the PC score plots for each variable as previously described. The results performed for functional clustering are presented in Fig. 10, which are mainly the dendrograms for each functional data variable cluster analysis. Some plots for LE and HDI have been omitted since they resulted to be very similar to those of MPI.

Table 2. Variance explanation results for functional principal components according to approximation parameters

Variable	Spline order	Basis dimension	FPC 1	FPC 2	FPC 3	Total
FR	8	59	84.5%	12.6%	1.4%	98.5%
GDP-GR	5	48	17.7%	16.5%	12.9%	47.1%
HDI	9	31	97.1%	1.2%	0.7%	99.0%
IMR	5	50	95.1%	3.7%	0.9%	99.7%
LE	8	59	92.5%	6.3%	0.8%	99.6%
MPI	9	29	97.6%	0.9%	0.6%	99.1%

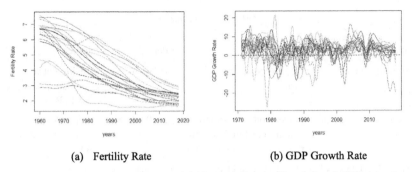

(a)   Fertility Rate   (b) GDP Growth Rate

Fig. 1. Approximations by B-spline method for variables fertility rate and GDP growth rate

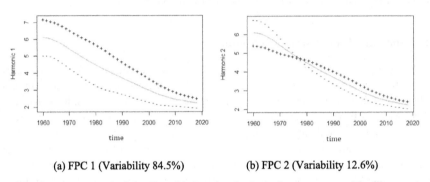

(a) FPC 1 (Variability 84.5%)   (b) FPC 2 (Variability 12.6%)

Fig. 2. Mean perturbations plot with functional principal components of fertility rate

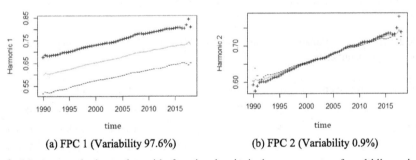

(a) FPC 1 (Variability 97.6%)   (b) FPC 2 (Variability 0.9%)

Fig. 3. Mean perturbations plot with functional principal components of multidimensional poverty index

4.3   Multivariate Principal Component Analysis

Furthermore, we present the results for the PCA using the covariance matrix S instead of the correlation matrix R, since S accounted for a bigger proportion of the variance explanation among the first two PC's. In fact, we consider the eigenvalue screeplots in Fig. 11, where this statement is depicted; the proportion of variance explained by the PC's corresponding to the first two eigenvalues is bigger than 90%. The resulting

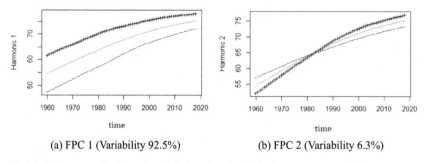

(a) FPC 1 (Variability 92.5%)   (b) FPC 2 (Variability 6.3%)

Fig. 4. Mean perturbations plot with functional principal components of life expectancy

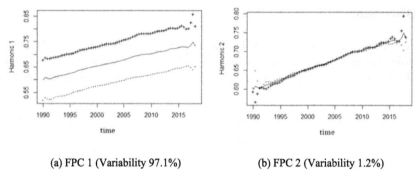

(a) FPC 1 (Variability 97.1%)   (b) FPC 2 (Variability 1.2%)

Fig. 5. Mean perturbations plot with functional principal components of human development index

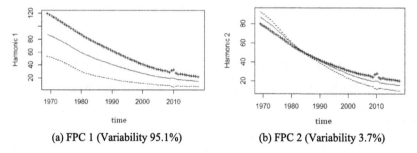

(a) FPC 1 (Variability 95.1%)   (b) FPC 2 (Variability 3.7%)

Fig. 6. Mean perturbations plot with functional principal components of infant mortality rate

biplot is described in Fig. 12. Finally, we present the dendrogram of the cluster analysis between the countries and variables considered, which is described in Fig. 13.

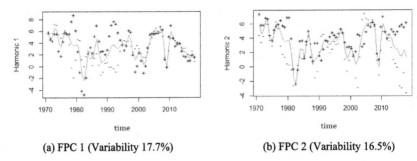

(a) FPC 1 (Variability 17.7%)   (b) FPC 2 (Variability 16.5%)

Fig. 7. Mean perturbations plot with functional principal components of GDP growth rate

5   Discussion

To begin with, we can observe in Fig. 1 accurate approximations of the FR and GDP-GR data using B-spline functions defined via a high-dimensional basis. After carrying out the FPCA, for variable FR, we present the two first FPC's which accounted for more

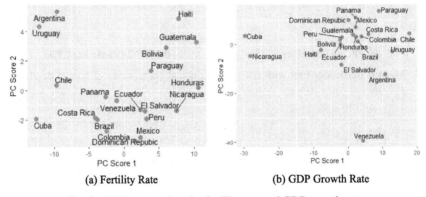

(a) Fertility Rate   (b) GDP Growth Rate

Fig. 8. FPCA score plots for fertility rate and GDP growth rate

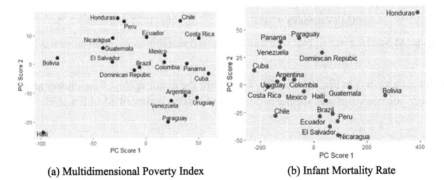

(a) Multidimensional Poverty Index   (b) Infant Mortality Rate

Fig. 9. FPCA score plots for multidimensional poverty index and infant mortality rate

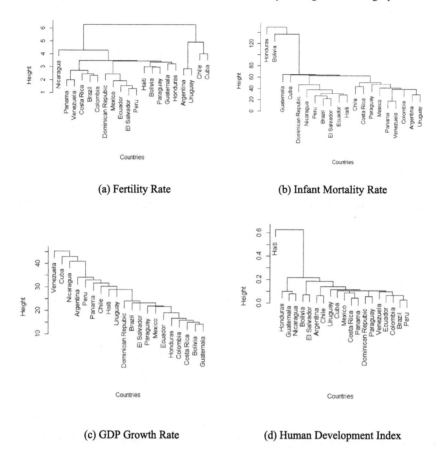

(a) Fertility Rate

(b) Infant Mortality Rate

(c) GDP Growth Rate

(d) Human Development Index

Fig. 10. Results for functional clustering dendrograms of demographic and economic variables

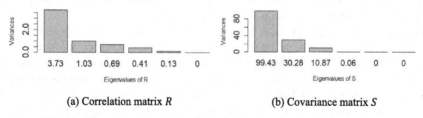

(a) Correlation matrix R

(b) Covariance matrix S

Fig. 11. Eigenvalue screeplots of classical PCA with the respective matrix

than 95% of the variance explained. In Fig. 2, we can observe that the first FPC has the greatest variability since the mean function perturbations plot indicates that most observations have greater variance among the year period until 2010, where the variance decreases proportionally with the mean function. In the second FPC, we note that there is an inverse relationship that flips around the year 1978. This is due to the fact that some countries have had sinusoidal rates before 1980. Finally, we do not retain further

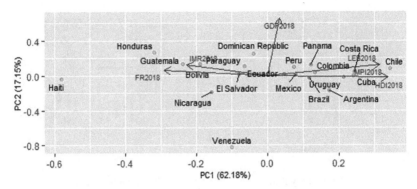

Fig. 12. PCA score biplot for demographic and economic variables with observations in 2018

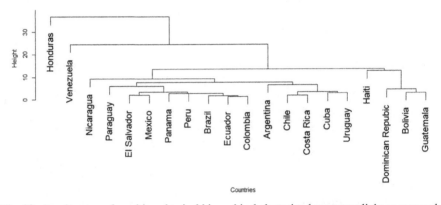

Fig. 13. Dendrogram of resulting classical hierarchical clustering by average linkage approach

components since there is not much relevant variance explanation; the perturbed mean functions are almost the same as the mean function itself.

In the FPC's presented in Figs. 2, 4 and 6, we note that there is an analogous behavior in the PC variance explanation, which yields a reduction of variance across the time intervals.[4] Most of it is accounted in FPC 1 whereas the other functions are not so relevant. Also, in Figs. 3 and 5 there is a homogeneous area of perturbation with respect to the mean function at each FPCA. Yet, in variables LE and IMR, there exists a flip in the perturbation incidence around the year 1980 which can be interpreted according to political and economic situations in a further expanded study. Likewise, this also has a tendency to increase MPI, as shown in Fig. 3.

The most surprising result is about the GDP-GR variable. We have, as noted in Fig. 7, that most variance is not explained by a relatively small amount of FPC's. In fact, it requires more than eight components to get a joint variance explanation of at

---

[4] Note that in Figs. 2 and 6, the functional variables tend to decrease in value at each time interval, whereas in Fig. 4 the variable increases. Nevertheless, we refer to the fact that in all these plots, there is evidence of lower variability among the data as the time increases in the intervals.

least 80%. This is the sole case with much difference among all variables, which can be due to the different nature of the GDP growth index and possible periodical behavior following economic cycles and other factors.

Furthermore, from Figs. 8 and 9, we analyze the observations relationship to each FPC's 1 and 2 through their respective PC scores. In the case of FR, there is some spreading degree among countries. For GDP-GR, there is an accumulation according to certain behavior of the index. Although the variance is not well explained by this approximation, there is enough data to discriminate the cases of Venezuela, Cuba and Nicaragua. For the IMR, there is a tendency to decrease in value for most countries, except for Honduras. Lastly, for the rest of demographic variables (MPI, LE and HDI) the behavior is similar since there is a general accumulation and tendency to increase. Nevertheless, the isolated case of Haiti is worth to mention which has low values on all three variables under this functional perspective. These assertions can be contrasted and confirmed with the dendrograms of the hierarchical cluster analysis where there is clear discrimination regarding the specific aforementioned cases. In variables MPI, LE and HDI, Haiti has the greatest linkage height among the rest of observations. Also, in the dendrogram for GDP-GR, there is a *scaled* clustering which confirms the different nature of the encountered phenomena. These explained statements are depicted in Fig. 10.

In the classical PCA, we observe that the considered observations, except for Honduras and Venezuela, share similar features among variables from Table 1. In fact, Venezuela shows the smallest value for GDP-GR in 2018, around -19.6%, which brings about its variability. In the case of Honduras, the data shows that even though this country shares similar rates with other observations, it has very small values for FR and IMR, as well as high values for LE, HDI, and MPI in 2018. This is well explained by the biplot in Fig. 12. Finally, from this same figure, we find that variables FR and IMR are negatively correlated with LE, HDI, and the MPI in 2018.

Moreover, GDP-GR in 2018 is almost independent of the rest of the variables considered. Thus, confirming again the different nature of this variable as a result of the proposed exploratory analysis.

Overall, the application of both, functional and classical, PCA methods help us to determine the importance of the variability of a particular observation in time with respect to the whole functional behavior of the variable. For instance, the particular observations in 2018 mentioned (FR and IMR for Honduras, and GDP-GR for Venezuela) have this distinctive explained feature in greater extent, as presented in the cluster analysis dendrogram from Fig. 13. Also, the case of Haiti in the functional PCA is worthy of comparison to present time observations in all variables.

6 Conclusions and Further Studies

Applications with an approach of analyzing data by considering its functional nature can exhibit important insights in comparison with classical methods. We conclude that in Ecuador, there are not many applications of FDA techniques for studying particular cases. By briefly reviewing the many fields of application, we encourage its expansion for more detailed and accurate analysis.

Regarding the demographic and economic data analyzed, this work provides preliminary insights to the variability of the observations and the correlation that may exist among the studied variables. The importance of FDA methods is based on the holistic approach that it allows. Specifically, FDA can be further used for forecasting studies, as stated by [17] about fertility rates and robust functional approaches. Also, we propose to perform analysis with aid of functional canonical correlation and functional regression methods, as well as considering different approximation basis, specifically for the case of GDP-GR. Lastly, we are interested in the effects of balancing the variability of the approximation with the goodness of fit criteria.

References

1. Wang, J., Chiou, J., Müller, H.: Review of functional data analysis. Ann. Rev. Stat. Appl. **3**(1), 257–295 (2015). https://doi.org/10.1146/annurev-statistics-041715-033624
2. Ramsay, J., Silverman, B.: Functional Data Analysis, 2nd edn. Springer, New York (2005). https://doi.org/10.1007/b98888
3. Grenander, U.: Stochastic processes and statistical inference. Ark. Mat. **1**(3), 195–277 (1950). https://doi.org/10.1007/BF02590638
4. Rao, C.R.: Some statistical methods for comparison of growth curves. Biometrics **14**(1), 1–17 (1958). https://doi.org/10.2307/2527726
5. Ullah, S., Finch, C.: Applications of functional data analysis: a systematic review. BMC Med. Res. Methodol. **13**(1), 43 (2013). https://doi.org/10.1186/1471-2288-13-43
6. Ros, J.: Poverty reduction in Latin America: the role of demographic, social and economic factors. CEPAL Rev. **2009**, 35–45 (2009). https://doi.org/10.18356/9350b5c9-en
7. Bongaarts, J.: Global population growth: demographic consequences of declining fertility. Science **282**(5388), 419–420 (1998). https://doi.org/10.1126/science.282.5388.419
8. Jacques, J., Preda, C.: Functional data clustering: a survey. Adv. Data Anal. Classif. **8**(3), 231–255 (2014). https://doi.org/10.1007/s11634-013-0158-y.hal-00771030
9. Ramsay, J., Silverman, B.: Applied Functional Data Analysis: Methods and Case Studies, 1st edn. Springer, New York (2002). https://doi.org/10.1007/b98886
10. Ramsay, J., Hooker, G., Graves, S.: Functional Data Analysis with R and MatLab, 1st edn. Springer, USA (2009). https://doi.org/10.1007/978-0-387-98185-7
11. Yao, F., Müller, H., Wang, J.: Functional linear regression analysis for longitudinal data. Ann. Stat. **33**, 2873–2903 (2005). https://doi.org/10.1214/009053605000000660
12. Ballari, D., Giraldo, R., Campozano, L., Samaniego, E.: Spatial functional data analysis for regionalizing precipitation seasonality and intensity in a sparsely monitored region: unveiling the spatio-temporal dependencies of precipitation in Ecuador. Int. J. Climatol. **38**, 3337–3354 (2018). https://doi.org/10.1002/joc.5504
13. Castillo-Páez, S., Flores, M., Herrera Enríquez, G.: Análisis de Datos Funcionales Aplicado al Riesgo Financiero: un Caso de Estudio en Cooperativas de Ahorro y Crédito Ecuatorianas. Latin Am. J. Comput. **4**(1), 9 (2017)
14. Ramsay, J.: Functional data analysis. http://www.psych.mcgill.ca/misc/fda/
15. Ramsay, J., Graves, S., Hooker, G.: Package 'fda' for R. CRAN Repository (2020)
16. Bande, M., Oviedo, M., Galeano, P., Nieto, A., Garcia, E.: Package 'fda.usc' for R. CRAN Repository (2020)
17. Hyndman, R.J., Ullah, M.S.: Robust forecasting of mortality and fertility rates: a functional data approach. Comput. Stat. Data Anal. **51**, 4942–4956 (2007). https://doi.org/10.1016/j.csda.2006.07.028

Assessment of Anthropometric Measurements for Obesity and Abnormal Body Fat Percentage Diagnosis Using k-means as Clustering Technique

Alexandra La Cruz[1]([✉]) [ID], Erika Severeyn[2] [ID], Jesús Velásquez[2] [ID],
Héctor Herrera[3] [ID], and Sara Wong[4] [ID]

[1] Faculty of Engineering, Ibagué University, Ibagué, Tolima, Colombia
`alexandra.lacruz@unibague.edu.co`
[2] Department of Thermodynamics and Transfer Phenomena,
Simón Bolívar University, Caracas, Venezuela
`{severeynerika,jmvelasquezf}@usb.ve`
[3] Department of Biological and Biochemical Process Technology,
Simón Bolívar University, Caracas, Venezuela
`haherrera@usb.ve`
[4] Department of Electronics and Circuits, Simón Bolívar University,
Caracas, Venezuela
`swong@usb.ve`

Abstract. The increased prevalence of overweight and obesity has become a major factor in public spending in countries around the world. The diagnosis of overweight and obesity is based on body mass index (BMI) and body fat percentage (BFP). The World Health Organization proposed BMI cut-off points to define overweight and obesity. Recently epidemiological studies established as normal BFP a BFP < 25 for men and BFP < 30 for women. A high correlation between a high BMI, abnormal BFP and skin thinness have been found in numerous studies. The aim of this work is to evaluate the k-means clustering algorithm using anthropometric measurements for the classification of subjects with overweight/obesity and abnormal BFP. Precision (P), accuracy (Acc) and recall (R) were calculated to evaluate the efficiency of the method to classify overweight/obesity and abnormal BFP. Results of this research suggest that the k-means method applied to anthropometric measurements can make an acceptable classification of overweight/obesity and abnormal BFP. The arm circumferences values show the best Acc, P and R (0.79, 0.84 and 0.71) compared to all other measurements for overweight/obesity diagnosis, otherwise, suprailiac and abdominal skinfolds values show the best Acc, P and R (0.73, 0.73 and 0.64) compared to all other measurements for abnormal BFP diagnosis. Results that are supported by studies asserting a strong relationship between arm circumferences, abdominal skinfold, suprailiac skinfold, BFP and BMI. Other machine learning techniques, such as neural networks and the support vector machine, will be studied in the future to assess the relationship between BMI, BFP and anthropometric measurements.

© Springer Nature Switzerland AG 2020
G. Rodriguez Morales et al. (Eds.): TICEC 2020, CCIS 1307, pp. 177–191, 2020.
https://doi.org/10.1007/978-3-030-62833-8_15

Keywords: Anthropometrics measurements · Skinfold thinkness · k-means clustering

1 Introduction

The increased prevalence of overweight and obesity has become a major factor in public spending in countries around the world [6]. Studies estimate that 57.8% of the world population will be overweight or obese by 2030 if current trends continue [6]. The obesity is commonly associated with several metabolic dysfunctions, such as insulin resistance [2,36], metabolic syndrome [29,35], increased blood glucose [1], dyslipidemia, hypertension and the development of other diseases such as type 2 diabetes, cardiovascular diseases [11,20] and atherosclerosis [1].

World Health Organization (WHO) has defined obesity as "an abnormal or excessive fat accumulation that presents a risk to health" [13]. Currently the diagnosis of overweight and obesity is based on body mass index (BMI). The WHO (2004) [37] proposed the cut-off points for defining underweight, normal weight, overweight and obesity in their different degrees. Among the limitations of BMI is the impossibility of discriminating between fatty tissue and muscle tissue, tending to produce false negatives in people with a high percentage of body fat but a normal BMI, and false positives in people with high BMI and high muscle tissue [3,23], because of this the use in concomitant of the body fat percentage (BFP) and BMI is recommended for a obesity diagnosis.

The BFP is calculated from several methods, among them are the bioelectric impedance and formula of Siri [33] that uses two, four and seven different skinfolds as variables, in these research the Siri formula with two skinfolds were used to compute the BFP [10]. Currently, there are no established limits for the abnormal BFP, mainly due to the limitation of the existing data around the world. Numerous studies have evaluated the relationship between overweight and obesity with BMI through skinfold thinness, finding a high directly proportional correlation between BMI, BFP and skinfold thinness [4,26].

Machine learning techniques to classify overweight and obesity have been already used [7]. Certain studies have used k-means to differentiate overweight and obesity from normal subjects using biochemical variables [21]. Some other studies use the k-means to detect overweight populations, based on anthropometric measures such as waist and hip circumference [9] and indicators of comorbidity such as diabetes, depression and atherosclerosis.

The aim of this work is to evaluate the k-means clustering algorithm using anthropometric measures to classify subjects with obesity and abnormal BFP. A database of 1053 subjects with anthropometric measurement (weight, height, arm circumferences, flexed arm circumferences, waist circumference, hip circumference, thigh circumferences, calf circumferences, triceps skinfolds, subscapular skinfolds, suprailiac skinfolds, abdominal skinfolds, thigh skinfolds, calf skinfolds, diameter of humerus and diameter of femur) values was used. In the following section the database and k-means method used in this investigation will be explained. In the Sects. 3 and 4 the results and discussion will be presented. And finally, in Sect. 5, conclusions and proposals for future work will be presented.

2 Methodology

2.1 Database

Between 2004 and 2012 [16], 1053 (male = 308) adult men and women from the district capital of Venezuela were recruited into the Nutritional Assessment Laboratory of the Simón Bolívar University. Anthropometric measurements such as: height, weight, height, arm circumferences, flexed arm cicumferences, waist circumference, hip circumference, thigh circumferences, calf circumferences, triceps skinfolds, subscapular skinfolds, suprailiac skinfolds, abdominal skinfolds, thigh skinfolds, calf skinfolds, humerus diameters and femur diameters were performed on each subject.

The diagnosis of overweight was made using the WHO guidelines which state that an overweight person has a BMI greater than or equal to 25. From the group of overweight subjects, 23 participants had a BMI greater than or equal to 30, indicating that they suffer from obesity [28]. Both overweight and obese subjects were placed in the same group for this study since we wanted to classify subjects with dysfunctional weight values.

Since there are no established limits for the abnormal BFP, the diagnosis of abnormal BFP were made according to [8,18,27] that established a cut off points of BFP < 25% for men and BFP < 30% for women as the limit of normality, above these limits are considered abnormal BFP.

All the procedures carried out in the study were in accordance with the ethical standards of the Bioethics Committee of the Simón Bolívar University and the 1964 Declaration of Helsinki and its subsequent amendments or comparable ethical standards. All subjects accepted the study by signing an informed consent form. Table 1 shows the characteristics of the dataset used, describing the values of each of the anthropometric variables by their mean and standard deviation of both normal and overweight subjects. While Table 2 shows the characteristics of normal and abnormal BFP subjects of the dataset used.

2.2 k-means Implemented

k-means [15] is a method that divide n observations into k clusters. In the k-means algorithm each observation is allocated to a cluster with the nearest centroid using a distance function, then, the centroids in each cluster are calculated again. This process is repeated until the centroids are the same between each step, and the final clusters are established.

In this study k-means were applied to each anthropometric measurement as separate variables (except height and weight because the BMI use them as

Table 1. Anthropometrics variables characteristics for obesity and overweight.

Anthropometrics variables	Normal weight Male = 246, n = 883	Overweight/obesity[c] Male = 62, n = 170
Age [years]	20.940 ± 2.773[b]	21.130 ± 2.919
Weight[a] [Kg]	56.125 ± 8.304	73.582 ± 10.174
Height [cm]	162.831 ± 8.521	163.274 ± 9.171
Right arm circumference[a] [cm]	25.762 ± 2.493	30.461 ± 2.373
Left arm circumference[a] [cm]	25.650 ± 2.425	30.432 ± 2.427
Right flexed arm circumference[a] [cm]	26.818 ± 2.717	31.381 ± 2.642
Left flexed arm circumference[a] [cm]	26.581 ± 3.109	31.119 ± 2.679
Waist circumference[a] [cm]	70.301 ± 7.095	84.824 ± 9.271
Hip circumference[a] [cm]	91.806 ± 5.471	103.539 ± 6.237
Right thigh circumference[a] [cm]	45.236 ± 2.370	49.594 ± 2.532
Left thigh circumference[a] [cm]	44.699 ± 2.565	49.093 ± 2.536
Right calf circumference[a] [cm]	33.736 ± 2.370	38.094 ± 2.532
Left calf circumference[a] [cm]	33.699 ± 2.565	38.093 ± 2.536
Right triceps skinfold[a] [mm]	13.593 ± 4.852	19.012 ± 5.634
Left triceps skinfold[a] [mm]	13.384 ± 4.788	18.861 ± 5.664
Right subscapular skinfold[a] [mm]	12.657 ± 3.991	20.512 ± 5.616
Left subscapular skinfold[a] [mm]	12.768 ± 4.005	20.658 ± 5.595
Right suprailiac skinfold[a] [mm]	11.837 ± 5.073	20.151 ± 6.451
Left suprailiac skinfold[a] [mm]	11.869 ± 5.102	20.216 ± 6.522
Right abdominal skinfold[a] [mm]	22.037 ± 5.073	30.351 ± 6.451
Left abdominal skinfold[a] [mm]	22.869 ± 5.102	31.216 ± 6.522
Right thigh skinfold[a] [mm]	19.899 ± 5.136	25.660 ± 6.019
Left thigh skinfold[a] [mm]	20.705 ± 5.219	26.282 ± 5.799
Right calf skinfold[a] [mm]	13.099 ± 5.136	18.860 ± 6.019
Left calf skinfold[a] [mm]	13.505 ± 5.219	19.082 ± 5.799
Right humerus diameter epicondylar[a] [cm]	5.973 ± 0.640	6.296 ± 0.634
Left humerus diameter epicondylar[a] [cm]	5.976 ± 0.635	6.301 ± 0.635
Right femur diameter epicondylar[a] [cm]	8.831 ± 0.661	9.588 ± 0.703
Left femur diameter epicondylar[a] [cm]	8.828 ± 0.660	9.595 ± 0.720
Body mass index [Kg/m^2][a]	21.106 ± 2.092	27.525 ± 2.349

[a]Statistically significant difference (p-value < 0.05) between control and overweight/obesity.
[b]Average and standard deviation.
[c]The database has 23 subjects with obesity.

variables in the case of obesity and overweight diagnosis; and triceps and subscapularis skinfolds in the case of abnormal BFP because Siri formula used them as variables); the number of groups was set to two (k = 2), to assess the ability of each variable to classify between obese/overweight and normal weight subjects, and between normal and abnormal BFP subjects. The Euclidean squared

Table 2. Anthropometrics variables characteristics for body fat percentage.

Anthropometrics variables	Normal BFP Male = 392, n = 949	Abnormal BFP Male = 16, n = 104
Age [years]	20.970 ± 2.790^{b}	20.960 ± 2.840
Weight[a] [Kg]	57.770 ± 9.950	69.640 ± 11.950
Height [cm]	163.210 ± 8.610	160.130 ± 8.280
Right arm circumference[a] [cm]	26.161 ± 2.820	29.840 ± 2.760
Left arm circumference[a] [cm]	26.050 ± 2.770	29.840 ± 2.800
Right flexed arm circumference[a] [cm]	27.220 ± 3.040	30.570 ± 2.870
Left flexed arm circumference[a] [cm]	26.930 ± 3.000	30.360 ± 2.800
Waist circumference[a] [cm]	71.570 ± 8.410	82.440 ± 10.250
Hip circumference[a] [cm]	92.730 ± 6.290	102.550 ± 7.690
Right thigh circumference[a] [cm]	45.630 ± 2.680	48.770 ± 3.120
Left thigh circumference[a] [cm]	45.100 ± 2.850	48.230 ± 3.180
Right calf circumference[a] [cm]	34.130 ± 2.680	37.270 ± 3.120
Left calf circumference[a] [cm]	34.100 ± 2.850	37.230 ± 3.180
Right triceps skinfold[a] [mm]	13.550 ± 4.680	22.880 ± 3.740
Left triceps skinfold[a] [mm]	13.330 ± 4.610	22.800 ± 3.610
Right subscapular skinfold[a] [mm]	12.790 ± 3.870	24.250 ± 4.040
Left subscapular skinfold[a] [mm]	12.900 ± 3.880	24.420 ± 3.930
Right suprailiac skinfold[a] [mm]	12.110 ± 5.220	22.900 ± 5.240
Left suprailiac skinfold[a] [mm]	12.140 ± 5.250	23.010 ± 5.260
Right abdominal skinfold[a] [mm]	22.310 ± 5.220	33.100 ± 5.240
Left abdominal skinfold[a] [mm]	23.140 ± 5.250	34.010 ± 5.260
Right thigh skinfold[a] [mm]	19.990 ± 5.070	28.490 ± 5.400
Left thigh skinfold[a] [mm]	20.790 ± 5.130	29.050 ± 5.190
Right calf skinfold[a] [mm]	13.190 ± 5.070	21.690 ± 5.400
Left calf skinfold[a] [mm]	13.590 ± 5.130	21.850 ± 5.190
Right humerus diameter epicondylar [cm]	6.020 ± 0.650	6.090 ± 0.610
Left humerus diameter epicondylar [cm]	6.020 ± 0.650	6.100 ± 0.590
Right femur diameter epicondylar[a] [cm]	8.900 ± 0.700	9.400 ± 0.780
Left femur diameter epicondylar[a] [cm]	8.900 ± 0.700	9.410 ± 0.790
Body mass index [Kg/m^2][a]	21.600 ± 2.660	27.050 ± 3.360
Fat body percentage [%][a]	22.610 ± 6.090	33.000 ± 3.220

[a] Statistically significant difference (p-value < 0.05) between normal BFP and abnormal BFP.
[b] Average and standard deviation.

distance were used to calculate the distance between each variable of data set with centroids and the process were replayed 10 times to prevent local minima. The silhouette coefficient (SC) was used to assess the assignment of the data set in the respective cluster [32].

2.3   Metrics Calculation

The confusion matrix [12, 31] is a table that contrasts the real classification with the classification made by the clustering model. In the Table 3 an example of confusion matrix is showed, the columns $(Class_1, ..., Class_n)$ represent the k-means classification and the rows represent the real classification. The numbers in the main diagonal $(A_{11}, ..., A_{nn})$ are the right k-means method classification and n is the amount of the total classes. In this study, the objective is to classify obese subjects from normal weight subjects, and normal BFP subjects from abnormal BFP subjects, as a consequence of that, the number of classes is two $(n = 2)$.

Table 3. Confusion Matrix.

True/predicted	$Class_1$	$Class_2$	...	$Class_n$
$Class_1$	A_{11}	A_{12}	...	A_{1n}
$Class_2$	A_{21}	A_{22}	...	A_{2n}
$\vdots$	$\vdots$	$\vdots$	$\ddots$	$\vdots$
$Class_n$	A_{n1}	A_{n2}	...	A_{nn}

The accuracy (Acc) [31] represents the rate between the correctly classified instances and the total. Equation 1 shows the expression of accuracy, where A_{ij} are the instances for $i = 1, ..., n$ and $j = 1, ..., n$, and n is the number of total classes.

$$Acc = \frac{\sum_{i=1}^{n} A_{ii}}{\sum_{i=1}^{n} \sum_{j=1}^{n} A_{ij}} \tag{1}$$

The precision (P_i) [31] of a $Class_i$ (see Eq. 2) represents the rate between of correctly classified instances of the $Class_i$ (A_{ii}) (true positives) and the total classifications of the $Class_i$ (A_{ji}). In this study the precision reported is the class precision average.

$$P_i = \frac{A_{ii}}{\sum_{j=1}^{n} A_{ji}} \tag{2}$$

The recall (R_i) [12] of a $Class_i$ (see Eq. 3) is the rate between the $Class_i$ (A_{ii}) correctly classified instances and the total number of instances that have the $Class_i$ as the true label (A_{ij}). The recall reported in this study is the average of the entire class recall.

$$R_i = \frac{A_{ii}}{\sum_{j=1}^{n} A_{ij}} \tag{3}$$

2.4   Statistical Analysis

To determine the differences between groups of two, the Wilcoxon non-parametric paired pair statistical test was used and a p-value $\leq 5\%$ was considered to be statistically significant [22].

3   Results

Table 1 reports the anthropometric measurements of the normal weight and overweight/obese subjects. The database consists of 1053 subjects, 83.86% belong to the normal weight subjects group and 16.14% are overweight/obese. The classification of overweight/obesity was made according to the WHO, all subjects with $BMI \geq 25$ were classified as overweight. The 13,5% of the subjects who belong to the overweight/obesity group have $BMI \geq 30$ indicating that endurance obesity. Table 2 reports the anthropometric measurements of the normal and abnormal BFP subjects. The classification of abnormal BFP group were made according to [18,27], that established as abnormal $BFP \geq 25$ in men and $BFP \geq 30$ in woman. The 9.88% of the subjects of the database presents an abnormal BFP and the 90.12% have a normal BFP; the subjects with abnormal BFP has a $BMI \geq 25$ indicating that they also belongs to the overweight/obesity group.

Table 4 and Table 5 show the confusion matrix of the variables with the best performance in the k-means non-supervising clustering for overweight/obesity and abnormal BFP classifications, respectively. In addition, the silhouette coefficient (SC), accuracy (Acc), precision (P) and recall (R) coefficient for overweight/obesity and abnormal BFP diagnosis was reported for $k = 2$ as it is shown in Table 6 and Table 7, respectively. Figure 1 shows the assignment of individuals to cumulus clusters for $k = 2$, using the anthropometric measurements. The character X represents the centroids of each cluster.

4   Discussion

Table 1 shows the descriptive and anthropometric measurements of the normal weight and the overweight/obese subjects. All parameters showed significant differences between the groups, except for age and height. All skinfolds showed higher values in overweight/obese subjects compared to normal weight subjects. On the other hand, Table 2 shows the descriptive and anthropometric measurements of the normal and abnormal BFP subjects. All parameters showed significant differences between the groups, except for age, height and epicondylar humerus diameter. All skinfolds showed higher values in abnormal BFP subjects compared to normal BFP subjects. All those facts are expected since obese and higher BFP subjects tend to have a thicker adipose panicle than normal weight and BFP subjects [17,34].

The k-means clustering method (Table 4) is capable of classifying obese subjects from normal weight subjects with the following anthropometric measures: right arm circumference, left arm circumference, right subscapular skinfold, left subscapular skinfold, waist circumference and hip circumference, with a $Acc \geq 0.78$, a $P \geq 0.78$, and a $R \geq 0.68$. On the other hand, k-means clustering demonstrated that is capable of classifying subjects with normal and abnormal

Table 4. Confusion matrix of k-means non-supervised classification of the variables with the best performance in the prediction of obesity and overweight

Anthropometrics measures	Confusion matrix		
	True/predicted	Normal weight $n = 883$	Overweight/obesity $n = 170$
Right arm circumference	Cluster 1	680^a $(77.01\%)^b$	14^c $(8.24\%)^d$
	Cluster 2	203 (22.99%)	156 (91.76%)
Left arm circumference	Cluster 1	681 (77.12%)	15 (8.82%)
	Cluster 2	202 (22.88%)	155 (91.18%)
Waist circumference	Cluster 1	677 (76.67%)	26 (15.29%)
	Cluster 2	206 (23.33%)	144 (84.71%)
Hip circumference	Cluster 1	659 (74.63%)	8 (4.71%)
	Cluster 2	224 (25.37%)	162 (95.29%)
Right subscapular skinfold	Cluster 1	698 (79.05%)	37 (21.76%)
	Cluster 2	185 (20.95%)	133 (78.24%)
Left subscapular skinfold	Cluster 1	695 (78.71%)	38 (22.35%)
	Cluster 2	188 (21.29%)	132 (77.65%)

[a] Number of subjects in the control group and classified in a respective cluster.
[b] Percentage of subjects in the control group and classified in a respective cluster.
[c] Number of subjects in the overweight/obesity group and classified in a respective cluster.
[d] Percentage of subjects in the overweight/obesity group and classified in a respective cluster.

BFP (Table 5) with the following anthropometric measures: right arm circumference, left arm circumference, waist circumference, hip circumference, suprailiac and abdominal skinfolds, with a $Acc \geq 0.73$, a $P \geq 0.73$, and a $R \geq 0.64$. Acceptable levels of accuracy and precision indicate that the method is capable of classifying subjects with the two pathologies. Slightly lower recall values indicate that the method is able to classify cases with the disease but gives a series of false negatives. It can also be seen that the silhouette coefficient (SC) is greater than 0.5 in all cases, indicating that all subjects were classified into a group for each of the parameters. In the parameters with the best Acc, P and R values, $SC \geq 0.55$ (Table 6 and Table 7).

Figure 1 shows that subjects with high skinfold values were located in cluster 2 (red) and subjects with lower skinfold values in cluster 1 (blue). Furthermore, the cluster 1 is where the highest percentage of normal weight and BFP subjects are found and the cluster 2 is where the highest percentage of overweight/obese and abnormal BFP subjects are found. This may be due to the fact that overweight subjects have a thicker adipose panicle and higher BFP than normal weight and BFP subjects [19,34]. The same fact is observed in the case of waist and hip circumference, where the method places the subjects with the largest hip and waist circumference in cluster 2, which is the group with the highest percentage of overweight/obese and abnormal BFP subjects. It should be noted

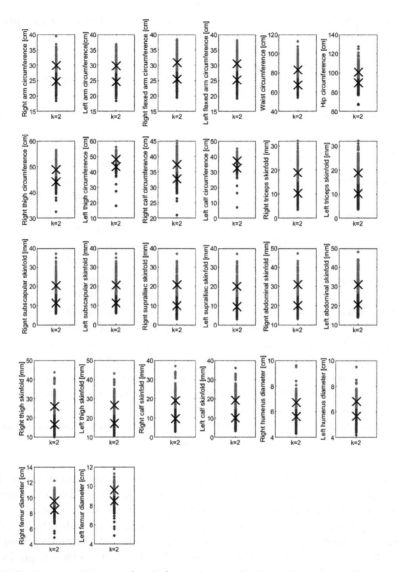

Fig. 1. Instance assignment (circles) to clusters for k = 2, using anthropometrics parameters. Red circles belong to cluster 1 and blue circles to cluster 2. Character X represents the cluster centroids. (Color figure online)

that waist circumference is strongly related to abdominal obesity and, in particular, it is used today as a risk factor for diseases such as cardiovascular disease and diabetes [5, 39].

Table 5. Confusion matrix of k-means non-supervised classification of the variables with the best performance in the prediction of abnormal BFP

Anthropometrics measures	Confusion matrix		
	True/predicted	Normal BFP $n = 949$	Abnormal BFP $n = 104$
Right arm circumference	Cluster 1	673^a $(71.00\%)^b$	21^c $(20.20\%)^d$
	Cluster 2	276 (29.00%)	83 (79.80%)
Left arm circumference	Cluster 1	674 (71.00%)	22 (21.20%)
	Cluster 2	275 (29.00%)	82 (78.80%)
Waist circumference	Cluster 1	675 (71.10%)	28 (27.00%)
	Cluster 2	274 (28.90%)	76 (73.00%)
Hip circumference	Cluster 1	652 (68.70%)	15 (14.40%)
	Cluster 2	297 (31.30%)	89 (85.6%)
Right suprailiac skinfold	Cluster 1	717 (75.60%)	10 (9.60%)
	Cluster 2	232 (24.40%)	94 (90.40%)
Left suprailiac skinfold	Cluster 1	670 (70.60%)	7 (6.70%)
	Cluster 2	279 (29.40%)	97 (93.30%)
Right abdominal skinfold	Cluster 1	717 (75.60%)	10 (9.60%)
	Cluster 2	232 (24.40%)	94 (90.40%)
Left abdominal skinfold	Cluster 1	670 (70.60%)	7 (6.70%)
	Cluster 2	279 (29.40%)	97 (93.30%)

[a] Number of subjects in the normal BFP group and classified in a respective cluster.
[b] Percentage of subjects in the normal BFP group and classified in a respective cluster.
[c] Number of subjects in the abnormal BFP cluster.
[d] Percentage of subjects in the abnormal BFP group and classified in a respective cluster.

In the case of overweight/obesity diagnosis the arm circumference values show the best *Acc*, *P* and *R* (0.79, 0.84 and 0.71) compared to the all other measures. The subjects with the largest arm circumference were placed in cluster 2, which is the group with the highest percentage of overweight/obese subjects (91.76%). This result indicates a strong relationship between high arm circumferences and high BMI values, corroborating some studies [5,24]. On the other hand, in the case of abnormal BFP diagnosis, the right abdominal and suprailiac skinfolds show the best *Acc*, *P* and *R* (0.77, 0.68 and 0.64) compared to the all other measures. The subjects with largest suprailiac and abdominal skinfold were placed in the cluster 2 (right skinfold 90.40% and left skinfold 93.30%). This results are in concordance with studies that correlate high body fat percentage with high abdominal fat accumulation [25,30], especially in subjects with insulin resistance and high risk of develop type 2 diabetes [14,38].

Table 6. Silhouette coefficient (SC), accuracy (Acc), precision (P) and recall (R) from k-means algorithm for overweight/obesity classification.

Anthropometrics variables	Silhouette	Metrics		
	Coefficient	Accuracy	Precision	Recall
Right arm circumference	0.60 ± 0.16	0.79	0.84	0.71
Left arm circumference	0.60 ± 0.17	0.79	0.84	0.71
Right flexed arm circumference	0.58 ± 0.18	0.75	0.82	0.68
Left flexed arm circumference	0.58 ± 0.19	0.77	0.81	0.68
Waist circumference	0.59 ± 0.19	0.78	0.81	0.69
Hip circumference	0.56 ± 0.18	0.78	0.84	0.70
Right thigh circumference	0.56 ± 0.17	0.77	0.81	0.69
Left thigh circumference	0.55 ± 0.18	0.73	0.80	0.67
Right calf circumference	0.56 ± 0.17	0.77	0.81	0.69
Left calf circumference	0.55 ± 0.18	0.73	0.80	0.67
Right triceps skinfold	0.56 ± 0.17	0.62	0.69	0.60
Left triceps skinfold	0.56 ± 0.18	0.62	0.68	0.60
Right subscapular skinfold	0.64 ± 0.19	0.79	0.79	0.68
Left subscapular skinfold	0.63 ± 0.18	0.79	0.78	0.68
Right suprailiac skinfold	0.60 ± 0.19	0.75	0.73	0.65
Left suprailiac skinfold	0.59 ± 0.19	0.73	0.74	0.64
Right abdominal skinfold	0.60 ± 0.19	0.75	0.73	0.65
Left abdominal skinfold	0.59 ± 0.19	0.73	0.74	0.64
Right thigh skinfold	0.58 ± 0.18	0.62	0.69	0.60
Left thigh skinfold	0.58 ± 0.18	0.62	0.70	0.61
Right calf skinfold	0.58 ± 0.18	0.62	0.69	0.60
Left calf skinfold	0.58 ± 0.18	0.62	0.70	0.61
Right humerus diameter epicondylar	0.62 ± 0.17	0.65	0.62	0.57
Left humerus diameter epicondylar	0.62 ± 0.17	0.68	0.60	0.56
Right femur diameter epicondylar	0.56 ± 0.17	0.67	0.71	0.62
Left femur diameter epicondylar	0.56 ± 0.18	0.66	0.71	0.61

Table 7. Silhouette coefficient (SC), accuracy (Acc), precision (P) and recall (R) from k-means algorithm for abnormal BFP classification.

Anthropometrics variables	Silhouette Coefficient	Metrics		
		Accuracy	Precision	Recall
Right arm circumference	0.60 ± 0.16	0.72	0.63	0.60
Left arm circumference	0.60 ± 0.17	0.72	0.62	0.60
Right flexed arm circumference	0.58 ± 0.18	0.67	0.60	0.59
Left flexed arm circumference	0.58 ± 0.19	0.67	0.60	0.59
Waist circumference	0.59 ± 0.19	0.71	0.61	0.59
Hip circumference	0.56 ± 0.18	0.70	0.63	0.60
Right thigh circumference	0.56 ± 0.17	0.69	0.59	0.58
Left thigh circumference	0.55 ± 0.18	0.64	0.57	0.57
Right calf circumference	0.56 ± 0.17	0.69	0.59	0.58
Left calf circumference	0.55 ± 0.18	0.64	0.57	0.57
Right suprailiac skinfold	0.60 ± 0.19	0.77	0.68	0.64
Left suprailiac skinfold	0.59 ± 0.19	0.73	0.66	0.62
Right abdominal skinfold	0.60 ± 0.19	0.77	0.68	0.64
Left abdominal skinfold	0.59 ± 0.19	0.73	0.66	0.62
Right thigh skinfold	0.58 ± 0.18	0.62	0.69	0.60
Left thigh skinfold	0.58 ± 0.18	0.61	0.59	0.59
Right calf skinfold	0.58 ± 0.18	0.61	0.59	0.59
Left calf skinfold	0.58 ± 0.18	0.61	0.59	0.59
Right humerus diameter epicondylar	0.62 ± 0.17	0.62	0.47	0.51
Left humerus diameter epicondylar	0.62 ± 0.17	0.65	0.48	0.51
Right femur diameter epicondylar	0.56 ± 0.17	0.61	0.53	0.55
Left femur diameter epicondylar	0.56 ± 0.18	0.61	0.52	0.55

5   Conclusions

The findings of this research suggest that the k-means method applied on anthropometric measurements can classify overweight/obese subjects and subjects with abnormal body fat percentage. The best anthropometric measurements to classify overweight and obesity on this research were: Arm circumferences, subscapular skinfolds, waist circumference and hip circumference. On the other hand, the best anthropometric measurements to classify abnormal BFP subjects in this research were: Arm circumferences, waist circumference, hip circumference, suprailiac and abdominal skinfolds.

Machine learning techniques, such as fully connected neural networks and the support vector machine, will be studied in the future to assess the relationship between BMI, BFP and anthropometric measurements. A machine learning technique would allow to evaluate how much influence have every antropometric variables over the classification, and would be possible to extract a spectrum to see which groups of subject are more vulnerable of suffering abnormal BFP.

Acknowledgment. This work was funded by the Research and Development Deanery of the Simón Bolívar University (DID) and the Research Direction of the Ibagué University. Full acknowledgement is given to David Powers, author of "Evaluation: From Precision, Recall and F-Factor to ROC, Informedness, Markedness & Correlation" (BioInfo Publications™).

References

1. Ahamad, M.G., Ahmed, M.F., Uddin, M.Y.: Clustering as data mining technique in risk factors analysis of diabetes, hypertension and obesity. Eur. J. Eng. Res. Sci. **1**(6), 88–93 (2016)
2. Altuve, M., Severeyn, E., Wong, S.: Unsupervised subjects classification using insulin and glucose data for insulin resistance assessment. In: 2015 20th Symposium on Signal Processing, Images and Computer Vision (STSIVA), pp. 1–7 (2015)
3. Altuve, M., Severeyn, E., Wong, S.: Adaptation of five indirect insulin sensitivity evaluation methods to three populations: metabolic syndrome, athletic and normal subjects. In: 2014 36th Annual International Conference of the IEEE Engineering in Medicine and Biology Society, pp. 4555–4558. IEEE (2014)
4. Bratke, H., et al.: Timing of menarche in Norwegian girls: associations with body mass index, waist circumference and skinfold thickness. BMC Pediatr. **17**(1), 138 (2017)
5. Chaput, J.P., et al.: Mid-upper arm circumference as a screening tool for identifying children with obesity: a 12-country study. Pediatr. Obes. **12**(6), 439–445 (2017)
6. Chooi, Y.C., Ding, C., Magkos, F.: The epidemiology of obesity. Metabolism **92**, 6–10 (2019)
7. DeGregory, K.W., et al.: A review of machine learning in obesity. Obes. Rev. **19**(5), 668–685 (2018)
8. Centers for Disease Control and Prevention: Quickstats: mean percentage body fat, by age group and sex–national health and nutrition examination survey, United States, 1999–2004 (2008)
9. Doménech-Asensi, G., Gómez-Gallego, C., Ros-Berruezo, G., García-Alonso, F.J., Canteras-Jordana, M.: Critical overview of current anthropometric methods in comparison with a new index to make early detection of overweight in Spanish university students: the normalized weight-adjusted index. Nutricion hospitalaria **35**(2), 359–390 (2018)
10. Durnin, J.V.G.A., Womersley, J.: Body fat assessed from total body density and its estimation from skinfold thickness: measurements on 481 men and women aged from 16 to 72 years. Br. J. Nutr. **32**(1), 77–97 (1974)
11. Farina, P.V.R., Severeyn, E., Wong, S., Turiel, J.P.: Study of cardiac repolarization during oral glucose tolerance test in metabolic syndrome patients. In: 2012 Computing in Cardiology, pp. 429–432. IEEE (2012)
12. Fawcett, T.: An introduction to ROC analysis. Pattern Recogn. Lett. **27**(8), 861–874 (2006)
13. Flegal, K.M., Carroll, M.D., Kit, B.K., Ogden, C.L.: Prevalence of obesity and trends in the distribution of body mass index among us adults, 1999–2010. Jama **307**(5), 491–497 (2012)

14. Genske, F., et al.: Abdominal fat deposits determined by magnetic resonance imaging in relation to leptin and vaspin levels as well as insulin resistance in the general adult population. Int. J. Obes. **42**(2), 183–189 (2018)
15. Hartigan, J.A., Wong, M.A.: Algorithm as 136: a k-means clustering algorithm. J. R. Stat. Soc. Ser. C (Appl. Stat.) **28**(1), 100–108 (1979)
16. Herrera, H., Rebato, E., Arechabaleta, G., Lagrange, H., Salces, I., Susanne, C.: Body mass index and energy intake in Venezuelan university students. Nutr. Res. **23**(3), 389–400 (2003)
17. Hung, S.P., Chen, C.Y., Guo, F.R., Chang, C.I., Jan, C.F.: Combine body mass index and body fat percentage measures to improve the accuracy of obesity screening in young adults. Obes. Res. Clin. Pract. **11**(1), 11–18 (2017)
18. Kim, J.Y., Han, S.H., Yang, B.M.: Implication of high-body-fat percentage on cardiometabolic risk in middle-aged, healthy, normal-weight adults. Obesity **21**(8), 1571–1577 (2013)
19. Krebs, N.F., Himes, J.H., Jacobson, D., Nicklas, T.A., Guilday, P., Styne, D.: Assessment of child and adolescent overweight and obesity. Pediatrics **120**(Supplement 4), S193–S228 (2007)
20. Ledezma, C.A., Perpiñan, G., Severeyn, E., Altuve, M.: Data fusion for QRS complex detection in multi-lead electrocardiogram recordings. In: 11th International Symposium on Medical Information Processing and Analysis, vol. 9681, p. 968118. International Society for Optics and Photonics (2015)
21. Li, L., Song, Q., Yang, X.: K-means clustering of overweight and obese population using quantile-transformed metabolic data. Diabetes Metab. Syndr. Obes. Targets Ther. **12**, 1573–1582 (2019)
22. Marusteri, M., Bacarea, V.: Comparing groups for statistical differences: how to choose the right statistical test? Biochemia Medica **20**(1), 15–32 (2010)
23. Mathew, H., Farr, O.M., Mantzoros, C.S.: Metabolic health and weight: understanding metabolically unhealthy normal weight or metabolically healthy obese patients. Metab. Clin. Exp. **65**(1), 73–80 (2016)
24. Mazicioglu, M.M., Hatipoglu, N., Öztürk, A., Cicek, B., Üstünbas, H.B., Kurtoglu, S.: Waist circumference and mid-upper arm circumference in evaluation of obesity in children aged between 6 and 17 years. J. Clin. Res. Pediatr. Endocrinol. **2**(4), 144 (2010)
25. Merrill, Z., Chambers, A., Cham, R.: Development and validation of body fat prediction models in American adults. Obes. Sci. Pract. **6**(2), 189–195 (2020)
26. Ojo, G., Adetola, O.: The relationship between skinfold thickness and body mass index in estimating body fat percentage on Bowen university students. Int. Biol. Biomed. J. **3**(3), 138–144 (2017)
27. Okorodudu, D., et al.: Diagnostic performance of body mass index to identify obesity as defined by body adiposity: a systematic review and meta-analysis. Int. J. Obes. **34**(5), 791–799 (2010)
28. World Health Organization: Physical inactivity: a global public health problem (2008)
29. Perpiñan, G., Severeyn, E., Altuve, M., Wong, S.: Classification of metabolic syndrome subjects and marathon runners with the k-means algorithm using heart rate variability features. In: 2016 XXI Symposium on Signal Processing, Images and Artificial Vision (STSIVA), pp. 1–6. IEEE (2016)
30. Philipsen, A., et al.: Associations between ultrasound measures of abdominal fat distribution and indices of glucose metabolism in a population at high risk of type 2 diabetes: the addition-pro study. PloS One **10**(4), e0123062 (2015)

31. Powers, D.M.W.: Evaluation: from precision, recall and f-measure to ROC, informedness, markedness and correlation. J. Mach. Learn. Technol. **2**(1), 37–63 (2011)
32. Rousseeuw, P.J.: Silhouettes: a graphical aid to the interpretation and validation of cluster analysis. J. Comput. Appl. Math. **20**, 53–65 (1987)
33. Siri, W.E.: The gross composition of the body. In: Advances in Biological and Medical Physics, vol. 4, pp. 239–280. Elsevier (1956)
34. Suclla-Velásquez, J.A., Smedts, C.: Obesity: a risk factor for infection after surgery. In: Weight Management. IntechOpen (2010)
35. Velásquez, J., Herrera, H., Encalada, L., Wong, S., Severeyn, E.: Análisis dimensional de variables antropométricas y bioquímicas para diagnosticar el síndrome metabólico. Maskana **8**, 57–67 (2017)
36. Vintimilla, C., Wong, S., Astudillo-Salinas, F., Encalada, L., Severeyn, E.: An aide diagnosis system based on k-means for insulin resistance assessment in eldery people from the Ecuadorian highlands. In: 2017 IEEE Second Ecuador Technical Chapters Meeting (ETCM), pp. 1–6. IEEE (2017)
37. Who, E.C.: Appropriate body-mass index for Asian populations and its implications for policy and intervention strategies. Lancet (Lond. Engl.) **363**(9403), 157 (2004)
38. Yang, H.R., Chang, E.J., et al.: Insulin resistance, body composition, and fat distribution in obese children with nonalcoholic fatty liver disease. Asia Pac. J. Clin. Nutr. **25**(1), 126 (2016)
39. Zhang, C., Rexrode, K.M., Dam, R.M.V., Li, T.Y., Hu, F.B.: Comparing groups for statistical differences: how to choose the right statistical test? Circulation **117**(13), 1658–1667 (2008)

A Comparative Review on Different Social Network Analytical Tools

Jacob P. Cherian[✉], Jubilant J. Kizhakkethottam, and Aneena Ann Alexander

Department of Computer Science and Engineering, Saintgits College of Engineering, Kottayam,
Kerala, India
cherianjacobp@gmail.com, jubilantjob@gmail.com,
aneenaalex@gmail.com

Abstract. With the evolution of Web 2.0, Social Networking sites like Facebook, Twitter, Instagram and similar platforms have gained wide popularity. They provide an in-depth of knowledge about users and the relationships between them. In order to analyse and extract meaningful information from these vast social network data, special graphical mining tools are needed that can efficiently model the characteristics of social networks. A variety of tools are available for Social Network Analysis, where raw network information can be formatted in an edge list, adjacency list, or adjacency matrix, often coupled with attribute information. We compare major tools and packages for analysing and visualising social networks that have a broad variety of applications covering genetics, economics, sociology, network theory, and several other domains. This work provides a comparison based on platform, license, file formats supported, layout and visualization and available metrics.

Keywords: Social networks · Tools · Metrics

1 Introduction

Social Network Analysis [1] is a methodology of quantitatively and qualitatively measuring and analyzing a social network. Social Network Analysis (SNA) is the method of analyzing social systems by use of networks and graph theory. It describes networked structures in terms of the nodes and the ties, edges, or links (interactions or relationship) that exist among them. SNA tools helps in identifying various relationships and changes in relationship between different entities. Entities or nodes may include computers, web pages, humans, group of authors collaborating on an article, organizations etc.

A famous example of connections among various nodes were described by Wayne W. Zachary who researched a social network of a karate club for a three-year period from 1970 to 1972. The network captures 34 karate club members, documenting connections between pairs of participants who interacted outside the club [2]. Our technological and economic systems have also become highly complex networks. This has made it harder to reason about their conduct and progressively dangerous to tinker with it. It made them vulnerable to disruptions spreading through the fundamental buildings of the network, sometimes turning localized breakdowns into cascading mistakes or financial crises (Fig. 1).

© Springer Nature Switzerland AG 2020
G. Rodriguez Morales et al. (Eds.): TICEC 2020, CCIS 1307, pp. 192–206, 2020.
https://doi.org/10.1007/978-3-030-62833-8_16

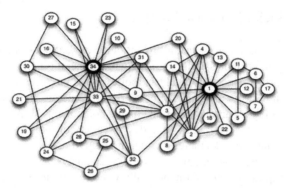

Fig. 1. The social network of friendships within a 34- person karate club (Zachary's Karate Club Dataset) [2]

Studying the various characteristics and prospective of a network has become a key research topic among social scientists. With the evolution of various tools for social network analysis, enormous amount of information has been gathered which influence the structure of the network thereby throwing light on marketing prospects, financial leaps, social exploration and so on. An interesting question is to why we should ever perform social media analytics? The answer lies in understanding the following aspects:

1. **Helps to understand the audience:** Knowing the social crowd can help maximize social media yields and help better conversions.
2. **Social data helps to create better content:** Tracking of a social network can help in identifying the content which drives traffic on a website.
3. **Help to understand competitors:** Your rivals also create content and execute policies on social media. This will result in their own unique information. You will be able to figure out what works and what isn't if you analyze this data.
4. **Social metrics can help you create a better strategy:** If you frequently study your social media analytics, you can find out what are the mistakes which resist your growth.
5. **Helps to identify the most influential node**: Many social network tools allow you to identify the key person in a network or the most influential node in a social graph.

All the above mentioned prospects of a social network can be well analyzed and studied by efficient tools. A wide variety of tools exist both to study the network structure of a social graph and understanding the structural and spatial characteristics of social data. In this paper, we focus on tools used to visualize and analyze the network structure of a social graph. Various tools like Gephi [3], Pajek [4], UCINET, Cytoscape [5], NetworkX [6] package, igraph package Graphviz [7], NodeXL [8] are to name a few.

2   Tools for Social Network Analysis

The social network analysis tool enables quantitative or qualitative study of social networks by defining the attributes of the social network, either through graphical or numerical representation [9]. A network analysis tool explores interactions and links within a dataset. Through network analysis, the networks are generated not by particular content types, but by relations among different content components. Typically, a network is made up of nodes and ties among these nodes. A variety of tools help in visualization and analysis of social networks thereby providing help to researchers in understanding how nodes are connected together in a network. Such analysis tools also aid in the creation of research questions and ultimately allow the researcher to reach conclusions. We have classified network analysis tools into two categories: Focused desktop tools and Developer tools. Focused desktop tools are standalone software tools which are primarily focused on network analysis and visualization. Developer tools are libraries or packages for network analysis which can be integrated along with another program.

2.1   Focused Desktop Tools

Cytoscape. Cytoscape is an open source software platform for the visualization and integration of molecular interaction networks and biological pathways with gene expression profiles, annotations and other state information. Although initially intended for biological studies, Cytoscape is now a general platform for complex analysis and visualization of networks [10]. Cytoscape was originally built by the Institute of Systems Biology in Seattle in 2002. Now, it is being developed by an internationally acclaimed consortium of free and open source software developers. The networks can be exported as ready to publish images with high quality. File formats like PDF, PS, SVG, PNG, JPEG, and BMP files are supported.

Gephi. Gephi is a free and open source tool primarily developed for Windows, Mac OS and Linux platforms. Gephi offers real time visualization with features for cartography, dynamic filtering and facilitation of logical reasoning. Gephi was initially developed by a group of students of the University of Technology, Compaigne in France. Gephi has been widely used in a number of research projects, journalism, academia and for examining traffic in Twitter networks. Gephi is widely used in Digital Humanities and various branches of social and political science. The purpose is to help data scientists make assumptions, intuitively discover patterns, isolate structure singularities or flaws during data sourcing. Gephi uses a 3D render engine to visualize large networks in real time and to accelerate the process of exploration [3].

Gephi is operated by its ad-hoc OpenGL engine, pushing the envelope on how customizable and effective network exploration can be. Networks that contain 100,000 nodes and 1,000,000 edges can be visualized using dynamic filtering Rich tools for constructive graph manipulation (Figs. 2 and 3).

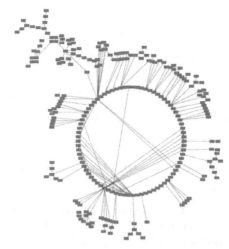

Fig. 2. Circular layout representation of a social network using Cytoscape

Fig. 3. Community detection using Gephi [11]

Pajek. Pajek is a program, for Windows, for visualization and analysis of large networks having thousands or millions of nodes. Pajek is useful in hierarchical data manipulation and provides powerful and accessible data manipulation functions. 3D visualization and its export in VRML are also available. 3 It can be used to analyze and visualize the large networks. It is developed by Vladamir Batagelj and Andrej Mrvar from the University of Ljubljana. Pajek is available freely, for noncommercial use. The key design aspects of Pajek was to facilitate the reduction of complex networks into smaller networks which can be further analyzed using sophisticated tools, to enable the user with powerful visualization tools, to implement a selection of efficient network algorithms [12] (Fig. 4).

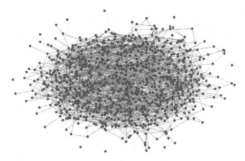

Fig. 4. Representation of a random network in Pajek using Fruchterman-Reingold layout

SocNetV. Social Network Visualizer (SocNetV) is a cross-platform, customer-friendly free software application for analysis and visualization of social networks. It provides tools for drawing social networks with a few clicks on a virtual canvas, loading field data from a folder in a compatible format, or browsing the internet to create a social network of related web pages. It also permits editing of actors and ties through point-and-click, analyze graph and social network properties, generates beautiful HTML reports and embed visualization layouts to the network (Fig. 5).

Fig. 5. Representation of Zachary's Karate Club using Kamada-Kawai layout model in SocNetV

2.2 Developer Tools

NetworkX. NetworkX is a Python language package for exploration and analysis of networks and network algorithms 4 NetworkX is appropriate for large-scale processing of real-world graphs, suitable for graphs reaching 10 million nodes and 100 million edges. NetworkX is a highly effective, exceptionally scalable, extremely mobile framework for social network analysis platform because it relies on a pure Python "dictionary" knowledge structure. With NetworkX, we can load and store networks in standard and non-standard data formats, create many types of random and traditional networks, analyze network composition, create network models, develop new network algorithms, formulate networks, and much more (Fig. 6).

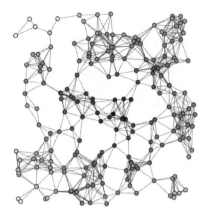

Fig. 6. Random geometric graph generated using networkx [13]

SNAP. Stanford Network Analysis Platform (SNAP) is a high performance, general purpose system for the manipulation and analysis of large networks. Graphs consists of nodes and directed, undirected or multiple edges between the nodes of the graph. Written in C++, the core SNAP library is designed for peak performance and concise graph representation. It is quickly scalable for large networks of hundreds of millions of nodes and billions of edges. Efficiently manipulates large graphs, measures structural properties, produces normal and random graphs, and supports node and edge attributes (Fig. 7).

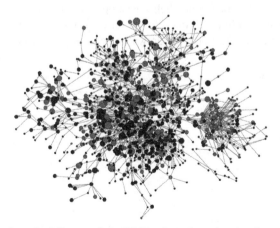

Fig. 7. Representation of a full network in SNAP, where the red nodes denote news media sites and the blue nodes denote blogs. (Color figure online)

iGraph. Igraph is a suite of network analysis tools focused on performance, portability & user-friendliness. Igraph is a free and open-source package. Igraph can be programmed in R, Python, Mathematica and C/C++. igraph can be used to generate graphs, compute centrality measures and path length based properties as well as graph components and graph motifs. It also can be used for Degree-preserving randomization. Igraph can read and write Pajek and GraphML files, as well as simple edge lists. The library contains several layout tools as well. Igraph consists of a large collection of generators that can be separated into two groups: deterministic and stochastic graph generators. With the same variables, deterministic generators create the same graph, whereas stochastic generators create a different graph. The igraph library was developed due to the lack of network analysis software which can handle complex graphs effectively, which can be embedded into a high level programming platform and which can be used both interactively and non-interactively [14] (Fig. 8).

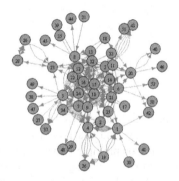

Fig. 8. Representation of a directed graph using igraph. [15]

sigma.js. Sigma is a JavaScript library devoted for drawing graphs. It allows easily publishable networks on Web pages, and helps developers to integrate network exploration in dynamic Web applications. Sigma offers a lot of different settings to make it simple to customize the way networks are drawn and connected. We can also directly add

Fig. 9. Representation of a social network using sigma.js [16]

functions to scripts for rendering nodes and edges the way we exactly want to. Custom rendering is provided in sigma.js with support for Canvas or WebGL (Fig. 9).

3   Evaluation

A wide variety of tools are available for social network analysis. In this paper, we have considered Pajek, SocNetV, Gephi, IGraph, NetworkX, Cytoscape and NodeXL for evaluation and comparison. The tools were selected purely based on the overall functionalities and ease of use provided by these tools. We have performed evaluation based on the following aspects:

a)   Popularity Trend of Search Term corresponding to the tools
b)   Metrics
c)   Layout & Visualization
d)   File Formats
e)   General Information (License, Platform, Type).

3.1   Popularity Trend

The popularity trend of search term corresponding to the tools mentioned above were performed on Google Trends. The search trend over a period spanning 15 years (2004 January to 2019 December) is as shown in Fig. 10. The search trend clearly indicates that NetworkX is the most popular network tool (since 2017) on search volume compared to the other tools, followed by Gephi. Pajek had been the favorite network analysis tool in the first decade of the 21st century. Worldwide search interest for the various tools are provided in Fig. 11. Geographic breakdown of search trend for each tool is provided form Fig. 12, 13, 14, 15 and 16. Table 1 provides information on country wise search percentages calculated out of searches for all five terms in various countries. Search trends for NodeXL and SocnetV were not considered due to their low search volume compared to the other tools.

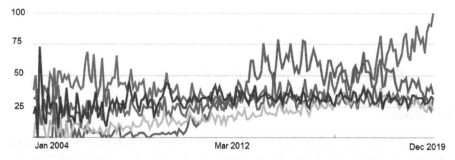

Fig. 10. Search trends for various tools from January 2004 to December 2019, Google Trends

● pajek   ● Gephi   ● Igraph   ● NetworkX   ● Cytoscape

Fig. 11. Worldwide search interest for different social network analysis tools from January 2004 to December 2019. The color intensity represent percentage of search volume. (Google Trends)

Fig. 12. Search interest for Pajek (Breakdown by Region), Google Trends

Fig. 13. Search interest for Gephi (Breakdown by Region), Google Trends

3.2 Metrics

Metrics or indices play a crucial role in identifying the most important nodes within a social graph. Identifying the most important person in a social network, identifying key infrastructure nodes on the internet, spreaders of epidemics are vital in network theory. This paper provides a comparative study on the different types of metrics available on the

Fig. 14. Search interest for IGraph (Breakdown by Region), Google Trends

Fig. 15. Search interest for NetworkX (Breakdown by Region), Google Trends

Fig. 16. Search interest for Cytoscape (Breakdown by Region), Google Trends

various tools in the study. The paper focus on centrality measures [17] like betweenness centrality, closeness centrality, degree centrality, eigen vector centrality, power centrality, eccentricity centrality, stress centrality and other indices like triads, cliques and page rank. It is observed that SocnetV and igraph package provide support to all the metrics under consideration. Betweenness centrality and closeness centrality measures can be calculated with all the tools under the study.

3.3 Visualization and Layout

The biggest challenges of graph exploration are geared towards high-level visualization. There are numerous ways in which a graph can be drawn and represented visually.

Table 1. Search percentages calculated out of searches for all five terms in various countries.

Country	Pajek	Gephi	IGraph	NetworkX	Cytoscape
Australia	0%	30%	18%	34%	18%
Brazil	13%	38%	15%	20%	14%
Canada	7%	26%	14%	26%	27%
China	16%	19%	13%	25%	27%
Germany	8%	26%	16%	31%	19%
India	5%	23%	11%	34%	27%
Norway	0%	26%	14%	26%	34%
Russia	5%	28%	14%	41%	12%
Sweden	0%	30%	17%	27%	26%
United States of America	5%	24%	17%	34%	20%

Table 2. Comparison of the metrics available on various tools

Indices	SocnetV	networkx	igraph	Cytoscape	Gephi	Pajek	NodeXL
Degree centrality	C	C	C	C		C	C
Betweenness centrality	C	C	C	C	C	C	C
Closeness centrality	C	C	C	C	C	C	C
Stress centrality	C		C	C			
Power centrality	C		C				
Eccentricity centrality	C	C	C		C		
Eigen vector centrality	C	C	C	C			C
Triad census	C	C	C			C	
Page rank	C	C	C	C	C		C
Cliques	C	C	C			C	

Each visualization layout has its own merits. In Table 3, a comparison on the different layout options available on the tools are provided. It is observed that not all the layout models considered are currently available in the tools under discussion. Each tool provides certain layout features as mentioned in the table. While most of the tools support Fruchterman Reingold layout and the circular layout, Sugiyama layout model is supported by igraph and nodexl.

Table 3. Comparison of the types of layout available on various tools.

Layout	SocnetV	networkx	igraph	Cytoscape	Gephi	Pajek	NodeXL
Fruchterman Reingold	C	C	C		C	C	C
Kamada Kawai	C	C	C			C	
Sugiyama			C				C
Spring layout	C	C		C			
Circular	C	C	C	C	C	C	C
Polar							C
Grid		C	C	C			C
Force atlas					C		
Random	C	C	C				C

3.4 File Formats

A social network graph can be represented in a variety of file formats. For example, a social graph can be represented in the form of an adjacency matrix, edge list, GML [18], GraphML [19] and various other formats. Table 4 identifies the different file formats that are supported by the major tools. The GraphML, GML and Pajek (.net) format is supported by most of the tools. However, adjacency matrix, edge list formats are supported only by SocnetV, networkx and igraph.

3.5 General Information

As a variety of tools are available for social network, it is always desirable to understand the general information pertaining to each tool such as the license, platform support and type of tool. This information is provided in Table 3. Most of the tools under discussion are updated and stable versions are released on a periodic basis. New features are being incorporated in every new release. Packages like networkx and igraph are available as part of R or Python Language whereas, socnetv, cytoscape and gephi are standalone softwares which can be downloaded and installed on any platform. Pajek is a standalone software designed especially for the Windows platform, while NodeXL is a windows based application integrated with Microsoft Excel.

Table 4. File formats supported by the various social networking tool

File format	SocnetV	networkx	igraph	Cytoscape	Gephi	Pajek	NodeXL
Graph ML	C	C	C	C	C	C	C
GML	C	C	C	C	C	C	
Pajek (.net)	C	C	C		C	C	C
UCINET (DL)	C						C
GEXF		C			C	C	
CSV					C	C	
DOT	C					C	
GXL						C	
LEDA		C					
JSON		C		C			
Adjacency matrix (.am)	C	C	C				
Edge list (.lst)	C	C	C				

4 Conclusion

Social Network Analytics is placed among various domains like sociology, mathematics, computer science, biological networks etc. Various types of visualization and analytical tools are available for different applications. How to choose a software varies from user to user. For example, Cytoscape is very efficient in visualization and integration of molecular interaction networks with genomic profiles and other state data. Pajek can be useful for analyzing complex networks with very large dataset but the user interface of Pajek is quite sophisticated. The igraph package and the networkx package are very useful from a command based GUI point of view. The igraph and networkx packages are updated periodically and built in algorithms are available for most of the graph operations. They are also very powerful for statistical computations.

SocnetV is an excellent tool for network analysis, given its clean and modern UI. It includes advanced features (Structural Equivalence, Hierarchical Clustering, and most Centrality metrics, FDP layouts), and primarily focus to help users understand what Social Network Analysis is. Tools like NodeXL (Microsoft) are very user-friendly and it only requires MS-EXCEL skills to handle medium-sized network datasets. NodeXL has the advantage of a simple UI design integrated with Microsoft Excel and provides facility to obtain the twitter datasets or facebook dataset of a user (Tables 2 and 5).

Thus, the choice of a social networking tool is up to the user, considering the type of application, complexity of the social network, ease of use or other parameters or features as already discussed in this paper.

Table 5. Information on license, type and platform

Tool	License	Type	Platform
SocnetV	GNU GPL3	Stand-alone	Multiple
networkx	BSD	Python package	Multiple
igraph	GNU GPL2	R package	Multiple
Cytoscape	GNU LGPL	Stand-alone	Multiple
Gephi	GNU GPL3	Stand-alone	Multiple
Pajek	Free for non commercial use	Stand-alone	Windows
NodeXL	Commercial user license	MS Excel integrated	Windows

References

1. Wikipedia: Social network analysis. https://en.wikipedia.org/wiki/Social_network_analysis
2. Easley, D., Kleinberg, J.: Cornell university: networks, crowds, and markets. In: Networks, Crowds, and Markets - Reasoning about a Highly Connected World. Cambridge University Press, July 2010
3. Bastian, M., Heymann, S., Jacomy, M.: Gephi: an open source software for exploring and manipulating networks. In: International AAAI Conference on Weblogs and Social Media, pp. 361–362 (2009)
4. Batagelj, V.: Pajek - program for large network analysis. Connections **21**(2), 47–57 (1988)
5. The Cytoscape Consortium: Cytoscape user manual 3.7.2. http://manual.cytoscape.org/en/stable/Navigation_and_Layout.html
6. Hagberg, A.A., Schult, D.A., Swart, P.J.: Exploring network structure, dynamics, and function using NetworkX. In: 7th Python in Science Conference (SciPy 2008) (SciPy), pp. 11–15 (2008)
7. Ellson, J., Gansner, E., Koutsofios, L., North, S., Woodhull, G.: Graphviz – open source graph.pdf, pp. 3–4 (2000)
8. Hansen, D., Shneiderman, B., Smith, M.A.: Analyzing social media networks with NodeXL. In: Insights from a Connected World. Elsevier, August 2010
9. Wikipedia: Social network analysis software. https://en.wikipedia.org/wiki/Social_network_analysis_software
10. Cytoscape Consortium: Cytoscape. https://cytoscape.org/what_is_cytoscape.html
11. Gephi: The open graph viz platform. https://gephi.org/features
12. Huisman, M., van Duijn, M.A.: Software for social network analysis. In: Models and Methods in Social Network Analysis, pp. 270–316 (2005)
13. NetworkX Developers: NetworkX: software for complex networks. https://networkx.github.io/documentation/stable/auto_examples/drawing/plot_random_geometric_graph.html
14. Csardi, G., Nepusz, T.: The igraph software package for complex network research. Inter-J. Complex Syst. **1695**(5), 1–9 (2006)
15. Toshkov, D.: Network visualization in R with the igraph package. http://re-design.dimiter.eu/?p=547
16. Jacomy, A.: SCIENCESPO - MÉDIALAB: Sigma JS. http://sigmajs.org/
17. Marsden, P.V., Elsevier: measures of network centrality. In: International Encyclopedia of the Social & Behavioral Sciences, pp. 532–539. Science Direct (2015)

18. Himsolt, M.: GraphEd: a graphical platform for the implementation of graph algorithms (extended abstract and demo). In: Tamassia, R., Tollis, I.G. (eds.) Graph Drawing. GD 1994. Lecture Notes in Computer Science, vol. 1190, pp. 233–240. Springer, Heidelberg (1996). https://doi.org/10.1007/3-540-58950-3_370
19. Brandes, U., Pich, C.: GraphML transformation. In: Pach, J. (ed.) GD 2004. LNCS, vol. 3383, pp. 89–99. Springer, Heidelberg (2005). https://doi.org/10.1007/978-3-540-31843-9_11

Text Mining Techniques Implemented to Extract Data from Transit Events in Twitter: A Systematic Literature Review

María-Inés Acosta-Urigüen⬤, Belén Arias⬤, and Marcos Orellana$^{(\boxtimes)}$ ⬤

Universidad del Azuay, Cuenca, Azuay 08544, Ecuador
{macosta,barias,marore}@uazuay.edu.ec

Abstract. The use of social networks generates large volumes of data that facilitates the communication and interaction of its users from different approaches and themes. In this context, Twitter is used to post short messages about traffic or transit in cities, becoming a means of direct communication for public and private users. The application of text mining techniques allows extracting relevant information in a specific place and time from this source. Performing a systematic literature review allows to obtain information related to the types of algorithms implemented, the used tools and the results achieved in the application of text mining. The methodology presented by Barbara Kitchenham was applied in order to collect, process, and analyze 456 scientific articles published in digital libraries and bibliographic databases. By using together both research questions and inclusion and exclusion criteria, the research articles were obtained and classified. Also, the assessment of the quality of the systematic literature review was determined based on the number of citations that each article has. The results show the most relevant algorithms, techniques, and tools used in the application of text mining to tweets related to vehicular traffic. This finding allows to expand the line of study both for the monitoring of the network and for the analysis of the messages.

Keywords: Text mining · Traffic · Transit · Systematic literature review

1 Introduction

Since the introduction of social networking sites such as Facebook and Twitter, millions of users have been attracted to use them as part of their daily activities [1]. One of the main features of these sites has been the portability they have, through devices such as smartphones and tablets[2, 3]. People continuously report their activities and feelings in private or public networks, which allows people to create an identity within a community with common interests. The result of a social network is the relationship its users maintain, sharing common interests in locating content and the knowledge issued by other users [4]. The penetration of social media, the appearing of data mining techniques and sentiment analysis has developed rapidly in recent years, however, only a few studies focus on the field of vehicular transportation and transit situations.

© Springer Nature Switzerland AG 2020
G. Rodriguez Morales et al. (Eds.): TICEC 2020, CCIS 1307, pp. 207–225, 2020.
https://doi.org/10.1007/978-3-030-62833-8_17

There are some proposals that link vehicular traffic with sentiment analysis, a concept that is known as the sentiment analysis for traffic (TSA); this tool has been transformed as a new theory [5]. The raw material or the source of information for the detection of events are the comments published on social networks; an event can be defined as an occurrence that happens in the real world in a specific time and space, which can be interpreted as congestion and traffic accident, for example [3]. The sentiment analysis of texts has also been called emotional polarity computation; it is a new area that has become a flourishing frontier of text mining adding the application of algorithms to analyze the emotional polarity contained in a text [6]. Text mining is a new technique that allows finding hidden patterns in unstructured data, such as texts expressed in a natural language (e.g., Spanish, English). The effectiveness of these methods is demonstrated through the acquisition of knowledge from the information expressed by users of the social network Twitter related to vehicular traffic problems in the city [7].

There are several microblogging services available on Internet. Twitter has become a very popular communication tool among Internet users and can be considered as one of the most popular social media resources [8], it allows users to share general information through character strings, called tweets [9]. These tweets are considered the raw data that can be processed using text mining techniques.

Text mining is a set of methods that, using the data emitted by users, obtains information and finds the most repeated topics, and allows categorizing users according to the information provided [10]. In text mining analysis, each opinion is treated as a particular document. Text mining is a technique that offers a solution with automatic systems, replacing or completing the work of people, regardless of the amount of text, finds unknown information, and determines patterns that would otherwise be complex to discover [11]. In addition, text mining techniques involve extracting useful information from unstructured documents and identifying interesting patterns of knowledge [12]. Text mining is an extension of data mining; many techniques used in data mining can be applied to it [13]. There are three main components of a data mining solution that can also be identified in the text mining field: the raw data, the feature representation extracted from the data, and the model or algorithm used to solve the problem [14]. In this context, it is necessary to identify, evaluate and interpret relevant articles and researches about this topic through a Systematic Literature Review (SLR) that allows to consolidate all the published scientific information.

2 Related Work

Twitter has been considered as one the most important social media platforms due to its capacity to attract a large number of works for topic discovery, event detection and content analysis [15].

From the reviewed articles, one systematic literature review (SLR) has been identified in the application of text mining in social media [16]; this article reports the different areas of application, among them: management and business, education, finance, government, health and medicine. However, it does not address the specific issue of traffic or vehicular transit. In parallel, other publications were identified that covered the topic of text mining, algorithms and tools used, highlighting the Naive Bayes algorithms [17–22], Support

Vector Machine (SVM) [18, 23], Random Forest (RF) [21, 23] and various types of tools without identifying one relevant.

Summarizing, there are a significant number of studies focused on text mining techniques and traffic separately; however, most of the studies that discuss the vehicular traffic or transit do not apply text mining techniques in order to identify hidden information and hidden patterns from tweets [24]. This fact creates a new field to study, a SLR can be considered as the first step to know the state of art, the most used techniques and tools, and some successful case studies.

3 Methodology

For the development of this systematic literature review, the methodology proposed by Barbara Kitchenham et al. [25] was used. It is composed of three phases: planning, development and reporting of the review. For the planning phase, five stages were developed related to the definition of the research questions, the design of the search process, the selection process, the evaluation of quality, and the analysis of data. The development and report of the review is covered in Sect. 4.

3.1 Research Questions

The main research question was to identify the techniques, tools and algorithms of text mining that have been used and applied to vehicular traffic in the social network Twitter and the proposed processes and methods to collect and clean the tweets. This question has been broken down into five sub-questions that allows to answer the question in a descriptive and analytic way:

- RQ1: What text mining algorithm was used?
- RQ2: Was the text mining technique a model of prediction, segmentation, association, or correlation?
- RQ3: What text mining tool was used?
- RQ4: What was the amount of processed data?
- RQ5: What algorithms, processes or methods were used to collect and clean the text of the tweets?

3.2 Search Process

Search Terms. In order to define the search string and obtain satisfactory results in the selected digital libraries, several items were considered, like the derivation of terms of the research questions, the identification of synonyms for main terms, the use of Boolean connectors *AND* and *OR* to link terms were taken into account [25]. The search string was applied in the selected different libraries and bibliographic databases, a filter for the title and/or the abstract was set; the definitive search string is: *((Data Mining OR Text Mining) AND (Social Media) AND (Twitter) AND (Traffic OR Transit)).*

The digital libraries that were used to look for primary studies are: Association for Computing Machinery (ACM), IEEE Xplore Digital Library, Springer Link, Science Direct; Scopus was the selected bibliographic database.

The search string was tested in the libraries described above in order to identify the characteristics of the personalized search strings of each library. The period reviewed included studies published from 2010 to 2019. The start date selected was based on the Pew Internet & American Life Project Report, "5 facts about Twitter at age 10", whose content showed the growth in the number of users of Twitter registering less than 50 million users in 2010 and more than 300 million accounts at the end of 2015 [26]. The use of the Application Programming Interface (API) for Twitter is important due the fact that it provides real-time tweet collection, keyword based search query, and returns the most recent tweets in one response and excludes tweets from users who opt for privacy [27]. Although, in 2008 Twitter added some API updates to include the update of the location field in a Twitter user's profile using Twitter, it was not until 2010 when Twitter included the Local Trends, which are mainly used these days [28].

3.3 Selection Process

In order to select articles, inclusion and exclusion criteria are generated to evaluate the relevance and applicability of each article according to the research questions on this SLR. The criteria are detailed below:

a) Inclusion Criteria: In this step, the review of titles and abstracts was performed, to include articles which abstract or title met at least one of the following inclusion criteria:

- Application of text mining techniques in vehicular traffic or transit in social networks.
- Application of text mining techniques on Twitter
- Articles that have been published between 2010–2019

b) Exclusion Criteria; In this step, articles which abstract or title met one of the following exclusion criteria were not considered:

- Duplicated articles.
- Articles that are extended abstract or short articles
- Books and book chapters.
- Articles that talk about text mining but there are outside the social media literature.
- Articles that address the problem of vehicular traffic without the need for text mining techniques.
- Articles that are not from journal or conferences.
- Articles without Digital Object Identifier (DOI).
- Articles that only present the abstract.
- Introductory articles for books or workshops.
- Articles that were not published in English or Spanish.
- Articles that have not been published between the years 2010 to 2019.

The process of selecting the documents was carried out by searching and obtaining the scientific articles in the selected digital libraries (step 1), these articles were reviewed in order to eliminate articles found in more than one database, and to apply the exclusion criteria in relation to the number of pages, year of publication and extension of the article (step 2).

A next step (3) consisted on reading the title and the abstract of each article, considering the inclusion and exclusion criteria to select or reject them. Each article was evaluated by two members of the research team to decide if both approved, both rejected or if there was discrepancy; in case of disagreement, a third member of the team joined the review, and as a result of the reading, a response was issued in acceptance or rejection of that article.

In step 4, each selected article in step 3 was examined in order to respond to the criteria regarding inclusion and exclusion. At this point, documents that do not reflect topics related to the research questions were excluded; once again, the criteria of validation by pairs was applied. The result of this step was the identification of the potential articles that were going to be read in order to respond the research questions.

The last stage (step 5) consisted in the generation of the data extraction matrix where the research questions were identified, recorded and registered in relation to their contents, value and impact, answering the determined research questions.

Figure 1 presents the implemented methodology which was taken and adapted from the articles "Systematic literature reviews in software engineering – A systematic literature review", "Lessons from applying the systematic literature review process within the software engineering domain", and "Investigating the effectiveness of technologies applied to assist seniors: A systematic literature review" [29–31].

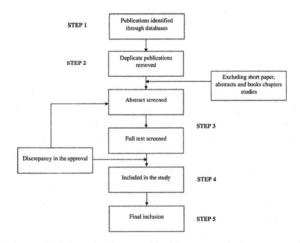

Fig. 1. Methodology implemented in this systematic literature review

3.4 Quality Assessment

In addition to general inclusion/exclusion criteria, it is necessary to evaluate the quality of the primary studies [31]. For this SLR, a data extraction matrix was created. It consisted of a double entry table that allowed quantifying the answer to each question numerically and the selected article. A 3 point Likert scale was used to indicate 1 when the article directly answers the research question, 0 when the article mentions that techniques, tools and/or text mining algorithms have been used but does not clearly identify them; and −1 when the article does not answer the research question [32]. For each research question, the name of the technique, tool and text mining algorithms, the number of tweets processed and the process of extracting and cleaning the information were registered using these criteria.

The number of citations in Scholar Google and Scopus was also included, and registered with 1 when the article has more than 5 citations; 0 when the article has between 1 to 4 citations; and −1 when the article does not have any citations. The thresholds were defined applying the quartiles for the mean of citations. The first group included articles without any citations, the second group included articles with 50% of the citations, and the last group included articles with 50% or more citations, being the values 0, 1–4 citations, and 5 or more citations. This last group represents the most relevant articles, evaluated with 1.

For each paper, the mean of the different scores was calculated. This value was used to identify the most representative studies. There are only four articles that registered a considerable score for the mean; these are: "From Twitter to detector: Real-time traffic incident detection using social media data", "Real-Time Detection of Traffic from Twitter Stream Analysis", "Scaling Big Data Mining Infrastructure: The Twitter Experience", and "A deep learning approach for detecting traffic accidents from social media data". The highest mean score of citations gotten in Scopus and Google Scholar were 164, 122, 88, and 86, respectively. The mean for the rest of articles showed values between 0 and 25 citations.

3.5 Data Analysis

In total, 456 articles were obtained. After applying the inclusion and exclusion criteria, the articles included to complete the data extraction matrix were 36 (7, 89%). It was found that 168 articles, 36,84% were obtained in two or more libraries; 9,65%, 44 articles were not selected after applying the inclusion/exclusion criteria; the abstract of 208 articles, 45,61%, were read; but only 36 abstracts included the criteria to answer the research questions. The number of Scopus and Google Scholar citations was also taken in account as a referent of the impact of the article due the fact that these information resources are recognized and accepted by the scientific community [33]. It is important to mentions that the citations were obtained on July 22, 2020.

The global number of articles for each database is listed in Table 1. Selected Articles.

Table 2 shows the 36 articles that were considered in the data extraction matrix, the library where each article was obtained, the year of publication, and the number of Scopus and Google Scholar citations.

The article "From Twitter to detector: Real-time traffic incident detection using social media data" has gotten 130 Scopus citations and 198 Google Scholar citations; it become the most relevant article for this SRL; the answers for all research questions were found in this paper. The article "A deep learning approach for detecting traffic accidents from social media data" has gotten 65 Scopus citations and 107 Google Scholar citations;

Table 1. Selected Articles.

Library	Frequency	Percent
Association for Computing Machinery (ACM)	84	18,42%
IEEE Xplore Digital Library	36	7,89%
Springer Link	88	19,30%
Science Direct	84	18,42%
Scopus	164	35,96%
TOTAL	456	100,00%

Table 2. Information of the selected articles.

#	ID	Tittle	Year	Library	Cites Scopus	Cites Google Scholar[a]
1	A16	From Twitter to detector: Real-time traffic incident detection using social media data	2016	ScienceDirect	130	198
2	A202	A deep learning approach for detecting traffic accidents from social media data	2018	ScienceDirect	65	107
3	A212	Transportation sentiment analysis using word embedding and ontology-based topic modeling	2019	ScienceDirect	19	20
4	A100	CITYPULSE: A Platform Prototype for Smart City Social Data Mining	2016	Springer	16	25
5	A330	Classification of posts Twitter traffic jam the city of Jakarta using algorithm C4.5	2018	Scopus	14	16

(*continued*)

Table 2. (*continued*)

#	ID	Tittle	Year	Library	Cites Scopus	Cites Google Scholar[a]
6	A400	Real-Time traffic classification with Twitter data mining	2017	Scopus	13	18
7	A90	Real-time crash prediction on freeways using data mining and emerging techniques	2017	Springer	11	15
8	A243	Real-time crash prediction on freeways using data mining and emerging techniques	2017	Springer	11	15
9	A413	Sensing and detecting traffic events using geosocial media data: A review	2018	Scopus	10	16
10	A163	Real Time Road Traffic Event Detection Using Twitter and Spark	2017	IEEE	9	12
11	A24	Mining and correlating traffic events from human sensor observations with official transport data using self-organizing maps	2016	ScienceDirect	9	10
12	A113	Real-Time Traffic Event Detection From Social Media	2017	Scopus	7	12
13	A123	Real-Time Traffic Event Detection From Social Media	2017	ACM	7	12

(*continued*)

Table 2. (*continued*)

#	ID	Tittle	Year	Library	Cites Scopus	Cites Google Scholar[a]
14	A7	Mining Complaints for Traffic-Jam Estimation: A Social Sensor Application	2015	IEEE	5	18
15	A110	Predicting Vehicle Recalls with User-Generated Contents: A Text Mining Approach	2015	Springer	4	5
16	A6	Jakarta Congestion Mapping And Classification From Twitter Data Extraction Using Tokenization And Naïve Bayes Classifier	2015	IEEE	3	7
17	A120	Exploration of Road Traffic Tweets for Congestion Monitoring	2016	Scopus	3	3
18	A91	Supporting geospatial privacy-preserving data mining of social media	2016	Springer	2	2
19	A409	Road traffic event detection using twitter data, machine learning, and apache spark	2019	Scopus	2	2
20	A166	Traffic Risk Mining From Heterogeneous Road Statistics	2018	IEEE	1	6
21	A320	An investigation on optimizing traffic flow based on Twitter Data Analysis	2018	Scopus	1	2

(*continued*)

Table 2. (*continued*)

#	ID	Tittle	Year	Library	Cites Scopus	Cites Google Scholar[a]
22	A181	Geospatial modeling of road traffic using a semi-supervised regression algorithm	2019	IEEE	1	1
23	A191	SNSJam: Road traffic analysis and prediction by fusing data from multiple social networks	2019	ScienceDirect	1	1
24	A192	Detection Traffic Congestion Based on Twitter Data using Machine Learning	2019	ScienceDirect	1	1
25	A326	ATAM: Arabic traffic analysis model for Twitter	2019	Scopus	1	1
26	A331	Classification of traffic related short texts to analyse road problems in urban areas	2017	Scopus	1	1
27	A1	Real-Time Detection of Traffic From Twitter Stream Analysis	2015	IEEE	0	244
28	A49	Scaling Big Data Mining Infrastructure: The Twitter Experience	2013	ACM	0	176
29	A284	A Text Mining Approach to Discover Real-Time Transit Events from Twitter	2019	Springer	0	1
30	A114	xTRoad: The Tweet Extraction Method For Profiling Road and Traffic Conditions	2017	Scopus	0	0

(*continued*)

Table 2. (*continued*)

#	ID	Tittle	Year	Library	Cites Scopus	Cites Google Scholar[a]
31	A119	Metropolitan Traffic Research and Analysis	2016	Scopus	0	0
32	A160	Identifying traffic event types from Twitter by Multi-label Classification	2019	IEEE	0	0
33	A317	An intelligent road traffic information system using text analysis in the most congested roads in Metro Manila	2019	Scopus	0	0
34	A324	Applying unsupervised and supervised machine learning methodologies in social media textual traffic data	2019	Scopus	0	0
35	A333	Congestion correlation and classification from twitter and waze map using artificial neural network	2018	Scopus	0	0
36	A390	Real Time Traffic Incident Detection by Using Twitter Stream Analysis	2019	Scopus	0	0

a. Number of citations obtained in July 2020

it answers three of the four research questions; it does not explain if it is a model for segmentation, prediction, association, or correlation[17, 34].

Analyzing the publication year, there is only one document published in 2013. From 2017 to 2019, 25 documents were published. It represents the 69,44%. Taking into account the source, Scopus contributes with 15 documents that represents the 42%; IEEE represents 19%; Science Direct, and SpringerLink represents 17% each, and finally ACM only represents a 2% of the selected articles.

4   Results

RQ1: What text mining algorithm was used?
The 36 selected articles describe various algorithms analyzed and implemented; the most used are Support Vector Machine (SVM) and Naïve Bayes being present in fourteen and eleven articles, respectively. SVM is based on a hyper-plane that distinguish clearly between two classes that are assigned to each object, the algorithm takes as input several parameters which modify the results performance[3, 35]. Naïve Bayes is based on a set of objects, each object belongs to a known class and has a known vector of variables, with this information, the algorithm classifies a new object to an existent class [36]. It is important to emphasize that the algorithms of Naïve Bayes and Support Vector Machine are supervised algorithms, they need to have had previous training in order to generate the model and classify a new element to the model [37]. The success of these algorithms is based on this training, while more data processed, they generate a more robust model [23, 38, 39]. The most used algorithms are presented in Table 3.

Table 3. Most used algorithms

Algorithm	Frequency	Article
Support Vector Machine (SVM)	14	A1, A90, A123, A191, A192, A202, A212, A284, A243, A324, A326, A390, A400, A409, A413
Naïve Bayes (NB)	10	A16, A1, A6, A7, A110, A212, A317, A326, A400, A409, A413
c4.5	3	A1, A110, A330
SLDA	3	A16, A113, A202
K-MEANS	3	A49, A100, A324
k-NN	3	A1, A331, A413
Random forest (RF)	2	A90, A317
PART	1	A1
Non-negative mamtrix factorizacion	1	A166
GEOCODER	1	A16
Vector Space Model	1	A160
Spatial clustering algorithm densitybased clustering algorithm (DBSCAN)	1	A91
Algorithm developed by its owner	1	A114

RQ2: Was the text mining technique a model of prediction, segmentation, association, or correlation?

There are 33 papers that answered the RQ2. The most useful techniques are related to models of prediction and segmentation. Although these techniques have not been directly described in the articles, the model was deduced based on the algorithm that was implemented. For example, the article "Real-Time Detection of Traffic from Twitter Stream Analysis" explains that data mining and machine learning algorithms (i.e., support vector machines (SVMs), decision trees, neural networks, etc.) are applied to the documents in the vector space representation, to build classification, clustering or regression models, but it does not explain specifically how to apply or perform the model [18].

RQ3: What text mining tool was used?

There are 16 papers that answered the RQ3. The implemented tools vary from tools developed by research groups, hybrid tools and known tools such as WEKA and MATLAB. WEKA is an open source software for data pre-processing and text mining elaboration where each user models the requirements according to his necessities, being difficult to assess the tool [18]. In the case of MATLAB, it has a specific library incorporated on the software; it is not flexible to adapt different models [23]. RapidMiner Studio is a software to apply predictive analytics, data mining, and text mining; it includes four machine learning algorithms (Naïve Bayes, Decision Tree, Random Forest, k-Nearest Neighbor) that can be implemented [37, 40].

The selected articles mention research procedures and results; they describe methods but not specific tools. This fact shows the lack of discussion in the community about the use of tools, the facilities for development, the interfaces, and the models they implement.

RQ4: What was the amount of processed data?

There are 18 papers that answered the RQ4. The amount of data processed is an important factor when evaluating the impact of a study; the results depend directly on the number of processed tweets and the successful classification percentages. In this context, the algorithms of Naïve Bayes and SVM are the ones that provide the best answers.

It is important to emphasize that not all articles report the amount of processed tweets. Of the few articles that do, the registered quantity varies singly, being impossible to establish a pattern of analysis.

The article "Jakarta congestion mapping and classification from twitter data extraction using tokenization and Naïve Bayes classifier" analyzes 224 tweets [19] compared to the article " Predicting Vehicle Recalls with User-Generated Contents: A Text Mining Approach " that analyzes 1,893,891 tweets [21]; it is important to consider the number of tweets since it influences the results; the more tweets the model processes, the more it acquires a better knowledge base and classifies the data in a better way.

It is also important to analyze specific functions to delimitate the period of time where the data was extracted. For example, [41] implemented the userTimeline function to pull the most recent 3,200 tweets from the social network. Table 4 describes the quantity of tweets processed for the most representative studies.

Table 4. Amount of Processed Tweets (most relevant studies)

ID	Tittle	Data (tweets)
A16	From Twitter to detector: Real-time traffic incident detection using social media data	10,542 (Pittsburgh) 11,658 (Philadelphia)
A24	Mining and correlating traffic events from human sensor observations with official transport data using self-organizing maps	63,407
A91	Supporting geospatial privacy-preserving data mining of social media	1,301,603
A110	Predicting Vehicle Recalls with User-Generated Contents: A Text Mining Approach	1,893,891 (toyotanation.com) 106,900 (cars)
A120	Exploration of Road Traffic Tweets for Congestion Monitoring	65,413
A191	SNSJam: Road traffic analysis and prediction by fusing data from multiple social networks	2,365,288
A192	Detection Traffic Congestion Based on Twitter Data using Machine Learning	15,181
A326	ATAM: Arabic traffic analysis model for Twitter	292,965
A400	Real-Time traffic classification with Twitter data mining	110,449

RQ5: What algorithms, processes or methods were used to collect and clean the text of the tweets?

There are 30 papers that mentioned the data collection process, and 27 papers presented the cleaning process implemented. Although some articles describe the processes implemented for data collection and cleaning; these are not clearly detailed. The data processing activities of tweets consist in applying cleansing, data transformation, data extraction, and the extraction of traffic information [42]. Table 5 presents the recorded data pre-processing techniques, among which are the elimination of irrelevant words, conversion to lowercase, elimination of special characters, reduction of words to their roots [43].

In relation to the techniques for data collection, the Twitter API has been used in 24 articles, compared with the others that present between 1 or 2 articles. The Twitter Api allow users to query tweets by keywords, user IDs, and time/date and it also allows to submit queries to retrieve recent or popular tweets [17] and also collects geotagged Twitter posts within a city thanks to the "locations" request parameter of the API [44].

Table 6 details the used techniques to collect Tweets.

Table 5. Pre-processing techniques

Algorithm	Frequency	Article
Tokenization	15	A1, A6, A110, A123, A163, A191, A192, A202, A212, A284, A317, A324, A326, A333, A390
Stop Word	10	A1, A110, A191, A212, A324, A331, A390, A400, A409, A413
Stemming	8	A1, A191, A212, A320, A324, A326, A390, A413
Lower case	6	A6, A163, A284, A320, A330, A400

Table 6. Used techniques to collect Tweets

Algorithm	Frequency	Article
Twitter API	24	A91, A16, A1, A6, A7, A113, A114, A119, A120, A123, A160, A202, A212, A284, A243, A317, A326, A330, A331, A333, A390, A400, A409, A413
Google Maps API	2	A191, A192
Own application	1	A100
Crawler	1	A110
Twint 2	1	A160
Enggement Library	1	A6
R	1	A326

5   Discussion

This section presents the discussion of the results and the analysis of the threats to validity for this SLR.

A) Conclusions on the state of the art. The research started with the inclusion of articles published in the libraries Association for Computing Machinery (ACM), IEEE Xplore Digital Library, Springer Link, and Science Direct. The quantity of articles was less than expected. This problem was corrected including the articles published by Scopus.

B) Conclusions for the implemented techniques, tools and algorithms of text mining. Different algorithms and techniques of text mining have been identified, as well as their application in areas that go beyond traffic or vehicular traffic. It is evident that the studies are diverse in terms of population sizes and data collection times; it is evident that the text mining techniques are acquiring a greater presence in the community, before the year 2013 a publication was registered, while to date there are 13 publications for the subject.

C) Threats to validity. During the process of this SLR, a number of threats to validity were found and different actions were carried out to minimize them.

1) Selections of the articles: The process of reading and selecting the articles was validated by two researches; it the case of discrepancy a third researcher resolved the inclusion or exclusion of the article. This activity allowed the team to discuss and classify the articles in conflict.

2) Search string: The search string was tested several times. This procedure allowed the team to identify false positives for the word "traffic" or "transit". The articles included these words but their meaning was not associated to vehicular issues. The search string was modified in order to control it.

   It was necessary to adapt the search string for each database; the same query could not be applied in all of them due the fact that the advanced search option did not have the same structure.

3) Time for the study: Several publications related to text mining techniques were published before the period selected for this study. It was taken as a started date the use of Twitter Api as a tool to collect data directly for Twitter.

6   Conclusions and Future Work

In this paper, the results of the systematic literature review about text mining techniques implemented to extract data from transit events in Twitter, 456 articles, were obtained but only 36 answered the research questions according to the algorithm, technique or tool implemented. It was found that there are not as many publications that discuss the use and application of text mining techniques for vehicular traffic or transit; however, it was identified the Support Vector Machine and Naïve Bayes as the most used algorithms and the Twitter API as the most popular data extraction tool.

In the case of data pre-processing techniques, a predominant technique could not be identified; a future study should be necessary in order to identify them due the fact that most articles did not include the description and process of the implemented techniques.

The future work is to extend this study including text mining techniques and sentimental analysis applied in different contexts such us politics, health, culture, on one side; and to compare the performance of different algorithms, techniques and tools through statistic results. It is evident that the majority of applications were implemented in English; for this situation, it is necessary to extend this SLR in order to obtain more information related to the challenge of applying natural language processing (NLP) techniques to identify meaningful information in tweets [45] in other languages such as Spanish.

A future research topic will include the analysis and application of real time detection of tweets obtained in the city of Cuenca in order to find traffic patterns related to people behavior with the aim of promoting the creation of new public policies.

Acknowledgment. This research was supported by the vice-rectorate of investigations of the Universidad del Azuay. We thank our colleagues from Laboratorio de Investigación y Desarrollo en Informática (LIDI) de la Universidad del Azuay who provided insight and expertise that greatly assisted this research

References

1. Conole, G., Galley, R., Culver, J.: Frameworks for understanding the nature of interactions, networking, and community in a social networking site for academic practice. Int. Rev. Res. Open Distance Learn. **12**(3), 119–138 (2011)
2. Atefeh, F., Khreich, W.: A survey of techniques for event detection in Twitter. Comput. Intell. **31**(1), 133–164 (2015)
3. D'Andrea, E., Ducange, P., Lazzerini, B., Marcelloni, F.: Real-time detection of traffic from twitter stream analysis. IJISET –Int. J. Innov. Sci. Eng. Technol. **2**(9), 2269–2283 (2015)
4. Tapiador, A., Carrera, D., Salvachúa, J.: Social stream, a social network framework. In: 1st International Conference Future Genereration Communication Technology FGCT 2012, pp. 52–57 (2012)
5. Cao, J., et al.: Web-based traffic sentiment analysis: methods and applications. IEEE Trans. Intell. Transp. Syst. **15**(2), 844–853 (2014)
6. Li, N., Wu, D.D.: Using text mining and sentiment analysis for online forums hotspot detection and forecast. Decis. Support Syst. **48**(2), 354–368 (2010)
7. Wang, S., et al.: Computing urban traffic congestions by incorporating sparse GPS probe data and social media data. ACM Trans. Inf. Syst. **35**, 4 (2017)
8. Pak, A., Paroubek, A.: Twitter as a corpus for sentiment analysis and opinion mining. In: Proceedings of the 7th International Conference Language Resources Evaluation Lr. 2010, December, pp. 1320–1326 (2010)
9. Wang, R.O., Sinnott, S.: Supporting geospatial privacy-preserving data mining of social media. Soc. Netw. Anal. Min. **6**(1), 1–15 (2016)
10. Che, D., Safran, M., Peng, Z.: From big data to big data mining : challenges, issues, and opportunities. In: 18th International Conference DASFAA, pp. 1–15 (2013)
11. Paquet, E., Viktor, H., Guo, H.: Big Data Analysis: New Algorithms for a New Society, vol. 16, pp. 159–175 (2016)
12. Deng, Q., Liu, Y., Deng, X., Zhang, H.: Semantic analysis on microblog data for emergency response in typhoon Chan-hom. In: Proceedings 1st ACM SIGSPATIAL International Workship Use GIS Emergency Management - EM-GIS 2015, pp. 1–5 (2015)
13. Tan, A.: Text mining : the state of the art and the challenges concept-based. In: Proceedings of the PAKDD 1999 Work, November 2000, pp. 65–70 (2011)
14. Lin, J., Ryaboy, D.: Scaling big data mining infrastructure: the twitter experience. ACM SIGKDD Explor. Newsl. **14**(2), 6–19 (2013)
15. Xu, Z., et al.: Social sensors based online attention computing of public safety events. IEEE Trans. Emerg. Top. Comput. **5**(3), 403–411 (2017)
16. Viviani, M., Pasi, G.: Credibility in social media: opinions, news, and health information—a survey, Wiley Interdiscip. Rev. Data Min. Knowl. Discov. vol. 7, no. 5 (2017)
17. Gu, Y., Qian, Z., Chen, F.: From Twitter to detector: real-time traffic incident detection using social media data. Transp. Res. Part C Emerg. Technol. **67**, 321–342 (2016)
18. Kumari, S., Khan, F., Sultan, S., Khandge, R.: Real-time detection of traffic from twitter stream analysis. IEEE Trans. Intell. Transp. Syst. **16**(4), 2269–2283 (2015)
19. Septianto, G.R., Mukti, F.F., Nasrun, M., Gozali, A.A.: Jakarta congestion mapping and classification from twitter data extraction using tokenization and naive bayes classifier. In: Proceedings - APMediaCast 2015 Asia Pacific Conference Multimedia Broadcast, pp. 23–25 (2015)
20. Georgiou, T., El Abbadi, A., Yan, X., George, J.: Mining Complaints for Traffic-Jam Estimation : A Social Sensor Application

21. Zhang, X., Niu, S., Zhang, D., Wang, G.A., Fan, W.: Predicting vehicle recalls with user-generated contents: a text mining approach. In: Chau, M., Wang, G.A., Chen, H. (eds.) PAISI 2015. LNCS, vol. 9074, pp. 41–50. Springer, Cham (2015). https://doi.org/10.1007/978-3-319-18455-5_3

22. Abhishek, K., Kashyap, R., Upadhyay, D., Singh, M.P.: Metropolitan traffic research and analysis. Asian J. Inf. Technol. **15**(24), 5106–5119 (2016)

23. You, J., Wang, J., Guo, J.: Real-time crash prediction on freeways using data mining and emerging techniques. J. Modern Transp. **25**(2), 116–123 (2017). https://doi.org/10.1007/s40 534-017-0129-7

24. PhridviRaj, M.S.B., Rao, C.V.G.: Mining top-k rank frequent patterns in data streams a tree based approach with ternary function and ternary feature vector. In: Proceedings Second International Conference Innovation Computer Cloud Computing - ICCC 2013, pp. 271–276 (2013)

25. Kitchenham, B., et al.: Systematic literature reviews in software engineering-a tertiary study. Inf. Softw. Technol. **52**(8), 792–805 (2010)

26. Desilver, D.: 5 facts about Twitter at age 10. (2016)

27. Purohit, H., Hampton, A., Shalin, V.L., Sheth, A.P., Flach, J., Bhatt, S.: What kind of #conversation is Twitter? Mining #psycholinguistic cues for emergency coordination. Comput. Human Behav. **29**(6), 2438–2447 (2013)

28. Jagroep, N., Brouwer, R.: Social Networking and Micro-Blogging Application Development : The Twitter API, pp. 1–8

29. Khosravi, P., Ghapanchi, A.H.: Investigating the effectiveness of technologies applied to assist seniors: a systematic literature review. Int. J. Med. Inform. **85**(1), 17–26 (2015)

30. Brereton, P., Kitchenham, B.A., Budgen, D., Turner, M., Khalil, M.: Lessons from applying the systematic literature review process within the software engineering domain. J. Syst. Softw. **80**(4), 571–583 (2007)

31. Kitchenham, B., Pearl Brereton, O., Budgen, D., Turner, M., Bailey, J., Linkman, S.: Systematic literature reviews in software engineering - a systematic literature review. Inf. Softw. Technol., **51**(1), 7–15 (2009)

32. Xu, J., Mei, T., Cai, R., Li, H., Rui, Y.: Automatic generation of social event storyboard from image click-through data. IEEE Trans. Circuits Syst. Video Technol. **28**(1), 242–253 (2018)

33. Torres-Salinas, D., álvaro Cabezas-Clavijo, Jiménez-Contreras, E.: Altmetrics: new indicators for scientific communication in web 2.0, Comunicar, **21**(41), 53–60 (2013)

34. Zhang, Z., He, Q., Gao, J., Ni, M.: A deep learning approach for detecting traffic accidents from social media data. Transp. Res. Part C Emerg. Technol., **86**, May 2017, pp. 580–596 (2018)

35. Chapelle, O., Vapnik, V., Bousquet, O., Mukherjee, S.: Choosing multiple parameters for support vector machines. Mach. Learn. **46**(1–3), 131–159 (2002)

36. Wu, X., et al.: Top 10 Algorithms in Data Mining, **14**, 1 (2008)

37. Kantardzic, M.: Data Mining: Concepts, Models, Methods, and Algorithms, vol. 36, no. 5 (2004)

38. Panda, M., Patra, M.R.: A comparative study of data mining algorithms for network intrusion detection. In: 2008 First International Conference Emergency Trends Engineering Technology, pp. 504–507 (2008)

39. Wang, D., Al-Rubaie, A., Clarke, S.S., Davies, J.: Real-time traffic event detection from social media. ACM Trans. Internet Technol. **18**(23), 1–23 (2017)

40. Bondoc, E.R.P., Caparas, F.P.M., MacIas, J.E.D., Naculangga, V.T., Estrada, J.E.: An intelligent road traffic information system using text analysis in the most congested roads in Metro Manila. In: 2018 IEEE 10th International Conference Humanoid, Nanotechnology, Information Technology Communication Control, Environment Management HNICEM 2018, pp. 1–6 (2019)

41. AlFarasani, A., AlHarthi, T., AlHumoud, S.: ATAM: arabic traffic analysis model for Twitter. Int. J. Adv. Comput. Sci. Appl. **10**(3), 328–336 (2019)
42. Wibowo, E.A., Winarko, A.: xTRoad: the tweet extraction method for profiling traffic and road conditions. ARPN J. Eng. Appl. Sci. **7**(12), 1–7 (2017)
43. Yang, L.H., Selvaretnam, L.C., Hoong, B., Tan, P.K., Howg, I.K.T.: Exploration of road traffic tweets for congestion monitoring. J. Telecommun. Electron. Comput. Eng. **8**(2), 141–145 (2016)
44. Giatsoglou, V., Chatzakou, M., Gkatziaki, D., Vakali, L." Athena; Anthopoulos, "CityPulse: a platform prototype for smart city social data mining, J. Knowl. Econ., **7**(2), 344–372 (2016)
45. Steiger, A., de Albuquerque, E., Porto, J.: Zipf Mining and correlating traffic events from human sensor observations with official transport data using self-organizing-maps. Transport. Res. Part C Emerg. Technol. **73**, 93–104 (2016)

NARX Neural Network for Imputation
of Missing Data in Air Pollution Datasets

Miguel Calle⊚, Marcos Orellana$^{(\boxtimes)}$ ⊚, and Patricia Ortega-Chasi⊚

Universidad del Azuay, Cuenca, Azuay 08544, Ecuador
miguicho@es.uazuay.edu.ec, {marore,portega}@uazuay.edu.ec

Abstract. Air pollutant sensors capture large amounts of data; some of this information is lost due to various causes, including sensor errors and human error. This work proposes a method for the imputation of missing data through a NARX neural network implemented in Matlab. Data pre-processing included standardization of input variables and removal of outliers. Subsequently, the value of the angle between the input variables' levels was calculated considering 10-min intervals. The neural network uses pollutants O3, CO, NO2, SO2, PM2_5, and temperature as input variables according to the previous analysis of interactions between contaminants. Data indicated that the method obtained the best results for the O3 and NO2 with values of R = 0.85 and R = 0.73, respectively.

Keywords: Palabras clave: Neural networks · Data mining · Data imputation · NARX neural network

1 Introduction

Air pollution has considerably affected humans' health. The leading cause is the exponential growth of urban land and industrialization in recent years [1]. This contamination causes health and environmental problems. A critical problem nowadays is phenomena such as the appearance of acid rains, the deterioration of the ozone layer, and global warming [13]. Exposures to pollutants, including particulate matter, carbon monoxide, sulfur dioxide, and other air gases, are problematic. They cause several public health issues, especially for children, due to their small respiratory organs are not completely developed yet, and to have low defenses in its mechanisms [6, 7].

The discipline of data mining allows the extraction of knowledge from a large amount of data, including data related to pollutants, allowing the study of their behavior [12]. Neural networks have been used in many projects to make predictions of pollutant behavior in different parts of the world [4, 15, 21]. This technique has been used, due to its certainty compared to other techniques that have the same functionality [21].

Neural networks have been applied in different fields within the discipline of data mining. For example, in predictions of meteorological behavior for decision-making in agricultural activities [9]. In urban environments such as Perugia, for predicting pollutants by monitored variables including sulfur dioxide, nitrogen oxides, PM10, benzene,

© Springer Nature Switzerland AG 2020
G. Rodriguez Morales et al. (Eds.): TICEC 2020, CCIS 1307, pp. 226–240, 2020.
https://doi.org/10.1007/978-3-030-62833-8_18

among others [21]. However, sometimes in the field of forecasts, it is complex to predict meteorological behavior due to a considerable variation of parameters and different behaviors that must be analyzed [11]. Once the neural network has been trained, it incorporates a faster analysis allowing more accurate time series to be predicted [14].

A large amount of data provides opportunities for information processing and observing its behavior. However, existing methods are often unsuitable for analyzing large volumes of data, resulting in searching for new forms of analysis [5]. The data mining discipline integrates various technologies, such as databases, statistics, machine learning, and high-performance computing. This combination of technologies provides mechanisms for modeling projects appropriately [16]. Neural networks are increasingly used in research topics related to air pollution [5]. In analyzing atmospheric pollutants, related studies have been developed using different data mining techniques, including neural networks, decision trees, and fuzzy logic [11]. However, the use of angular values as input data for predicting atmospheric pollutants could not be evidenced in previous studies. In this study, the angular values are formed between the initial and final values of each contaminant.

Several studies related to air quality in the city of Cuenca have been carried out at the Universidad del Azuay in collaboration between the LIDI (Laboratorio de Investigación y Desarrollo en Informática) research group and the IERSE department (Instituto de Estudios de Regimen Seccional del Ecuador). These projects have common issues related to the considerable amount of data loss due to diverse circumstances, including sensor failures. For this reason, it is necessary to address the imputation of lost data. The study's purpose was the experimentation through neural networks, combined with angular value inputs to obtain adequate predictions for the data imputation in the positions of the missing values.

2 Related Studies

Several studies have addressed air pollution using neural network techniques to make predictions in different parts of the world. Kurt [15] applied neural networks to prepare forecasts for the next three days of air pollution in the Istanbul metropolitan area. In the agricultural field, Neural networks also have been applied for different purposes. For example, in the study carried out by Fuentes [9] used neural networks to predict the next day's temperature in central Chile to detect frost to prevent crop losses. Other studies have focused on predictions, such as the survey realized in Perugia, to obtain prognoses of pollutants in the short, medium, and long term [21].

Similarly, in Malaysia, air pollutants' predictions are obtained, focusing on pattern recognition [4]. The study conducted in Hong Kong focusing on prediction adapted the Particle Swarm Optimization Algorithm (PSO) to improve the results of the forecast of NO2 and NOX pollutants in a time of three days [16]. These studies have been developed using neural networks to make predictions, directly applying them or with the joint incorporation of other techniques. However, they differ either by software, inputs, outputs, and places where the studies were conducted.

Fuentes [9] conducted a study aimed at forecasting the minimum temperature for the following day. The data used in this study consisted of climate data collected for approximately eight years, including temperature, relative humidity, radiation, precipitation, wind speed, and direction, as input variables. For the study in Malaysia [4], eight parameters CO, O3, PM10, methane, SO2, NO2, non-metallic hydrocarbons, and total hydrocarbons were considered input variables. The data were collected every hour for seven years from 10 stations. The study conducted in Istanbul [15] evaluated different inputs for training the neural network. These inputs included the day temperature, condition, night temperature, humidity, pressure, speed, and wind direction to obtain predictions of SO2, PM10, CO pollutants.

The use of angular values as input variables for the neural network training proposed in the present study has not been evidenced in the literature. In this study, in addition to the variables O3, NO2, SO2, CO, PM2.5, and the meteorological temperature variable, it is proposed the inclusion of the angular values obtained from the initial and final levels of each input parameter and the date, as input parameters for training a NARX neural network. Related studies focused on predicting future values to visualize the behavior of both pollutants and minimum temperatures [4, 9, 15, 16, 21]. In contrast, we propose applying predictions for imputing missing data from the set of air pollutants.

3   Method

Figure 1 shows the methodology comprised three phases developed sequentially to achieve the objective of the study. The first phase consisted of data pre-processing, later the generation of the predictive model. Finally, the third phase is the evaluation of results.

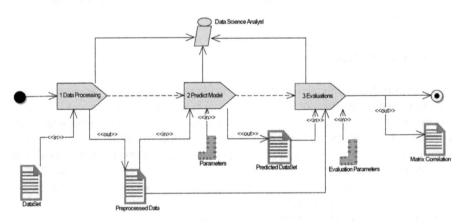

Fig. 1. Methodology scheme.

3.1   Data Processing

The tasks performed during the Data Processing phase included data understanding and data preparation. These processes aim to obtain the pre-processed data to adapt the information to the Predict Model phase. The tasks performed are described below.

Understanding Data. The data used in this study was provided by IERSE. The data was collected by the Municipio de Cuenca air monitoring station in Cuenca-Ecuador. The supplied information consists of time data, air pollutant data (taken every minute), and meteorological variables (taken every 10 min). The difference in the time granularity of the variables mentioned earlier required a process for averaging the pollutant variables' values every 10 min. The data set comprises the period from January 1, 2018, to November 31, 2018, accounting for 48,095 records.

Data Preparation. The data preparation step comprised the adaptation in several stages. These stages included data selection, data cleaning, data structuring, and data integration. These processes yielded consistent data, ready for adapting the information needed to be used in the Predict Model phase. Each of the stages is described in more detail in the following sections.

Data Selection. Studies related to air quality previously conducted in Cuenca evidenced the relationship between pollutants and meteorological variables [2, 20] (See Table 1). The creation of a new data set was based on analyzing these relationships and including only the information required for the study, eliminating all irrelevant information (See Table 2).

Table 1. Interaction between Atmospheric Pollutants and Temperature

Pollutant	O3	NO2	SO2	CO	PM2_5	TEMP
O3		X	X	X		X
NO2			X	X	X	X
SO2				X	X	X
CO	X		X		X	
PM2_5			X	X		X

Table 2. Modified Dataset

EC_TIME_STAMP	Day_week	O3	CO	NO2	SO2	PM2_5	TEMPAIRE_AV
1/1/2018 0:10	1	9.465	1.011	54.869	21	43	12.2
1/1/2018 0:20	1	10.733	1.015	54.548	24	43	12.4
1/1/2018 0:30	1	12.662	0.960	53.897	35	43	12.5

Data Cleaning. Consistency is a fundamental aspect of data cleaning for avoiding altering the results. Therefore, it was necessary to eliminate missing values and to handle outliers [19]. Missing values suppose the suppression of records in the predictor inputs. In this way, the absent values will be filled with the predictions obtained. Table 3 shows the current number of records for each data set after removing missing values. It also presents the percentage each set represents from the initial set consisting of 48,095 records.

Table 3. Number of Current Records

Pollutants	Current Records	Percentage %
O3	35.235	73.26
CO	42.542	88.85
NO2	38.015	79.04
SO2	38.898	80.87
PM2_5	38.711	80.48

Outliers are values outside the normal range of the data and can cause problems when processing information. For the treatment of outliers, the Z-scoring method was applied. This method is based on the normal distribution, using the average and standard deviation. The rule indicates that Z's calculated absolute values greater than three standard deviations are outliers [10]. In Eq. (1) [10], χ represents the original data, μ the average, and σ the standard deviation.

$$Z = \frac{\chi - \mu}{\sigma} \tag{1}$$

Table 4. Outliers results

Pollutant	Average	Standard Deviation	Variation coefficient	# Outliers	Percentage %
O3	24.02	17.30	72.04	270	0.76
CO	0.80	0.40	49.00	672	1.57
NO2	17.00	11.00	63.00	250	0.65
SO2	10.00	9.10	90.00	691	1.77
PM2_5	10.00	7.70	76.00	530	1.36

Outlier detection results are shown in Table 4, including the number of outliers classified by pollutants and their percentage within the complete dataset.

Structuring Data. The data set comprised of meteorological and pollutant variables has different scales. The temperature values are expressed in Celsius, the particulate matter (PM2.5) in micrograms per cubic meter, and Ozone (O3), Carbon Monoxide (CO), Nitrogen Dioxide (NO2), and Sulfur Dioxide (SO2) in parts per billion. Hence, the standardization was performed with Eq. (1) [3], where Z represents the standardized value. Tables 5 and 6 show an example of the result of unstandardized and standardized data.

Table 5. Unstandardized variables

EC_TIME_STAMP	Day week	CO	NO2	SO2	TEMP.AIR_AV	O3
1/1/2018 0:20	1	1.016	54.55	24	12.4	11
1/1/2018 0:30	1	0.961	53.90	35	12.5	13
1/1/2018 0:40	1	1.187	59.71	33	12.5	13

Table 6. Standardized variables

EC_TIME_STAMP	Day week	CO	NO2	SO2	TEMP.AIREAV	O3
1/1/2018 0:20	1	0.672	3.443	1.6	−0.8256	11
1/1/2018 0:30	1	0.528	3.383	2.8	−0.7930	13
1/1/2018 0:40	1	1.121	3.920	2.6	−0.7930	13

Data Integration. This step comprised integrating new fields to the dataset to comply with the predict model phase requirements. The data fields included are start date, end date, levels of pollutants, and angular values. Table 7 and Table 8 show the resulting record.

Table 7. Date fields added

Start date	End date	Day week
1/1/2018 0:10	1/1/2018 0:20	1
1/1/2018 0:20	1/1/2018 0:30	1
1/1/2018 0:30	1/1/2018 0:40	1

Table 8. Pollutants fields added

O3 Ini	O3 Fin	Angle	SO2 Ini	SO2 Fin	Angle	PM2_5 Ini	PM2_5 Fin	Angle
−0.807	−0.733	0.424	1.179	1.554	2.146	4.338	4.338	0.00
−0.733	−0.621	0.645	1.554	2.803	7.118	4.338	4.328	−0.06
−0.621	−0.602	0.108	2.803	2.587	−1.235	4.328	4.300	−0.15

3.2 Predict Model

The neural network was created at this stage, with the data previously processed. For the creation of the network, a supervised network model was used (Fig. 2). Selecting the type of network was determined by the availability of the output values for the comparison. The neural network specifically was a closed-loop NARX (Nonlinear Autoregressive Exogenous Model) to perform the training, which is also a retro propagation network [18].

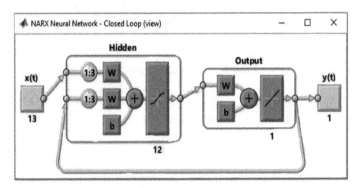

Fig. 2. NARX.neural network

Figure 3 shows the structure of the network. The diagram shows the input layers and the output layer, specifically, the neural network architecture for ozone predicting. The configuration of the networks for the remaining pollutants to be predicted works similarly. The input layers are the time, angular values, and pollutants' values that intervene to predict the specific pollutant. Table 1 describes the interrelation between pollutants and if the temperature variable is also related to the pollutant.

Adequate network training depends on the definition of several parameters, including the number of hidden layers, type of algorithm, and waiting time. Several tests, applying different algorithms (Bayesian Regularization, Scaled Conjugate Gradient, and Levenberg Marquardt), were performed to select each network training element. Levenberg Marquardt algorithm performed better in comparison to the other algorithms.

Following the criteria used in related studies on imputation or prediction, the data was divided into three sets: 70% for training, 15% for validations, and the remaining 15% for testing [8].

The best training results were obtained by the trial-error method. Noteworthy that each time the network is trained, even if they are the same parameters, different results are obtained in each training. The interpretation of the Performance and the Input-Error Cross-Correlation graphs is central for analyzing the training results. Figure 4 shows the neural network performance with the defined parameters. The closer the validation and test lines are to each other, the better trained the network is, without presenting over-adjustments [17].

The Input-Error Cross-Correlation (Fig. 5) graph allows observing the correlation error with the input values. A model can be determined as correct when the values are within the ranges belonging to the broken lines. Otherwise, it is indicative that the training parameters should be changed to improve these results, mainly the delays to adapt better to the model [17].

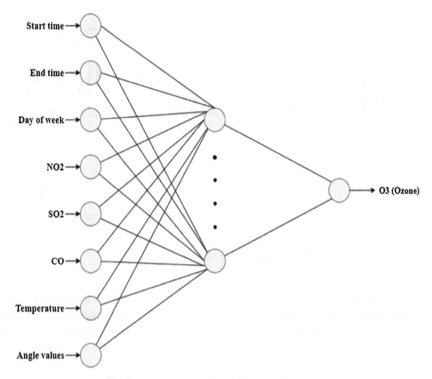

Fig. 3. Neural Network Architecture for Ozone.

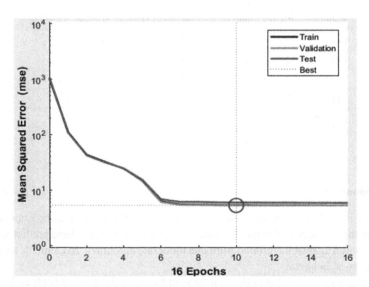

Fig. 4. Network performance for NO2.

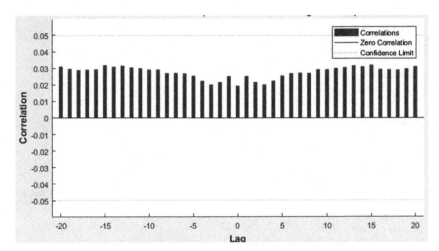

Fig. 5. Input-Error Cross-Correlation.

Table 9 shows the parameters that were used for the creation of each neural network. The number of entries depends on each pollutant. The remaining parameters were assessed using various tests to define each network's appropriate arguments, considering the graphs above for each of the cases.

Table 9. Parameters for the creation of each neural network

Pollutant	Inputs	InputDelays	FeedbackDelays	HiddenLayerSize
O3	15	1:3	1:3	12
CO	12	1:4	1:5	4
NO2	15	1:3	1:3	7
SO2	12	1:3	1:4	4
PM2_5	12	1:3	1:3	3

3.3 Evaluation

Evaluation is the last task to carry out in the Predict Model phase. This task consisted of analyzing the predictions for specific values obtained randomly. These predicted values were compared against the ground truth in a moderate amount of 20 elements to analyze the two curves' behavior.

The graph in Fig. 6 shows the comparison between the ground truth and the data predicted with the neural network for ozone using the 20 values obtained randomly.

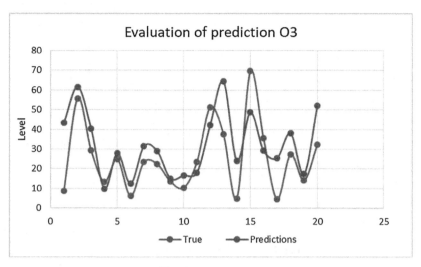

Fig. 6. Data behavior.

4   Results and Discussion

This section presents the analysis for the predictions of each pollutant. The test set was used to evaluate the results by contrasting the ground truth against the predictions obtained. Adjusted R was calculated to evaluate the closeness between the ground truth and the predicted values. Table 10 shows the results for each pollutant.

Table 10. Adjusted R results

Pollutant	Adjusted R
O3	0.85
CO	0.53
NO2	0.73
SO2	0.49
PM2_5	0.55

The line graphs allow visualizing the prediction results to understand the behavior of the data better. Figure 7 shows how a missing data section of O3 is filled. In the graph, the data imputed is represented in black and the existing data in green. At first glance, logically, it is evident that the imputed data adapt to the ground truth values, following a logical sequence in the dataset.

A large amount of information was a problem for the visualization of the behavior of the data, for which it was necessary to find a way to analyze all the values and allow a better interpretation of the results. For better visualization, data were divided by months for their representation.

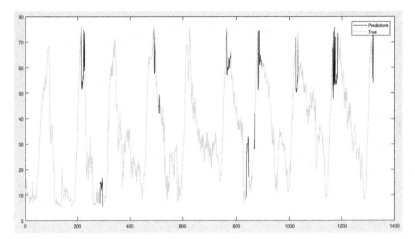

Fig. 7. Full set data imputation - O3.

The graph in Fig. 8 corresponds to the first ten days of October for O3. In this case, the existing data is represented in blue, while the predictions in red. This graph shows the behavior of the curves more clearly.

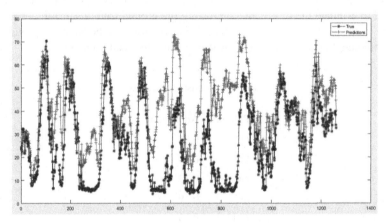

Fig. 8. October data – O3.

Figure 9 shows how the missing data is filled in the section taken from October. November is one of the months with the least amount of data; this allows observing the data's behavior in each of the pollutants (see Fig. 10).

NO2 evidenced a vast amount of lost data at the end of May and the beginning of June (see Fig. 11). Nevertheless, the results showed a high Adjusted R-value for NO2. Figure 12 shows how all these missing values were imputed.

Even though the adjusted R-value of CO did not have similar values to O3 and NO2, the graph (Fig. 13) shows a certain similarity between the lines representing the imputed

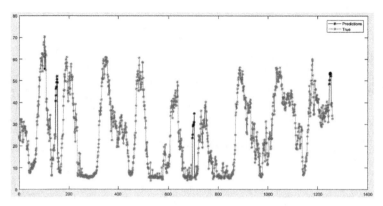

Fig. 9. Imputation of data in the month of October - O3.

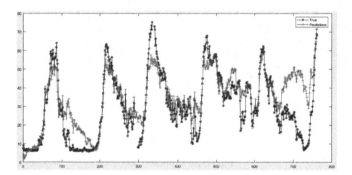

Fig. 10. November data - O3.

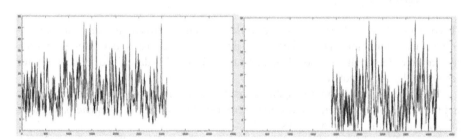

Fig. 11. May and June data set - NO2.

values and the truth. It can be seen that although they are not so close to the ground truth values, they have a certain similarity in their behavior.

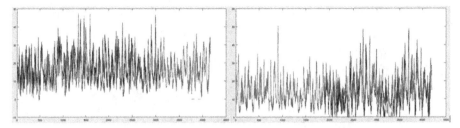

Fig. 12. Imputation May - NO2.

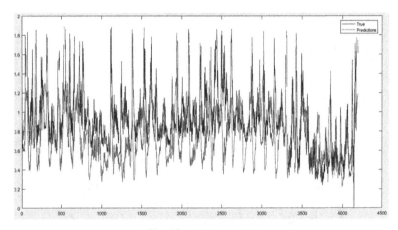

Fig. 13. October - CO.

5 Conclusions

This paper presented a NARX neural network's implementation for missing data imputation on an air pollutant dataset. The method describes three phases (data pre-processing, generation of the predictive model, and evaluation of results) developed sequentially for designing the neural network.

The selection of the input variables considered the interrelation between pollutants and the temperature. Several algorithms were tested to define the adequate parameters for configuring the neural networks.

The results yielded the best prediction for O3 with an R of 0.85 and the NO2 with an R of 0.73. The remaining pollutants of CO, PM2_5, and SO2, obtained an R-value of 0.53, 0.55, 0.49 correspondingly.

Future works could develop comparisons between the proposed method and other studies that make predictions to fill in data with different techniques. Another work line could analyze the pollutants' behavior in other cities to examine whether the method yields similar or different results in each case. For any of these, it is recommended to use a significant amount of information.

References

1. Alvarez, I., Méndez Martínez, J., Bello Rodríguez, B.M., Benítez Fuentes, B., Escobar Blanco, L.M., Zamora Monzón, R.: Influencia de los contaminantes atmosféricos sobre la salud. Revista Médica Electrónica, **39**(5), 1160–1170 (2017). http://scielo.sld.cu/scielo.php?script=sci_arttext&pid=S1684-18242017000500017
2. Andrade, P.S.: Aplicación de minería de datos en el análisis de contaminantes atmosféricos y variables meteorológicas (2018)
3. Avila, R.M., De Hernández, G., Rodríguez Pérez, V., Caraballo, E.A.H.: Predicción Del Rendimiento De Un Cultivo De Plátano Mediante Redes Neuronales Artificiales De Regresión Generalizada. Publicaciones En Ciencias y Tecnología, **6**(1), 200702–202730 (2012)
4. Azid, A., et al.: Prediction of the level of air pollution using principal component analysis and artificial neural network techniques: a case study in Malaysia. Water Air Soil Pollut. **225**(8), 1–14 (2014). https://doi.org/10.1007/s11270-014-2063-1
5. Bellinger, C., Mohomed Jabbar, M.S., Zaïane, O., Osornio-Vargas, A.: A systematic review of data mining and machine learning for air pollution epidemiology. BMC Public Health **17**(1), 1–19 (2017). https://doi.org/10.1186/s12889-017-4914-3
6. Cevallos, V.M., Díaz, V., Sirois, C.M.: Particulate matter air pollution from the city of Quito, Ecuador, activates inflammatory signaling pathways in vitro. Innate Immunity **23**(4), 392–400 (2017). https://doi.org/10.1177/1753425917699864
7. Estrella, B., Sempértegui, F., Franco, O.H., Cepeda, M., Naumova, E.N.: Air pollution control and the occurrence of acute respiratory illness in school children of Quito, Ecuador. J. Public Health Policy **40**(1), 17–34 (2019). https://doi.org/10.1057/s41271-018-0148-6
8. Fernanda, P., Logroño, B.: ESCUELA SUPERIOR POLITÉCNICA DE CHIMBORAZO METEOROLÓGICA CHIMBORAZO (2018)
9. Fuentes, M., Campos, C., García-Loyola, S.: Application of artificial neural networks to frost detection in central Chile using the next day minimum air temperature forecast. Chilean J. Agric. Res. **78**(3), 327–338 (2018). https://doi.org/10.4067/s0718-58392018000300327
10. Garcia, F.: Tests to identify outliers in data series. Pontifical Catholic University of Rio de Janeiro, 1–16 (2012). http://habcam.whoi.edu/HabCamData/HAB/processed/OutlierMethods_external.pdf
11. Geetha, A., Nasira, G.M.: Data mining for meteorological applications: decision trees for modeling rainfall prediction. In: 2014 IEEE International Conference on Computational Intelligence and Computing Research, IEEE ICCIC 2014, 0–3 (2015). https://doi.org/10.1109/ICCIC.2014.7238481
12. Gore, R.W., Deshpande, D.S.: An approach for classification of health risks based on air quality levels. In: Proceedings - 1st International Conference on Intelligent Systems and Information Management, ICISIM 2017, 2017-Janua, pp. 58–61 (2017). https://doi.org/10.1109/ICISIM.2017.8122148
13. Kingsy, G.R., Manimegalai, R., Geetha, D.M.S., Rajathi, S., Usha, K., Raabiathul, B.N.: Air pollution analysis using enhanced K-Means clustering algorithm for real time sensor data. In: IEEE Region 10 Annual International Conference, Proceedings/TENCON, (August 2006), pp. 1945–1949 (2017). https://doi.org/10.1109/TENCON.2016.7848362
14. Kukkonen, J., Partanen, L., Karppinen, A., Ruuskanen, J., Junninen, H., Kolehmainen, M., Cawley, G.: Extensive evaluation of neural network models for the prediction of NO2 and PM10 concentrations, compared with a deterministic modelling system and measurements in central Helsinki. Atmospheric Environ. **37**(32), 4539–4550 (2003). https://doi.org/10.1016/S1352-2310(03)00583-1
15. Kurt, A., Gulbagci, B., Karaca, F., Alagha, O.: An online air pollution forecasting system using neural networks. Environ. Int. **34**(5), 592–598 (2008). https://doi.org/10.1016/j.envint.2007.12.020

16. Li, S.T., Shue, L.Y.: Data mining to aid policy making in air pollution management. Expert Syst. Appl. **27**(3), 331–340 (2004). https://doi.org/10.1016/j.eswa.2004.05.015
17. MATLAB: Shallow Neural Network Time-Series Prediction and Modeling (2018). https://www.mathworks.com/help/deeplearning/gs/neural-network-time-series-prediction-and-mod eling.html
18. MATLAB and Simulink: Design Time Series NARX Feedback Neural Networks. MathWorks Deutschland. Retrieved from MATLAB Documentation website (2019). https://de.mathwo rks.com/help/deeplearning/ug/design-time-series-narx-feedback-neural-networks.html;jse ssionid=44f1e9acc4fc3d65278ab59a923f
19. Matute Rivera, M.A.: Evaluación de las herramientas de minería de datos en variables de contaminación atmosférica. 100 (2018). http://dspace.uazuay.edu.ec/handle/datos/8203
20. Ortega, J.J.: Impacto de la aplicación de algoritmos de minería de datos en variables de contaminación del aire. Director, **15**(2), 2017–2019 (2018). https://doi.org/10.22201/fq.187 08404e.2004.3.66178
21. Viotti, P., Liuti, G., Di Genova, P.: Atmospheric urban pollution: applications of an artificial neural network (ANN) to the city of Perugia. Ecol. Model. **148**(1), 27–46 (2002). https://doi.org/10.1016/S0304-3800(01)00434-3

ICT's Applications

Use of the Heuristic Model and GIS to Zone Landslide Hazards in the Mira River Basin, Ecuador

Mauricio David Reyes Pozo[1] ⓘ, Victor Julio Moreno Izquierdo[1] ⓘ,
Adriana Carolina López Alulema[1] ⓘ, Lorena del Pilar Lasso Benítez[2] ⓘ,
Verónica del Rocio Suango Sanchez[1] ⓘ, and Theofilos Toulkeridis[3](✉) ⓘ

[1] Instituto Geográfico Militar, Quito, Ecuador
[2] Universidad Central, Quito, Ecuador
[3] Universidad de las Fuerzas Armadas ESPE, Sangolquí, Ecuador
ttoulkeridis@espe.edu.ec

Abstract. The lack of geo-information related to important types of natural hazards such us landslides, leads to use quick and inexpensive methodologies in models that indicate the reality, this with the purpose of the acquisition of information for planning and development of the territory. The main objective of this study has been to determine landslides hazard zones along the Mira river basin in northern Ecuador. The delimitation of these zones has been performed through geographic information systems (GIS), which supported to collect, process and interrelate the information of conditional factors (land cover, lithology and slope) with triggering factors (seismic and precipitation records). These factors have been weighted with a heuristic model for their subsequent combination through the use of double-entry matrices. The result of the model application delivered five hazard categories of landslides being high, medium, low, none and not applicable category (water bodies and units without geomorphological characterization). Therefore, if the slope of a surface increased and it had soils that have poor vegetation or has been related with non-consolidated or fractured lithologic material, during the occurrence of strong precipitations (the principal triggering factor), all of it creates favorable scenarios for the generation of landslides. Therefore, for the territorial development in the Mira River basin, there is the need of the implementation of correct practices in places with adequate slopes, as this appeared to be the most important conditioning factor.

Keywords: Landslide · Hazard · Zonification · Mira river basin · GIS

1 Introduction

Landslides are a type of hazard or risk that causes economic loss, property damage and high maintenance costs, as well as injuries or fatalities [1–4]. They are responsible for approximately 17% of all world deaths, especially in mountainous regions and areas where unplanned urbanization takes place [5–8]. In order to mitigate landslide hazards,

© Springer Nature Switzerland AG 2020
G. Rodriguez Morales et al. (Eds.): TICEC 2020, CCIS 1307, pp. 243–257, 2020.
https://doi.org/10.1007/978-3-030-62833-8_19

it is necessary to understand the processes and factors that lead to landslides and subsequently to conduct their mapping [9, 10]. This task will serve as a guide in order to establish the risk management bases and the subsequent creation of safety measures with the purpose of avoiding partial or total losses of strategic infrastructure and lives [3, 11–13].

Ecuador has a diversity of landscapes resulting from the influence of its water systems, which are delimited in river basins, the same ones that due to population growth or demographic pressure suffer constant changes in their natural conditions due to new human settlements or farms [14–16]. The country also has a great diversity of hazards of natural origin such as landslides, earthquakes, droughts, floods, tsunamis and active volcanism [17–33]. These geomorphological, geological and climatic circumstances are related due to Ecuador's geodynamic setting being part of the Pacific Ring of Fire, with active plate tectonic movements [34–40]. There are a variety of catastrophic events of mass movements that have been the cause of disasters with fatal consequences in the country, such as the disappearance of the population of Cacha Canton with some 5,000 fatalities, the collapse of La Josefina with some 50 victims and economic damages of around 147 million dollars [41–43].

Nonetheless, a reduction of such risks and hazards, may be the application of a certain zoning of such areas, which, if they reflect as close as possible the natural given conditions, they may mark the areas with different degrees of risks of landslides. This shall help to obtain technical information that supports the decision making in the territorial planning and risk mitigation. Therefore, the current work is a case study which includes hazard zoning of landslides in the Mira River basin, northern Ecuador, based on the interaction of conditioning factors and triggers (earthquakes and rainfall), through the use of a heuristic model.

2 Study Area

The study area has been the Mira River basin, which is located in northern Ecuador, covering an area of approximately 656,092.90 ha [44]. It is one of the ten largest river basins in the country, situated in altitudes between 500 and 5,000 m above sea level, representing a highly biodiverse region [45, 46]. Such area, between the provinces of Carchi and Imbabura, the temperatures range between 8 to 24 °C (Fig. 1). Approximately 522,732 people live within the basin, who are mostly dedicated to agricultural work and commercial activities [47].

The lithology of the basin is composed of andesitic rocks, which are covered with recent pyroclastic projections, ashes and lapillis that have resulted in the formation of soils [16, 48]. Such layer has been the one that supports the constant precipitation that easily infiltrates, saturating the material, making the soil heavier and weaker, increasing the susceptibility of occurrence to a landslide [49–51]. The soils formed from this allophanic material, with special characteristics such as thixotropy, bulk density with less than 0.8 g/cm^3, high content of organic matter and high porosity and water retention capacity greater than 50% [52]. These predispose the surface layer to the development of a landslide, causing significant problems at the time of construction or agricultural operations [53, 54].

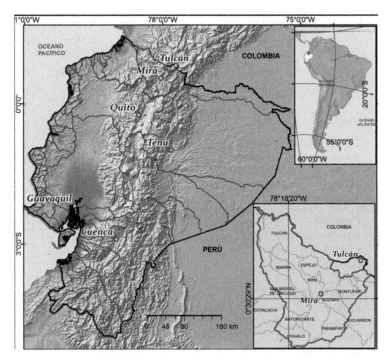

Fig. 1. Location of the Mira river basin.

3   Methodology

The qualitative or quantitative zoning of risks or hazards, is strictly related to the available data set and does not depend on the level of complexity of the analysis Cascini [55]. For the zoning of the risks due to landslides, the heuristic (expert) method and the multi-territory analysis were used, adapting to the accessibility and availability of the data [4, 56]. The analyzed variables such as slope, vegetation cover, lithology, earthquakes and precipitation, have intervened both in quantitative and qualitative studies and are recognized as basic for the development of this type of mass movements [7, 11, 42, 49–51, 57–65]. These variables were evaluated, reclassified and weighted, while the values were assigned according to their degree of influence [66].

Data on conditioning factors were acquired from the national geoinformation generation project at the national level [67]. The slope (S) was grouped into six ranges, adapting the information in the databases [50, 51]. The slopes less than 12% were grouped and qualified as none (null), as on slopes with a degree of less than 7° (approximately 12%), such type of movement has not been generated [50, 51]. The lithology (L) was classified according to the degree of consolidation of the different types of rock [57]. The vegetation cover of the soil (C) was grouped according to the similar characteristics of soil protection [51, 68] (Table 1).

The Weight column is assigned as the rating or weighting values, which correspond to each of the factors separately. That is, the weighting performed is given for each of the variables, one independent of the other. In the database, all the possible combinations

Table 1. Reclassification and weighting of conditioning and triggering factors

Conditioning factors			Triggering factors			
Range of slopes (%) (S)	Lithology (L)	Plant coverage (C)	Precip. (mm) (TP)	Quakes (richter) (TS)	Weight	Category
0 a 12	N.A.	N.A.	N.A.	<3,5	0	None
13 a 25	Tillites, lavas, gravels and blocks of variable composition	Without coverage, Agricultural land	<100	3,5–4,4	1	Very low
26 a 40	Pyroclastic flows, tobaceous sediments, massive volcanoclastic conglomerates, granites, granodiorites and quartzdiorites	Crops	100–150	4,5–5,9	2	Low
41 a 70	Sands, gravels, tuffs, pumice, silts, clays, phyllites, graphite and quartzite interspersed with quartz veins, shales	Crops and shrub vegetation	151–200	6,0–6,9	3	Medium
71 a 100	Sands, gravels, tuffs, pumice, silts, clays, phyllites, graphite and quartzite interspersed with quartz veins, shales	Pastures and forests	201–250	7,0–7,9	4	High

(continued)

Table 1. (*continued*)

Conditioning factors			Triggering factors			
Range of slopes (%) (S)	Lithology (L)	Plant coverage (C)	Precip. (mm) (TP)	Quakes (richter) (TS)	Weight	Category
>101	Sands, gravels, tuffs, pumice, silts, clays, phyllites, graphite and quartzite interspersed with quartz veins, shales	Paramos	>250	>7,9	5	Very high

occur within the study area for each unit of analysis (geomorphological delimitation), and, each record will have a column in which the weighting value will be placed. Detonating or triggering factors (earthquakes -TS- and precipitation -TP-) have the ability to cause the event [57]. In the first case, the data were obtained from the seismic catalog prepared by the Geophysical Institute of the National Polytechnic School, with a total of 13,863 records -from the year 1901-, of which 1,580 were used to obtain the Earthquake mapping modeling [69].

In order to determine the sample size, for validation and interpolation, the program Decision Analyst STATS was used, with an acceptable error rate of 5% and a confidence level of 95%, through the which obtained a sample size for the validation of the 70 records model and the rest for interpolation (1510 records) [70]. For the selection of the data and with the purpose of better zoning the interpolation values, a grid of 120 units has been performed, which has been obtained based on the minimum and maximum coordinates of the basin. This resulted in 91 effective grids containing more than one magnitude data (one to model, another to validate, as required in the sample size), while those of greater magnitude are selected for interpolation.

Regarding precipitation by rainfall, the data was obtained from [71], where weather stations registered the maximum rainfall in 24 h for about 245 mm, for a return period of 100 years. For the modeling of the mapping we used a total of 101 weather stations with the corresponding maximum rainfall information. The interpolation was conducted by the ILWIS 3.3 Academic program using the mobile surface interpolation method, with parameters for weight function, inverse distance, and second degree polynomial surface, as that interpolator yields the best results in the generation of geo-spatial models [72].

In order to handle the different raster and vector formats, the GIS ArcGis 10.3 tools were used. The geomorphological delimitation was obtained in shapefile format, in which the conditioning factors (slope, lithology and the predominant vegetation cover) are characterized. The information of the triggering factors (earthquakes and precipitation) were obtained in Raster format. The raster information was introduced into the vector by using the Zonal Statistics as Table tool, which allowed to summarize the values of a raster within the limits of another data set and report the results in a table [73]. Hereby, the value of the raster cell that occurs most frequently (majority statistical option) has been obtained within the same area as in the output polygon. In this way we obtained the highest value of precipitation as well as for earthquakes within each polygon, avoiding the superposition of layers or algebra of maps and keeping intact the unit of analysis delimited by geomorphology.

HAZARD LANDSLIDE DETERMINATION

Conditioning factors

CxCL — Lithology weighting (CL), rows: Vegetation coverage weight (C)

	1	2	3	4	5
1	1	2	2	2	3
2	2	2	2	3	3
3	3	3	3	3	4
4	4	4	4	4	4
5	5	5	5	5	5

↓

CSxCCL — (CCL), rows: Slope weighting (CS)

	1	2	3	4	5
0	0	0	0	0	0
1	1	1	2	2	2
2	2	2	2	3	3
3	3	3	3	3	5
4	3	3	3	4	4
5	4	4	5	5	5

Triggering factors

TPxTS — Seismicity weighting (TS), rows: Precipitation weighting (TP)

	0	1	2	3	4	5
1	1	1	2	2	3	3
2	2	2	2	3	3	4
3	3	3	3	3	3	4
4	4	4	4	4	4	4
5	5	5	5	5	5	5

↓

SxD — Triggering weight, rows: Suscebility weight (TSU)

	1	2	3	4	5
0	0	0	0	0	0
1	1	1	2	3	3
2	2	2	2	3	3
3	3	3	3	3	4
4	4	4	4	4	5
5	5	5	5	5	5

Category
0: none; 1: very low; 2: low; 3: medium; 4: high; 5: very high

→

Fig. 2. Matrix analysis

The calculation of the degree of susceptibility (Su), triggers (T) and hazards has been conducted by using double-entry matrices with weighted values of the conditioning factors (S, L and C), which allowed to control the degree of influence of each of the factors [74]. The first matrix is obtained by performing the combination of L with C, obtaining the degree of susceptibility between the type of rock and the cover present in the soil (CL). The resulting values of the combination between the factors were assigned taking into account that the landslide occurs in the soil covered by the vegetation and not in the consolidated rock [50, 57, 75]. Then, the combination of the result of the matrix CL is performed, with the weighting values of C.

The assigned value, the result of the combination of the first LC matrix by S, is directly proportional to the increase in S due to the enormous importance of increasing this factor in the development of landslides [7, 42, 50, 51, 57, 62, 65, 76–78]. With the triggers, in the same way, a double input matrix is made to interact with the Trigger factors (TS and TP). Finally, for the determination of the value and the degree of risk

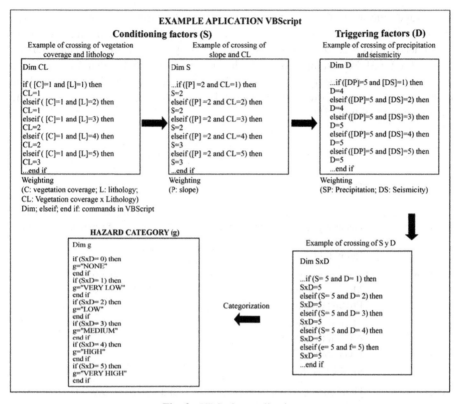

Fig. 3. VBScript application

to landslides, the resulting matrices are crossed (C versus T), in which it is possible to control the interaction of the factors based on logical and expert knowledge (Fig. 2).

In order to automate the crossing of matrices, an order file or processing file (script) was prepared in the *Visual Basic Script* programming language (VBScript), in which the crossings of conditioning factors and triggers developed in the matrices were conducted. The examples of some combinations can be seen in Fig. 3. Starting with the crossing of the weighted values of the coverage (CP) and the lithology (L). The results (CL) of these combinations are crossed with the weighted values of the Slope (S), obtaining the total values of the Conditioners (C). Likewise, the total values of the triggers (T) are obtained, in the example the interaction of the weighted values such as 5 of the Detonator by Precipitation is carried out with each of the weights of the Seismic Detonator (TS). This same procedure is repeated for each of the possible combinations of the conditioning and triggering factors. Finally, the combinations of the conditioning and detonating values are performed to categorize them (0: null; 1 and 2: low; 3: medium; 4 and 5: high).

4   Results and Discussion

The interaction of the conditioning and trigger factors yielded five categories of risk to landslides (Table 2). The category with the highest percentage of occupation has been the average with about 62.04% (Fig. 4). This coincides with previous studies, which categorized the Mira canton with a relatively high degree of hazards, mainly due to pronounced slopes [42, 79, 87]. Likewise, each category presents ranges of characteristic slopes [7, 62, 65]. For example, in the high category slopes higher than 71% or in the low category outstanding from 13 to 40%, determining that as the slope increased the hazard category changed, due to the high correlation of the slope and the increase in the phenomenon of sliding [51].

Table 2. Landslide threat categories

Hazard category	Main features	Surface	
		ha	%
High	Generally slopes greater than 70% Strong earthquakes (7 to 7.9 Ms) Rainfall higher than 250 mm	51.610,53	7,87
Medium	Generally slopes greater than 41% Medium Earthquakes (Ms up to 6.9) Precipitation less than 200 mm in 24 h	407.059,93	62,04
Low	Mainly on slopes greater than 13% Low and very low earthquakes (Ms 3.5 to 5.9) Precipitation, mostly less than 150 mm	101.902,98	15,53
None	Slopes less than 12%	85.610,46	13,05
Not applicable	Units corresponding to populated areas and water bodies	9.909,00	1,51
Total		**656.092,90**	**100,00**

The vegetation cover directly influences the occurrence of a landslide [58]. In the study area it was classified into 5 protection ranges being 1. Very low (e.g. agricultural land at rest -used periodically in the agriculture and livestock-; 2. Low (e.g. crops); 3. Medium (e.g. shrub vegetation); 4. High (e.g. forests) and 5. Very high (e.g. native forest), based on the protection it exercises each type of cover, acting as a slope stabilizer and protective mattress against the erosive effects of runoff water [50, 51, 68]. There are areas that despite if they have soils protected by abundant vegetation cover, they show landslides, according to [50], the stability given by the vegetation is strongly conditioned by the effect of climate and topography, that is, in areas with strong winds and slopes, they destabilize the trees, which you see generate removal of the ground through its roots.

As for the trigger factors, 5 precipitation ranges were categorized: a) < to 100 mm; b) from 100 to 150 mm; c) 151 to 200 mm; d) 201 to 250 mm; d) > to 250 mm, determining that the Mira River basin, for the most part, is a humid zone, because it has no water deficit, since its rainfall is greater than the actual evapotranspiration [42]. Likewise, as rainfall increases, the threat category increases, due to the strong correlation between the fall of rain and the occurrence of landslides [51, 58]. The areas with the highest rainfall

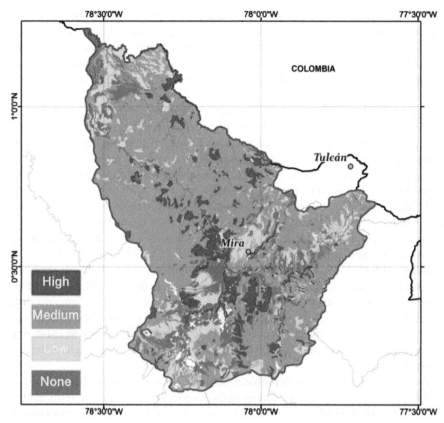

Fig. 4. Zoning of hazards of landslides in the hydrographic basin of the Mira river, northern Ecuador

(medium, high and very high categories) are located mainly in the center and south of the river basin and easily exceed 151 mm, directly influencing the occurrence of landslides, being an area with high rainfall or heavy rains that, when falling, saturate the soil mass and give off lithological materials that are not consolidated, causing a movement of land [49, 59].

The second trigger factor (the earthquakes) was categorized into 6 ranges, according to the Richter scale: Null (< to 3.5); very low (3.5 to 4.4); low (4.5 to 5.9); medium (6 to 6.9); high (7 to 7.9) and very high (>7.9), based on the classification developed by [67], who categorize Mira within a space with a category of threat to earthquakes slightly high and when presenting seismic movements influence the slopes for the production of a landslide [62, 88].

Landslides cause high damage in terms of material and human losses [51, 61, 81], the Mira River basin is no exception, in areas classified as medium and high, the amount of infrastructure and population that could be affected is approximately 522,732 people [47]. Likewise, the zoning carried out serves as a guide for the elaboration of territorial planning at the level of Municipal Decentralized Autonomous Government, in a fast, reliable and cheap way, as well as several categorical analysis methods [62, 80, 82–84], including quantitative techniques, with different slope calculation methods and qualitative techniques with probabilistic, statistical or deterministic. The resulting areas with threat levels categorized as low or null, would be the most conducive to the development of farms or construction activities, due to their lithological consolidation or flat slopes [85].

The information generated in the country on mass movements is framed within cantonal or provincial boundaries, the present work analyzed the threat of landslide in the land unit (delimited by the geomorphological unit), that is, that each polygon has its rating in terms of slope, type of rock, vegetation cover, category due to earthquake damage and precipitation, due to the use of the complex physical geography or landscape geography approach within a river basin [64].

Studies of [51, 86], ensure that there is still no conclusion as to whether the quantitative techniques with slope stability calculation or the qualitative techniques with probabilistic data, statistics or deterministic approaches, is a better than the other. The important issue is that the model used is in accordance with reality regardless of the use of any GIS [58]. The most important point in heuristic methodology is the expert qualification of the variables, since the applied weights are indicators of the importance of each of the conditioning or triggering factors [74]. Thus the areas of greatest threat have mostly the highest weights, which results from the crossing of the double entry matrices, in which those that are directed to each of the land units towards an established category, which, despite applying weighted averages, assigns greater weight to the most important factors [3].

The methodology used avoids problems generated by using map algebra (topological problems resulting from the overlapping of the layers), since the analysis units are kept intact (geomorphological units), in which their components, in our case variables of conditioning and detonating factors, form a single integral on the earth's surface and have its spatial manifestation in a certain relief [64].

5   Conclusions

The interaction of the conditioning and triggering factors, through the application of the heuristic methodology, determined four categories of landslides hazards within the basin, of which the average category has been the dominant one by surface. Likewise, it was determined that the slope and precipitation are the conditioning and triggering factors, respectively, that most influence the occurrence of a landslide.

The constant precipitation and the special characteristics of the soil, due to its volcanic genesis, such as thixotropy or high water retention causes the basin, for the most part, to possess high humidity, which is directly predisposing the surface layer for the development of a landslide.

A variety of towns are located in areas categorized with the greatest risks to landslides. Such information is essential in the generation of land planning issues, preventing and avoiding potential future possible catastrophes. In addition, it is also recommended that this delimitation be used to minimize inappropriate land use in places that present a high threat of landslides and in places where cadastral information is available, it would be possible to quantify possible damages.

The purpose of preparing cartography at a semi-detailed level has been to examine a large area of territory at low costs and as early as possible. Hereby, the use of multicriteria analysis is essential for the analysis and processing of available information. The use of double-input matrices confer control on the generation of predictions, thus avoiding results that are not consistent with reality. Finally, the use of weights offers a certain mathematical foundation in the importance of each variable that enters into analysis.

References

1. Das, I., Sahoo, S., van Westen, C., Stein, A., Hack, R.: Landslide susceptibility assessment using logistic regression and its comparison with a rock mass classification system, along a road section in the Northern Himalayas (India). Geomorphology 114(4), 627–637 (2010)
2. Guo, H.: Understanding global natural disasters and the role of earth observation. Int. J. Digit. Earth 3(3), 221–230 (2010)
3. Feizizadeh, B., Blaschke, T., Nazmfar, H.: IS-based ordered weighted averaging and Dempster-Shafer methods for landslide susceptibility mapping in the Urmia Lake Basin, Iran. Int. J. Digit. Earth 7(8), 688–708 (2012)
4. Paz, J., Gonzáles, R., Gómez, M., Velasco, J.: Metodología para elaborar mapas de susceptibilidad a procesos de remoción en masa, análisis del caso ladera sur de Tuxtla Gutiérrez, Chiapas. Investigaciones Geográficas 92, 128–143 (2017)
5. Kanungo, D., Arora, M., Sarkar, S., Gupta, R.: A comparative study of conventional, ANN black box, fuzzy and combined naural and fuzzy weighting procedures for landslide susceptibility zonation in Darjeeling Himalayas. Eng. Geol. 85(3–4), 347–366 (2006)
6. Goetz, J., Guthrie, R., Brening, A.: Integrating physical and empirical landslide susceptibility models using generalized additive models. Geomorphology 129(2011), 376–386 (2011)
7. Pourghasemi, H., Mohammady, M., Predhan, B.: Landslide susceptibility mapping using index of entropy and conditional probability models in GIS: Safarood Basin, Iran. CATENA 97, 71–84 (2012)
8. Castelo, C.A.J., Cruz, M., Almeida, O.P., Toulkeridis, T.: Comparative determination of the probability of landslide ocurrences and susceptibility in Central Quito, Ecuador. In: 2018 International Conference on eDemocracy & eGovernment (ICEDEG), pp. 136–143. IEEE (April 2018)
9. Vallejo, R.Z., et al.: Numerical probability modeling of past, present and future landslide occurrences in Nothern Quito, Ecuador. In: 2018 International Conference on eDemocracy & eGovernment (ICEDEG), pp. 117–125. IEEE (April 2018)
10. Orejuela, I.P., Toulkeridis, T.: Evaluation of the susceptibility to landslides through diffuse logic and analytical hierarchy process (AHP) between Macas and Riobamba in Central Ecuador. In: 2020 Seventh International Conference on eDemocracy & eGovernment (ICEDEG), pp. 201–207. IEEE (April 2020)
11. Varnes, D.: Landslide Hazard Zonation: A Review of Principles and Practice. UNESCO, Paris (1984)
12. Yilmaz, I.: Comparison of landslide susceptibility mapping methodologies for Koyulhisar, Turkey: conditional probability, logistic regresion, artificial neural networks, and support vector machine. Environ. Earth Sci. 61(4), 821–836 (2010)
13. Althuwaynee, O.F., Pradhan, B., Lee, S.: Application of an evidential belief function model in landslide susceptibility mapping. Comput. Geosci. 44, 120–135 (2012)
14. Sánchez, A., García, R., Palma, A.: La cuenca hidrográfica: unidad básica de planeación y manejo de recursos naturales. Secretaria de Medio Ambiente y Recursos Naturales, Tlalpan (2003)

15. Arce, E., Sandoval, W., Toulkeridis, T., Carrera, D., Merizalde, M.J.: Ecological flows for Ecuadorian basins determined by the slope method of the mass-curve. In: IOP Conference Series: Earth and Environmental Science, vol. 191, no. 1, p. 012118. IOP Publishing (2018)
16. Winckel, A., Zebrowski, C., Sourdat, M.: Las regiones y paisajes del Ecuador. Talleres gráficos del IGM del Ecuador, Quito (1997)
17. Toulkeridis, T., Buchwaldt, R., Addison, A.: When volcanoes threaten, scientists warn. Geotimes **52**, 36–39 (2007)
18. Padrón, E., et al.: Fumarole/plume and diffuse CO_2 emission from Sierra Negra volcano, Galapagos archipelago. Bull. Volcanol. **74**, 1509–1519 (2012)
19. Chunga, K., Toulkeridis, T.: First evidence of paleo-tsunami deposits of a major historic event in Ecuador. Sci. Tsunami Hazards **33**, 55–69 (2014)
20. Toulkeridis, T., et al.: Evaluation of the initial stage of the reactivated Cotopaxi volcano - analysis of the first ejected fine-grained material. Nat. Hazards Earth Syst. Sci. **3**(11), 6947–6976 (2015)
21. Toulkeridis, T., Simón Baile, D., Rodríguez, F., Salazar Martínez, R., Arias Jiménez, N., Carreon Freyre, D.: Subsidence at the "trébol" of Quito, Ecuador: an indicator for future disasters? In: Proceedings of the International Association of Hydrological Sciences, 12 November 2015, vol. 372, pp. 151–155 (2015b)
22. Rodriguez, F., et al.: The economic evaluation and significance of an early relocation versus complete destruction by a potential tsunami of a coastal city in Ecuador. Sci. Tsunami Hazards **35**(1), 18–35 (2016)
23. Toulkeridis, T.: Unexpected results of a seismic hazard evaluation applied to a modern hydroelectric plant in central Ecuador. J. Struct. Eng. **43**(4), 373–380 (2016)
24. Toulkeridis, T., et al.: Causes and consequences of the sinkhole at El Trébol of Quito, Ecuador - implications for economic damage and risk assessment. Nat. Hazards Earth Sci. Syst. **16**, 2031–2041 (2016)
25. Rodríguez Espinosa, F., et al.: Economic evaluation of recovering a natural protection with concurrent relocation of the threatened public of tsunami hazards in central coastal Ecuador. Sci. Tsunami Hazards **36**, 293–306 (2017)
26. Rodriguez, F., Toulkeridis, T., Padilla, O., Mato, F.: Economic risk assessment of Cotopaxi volcano Ecuador in case of a future lahar emplacement. Nat. Hazards **85**(1), 605–618 (2017)
27. Toulkeridis, T., Zach, I.: Wind directions of volcanic ash-charged clouds in Ecuador – implications for the public and flight safety. Geomat. Nat. Hazards Risks **8**(2), 242–256 (2017)
28. Mato, F., Toulkeridis, T.: The missing link in El Niño's phenomenon generation. Sci. Tsunami Hazards **36**, 128–144 (2017)
29. Toulkeridis, T., et al.: The 7.8 M_w earthquake and tsunami of the 16th April 2016 in Ecuador - seismic evaluation, geological field survey and economic implications. Sci. Tsunami Hazards **36**, 197–242 (2017)
30. Toulkeridis, T., et al.: Contrasting results of potential tsunami hazards in Muisne, central coast of Ecuador. Sci. Tsunami Hazards **36**, 13–40 (2017)
31. Chunga, K., Toulkeridis, T., Vera-Grunauer, X., Gutierrez, M., Cahuana, N., Alvarez, A.: A review of earthquakes and tsunami records and characterization of capable faults on the northwestern coast of Ecuador. Sci. Tsunami Hazards **36**, 100–127 (2017)
32. Suango Sánchez, V.D.R., et al.: Use of geotechnologies and multicriteria evaluation in land use policy – the case of the urban area expansion of the city of Babahoyo, Ecuador. In: 2019 6th International Conference on eDemocracy and eGovernment, ICEDEG 2019, pp. 194–202 (2019)
33. Toulkeridis, T., et al.: Climate change according to Ecuadorian academics–perceptions versus facts. La Granja **31**(1), 21–49 (2020)

34. Toulkeridis, T., Mato, F., Toulkeridis-Estrella, K., Perez Salinas, J.C., Tapia, S., Fuertes, W.: Real-time radioactive precursor of the April 16, 2016 Mw 7.8 earthquake and tsunami in Ecuador. Sci. Tsunami Hazards **37**, 34–48 (2018)
35. Mato, F., Toulkeridis, T.: An unsupervised K-means based clustering method for geophysical post-earthquake diagnosis. In: 2017 IEEE Symposium Series on Computational Intelligence (SSCI), pp. 1–8 (2018)
36. Navas, L., Caiza, P., Toulkeridis, T.: An evaluated comparison between the molecule and steel framing construction systems – implications for the seismic vulnerable Ecuador. Malays. Construct. Res. J. **26**(3), 87–109 (2018)
37. Celorio-Saltos, J.C., García-Arias, J.M., Guerra-Luque, A.B., Barragan-Aroca, G., Toulkeridis, T.: Vulnerability analysis based on tsunami hazards in Crucita, central coastal of Ecuador. Sci. Tsunami Hazards **38**(3), 225–263 (2018)
38. Matheus-Medina, A.S., Toulkeridis, T., Padilla-Almeida, O., Cruz-D'Howitt, M., Chunga, K.: Evaluation of the tsunami vulnerability in the coastal Ecuadorian tourist centers of the peninsulas of Bahia de Caráquez and Salinas. Sci. Tsunami Hazards **38**(3), 175–209 (2018)
39. Chunga, K., Mulas, M., Alvarez, A., Galarza, J., Toulkeridis, T.: Characterization of seismogenetic crustal faults in the Gulf of Guayaquil, Ecuador. Andean Geol. **46**(1), 66–81 (2019)
40. Toulkeridis, T., et al.: Two independent real-time precursors of the 7.8 Mw earthquake in Ecuador based on radioactive and geodetic processes—powerful tools for an early warning system. J. Geodyn. **126**, 12–22 (2019)
41. Harden, C.: Sediment movement and catastrophic events: the 1993 rockslide at La Josefina, Ecuador. Phys. Geogr. **22**(4), 305–320 (2001)
42. D'Ercole, R., Trujillo, M.: Amenazas, vulnerabilidad, capacidades y riesgo en el Ecuador. Los desastres un reto para el desarrollo. Ekseption, Quito (2003)
43. Morris, A.: Understandings of catastrophe: the landslide at La Josefina, Ecuador. In: Natural Disaster and Development in a Globalizing World, pp. 173–185. Routledge (2003)
44. SENAGUA: Servicio de descargas de Geoinformación. Secretaría del Agua. Accedido el 10 de marzo de 2017 (2002)
45. Myers, N., Mittermeier, R., Mittermeier, C., da Fonseca, G., Kent, J.: Biodiversity hotspots for conservation priorities. Nature **403**, 853–858 (2000)
46. Ramsay, P., Oxley, E.: An assessment of aboveground net primary productivity in andean grasslands of central Ecuador. Mt. Res. Dev. **21**(2), 161–167 (2001)
47. INEC: Población por sexo, según Provincia, Parroquia y Cantón de empadronamiento. Instituto Nacional de Estadísticas y Censos (2017)
48. Espinosa, J., Moreno, J., Bernal, G. (eds.): The Soils of Ecuador. WSBS. Springer, Cham (2018). https://doi.org/10.1007/978-3-319-25319-0_6
49. Alcantara, I.: Landslides: Deslizamiento o movimientos del terreno? Definición, clasificaciones y terminología. Investigaciones Geográficas **41**, 7–25 (2000)
50. Lara, M., Sepúlveda, S.: Remociones en masa. Apunte del curso. Santiago de Chile, Departamento de geologia, Chile (2008)
51. Hadji, R., Boumazbeur, A., Limani, Y., Baghem, M., Chouabi, A., Demdoum, A.: Geologic, topografic and climatic controls in landslide hazard assessment usin GIS modeling: a case study of Souk Ahras region, NE Algeria. Quat. Int. **302**, 224–237 (2013)
52. Vallejo, L.: Suelos del Ecuador. IGM, Quito (1997)
53. Bathrellos, G.D., Gaki-Papanastassiou, K., Skilodimou, H.D., Skianis, G.A., Chousianitis, K.G.: Assessment of rural community and agricultural development using geomorphological–geological factors and GIS in the Trikala prefecture (Central Greece). Stoch. Environ. Res. Risk Assess. **27**(2), 573–588 (2013)

54. Guzzetti, F., Mondini, A.C., Cardinali, M., Fiorucci, F., Santangelo, M., Chang, K.T.: Landslide inventory maps: new tools for an old problem. Earth-Sci. Rev. **112**(1–2), 42–66 (2012)
55. Cascini, L.: Applicability of landslide susceptibility and hazard zoning at different scales. Eng. Geol. **102**(3), 164–177 (2008)
56. Díaz, J., López, J.: Evaluación del potencial para acuacultura costera de camarón en el entorno de la laguna de Mar Muerto, mediante la aplicación de técnicas de análisis multicriterio con un SIG. Ekseption, Quito (2000)
57. Mora, C., Vahrson, W.: Macrozonation methodology for landslide hazard determination. Environ. Eng. Geosci. **31**(1), 49–58 (1994)
58. Chau, K., Sze, Y., Fung, M., Wong, W., Fong, E., Chan, L.: Landslide hazard analysis for Hong Kong using landslide inventory and GIS. Comput. Geosci. **30**(4), 429–443 (2003)
59. Castellanos, E., Van Westen, C.: Qualitative landslide susceptibility assesment by multicriteria analysis: a case study from San Antonio del Sur, Guantanamo, Cuba. Geomorphology **94**(3–4), 453–466 (2007)
60. PMA GCA: Movimientos en masa en la región andina: Una guía para la evaluación de amenazas. Proyecto Multinacional Andino: Geociencias para las Comunidades Andinas (2007)
61. Fell, R., Corominas, J., Bonnard, C., Cascini, L., Leroi, E., Savage, W.: Guidelines for landslide suscetibility, hazard and risk zoning for land use planning. Eng. Geol. **102**(3), 85–98 (2008)
62. Kamp, U., Growley, B., Khattak, G., Owen, L.: GIS-based landslide susceptibility mapping for the 2005 Kashmir earthquake region. Geomorphology **101**(4), 631–642 (2008)
63. Aleotti, P., Chowdhury, R.: Landslide hazard assessment: summary review and new perspectives. Bull. Eng. Geol. Environ. **58**, 21–44 (1999)
64. Bocco, G., Mendoza, M., Priego, A., Burgos, A.: La cartografía de los sistemas naturales como base geográfica para la planeación territorial. Universidad Nacional Autónoma de México, México (2009)
65. Raman, R., Punia, M.: The application of GIS-based bivariate statistical methods for landslide hazards assessmets in the upper Tons river valley, Western Himalaya, India. Georisk: Assess. Manag. Risk Eng. Syst. Geohazards **6**(3), 145–161 (2012)
66. Chacón, J., Irigaray, C., Fernandez, T., El Hamdouni, R.: Engineering geology maps: landslides and geographical information systems. Bull. Eng. Geol. Environ. **65**(4), 341–411 (2006)
67. MIDENA, SENPLADES, IEE, MAGAP: Memoria técnica de amenazas a movimientos en masa del cantón Mira. Ministerio de Defensa Nacional, Secretaría Nacional de Planificación y Desarrollo, Instituto Espacial Ecuatoriano, Ministerio de Agricultura, Ganadería, Acuacultura y Pesca (2013)
68. Gómez, A., Goulart, C., Queiroz, G.: Evaluation of landslide susceptibility of Sete Cidades volcano (S. Miguel Islands, Azores). Nat. Hazards Earth Syst. Sci. **5**(3), 251–257 (2005)
69. IGEPN: Catálogo sísmico Homogeneizado hasta el 2009. Instituto Geofísico Escuela Politécnica Nacional. Solicitud de datos. Accedido el 10 de marzo de 2017 (2017)
70. Hernández, R., Fernández, C., Baptista, P.: Metodología de la investigación. McGraw-Hill, México (2006)
71. INAMHI: Anuario meteorológico. Instituto Nacional de Meteorología e Hidrología (2017)
72. Moreno, J., et al.: Validación de modelos geo-espaciales para cuantificar la fijación de carbono en el suelo. Subcuenca de Guayllabamba-Ecuador. Ecuador es calidad. Revista científica ecuatoriana **5**(1), 32–39 (2018)
73. ESRI: ArcGis for Desktop. Environmental Systems Research Institute. ESRI, California (2016)

74. Márquez, H.: Métodos matemáticos de evaluación de factores de riesgos para el patrimonio arqueológico: una aplicación GIS del método de jerarquías analíticas de T.L. Saaty. SPAL **6**(8), 21–37 (1999)
75. Selby, M.: Hillslope Materials and Processes. Oxford University Press, New York (1993)
76. Keefer, D.: Landslides caused by earthquakes. Geol. Soc. Am. Bull. **95**(4), 406–421 (1984)
77. González-Díez, A., Remondo, J., Díaz de Terán, J., Cendrero, A.: A methodological approach for the analysis of the temporal current and triggering factors of landslides. Geomorphology **30**(2), 95–113 (1999)
78. Rodríguez-Pineda, C.E., Yepes-Heredia, J.: Probabilistic landslide hazard for El Salvador. In: Margottini, C., Canuti, P., Sassa, K. (eds.) Landslide Science and Practice. Springer, Heidelberg (2013). https://doi.org/10.1007/978-3-642-31325-7_43
79. MIDENA, SENPLADES, IEE, MAGAP: Geoportal Proyecto: Generación de Geoinformación para la Gestión a Nivel Nacional. Ministerio de Defensa Nacional, Secretaría Nacional de Planificación y Desarrollo, Instituto Espacial Ecuatoriano, Ministerio de Agricultura, Ganadería, Acuacultura y Pesca (2016)
80. Fell, R.: Landslide risk assessment and acceptable risk. Can. Geotech. J. **31**(2), 261–272 (1994)
81. Margottini, C., Canuti, P., Sassa, K. (eds.): Landslide Science and Practice. Springer, Heidelberg (2013). https://doi.org/10.1007/978-3-642-31337-0
82. Schuster, R., Fleming, W.: Economic losses and fatalities due to landslides. Bull. Assoc. Eng. Geol. **23**(1), 11–28 (1986)
83. Brabb, E.: The world landslide problem. Episodes **14**(1), 52–61 (1991)
84. Schuster, R.L., Highland, L.: Socioeconomic and Environmental Impacts of Landslides in the Western Hemisphere. US Department of the Interior, US Geological Survey, Denver (2001)
85. Galacho, F., Arrebola, J.: Modelo de evaluación de la capacidad de acogida del territorio con SIG y técnicas de decisión multicriterio respecto a la implantación de edificaciones en espacios rurales. Investigaciones Geográficas **60**(1), 69–85 (2013)
86. Carrara, A., Cardinali, M., Detti, R., Guzzetti, F., Pasqui, V., Reichenbach, P.: GIS techniques and statistical models in evaluating landslide hazard. Earth Surf. Process. Landf. **16**(5), 427–445 (1991)
87. SGR: Escenario de probabilidad de generación de movimientos en masa Octubre - 2016. Secretaría de Gestión de Riesgos (2016)
88. Baiocchi, V., Dominici, D., Ferlito, R., et al.: Test of a building vulnerability model for L'Aquila earthquake. Appl. Geomat. **4**, 95–103 (2012). https://doi.org/10.1007/s12518-011-0065-x

GeoGebra as a Technological Tool in the Process of Teaching and Learning Geometry

Abdón Pari Condori[1](✉) (iD), Derling Jose Mendoza Velazco[2](✉) (iD),
and Roxana Auccahuallpa Fernández[2](✉) (iD)

[1] Universidad Adventista de Bolivia UAB, 528, Cochabamba, Bolivia
apariducho@gmail.com
[2] Universidad Nacional de Educación UNAE, Chuquipata 030154, Ecuador
derling969@gmail.com, roxana.auccahuallpa@unae.edu.ec

Abstract. The objective of the study was to determine the level of understanding and characterize the type of ideal geometric thinking that teachers demonstrate in solving problems with the use of the GeoGebra software. The research was of mixed character, with sequential exploratory design. It was structured in two phases. The population was made up of 120 teachers who attended the course entitled: Innovate and transform the teaching of mathematics with GeoGebra. The virtual course was developed by the National University of Education during the period 2019–2020. In the first phase of the quantitative phase, a diagnostic questionnaire of descriptive analysis was applied. The second qualitative phase applied an analytical questionnaire on the polygons issued by the participants. The results show that the participants understood the activities in a dynamic way. To learn geometry, the level of understanding was very good when using the GeoGebra. It was possible to characterize that 15% of the participants developed a basic geometric representation without connection, demonstrating a submissive and linear style in the development of activities. 35% of the participants worked on contrasting geometric polygons, representing a constructivist design of visual variables. Finally, 50% of the participants designed axial geometric polygons, representing a higher level of complexity and totalitarian figuration. In conclusion, the software generated a great interest and motivation in the pedagogical activities. With the use of GeoGebra a level of effective understanding is acquired in the development of geometry.

Keywords: GeoGebra · Teaching and learning of mathematics · Technological innovation · Geometry · Continuous training

1 Introduction

Never before has information and communication technology (ICT) had such an impact on individual and collective development in the field of education. According to [1], before the Covid-19 pandemic, several countries were going through a period of digital transformation, but at different speeds and in different ways depending on social strata, geographical location or sectors of activity.

© Springer Nature Switzerland AG 2020
G. Rodriguez Morales et al. (Eds.): TICEC 2020, CCIS 1307, pp. 258–271, 2020.
https://doi.org/10.1007/978-3-030-62833-8_20

In the case of Ecuador, education was aware of this transformation. There was a change in communication habits, business, and access to services. From this perspective, the Ecuadorian Institute of GeoGebra, based at the National University of Education (UNAE), is developing training courses in the use of GeoGebra as a teaching resource for mathematics. Courses are directed to basic education within the Continuous Training Program for in-service teachers. The course is developed in a bimodal way: a classroom part and a virtual part.

With the pandemic caused by VOC-19 and confinement status, people's dependence on technology has increased [1]. The current situation requires teleworking activities and virtual classes. In view of this situation, based on the experience gained in the bimodal course, a continuing education course was offered entitled: "Innovate and transform the teaching of mathematics with GeoGebra" (ITEMG). The course [2] has 200 free places for in-service teachers. Finally, only 120 places were occupied.

The ITEMG course consists of nine units, covering different topics. Each unit is developed separately during fifteen days with a virtual introduction through the zoom, after applying autonomous and cooperative works among teachers and the feedback of the facilitators. ITEMG allows for consideration of the demands, challenges and difficulties faced by teachers in their pedagogical practice and teacher training [2].

This study is part of a research project entitled "The impact of the use of GeoGebra in the teaching and learning process of mathematics in Ecuadorian teachers" developed by the Institutional Research Group Eureka 4i with interdisciplinary, intercultural, international and innovative studies [3].

1.1 General Objective of the Research

Determine the level of understanding that students have with the use of the GeoGebra software. Then, characterize the type of geometric thinking that teachers demonstrate in solving problems with the use of GeoGebra.

1.2 Specific Objectives

1. Perform a theoretical, pedagogical and didactic analysis issued by different authors when using GeoGebra in the process of teaching and learning mathematics
2. Design and develop a descriptive diagnostic questionnaire
3. To determine the level of understanding that participants acquire in the ITEMG course
4. Characterize the type of geometric thinking emitted by ITEMG course participants in solving problems with the use of the GeoGebra software

2 Background

2.1 Information and Communication Technologies

In 1983, the Center for Educational Technology at Harvard University began using information and communication technologies (ICTs) in learning mathematics and science in primary and secondary education. In this context, the use of ICTs is widely accepted in different areas of today's society. Likewise, with respect to teaching and learning mathematical content, various researches indicate that the implementation of ICTs offers opportunities for students. Opportunities to develop activities that favour exploration, formulation of conjectures, verification, discovery of properties and generalisation of results. However, such technologies have not been installed in formal education as naturally as they are in other areas such as economics, medicine, and communication, among others [4].

According to [5, 6], learning mathematics is effective only when the student is able to identify conditions for the use of mathematical knowledge in new situations. Although mathematics has been taught and learned for millennia, the nature and quality of mathematical teaching and learning has not been seriously studied until the last century. Learning mathematics is considered to be related to problem solving, because the heart of mathematics is problem solving and is a means of identifying, exploring, testing, and communicating solution strategies. In other words, when a person solves problems, he or she enters into a process of exploring different representations, searching for patterns, invariants and relationships between mathematical objects, which allow the presentation of arguments, communication of results, formulation of questions and setting out of new problems.

On the other hand, in the last decades the integration of ICTs has opened new paths in the process of teaching and learning mathematics. These routes have aroused great interest from great mathematicians, researchers in mathematical education and mathematics teachers [7].

However, the integration of ICT alone is not enough, software already has an important place in innovative development, it can also have a significant potential for implementation in mathematics learning [8]. The implementation of mathematical software requires development, research and more detailed study. The appropriate and effective use of ICT can increase the level of visualization in mathematics and improve student learning, and its implementation can contribute to improving the quality of education [9].

Visualization of digital learning resources in lectures and practices allows students to better understand mathematical concepts and processes for meaningful learning [10]. Didactic resources strengthen communicative competence for both students and teachers. One of the ways to improve the visualization of abstractions in Mathematics is an effective and appropriate pedagogical and didactic application supported by ICTs [11].

2.2 GeoGebra

There are a variety of digital resources for teaching mathematics related to geometry, for example, the use of a Dynamic Geometry System (DMS), Geometr's Sketchpad and Cabri. But many of these software applications were not created with a particular pedagogical approach, nor are they all freely available or suggested in the curriculum for mathematics teaching.

GeoGebra software is a free open source program that combines features of dynamic geometry software, computer algebra systems and spreadsheet programs [12]. GeoGebra was created by Markus Hohenwarter as part of his Master's thesis in Mathematics

Education at the University of Salzburg (Austria) in 2002. With its unique ability to illuminate both algebraic and geometric concepts. GeoGebra provides a mechanism to improve how mathematics is taught and learned in classrooms at all levels of the education system [13].

According to [14], an important tool during exploration within GeoGebra is dragging. The basic principle of dragging an object from a figure is that the figure should keep all its properties as it was built. That is to say, it is the one that differs from a mathematical object constructed from a drawing. Because it is possible to observe how the attributes, length of a segment, area, amplitude of one or several angles change. of the mathematical objects involved. The importance of this dragging tool is that it allows observing invariants and patterns among the elements of a constructed figure [15].

2.3 Continuing Education of Teachers

According to [16] one of the problems in integrating ICTs and mathematics is teacher training. [17, 18] They say that teachers are considering using GeoGebra, emphasizing that the education system is changing from traditional to new, from analog to digital.

Similarly, [19] they say, there is a general tendency for teachers to evaluate themselves as not being trained to use ICTs and that they have them available in educational institutions. They are trained to handle them technically, although their level depends on the novelty of the technology. They claim that they handle them at home, but not in educational institutions.

In addition, according to [20], they indicate that they have little training in the design and production of media, other than in their didactic use. Regardless of variables such as age and gender, teachers generally show great interest in being trained to use these didactic instruments. Although it is logical, as it happens with other variables, younger teachers are more concerned about their incorporation, use and training than older ones. They admit that they have not received a real qualification throughout their studies, to incorporate into their professional practice.

Research on the use of ICTs in teacher training is abundant. However, very little addresses the use of GeoGebra in teacher training, especially as it relates to Ecuadorian teachers. Therefore, the research emphasizes the use of GeoGebra software in the teaching and learning process of geometry in Ecuadorian teachers.

2.4 Ecuadorian Institute of GeoGebra

The Ecuadorian Institute of GeoGebra (IEG) is based at the National University of Education (UNAE). It was officially constituted on April 24, 2018, on the occasion of the celebration of the 6th Ibero-American GeoGebra Day. The objective of creating the Ecuadorian Institute of GeoGebra is to contribute to the purposes and functions of the International Institute of GeoGebra. The functions of the institute are to motivate, promote, support, and disseminate the use of GeoGebra as a powerful tool to innovate and transform the teaching of mathematics at all educational levels in Ecuador. GeoGebra is more than just dynamic mathematics software; it is an educational program that links the Science Technology, Engineering and Mathematics STEM project.

3 Research Method

3.1 Research Focus

The methodology of the research was of a mixed or multi-method type. The research design was "Field study". A theoretical review and documentary analysis was applied. These reviews allowed to complement, define and describe the object of study. It was possible to analyse and distribute the research time, without having to influence the variables involved. In this way, the use of the quantitative and qualitative paradigm is implied, a method recommended by [21].

3.2 Research Design

There are many multi-method research designs. The authors applied the Deplix method, defined by [22] as a sequential exploratory design. This design is done in two phases. In the first phase of a quantitative nature, numerical data are collected. Then the results are analyzed in an explanatory way. Based on the numerical data, the second phase begins. In the second phase, complementary qualitative data is collected and interpreted to meet the objectives set.

3.3 Population and Sample

The study population corresponds to the participants of the continuing education course "ITEMG" for the four-month period May-August 2020. Directly, the sample was 120 teachers (62 females and 48 male). All the participants in the course represented 17 provinces of Ecuador. The provinces of Azuay, Bolivar, Cañar, Carchi, Chimborazo, El Oro, Esmeraldas, Guayas, Loja, Los Ríos, Manabí, Napo, Orellana, Pastaza, Pichincha, Santo Domingo and Tungurahua. A non-probabilistic, purposive sample was established for the sample, no statistical formula was applied and all participants were chosen for the study [23].

3.4 Research Instruments

In order to respond to specific objective 2, a descriptive diagnostic questionnaire was designed. The questionnaire allowed the collection of data in the quantitative phase. The questionnaire measures the ease and understanding that GeoGebra provides in mathematics education. The questions were sent by e-mail to all the participants of the study. The answer options were of a scalar type. The very poor option has the lowest value with 1 PV point. Then the poor option has a value of 2 "D" points. The regular option was the intermediate level with 3 "R" points. The very good option had a score of 4 "VG". Finally, the excellent option with the score greater than 5 "E" points (see Table 1). A pilot test was applied to 5 participants to evaluate the level of reliability of the instrument. Cronbach's alpha coefficient was applied to the instrument for reliability analysis. The statistical value was 0.838 as [24] it is demonstrated that it is a reliable instrument.

Table 1. Table 1. Diagnostic questionnaire applied to ITEMG course participants.

Universidad Nacional de Educacion Docente del Grupo de Investigación Institucional EUREKA 4i	UNAE

Dear Teacher, This questionnaire aims to determine teachers' perceptions about learning mathematics with the use of the GeoGebra® software from the development of the course "Innovate and transform math teaching with GeoGebra®". The information you provide is an important contribution to further improve the development of the course. We kindly ask for your participation and guarantee the anonymity of your answers.

Items	On a scale of 1 to 5, how do you rate the premise 'The use of GeoGebra software favours:'?	1 VP	2 D	3 R	4 VG	5 E
		Options				
1	Understanding math concepts					
2	The development of critical and analytical thinking					
3	Mathematical logical reasoning					
4	Numerical reasoning					
5	Mathematical demonstrations in a dynamic way					
6	The verification of conjectures and mathematical postulates					
7	The discovery of objects and mathematical concepts					
8	Meaningful learning of mathematics					

Items	On a scale of 1 to 5, how do you rate the premise 'When using the GeoGebra® in the classroom the software allows	1 VP	2 D	3 R	4 VG	5 E
		Options				
9	To awaken students' interest and motivation in mathematics					
10	The development of skills for teamwork/collaborative work					
11	Understanding math concepts					
12	Develop positive and supportive attitudes towards learning mathematics					
13	The discovery of objects and mathematical concepts in the classroom.					
14	Understanding mathematics in a dynamic way					
15	The verification of postulates and concepts of abstract mathematics.					
16	A creative and dynamic construction of mathematical concepts					

The data obtained from the questionnaire were analysed in a descriptive manner. Based on the results, a second instrument of qualitative analysis is designated. The participants were asked to create from any polygon, to build a new polygon on one side less and whose area is equal to the initial polygon. In this way, it was possible to analyze and characterize the type of geometrical thinking emitted by the participants of the ITEMG course (see Table 2).

Table 2. Qualitative analysis questionnaire applied to ITEMG course participants

Universidad Nacional de Educacion Docente del Grupo de Investigación Institucional EUREKA 4i	▉ UNAE
Dear teacher, the purpose of this application is to identify the most common geometric models suitable for use with GeoGebra® software, based on the development of the course "Innovating and transforming mathematics teaching with GeoGebra®". The information you provide is an important contribution to further improve the development of the course. We kindly ask for your participation and guarantee the anonymity of your answers.	
Geometrical development	Figure
From any polygon, build a new polygon on one side less and whose area is equal to the initial polygon.	

The analysis of the activity proposed in Table 2 was developed in an interpretative way. The researchers developed the triangulation of analytical and theoretical data from different authors on the figures designed by the participants. The results are presented below.

4 Analysis of the Results

4.1 Diagnostic Phase - Quantitative

After developing the ITEMG course, the researchers applied the Diagnostic Questionnaire (see Table 1). The results of the premise "The use of the GeoGebra software favors" are shown in Fig. 1. The results of each item were averaged through an arithmetic mean, the highest average being the "very good" option with an average of 42.08%. Second, the regular option with an average of 35.72%. The excellent option averaged 16.14%. Then the poor option with an average of 5.41% and the lowest was 0.62% for the very poor option.

Finally, it can be indicated that the majority of participants consider that the use of GeoGebra greatly favors demonstrating and applying mathematical concepts. Similarly for [25], the development and didactic use of GeoGebra facilitates the generation of user-specific concepts. The manipulation of its graphic representation; later, through the identification of regularities observed in the graph, the algebraic expression is constructed as a way to represent the relationships between the quantities that intervene in the quantities of the situation.

This type of sequence is important because mathematical concepts such as the function are introduced with the graphical representation, based on experimentation with the software. GeoGebra offers algebraic representations that facilitate the development of critical and analytical thinking. According to [26], the GeoGebra system is a phenomenon that allows mathematical demonstrations to be made dynamically. Tools such as the GeoGebra software are useful resources in the mathematics classroom because

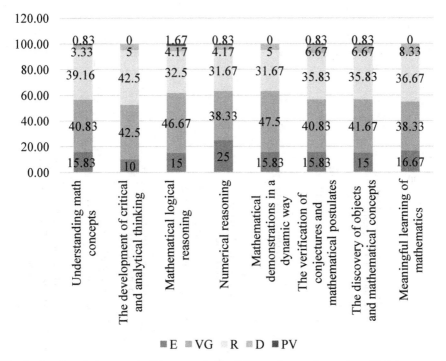

Fig. 1. Results of the premise'The use of GeoGebra software favours' applied to research participants.

they allow students to show, by putting into practice their previous knowledge, what they have been able to internalize so far.

The second premise, "Using the GeoGebra® software in the classroom allows", focused on the understanding and motivation that the software generates in the students. Similarly, when applying an average of the items, the first result was 46.77% considered very good. In second place the excellent option with an average of 26.87%. Then, the regular option with an average of 21.45%. The deficient option with an average value of 4.47%, the option with the lowest average was "very deficient" with a value of 0.41%. In this way, it can be described that the use of geography awakens interest and motivation in the student body. Like [14], it is established that geography is a dynamic component of exposure to and understanding of mathematical content. Creative construction depends on the teacher and his or her development, that is, the teacher must possess the basic skills of use in order to develop dynamic activities (see Fig. 2).

The dynamic activities in the mathematics classroom facilitate understanding [27]. For the researchers of the ITEMG course the results show that motivation improves academic performance. Students' performance can be positively affected by improving the development of their mathematical thinking and the level of competence in responding to problems associated with calculus and algebra. Finally, the third specific objective is answered, determining that the level of understanding acquired by ITEMG course

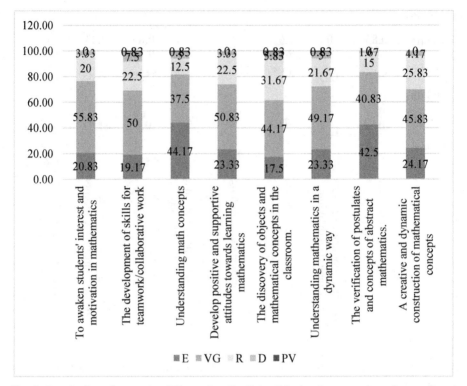

Fig. 2. Results from the premise 'When using GeoGebra® in the classroom the software allows' applied to research participants.

participants is very good. The "very good" level covers the competencies of developing critical thinking, logical reasoning, meaningful learning, dynamic creative teaching, motivation and understanding in the process of teaching and learning through the use of the GeoGebra software.

4.2   Qualitative - Interpretative Phase

After determining the level of understanding of the participants, the qualitative analysis questionnaire was executed to answer specific objective 4. In Table 2, it can be seen that the proposed activity was to design from any polygon, a new polygon on one side less and whose area is equal to that of the initial polygon. The analysis of the development of the activity as the geometric representation was presented with the following results:

Basic Geometric Representation without Connection

15% of the participants drew two polygons, so the second polygon has a smaller side than the first and its areas are equal. But by moving any of the free points of the polygons, the equality of area is no longer achieved. As shown below (See Fig. 3) (Table 3).

Graphic representation is understood more in line with the current concept of "meaning", which includes the emotional, social and cultural dimensions of the designer [28].

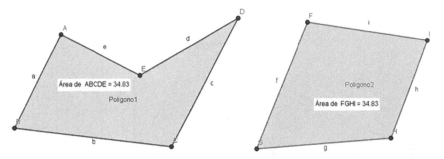

Fig. 3. Polygons drawn by participants with distant and unconnected geometric figures.

Table 3. Number of attempts to construct polygons with equal area

Number of attempts	Difficulties	Percentage
Those who managed on the first attempt	They had no difficulty	45%
Those who managed on the second attempt	Most have drawn and not built or were not related to each other	30%
Those who managed on the third attempt	For them, a second feedback was necessary	20%
Those who didn't make it	Despite the suggestion, they did not manage to carry out the activity as requested	5%
TOTAL		100%

In a certain sense, both terms could even be considered synonyms, although on this occasion the authors apply the representation of polygons in an interpretative manner with respect to their model of geometric thought in order to avoid confusion.

The two polygons in Fig. 3 represent a basic differentiation and organization from the topological point of view. The two polygons are distant and are characterized in the unconscious plane of a simple model. The teacher represents aspects of behaviorism and linear thinking, i.e., he only designs the requested figures without adding links between the polygons.

Contrast Geometric Representation. Another characteristic of the teachers in the development of the proposed activity was the use of connection or contrast by means of the vertices. It has been observed that 35% of them use the more classic or common figures such as the square and the triangle, that is, they lack that generalized understanding of any polygon. As shown in Figs. 4 and 5.

Contrast geometry is defined by the interposition of two or more figures, also when placing an image in front of or behind another one [29]. In Fig. 4, the participants placed contrasting polygons, between a square and a triangle, the figures are unified in common side GB and vertex B. Similarly, in Fig. 5, participants contrasted a triangle and

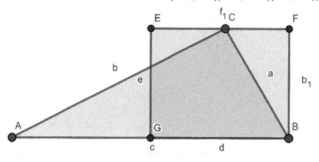

area of (5.42, -1.2)(8.88, -1.22)(8.9, 1.43)(5.44, 1.45) = 9.17

area of (1.96, -1.18)(8.88, -1.22)(7.3, 1.44) = 9.17

Fig. 4. Equal area of square and triangle developed by IEMTEG participants

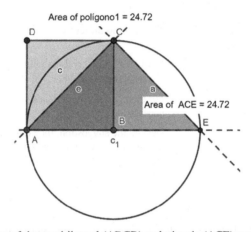

Fig. 5. Equal area of the quadrilateral (ABCD) and triangle (ACE) contrasted in a circle

a square, both circled by a circle. As for the perception of objects and levels of perception, the author demonstrates the qualities of geometric abstraction even if modifications are made. The author generates visual variables by establishing new parameters in his design. In the same way, at a constructivist level the author complies with the requirement of equality of areas, but his sides and vertices are interconnected in a dependent way. These two examples show the creativity generated by the author when applying GeoGebra. The perceptive constancy of form and value can also be appreciated by looking for models that are different from the common patterns of separate figures.

Axial Geometric Representation. Finally, 50% of the figures were of axial geometric design (see Fig. 6).

The level of axial geometric representation is constituted by the connection between the brain and the world, whether with respect to nature, others and oneself [30]. Figure 6 leads to an objective representation of the geometric continuity of polygons. It is perceived that the author has the capacity to justify two or more figures around two axial

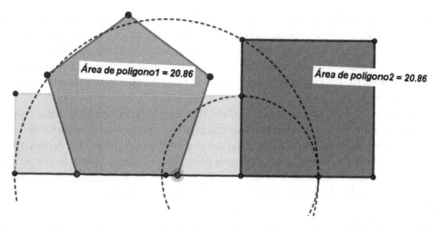

Fig. 6. Axial geometric representation in the equal area of three polygons (Color figure online)

axes. The polygons emitted by the activity were the pentagon and the square with equal area, but, to establish their design a green rectangle was added. All subscribed to a common axis.

Within the thematic part it is necessary to structure that the polygons are visually connected and they can be moved without difficulty that there is a division between them. These geometric designs represent a hierarchy of complexity and depth. At a cognitive level, the order and dynamic sequence of the course object is perceived. An order is also established to emphasize one or several structures that link polygons and other figures that are attached.

5   Conclusions

In conclusion, GeoGebra is one of the most important software since it facilitates and helps teachers to interact dynamically with thematic contents in the area of mathematics; this program is one of the technological options that enriches the quality of research and visualizes mathematics from different perspectives, supporting feedback; it also offers teachers strategies for instruction according to the needs of students. It also facilitates learning through virtual representations that are representations of reality and concentrates pedagogical benefits.

After analyzing the results in the quantitative phase, it is possible to describe that the participants acquire a level of effective understanding in the development of geometry. It has been proved that learning environments are not only physical spaces, tools or time distributions, but the result of the teacher-learner relationship from a digital didactic environment, versatile and according to the participants' degree of maturity, rich in significant activities with permanent changes, multiple resources and completely dynamic. GeoGebra also provided the motivation in students during the course, establishing a digital connectivity between teachers and students.

An effective and sustainable education is an innovative education that uses ICT and other means to improve the teaching and learning process in general and in mathematics in particular. At the same time, it seeks to meet the needs of current and future generations in relation to motivational, social and environmental aspects. In this way, teachers are motivated in their learning and continuous training not only in the use of GeoGebra, but in different areas or dimensions such as disciplinary, pedagogical, technological and human relations for the sustainable use of ICTs to raise the quality of education and life in the long term.

With respect to the characterization of the type of geometric thinking, three groups were structured. 15% designed basic unconnected geometric representations, demonstrating a submissive and linear style in the development of activities. 35% of the participants worked on contrasting geometric polygons, representing a constructivist design of visual variables. Finally, 50% of the participants designed axial geometric polygons, representing a higher level of complexity and totalitarian figuration.

References

1. García, F.: El sistema universitario ante la COVID-19: Corto, medio y largo plazo. En Universidad (2020). https://bit.ly/2YPUeXU
2. Universidad Nacional Abierta: Curso virtual, "Innovar y transformar la enseñanza de las matemáticas con GeoGebra (2020). https://oeiecuador.org/uploads/files/news/OEI-Educat ion/135/curso-de-GeoGebra-formacion-continua-unae.pdf
3. Universidad Nacional de Educación UNAE: Eureka 4i (2016). https://unae.edu.ec/oferta/eur eka-4i/
4. Artigue, M.: Tecnología y enseñanza de las matemáticas: desarrollo y aportaciones de la aproximación instrumental. Cuadernos de Investigación y Formación en Educación Matemática 6(8), 13–33 (2011)
5. Kilpatrick, J.: History of research in mathematics education. Encyclopedia of Mathematics Education, Springer, Cham (2020)
6. Schoenfeld, A.: Mathematics Problem Solving. Academic Press, New York (1985)
7. Pari, A.: El impacto de GeoGebra en el Desarrollo profesional del profesorado de matemáticas. Publisher UNAE, Ecuador (2019)
8. Mendoza, D.J., Mendoza, D.I.: Information and communication technologies as a didactic tool for the construction of meaningful learning in the area of mathematics. Int. Electro. J. Math. Edu. 13(3), 261–271 (2018). https://doi.org/10.12973/iejme/3907
9. Mendoza, D., Nieto, Z., Vergel, M.: Technology and mathematics as a cognitive component. J. Phys: Conf. Ser. 1414, 012007 (2019). https://doi.org/10.1088/1742-6596/1414/1/012007
10. Ballester, A.: Meaningful Learning in Practice. J. Educ. Hum. Dev. 3(4), 199–209 (2014)
11. Fernández, R., Delgado, L.: La realidad aumentada como recurso didáctico para la enseñanza de las matemáticas. Ciencias Aplicadas 10(7), 2560 (2020)
12. Sarmiento, W., Luna, K.: GeoGebra application of software in mathematics practices under a constructivist methodology. Revista Killkana Sociales 1(2), 45–50 (2017)
13. Zengin, Y.: Incorporating the dynamic mathematics software GeoGebra into a history of mathematics course. Int. J. Math. Educ. Sci. Technol. 49(7), 1083–1098 (2018). https://doi.org/10.1080/0020739X.2018.1431850
14. Iiris, A., Kjell, B., Mirko, R.: Generating the patterns of variation with GeoGebra: the case of polynomial approximations. Int. J. Math. Educ. Sci. Technol. 47(1), 45–57 (2016)
15. Umit, K.: Turkish mathematics teachers' experiences with GeoGebra activities: changes in beliefs. Res. Math. Educ. 14(3), 293–294 (2012)

16. Llorente, M.: Aspectos Fundamentales de la Formación del Profesorado en TIC. En Pixel-Bit. Revista de Medios y Educación **31**, pp. 121–130 (2008) https://idus.us.es/bitstream/handle/11441/14245/file_1.pdf?sequence=1
17. García, A., Tejedor, J.: Condiciones (actitudes, conocimientos, usos, intereses, necesidades formativas) a tener en cuenta en la formación del profesorado en TIC. Enseñanza **23**, 115–142 (2005)
18. Monedero, J.: Uso y evaluación de materiales educativos durante el desarrollo del curriculum: ¿Qué hacen los profesores?, ¿Qué pueden hacer? Pixel-Bit **12**, 55–64 (1999)
19. Carrillo, A., Llamas, I.: GeoGebra. Mucho más que geometría dinámica. Alfaomega Ra-Ma, México (2009)
20. Fernández, M., Cebreiro, B.: La integración de los medios y nuevas tecnologías en los centros y practicas docentes. Pixel-Bit **20**, 33–42 (2003)
21. Yanez, S., Martinez, M., Mendoza, D., Lucano, S., Sanchez, H., Barros, R.: The solitary and hatred within social media. Acad. J. Interdisc. Stud. **8**(3), 71–80 (2019)
22. Hernández, R., Fernández, C., Baptista, P.: Metodología de la investigación. McGraw Hill, México (2010)
23. Wright, S., Noble, R., Bailer, A.: Equal-precision allocations and other constraints in stratified random sampling. J. Stat. Comput. Simul. **77**(12), 1081–1089 (2007). https://doi.org/10.1080/10629360600897191
24. Pranav, D., Naved, A., Divya, G.: Genetically modified organisms: Reliability analysis and perceptions. J. Inf. Optim. Sci. **39**(7), 1401–1415 (2018)
25. Royati, A., Ahmad, F., Rohani, A.: The effects of GeoGebra on mathematics achievement: enlightening coordinate geometry learning. Procedia Soc. Behav. Sci. **8**, 686–693 (2010)
26. Martin, D.: Student's Guide to the Study, Practice, and Tools of Modern Mathematics. Chapman and Hall/CRC, New York (2010)
27. Gallego, F., Granados, H., Sanchez, O.: Influence of GeoGebra in the motivation and self-regulation of the learning of calculus and algebra in universities. Espacios **39**(17), 7–20 (2018)
28. Asghar, J., Mohammad, K., Mansour, K.: Representational approaches in graphic design. Bagh- e Nazar **14**(50), 49–56 (2017)
29. Monedero, J.: Simulación visual de materiales: teoría, técnicas, análisis de casos. Publicacions Academiques Digitals de la UPC, Barcelona (2015)
30. Castellaro, M.: El concepto de representación mental como fundamento epistemológico de la psicología. Límite **6**(24), 55–67 (2011)

A Data as a Service Metamodel for Managing Information of Healthcare and Internet of Things Applications

Priscila Cedillo$^{(\boxtimes)}$ ⓘ, Wilson Valdez$^{(\boxtimes)}$ ⓘ, Paúl Cárdenas-Delgado$^{(\boxtimes)}$ ⓘ, and Daniela Prado-Cabrera$^{(\boxtimes)}$ ⓘ

Universidad de Cuenca, Cuenca Av 12 de Abril S/N, Cuenca, Ecuador
{priscila.cedillo,wilson.valdezs,paul.cardenasd,
daniela.pradoc}@ucuenca.edu.ec

Abstract. Internet of Things (IoT) applications nowadays generate a large amount of data, which are continually requiring adequate treatment and services on the Cloud to be available to stakeholders. Healthcare applications manage critical data from different sources as patient charts, Electronic Health Record (EHR), and devices which need security levels, data formatting, and quality of data due to their importance and sensitivity. Data as a Service (DaaS) is a data management framework provided though services on Cloud to bring data storage, integration, processing, analysis services, security, availability, elasticity, and quality characteristics to the data concerning the stakeholders. In this context, this paper proposes a data management solution deployed as DaaS for the healthcare domain presented through a metamodel focused on the federation pattern of data based on an Extract-Transform-Load (ETL) model for data classification; and considering a brief analysis of the non-functional characteristics proper of the DaaS domain as the security, confidentiality, priority, and availability. The metamodel is validated through an instantiation process using the MOntreal Cognitive Assessment (MOCA) test as the entry. Finally, it is presented a discussion from four stakeholder perspectives (e.g., data engineer, IoT solution developer, data quality analyst, health professional) about the solution.

Keywords: Data as a service · Internet of things · Ambient assisted living · Healthcare · Metamodel · Model-Driven engineering

1 Introduction

Nowadays, organizations have made significant progress due to the emergence and impact of important paradigms as Cloud Computing, Data Analysis, and the Internet of Things (IoT) [1–5]. IoT is a global network of interconnected machines and mobile devices that interact among them, where that interaction is one of the essential bases for the technology advances [6]. Application areas, research, and challenges of this paradigm are expanded to many fields such as healthcare systems, Ambiental Intelligence, and emerging from them, Ambient Assisted Living (AAL) systems [7, 8]. Therefore, the

© Springer Nature Switzerland AG 2020
G. Rodriguez Morales et al. (Eds.): TICEC 2020, CCIS 1307, pp. 272–286, 2020.
https://doi.org/10.1007/978-3-030-62833-8_21

healthcare industry is one of the most benefited because of technological developments related to IoT [1, 9, 10]. Consequently, the improvement of the infrastructure, communications advances, medical solutions, and devices connected generate a huge amount of data. Particularly, in the healthcare domain, the information that comes from devices, web or mobile applications, patient charts, or Electronic Health Records (EHR) is dispersed in autonomous and heterogeneous information systems due to locations, formats, and types of data treatment. Hence, this diversity causes the decentralization of information and disparity in format, security levels, and quality of data [11, 12].

IoT and AAL are widely accepted technological paradigms in the healthcare field [8, 13]. AAL are living environments focused on monitoring and supporting daily user activities by sensing and reacting to defined actions to support patients by creating context-awareness systems and also managing the obtained information [6]. The combination of these and other technologies in the health domain during the time has derived in the term of e-Health, which is defined by Ahern et al. [14] as an emerging field at the intersection of medical informatics, public health, and business, which refers to the services of health and information delivered or improved through the Internet and related technologies. In a broader sense, the term characterizes not only a technical development but also a state of mind, a way of thinking, an attitude, and a commitment to global networked thinking to improve health care at the local, regional, and worldwide [15–17]. e-Health encompasses fields such as EHR, electronic medical records (EMR), telehealth, telemedicine, health information systems, health IT data consumer, and mobile Health (m-Health). The heterogeneity of the sources from where these data are obtained require standardization in their formats, to describe, store, and protect them. Moreover, since the sanitary point of view, the patient registry must contain uniform information about his/her individual characteristics, which must be systematically and comprehensively collected to serve the previously established research goals, clinical practices, or health policy objectives [18].

The rise up of IoT applications in the healthcare field has increased the number of connected devices in an AAL such as sensors, devices, applications, and thus, the amount of collected data [19]. The study presented in [20] shows that the amount of data generated by approximately 41.6 billion connected IoT devices in 2025 will generate 79.4 zettabytes (ZB) of data. For this reason, data standardization in e-Health systems is essential for an optimal sharing and management of information. Then, several existing formats can be used in this domain [21].

Nowadays, there is a growing trend to move towards service-oriented architectures that have been encompassed into Cloud Computing paradigms (e.g., Infrastructure as a Service, Platform as a Service, Software as a Service, Data as a Service) [22]. Data as a Service (DaaS) is considered a data management strategy that uses the Cloud to offer data storage, integration, processing, and analysis services [22]. The intrinsic characteristics of DaaS provide users security, availability, elasticity, and quality characteristics offered by Cloud environments [23]. In summary, DaaS brings a service focused on efficient data storage and processing. Here, data are raw material, which is obtained from devices, or applications, and are offered to domain experts and users for helping them in taking decisions [22]. DaaS adopt a set of information service patterns proposed by IBM, which is divided into three components: i) pattern data federation, ii) data consolidation pattern, and iii) data cleansing pattern [24].

In a previous study [25] was presented the adaptive solution of a middleware architecture located between smart devices and Cloud Computing to enhance the management of the heterogeneity of data providing from IoT devices in AAL environments. That middleware provides configuration options, adaptability, and bearability for different environments. Also, it gets data but does not manage the information beyond the context of its architecture. Thus, in this paper, it is proposed: i) a data management solution deployed as DaaS for the healthcare domain; ii) a metamodel focused on the federation pattern of data based on an Extract-Transform-Load (ETL) model for data classification; iii) a brief analysis of the non-functional characteristics proper of the DaaS domain (e.g., security, confidentiality, priority, availability); and iv) a first approach towards a data classification into categories for further use to provide insights to final users and domain experts.

Therefore, to demonstrate the feasibility of the solution, a medical record is instantiated by using the metamodel. This medical record provines from a neuropsychological test used to a neurocognitive intervention in an AAL environment. This test generates different data formats that will be aligned to a unique classification using the model.

Finally, the structure of this paper is as follows: Sect. 2 presents related work. Section 3 presents the DaaS framework. Also, Sect. 4 presents the DaaS metamodel for healthcare. Section 5 shows the instantiation of the metamodel. Then, Sect. 6 discusses the metamodel from four different stakeholder perspectives (i.e., data analytics, data quality, IoT, medical). And, Sect. 7 presents conclusions and further work.

2   Related Work

In this section, there are described several studies that address DaaS solutions or conceptual models related to data generated by IoT, AAL, and e-Health domain.

Rajesh et al. [22] present a study about the importance of the implementation and the challenges of DaaS. It proposes one of the first approaches to data treatment and to conceive it as a service. Hence, it presented a group of steps to develop a DaaS model based on the data value chain. Finally, it shows some use case examples such as secondary use of personal health data, data governance, among others. Thence in the context of health, the importance of adequate data management generates some advantages such as monitoring the health of the population, determine the effectiveness of treatment, quantify prognosis, assess the usefulness of preventive strategies, support administrative functions, monitor the adequacy of care, among others. Hereof, the importance of addressing data management techniques aligned to new solutions such as DaaS in e-health is evident, to benefit stakeholders in this domain.

Valdez et al. [26] present a metamodel of data infrastructure for managing information obtained from AAL environments. That metamodel provides the data flow starting from records obtained in the IoT devices and ends on the Cloud crossing Fog Computing layers. Moreover, it includes communication protocols, security features, and the relationship between elements in AAL environments. The metamodel was evaluated, instantiating the classes, and then verifying the relationships between those classes and the data structures. While, it presents a data infrastructure for AAL, where data comes from sensors; however, there are two concerns: on the one hand, the metamodel does not consider other sources of data as EHR, EMR, or e-Health applications; and on the other hand, data is not stored considering DaaS models.

Concerning healthcare, Boonma et al. [24] present a distributed DaaS framework; which helps to assure the level of data quality and improves the performance of data analytics. That DaaS framework consists of two parts: Firstly, a distributed DaaS infrastructure, which handles data processing, such as ETL, data quality checking, and caching. Secondly, a client data adapter, which is connected to the first part to retrieve and format data into a representative structure suitable for the client application. The model is a complete DaaS infrastructure for health systems, which is focused on improving data quality and system performance. However, the study does not consider other sources of data like EHR, EMR, sensors, or devices.

Besides, Amarouche et al. [27] propose an architecture for the automatic composition of DaaS Web services about EHR published by heterogeneous health information systems, which employs different data standards and proposes a two-level ontology. The first level models the generic data concepts and their inter-relationships; the second level allows the specification of a concept of the first level that is represented in different health ontologies and data standards. On the one hand, those ontologies are used to specify EHR DaaS and mediation services; on the other hand, they specify user queries. However, the study does not solve the complex data transformations between input and output parameters of EHR DaaS, and also it does not include data quality aspects.

Consequently, the metamodel proposed in this paper presents a solution based on DaaS, which considers quality characteristics at the moment of collecting and delivering data to users by taking into account all the possible data sources and data stakeholders in healthcare applications that include IoT technologies. Moreover, to structure a solution that considers non-functional requirements, security levels, and providing data service according to the need of data of a specific user in this kind of application.

3   DaaS Framework

Data as a Service (DaaS) is a new service model that has emerged from Cloud Computing technologies. DaaS architectures aim to offer data services following the pay-as-you-go service model [28]. DaaS offers a framework where the analysis and insurance of data quality (e.g., reliability, accessibility, precision, consistency, security), cleansing, and enriching data is made in a centralized place. Then, these data are offered to different systems, applications, or users with elastic access to data, scalability, high availability, and system performance by demand irrespective of the location of the organization or network [22]. Those properties are necessary to provide reliable information that allows a proper analysis and processing of data. From this, the DaaS solution offers the following advantages *(i)* A*gility and simplicity* of the data access and ease of making changes according to customer requirements. *(ii)Cost-effectiveness*, the performance improves despite higher demand. *(iii) Data quality* is the main benefit of DaaS concerning better data delivery users.

Moreover, all the benefits presented by a DaaS model depend on the non-functional characteristics of the data, such as reliability, accessibility, accuracy, con-sistency, security, scalability, among others. DaaS model aims to guarantee a better quality of data service, improving all of these non-functional characteristics. Thereof, some of the most important non-functional characteristics of data quality within a DaaS model are described in detail in the ISO 25012 [29] standard.

3.1 DaaS in Healthcare and IoT Technologies

According to the World Health Organization (WHO), data reliability and precision play an important role in the health system [30]. Mostly data provining from health and IoT systems are found in formats such as CSV, XML, JSON, or others [31]. Those formats, although they are useful for several consumers, they are not appropriate for all the solutions, because it represents a problem when accessing and consuming the information in non-standardized formats.

Figure 1 shows a representation of stakeholders that consumes data from DaaS in healthcare IoT applications (i.e., health professional, external consumer, data quality analyst, data engineer, patient, IoT solution developer, administration and legal staff).

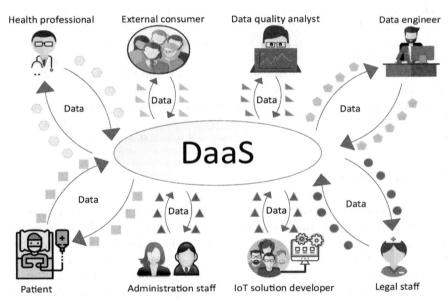

Fig. 1. DaaS model from the perspective of stakeholders in a health system and IoT

On the other hand, Fig. 2 represents the data sources in DaaS architecture in an IoT healthcare system. As it is shown, the system may have several data sources or data providers and, additionally, several types of data consumers. Sometimes, several stakeholders accomplish several roles at a time, such as data providers and consumers (e.g., a doctor who enters a medical record and subsequently consults data from other patients). Another example is a device with sensors (source) and actuators (consumer) within an AAL environment. All of them, coexisting within an ecosystem of a healthcare IoT application.

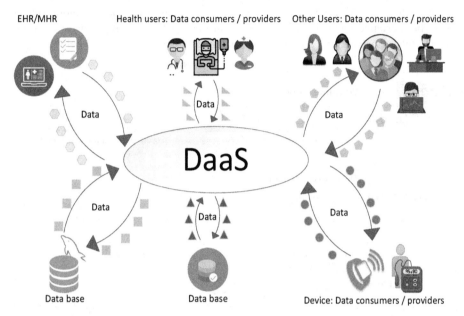

Fig. 2. DaaS model from the perspective of data sources in a health system and IoT.

The DaaS model allows users to enter data in the format they handle; and, in turn, consume the same or other data in a suitable format. In summary, stakeholders can retrieve data in the format that they choose. Also, it is essential to emphasize the importance of the non-functional characteristics related to data quality. Access to data always is validated by a data service, which allows or denies the data access according to confidentiality and authorization constraints.

3.2   Data Federation and Extract-Transform-Load (ETL)

As already mentioned, in a healthcare IoT application, data can be gathered from different sources, and therefore in a variety of formats. Then, in this paper, the ETL process is considered. DaaS carried out ETL automatically; therefore, users can access data as a service. The ETL process is used by several proposals [32–35] and consists of a set of patterns divided into three parts: i) data federation, ii) data consolidation, and iii) data cleaning [24, 27].

The Data federation aims to integrate multiple heterogeneous data sources with efficient and low redundancy way. On the other hand, the data consolidation pattern focuses on solving conflicting data from multiple sources and creates a standard data model. Finally, the data cleaning pattern improves the consistency and quality of data based on that data model [24].

4   DaaS Metamodel for Healthcare

This section presents an initial proposal of a DaaS metamodel of the IoT healthcare domain for AAL. The provided services for this DaaS metamodel could be configuration, data auditing, network access, temporary storage, data transformation, among others [24]. The presented metamodel is aligned with the three ETL components (i.e., *data extract, data transform,* and *data load*) as shown in Fig. 3, and described below:

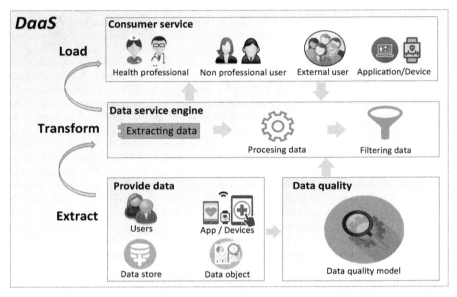

Fig. 3. DaaS model from the ETL perspective in a health system and IoT.

Data Extract: It loads data from all different sources in their original format. These data can be stored in the database with JSON format and accessible from the network.

Data Transformation: It combines the data from the data extractor into a single data set. Further, this procedure transforms the data extractor format from different sources in the data load format; and it assigns the correct format to each stakeholder. Thus, this procedure analyzes the data's non-functional characteristics and service quality.

Data Load: It receives requests from service clients, and pass this request to the transformation procedure, for later assign and load the data to different stakeholder. Further, this procedure analyses the quality data previously to delivery to data clients..

In this metamodel, the *extraction* component receives data in a JSON format from different sources, and processes those data; then, this component carries out an analysis of the quality through a data quality model. Then, it performs the transformations and data processing. These transformations are left as further work. Finally, it is considered the process which provides data to the different types of users through the *load* activity.

The metamodel aims to deal with problems emerging from the AAL applications due to the diversity of data sources and types generated by IoT devices and customers. These problems can affect data quality, system performance, and data access. Thus, the model is focused on managing the different data sources or providers (e.g., prototypes, devices, tests, medical signals, data consumers) that may exist in an AAL environment. The model has two main parts: i) a data quality model and ii) a data service model. The second part depends directly on the first since it considers non-functional characteristics related to the data quality before being used in the data service engine.

Also, the model presents the monitoring and operationalization requirements used in the DaaS process. Figure 4 shows the metamodel and, thus, the metaclasses for the DaaS quality model, whose first part is based on the SaaS quality model presented in [26]. The quality model is aligned with the ISO 25010 [36] and ISO 25012 [29] standards. This model allows the definition of the entire set of characteristics, sub-characteristics, and attributes for the proposed system's classes. Moreover, the *Data Analisys Model* metaclass represents both the federation process and the consolidation of the data (see Fig. 4). Likewise, the metamodel considers a service quality analysis, which, in a certain way, serves as an instrument for validating data cleanliness.

The *operationalization* metaclass allows the measurement by applying a metric and considers the different cloud levels (SaaS, PaaS, IaaS, DaaS). In this case, the metamodel prioritizes the DaaS level; this is useful because there are several non-functional requirements for data (e.g., scalability, elasticity, security) that need to be monitored at different levels of the stack of the services [37]. These requirements are also used by *data* metaclass, which has attributes related to data characteristics, and the non-functional requirements. Moreover, it is essential to specify the stakeholder's perspective using the monitoring information; in this case, it will only be focused on the provider, data sources, and the consumer of the data. The *Service Consumer* metaclass includes the users' characteristics and the data formats to be requested.

The information contained in this metamodel is useful for data management according to the perspective of quality and service consumption. The *DirectMetric-Operationalization* metaclass represents a measure of an attribute that does not depend on any other measure; meanwhile, the *IndirectMetricOperationalization* metaclass represents measures that are derived from other *DirectMetricOperationalizations* or *IndirectMetricOperationalizations*. The *Platform* and *MeasurementMethod* metaclasses represent a form of measure the Quality of DaaS and the data characteristics [30].

The metamodel includes classes that represent the data sources (e.g.., sensors, applications, users). Users have their privileges categories for accessing to data. Also, there are considered the types of data, and the different health formats (e.g., NH7, FHIR, EHR, EMR), which can be used in the system and are aligned to an extensive list of existing medical standards. An important metaclass is *Service Consumer*; this class presents attributes to know characteristics of consumer type, like the required format, consumer role, privileges, among other. The enumeration *Consumer Authorization*, shows the types of authorization have been proposed by following the classification of authorization for users presented in [38] and the data security features outlined in ISO 25012.

Moreover, the *Data Analisys Model* metaclass represents the engine for managing data. At the moment far, we do not present a specific processing system for the DaaS

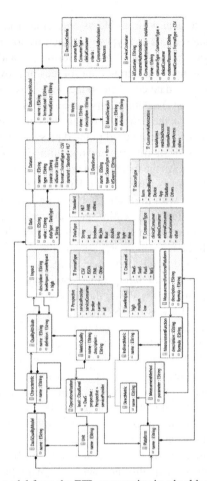

Fig. 4. DaaS model from the ETL perspective in a health system and IoT

service. However, according to the characteristics of the analyzed system and the proposed model, it is possible to use grouping techniques, data mining, or classification techniques which will be addressed as future work.

5   Instantiation of the Metamodel

To evaluate the feasibility of the presented metamodel is made an instantiation about a particular healthcare solution, by using the implementation tools (Java Eclipse design tools). This instantiation aims to evaluate the correct relationship between the metaclasses and the inclusion of the needed components for the traceability of data from different sources. In this case, an excerpt from the MOntreal Cognitive Assessment (MOCA) [39] test was used as a data source from healthcare (see Fig. 5). This test evaluates the cognitive functions and the mental state of people. Remarkably, the mild cognitive impairment by measuring cognitive domains such as concentration, attention, executive functions, among others.

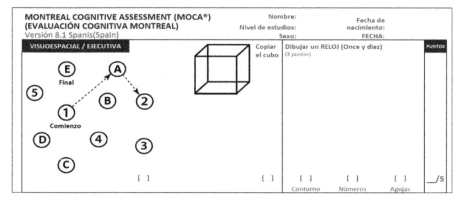

Fig. 5. Excerpt of MOCA test [39].

Then, from the MOCA test, two dynamic instances were generated. On the one hand, an instance that is based on the *"Data Analysis Model"* primary metaclass, as shown in Fig. 6, which represents the complete infrastructure and displays all the metaclasses contained in the DaaS metamodel. On the other hand, an instance generated from the DaaS quality model module, where the *"DaaS Quality Model"* metaclass was taken as the container. Below, the complete representation with all its classes deployed is shown.

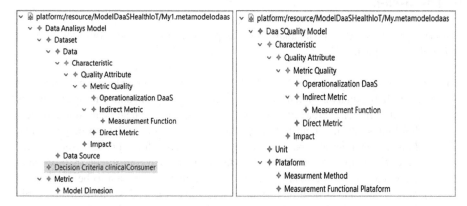

Fig. 6. Metamodel Instantiation

Finally, in order to instantiate it with values and show how the metamodel should be used; it was entered the attributes of each class with different types of data regarding the MOCA test. Thereof, different data types extracted from the visoespacial activity of the excerpt of the test (e.g., string, date, image, integer) were entered as an example (See, Fig. 5, Fig. 7 a–d, Fig. 7 e-f, Fig. 7 g-h). In this sense, the validity of the metamodel could be verified.

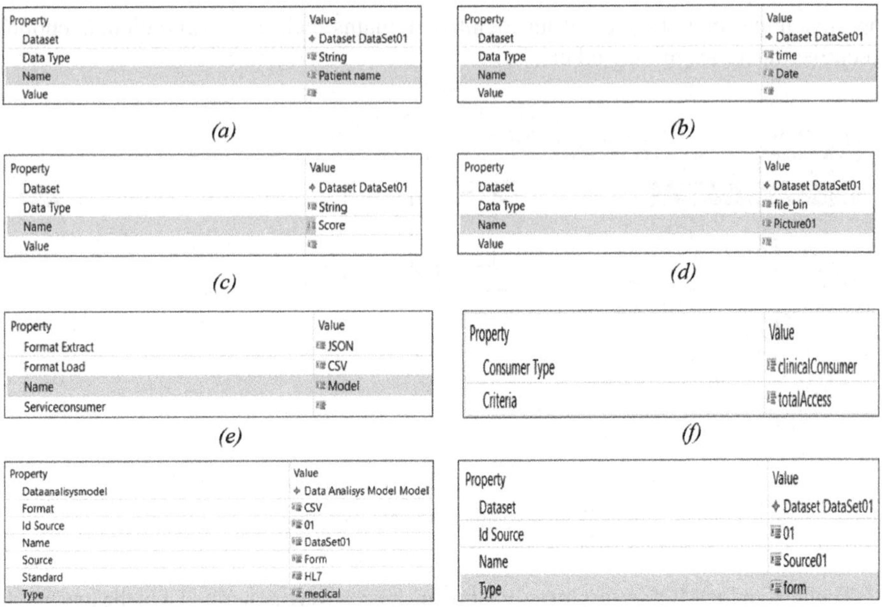

Property	Value
Dataset	Dataset DataSet01
Data Type	String
Name	Patient name
Value	

(a)

Property	Value
Dataset	Dataset DataSet01
Data Type	time
Name	Date
Value	

(b)

Property	Value
Dataset	Dataset DataSet01
Data Type	String
Name	Score
Value	

(c)

Property	Value
Dataset	Dataset DataSet01
Data Type	file_bin
Name	Picture01
Value	

(d)

Property	Value
Format Extract	JSON
Format Load	CSV
Name	Model
Serviceconsumer	

(e)

Property	Value
Consumer Type	clinicalConsumer
Criteria	totalAccess

(f)

Property	Value
Dataanalisysmodel	Data Analisys Model Model
Format	CSV
Id Source	01
Name	DataSet01
Source	Form
Standard	HL7
Type	medical

(g)

Property	Value
Dataset	Dataset DataSet01
Id Source	01
Name	Source01
Type	form

(h)

Fig. 7. (a-d) Data class attributes with different types of data (e) DataAnalisysModel class attributes (f) DecisionCriteria class attrbutes (g) ServiceConsumer class attributes (h) Data Source class attributes

6   Discussion

In this section, it is presented an analysis of the proposed metamodel from four different stakeholder perspectives:

(i) *Data engineer stakeholder.* Nowadays, the extraction of knowledge or detection of patterns in big data through the use of machine learning and data mining techniques is essential in many areas of science and industry. In the healthcare domain, new technologies advancement has caused massive amounts of data to be generated, and thus, its sources also become heterogeneous. Therefore, it is necessary to have services that help the accessibility of data for all types of consumers. In the context of data analysis, it is crucial to have a service that allows data to be obtained in an appropriate and structured format, as this makes the analysis more manageable and much faster the data preprocessing and data preparation. When analyzing data, it is always essential to have a domain expert, many times the access to the data and the format in which it is presented for a data mining or machine learning process are not easy to understand (e.g., doctor), but this domain expert must help data engineers in understanding the context of data. Therefore, technology such as DaaS bridges the activities between a data engineer and an expert in the domain. Moreover, it provides data in a format suitable for their pertinent purposes.

(ii) *IoT solution developer stakeholder.* A concern within an IoT application is the collection and the communication of data with the analysis platform. Thus, adequate control of the data flow is necessary due to the need to process the information in real-time and deliver information opportunely to application analysts or another stakeholder through dashboards for decision making. In this case, the high availability of the data services is a fundamental base and even more if there are certain conditions established on the Service Level Agreements (SLA). Therefore, the presentation of this metamodel shows a promising framework for proper data management in a Healthcare IoT application.

(iii) *Data quality analyst stakeholder.* Quality characteristics are necessary when storing data. High-quality data contribute to health personnel in making decisions. However, for the use of collected data, it should be accurate, timely, and available when it is needed. Moreover, the information generated from data must meet the real world and the patient's status. Several standards should be considered (i.e., IEEE 25012), which shows the necessary characteristics, sub characteristics, and attributes that must be considered while data is being collected.

(iv) *Health professional stakeholder.* Data collected from patients in health care is essential to establish medical records. The benefits for health personnel of efficiently accessing patients' clinical information are multiple (e.g., improving patient health care, including safety, patient-centeredness, communication between professionals, doctor-patient relationship, timeliness, equity). Concentrating data in a database contributes significantly to health professionals due to help in taking better solutions related to diagnosis and therapeutic issues. When health care personnel have access to complete and accurate information, patients receive better medical care be-cause professionals can improve the ability to diagnose diseases and reduce or prevent medical errors. Medical errors are a public health problem, and it is a challenge to discover its origin. However, with a complete data record and efficient and effective access, the occurrence of adverse events can be identified and recognized; with this information, health personnel can make decisions based on learning to prevent the occurrence of future adverse events. Managing information system supports health personnel with timely feedback about patients' health condition, especially on groups that suffer from a specific clinical condition or disability, or who are taking specific medicines ad need for specific preventive measures. Also, it saves costs and efforts in diagnostic tests that can be redundant.

7 Conclusions and Future Work

Internet of Things applications nowadays generate a large amount of data which are continually requiring adequate treatment and services on Cloud to the right distribution to stakeholders. Healthcare applications manage critical data from different sources as patient charts, EHR, and devices which need security levels, data formatting, and quality of data due to their importance and sensitivity. DaaS is a data management framework provided though services on Cloud to bring data storage, integration, processing, analysis services, security, availability, elasticity, and quality characteristics to the data concerning the stakeholders. In this context, this paper proposes a data management solution deployed as DaaS for the healthcare domain presented through a metamodel focused on the federation pattern of data based on an ETL model for data classification; and considering a brief analysis of the non-functional characteristics proper of the DaaS domain as the security, confidentiality, priority, and availability. The metamodel is validated through an instantiation process using a MOCA test as the entry. Finally, it is presented a discussion from four stakeholder perspectives (e.g., Data engineer, IoT solution developer, Data quality analyst, Health professional) about the solution. These points of view agree that obtaining application information in a data format consistent with expertise is timely for the tasks that are incumbent on stakeholders. Thus, this solution is useful from any of the points of view presented.

For future work, it is mentioned the implementation of this metamodel in a solution deployed on the Cloud. Then a validation of the implementation in a real AAL application and obtain feedback from stakeholders through experimental evaluations when using the implemented data service.

Acknowledgment. The authors would like to thank to Corporación Ecuatoriana para el Desarrollo de la Investigación y Academia–CEDIA, for the partial financial support given to the present research, development, and innovation work through its CEPRA program, especially for the "CEPRA XIV-2020- 07 Adultos Mayores" fund.

Moreover, this work is part of the research project: "Design of architectures and interaction models for assisted living environments for elderly people. Study case: ludic and social environments", winner of the Call for Research Projects DIUC XVIII; Hence, we thank "Dirección de Investigación de la Universidad de Cuenca-DIUC" for its academic and financial support.

References

1. Thimbleby, H.: Technology and the future of healthcare. J. Public Health Res. **2**(3), 28 (2013)
2. Chandra, A., Skinner, J.: Technology growth and expenditure growth in health care. J. Econ. Lit. **50**(3), 645–680 (2012)
3. Padhy, R.P., Patra, M.R., Satapathy, S.C.: Cloud computing: security issues and research challenges. Int. J. Comput. Sci. Inf. Technol. Secur. (IJCSITS) **1**(2), 136–146 (2011)
4. Marston, S., Li, Z., Bandyopadhyay, S., Zhang, J., Ghalsasi, A.: Cloud computing - the business perspective. Decis. Support Syst. **51**(1), 176–189 (2011)
5. Lasi, H., Fettke, P., Kemper, H.-G., Feld, T., Hoffmann, M.: Industry 4.0. Bus. Inf. Syst. Eng. **6**(4), 239–242 (2014). https://doi.org/10.1007/s12599-014-0334-4
6. Lee, I., Lee, K.: The internet of things (IoT): applications, investments, and challenges for enterprises. Bus. Horiz. **58**(4), 431–440 (2015)
7. Kabene, S.M.: Healthcare and the effect of technology: developments, challenges and advancements: developments, Challenges and Advancements. IGI Global, Hershey (2010)
8. Memon, M., Wagner, S.R., Pedersen, C.F., Hassan, F., Beevi, A., Hansen, F.O.: Ambient assisted living healthcare frameworks, platforms, standards, and quality attributes. Sensors **14**(3), 4312–4341 (2014)
9. Yin, Y., Zeng, Y., Chen, X., Fan, Y.: Journal of Industrial Information Integration The internet of things in healthcare: An overview. J. Ind. Inf. Integr. **1**, 3–13 (2016)
10. Patel, A., Singh, N.M., Kazi, F.: Internet of Things and Big Data Technologies for Next Generation Healthcare. vol. 23, October 2017

11. Mathew, P.S., Pillai, A.S.: Big data solutions in healthcare: problems and perspectives. In: 2015 IEEE International Conference on Innovations in Information, Embedded and Communication Systems, ICIIECS 2015 (2015)
12. Berndt, D.J., Fisher, J.W., Hevner, A.R., Studnicki, J.: Healthcare data warehousing and quality assurance. Comput. (Long. Beach. Calif) **34**(12), 56–65 (2001)
13. Yin, Y.: The internet of things in healthcare: an overview. J. Ind. Inf. Integr. **1**, 3–13 (2016)
14. Ahern, D.K., Kreslake, J.M., Phalen, J.M.: What is eHealth (6): Perspectives on the evolution of eHealth research. J. Med. Internet Res. **8**(1), e4 (2006)
15. Hill, J.W., Powell, P.: The national healthcare crisis: is eHealth a key solution? Bus. Horiz. **52**(3), 265–277 (2009)
16. Gibbons, M.C.: eHealth Solutions for Healthcare Disparities. Springer, New York (2008). https://doi.org/10.1007/978-0-387-72815-5
17. Wernhart, A., Gahbauer, S., Haluza, D.: eHealth and telemedicine: practices and beliefs among healthcare professionals and medical students at a medical university. PLoS ONE **14**(2), e0213067 (2019)
18. Gliklich, R.E., Dreyer, N.A., Leavy, M.B.: Patient Registries. Agency for Healthcare Research and Quality (US) (2014)
19. Linchpin, S.E.O.: Guide To The Connected Healthcare Device Market and Growing Market Share (2020). https://linchpinseo.com/guide-to-connected-healthcare-device-market/. Accessed 07 Jul 2020
20. IDC, The Growth in Connected IoT Devices Is Expected to Generate 79.4ZB of Data in 2025, According to a New IDC Forecast (2019). https://www.idc.com/getdoc.jsp?containerId=prUS45213219. Accessed 29 May 2020
21. Abouelmehdi, K., Beni-Hessane, A., Khaloufi, H.: Big healthcare data: preserving security and privacy. J. Big Data **5**(1), 1–18 (2018). https://doi.org/10.1186/s40537-017-0110-7
22. Rajesh, S., Swapna, S., Shylender Reddy, P. Dr.: Data as a service (Daas) in cloud computing. Glob. J. Comput. Sci. Technol. September 2012
23. Liu, F., Mao, J., Bohn, R., Messina, J., Badger, L., Leaf, D.: NIST cloud computing reference architecture. NIST **500**, 35 (2011)
24. Boonma, P., Natwichai, J., Khwanngern, K., Nantawad, P.: DAHS: a distributed data-as-a-service framework for data analytics in healthcare. In: Xhafa, F., Leu, F.-Y., Ficco, M., Yang, C.-T. (eds.) 3PGCIC 2018. LNDECT, vol. 24, pp. 486–495. Springer, Cham (2019). https://doi.org/10.1007/978-3-030-02607-3_45
25. Cedillo, P., Riofrío, X., Orellana, M.: A Middleware for Managing the Heterogeneity of Data Provining from IoT Devices in Ambient Assisted Living Environments
26. Valdez, W., Cedillo, P., Trujillo, A., Orellana, M.: A data infrastructure for managing information obtained from ambient assisted living. In: Proceedings - 2019 International Conference on Information Systems and Computer Science, INCISCOS 2019, pp. 57–61 (2019)
27. Amarouche, I.A., Benslimane, D., Barhamgi, M., Mrissa, M., Alimazighi, Z.: Electronic health record data-as-a-Services composition based on query rewriting. In: Hameurlain, A., Küng, J., Wagner, R., Böhm, C., Eder, J., Plant, C. (eds.) Transactions on Large-Scale Data- and Knowledge-Centered Systems IV. LNCS, vol. 6990, pp. 95–123. Springer, Heidelberg (2011). https://doi.org/10.1007/978-3-642-23740-9_5
28. Badidi, E., Routaib, H., El Koutbi, M.: Towards data-as-a-service provisioning with high-quality data. In: El-Azouzi, R., Menasché, D.S., Sabir, E., Pellegrini, F.D., Benjillali, M. (eds.) Advances in Ubiquitous Networking 2. LNEE, vol. 397, pp. 611–623. Springer, Singapore (2017). https://doi.org/10.1007/978-981-10-1627-1_48
29. ISO/IEC, ISO/IEC 25012 - Quality of Data Product Standard (2019)
30. Mphatswe, W., et al.: Improving public health information: a data quality intervention in KwaZulu-Natal, South Africa. Bull. World Health Organ. **90**, 176–182 (2012)

31. Mphatswe, W., et al.: Amélioration des informations sur la santé publique: Une intervention sur la qualité des données dans le Kwazulu-Natal (afrique du sud). Bull. World Health Organ. **90**(3), 176–182 (2012)
32. Segura, A.M., Cuadrado, J.S., De Lara, J.: ODaaS: Towards the model-driven engineering of open data applications as data services. In: Proceedings - IEEE International Enterprise Distributed Object Computing Workshop, EDOCW 2014, pp. 335–339 (2014)
33. Bansal, S.K.: Towards a semantic extract-transform-load (ETL) framework for big data integration. In: Proceedings - 2014 IEEE International Congress on Big Data, BigData Congress 2014, pp. 522–529 (2014)
34. Bansal, S.K., Kagemann, S.: Integrating big data: a semantic extract-transform-load framework. Computer **48**(3), 42–50 (2015)
35. Nath, R.P.D., Hose, K., Pedersen, T.B.: Towards a programmable semantic extract-transform-load framework for semantic data warehouses. In: DOLAP: Proceedings of the ACM International Workshop on Data Warehousing and OLAP, vol. 23 October 2015, pp. 15–24 (2015)
36. ISO/IEC, ISO/IEC 25010 Systems and Software Quality Requirements and Evaluation (SQuaRE) – System and software quality models (2011)
37. Cedillo, P.: Monitorización de calidad de servicios cloud mediante modelos en tiempo de ejecución. Universitat Politècnica de València (2016)
38. Mrissa, M., Tbahriti, S.E., Truong, H.L.: Privacy model and annotation for DaaS. In: Proceedings - 8th IEEE European Conference on Web Services, ECOWS 2010, pp. 3–10 (2010)
39. Hobson, J.: The Montreal Cognitive Assessment (MoCA). Occup. Med. (Chic. Ill). **65**(9), 764–765 (2015)

Teaching Botany for Adults with the Blended Learning Modality

Jaime Naranjo-Morán[1,3]($\boxtimes$), Marcos Vera-Morales[1,3], Vanessa Sánchez-Rendón[3],
and Andrea Pino-Acosta[2,3]

[1] Escuela Superior Politécnica del Litoral, ESPOL, ESPOL Polytechnic University, Campus
Gustavo Galindo Km. 30.5 vía Perimetral, P.O. Box 09-01-5863, Guayaquil, Ecuador
{jaianara,mxvera}@espol.edu.ec
[2] Escuela Superior Politécnica del Litoral, ESPOL. Facultad de Arte, Diseño y Comunicación
Audiovisual, FADCOM, Bosque Protector "La Prosperina", ESPOL Polytechnic University,
Campus Gustavo Galindo Km. 30.5 vía Perimetral, P.O. Box 09-01-5863, Guayaquil, Ecuador
ypino@espol.edu.ec
[3] Red de Bosques Secos, REBS, Km. 30.5 vía Perimetral, P.O. Box 09-01-5863,
Guayaquil, Ecuador
vsanche@espol.edu.ec

Abstract. In the area of biological sciences, teaching botany constitutes a fundamental contribution to understand the dynamics of living systems. Traditionally,
this process has done in person with the help of field trips, visits to the herbarium
and simulations in the classroom. However, little is known about how new information and communications technology would promote digital teaching environment
for the development of academic skills. The present study focused on a training
course on the introduction to botany of vascular plants present in the tropical dry
forest, which used blended learning supported in constructivist activities using
digital tools. Overall, the study showed that digital tools are used by participants
in the development of autonomous and previous work. However, young adults
showed low participation, being mature and older adults are the ones who stood
out, regarding the development of activities and work in the blended learning
modality. In addition, it was evidenced that older adults are who develop activities that demand a higher level of cognitive complexity. The results showed that
there are few students who dropped out during their development. In conclusion,
the results provide a basis for promoting digital instruction using blended learning. Furthermore, the study shows the effectiveness of digital tools for teaching
botanical science.

Keywords: Botanical education · Digital education · Blended learning · Digital
tools

1 Introduction

Universities are increasingly neglect taxonomic education, which means that new generations will not be able to identify plant specimens, even in their locality [1]. In the

© Springer Nature Switzerland AG 2020
G. Rodriguez Morales et al. (Eds.): TICEC 2020, CCIS 1307, pp. 287–301, 2020.
https://doi.org/10.1007/978-3-030-62833-8_22

educational field, there are some researchers who argue that " the disinterest of the students is probably due to the teaching way and the lack of didactic resources in the classrooms [2] ". It may be true, for sure, but the environmental variables from the classroom are many and sometimes they are not considered.

Blended learning is of great importance to the training of professionals, given the context of virtual education and learning through interactive online technologies, these tools are necessary for a developing country like Ecuador, since the student shows autonomy and independence to acquire new knowledge [3]. Continuous or permanent learning implies breaking paradigms in the training to professionals in the biological sciences, since these become entrenched in the kinesthetic activities of the student, with experimentation and practice. In this sense, reasoning based on modeling becomes a powerful tool in the development of scientific process skills [4]. The allows us to structure new strategies in continuous learning, making use of innovative plans that adopt learning combined with digital resources to teach students [5]. Therefore, well-designed courses that include synchronous and asynchronous communication can be as effective as traditional classroom courses [6].

Blended learning combines face-to-face and online technology-based instruction [7], widely used in current university teaching [8]. Blended learning has been used with names such as hybrid, blended mode, flexible learning. It is a system that results in a learning environment consisting of a content, communication and constructive component [9]. So, research shows that blended learning is a ubiquitous definition [10]. The activities developed through this educational methodology provide students with various possibilities to do, create, research and experiment in a way that enhances the teaching-learning process for students and professionals in any area of science, technology, engineering and mathematics [11]. These students learn to interact, look for information, select activities, ask questions, and argue in a pertinent way the instructions given by the facilitator [12].

Although programs in the field can improve students' attitudes and knowledge of botanical science [13–15], with the application of adequate teaching methods, favorable results can be obtained in student attention and learning [16]. As well as the implementation of virtual tools that allow to carry out practices, training and evaluations of learning based on theoretical constructs of botanical science [17, 18].

Currently, with the invasion of technologies, classes must be flexible, allowing immediate alternatives in the learning process. Therefore, the activities should provide opportunities for students to acquire skills while building their knowledge [19]. Given that the blended learning environment is different from the traditional one, it is necessary to focus attention on techniques and strategies that meet the needs of the adult [20], in this sense, active learning methodologies based on research that can make students transit towards complex operations of thought [21].

The teaching of botanical science must be fundamental in the training of academics in the area of biological and related sciences, since their understanding allows us to reveal the impacts on biodiversity and mitigate threats to food security [22, 23]. For this, tools must be sought to improve the teaching and learning processes. However, very little is known about how mixed instruction affects the teaching process in adults. Therefore, the objective of this research was to apply the blended learning methodology in the training of professionals in the biological sciences using search and interpretation tools for the identification of plant specimens.

2 Theoretical Framework

2.1 Teaching of Botanical Science

In botanical education students can develop scientific competencies, providing solutions to real-life problems such as the making of herbaria, orchards, drawings, photographic and specimen collections. Seen in another way, people who study flora have an innate passion that transcends by visualizing other ecological relationships in their environment and this strengthens the evidence of role models as internal questions arise in students about the subject and the knowledge they possess. Botany being related to other sciences allows the development of critical thinking from its historical compilation and useful knowledge associated or not with the botanical environment, being a science that has allowed itself to be adapted to different pedagogical scenarios [24]. The typical botanical excursion is of great relevance since it allows to guide and direct actions within a course [25], however, mixed learning allows to carry out an autonomous in-house simulation, the same one that makes possible a subsequent diagnosis of the specimens and the environment where they live. The botanical description of medicinal plants and edible species are a great strategy to encourage and promote the environmental conservation of vulnerable species, since students distinguish their main uses and functions in the ecosystem [26].

2.2 Teaching with Digital Technology

The new way for students to develop basic and complex thinking operations is under-pinned by research on learning theories. Several of the theories are: sociocultural theory based on the Vygotsky Proximal Development Zone, constructivist theory, connectivity theory, all these theories based on student-centered learning methodologies, making their role more protagonist in the process to produce and share knowledge and experiences. Technologies offer these students tools that can be used to represent their knowledge through mind facts, conceptual or mental maps, images, infographics, etc.

The successful incorporation of technologies in the teaching process may be subject to the context and needs of the process [27]. However, teaching practice is increasingly influenced by technologies, as society has a closer approach to mobile devices [28], tablets [29] and laptops, which constitute new challenges and opportunities for teachers. Digital technologies provide teachers with greater breadth in the use of different tools to support their educational practice [30] and students a greater approach in the management of data and information [31], which could favor the construction of knowledge.

2.3 Digital Virtual Tools as Means of Disseminating Knowledge

Digital resources have generated new communication environments understood as systems of construction, socialization and evaluation of knowledge within the teaching-learning process, but the innumerable applications of digital tools also open new fields of analysis in the digital literacy skills of teachers

In traditional education, the linear communication model is promoted where students are recipients of instructions and the teacher is the face-to-face transmitter that promotes communication of the activity [32]. Today we find a receiver-user (student) that transforms linear communication into a dynamic form of learning using digital tools. Consolidating in them the opportunities to promote their communication skills and presenting new open and shared knowledge according to their interests, that is, they went from being consumers of passive information to active creators of "prosumer" content [33].

The conjunction of education and digital tools have given way to a type of "participatory architecture" where the recipients-users build information about society and not about technologies [34]. The impulse of this culture of knowledge has been promoted under the perspective of the evolution of the web, ICT (Information and Communication Technologies) and the internet, presenting a new opportunity in online education and training "e-learning".

With the arrival of the internet, the drive from a linear one-way model and without updating (web 1.0) to its first approaches to the social and participatory web (web 2.0), where the virtual community appears, followed by the accessibility of information without a browser, is evident. (web 3.0), being undeniable to highlight the level of intervention and evolution in the linear communication model to circulate where new technologies provide value to these prosumers, facilitating access to content and resources (see Fig. 1).

Fig. 1. Evolution of the website and its objectives. Authors' own elaboration.

However, the advantages that 7.0 (sensory network and emotional network) present in the new web updates, points out to a student-user that they have many more tools, but without the ability to be motivated to the learning process at levels of attention, effort and work. This scenario shows the dissociation of the objective in the teaching-learning process and the use of digital tools, where the technological process is adopted first to the pedagogical one, that is, we speak of an ICT teaching and not a process of learning with ICT.

The internet has built a new scenario where hypertextuality establishes connections between the different elements of information, expanding the types of representation of the text and with it, presents new demands in relation to understanding. The diversity of discourse presentation in education is shown in letters, but nowadays it is complemented as a story with multimedia resources (images, videos, audios), giving way to leaps to find what is necessary, ceasing to understand the words, to read alone. What interests us, persuades and attracts.

The challenge in education and the application of digital tools is not only in their implementation, but also in self-regulating new media literacy strategies where the user is a reader capable of issuing and generating information selection criteria using ICT tools, transformed the representation of space, time and society.

2.4   The Dry Forest Network (REBS)

The Dry Forest Network (REBS) is an initiative of the Institutional Program of Protective Forests "La Prosperina" of the Escuela Superior Politécnica del Litoral, in alliance with the Ministry of the Environment, Provincial Directorate of Guayas. It was created on February 18, 2020, with the aim of working together to plan prevention and conservation actions, share information, promote research regarding the biodiversity of dry forests; and execute activities related to the responsible and sustainable management of the natural resources of our forests.

It is made up of representatives of different Dry Forests of the Costa Region, professionals, students and the general public interested in the conservation, protection and research carried out in the coastal ecosystems of Ecuador; Its creation stems from the need to communicate to sensitize society to environmental problems, coordinate and execute joint actions in favor of the biodiversity of dry forests; as well as establishing strategic alliances to obtain external financing and execute research and/or linkage projects.

Among the programmed activities related to the transfer of knowledge, the members of the REBS considered through a cooperative work, the execution of the course of introduction to botany of vascular plants which arises due to the need to strengthen skills and abilities. in the identification of plants located in tropical dry forest areas.

3   Materials and Methods

The module of introduction to the botany of vascular plants present in the tropical dry forest taught by the REBS, incorporated aspects of anatomy, morphology, physiology of the plants, as well as tools for the identification of specimens, ecology and floristic composition. The classes were conducted through the Zoom platform with 27 participants from REBS. These students have previous experience in basic elements of botany, there were a total of 8 undergraduate students in the biological area with ages between 20–25 years and 16 professionals with ages between 26–70 years. The undergraduate students have passed the botany course and some of the professionals have previous experience in flora sampling.

The module was about 20 h divided into 10 h of synchronous communication and 10 h of autonomous practical work. The module was prepared with the application of new methods, with interaction with the participants and previous instructor training [35]. Practical exercises (PE) and comprehension activities (CA) were used. The virtual classes were five, segmented every 48 h. Classes contained, opening with remembrances, orientations, and activities like the game of roulette (https://wheelofnames.com/) to recreate an atmosphere of empathy. Starting from the simple and gradually to the complexity of the topics covered [36]. Then the facilitator gave the lecture, culminating with information on the activities and advice regarding the works that were used as practical and autonomous works, which were developed in classes with the help of the tutor and using technological tools: Cmaptools, Nubedepalabras.es, kvetnidiagram, Easelly, Plantidtools.

The training program prioritized five key themes: plant overview, vascular plant morphology and tools for identifying plant specimens, morphological identification of plant specimens, landscaping, and floristic composition. In each of the topics, two practical works were carried out and two autonomous tasks were sent.

The first topic contained the following activities: field file using elements of the observational technique (PE), conceptual map of plant morphology (PE), reflection of 100 words on the importance of Ecuadorian botany (CA) and search for two publications prioritizing the plant diversity of the tropical dry forest (CA).

Second topic: investigation of leaf shapes (PE), word cloud of the characteristics of the stem (PE), floral diagram and the particular characteristics of the plant family (CA) and, 250-word summary of the flora endemism with introduction, objectives, methodology, results and conclusions (CA).

Third topic: drawing of the morphology of a plant (PE), high-level questions and answers analyzing a scientific article from the BBC (PE), reflection of 80 words that shows the importance of studying this endemic species in the Tumbesian Region of the forest tropical dry (CA) e, identification of a species in digital herbarium (CA).

Fourth topic: advantages and disadvantages of digital herbaria and mobile apps (PE), infographic of the Raunkiær classification (PE), recognizing in five words five plant families highlighting their importance (CA), and botanical description of two plant species, evidencing its agricultural and ecological utility (CA).

Fifth topic: with a field card three describe species of their preferred diet (PE), a reflection of 80 words: What do you think of mycorrhizal networks and the adaptation processes of plant species in the tropical dry forest? (PE), create a species list of three typical Ecuadorian dishes (CA) and make six slides describing the plant species of your favorite dish (CA). The fulfillment of the activities was qualified by assigning categorical data 1 complies and 0 does not comply, to ask about the preference of the selected activity. The activities of the virtual classes and the level of complexity were established without the prior knowledge of the participant. At the end of the training, the students took a multiple-choice test, which was developed on the Quizizz platform to learn about the new learning acquired during the process.

Finally, a questionnaire of perceptions regarding the module was sent to the emails of each student. They were asked to rate on a scale of 1 (minimum) to 5 (maximum) the content, the didactic process, the planning and organization of the introductory module to the basic botany of vascular plants present in the tropical dry forest.

The quantitative data collected from the didactic activities were analyzed using the InfoStat v. Software. 1.2.0 (2017), where the analysis of variance (ANOVA) and the Tukey test were performed with p values <0.05 for the variables studied. In addition, a correspondence analysis was applied on the results of categorical data of the different activities.

4   Results

Of the 27 participants registered prior to the start of the course, 24 of them completed, completing all activities, while three of them withdrew during the course.

To know the participation of the students in the autonomous and previous works, of the five classes under the blended learning modality, the data were distributed according to their level of categorical complexity (low, medium and high) and delivery. The works with the highest participation were: a reflection of 50 words, identification of the shape of the leaf, a drawing, the advantages and disadvantages between herbaria and mobile applications, and creating a list of species of a typical dish in Table 1.

Table 1. Didactic content of the virtual sections of the module.

Autonomous and previous works	Virtual classes	Complexity	Number
1. Observation sheet	1st	L	19
2. Conceptual map	1st	H	8
3. 50 word reflection	1st	L	20*
4. Critical transfer of scientific article	1st	M	10
5. Leaf shape ID	2nd	L	23*
6. Word cloud	2nd	M	13
7. Floral diagram	2nd	H	15
8. Specialized article	2nd	M	11
9. Botanical drawing	3rd	L	19*
10. Prosumer role of questions and answers	3rd	H	8
11. 80 word reflection	3rd	M	14
12. Search for species in digital herbaria	3rd	H	13
13. Advantages and disadvantages of digital herbs VS Apps	4th	M	19*
14. Raunkiær classification infographic	4th	H	9
15. Recognition of main plant families	4th	M	9
16. Botanical description of Agricultural and Ecological species	4th	L	18
17. Field tab	5th	M	10
18. Mycorrhizal networks video	5th	L	17
19. Create species list of the typical dish	5th	H	23*
20. Slides of the species present in the favorite dish	5th	H	5

* Works with more participants, L = Low, M = Medium, H = High, Own elaboration, 2020

To evaluate the activities elaborated by the participants, a statistical analysis of correspondences was made, taking as base of classification the ages according to they are young adults (20–40 years), mature adults (40–60 years) and older (more than 60 years). The data reveal that there is a greater participation of mature and older adults, in the realization of autonomous and practical work (see Fig. 2). In addition, the older adults were the ones who developed the activities that demanded the highest level of cognitive complexity (such as concept map, flower diagram, prosumer role, search for herbarium species, creating species list and slides of the species present in the typical dish). These results can be considered as a product of the academic level of mature and older adults, for being all third and fourth level professionals. In addition, the older adults have experience in sampling flora in different regions of the country. Meanwhile, the young adults are all undergraduate students and despite having a greater approach to technologies, they were not able to integrate these experiences in the presentation of well-prepared papers. While the digital immigrants with the follow-up of the teacher were able to elaborate ingenious tasks, product of their imagination, complemented with the technological tools.

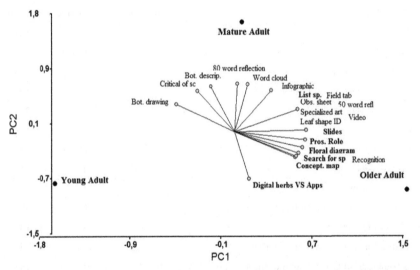

Fig. 2. Statistical analysis of correspondences to determine the degree of participation in the different constructivist activities, considering the ages of the participants and classifying them into young adults (20–40 years), mature adults (40–60 years), adults older than 60 years. Authors' own elaboration.

The evidence collected at the level of complexity has significant differences for low-level activities (see Fig. 3), while medium and high-level activities did not differ. Therefore, the application of the blended learning methodology allows the participants to develop basic operations of thought, thus achieving a conceptual understanding of the basic contents of the botany of vascular plants.

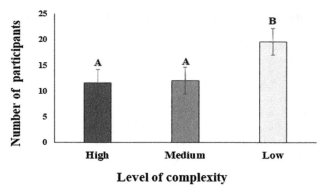

Fig. 3. Acceptance of the participants according to the level of complexity of the performed activities. Different letters on the bars indicate the significant statistical differences according to the Tukey test ($p < 0.05$). Authors' own elaboration.

On the other hand, if we consider that the results are true, we can infer that in the different virtual classes through the application of the blended learning methodology the students presented discrepancies in the development of their activities, showing greater interest in identifying the types and shapes of leaves of plant specimens. (see Fig. 4).

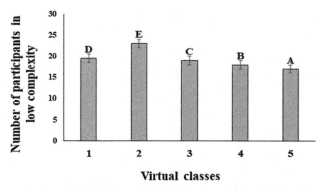

Fig. 4. Low complexity activities of virtual blended learning classes. Different letters on the bars indicate the significant statistical differences according to the Tukey test ($p < 0.05$). Authors' own elaboration.

At a qualitative level, the virtual module met the proposed objectives and allowed professionals to develop new skills, such as the botanical identification of vascular plants. In addition, the participants rated the academic content, activity methodologies and general organization of the virtual module very well. Most of the academic performance was acceptable above 50% of the minimum fulfillment of the activities to achieve a certificate of participation and approval Table 2. Participants who performed more activity received a certificate of honor, since it exceeded expectations of the initial policies of the module.

Table 2. Didactic content of the virtual sections of the module

Participants	Sex	Qualification %
1	M	50
2	M	50
3	F	65
4*	F	100
5	M	55
6	M	60
7	M	50
8*	M	85
9	M	60
10	F	60
11	F	50
12	M	60
13	M	50
14	M	55
15	F	50
16*	F	95
17	F	50
18	M	55
19	F	55
20	F	50
21	M	50
22	M	50
23	F	55
24	M	50

*Participants with the best scores, M = Male, F = Female

Activity Comments: "Slides of the species present in the favorite dish"

"Finally, it is important to understand the origin of our food, some of which are our favorites, to know which family they belong to and their gender. In addition, it is very helpful to know the family of vegetables that we consume daily because in that way we know the nutritional benefits that it brings us and as a result we would have a balanced diet and very beneficial in nutrients."

"Creole crabs in their preparation include 5 families of vegetables, corresponding to 7 genera and 8 species, being from the AMARYLLIDACEAE families with one genus and two species of the APIACEAE family with two genera and the other three families. They have one representative each. The vegetables present in the preparation of Creole crabs are from different types of ecosystems, being these from tropical dry forest of the western coast or region and the Andean highlands or central regions."

"The identification of the characteristics at the family level by reviewing the leaves, the stems, the fruits, I consider to be a very important starting point, which with practice allows developing at the field level the experience to be able to identify plant species."

Students give an important rating to the activity of describing the species present in their favorite typical dish, belonging to their locality. This activity has allowed them to put into practice the learning acquired in the module, and taxonomically identify the vascular plants that belong according to their preferred food.

The participants find it interesting that the nutritional benefits provided by each of the vegetables consumed during their diet are also included within the systematic identifications, which can help them differentiate the nutritional requirements of their diets. Likewise, they consider the diversity of plants that they may have in their typical dish and contrast the specimens with other ecosystems belonging to the different regions of Ecuador.

Regarding the perception's surveys in Fig. 5, a total of 18 multiple-choice questions were asked where the students rated on a scale of 1 (minimum) to 5 (maximum), planning, the teaching process and the facilitator. From the results obtained, it was evident that over 90% consider the development of the training relevant (maximum grade). From the observations presented in the comments to improve, the participants consider that more interaction should be allowed, that means, develop more group or collaborative work.

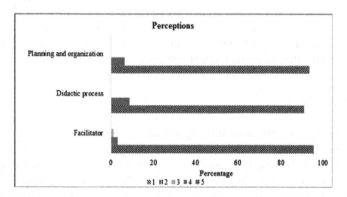

Fig. 5. Evaluation results of perception by participants. Authors' own elaboration.

5   Discussion

In this study, the mixed learning modality was applied to a training module about the introduction of vascular plants of the tropical dry forest. The results shown the active participation of the students in several of the proposed activities. This same type of achievement has been shown in the results of the university students in STEM education, when mixed modality where applied. [37, 38].

In the present study, it was possible to show that the application of technologies in the area of botany can encourage to the students to become interested by doing various activities that will help them to strengthen their skills and build their knowledge. The use of technological resources is increasingly used by students in their learning process [39].

During the development of the module, a low dropout rate was evident, so there is a positive effect of the mixed modality, as described in a previous study, where it is shown that ICT provide to the trainers and students a learning environment that stimulates the teaching process to remain successful until completion [40, 41]. In general, studies using human beings leads to very specific results because many factors may affect human performance. For example, local culture and personal context may affect reasoning, understanding, and feelings. So, the same aspects tested may find different results, for example, in management students, the application of blended learning increased the dropout rate [42].

Due the activities developed by the participants, from the different levels of complexity: low, medium and high, it is possible that they achieve a conceptual understanding of the aspects related to the basic principles of botany. This shows that students can achieve basic and complex thinking operations (recognize, remember, apply, analyze, evaluate and create) of Bloom's taxonomy [43]. For the dynamic and interactive nature that technologies provide could help students reinforce their learning about the general aspects of biological science [44–47].

The scores obtained by the presentation of the different works, evidence that many of the participants could successfully passed the training. The module design has allowed the activities to being innovative, motivating to the students in their development and presentation. Therefore, in order to increase interest in botany, it is necessary to focus on the material that is designed in the training [48], integrating innovative strategies that allow harmonizing the curricular contents [49, 50].

6 Conclusions

Blended learning is an effective learning modality that helps as a complement to the construction of knowledge for academics in the biological sciences, since it enables an appropriate space for people to discuss, learn and provide useful feedback in the professional field of science botany. With the application of the blended learning modality, the participants externalized a perception of complacency and highlighted the high professional level of the facilitator and the coordinators of the virtual module, making this an ideal setting for the future training of validated environmental interpreters in the field of botany by REBS, academic and government institutions. In conclusion, this research provides useful information on the applicability of blended teaching in the area of biological sciences, specifically in systematic botany. However, it is important to continue with studies where these blended learning methodologies are applied in other branches of biology to integrate and complement the results. New studies should include activities such as gamification or serious games, to challenge to the participants in a constructivist learning environment.

References

1. Stagg, B.C., Donkin, M.: Teaching botanical identification to adults: experiences of the UK participatory science project 'Open Air Laboratories'. J. Biol. Educ. **47**(2), 104–110 (2013). https://doi.org/10.1080/00219266.2013.764341
2. Wandersee, J., Sundberg, E.E.: Toward a theory of plant blindness. Plant Sci. Bull. **47**, 2–9 (2001)
3. Martí, J.: Aprendizaje mezclado (B-Learning) modalidad de formación de profesionales. Revista Universidad EAFIT **45**(154), 70–77 (2009)
4. Quillin, K., Thomas, S.: Drawing-to-Learn: a framework for using drawings to promote model-based reasoning in biology, CBE Life Sci Educ. **14**(1), (2015). https://doi.org/10.1187/cbe.14-08-0128
5. Gambari, A.I., Shittu, A.T., Ogunlade, O.O., Osunlade, O.R.: Effectiveness of blended learning and elearning modes of instruction on the performance of Undergraduates in Kwara State, Nigeria, Malaysian. J. Educ. Sci. **5**(1), 25–36 (2017)
6. Biel, R., Brame, C.J.: Traditional versus online biology courses: connecting course design and student learning in an online setting. J. Microbiol. Biol. Educ. (2016) https://doi.org/10.1128/jmbe.v17i3.1157
7. Graham, C.R.: Emerging practice and research in blended learning. Routledge Handbooks Online (2012)
8. Wang, S.C., Cowie, B., Jones, A.: Benefits? or Challenges? University student perception of e-learning. J. Internet Technol. **10**(5), 5 (2009)
9. Kerres, M., Witt, C.: A didactical framework for the design of blended learning arrangements. J. Educ. Media, **28**, pp. 101–114 (2003). https://doi.org/10.1080/1358165032000165653
10. Smith, K., Hill, J.: Defining the nature of blended learning through its depiction in current research. Higher Educ. Res. Dev. **38**(2), 383–397 (2018). https://doi.org/10.1080/07294360.2018.1517732
11. Chirikov, I., Semenova, T., Maloshonok, N., Bettinger, E., Kizilcec, R. F.: Online education platforms scale college STEM instruction with equivalent learning outcomes at lower cost. Sci. Adv. **6**(15), p. eaay5324 (2020) https://doi.org/10.1126/sciadv.aay5324
12. Camacho, J.A., Chiappe, A., López, C.: Blended learning y estilos de aprendizaje en estudiantes universitarios del área de la salud. Educación Médica Superior **26**(1), 27–44 (2012)
13. Cetin, G.: Field trip to Kazdagi National Park: views of prospective biology teachers. ERR. **9**(19), 823–833 (2014). https://doi.org/10.5897/err2014.1918
14. Fančovičová, J., Prokop, P.: Plants have a chance: outdoor educational programmes alter students' knowledge and attitudes towards plants. Environ. Educ. Res. **17**(4), 537–551 (2011). https://doi.org/10.1080/13504622.2010.545874
15. Scott, G.W., Goulder, R., Wheeler, P., Scott, L.J., Tobin, M.L., Marsham, S.: The value of fieldwork in life and environmental sciences in the context of higher education: a case study in learning about biodiversity. J. Sci. Educ. Technol. **21**(1), 11–21 (2012). https://doi.org/10.1007/s10956-010-9276-x
16. Strgar, J.: Increasing the interest of students in plants. J. Biol. Educ. **42**(1), 19–23 (2010)
17. Conejo, R., Garcia-Viñas, J.I., Gastón, A., Barros, B.: Technology-enhanced formative assessment of plant identification. J. Sci. Educ. Technol. **25**(2), 203–221 (2015). https://doi.org/10.1007/s10956-015-9586-0

18. Jacquemart, A.L., Lhoir, P., Binard, F., Descamps, C.: An interactive multimedia dichotomous key for teaching plant identification. J. Biol. Educ. **50**(4), 442–451 (2016). https://doi.org/10. 1080/00219266.2016.1150870

19. Biggs, J.B.: Teaching for quality learning at University: what the student does. McGraw-Hill Education (UK) (2011)

20. Huang, H.M.: Toward constructivism for adult learners in online learning environments. Br. J. Edu. Technol. **33**(1), 27–37 (2002). https://doi.org/10.1111/1467-8535.00236

21. Gardner, J., Belland, B.R.: A conceptual framework for organizing active learning experiences in biology instruction. J. Sci. Educ. Technol. **21**(4), 465–475 (2012). https://doi.org/10.1007/ s10956-011-9338-8

22. Drea, S.: The end of the botany degree in the UK. Biosci. Educ. **17**(1), 1–7 (2011). https:// doi.org/10.3108/beej.17.2

23. Wise, M.J.: A field investigation into the effects of anthropogenic disturbances on biodiversity and alien invasions of plant communities. Bioscene: J. College Biol. Teaching. **43**(2), 4–14 (2017)

24. Rodríguez, D.S.: La Botánica en el marco de las ciencias naturales: diversas miradas desde el saber pedagógico pág: 35-50, Bio-grafía. **4**(6), 6 (2011) https://doi.org/10.17227/20271034. vol.4num.6bio-grafia35.50

25. Hernández-Peña, A.M., Martínez-Pérez, C.M., Torres-Torres, I.C., Hernández-Pérez, A.: La enseñanza-aprendizaje de la botánica II mediante la excursión integradora. Ciencias Holguín. XVII **I**(3), 1–13 (2012)

26. Ospino, Y. R.: Las plantas medicinales como estrategia pedagógica para la conservación del Medio Ambiente, Cultura Educación y Sociedad. **9**(2), 129–136 (2018). https://doi.org/10. 17981/cultedusoc.9.2.2018.12

27. Quaicoe, J.S., Pata, K.: Basic school teachers' perspective to digital teaching and learning in Ghana. Educ. Inf. Technol. **23**(3), 1159–1173 (2017). https://doi.org/10.1007/s10639-017-9660-8

28. Selwyn, N., Nemorin, S., Bulfin, S., Johnson, N.F.: Left to their own devices: the everyday realities of one-to-one classrooms. Oxford Rev. Educ. **43**(3), 289–310 (2017). https://doi.org/ 10.1080/03054985.2017.1305047

29. Ditzler, C., Hong, E., Strudler, N.: How tablets are utilized in the classroom. J. Res.Technol. Educ. **48**(3), 181–193 (2016). https://doi.org/10.1080/15391523.2016.1172444

30. Walan, S.: Embracing digital technology in science classrooms—secondary school teachers' enacted teaching and reflections on practice. J. Sci. Educ. Technol. **29**(3), 431–441 (2020). https://doi.org/10.1007/s10956-020-09828-6

31. Dawson, V.: Use of information communication technology by early career science teachers in western Australia. Int. J. Sci. Educ. **30**(2), 203–219 (2008). https://doi.org/10.1080/095 00690601175551

32. Skinner, B.F.: Tecnología de la Enseñanza. Labor S.A, Barcelona (1970)

33. Islas, O., Arribas, A., Gutiérrez, F.: La contribución de Alvin Toffler al imaginario teórico y conceptual de la comunicación. Revista Latina de Comunicación Social **73** (2018)

34. Cobo, C., Pardo H.: Planeta Web 2.0. Inteligencia colectiva o medios fast food. México. Barcelona/México DF.: Grup de Recerca d'Interaccions Digitals, Universitat de Vic. Flacso, (2016)

35. Crawford-Ferre, H.G., Wiest, L.R.: Effective online instruction in higher education. Q. Rev. Distance Educ. **13**(1), 11–14 (2012)

36. Bain, K.: What the Best College Teachers Do. Harvard University Press, London (2004)

37. Bazelais, P., Doleck, T.: Blended learning and traditional learning: a comparative study of college mechanics courses. Educ. Inf. Technol. **23**(6), 2889–2900 (2018). https://doi.org/10. 1007/s10639-018-9748-9

38. Bazelais, P., Doleck, T.: Investigating the impact of blended learning on academic performance in a first semester college physics course. J. Comput. Educ. **5**(1), 67–94 (2018). https://doi.org/10.1007/s40692-018-0099-8

39. Stagg, B.C., Donkin, M.E.: Apps for angiosperms: the usability of mobile computers and printed field guides for UK wild flower and winter tree identification. J. Biol. Educ. **51**(2), 123–135 (2016). https://doi.org/10.1080/00219266.2016.1177572

40. Bernard, R.M., Borokhovski, E., Schmid, R.F., Tamim, R.M., Abrami, P.C.: A meta-analysis of blended learning and technology use in higher education: from the general to the applied. J. Comput. Higher Educ. **26**(1), 87–122 (2014). https://doi.org/10.1007/s12528-013-9077-3

41. López-Pérez, M.V., Pérez-López, M.C., Rodríguez-Ariza, L.: Blended learning in higher education: students' perceptions and their relation to outcomes. Comput. Educ. **56**(3), 818–826 (2011). https://doi.org/10.1016/j.compedu.2010.10.023

42. Deschacht, N., Goeman, K.: The effect of blended learning on course persistence and performance of adult learners: a difference-in-differences analysis. Comput. Educ. **87**, 83–89 (2015). https://doi.org/10.1016/j.compedu.2015.03.020

43. Anderson, L.W., Krathwohl, D.R., Bloom, B.S.: A taxonomy for learning, teaching, and assessing: a revision of Bloom's Taxonomy of educational objectives (2000)

44. Goff, E.E., et al.: Efficacy of a meiosis learning module developed for the virtual cell animation collection, CBE Life Sci Educ. **16**(1), (2017) https://doi.org/10.1187/cbe.16-03-0141

45. Goff, E.E., et al.: Investigation of a stand-alone online learning module for cellular respiration instruction, J Microbiol Biol Educ. **19**(2), (2018) https://doi.org/10.1128/jmbe.v19i2.1460

46. McClean, P., et al.: Molecular and cellular biology animations: development and impact on student learning. Cell Biol. Educ. **4**(2), 169–179 (2005). https://doi.org/10.1187/cbe.04-07-0047

47. O'Day, D.H.: The value of animations in biology teaching: a study of long-term memory retention. CBE Life Sci. Educ. **6**(3), 217–223 (2007). https://doi.org/10.1187/cbe.07-01-0002

48. Bonser, S.P., de Permentier, P., Green, J., Velan, G.M., Adam, P., Kumar, R.K.: Engaging students by emphasising botanical concepts over techniques: innovative practical exercises using virtual microscopy. J. Biol. Educ. **47**(2), 123–127 (2013). https://doi.org/10.1080/0021 9266.2013.764344

49. Tanner, K., Allen, D.: Approaches to biology teaching and learning: on integrating pedagogical training into the graduate experiences of future science faculty. LSE. **5**(1), 1–6 (2006). https://doi.org/10.1187/cbe.05-12-0132

50. Wood, W.B.: Innovations in teaching undergraduate biology and why we need them. Annu. Rev. Cell Dev. Biol. **25**(1), 93–112 (2009). https://doi.org/10.1146/annurev.cellbio.24.110 707.175306

Industry 4.0

Magnetic Control of DC-DC Converters for LED Drivers Applications

Héctor F. Chinchero$^{(\boxtimes)}$ ⓘ and J. Marcos Alonso ⓘ

Electrical Engineering Department, University of Oviedo, Campus de Viesques, 33204 Gijón, Asturias, Spain
UO248474@uniovi.es

Abstract. In this paper a research on magnetic control of DC-DC converters applied to LED Lighting Drivers is presented. The proposed control method is based on the modulation of the effective inductance in the input filter of the DC-DC converter operated in discontinuous conduction mode (DCM). Thus, by using a variable inductor (VI), the converter output can be controlled in order to regulate the current through the LED. This work demonstrates how the method of magnetic control can effectively be used to control DC-DC converters with an LED load, as well as be combined with other control parameters as duty cycle or switching frequency to improve the converter performance. An experimental prototype has been built to test the control method analysis and modeling methodology, and to verify its feasibility and possibilities.

Keywords: Light Emitting Diode (LED) · Variable Inductor (VI) · DC-DC Converter · Magnetic Control (MC) · Discontinuous Conduction Mode (DCM)

1 Introduction

Consumption of energy in the world is mainly linked to population growth, the development of new infrastructure in cities, transport, new production processes in industry, as well as the dizzying increase in urban environments, among other factors, including those related to climate change.

The high level of energy consumption is one of the largest contributors to climate change, accounting for about 60% of global greenhouse gas emissions. In this sense, the lighting related to residential and working environments corresponds to 20% of the total consumption of the energy produced and 23% of the electricity consumed in the building, which is associated with the type of lamp, its efficiency and mode of use, among other aspects [1].

The three types of lighting lamps in today's industry are halogen light lamps, compact fluorescent light, and LED lamps. Several studies have also found that LED lamps require less power compared to halogen or fluorescent lamps. Thus, the new LED lighting systems have become one of the best lighting sources used today, owing to their high luminous efficiency [1, 2].

© Springer Nature Switzerland AG 2020
G. Rodriguez Morales et al. (Eds.): TICEC 2020, CCIS 1307, pp. 305–318, 2020.
https://doi.org/10.1007/978-3-030-62833-8_23

LED lighting is increasingly one of the most used lighting technologies in residential environments, commercial buildings, public roads, parks, industry buildings, academic campus, hospitals, hotels, etc. Many luminaire manufacturers are developing new encapsulation technologies and above all implementing new control technologies, drivers and optimized methodologies for LED Lighting Systems.

Basic control of an LED diode is done by using linear dimming sources and power regulation. The linear current source allows for a current regulation of the LED diode, being one of the simplest methods, low cost and with few components. In addition, it does not have EMI generation, although it is inefficient [2, 9, 10].

Figure 1a shows the circuit diagram of a linear current source, where the LED current is controlled by a control signal acting on the basis of a transistor operating in the active region. On the other hand, in the control by switching power converters shown in Fig. 1b, a larger number of components is included and therefore has a higher cost. In addition, it has high efficiency and low power loss. The main disadvantage is that it presents EMI generation; however, it is very efficient in LED light control applications [2, 9].

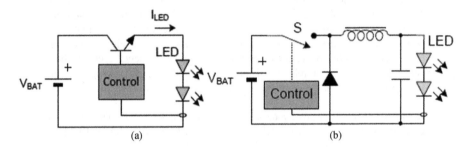

Fig. 1. LED control. (a) Linear source control. (b) Power converter control

DC-DC converters are generally used for LED lighting control, which work at different operating points according to the modification of parameters such as duty cycle, frequency, etc. One emerging method for controlling DC-DC converters is Magnetic Control (MC) [3]. In MC it is possible to regulate the conditions of the converter output based on the variation of the converter filter inductance. The variation of inductance is performed by the use of a variable inductor (VI) which changes according to the effect produced by an auxiliary winding through which a polarization current circulates [3–7, 11–13].

In this paper, a new concept on DC-DC converters with MC for LED Lighting applications employing the buck converter topology is introduced based on the use of a variable inductor as a controllable element in the input filter of the converter.

In conventional DC-DC converters the inductance should be designed lower than the critical inductance with which the DC-DC buck operates in Discontinuous Conduction Mode (DCM) at the maximum input voltage, minimum output voltage and full load current. With a fixed inductance, the inductor current ripple will be quite large when the DC-DC buck converter operates with lower input voltage but higher output voltage, leading to higher switching and conduction losses. However, with the controllable inductor the inductance can be adaptively varied with the input voltage or load current, contributing to lower current stress and higher conversion efficiency with respect to the converter working at the same input voltage or load current but with a fixed inductance.

2   Magnetic Control for LED Drivers

2.1   Magnetic Control of DC-DC Converters

MC for DC-DC Converters is performed modifying the inductance value in the converter LC filter using a VI [3–7]. MC in DC-DC converters is performed when the converter is working in DCM [8, 9]. Figure 2 shows the current waveform through the inductor of a buck converter operating in DCM with two different inductance values, L_1 and L_2. The inductor has a direct effect on the average output current and the average output voltage. As the inductance value increases, the average current and output voltage will decrease [9].

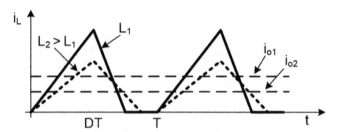

Fig. 2. Buck converter waveforms on DCM operation.

From the studies presented in [8] it is possible to obtain the output characteristics of the different converters operating in DCM under MC. For this purpose, the normalized inductance of the buck converter is defined as follows:

$$L_n = \frac{L}{R/2f} \tag{1}$$

where L is the inductance of the converter, R represents the load resistance and f is the switching frequency of the converter.

The static characteristics of the buck converter operating in DCM with MC can be obtained from the normalized characteristics given by:

$$M = \frac{V_o}{V_i} = \frac{2}{1 + \sqrt{1 + \frac{4}{D^2}L_n}} \quad if \quad L_n \le 1 - D \tag{2}$$

by replacing the normalized inductance at (2) given by (1), the following expression is obtained for the voltage gain of the buck converter operating in DCM [6, 7]:

$$M = \frac{V_o}{V_i} = \frac{2}{1 + \sqrt{1 + \frac{8fL}{D^2R}}} \quad if \quad L \le (1 - D)\frac{R}{2f} \tag{3}$$

In (3), the voltage gain of the converter in DCM M is a direct function of the inductance. In this way, MC provides a control parameter against traditional methods.

Variable Inductors Implementation. The VI is basically a main winding on a magnetic core, in which the inductance depends on the geometric parameters and the permeability of the material with which it is constructed. VIs have been extensively studied in preliminary literature [3, 4]. These devices are able to provide an inductance value that can be controlled by a DC current injected into one or more auxiliary windings. Figure 3 shows the most common VI scheme; the VI double-E structure. This structure has previously been studied in [3–7, 11–15], where it is possible to find information on how to analyze, design and simulate this type of VI.

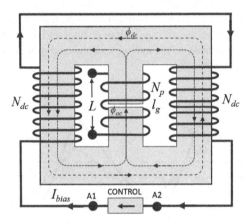

Fig. 3. VI double-E structure.

For a null control bias current I_{bias}, the inductance L associated with the main winding N_p is at its maximum value, L_{max}. If the bias current I_{bias} increases, this value decreases progressively until a minimum value L_{min}. If the core is completely saturated there will be a low limit value for this inductance. In this way, the use of a VI in power converters allows the designer to employ an additional degree of freedom to perform current regulation at the converter output.

2.2 DC-DC Buck Converter with Magnetic Control for LED Load

In order to evaluate the possibilities of CM to DC-DC converters operating in DCM and applied to LED loads, this section will carry out a case study for the Buck converter.

The basic topology of the DC-DC Buck Converter with LED load is shown in Fig. 4, which consists of a controlled switch S, a diode D, a variable inductor (VI) L, a C capacitor and an LED load. Inductance value control is performed through a bias current I_{bias} that is related to magnetic field force variation H_{bias} of the VI core [3, 4]. This allows the system to vary the value of the inductance of the buck converter when working in DCM mode [8, 9], thus modifying the average value of the output current circulating through the LED.

Static Analysis of the DC-DC Buck Converter with MC for LED Load. Considering that in this study the type of load is an LED, so that the output voltage on the LED channel

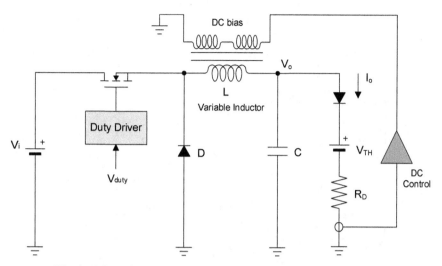

Fig. 4. DC-DC buck converter with MC for LED lighting applications.

is determined by $V_o = V_{TH} + R_D * I_o$ [8–10] where V_{TH} is the LED threshold voltage and R_D is the LED dynamic resistance, it is possible to write:

$$R = \frac{V_o}{I_o} = \frac{V_{TH}}{I_o} + R_D \tag{4}$$

Using the expression (4) in (3) and clearing L, the expression for the inductance is:

$$L = \frac{D^2}{8f} \cdot \left(\frac{V_{TH}}{I_o} + R_D \right) \cdot \left[\left(\frac{2V_i}{V_{TH} + R_D I_o} - 1 \right)^2 - 1 \right] \tag{5}$$

As can be inferred from (5), to operate in a range of I_o values, the converter must work in a range of L inductance values, which provides the starting point for the VI design, considering a certain LED operating point [2].

2.3 Case Study: Magnetic Control of the DC-DC Buck Converter with LED Load

The proposed control scheme of the DC-DC Buck Converter operating in DCM mode with MC for an LED load is illustrated in Fig. 5. As can be seen, the main switch S works with duty cycle and frequency set by a driver circuit.

The output current is measured by a series resistance R_s and a low pass filter implemented by the operational amplifier (OA) U1 and it is introduced into a proportional integral compensator (PI) implemented by the OA U2, which drives the bipolar transistor Q to generate the required bias current i_b for the VI.

2.4 Implemented Prototype

As an example of implementation, this section presents the performance of a DC-DC Buck Converter operating with a duty cycle of 0.5 and a switching frequency of 100 kHz.

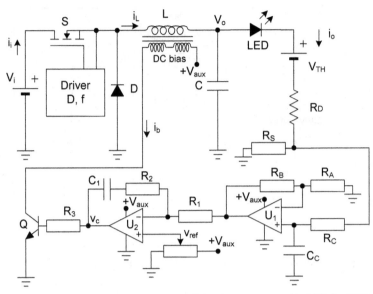

Fig. 5. Proposed control scheme of the DC-DC Buck converter with MC for LED lighting applications.

The implemented VI ranges from 27 μH to 60 μH with the parameters shown in Table 1. Figure 6 shows the inductance characteristic versus the bias current of the implemented VI.

The DC-DC Buck Converter is powered by an input voltage of 48 V and an LED load made up by a Bridgelux BXRA-C4500, which has a rated voltage of 25.4 V and a rated current of 2.1 A. The capacitance of the output filter of each channel is 33 μF, implemented with a film capacitor so that its series resistance can be neglected. Table 2 summarizes the parameters of the implemented converter prototype.

Table 1. Implemented VI Parameters.

Parameter	Type/Value
Structure	Doble E
Core and magnetic material	EFD34/17/11, N87
Main winding	$N_p = 20$, 66×0.08 mm (litz)
Air gap	1 mm
Bias winding	$2 \times N_b = 22$, 1×0.75 mm
Main inductance range	27 μH–65 μH
Bias winding effective series inductance and resistance	0.139 mH/0.25 Ω @ 10 kHz
Bias winding transistor and output admittance	BD139/$h_{oe} = 0.1667\Omega^{-1}$
Bias winding transistor base resist.	4.7 kΩ

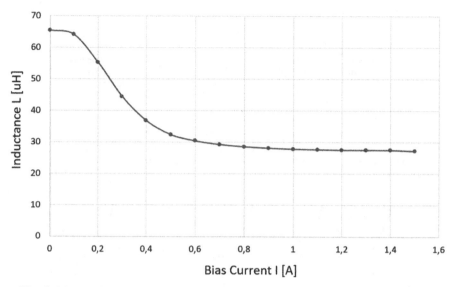

Fig. 6. Measured characteristic of inductance versus Bias current of the implemented VI.

Table 2. Implemented DC-DC Buck Converter with MC for LED Lighting Parameters.

Parameter	Type/Value
Nominal input voltage	48 V
Output voltage	25.4 V
Duty Cycle	0.5
Switching Frequency	100 kHz
Variable Inductor	27 μH–65 μH
Capacitor	33 μF
LED Diode	Bridgelux BXRA-C4500
Dynamic resistance	1.4 Ω
Threshold voltage	22.5 V
Power switch	IRF540
Power diode	MUR849
LED current sensor series resistance	1 Ω

2.5 Experimental Verification

Figure 7 shows the experimental waveforms of input voltage to the LC filter of the DC-DC buck converter and current through the VI at two different operating points. As can be seen, the converter works in DCM although in the waveforms shown in Fig. 7b is already on the border between DCM and CCM.

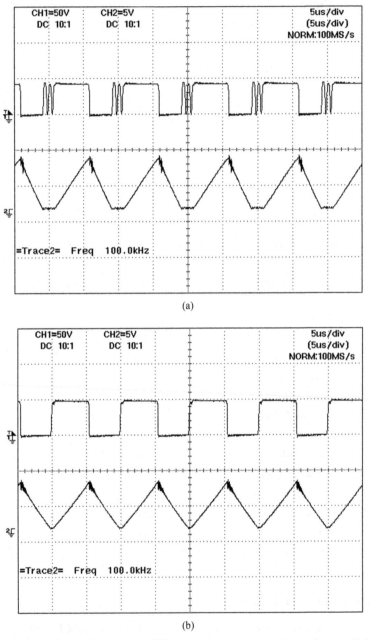

(a)

(b)

Fig. 7. Experimental waveforms at two different operating points. Above: input voltage to the LC filter of the buck converter. Down: current through the VI. Scales: 50 V/div, 1 A/div, 5 μs/div. (a) Operating in DCM. (b) Operating on the boundary between DCM and CCM.

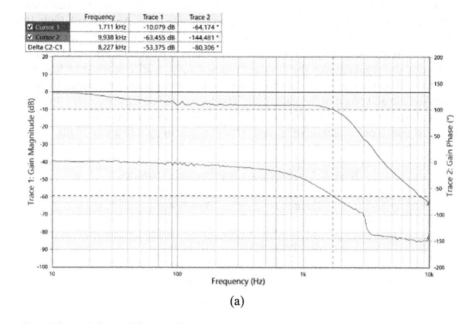

	Frequency	Trace 1	Trace 2
Cursor 1	1,711 kHz	-10,079 dB	-64,174 °
Cursor 2	9,938 kHz	-63,455 dB	-144,481 °
Delta C2-C1	8,227 kHz	-53,375 dB	-80,306 °

(a)

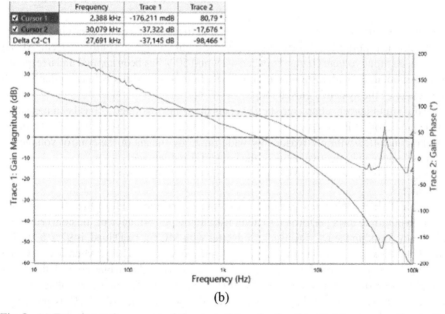

	Frequency	Trace 1	Trace 2
Cursor 1	2,388 kHz	-176,211 mdB	80,79 °
Cursor 2	30,079 kHz	-37,322 dB	-17,676 °
Delta C2-C1	27,691 kHz	-37,145 dB	-98,466 °

(b)

Fig. 8. (a) Experimental response of the control transfer function $G_o(s)$ corresponding to the buck converter implemented with MC for LED supplying. (b) Open loop gain and phase obtained experimentally with a PI compensator.

Other test performed on the prototype was to measure the system dynamics by acquiring the bode diagram of the system transfer function $G_{o(s)}$. An Omicron Bode 100 analyzer has been used for this operation. The Fig. 8a shows the obtained results. As can be seen, the response corresponds to a two-pole system at frequencies in the kHz range.

To test the regulation of the system in closed loop, a PI compensator has been designed as illustrated in Fig. 5. Table 3 shows compensator parameters. Figure 8b shows the magnitude and phase of the gain of the T(s) loop obtained experimentally from the DC-DC Buck Converter with MC when the PI compensator is used. The system is well stabilized with a phase margin of around 80° and a gain margin of about 25 dB.

Table 3. PI Compensator Implemented Parameters.

Parameter	Type/Value
High Frequency Gain	0 dB
Zero Frequency	1.7 kHz
Operational Amplifier	LM358
Resistances R_1, R_2	10 kΩ
Capacitor C_1	10 nF

Figure 9 shows the experimental responses of the buck converter operating in closed loop with the proposed MC corresponding to the input voltage and output current. As can be seen, an input voltage change between 44 V and 50 V has been applied and a response has been obtained with a stabilization time of about 4 ms, which is in accordance with the design of the system's closed loop.

The output current characteristic I_o versus the control voltage v_c has been measured in the laboratory. Figure 10 shows the obtained result. As can be seen, the output current can be controlled within a reasonably wide range by means of the control voltage v_c, which changes the effective value of the converter inductance.

Figure 11 shows the working environment with the prototype implemented in laboratory.

Table 4 shows the experimental measurements and the result of the efficiency calculations in three tests performed to demonstrate the performance of the converter. The efficiency found in the DC-DC Buck Converter with MC for LED load, is 97.2%, 95.7% and 96.6% for input voltages of 42 V, 48 V and 53 V respectively, when losses in the winding bias are not considered. Taking into account losses due to bias control, the effective efficiency of the converter is 90.7%, 90.0% and 95.0% for the same voltage values indicated above. It should be considered that the performance of 95.1% is presented because at this point of operation the converter has lower losses due to the bias winding.

Finally, a cost analysis has been carried out for the implemented prototype. Since the LED driver with MC has conventional electronics elements and integrated circuits (ICs), a low cost of 15 USD has been found for all materials and accessories.

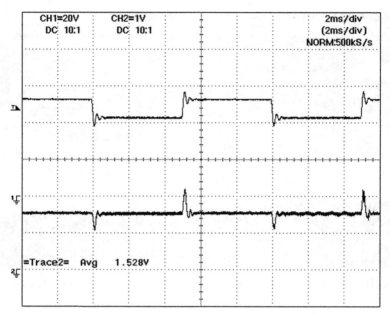

Fig. 9. Experimental response in closed loop of the magnetically controlled buck converter with a PI compensator. Up (CH1): input voltage showing a voltage step between 44 V and 50 V. Down (CH2): output current by LED. Scales: 20 V/div, 1 A/div, 2 ms/div.

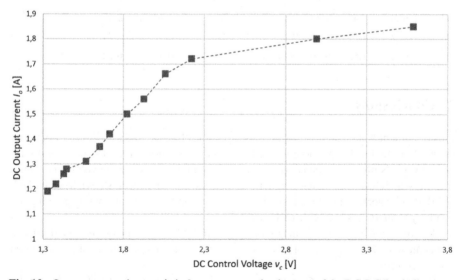

Fig. 10. Output current characteristic I_O versus control voltage v_C of the DC-DC Buck Converter with MC for LED load.

Fig. 11. Prototype of DC-DC Buck Converter with MC for LED Drivers Applications.

Table 4. Efficiency of DC-DC Buck Converter with MC for LED load.

V_i [V]	P_i [W]	I_o [A]	P_o [W]	η w/o bias%	V_{bias} [V]	I_{bias} [A]	P_{bias} [W]	η w/bias%
42	38.8	1.45	37.73	97.2	2.0	1.40	2.80	90.7
48	42.2	1.51	39.56	95.7	2.0	0.87	1.74	90.0
53	41.2	1.52	39.80	96.6	2.0	0.35	0.70	95.1

3 Conclusions

This document has presented magnetic control for a DC-DC Buck Converter operating in DCM applied to LED load control. It has also been shown that it is possible to use the converter's filter inductance as a control parameter to regulate the voltage or output current, which has been called magnetic control (MC). It has been shown how the DC-DC Buck Converter can be analyzed both statically and dynamically with enough good accuracy to model its behavior under MC.

The dynamic model of the magnetically controlled buck converter is very similar to that achieved with other control methods, such as voltage mode control or programmed current control.

Because the converter operates in DCM, it maintains its first-order behavior by displaying a main pole given by filter capacitance and equivalent load resistance. The MC introduces a second pole given by the effective inductance of bias winding and by the resistance resulting from adding the output resistance of the current source used to handle bias winding and serial resistance of the same bias winding.

Experimental results have demonstrated the theoretical model of the MC buck converter. It has also been demonstrated how the converter can be controlled in closed loop with a simple PI compensator that can be designed based on conventional design methods. Experimental measurement of the converter loop gain and input voltage step response are fully consistent with the closed loop design.

In addition, one of the drawbacks found on MC for LED lighting drivers is the extra power losses in the auxiliar windings of the VI, which makes it necessary to improve the control system of the bias driver.

It is possible to combine several techniques simultaneously to improve the behavior of the converter in future works. Likewise, this technique can be used in a variety of applications where DC-DC converters are required as solar PV generation, battery chargers, electric vehicle converters, etc. However, each application must be analyzed theoretically preliminarily considering all its components in order to properly develop the necessary control technique.

References

1. United Nations: The Sustainable Development Goals Report 2017. United Nations Publications, pp. 1–7, NY (2017)
2. Wang, Y., Alonso, J.M., Ruan, X.: A review of LED drivers and related technologies. IEEE Trans. Ind. Electron. **64**(64), 5754–5765 (2017)
3. Perdigão, M., Menke, M., Seidel, A., Pinto, R., Alonso, J.M.: A review on variable inductors and variable transformers: applications to lighting drivers. IEEE Trans. Ind., App (2016)
4. Medini, D., Ben-Yaakov, S.: A current-controlled variable-inductor for high frequency resonant power circuits. In: Application Power Electronic Conference and Exp., vol. 1, pp. 219–225 (1994)
5. Alonso, J.M., Perdigão, M., Vaquero, D., Calleja, A., Saraiva, E.: Analysis, design, and experimentation on constant-frequency DC-DC resonant converters with magnetic control. IEEE Trans. Power Electr. **27**(3), 1369–1382 (2012)
6. Alonso, J.M., Perdigão, M., Dalla Costa, M.A., Martínez, G., Osorio, R.: Analysis and design of a novel variable-inductor-based LED driver for DC lighting grids. In: Industry Applications Society Annual Meeting Conference (2016)
7. Alonso, J.M., Martínez, G., Perdigão, M., Cosetin, M.R., do Prado, R.N.: A systematic approach to modeling complex magnetic devices using SPICE: application to variable inductors. IEEE Trans. Power Electr. **31**(11), 7735–7746 (2016)
8. Kazimierczuk, M.: Pulse Width Modulated DC-DC Power Converters. Wiley, Chichester (2008)
9. Alonso, J. M.: LED Lighting and Drivers. Amazon KDP (2019)
10. Schubert, E.F.: Light Emiting Diodes. Cambridge (2006)
11. Kislovski, A.S.: Quasi-linear controllable inductor. Proc. IEEE **75**(2), 267–269 (1997)
12. Alonso, J.M., Perdigão, M., Dalla Costa, M.A., Zhang, S., Wang, Y.: Analysis and experimentation of the quad-U variable inductor for power electronics applications. IET Power Electr. **11**(14), 2330–2337 (2019)
13. Alonso, J.M., Perdigao, M., Abdelmessih, G.Z., Dalla Costa, M.A., Wang, Y.: SPICE modeling of variable inductors and its application to single inductor LED driver design. IEEE Trans. Ind. Electr. **64**(7), 5894–5903 (2017)

14. Pinto, R.A., Alonso, J.M., Perdigao, M.. Da Silva, M.F., Do Prado, R.N.: A new technique to equalize branch currents in multiarray LED lamps based on variable inductor. In: Industry Applications Society Annual Meeting, pp. 1–9 (2014)
15. Alonso, J.M., Perdigao, M., Dalla Costa, M.A., Martínez, G., Osorio, R.: Analysis and experiments on a single-inductor half-bridge LED driver with magnetic control. IEEE Trans. Power Electr. **32**(12), 9179–9190

Integrated Approach for Planning of Intermodal Food Transport Chains Considering Risk Factors

Ludmiła Filina-Dawidowicz$^{(\boxtimes)}$ (ID), Daria Możdrzeń(ID), and Sara Stankiewicz(ID)

Faculty of Maritime Technology and Transport, West Pomeranian University of Technology, al. Piastów 41, 71-065 Szczecin, Poland
{ludmila.filina,daria.mozdrzen}@zut.edu.pl,
stankiewicz-sara@wp.pl

Abstract. Nowadays, the growing demand for intermodal food transport is observed. During transportation of food products the ensuring of special storage conditions inside refrigerated containers is required. These products may lose their quality during transportation process under risk factors influence. Different methods could be applied for risk analysis and prevention, however, forwarders sill face challenges while planning transport chains of food in refrigerated containers. The article aims to present the integrated approach for planning of intermodal food transport chains considering risk factors influence. It was proposed to analyze different risk factors influence on cargo quality during implementation of particular links of intermodal transport chains, as well as integrate different risk assessment approaches and methods within one decision-making tool. Additionally, the opinions of forwarders operating in Poland on risk factors occurrence were considered. It was stated that due to forwarder's opinion, refrigerated containers handling at seaports is dealing with the highest risk of cargo quality loss. The research results allow to improve information analysis and decision-making processes related to shaping and planning of intermodal transport chains implemented for food products deliveries.

Keywords: Intermodal transport · Refrigerated container · Food · Risk factors · Logistics

1 Introduction

Nowadays, the growth of food transportation in refrigerated containers is observed worldwide. Due to analysis shown in the report prepared by Drewry Maritime Research [1], in 2019 the volume of seaborne reefer trade increased by 1,7% (to 130.5 million tons) compared to the previous year. It turned out that this growth was lower compared to an increase of 3% in 2018. The weaker development of trade was influenced by the slowdown in shipments of such products as deciduous and citrus fruits due to extreme weather conditions in Europe, drought in South Africa and Chile and other factors. Despite slowdown in the global maritime trade, Drewry forecasts that global seaborne

© Springer Nature Switzerland AG 2020
G. Rodriguez Morales et al. (Eds.): TICEC 2020, CCIS 1307, pp. 319–332, 2020.
https://doi.org/10.1007/978-3-030-62833-8_24

traffic of perishable reefer goods will continue to expand at rate of 3.7% a year up to 2024. The share of containerized reefer trade will increase from 87% in 2019 to 92% by 2024, but breakbulk reefer shipping will continuing contraction [1].

Food products (e.g. fruit, vegetables, meat, fish, etc.) should be transported under set conditions (e.g. temperature, air humidity, ventilation etc.) and require fast deliveries due to its limited shelf life [2–5]. This type of cargo is susceptible to quality loss in case the required transport conditions are not assured under extraordinary events occurrence [6–8].

The specificity of perishable products is taken into account by forwarders or logistics operators, who plan and organize intermodal food transport chains. Awareness of possible deterioration of cargo quality influence the decisions related to planning of transport process [9, 10]. In order to deliver cargo safely, such decisions should take into consideration the risk factors influence on cargo during its transportation.

Different approaches to analyze the risk related to perishable food transport are developed and presented in the available literature [4, 6, 11–15]. These approaches consider various risk factors occurrence, as well as different methods to analyze the available data are proposed [9, 16–18]. However, these approaches mainly examine individual cases and do not include the comprehensive view on planning of food deliveries in refrigerated containers considering risk factors appearance.

Therefore, the article aims to develop the integrated approach for planning of intermodal food transport chains considering risk factors influence. Moreover, it aims to study opinions of forwarders related to their perception of risk occurring during implementation of particular links of intermodal transport chains of food products. In order to do this, questionnaire survey was carried out among forwarders operating in Poland and collected results were analyzed.

The article includes literature review, description of used methodology, proposed approach and survey results. In order to sum up the conclusions have been drawn and further research directions have been presented.

2 Literature Review

Contemporary problems of intermodal transport are wieldy analysed in the available literature [10, 19–24]. These problems among other issues are related to transport of food products in refrigerated containers [6, 12, 25–28]. Transport of food inside such containers' type allow to deliver cargo from sender to recipient assuring required transport conditions [4].

Intermodal transport chains are planned by forwarders, logistics operations or other responsible person, who have to take into account various circumstances of perishable food transport. One of the main challenges of forwarders is ensuring appropriate cargo storage conditions during its transportation and undertaking various actions in order to prevent cargo quality loss [29, 30].

Transport chains of refrigerated containers may involve different links, including maritime, road, rail and air transport, as well as cargo service at transhipment terminals (e.g. located in seaports) [27, 28, 31]. International intermodal transport chains of food products very often are performed using maritime and road transport. While planning of intermodal transport chains the available infrastructure and vehicles are analysed in detail in order to choose appropriate ones [5, 19]. This is connected with the need to plug the refrigerated containers to electrical supply during execution of certain links of transport chain [12]. Container may be plugged to terminal's, vehicle's supply systems or to portable power generator (GenSet) [13].

It should be noted that available literature widely investigates the issues of risks occurring during performance of perishable food transport chains [4, 8, 14, 15, 30, 32–34]. The influence of different risk factors on cargo quality is considered. These factors may be connected with human mistakes, failure of technical devices, as well as impact of unfavourable environmental conditions [35–37]. Risk factors can occur during particular links of transport chains and may have negative effect on transport process (e.g. decrease of cargo quality, increase of costs and time of cargo delivery, etc.). These risks may be equipment-related, organizational and policy-related, deal with failure to assure cargo cooling or freezing, etc. [4]. Current publications discuss various types and number of risk factors occurring during transport of food [4, 7, 8, 14, 15, 30, 34].

Moreover, different risk assessment methods are presented in the literature. These methods are based i.a. on collecting experts opinions, statistical data analysis, etc. The most common approach considers risk as multiplication of probability (likelihood, possibility, intensity, etc.) of unfavourable situation occurrence and possible losses (their costs) [34]:

$$R = P(V) \cdot C(V) \leq R_{acc}, \tag{1}$$

where:

$P(V)$ – probability of cargo quality loss $[0 \div 1]$,
$C(V)$ – amount of losses in case of cargo quality loss (depends on the type of containerized cargo) [USD],
V – conditions of cargo service,
R – calculated risk [USD],
R_{acc} – accepted risk [USD]

In the available studies the steps used to analyze risks are discussed (e.g. risk identification, analysis and evaluation, strategies and treatment, etc.), as well as risk strategies implemented by decision-makers (e.g. risk prevention, reduction, transfer, etc.) are proposed [4]. Low, moderate and high risks are distinguished [34].

On the basis of literature analysis it could be stated that the number of approaches to evaluate risk level have been developed [4, 15, 32–34]. Particular approaches show different ways to assess and analyze risks that may be difficult to implement by forwarders or logistics operators to facilitate their decision-making processes. Therefore, integrated approach could be developed for planning of intermodal food transport chains to support decision-making and obtain information favourable to making rational decisions. This approach have to enable integration of various available methods and approaches within one decision-making tool.

3 Methodology

On the basis of literature analysis, as well as observations of the methods used in carrying out food transport, an approach has been developed for planning of intermodal transport chains of food products considering risk factors influence. It was assumed that:

- the approach allows to select rational shape of intermodal transport chain of food,
- the approach considers risk level among other decision-making criteria,
- the impact of particular risk factors occurring during the implementation of certain links of intermodal transport chains is analysed,
- different available methods to calculate the risk level are integrated.

Having regard to set assumptions the appropriate methodology have been elaborated and the stages of its implementation were determined and described.

In order to obtain the information about links of transport chains that may deal with the risk of cargo quality loss, the questionnaire was developed and survey was carried out among freight forwarders operating in Poland. The questionnaire in electronic form was sent in January 2020 to 30 selected companies operating in Poland that deal with planning of intermodal transport chains for food deliveries. The respondents were asked two questions:

- what links of intermodal transport chains are vulnerable to risk of food quality loss?
- what is the influence of particular risk factors groups on quality loss of food transported in refrigerated containers?

The questionnaire was filled by 23 respondents. The achieved results were analysed that allowed to draw the conclusions.

4 Results

4.1 An Approach for Planning of Intermodal Food Transport Chains

An approach proposed for planning of intermodal transport chains of food in refrigerated containers is shown in Fig. 1. After receiving the order for food transportation, the preliminary analysis of transport task should be carried out. Development of possible transport chains have to take into consideration the possibility of transport modes interaction. It means the availability of infrastructure, for example plugs, temperature monitoring systems, information management etc. Then particular transport chains are analyzed in details. The essential part of the presented approach deals with the need to analyze risk factors that can influence the cargo quality loss during implementation of particular links of transport chain.

The procedure for selecting the rational shape of intermodal transport chain of perishable food using the proposed approach may consist of the following stages:

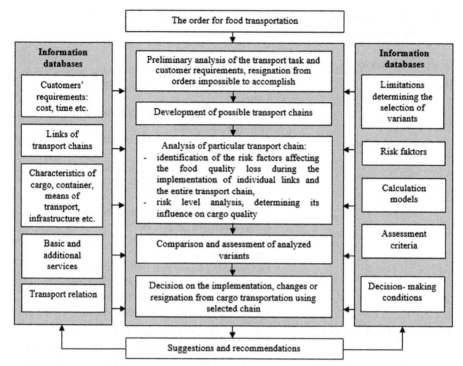

Fig. 1. An approach for planning of intermodal food transport chains considering risk factors influence (own elaboration based on [13]).

1. Analysis of the research problem. During this stage necessary information is collected and information databases are created. These databases may contain information related to customers' requirements, used intermodal loading units, perishable cargo types and its specific features, links of transport chains, used vehicles and infrastructure, basic and additional services needed during transportation, etc. These databases have to be filled with required data.

The example of part of database containing risk factors is shown in Table 1. It should be noted that this database may include different factors appropriate for the analyzed cargo and geographic area of its transportation. Such factors may be relevant to link of transport chain (e.g. maritime transport) or could belong to entire transport chain (e.g. unsatisfactory condition of the refrigerated container). Some risk factors may appear only on the selected routes (e.g. there are maritime routes where sea icing or other extreme weather conditions do not appear). Such database should be flexible in order to make it possible to add or delete risk factors. Experts opinions may be used to select risk factors applicable to particular transport chain and its links.

Moreover, a preliminary analysis of requirements for the transportation of selected cargo is carried out during this stage.

Table 1. The example of part of database on risk factors affecting the food transported in refrigerated container (own elaboration based on [13]).

Group of risk factors	Risk factors examples
Human factor	• Inappropriate behaviour of road users, etc. (road transport), • Inappropriate behaviour of sea traffic participants, etc. (maritime transport), • Improper behaviour of people at railway crossings, etc. (rail transport), • Trespassing the port by unauthorized persons, failure to plug container to power supply etc. (transshipment at terminal (e.g. seaport)), • Individual mental and psychological factors: poor health, employee fatigue, etc., • Individual professional factors: e.g. insufficient qualification, etc., • Factors of improper organization of transport: insufficient number of employees, improper information exchange, imprecise tasks, etc., • Social factors: thefts, strikes, epidemics, terrorism, etc.
Technical and technological factors	• Unsatisfactory technical condition of GenSet, • Unsatisfactory condition of the refrigerated container: refrigeration unit's failure, container's frame damage, etc., • Unsatisfactory condition of transport means: unreliability of vehicles, transhipment devices, etc., • Unsatisfactory condition of transport infrastructure: poor condition of road surfaces, storage areas, etc., • Incorrect container handling technology: insufficient number of handling devices, etc.
Environmental factors	• Adverse seismic conditions: earthquakes, etc. (road, maritime transport and transshipment at terminal), • Adverse hydrological conditions: tsunami, waves, floods, etc. (maritime transport and transshipment at terminal), • Adverse climatic and atmosphere conditions: strong winds, snow, rains, hurricanes, tornados, etc.

2. Determining variants of intermodal transport chains. After a preliminary analysis of transport task for selected food products, having regard to links of transport chains and their possible connections, the variants of intermodal transport chains are designed. These variants are created based on the requirements for food transport indicated by cargo owner (e.g. places of shipment and delivery of cargo, time and financial framework of transport, etc.), taking into account the available infrastructure and transport means operating on the selected route, as well as standards and other requirements for cargo service. At this stage initial selection of possible chains is also carried out, as well as chains that do not meet the guidelines of the transport task, including time and cost, are rejected. After selecting the acceptable variants of cargo transportation, individual chains are subjected to further detailed analysis.

Set of intermodal transport chains accepted for further analysis could be presented as follows:

$$TC = \{tc_i : i = 1, 2, \ldots, I\}, \ i \in \aleph^+, \tag{2}$$

where:

TC – a set of intermodal transport chains,
tc_i – a selected chain, $i = \{1, 2, \ldots, I\}$,
I – number of analyzed chains

3. Analysis and evaluation of individual variants according to selected criteria. The analysis of selected variants may be carried out considering different criteria. These criteria may involve cost and time of cargo transportation, environmental aspects of transport activity, as well as risk level related to cargo quality loss. The set of criteria that will facilitate decision-making may be formulated as follows:

$$CR = \left\{cr_j : j = 1, 2, \ldots, J\right\}, \ j \in \aleph^+, \tag{3}$$

where:

CR – a set of decision-making criteria,
cr_j – a selected criterion, j = $\{1, 2, \ldots, J\}$,
J – number of criteria in a set of decision-making criteria

Particular links of selected transport chain may be analyzed considering conditions of their performance. Set of links of intermodal transport chain may be presented as follows:

$$LTC = \{ltc_k : k = 1, 2, \ldots, K\}, \ k \in \aleph^+, \tag{4}$$

where:

LTC – a set of links of intermodal transport chain,
ltc_k – a selected link, $k = \{1, 2, \ldots, K\}$,
K – number of links in set of links of intermodal transport chain

The links of transport chain may be analyzed considering the set of decision-making criteria, including risk level. In order to analyse risk level, the risk factors occurring during cargo transportation should be determined. Set of risk factors influencing the cargo quality loss during implementation of transport chains could be described using formula:

$$RF = \{rf_n : n = 1, 2, \ldots, N\}, \ n \in \aleph^+, \tag{5}$$

where:

RF – a set of risk factors,
rf_n – a selected risk factor, $n = \{1, 2, \ldots, N\}$,
N – number of risk factors in a set of risk factors

Risk factors may be divided into groups, e.g. human factor, technical and techno-logical factors, environmental factors, etc. It is necessary to identify all possible risk factors that may influence the transportation process. For that reason data obtained from literature and experts' opinions may be used.

Moreover, the set of relations between risk factors and certain links of transport chains should be determined:

$$RRL = \{rrl_m : m = 1, 2, \ldots, M\}, \ m \in \aleph^+, \tag{6}$$

where:

RRL – a set of relations between risk factors and links of intermodal transport chains,
rrl_m – a selected relation between risk factor and link of transport chain, $m = \{1, 2, \ldots, M\}$,
M – number of relations in a set of relations between risk factors and links of transport chains

During the analysis of selected transport chains the influence of particular risk factors rf_n on cargo during implementation of ltc_k link of intermodal transport chain tc_i is analyzed. This analysis is carried out based on information contained in databases, using appropriate calculation models. Therefore, the set of approaches and methods that may be implemented to assess the risk factors influence on transported cargo could be determined:

$$MRL = \{mrl_l : l = 1, 2, \ldots, L\}, \ l \in \aleph^+, \tag{7}$$

where:

MRL – a set of methods to analyze risk level,
mrl_l – a selected method, $l = \{1, 2, \ldots, L\}$,
L – number of methods in a set of methods to analyze risk level

The integrated approach considers that different methods for risk level assessment may be applied within one decision-making tool. For example the risk level may be calculated using i.a.:

- methods of probability theory, in case the statistical data are available,
- methods of multivalued logic theory,
- methods of fuzzy logic theory, when statistical data are unavailable,
- experts' evaluation of particular factors, used when experts assess the possible influence of risk factors on cargo, based on their professional experience (e.g. it could be done using Likert scale [38] or indicating percentage of possible cargo quality loss), etc.

The implementation of particular method may require gathering the necessary information and creation of separate databases and data sets.

Within the approach the way to analyze risk level occurred during particular links and entire transport chain should be determined. The risk level of transport chain may be performed as follows:

$$PR_{tc_i} = \max\left(PR_{ltc_k}\right), \tag{8}$$

where:

PR_{ltc_k} – a risk level occurring during link of transport chain,
PR_{tc_i} – a risk level occurring during implementation of selected i transport chain

Moreover, the integrated approach should give the possibility to compare calculation results received using different methods. Therefore, the reference methodology of achieved calculation results should be elaborated.

4. Deciding on the selection of chain based on the obtained calculation results. After detailed analysis of selected variants, a decision is taken regarding the choice of the intermodal transport chain. Selected transport chains are compared considering set criteria. The final decision on the shape of this chain is taken by the decision-maker based on one or several criteria analysis. Among decision-making criteria the minimization of risk level of cargo quality loss could be applied:

$$PR_{tc} \rightarrow \min\left(PR_{tc_i}\right), \tag{9}$$

where:

PR_{tc} – a risk level occurring during implementation of transport chain

It is important to select the transport chain with the lowest risk level among other analyzed variants.

Weigh coefficients of individual criteria and the ranges of their acceptance have to be specified to improve decision-making. Examples of ranges received using different calculation methods are shown in Table 2. These ranges may be referred to low (highly

Table 2. Sample ranges of acceptance of risk level calculated using different methods.

Method	Highly acceptable	Acceptable	Conditionally acceptable	Unacceptable
Method 1	$PR_{tc} \leq 0,05$	$0,05 < PR_{tc} \leq 0,3$	$0,3 < PR_{tc} \leq 0,6$	$PR_{tc} > 0,6$
Method 2	$PR_{tc} \leq 2$	$2 < PR_{tc} \leq 6$	$6 < PR_{tc} \leq 10$	$PR_{tc} > 10$
Method 3	$PR_{tc} \leq 100$	$100 < PR_{tc} \leq 2000$	$2000 < PR_{tc} \leq 5000$	$PR_{tc} > 5000$

acceptable and acceptable risk level), moderate (conditionally acceptable risk level) and high (unacceptable) risk.

Taking into account the results of the obtained assessments the appropriate decisions could be taken. Set of possible decisions is presented as follows:

$$DTC = \{dct_o : o = 1, 2, \ldots, O\}, \quad o \in \aleph^+, \tag{10}$$

where:

DTC – a set of decisions related to transport chain,
dct_o – a selected decision, $o = \{1, 2, \ldots, O\}$,
O – number of decisions in a set of decisions related to transport chain

This set may be filled with new decisions and new solutions. The examples of possible decisions may be as follows:

- transport performance based on a selected chain (in case of highly-acceptable and acceptable risk level),
- introducing changes in the implementation of the chain aiming to improve it (conditionally acceptable risk level), including:

  - chain-shaped changes,
  - changes in organization or the technology used to transport the cargo,
  - changes in the guidelines for the goods carriage, etc.

- resignation from the implementation of the transport chain according to requirements determined in the order for cargo transport (unacceptable risk level).

On that basis the suggestions and recommendations may be developed for further analysis of transport chains, as well as changes in the existing databases may be introduced.

4.2 Survey Results Analysis

In order to collect necessary data, the opinions of forwarders were analysed. On the basis of the collected opinions of 23 forwarders operating in Poland, it was possible to analyse their perception on risk factors occurring during transport of food in refrigerated containers.

The forwarders answered the question "What links of intermodal transport chains are vulnerable to risk of food quality loss?" (Fig. 2). The respondents had to grade the links in Likert scale from 1 to 5, where 1 – there is no risk, 5 – there is a high risk.

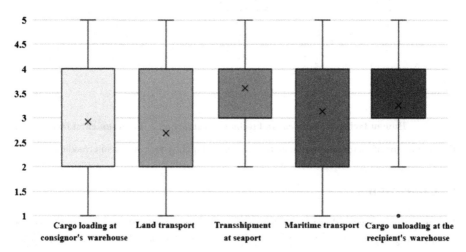

Fig. 2. The forwarders' opinions on links of the intermodal food transport chains, during which the risk of food quality loss may occur.

Analysed group of respondents stated that refrigerated containers transhipment at seaport is dealing with the highest risk of cargo quality loss (with mean score – 3.61). Then, cargo unloading at the recipient's warehouse (3.26), maritime transport (3.13) and cargo loading to the container (2.91) were set. The land transport of cargo (mainly road transport) seems to be less risky (mean score – 2.7). It may be influenced by short distances performed by land transport means on routes organized by forwarders.

The respondents also answered the question related to groups of factors that in their opinion generate the risk of cargo quality loss while transporting the cargo in refrigerated containers (Fig. 3). Forwarders were also asked to assess the factors' groups in Likert scale from 1 to 5, where 1 – group of factors do not generate risk, 5 – generate high risk.

The respondents expressed the opinion that human factor to the greatest extent contributes to the occurrence of risk of cargo quality loss (mean score 3.67). Then, technical and technological factors (mean score 3.22) and environmental factors (mean score 2.91) were placed. The results prove that human mistakes and incorrect decisions essentially influence goods quality losses. The negative influence of other factors is lower.

The obtained data may be useful for databases creation while assessing the influence of risk factors on food quality loss during its transportation.

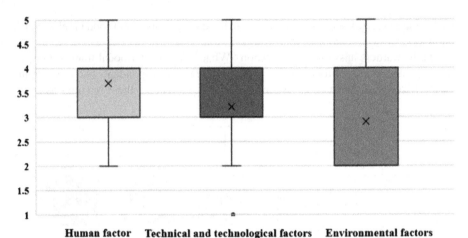

Human factor   Technical and technological factors   Environmental factors

Fig. 3. Groups of factors that generate the risk of food quality loss during intermodal transport.

5   Conclusions

The proposed integrated approach for planning of intermodal transport chains of food products highlights the necessity to analyze the risk factors influence on transported cargo. It shows the preliminary research results that will be developed in more details. Its main idea is to create a possibility to analyze and compare risk level calculated using different methods. The research results may form the basis to create IT tool that will facilitate forwarders in decision-making and give them the opportunity to reach decisions faster and more efficiently.

The results of the survey conducted among freight forwarders operating in Poland proved that there is a risk dealing with transport of food in refrigerated containers. The level of risk occurring during particular links of intermodal transport chain is diverse and particular groups of factors show different influence on transported cargo. Due to forwarders' opinion refrigerated containers handling at seaports is dealing with the highest risk of cargo quality loss comparing to other links of transport chain.

The research results may be of interest for logistics operators and other persons who plan and organise the intermodal food transport chains. The elaboration of methodology allowing to compare calculation results of risk level using different methods, as well as detailed analysis of risk factors occurring during refrigerated containers carriage within intermodal transport chains will form the directions of our further research.

Acknowledgement. The authors would like to acknowledge certain forwarders who shared their opinion and agreed to complete the questionnaire. Moreover, the authors would like to thank the reviewers for helpful comments and suggestions on the draft of the manuscript.

References

1. Drewry Maritime Research. Reefer Shipping Annual Review and Forecast 2020/2021 (2020)
2. Panozzo, G., Cortella, G.: Standards for transport of perishable goods are still adequate?: connections between standards and technologies in perishable foodstuffs transport. Trends Food Sci. Technol. **19**(8), 432–440 (2008)
3. Rodrigue, J.P.: Reefers in North American cold chain logistics: evidence from Western Canadian supply chains. The Van Horne Institute, University of Calgary (2014)
4. Tseng, W.J., Ding, J.F., Chou, C.C., Hsu, F.T., Wang, Y.M., Liu, Y.N., Chang, N.W., Wu, Y.W.: Risk analysis of cargos damages for aquatic products of refrigerated containers: shipping operators' perspective in Taiwan. Inf. Manag. Bus. Rev. **4**(2), 86–94 (2012)
5. Gajewska, T., Lorenc, A.: The impact of trailer conditions on the quality of refrigerated food transport services – a case study. Transp. Prob. **14**(3), 97–107 (2019)
6. Ma, Q., Wang, W., Peng, Y., Song, X.: An optimization approach to the intermodal transportation network in fruit cold chain, considering cost, quality degradation and carbon dioxide footprint. Pol. Maritime Res. **25**(1), 61–69 (2018)
7. Molina-Besch, K., Pålsson, H.: A simplified environmental evaluation tool for food packaging to support decision-making in packaging development. Pack. Technol. Sci. **33**(4–5), 141–157 (2020)
8. Ackerley, N., Sertkaya, A., Lange, R.: Food transportation safety: characterizing risks and controls by use of expert opinion. Food Prot. Trends **30**(4), 212–222 (2010)
9. Broaddus, A., Cervero, R.: Transprtation planning. United States: The Routledge Handbook of International Planning Education, pp. 253–264 (2019)
10. Holz-Rau, C., Scheiner, J.: Land-use and transport planning – a field of complex cause-impact relationships. Thoughts on transport growth, greenhouse gas emissions and the built environment. Transp. Pol. **74**, 127–137 (2019)
11. Basada, C., Gil, R., Fathi, A., Navarro, P., Salvador, A.: Effect of transport temperature on persimmon fruit quality. Acta Hort. **1256**, 355–359 (2019)
12. Filina, L., Filin, S.: An analysis of influence of lack of the electricity supply to reefer containers serviced at sea ports on storing conditions of cargoes contained in them. Pol. Maritime Res. **4**, 96–102 (2008)
13. Filina-Dawidowicz, L.: Wspomaganie podejmowania decyzji w zakresie kompleksowej obsługi kontenerów chłodniczych w zintegrowanych terminalach transportowych. Oficyna Wydawnicza Politechniki Warszawskiej, Warszawa (2018). (in Polish)
14. Yaacob, T.Z., Rafman, F.A., Jaafar, H.S.: Risk categories in halal food transportation: A preliminary finding. Int. J. Supp. Chain Manag. **7**(6), 453–461 (2018)
15. Tseng, W.J., et al.: Transport risks analysis of temperature-controlled cargoes for airfreight forwarders in Taiwan: case study of the orchids. Afr. J. Agric. Res. **6**(27), 5992–5998 (2011)
16. Martinadale, W., Duong, L., Hollands, T.Æ., Swainson, M.: Testing the data platforms required for the 21st century food system using an industry ecosystem approach. Sci. Total Environ. **724**, 137871 (2020)
17. Jedermann, R., Praeger, U., Geyer, M., Lang, W.: Remote quality monitoring in the banana chain. Philos. Trans. Roy. Soc. A: Math., Phy. Eng. Sci. **372**(2017), 20130303 (2014)
18. Lorenc, A., Kuźnar, M.: The impact of cargo monitoring systems usage on intermodal transport risk and costs. World Rev. Intermodal Transp. Res. **6**(4), 336–351 (2017)
19. Baccelli, O., Morino, P.: The role of port authorities in the promotion of logistics integration between ports and the railway system: the Italian experience. Res. Transp. Bus. Manag. 100451 (2020)
20. Chen, Y., Liu, Y., Gou, D., Chen, Z., Li, X.: Freight transit assignments for an integrated network of road transportation and underground logistics systems. J. Pepeline Syst. Eng. Pract. **11**(2), 434 (2020)

21. Ma, Y., Chang, D., Wang, F.: Integrating business processes of container sea-rail combined transport. Int. J. Internet Manuf. Serv. **6**(1), 48–63 (2019)
22. Gnap, J., Varjan, P., Ďurana, P., Kostrzewski, M.: Research on relationship between freight transport and transport infrastructure in selected European countries. Transp. Prob. **14**(3), 63–74 (2019)
23. Kostrzewski, M., Kostrzewski, A.: Analysis of operations upon entry into intermodal freight terminals. Appl. Sci. **9**(12), 2558 (2019)
24. Mańkowska, M., Kotowska, I., Pluciński, M.: Seaports as nodal points of circular supply chains: opportunities and challenges for secondary ports. Sustainability **12**(9), 3926 (2020)
25. Castelein, B., Geerlings, H., Van Duin, R.: The reefer container market and academic research: a review study. J. Clean. Prod. **256**, 120654 (2020)
26. Filina-Dawidowicz, L., Gajewska, T.: Customer satisfaction in the field of comprehensive service of refrigerated containers in seaports. Periodica Polytech. Transp. Eng. **46**(3), 151–157 (2018)
27. Cheng, T.: Optimization plan of refrigerated container refueling strategies in transit. In: ICTE 2015 - Proceedings of the 5th International Conference on Transportation Engineering, Dalian, pp. 3238–3250 (2015)
28. Liu, S., Shao, Y., Peng, Y.: Optimization of multimodal transport paths for refrigerated containers under carbon emission restriction. Appl. Math. Mech. **41**(2), 204–215 (2020)
29. Rech, S., Finco, E., Lazzaretto, A.: A multicriteria approach to choose the best renewable refrigeration system for food preservation. Renew. Energy **154**, 368–384 (2020)
30. Rong, A., Akkerman, R., Grunow, M.: An optimization approach for managing fresh food quality throughout the supply chain. Int. J. Prod. Econ. **131**(1), 421–429 (2011)
31. Leleń, P., Wasiak, M.: The model of selecting multimodal technologies for the transport of perishable products. Arch. Transp. **50**(2), 17–33 (2019)
32. Lakehal, A., Tachi, F.: Probabilistic assessment of road risks for improving logistics processes. MATEC Web Conf. **183**, 139366 (2018)
33. Hachicha, W., Elmsalmi, M.: An integrated approach based-structural modeling for risk prioritization in supply network management. J. Risk Res. **17**(10), 1301–1324 (2014)
34. Filina-Dawidowicz L.: Rationalization of servicing reefer containers in sea port area with taking into account risk influence. Pol. Maritime Res. **2**(82)21, 76–85 (2014)
35. Chou, S.-F., Horng, J.-S., Sam Liu, C.-H., Lin, J.-Y.: Identifying the critical factors of customer behavior: An integration perspective of marketing strategy and components of attitudes. J. Retail. Consum. Serv. **55**, 102113 (2020)
36. Dai, T., Yang, Y., Lee, R., Fleischer, A.S., Wemhoff, A.P.: Life cycle environmental impacts of food away from home and mitigation strategies—a review. J. Environ. Manag. **265**, 110471 (2020)
37. Cepolina, E.M., Cangialosi, E., Giusti, I., Aquaro, D., Caroti, G., Piemonte, A.: Impact of RFID-TTI technologies on the efficiency of perishable products logistics. In: 5th International Food Operations and Processing Simulation Workshop, FoodOPS 2019; Lisbon; Portugal, 151965 (2019)
38. Joshi, A., Kale, S., Chandel, S.K., Pal, D.K.: Likert scale: explored and explained. Br. J. Appl. Sci. Technol. **7**, 396–403 (2015)

Towards an Architecture for Monitoring and User Experience in an Educational Robotics Context

Julian Galindo$^{(\boxtimes)}$ (iD), Henry Paz-Arias(iD), and Lesly Tello(iD)

Escuela Politecnica Nacional, Quito, Ecuador
{julian.galindo,henry.paz,lesly.tello}@epn.edu.ec

Abstract. User experience (UX) has become the main key to support project development to improve user understanding in many contexts. Distinctly, in education, teachers make a strong e ort to monitor the learning process by using manual methods like questionnaires. However, the observation of UX is challenging as data needs to be captured in real-time to have a more clear student's response during the interaction. This article shows an architecture that seeks to monitor and visualize the UX of learning in an educational context in real-time. The architecture, E-catcher, is composed of 4 components: the information gathering, the process, the results, and the monitoring learning. Moreover, the article also shows the creation of a prototype based on our architecture. This prototype is designed as a web application. It uses a facial recognition API and it analyzes emotions, age and gender through detected facial photos. This prototype was tested in a promising experiment. It involved an educational robotics workshop for children by using the Lego Wedo platform. The results showed that it is feasible to observe and visualize user data as emotions, age, and gender in an educational context in real-time by using E-catcher.

Keywords: UX education context monitor architecture · Facial recognition emotions web application WeDo

1 Introduction

User experience (UX) is defined as the mixture of all aspects of the user's interaction with the product or service: how it is perceived, learned, and used [1] as well as users properties such as emotions, preferences, beliefs perceptions, physical and psychological responses, behaviors that happen before, during and after use [6]. It means, the experience of use which can be conceived as user reactions during the interaction in many contexts such as education, marketing, social, among others [1]. Particularly, Education is essential to improve social life and sustainable development. Here, kids and teenagers have an important role to achieve these goals.

System education has serious aws and students memorize but they do not learn. Moreover, according to Unesco's 2017 report, poor quality of education [18] is a common problem in the world. Even more, each person learns in a di erent way being evaluated

© Springer Nature Switzerland AG 2020
G. Rodriguez Morales et al. (Eds.): TICEC 2020, CCIS 1307, pp. 333–347, 2020.
https://doi.org/10.1007/978-3-030-62833-8_25

some times as a group rather than as individual. This could lead to incorrect evaluations about the learning process which can affect the individual process of learning. A common way to measure the level of knowledge is using quizzes. This model limits some student's process learning as quizzes may not be created with dynamic and multimedia content. This approached shows that teaching techniques are not enough to get a good level of education.

To overcome these issues, teachers are using new material tools such as slides, videos, and websites. Besides, they monitor students by checking whether every-one is doing the proposed activity. However, all these evaluation techniques are manual and can not be done every day and through all classes. Another way to carry out the learning monitoring process is through an automated procedure. It can analyze implicit data (detected user signals) from several students at once and in real-time. For instance, video recognition allows teachers to examine the results obtained easily, by analyzing expressions of students such as facial, gestures, or even speech recognition. In this context, the detected signals can be analyzed to retrieve expressive reactions such as emotions. They have the potential to measure such reactions which may uncover the user experience.

In this context, this paper shows an architecture called e-catcher (Emotion catcher) to monitor UX in a learning process by using emotions. This architecture attempts to be independent of technology. It can get data from a user and infers vital signs, face attributes, emotions, and basic data like age and gender. Hence an important part of this project is to design a Software system prototype that interacts with new technologies like facial recognition to monitor UX. The prototype collects information in an educational robotics workshop with children between 9 and 10 years old with a camera. In the workshop, there are three learning stages provided by LEGO education: explore, create, and share [10]. Teachers show a problem to be explored by children so that they can figure out solutions to it by using a robotic Lego kit like Wedo 2.0. Finally, children share their solutions with others. The e-catcher prototype analyses facial expressions to retrieve eight emotions: neutral, fear, sadness, contempt, anger, happiness, disgust, surprise, and also gender and age through the workshop phases of learning [16].

The remainder of this paper is the following: the Sect. 2 presents related work about architectures used measuring emotion in other contexts. The Sect. 3, presents an explanation of the architecture design proposed called E-catcher. The Sect. 4 describes the prototype design based on our architecture and how it was tested in a robotic workshop. The Sect. 5, summarizes the results and finally, last section shows conclusions and future work.

2   Related Work

In [5], an adaptive interface design is presented with to customize interfaces to the needs of the user. The architecture of this type of system is based on dividing the tasks to be performed into modules. Data capture is done in real-time through the use of sensors. The user characteristics captured are both dynamic and static. The dynamic characteristics are movement patterns and their relationship with their mental state. The static characteristics are age, gender, language, etc. The limitations would be that it does not have an image correction stage. It does not decide if the data taken is valid or not without storing it. Moreover, it also does not have graphics, statistical analysis, and multi-user.

[11] presents an adaptive system architecture designed to perceive the user's emotional and active states through three multi-modal subsystems: Visual through facial images and videos, Kinesthetic through autonomic nervous system signals and Auditory through speech. The results of the system's detection are integrated into the agent's multi-modal perceived anthropomorphic interface, and then it adapts its interface by responding in the most appropriate way to the user's current emotional states and provides intelligent multi-modal feedback to the user. The limitations is related to user analysis. It asks the user for an initial state and then a different one. No analysis is shown during the transition, it does not present analysis by multi-user so that it is limited to one person at the time.

In [2] it should be noted that sensory-motor control and learning are fundamental requirements for cognitive development in humans and animals. Human behavior and neuroscience researchers agree that brain and motor development are intertwined with the process of exploration, where body representations are created and maintained, to guide our movements. This work focuses principally on the autonomous motor and mental development to bring together the latest advances in studies on exploration, behavior, internal body representations, and the process of sensory and motor simulations. It does not focus on other stages than exploration, neither does it take data through a real-time camera.

In [14], presents an architecture capable of adapting to changes in context without losing usability. The architecture presents three main processes: data capture, data analysis, and interface change management. Another feature is the capture of data in real-time using various tools such as network speed meters, light intensity, etc. The limitations of this architecture would be the lack of an image correction stage. The architecture is based on considering different sources, so an invalid photo is not given special treatment. Another limitation would be the low storage. This system is based on processing the current data and not the storing of the already processed data. This limitation means that the behavior of the data can not be plotted and there is no statistical analysis. The system is based on capturing environmental attributes and does not analyze or take user data at any time. In [3] for the analysis of human affective states, the electroencephalogram (EEG) and peripheral physiological signals of 32 participants were used. These were recorded while each participant watched 40 one-minute extracts from music videos. Participants rated each video in terms of levels of taste, disgust, mastery, and familiarity among others. The front side of the participants was also recorded. There is not a process to support images correction in the case of such activity is required. Finally, multi-user analysis is not performed.

Finally Table 1 shows a comparison between all the architectures presented. Mainly, it is clear that there is a lack of an image correction process, storing data, and multi-variable analysis since only one of them supports multi user analysis. Moreover, real-time is not a generalized feature. Thus, these ongoing features lead us to move forward to do a deep exploration in monitoring and visualizing UX with multiple variables at real-time.

The next section will describe the proposed architecture, taking the best strategies from other ones.

Table 1. Comparative table of the related work

Related work					
Features	[5]	[14]	[2]	[3]	[11]
Modularity	+	+	+	+	+
Image Correction	−	−	−	−	−
Real Time	+		+		
Storage Information			−		
Graphs				+	−
Statistic analysis			+	+	+
Multi-user analysis			+	+	+

3   Architecture E-Catcher

We designed an architecture of the educational robotics system called E- catcher (Emotion catcher) to monitor and visualize UX at real time. It attempts to reuse the best-found features of all the valuable works shown in the related work. It is illustrated in Fig. 1 which is composed of four components: information gathering, process, results and the monitoring learning. The rst component is the information gathering stage, made up of explicit information and user data captured by sensors. The bene t of this user data is to have a user representation or user model as shown in the General User Model Ontology [9]. This sensor data involves user variables such as Ekman emotions (anger, contempt, disgust, fear, happiness, neutral, sadness and surprise) [8, 7], gender, age, and other user

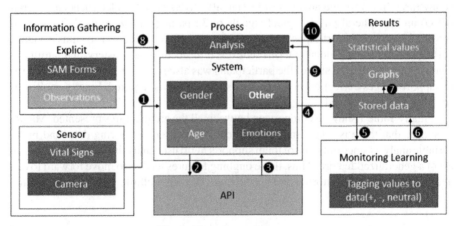

Fig. 1. E-catcher architecture.

features such as face rectangle, shape and size of the nose, facial hair and accessories as glasses or hats [12].

These data are sent to the system (1). In the process component, the system that receives the data from the sensors is processed using an API (2). The output values of the API are returned to the system. (3) These values are stored in the result component, which is responsible for loading, storing, and displaying the data generated by the process component (4). The data stored in the rst instance is tagged as positive, negative, or neutral in the last component (the Monitoring Learning) (5). These data are returned to the results stage to be stored in a new data collection (6). The same data is used by the system to generate graphs according to the different measures obtained by the system (7). Besides this information gathered by sensors, e-catcher is able to collect explicit information (e.g. observations of the user experience by using Self Assessment Manikin (SAM)) during the interaction (8). This information along with the stored data is analyzed by the process (9) and send to the results component to compute statistical values like average of emotions (10). This architecture aims to cover the features of real-time detection and graphics.

4   Experimental Study

Following the E-catcher architecture, explained in the section above, a prototype was implemented. It used Java-script to full functionality and Maqetta for design user interfaces (UI). Further, Microsoft face-recognition API and Firebase as database and storage. We conduct an experimental study which allows us to understand how the prototype can be used to monitor the User experience by detecting user variables such as gender, age and emotions. Particularly, emotions are seen as user responses during the interaction [4].

4.1   Goal and Hypothesis

The objective of this experiment is to examine whether E-catcher is able to detect and visualize user data (emotions, gender and age) in an educational context during the interaction. This information is collected in real-time using the software prototype of the e-catcher architecture while students participate in a educational robotics (RE) workshop. The workshop involves three stages: exploring, creating and sharing. Children explore the problem, create a solution with a robotic Lego kit like Wedo 2.0 and show it to all the class. Hence, the experiment hypothesis is:

H_0: E-catcher is able to infer and visualize emotions (neutral, fear, sadness, contempt, anger, happiness, disgust and surprise), gender and age in real-time for a RE workshop per each stage of a learning process (explore, create and share).

4.2   Experimental Method

A web interface was developed aligned to the e-catcher architecture to monitor user experience as shown in Fig. 2. This web prototype has 2 roles: administrator (instructor) and participants (children). The rst one can manage all options in the prototype which

Fig. 2. e-catcher prototype

is used by the instructor. The participants interact with Lego Wedo 2.0 software while following instructions of the administrator.

In terms of technology, Microsoft Face Recognition was included in E-catcher prototype. It was the tool used to detect emotions and the other features. Participants interact with The Wedo 2.0 LEGO software that allows simple programming such as allowing movement [10]. The Lego kit is part of the Education WeDo 2.0 Core Set which is used by children to build a lego project.

The prototype includes four modules: administrator, stage, data collection, and visualization. In the administrator module, a new participant can be added and complete his/her data. Also, it is possible to modify the personal information about children or delete. Create, modify and delete are functions of the administrator. The Module stage is the main part of the software application web. Administrator can select the workshop and participants for it. Then, children saves that information on the database. Next, there is a list of learning's stages, which can be chosen by the administrator. Finally, the administrator does a click on button 'start' and data will be collected until button 'stop' is clicked. The Module Data collection takes photos and plots all the information inferred by Microsoft API recognition tool. During the workshop, children did not realize the exact moment when a photo was taken. Moreover, there was not any restriction for children, they were free to move, so, if a they wanted to change places with one another, they did it. Besides, each image was taken by a camera which was stable and static (xed position). In the execution of the prototype of the software system E-catcher, con icts were obtained with the extraction of the URL of the captured image. To solve this limitation in images storage, rebase was used as data storage to simplify the extraction process. Cloud Storage helps to design quickly and easily store and save photos and videos. Since this, the system was able to send the image to the API free version to get back the user data every 20 s (API limitations).

Procedure, tasks and participants The experiment sample included 8 participants (children): 50% male and 50% female from 9 to 10 years old (mean age 9). Each participant was assigned to one workshop. To recall, there are three learning stages provided by LEGO education: explore, create, and share [10]. There were two sessions for each workshop. On the rst session (Monday), the instructor explained to the participants the objective of the workshop, and a brief explanation was given about a science problem. In this case, the workshop was about the understanding of frog metamorphosis. The rst stage carried out was the Exploration stage, each child listened to the indications and participated with the instructor, through questions and answers. Once this stage was nished, we proceeded to the Creation stage, in which the children got to know the different components of the Legos Kit and the functioning of the Wedo2.0 software to build a frog with lego. The students selected the workshop indicated by the instructor "Metamorphosis of the Frog" in the Wedo2.0 software. The software instructed them step to step how to assemble the frog, with each child placing a piece of lego at a time. If any doubts arose then the instructors were responsible for solving them. The rst part of this stage ended with the Frog Metamorphosis without any functionalities, ending the photo session, and concluding the rst session. The built frog is illustrated in Fig. 3. The rst figure shows the frog construction without front legs while the second one is the improvement including the missing legs in the previous model.

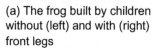

(a) The frog built by children without (left) and with (right) front legs

(b) The code associated with the lego frog implemented by children

Fig. 3. The built frog and its code.

In the second session (Thursday), once the students were located at the workplace, the team resumed the creation stage and activated the photo session. The instructors indicated which components of the Wedo2.0 software should be used for the frog to have motion functionality, then the students dragged the components to the built frog to create motion. Figure 3 shows the resulting code to make the frog moves. It provides motion to the frog by a Bluetooth connection between the PC and the Bluetooth lego device. Essentially, it moves the lego motor once to allow the back legs motion of the frog in Fig. 3. Fifteen minutes were given for the students to modify the frog to their liking in both appearance and functionality, the working group continued with the change of the frog parts, giving it new functionalities such as sound, undefined movement, etc. Creation stage was nished. Next, the sharing stage is initiated, the instructor asks a series of questions to each member of the working group, each student shares his or her experience with others, ending the sharing stage and concluding the photo-detection. Finally, the students disarm their creation, and the instructors and data collection sta thank the students for their collaboration.

Interaction Data and Images Correction During the experiment using the implemented software system prototype, several images were captured per user. There was an agreement to take these photos so that this private information is only for academic purposes and it is only available for the institution where the workshop takes place. The images provided this set of information: detected emotions (sadness, contempt, happiness, disgust, surprise, neutral, fear and anger), his/her gender, and an estimation of the age from the physical features. The capture of the images was done in two sessions (2 h per session) with a total of 298 images (facial pictures). On the rst session (Monday) the stage of exploring and creating, while on the second session (Thursday) the stage of creating and sharing. There were organization activities and explanations to children before starting each stage to clarify the workshop without data detection.

After the images were captured during each learning stage, a selection of valid images was made automatically as the system releases a detection error with invalid images. To determine a valid image, it must contain a greater focus of the user's face as can be seen in Fig. 4.

(a) Valid Image   (b) Invalid image

Fig. 4. Valid and Invalid image.

In this picture, it is possible to detect the whole face of the child in the central part, and he is looking directly at the camera. Further, the girl on the left side, although she is not looking directly at the computer, the camera can detect her whole face, allowing the analysis through the API.

To determine an invalid image, it must have a bad facial focus of the user and even show parts of the body not related to the user's face as shown in the following Fig. 4. As you can see in the picture, it is not possible to detect the children's faces because they are outside the range covered by the camera. Also, there are parts of the body such as the arm and body of the children that do not give any valid information for later analysis. This makes the analysis through the API di cult.

As shown in Table 2, on Monday, a total of 57 photos were captured for the exploration stage: 54 photos of them are valid, with a percentage of 94.74%, and a total of

Table 2. Photo collection.

Photos				
Day of work	Stage	Total photos	Total valid photos	Percentage
Monday	Explore	57	54	94,74%
Monday	Create	125	119	95,20%
Thursday	Create	89	81	91,01%
Thursday	Share	27	20	74,07%
Total		298	274	91.95%

125 photos for the creation stage, of which 119 are valid, with a percentage of 95.20%. Finally, on Thursday a total of 89 photos were captured for the create stage of which 81 are valid with a percentage of 91.01% and a total of 27 photos for the share stage of which 20 are valid with a percentage of 74.07%. The data that attracts the most attention is in the sharing stage because it has a relatively low percentage compared to the other stages. This is due to the fact that in this stage, as its name indicates, the children had to share her/his experience with other ones. Therefore, they had to stand up from their seats and explain in front of their classmates. The range covered by the camera does not manage to capture their faces, which is why we have a greater number of invalid images causing their percentage to decrease accordingly.

4.3   Measure and Methods

As the goal is to monitor the user during a learning experience, the measures involve user interaction data: detected emotions which are categorized based on [15] as positive (happiness), negative (fear, sadness, contempt, anger, happiness, disgust), neutral and surprise (which can be interpreted as positive or negative [17]), detected emotion average (e.g. total happiness/number of detected pictures), facial pictures, date and time detection, image URL, gender and age [12]. The pictures were taken at an interval of 20 s during the development of the practice with the robotics kit as a considerable time limit of the free version of the API [12]. Each picture that was taken by the E-catcher system by using Microsoft's Face API. The Microsoft API integrates face detection, emotion recognition, and different characteristics of a person's face. Both the data collection and its analysis were done in real-time so it was necessary to have a testing period before using the system in the workshop.

4.4   Prototype Tests

The web prototype was tested to check a correct functionality. The main objective of the tests was to check the integration of all its components: the Storage of the photos in the database, the gathering of the URL through Firebase Firestore, the Capture of the data generated by the API and the Generation of graphs from the data obtained by the system.

In the case of storage, it is veri ed that the photos are uploaded with the speci ed format name of "image taken + date + time" in the respective collection for each stage. The obtaining of the URL is veri ed by the response from the Microsoft Facial Recognition API. The capture of the data generated by the API is validated by database queries. The graphics generated in real-time are tested using the photos captured by the system. The testing phase took place before the workshop. Each member of the development team used the system to simulate di erent emotions. In total, 180 photos were taken. Detected emotions, gender and age were gathered. The rst photos are directly seen to the camera and then, simulating situations in which there is no full-face or covering certain parts of the face. The second test, detected if the facial recognition tool is able to analyze more than one person in the photo. There was not error during test phase and all the photos and data related were stored at Firebase. After verifying the functionality of each of the components, the complete system was tested. The correct functionality of the system consisted in the execution for a long period time. The test consisted of a simulation of the workshop carried out. The estimated times were 20 min for the Explore stage, 50 min for the Create stage and 10 min for the Share stage. The system works well at integrating all components across the three learning stages.

5   Results

5.1   Ho: E-Catcher Is Able to Infer and Visualize Emotions, Gender, and Age in Real-Time for a RE Workshop Per Each Stage of the Learning Process

The Fig. 5 shows a comparison between a photo taken on the day of the workshop and its respective emotion analysis with the API. We can see that in the image the face of the girl in the middle shows a certain level of surprise and e-catcher prototype shows 95.9% of the emotion surprise along with less than 5% for the others.

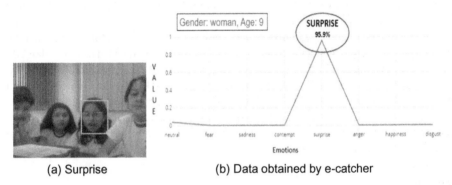

(a) Surprise   (b) Data obtained by e-catcher

Fig. 5. Comparative of the captured image and its analysis I

On the other hand the Fig. 6 and Fig. 7 show images where a child evokes mainly emotions like happiness (0.9) and neutral (0.698) respectively. Each of these images has its detection analysis. We can see that what is obtained with the API is not different from the expressions that the children manifest in these images.

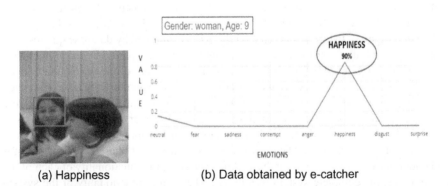

(a) Happiness   (b) Data obtained by e-catcher

Fig. 6. Comparative of the captured image and its analysis II (Color figure online)

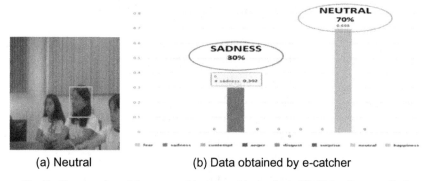

(a) Neutral   (b) Data obtained by e-catcher

Fig. 7. Comparative of the captured image and its analysis III (Color figure online)

The results show a clear predominance of "neutral" emotion over all other emotions for Monday (rst session) as we can see in the emotions graph over the time in Fig. 8. Table 3 show us the averages of the emotions for Mondays in this table the neutral emotion has an average of 77.61%. Similarly, the graph of emotions vs time for Thursday (Fig. 8) show us a clear predominance of "neutral" emotion over all other emotions as shown in the Table 3 where the averages of the emotions are shown. In this table the neutral emotion has an average of 73.91%. Remarkably, it is clearly seen that there are differences in the trend lines of emotions for both Figures 6 and 7. For instance, the red trend line (surprise levels) is bigger on Monday than Thursday inferring that children have less surprise as they have more familiarity with the learning activity.

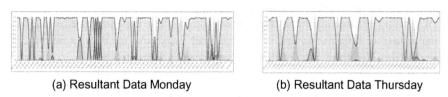

(a) Resultant Data Monday   (b) Resultant Data Thursday

Fig. 8. Neutral detected emotion (green) in Monday and Thursday (Color figure online)

On the other hand, the e-catcher prototype was able to detect and visualize gender and age for all participants (Fig. 6 and Fig. 5). However, there were almost 30% of error at finding the users gender and age. For instance, a boy aged 9 was actually detected 12 years old with a woman detected label. It means a low accuracy detection for these both variables by the API. Overall, these results show that it is feasible to monitor and visualize user data (emotions, gender and age) during the workshop by using e-catcher prototype which validates Ho.

Table 3. Emotion average on Monday and Thursday.

Emotion average		
Emotion	Monday	Thursday
Happiness	10.4%	12.4%
Anger	2.2%	0.59%
Surprise	3.4%	0.78%
Fear	0.8%	0.13%
Sadness	2.62%	0.91%
Neutral	77.61%	73.91%
Contempt	2.22%	1.11%
Disgust	0.31%	0.11%

5.2 Discussion

The development of a prototype system based on the E-catcher architecture and the capture of emotions, gender and age carried out by the prototype was successful. Particularly, the manner of visualize user data at real-time such as emotions reactions as trend lines to uncover UX. This can be helpful for teachers or even fathers to understand how students are responding during learning activities [2, 11].

During the development of the workshop, the students' data were obtained in real-time. The emotions obtained were graphed in order to observe the evolution of the emotions during the development of the workshop.

According to the comparative Table 4, we observed that the great shortcomings are in the storage of information and in the statistical analysis of the data carried out. To overcome this, E-catcher captures the data permanently in a database.

Table 4. Comparative table with E-catcher

Camparative table						
Features	[5]	[14]	[2]	[3]	[11]	E-catcher
Modularity	+	+	+	+	+	+
Image correction	−		−	−	−	+
Real time	+		+	+		+
Storage Information			−			+
Graphs				+	−	+
Statistic analysis				+	+	+
Multi-user analysis		+		−	−	+

The big limitation we found was that the users moved freely. This causes some photos to be invalid for analysis. However, it allows getting very truthful data without any influence on the users. Moreover, even when the e-catcher prototype was tested successfully in a real experience (workshop) involving instructors and children, it should be necessary a formal evaluation of the architecture to compare key features with other architecture prototypes such as time detection, detection accuracy, valid taken images, system latency and others. One limitation to achieve this evaluation is that not all architectures shown in the related work provides such information or a prototype (architecture implementation).

In terms of detection accuracy, e-catcher is linked to the API for the detection. The experiment used microsoft api with an accuracy of 90–95% on emotions [12]. The gender and age detection needs to be improved to have a better accuracy. Although our goal is to monitor and visualize UX, it could affect UX interpretation as the instructor could de ne inappropriate instructions or educational content to guide students based on a misleading age which could lead to a negative UX. Moreover, a 20 s of time detection may lead to a lack of UX as users evoke multiple expressions per second [13]. An e-catcher test with the paid version of the API may lead to a more precise UX monitoring.

User satisfaction is linked to the degree of user familiarity with an object (workshop) [17]. It may be inferred with e-catcher as children had less surprise on the second session so that they may have a more pleasant feeling. It was re effected by lower trend lines (surprise levels) on Thursday.

6 Conclusions and Future Work

This paper presents an architecture named E-catcher (Emotion catcher) for monitor and visualize UX in real-time by gathering user data. A prototype of the architecture was implemented. It was used in a promising experiment associated with an educational robotics workshop for children. The preliminary results validate that it is feasible to infer gender, age, and, particularly, visualize emotions over a learning process in an educational context in real-time. More experiments will be necessary to prove the effectiveness of the presented architecture with all kind of user data.

E-catcher manages to effectively integrate the monitoring and visualization of images in real-time through a developed prototype. It allows the capture of photos by a camera, to extract user data: emotions, gender and age across the learning phases. The prototype works well but it can be improved in some aspects as: security, more detected photos, more precise detection time, and more multidimensional data such as speech recognition or body gestures.

In the data collection, some captures do not show any results. This was due to the children covered their faces, putting their hands on the. The data obtained by these captures are null, however, the data obtained in each valid capture indicates that there exist emotion differences. Besides, there is an influence of external factors on UX such as the team working, instructors, teachers and data collection sta. This makes the results to lose precision.

Moreover, being able to quantify data as emotions generates a great opportunity to statistically analyze the influence of these not only in the area of education but also in areas where a user-centered approach is a key element: marketing, psychology, medicine, and others. The non-invasive method and the fact that users were not aware of the data collection has given us more real and reliable data for analysis. In spite of the architecture limitations, this is a valuable step to go beyond traditional methods to monitor and visualize UX in an educational context in real-time.

References

1. Albert, W., Tullis, T.: Measuring the User Experience: Collecting, Analyzing, and Presenting Usability Metrics. Newnes, May 2013. google-Books-ID: bPhLeM-BLEkAC
2. Biswas, P., Bhattacharya, S., Samanta, D.: User model to design adaptable interfaces for motor-impaired users. In: TENCON 2005 2005 IEEE Region, vol. 10, pp. 1–6. IEEE (2005). http://ieeexplore.ieee.org/xpls/absall:jsp?arnumber=4085088
3. Calvary, G., et al.: Plasticity of user interfaces: A revisited reference frame-work. In: Task Models and Diagrams for User Interface Design. Citeseer (2002). http://citeseerx.ist.psu.edu/viewdoc/summary?doi=10.1.1.13.3312
4. Cernea, D., Weber, C., Ebert, A., Kerren, A.: Emotion scents: a method of representing user emotions on gui widgets. In: IS&T/SPIE Electronic Imaging, pp. 86540F–86540F. International Society for Optics and Photonics (2013), http://proceedings.spiedigitallibrary.org/proceeding.aspx?articleid=1568718
5. Conati, C., Chabbal, R., Maclaren, H.: A study on using biometric sensors for monitoring user emotions in educational games. In: Workshop on assessing and adapting to user attitudes and a ect: Why, when and how. Citeseer (2003)
6. DIS, I.: 9241-210: 2010. Ergonomics of human system interaction-Part 210: Human-centred design for interactive systems. International Standardization Organization (ISO). Switzerland (2009)
7. Ekman, P.: Emotions revealed: Recognizing faces and feelings to improve communication and emotional life. Macmillan (2007)
8. Ekman, P., Keltner, D.: Universal facial expressions of emotion. California mental health research digest **8**(4), 151–158 (1970). https://www.paulekman.com/wp-content/uploads/2013/07/Universal-Facial-Expressions-of-Emotions1.pdf
9. Heckmann, D., Schwartz, T., Brandherm, B., Schmitz, M., von Wilamowitz-Moellendor, M.: Gumo{the general user model ontology. In: User modeling 2005, pp. 428–432. Springer (2005). http://link.springer.com/chapter/10.1007/1152788658
10. lego.com, L.: WeDo 2.0 Teacher Guides { Support { LEGO Education (2016). https://education.lego.com/en-us/support/wedo-2/teacher-guides
11. Lisetti, C., Bastard, G., MAUI, I.I.: MAUI: a Multimodal A ective User Interface Sensing User's Emotions based on Appraisal Theory-Questions about Facial Expressions.http://www.eurecom.fr/fr/publication/1800/download/mm-lisech-040601.pdf
12. Microsoft.com: Computer Vision API for Microsoft Cognitive Services (2020). https://docs.microsoft.com/en-us/azure/cognitive-services/computer-vision/home
13. Noldus.com: FaceReader (2020). https://www.noldus.com/facereader
14. Partala, T., Kallinen, A.: Understanding the most satisfying and unsatisfying user experiences: Emotions, psychological needs, and context. Interacting with computers **24**(1), 25–34 (2012). publisher: Oxford University Press Oxford, UK
15. Posner, J., Russell, J.A., Peterson, B.S.: The circumplex model of a ect: an integrative approach to aective neuroscience, cognitive development, and psychopathology. Development and psychopathology **17**(03), 715–734 (2005). http://journals.cambridge.org/abstractS0954579405050340

16. Schutz, P.A., Pekrun, R.: Introduction to emotion in education. In: Emotion in education, pp. 3–10. Elsevier (2007)
17. Steunebrink, B.R., et al: The Logical structure of emotions (2010). http://dspace.library.uu.nl/handle/1874/43581
18. UNESCO: More than one-half of children and adolescents are not learning worldwide (2017). publisher: UNESCO Institute for Statistics Montreal, QC

Real-Time Augmented Reality Application for Visualizing Variables in Industrial Processes

Juan Carlos Molina$^{(\boxtimes)}$, Gabriela Chiliquinga , Morelva Saeteros ,
and Gustavo Caiza

Universidad Politécnica Salesiana, Quito, Ecuador
{jmolinaa1,gchiliquinga}@est.ups.edu.ec,
{csaeteros,gcaiza}@ups.edu.ec

Abstract. In recent years there has been an increase in the use of virtual tools in different areas such as: education, tourism or industry. The augmented reality (AR) enables the correlation of the real world with virtual objects so that users have additional information of the surrounding environment supplementing the learning and experience of the user. The present work shows the development of an AR application, which characterizes and sends information of the industrial sensors in real time; the recognition of objects utilized a three-dimensional analysis due to the holographic geometry of the MPS PA Compact Workstation, the mobile application combines various development platforms such as: Visual Studio, Android Studio Unity and Vuforia. The data of the sensors arrive to a public URL address which enables visualizing its status in real time, the Android application accesses the particle cloud server via WiFi enabling visualizing the information of the sensors in the smartphone.

Keywords: Augmented reality · Wireless communication · Industrial sensors · AR application · Object recognition

1 Introduction

At present, the use of virtual tools shows a great development in entertainment, tourism and education. The augmented reality takes part in the tools that enable combining the real world with virtual data, enhancing the senses with which reality is perceived, this is achieved through the information there is in the digital world, by means of different technological supports such as tablets and mobile telephones, thus acting as a lens with which the world is seen [1, 2]. In addition, various studies have been carried out which investigate the impact on the learning of people and it has been demonstrated that it facilitates the long-term understanding and retention [3].

Integrating the experience of the real world with virtual channels enables improving the acquisition of information in real time [2]. In addition, due to the emergence of smart phones, it has been developed applications to interact with Augmented Reality that help the user to recognize objects in their surrounding by means of cameras and

© Springer Nature Switzerland AG 2020
G. Rodriguez Morales et al. (Eds.): TICEC 2020, CCIS 1307, pp. 348–362, 2020.
https://doi.org/10.1007/978-3-030-62833-8_26

software to obtain real information, and supplement it with additional virtual information in the screen of their mobile device [4]. The Industrial Augmented Reality (IAR) is one of the technologies that provide support tools to the operators to undertake tasks, helping in the mounting, assistance, visualization, interaction, quality control and materials management [5]. On the other hand, this technology may be applied to project the visual appearance of a prototype by directly focusing on a physical model [6], it may be also presented additional and dynamic information to the operators and technical staff, and besides create applications for the maintenance, programming and assembly of equipment [7]. In the area of maintenance, it should be taken into account the complex environmental, regulatory and economic requirements that must be fulfilled by support applications with Augmented Reality [5]. At present, there are relatively few researches works in the development of AR applications focused in the characterization of industrial equipment and real-time data acquisition. The purpose of the characterization is to determine the functioning of an element to know the technical data of the manufacturer to operate them in a correct and safe manner [8].

The present work develops an AR application that enables characterizing industrial elements through the recognition of objects, and at the same time presents process data in real time. The application was tested in the MPS PA Compact Workstation module, which enables implementing real industrial processes, has analog or digital sensors and actuators, a PLC that enables implementing various control systems such as: level, flow, pressure or temperature control. The software Vuforia, Unity, Visual Studio and Android Studio were utilized for the recognition of images and the generation of AR elements, while an IoT development electronic board, known as particle photon, was utilized for data acquisition; data from analog and digital sensors are acquired during the process, which are sent through a Wi-Fi connection to the Particle Cloud to be visualized in a smartphone or in virtual reality glasses, and once the object has been recognized, the AR application displays the name of the element and the values of the variables obtained in real-time. In addition, by means of an information button a brief characterization of the technical data of the sensor is accessed, with the purpose of providing the user a global perspective of the identified element.

The paper is organized in the following manner: Sect. 2 describes the utilized materials and methods, the design and implementation are shown in Sect. 3, Sect. 4 shows the results and finally Sect. 5 provides the conclusions.

2 Technological Framework

2.1 Augmented Reality

The augmented reality combines the physical world with virtual objects and increases the perception of the world for the user, in this way, a realistic perspective of both scenarios is externalized as if it were real elements [9]. It enables that the users have additional information of real environments, thus becoming a useful tool for the programming, maintenance, training, safety and prevention in particular working environments [10]. Similarly, it is related to the virtual reality technology that exhibits some common features, such as the incorporation of 2D (two-dimension) and 3D (three-dimension) graphical virtual models.

2.2 Vuforia Development

Vuforia is a web environment where the users can create and manage their bookmarks. This software is capable of creating 3D objects and texts that are stored in the cloud of the users. Some of its functionalities are detailed in the following [11]:

Image Recognition. The selected frames were subjected to a reference point in their ability to recognize flat images.

Target-Star Rating. Image targets are detected based on the natural features that are extracted from their destination to compare them in run time with features of the live images. The star rating of a target ranges between 1 and 5 stars. In order to obtain the best results, it is necessary to aim for targets with 4 or 5 stars (Table 1).

Table 1. Attributes for the target-star rating [11].

Attribute	Example
Rich in detail	Street scene, group of people, collages and mixtures of items or sport scenes
Good contrast	Has bright and dark regions, is well-lit, and does not have brightness nor color
Without repetitive patterns	Grass field, the front of a modern house with identical windows, and other regular grids and patterns

Object Recognition. It is a digital representation of the features and the physical geometry of an object, as opposed to the image recognition which requires the use of a flat source image, this type of recognition is ideal for rigid 3D objects. The object subject to analysis must be opaque, rigid, contain few moving parts, be indoor with moderately bright and diffuse light, the surface of the object must be uniformly illuminated and should not contain shadows.

2.3 Unity

It is a multiplatform engine developed by Unity Technologies. It utilizes the languages C, C++ and C Sharp compatible with Microsoft. Unity has available script sections with multiple libraries for graphic design. Once a project is created in Unity various folders are generated: library (stores the libraries utilized), project Settings (includes configuration files of the Unity Mecanims), obj (files related with the compiler), assets (files of the scenes created by the developer) [12].

2.4 Visual Studio

Visual Studio is an Integrated Development Environment (IDE) programmed in C++ and Microsoft C Sharp. It may be installed in Microsoft Windows and Mac OS systems. It supports programming languages such as C++, C#, Visual Basic .NET, F#, Java, Python, Ruby, PHP and ASP.NET, among others. Unity 3D has the capability of working with Visual Studio Community [13]. Visual Studio enables creating web applications in any environment that supports the .NET platform, which provides a high-level language that generates the grammar to communicate with the computer [14]. The more important aspects of the coding of a program in Visual Studio are: instructions (individual steps to be executed), flow control instructions (they enable creating loops, conditions and branching in the code), variables (containers of data that, in general, may be texts, numbers or Booleans), assignment (place the name of a variable to the left of an assignment operator so that the data is stored in that variable), function calls (function blocks previously written, encapsulated in a single name) [13].

2.5 MPS PS Compact Workstation

MPS PA is a Workstation for technical training that utilizes practical problems of real operational applications. At the same time, it provides the perfect platform to analyze, understand and master the interaction of the mechanics, the pneumatics, the electrical engineering, the control technology and the communication interfaces [15]. The digital and analog sensors and actuators together with the PLC provide four closed control loops that include: level, flow, pressure and temperature control. The functionalities of each closed-loop system are the result of the manual combination of valves and PLC programming [16] (Fig. 1).

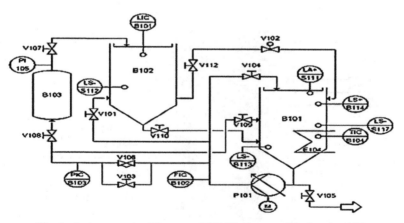

Fig. 1. Instrumentation Diagram - MPS PA Compact Workstation.[17]

The most important technical data of the sensors and actuators utilized in the AR application are detailed in Table 2.

Table 2. Values of voltage and current of the sensors and actuators.

Element	Description
Capacitive sensor	Operation: – Digital (0/24) Vdc
Ultrasonic sensor	Operation: – Analog (0–10) Vdc
Temperature sensor	Incorporates a PT100, has analog operation: (0–10) Vdc linearly related with temperature (0°–100°) C
Pump	Operation: – Analog (0–10) Vdc – Digital (0/24) Vdc
Heater	Operation: – Analog (0–10) Vdc – Digital (0/24) Vdc

2.6 Particle Photon

It is an IoT development board, which has an ARM Cortex M3 microcontroller of 120 MHz with a chip Broadcom Wi-Fi of small size. Particle Photon provides a free service in the Particle Cloud, it has an API REST compatible with web and local IDEs. It has 18 mixed-signal GPIOs, and also a LED RGB indicator of the status of the connection of the board. The energy is supplied to the Photon through a VIN pin, and the voltage must be regulated in the range 3.6VDC-5.5VDC. The average current consumption is 80 mA when the Wi-Fi is active. It has a 12-bit ADC [18] (Fig. 2).

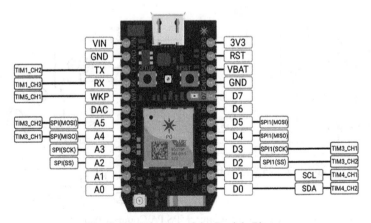

Fig. 2. Pin Diagram of the Particle Photon.

3   Design

The process initiates with the acquisition of data from the industrial sensors, which operate in voltage ranges higher than those of the microcontroller; for this reason, a signal conditioning stage was designed through a voltage divider that enables obtaining 3 Vdc in the digital sensors and a voltage range (0–3.27) Vdc in the analog sensors.

For the development of the AR application it was utilized a computer with the following tools: Unity enables developing the graphic environment; Visual Studio Community enables the programming in C language to create various screens or animations; Vuforia Development enables generating the recognition of objects, Android Studio the creation of an application installable in a mobile device compatible with Android, Particle Photon takes and processes the signals from the industrial sensors, sends them through WiFi to Internet and presents the acquired data. (Figure 3) describes the general process for the application development.

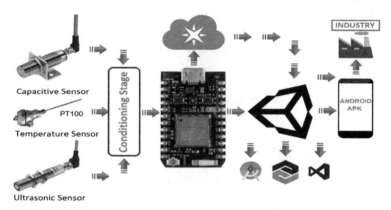

Fig. 3. Diagram of the execution process – AR application.

3.1   Recognition of Objects

For this case it was utilized a three-dimensional analysis through the Vuforia Scanner, the plane performs as a marker, i.e., a surface for recognizing 3D objects on which the X, Y, Z axes of the scanner coordinate system are observed. Through the use of the "scanner" application of Vuforia, the camera recognizes the surface of the object, identifying the recognition patterns of the three-dimensional geometry of the element analyzed (points); "scanner" has 2 buttons, TEST and CONT SCAN, that enable opening the camera again to make a test about the identification of the object, and knowing if it was successful.

3.2   Recognition of Images

The QR codes are utilized as bookmarks that give access to the virtual information, a QR code is assigned to each sensor utilized in the AR application. The design of the AR application in 2D is based on the recognition of images in two-dimensions; the

Vuforia Image Target tool is utilized to perform this process, where the QR codes are imported from which various points are taken to enable recognizing the pattern of the image recognition.

3.3 Particle Photon Configuration

The Photon development board utilizes a mobile or fixed network that establishes a wireless connection between the microcontroller and the computer, with the purpose of accessing to the API REST of Particle Cloud where the instructions to be executed are programmed, creating a URL address which will be utilized in the acquisition of data. Particle Photon is capable of handling up to 20 analog and/or digital variables, i.e., it generates up to 20 URLs that enable visualizing the reading of the variables. Once the connection to Internet is established, a token must be generated. With the assigned token and the device ID a reading of the variable is carried out, and by means of the assignment of a name the value of the variable is accessed, which delivers a favorable response (true) indicating a successful result (Fig. 4).

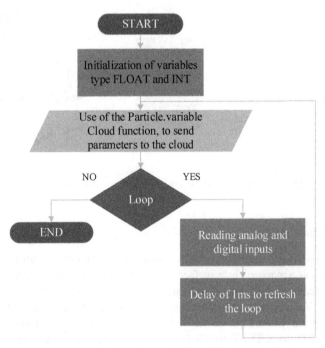

Fig. 4. Flowchart for the acquisition of data in the cloud.

3.4 Unity Configuration

It is selected the Android platform that enables compiling the APK (Android application package), and then the extensions of Vuforia and Visual Studio compatible with Android are enabled so that the application may carry out a 2D and 3D scanning. Using 3D texts, it was added a script called "Reading" which enables acquiring the data from the Particle Cloud, establishing a Wi-Fi wireless communication to visualize the data in the smartphone.

For the characterization, it is utilized a script that enables opening a new scene which indicates the most important technical information of each sensor, either analog or digital. It is important to remark that this button only appears after the application has executed the recognition of objects.

3.5 Three-Dimensional Animations

The implementation of animations enables the augmented reality application to be interactive, and for this reason a three-dimensional animation was included for each sensor; Unity Assets Store was utilized to represent the animations. The representation of the water level was made through the asset Easy Water, the variation of this animation depends on the change in the ultrasonic sensor; animations shaped as particles of smoke were used to represent the temperature. Finally, the change in the logical state of the digital sensor when this is in 1L, was represented through a sphere. The configuration was carried out through a script that generates RGB colors. Once the application is finalized all the scenes must be included in the platform; each scene corresponds to a window created that contains the information of scripts, 3D shapes, texts, 2D analyses, animations, objects, images, effects and buttons, that will be executed when the APK is generated.

The elements utilized in the creation of the AR application are visualized on (Fig. 5); it has buttons for screen, information and gallery capture. The augmented reality cube of Vuforia corresponds to the three-dimensional analysis on which labels, three-dimensional objects, colors, texts or numbers are added. The numerical texts present the values acquired in real time from the sensors.

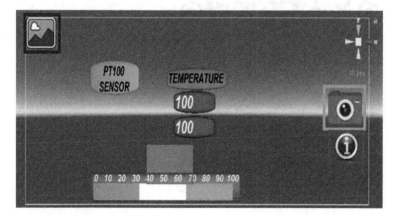

Fig. 5. Scene of development of the AR –Unity application. (Color figure online)

3.6   AR Application in Virtual Reality Glasses

To implement the AR application in the Virtual Reality glasses, it was inserted an image in Unity that enables dividing the screen in two sub-screens, which will be adjusted to the size of the canvas. Two virtual cameras that divide the AR camera (main) were utilized to simulate the virtual environment of the glasses; these correspond to each of the lenses of the viewer (left and right).

4   Results

4.1   Analysis of Recognition of Objects and Images

It was decided to carry out an analysis in two dimensions through Image Target (recognition of flat images or in two dimensions) and a three-dimensional analysis through Object Target (recognition of three-dimensional objects). Object Target enabled recognizing the sensors utilized in the application, this tool is sensitive to the variations of light which causes that the recognition of the object takes more time when this type of variations occur; taking into account that in an industrial environment the variations of the light may be significant, it was implemented QR codes that were analyzed with Image Target, the advantage of these codes is their unique pattern that generate an excellent target-star rating, making it ideal for working in environments which have a high variation of the light such as the industrial environments.

In (Fig. 6) QR codes it was detected a great amount of patterns, obtaining a target-star rating equal to five, i.e., it was obtained the maximum rating regarding the detail of the image.

QrTemperatura

Fig. 6.   Target-Star rating for 2D Analysis.

(Figure 7) shows the green areas detected by the scanner as the ones with more detail, such areas generated 254 points. The features present in the three-dimensional recognition make this option the best alternative when detecting objects, and for this reason this project utilized the 3D analysis.

Name

Temperature

Last Modified

dic. 11, 2019 14:39

File Size

6.1 MB

Points

254

Fig. 7. Areas of Greatest recognition. (Color figure online)

(Figure 8) shows the 3D analysis, the blue sections indicate the areas that obtained the smaller rating regarding the detail, while the orange sections indicate objects or areas with more quality of detail. This area corresponds to the pipeline system of the MPS PA station. The greatest area of recognition was on the pipelines since Vuforia generates the greatest amount of points of identification on the areas that present more detail.

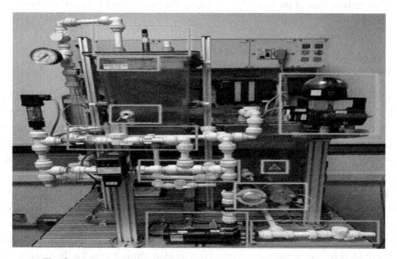

Fig. 8. Areas of Recognition for 3D Analysis. (Color figure online)

Since the pipelines have elbows, valves and notches they become a surface rich in detail, and therefore they highlight from the rest of the elements of the industrial plant.

In the following, a comparison chart of the water levels is shown, the blue series represents the data acquired in the AR application, while the orange series presents the real data of water level measured in the tank. The real values of water level measured in the tank, the values obtained in the AR application and there is an average percentage error of 1.91% due to a human failure at the moment of acquiring the data, also influenced by the time required to recognize the object, process and send the information (Fig. 9).

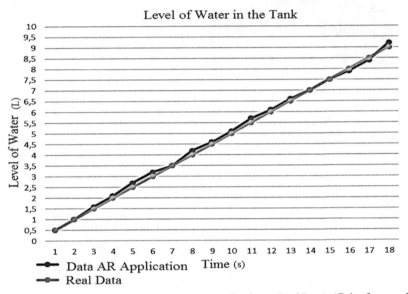

Fig. 9. Comparison chart of the Water Level (AR Application vs Real Data). (Color figure online)

4.2   Final Result of the AR Application

The implementation of animations enables that "Fig. 17" shows the result obtained in the AR application for the digital capacitive sensors, which has elements of augmented reality such as: three-dimensional objects that constitute labels, texts to show the name of the sensor and the state of the water level in the tank, three-dimensional animations (spheres that change color according to the logical state of the sensor, red for 0L and green for 1L), numerical text (indicates the logical state of the sensor) (Fig. 10).

(Figure 11) indicates the result obtained in the AR application for the analog temperature sensor, which has elements of augmented reality such as the described in the digital sensors; however, the numerical texts indicate the value of temperature in real time, both in Celsius and Fahrenheit degrees. The data are of type float to capture all the information provided by the sensor sensitivity; it was also implemented a three-dimensional animation to represent the water temperature shaped like smoke.

Fig. 10. Final result of the AR application (Capacitive Sensors). (Color figure online)

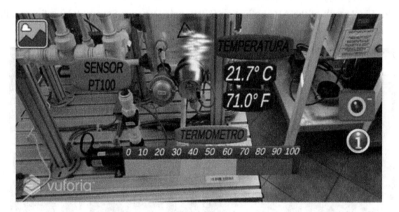

Fig. 11. Final result of the AR application (Temperature Sensor).

On the other hand, "Fig. 19" corresponds to the ultrasonic distance sensor, which has a configuration very similar to the configuration of the temperature sensor, with the difference that the animations are not fixed, i.e., every time that the water level in liters goes up, the water animation is seen in real time and represents the increase proportional to the amount of liquid.

4.3 Result AR Application with Virtual Reality Glasses

"Figure 20" divides in two sub-cameras that are adjusted to the lenses of the virtual reality viewer to generate a surround perspective of the virtual environment, unlike "Fig. 19" which shows the result of the AR application in the smartphone (Fig. 13).

Fig. 12. Final result of the AR application (Ultrasonic Distance Sensor) (Color figure online)

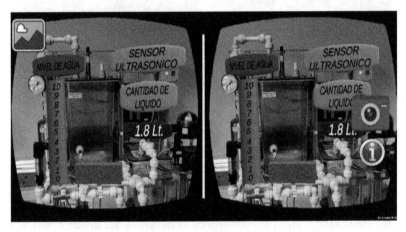

Fig. 13. Final result of the AR application with VR Glasses.

5   Conclusions

The main difficulty in the implementation of augmented reality in a MPS PA module is the existence of areas of difficult access for the scanner, and elements that do not have enough detail in the surface subject to analysis; in "Fig. 12", the blue sections indicate the areas in which it is not recommended the AR implementation, while in the orange sections this type of technology is very applicable, besides the recognition of the sensors was carried out by means of Object Target. This option is ideal for industrial elements because it analyzes volume, depth and amount of light, thus being the most viable option for this technology.

The URL address provided by Particle Cloud is configured as public, such that if a mobile device accesses the URL address, it will be able to see the state of the sensors in real time and in Json format; the error obtained is 1.91% which indicates the reliability of the mobile application in data acquisition. This error is due to human failures at the moment of acquiring the data and the time required by the application to execute the whole process, from the acquisition of the data from the sensor to the presentation of the values in the AR application.

References

1. Besbes, B.: An interactive augmented reality system : a prototype for industrial maintenance training applications. In: 2012 IEEE International Symposium on Mixed and Augmented Reality, pp. 269–270 (2012)
2. Castillo-Vergara, M., Pizarro-Guerrero, J., Espinoza-Vera, E., Alvarez-Marin, A.: Realidad Aumentada como Apoyo a la Formación de Ingenieros Industriales. Formación Universitaria, Lima (2016)
3. Diaz, D.M.S.: Creating educational content with Augmented Reality applying principles of the cognitive theory of multimedia learning: comparative study to teach how to fly a drone (quadcopter), pp. 456–462 (2015)
4. Tatic, D., Tesic, B.: Improvement of occupational safety systems by the application of augmented reality technologies. In: 2015 23rd Telecommunications Forum, TELFOR 2015, pp. 962–965 (2016)
5. Bohórquez, I.M.M.: Realidad aumentada y aplicaciones, TIA, Bogotá (2018)
6. Lorenz, M.: Industrial augmented reality: requirements for an augmented reality maintenance worker support system. In: 2018 IEEE International Symposium on Mixed and Augmented Reality Adjunct, pp. 151–153 (2018)
7. Georgel, P.: Photo-Based Industrial Augmented Reality Application Using a Single Keyframe Registration Procedure, pp. 187–188 (2009)
8. Fombuena, V., Fenollar, O.Á., Montañés, N.: Caracterización de materiales Polimericos. In: Caracterización de materiales Polimericos, Primera, Universitat Politécnica de Valéncia, Ed. Valencia, p. 2 (2016)
9. Torres, D.R.: La Realidad Aumentada. In: La Realidad Aumentada, Primera, Ediciones Trea, Ed. Asturias, pp. 17–18 (2013)
10. Herpich, F., Guarese, R.L.M., Tarouco, L.M.R.: A comparative analysis of augmented reality frameworks aimed at the development of educational applications. Creat. Educ. 08(09), 1433–1451 (2017)
11. Vuforia: Optimizing Target Detection and Tracking Stability. https://library.vuforia.com/articles/Solution/Optimizing-Target-Detection-and-Tracking-Stability.html?fbclid=IwAR179HdA4mt6bo3U7Qz42qGqigOW0sslt1-BSgrjeezI6lJPGveTMKX6goA. Accessed 03 July 2019
12. Martín-Maldonado Jiménez, D., Ferrandis, J.S.: Desarrollo y edición de juegos serios con Unity y E-Adventure (2017)
13. Tim, P.: Programación con Visual Basic 2008. In: Luna, M.A. (ed.) Programación con Visual Basic 2008, 1ra ed., pp. 33–34. McGrawHill Editions (2010)
14. Marín, J.L., García, A.: Solución integral para pc, tablet y smartphone dirigida a la gestión y lectura de libros electrónicos implementado en C # y XAML. DIRECTOR: Autor, p. 17 (2015)
15. Helmich, J., ADIRO: MPS PA Compact Workstation Manual. System, no. 5. pp. 1–9 (2006)
16. Santacana, J., Coma, L.: El m-learning y la educacion patrimonial, 1ra edn. Ediciones Trea, España (2014)

17. Caiza, G., Saeteros, M., Pillajo, C., Arévalo, G.: Development of an IEC-61499 PID control for industrial processes applications. In: Proceedings of the 2018 IEEE Colombian Conference on Communications and Computing, COLCOM 2018 (2018). https://doi.org/10.1109/colcom con.2018.8466706
18. Particle: Photon Datasheet. https://docs.particle.io/datasheets/boron/boron-datasheet/. Accessed 13 Feb 2020
19. Naranjo, J.E.: An approach of training virtual environment for teaching electropneumatic systems. IFAC-PapersOnline **52**(9), 278–284 (2019)
20. Caiza, G., Bologna, J.K., Garcia, C.A., Garcia, M.V.: Industrial training platform using augmented reality for instrumentation commissioning. In: De Paolis, L.T., Bourdot, P. (eds.) AVR 2020. LNCS, vol. 12243, pp. 268–283. Springer, Cham (2020). https://doi.org/10.1007/978-3-030-58468-9_20

Stock Markets Risk Analysis Performance by Self Organized Maps AI Techniques: Comparison and Implementation of Three SOM Methods

Gissela E. Pilliza[1,2]([⊠]), Luis Zhinin-Vera[1,2], Rafael Valencia-Ramos[1,2], and Ronny Velasteguí[1]

[1] School of Mathematical and Computational Sciences, Yachay Tech University, 100650 Urcuqui, Ecuador
gissela.pilliza@gmail.com
[2] MIND Research Group - Model Intelligent Networks Development, Urcuquí, Ecuador
http://www.mind-researchgroup.com

Abstract. Despite the exponential increase in the use of AI tools, the financial field has become a target just in the latest years. The stock markets meant a decisive factor for economic growth as it works as a management mechanism for money generated by the industrial force of the countries. In order to obtain the improved algorithm, this work focus on establishing the best SOM architecture for stock market treatment in an initial step. Therefore, after the literature review, the data extraction was performed using Yahoo Finance open source to get the historical data of the selected financial index. The ISOM SP40 proposed in this work uses an adequate combination of hexagonal SOM architecture and neighbor function based on Manhattan distance. Moreover, two SOM methods more denominated SOM IBEX35 and SOM NYSE were tested by the same conditions for compare, and determinate the best scenario for SP Latin America 40 data set. Thus the risk investment was analyzed with density correlations of profit, industrial area, and geography detected with an 80% of success rate using the top 9 companies in the stock index, also it was verified in a time-frequency analysis developed here with the top 6 companies reference companies from 2014–2019. The training time in the proposed ISOM SP40 method also improves two decimal places in comparison with the other tested techniques. In this sense, there is appropriated to establish that the improved algorithm was found, and it succeeds in the adaptation to SP Latin America 40 index data set.

Keywords: Self Organized Maps · Stock market · Stock index · S&P Latin America 40 · IBEX35 · NYSE · NASDAQ · Investment risk

1 Introduction

Risk analysis for stock exchange markets investment, in any region, means a relevant issue when huge amounts of money are circulating and producing around the world

© Springer Nature Switzerland AG 2020
G. Rodriguez Morales et al. (Eds.): TICEC 2020, CCIS 1307, pp. 363–374, 2020.
https://doi.org/10.1007/978-3-030-62833-8_27

directly affected by economic, social, and even political events [4]. The stock exchange market or bursal field is a financial mechanism that allows to the brokers and trades the exchange and negotiation of different financial instruments just as bonds, titles, stocks, among others. Thus, the risk analysis for this purpose is conceptualized as the process in which the investors evaluates probabilistic the incidence of negative episodes on the transactional movements of capitals to avoid significant losses and perform the purchases-sells at the right time for the company [14]. Most of those analyses have been treated by traditional statistical approaches [15].

2 Related Works

Within the AI increasing area, several sub-branches have been born, being applied almost in any field. Thus, the complex modeling of the behavior of the markets makes necessary the use of complex and integral forecasting and prediction tools as artificial intelligence tools. This section of the current work analyzes some of the existing methods applied in the finances field to find the best adaptation and make the final architecture selection for the optimization and comparison if this study. Despite there are several methods implemented before, just the methods which have shown results kindred to the project objectives and good approximations were reviewed and listed below:

2.1 Bayesian Network and ANN Hybrid Method

The work developed on Bayesian Network and ANN fits in the category of AI-ANN-machine learning (ML) method, which uses a Back Propagation Learning (BPL) algorithm and Directed Acyclic Graph (DAG) structure for analyzing the bank liquidity risk [13].

When the methods approximate risk function have some troubles estimating the distribution function, but as the BN has good results clustering qualitatively, it achieves good approximations. On the other hand, as the input data were statically selected, they do not count with a dynamic setting that limits the realistic behavior closer to the bank liquidity risk [13].

2.2 Recurrent Neural Networks (RNNs) with Transfer Learning and Long-Term Memory

The method applied by Kraus and Feuerriegel in 2017 is an AI-ML-ANN method, which uses specific hierarchical structures and a large number of hidden layers to support financial decision [7]. It takes as an input financial disclosure documents containing sequences of words which allow its superficial analysis. After the process, the predictor target is the obtaining of the return or the tendency of the price change [7]. The main finding appears when long short-term-memory (LSTM) is applied. The approximation of the trend shows a better accuracy achieving 5.6% points according to figure. On the other hand, the method sub-utilizes the deep learning benefits as it "computes word tuples instead of processing the raw text" and at the same time, the used RNNs fail to improve the efficiency against the classic DL techniques.

2.3 Long Short-Term Memory Networks

Meanwhile, in 2018 Fisher and Krauss applied an AI-ML-RNN method Long short-term memory (LSTM) to predict "directional movements for the constituent stocks of the SP 500 from 1992 until 2015" [3]. As input data, it uses the monthly constituent list of Thomson Reuters enterprise from the SP 500 index in the time interval from 1989 to 2015. The purposed method can overcome the vanishing gradient problem by exploding different gradients. This paper summarizes other applications of AI technologies in several domains of business administration.

2.4 Neurocomputing

It is an AI-ML/aNN/DL method using a descriptive model for business computing has made considerable progress and offered a new opportunity for academic research and applications in many fields, especially for business activities and enterprises development. Very general and spread. This paper summarizes different applications of AI technologies in several domains of business administration. Finance, retail industry, manufacturing industry, and enterprise management are all included. In spite of all the existing challenges, we conclude that the rapid development of AI will show its significant impact on more fields worked in 2018.

2.5 Chartist Analysis

It is a method of statistical nature. An example of a chartist analysis is to establish that the market, concerning to a specific title, can be in an upward or downward trend. Thus, based on the past contribution behavior for similar situations, we can establish that to pass to specific predetermined phase.

2.6 Oscillators Analysis

It is a statistical smoothness method. The simplest example of an oscillator (and one of the most used) is the mobile average. The moving average of a period is the average of the prices of a particular title during this period. By smoothing the price curve, it is a more straightforward way to observe market trends.

2.7 Automatic Traders and Talentum

It is a method AI method which uses "automated trading systems, or automatic traders allow you to establish a series of automatic rules that dictate when to perform an operation and when to close it, so that it is executed autonomously without further human intervention. The programmed rules in these can be relatively simple, like the half-mobiles that we saw earlier, or much more complex".

3 Self Organized Maps

In 1981 the professor Teuvo Kohonen proposed this model motivated with the idea of "abstract feature maps found in the biological central nervous systems". This model is presented as an alternative for data sets that can not be linearly modeled, and the calibration as input works even there is a big amount of data or not. The idea of SOM is cluster and abstract the data dimensionality, to become one of the most popular unsupervised neural network techniques [6]. In general terms, a SOM is one 2D structure used as an input layer of an ANN (Fig. 1), that could have multidimensional input space. The SOM units grid is associated with the vector model in an ANN. The mapping performed in the learning process uses the topological distance between the patterns according to their similarity [1].

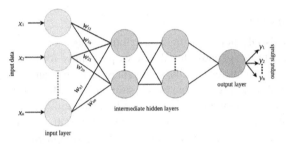

Fig. 1. Artificial neural network classic architecture *Source: [11]*

The SOM capability to detect relations in data patterns and variables of different dimensions without labeling caused that SOM is used in different areas such as chemical models [12], manufacturing process [8], biometric systems, robotics [5], and much more others [2].

SOM structure comes from the concept of ANN with an interconnection layer to layer defined by a winner model. Once the significant patterns are detected, they are located on a map according to an established geometry and distance obtained by the network. The output number and distribution depend on the number of relevant clusters catch by the network Fig. 2.

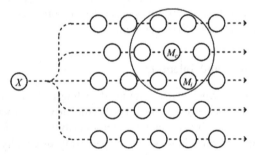

Fig. 2. Illustration of a self-organizing map. An input data item X is broadcast to a set of models Mi, of which Mc matches best with X. All models that lie in the neighborhood (larger circle) of Mc in the grid match better with X than with the rest. *Source: [6]*

4 S&P Latin America 40

In the stock markets field, there is important to emphasize that a stock market is not the same as a stock market index. While the first one is a group of companies listed in the same stock market, the second measure the performance of a group of enterprises that can be part of different stock markets. From the S&P Dow Jones series indexes arises the S&P Latin America 40, which concentrates the 70% of the capitals in Latin America.

For this work, the daily data from April of 2014 to April 2019 were extracted to being analyzed. All of them downloaded in .*csv* the format compatible with readers or processors of spread-sheets. Using a Self Organized Maps method, SP Latin America 40 stock exchange prices are going to be analyzed. These results are going to be compared with the other two SOM methods, which show acceptable results in the stock exchanges according to the studies [10], and [16].

5 Data Verification

To verify the modeling of **SP Latin America 40**, two additional data sets were selected due to its reliability in previous studies in terms of quantity and quality necessary to perform a study with Self Organized Maps. The **IBEX35** and **NIKKEI** indexes were selected to feed three different SOM due to they have more than 20 enterprises with historic data at least one year. Also, the three data sets are considered the most robust indexes in their corresponding region [11].

6 Proposed ISOM Approach

For the model to be implemented, it is expected that follows the hexagonal structure of the IBEX35 approach developed in previous risk analysis paper [10], but the hyper-parameters are fixed for a different test, and in the neighbor, mechanism is modified whit the Manhattan distance. Then, it would use the Eqs. 1, 2, 3, and 4, but in the weights update step according to the mathematical formula improvement, it could be applied building a topological structure representing the original surface of the system adapting the mesh organization [9]. Meanwhile, there is the automation in the initialization scheme of data the data set, through the "python prepossessing algorithm" to be entered after in Matlab, phyton was used as it shows optimal simple handling of documents preprocessing. Matlab is going to be the IDE used in the whole AI project because of the dynamic handling of the modules to build the project being compatible without the need for auxiliary algorithms with the data matrixes. In contrast with existing libraries in the traditional programming languages as C or C++ which need of auxiliary scripts and time to implement them. The general flowchart of the proposed approach is depicted in Fig. 3.

6.1 Proposed SOM Pseudo-code

Weights Initialization:

$$w(0) = random([a, b], [n, m, o]) \tag{1}$$

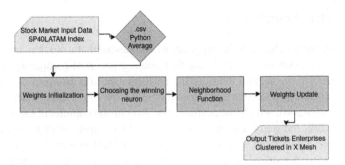

Fig. 3. Improved SOM flow Chart *Source: [11]*

Choosing the winning neuron:

$$G(x(p)) = argmin_{\forall i}\{\|x(p) - w_i(p)\|\}\forall i = 1, 2, 3, .., n \times m \qquad (2)$$

Neighborhood Function:

$$\Lambda(P_j, P_k) = Sum(Abs((P_j - P_k))) \qquad (3)$$

Weights Update:

$$w_i(p+1) = w_i(p) + \eta(p)\Lambda(P_r, P_i)(x(p) - w_i(p)) \qquad (4)$$

6.2 Training Models and Resources

- The data will be prepossessed in the same way described in the above section; for the three cases, they will be introduced equally in the three algorithms IBEX35, NYSE-NASDAQ, and SPLatam40.
- Each algorithm uses its routine for training and cluster as the schemes explained before in the methodology section.
- The whole process will be run in Matlab IDE, including the prepossessing and training, and with an available in a Laptop Dell core i5 from 4*th* generation and Ubuntu operative system.

6.3 Performance Metrics

For the present work, the metrics that will allow us to measure the results in a standard manner to compare the three methods refereed before are going to be:

Topological Distance. The SOM algorithms major clustering tools are based on distances, one of the most wide distances, and one that could be applied to the three selected models is the Euclidean distance. Still, as the project goal involve the modification of this function, the Manhattan distance is applied. Thus, the tautological distance metric will impact the accuracy expected in the density correlations described bellow.

Euclidean Distance. The SOM algorithms major clustering tools are based on distances, the one of the most widely distances and one that could be applied to the three selected models is the Euclidean distance. It will be a quantitative metric and in this project will be calculated as follow [10]:

$$d(P_j, P_k) = \sqrt{(P_{j1}, P_{k1})_2 + (P_{j2}, P_{k2})_2} \tag{5}$$

$\forall k = 1, 2, 3, \dots, M.$

where:
P_j is the treated company,
P_k is the k-st company to get the distance, and
M is the total number of companies.

Density Correlations. The density correlations [11] are qualitative metrics that are identified as areas of the graphics generated by the algorithms in each case, as is shown in Fig. 4. Therefore, codes could be adapted to analyze the correlation areas by:

– General Company Tickets: distribution of the companies with more profit in the SOM structure.
– Geographical Distribution: distribution into the SOM of companies that belong to the same country.
– Industrial Areas: distribution of companies associated with the same business line such as banking, energy, food, chemicals, oil, and many others.

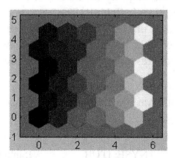

Fig. 4. SOM density correlation illustration *Source: [11]*

Training Time. This quantitative metric is referred to the time that the Matlab program is going to take to measure the model construction with the data set. The project will be quantified by the tic-toc function integrated into Matlab that, according to its documentation, in summary, measures the time until the program completes the last operation.

– From the three algorithms, the same result features will be extracted under the metrics founded before.
– After the three algorithms were run the Topological distance for density correlations, Training Time, will be crossed to detect the differences between the three methods.
– At the same time, the metrics will be widely analyzed to determine if the method it's efficient in the adaptation to the SP40 LATAM data set.

7 Results

The result is presented to determine the points of interest in the comparisons of ISOM SP40, SOM IBEX35, and SOM NYSE. Also, the analysis of the facts that can be deduced from the newly available information will be explored in detail. Three subsections a table is provided with three columns: the number of iterations, accuracy of the top 8 enter prices, and the execution time in seconds. The content of that columns is over understood except for the top 8 accuracies, it is about how every clustering test has its graphical result in the correspondent SOM. Thus it was affirmative if those eight companies were near or negative if they not. The Yes/No case represents a particular distribution in which the companies, even all the top 8 enterprises, were no close enough; the SOM distribution represents a relation between them in subsections. The second source is the SOM graph generated by the models and analyzed thoroughly bellow. Moreover, for the last experiment, three graphs are provided to an overall analysis trough the time [11].

7.1 Experiment

This initial experiment was developed with two objectives: first, to calibrate the parameters correctly in the proposed model, and to measure the metrics for being compared.

The first idea that can be extracted for Table 2 has a relation with the execution training time; it was found a significant improvement while the number of iterations was reduced. The referent number of iterations took form the previous studied tends to over-fitted the model. In the majority of the cases, it did no established a uniform relation of the top nine enterprises in Table 1. The best approximation was 0,579 s, and it represents almost two decimal places of difference with the worst-case founded in the NYSE SOM method analyzed later. In further cases, those two decimals are essential to take advantage of the hardware resources in studies with much more amount of data.

Table 1. SP40 Latin America Top 9 strongest companies *Source: [11]*

ID	Company name	Ticker symbol	Industry	Country
31	Itaú Unibanco	NYSE: ITUB	Banking Brazil	Brazil
39	Vale	NYSE: VALE.P	Mining Brazil	Brazil
03	Banco Bradesco	NYSE: BBD	Banking Brazil	Brazil
34	Petrobras	NYSE: PBR.A	Oil Brazil	Brazil
06	Banco do Brasil	B3: BBAS3	Banking Brazil	Brazil
17	AmBev	NYSE: ABEV	Beverages Brazil	Brazil
02	América Móvil	BMV: AMX L	Telecommunications Mexico	Mexico
27	FEMSA	BMV: FEMSA UBD	Beverages Mexico	Mexico
32	Itaúsa Investimentos Itau	B3: ITSA4	Banking Brazil	Brazil

At the same time, in Fig. 5, the red points represented the top nine enterprises listed in Table 2. Here the *a*) part of the figure presents a complete overview of the SOM distribution. The verification points are well accurate clustered as at least the top 6 enterprises in part *c*) and *b*) of the graph are inside a three-range of neighborhoods. That means that from each hexagon corner, there are maximum three corners of separation. There, an explanation can be verified with the fourth experiment for the three essential points outside of the profit area, and it could be related to their position in the top 9 list.

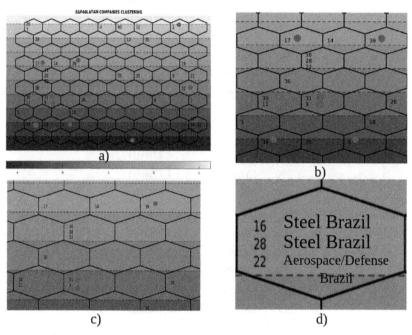

Fig. 5. Clustering and density results for ISOM SP40 algorithm *Source: [11]* (Color figure online)

On the other hand, the enterprises in the profit area that were not in the top 9 list, this time were zoom in part *d*) of the graph. Thus, verifying this behavior with the other two density correlation metrics, and there was quick to detect that they belong to the same industrial area, the metallurgic and more much consistent in the same geographical location Brazil.

In the first moment, the background colors in all graphs are expected to detect concentration areas of profit or looses, but at the end with the experimental repetitions, just the 50% of them correspond to a correct association, which that percentage it is not considered relevant. The situation for this data set and algorithm is that with a smaller size of iteration, they always find good approximations. Still, its worst fact is that two of five in the repetitions in this experiments, the relationships are somehow ambiguous [11].

Table 2. Execution time comparison and qualitative results for ISOM SP40 algorithm. *Source:* *[11]*

N. Iter.	Accuracy top 8	Time (s)
10	Yes	5,79E−01
10	Yes/No	5,95E−01
10	Yes/No	5,77E−01
10	Yes	5,71E−01
10	Yes	5,79E−01
50	No	2,91E+00
50	Yes/No	2,94E+00
50	Yes/No	2,95E+00
50	Yes/No	2,96E+00
50	No	3,05E+00
200	No	1,23E+01
200	Yes/No	1,17E+01
200	No	1,83E+01
200	No	1,78E+01
500	No	3,25E+01
500	Yes/No	3,12E+01
500	Yes/No	3,39E+01
500	Yes/No	3,32E+01
500	No	3,14E+01

8   Conclusions

Broadly speaking, the implementation of an improved SOM algorithm for the SP40 Latin America data set was achieved successfully in terms of time execution reduction and accuracy of the density correlations. The relationships among the top nine companies of the index were corroborated in the SOM map distributions and a final time-frequency analysis [11]. Being precise in technical terms and specific metrics, there is concluded that:

- The prepossessing of the data sets were improved with practical tools as Python libraries *panda* and *numpy*, which allows the automatizing of data treatment and concatenation in different formats and compatible with multiple programming languages and development environments.
- The hexagonal architecture of the SOM have demonstrated a good performance in all the studies reviewed, specifically in the financial field for stock market prediction and clustering. Also, the algorithm implemented used this structure for being compared

with the good performance of the hexagonal architectures of [10] and [16] studies showing positive results.
- The design of the SOM architecture comes along with the improvement of the topological distance used in the neighborhood function. This work demonstrated that besides the classic Euclidean distance, there is the Manhattan Distance, which reduces the machine operations without affecting the accuracy of the densities correlations and being adaptable to the SP40 Latin America index market.
- The performance of the three methods with the SP40 LATAM data set was compared, showing that the adequate algorithm for those companies is the ISOM SP40 proposed algorithm. This is corroborated with the metrics selected for the comparison execution time and the different density correlations. Thus, the higher accuracy corresponds to the proposed method with 80% overall in all the experiments against the 10%, and 5% of the other two methods.
- The execution time was reduced in almost two significant decimals having $5,79E - 01(s)$ as the minimum time in the experiments with ten iterations and well-sorting distribution in SOM. In contrast, the IBEX35 method, which even with the ten iterations it achieves at least $6,15E + 00(s)$ time of execution.
- The density correlations were pointed out by the Fig. 5 with the top nine enterprises and the time-frequency analysis among the companies ITUB, VALE, BBD, PBRA, the profit analysis is done. Then, the geographic and business sector were also verified in the amplified cell, which group SID, ERJ, and GGB three metallurgic enterprises from Brazil.

As future works, first, with the whole information generated and the interpretations of the study, these can be transformed in a more customer oriented tool with a graphical interface in which any user with non programming skills can easily set the parameters. It should be very visual and owns interactive indicators such as set combinations of the different data sets and methods of being presented with a click. If the use of this tool become real, the risk of investment would be minimized.

References

1. Afolabi, M.O., Olude, O.: Predicting stock prices using a hybrid Kohonen self organizing map (SOM). In: 2007 40th Annual Hawaii International Conference on System Sciences, HICSS 2007, p. 48, January 2007
2. Deboeck, G., Kohonen, T.: Visual Explorations in Finance with Self-Organizing Maps, January 1998
3. Fischer, T., Krauss, C.: Deep learning with long short-term memory networks for financial market predictions. Eur. J. Oper. Res. **270**(2), 654–669 (2018)
4. Hu, H., Tang, L., Zhang, S., Wang, H.: Predicting the direction of stock markets using optimized neural networks with Google trends. Neurocomputing **285**, 188–195 (2018)
5. Kohonen, T., et al.: Engineering applications of the self-organizing map. Proc. IEEE **84**(10), 1358–1384 (1996)
6. Kohonen, T.: Essentials of the self-organizing map. Neural Netw. **37**, 52–65 (2013). Twenty-Fifth Anniversary Commemorative Issue
7. Kraus, M., Feuerriegel, S.: Decision support from financial disclosures with deep neural networks and transfer learning. Decis. Supp. Syst. **104**, 38–48 (2017)

8. Li, Y., Pan, F.: Application of improved SOM neural network in manufacturing process quality control, March 2013
9. Oyana, T.J., et al.: A mathematical improvement of the self-organizing map algorithm. In: Mwakali, J., Taban-Wani, G. (eds.) Proceedings from the International Conference on Advances in Engineering and Technology, Oxford (2006)
10. Pilliza, G.E., Román, O.A., Morejón, W.J., Hidalgo, S.H., Ortega-Zamorano, F.: Risk analysis of the stock market by means self-organizing maps model. In: 2018 IEEE Third Ecuador Technical Chapters Meeting (ETCM), pp. 1–6, October 2018
11. Pilliza, G.: Risk analysis of stocks markets by a merged unsupervised model, time evolution comparison, and optimization (2020)
12. Reker, D., Rodrigues, T., Schneider, P., Schneider, G.: Identifying the macromolecular targets of de novo-designed chemical entities through self-organizing map consensus. Proc. Natl. Acad. Sci. **111**, 4067–4072 (2014)
13. Tavana, M., Abtahi, A.R., Caprio, D.D., Poortarigh, M.: An artificial neural network and Bayesian network model for liquidity risk assessment in banking. Neurocomputing **275**, 2525–2554 (2018)
14. Times, T.E.: Definition of 'investment risk' (2019)
15. Tkáč, M., Verner, R.: Artificial neural networks in business: two decades of research. Appl. Soft Comput. **38**, 788–804 (2016)
16. Wu, M.H.: Financial market prediction. Preprint submitted to arXiv (2015)

Smart Cities

Using Virtual Reality to Detect, Assess, and Treat Frustration

Fernando Paladines-Jaramillo[1]([✉]), Veronica Egas-Reyes[1,2] [iD],
Diego Ordonez-Camacho[3] [iD], Juan Salazar[1], Veronica Realpe[1], and Ivan Terceros[4]

[1] Facultad de Psicología, Pontificia Universidad Católica del Ecuador, Quito, Ecuador
{mpaladines001,megas776,vrealpe663}@puce.edu.ec,
juanzjck1996@gmail.com
[2] Centro de Psicología Aplicada, Pontificia Universidad Católica del Ecuador, Quito, Ecuador
[3] Grupo de Investigación en Informática, Universidad UTE, Quito, Ecuador
dordonez@ute.edu.ec
[4] Medialab CIESPAL, Quito, Ecuador
iterceros@medialabuio.org

Abstract. Frustration is an inherent component of the day-to-day of human activity. Any blockage to reach a goal causes frustration. One of the problems we are currently facing is that tolerance to frustration in children and young people is increasingly lower, and non-adapted behavior caused by low tolerance to frustration is seen more often in the workplace. The first step to avoid this problem is an appropriate detection of the capacity to adapt constructively to frustration. Among the most used tools is the Rosenzweig frustration test; although it is one of the most used tests at the moment when evaluating frustration, it shows a technological gap: it is presented as drawings on paper, in the style of a comic strip. Adolescents and young people of the last generations are used to much more dynamic representations of reality, therefore they see the test as outdated and do not react well to it. This project attempts to tackle these problems by adapting the Rosenzweig frustration test to the current technological needs, reinterpreting it into Virtual Reality scenes, a technological trend that has been successfully used today in many related fields. Besides the work with the Rosenzweig's test, the project used the Frustration Discomfort Scale as a tool to compare frustration levels and to control and validate the results.

Keywords: Virtual reality · Frustration · Rosenzweig's frustration test · Picture frustration test · Frustration discomfort scale · Aggression

1 Introduction

Frustration is intrinsically a part of the human being and it shows up when it is not possible to reach some goal or objective. There is a clear tendency nowadays towards lower tolerance for frustration, especially in children, adolescents, and young people. Frustration mishandling is leading this population to greater problems like being prone

© Springer Nature Switzerland AG 2020
G. Rodriguez Morales et al. (Eds.): TICEC 2020, CCIS 1307, pp. 377–390, 2020.
https://doi.org/10.1007/978-3-030-62833-8_28

to aggressiveness, and even attacking others, among other behaviors exceeding social norms.

To effectively avoid these frustration mishandling problems, the first step is proper detection. Rosenzweig et al., [1] built a projective psychological tool to quantify and qualify frustration, the Picture Frustration Test (PFT), widely used today. This test assesses the tolerance or intolerance to frustration of an individual, as well as identify where that aggression is going (towards himself or others). Despite its effectiveness, it shows signs of a technological lag since it is presented on paper and drawn in the style of a vignette in a comic strip. This provokes that, especially in adolescents and young people, accustomed to more dynamic representations of reality, it is perceived as outdated and not given enough attention, hindering its goals. The original design of the PFT, then, shows limitations in its capacity for motivation and stimulation, when compared with all the available computational alternatives nowadays.

This work is part of an inter-institutional research project on the use of Virtual Reality (VR) to assess the level of frustration and its handling mechanisms in university students. It combines techniques and methods from the fields of Information and Communication Technologies (ICT) and Psychology. It seeks to treat an increasingly pressing current problem, such as the inadequate management of frustration. Frustration is not detected properly and, therefore, is not treated effectively.

Taking the original PFT as a starting point, it is proposed to build an updated technique that allows a stimulating interaction, according to the expectations of adolescents and young adults. The subjects are introduced in an interpellation situation from their own point of view and with their own language.

It is assumed that through VR, the young person feels more comfortable and confident, given that these environments are already familiar. This is a stimulating factor that promotes a less resistant or less controlled reaction of the functions of the Id, and therefore the reaction would be less defensive, and more truthful information would be obtained on some aspects of his personality, especially the impact and management of the frustration. The type of stimuli offered by the VR could favor the manifestation of unconscious defense mechanisms and reduce conscious control, allowing an authentic, immediate, and not so elaborate (not so calculated) response to be shown. This would cause that, thanks to the use of new technologies, the psychologist determines more precisely the intensity, mode and type of reactions related to frustration.

As far as it has been possible to investigate in specialized literature, no other work has proposed an adaptation of the Rosenzweig test to VR. In fact, we have not been able to find projective tests adapted to VR, only software helping with data processing. In general, VR linked to Psychology, has been used mainly for the treatment of phobias, anxiety, panic crisis, social maladjustment, etc. As for the tests that allow the detection of psychological problems, the closest case is related to the anxiety detection test, Mini Spin [2], which was reinterpreted in VR by Egas-Reyes, Hinojosa and Ordóñez-Camacho [3].

Among the many advantages that the use of VR could entail, it makes the application of the test much friendlier, minimizing interference caused by people's resistance or defenses. The use of VR could shorten the gap between generations, bringing those called "millennials and centennials" closer to previous generations that handle other types of devices, social dynamics, and logic. In the same way, it makes available to psychologists a practical means of diagnosis and research and validates the integration between ICT and Psychology.

2 Related Work

Based on the PFT, many scales have been built around the evaluation of frustration, and it is worth mentioning the work of Hornsveld, Nijman, Hollin, and Kraaimaat [4], who created an adaptation of the PFT to detect hostile thoughts in patients with behavioral and antisocial personality disorders. This relationship between frustration intolerance and emotional behavioral problems is verified in the work of Filippello, Harrington, Buzzai, Sorrenti and Costa [5]. Also, Keertish and Sharma [6], using the PFT, study the reactions of adolescents with conversion disorder and find that they worry excessively about the situation that causes frustration, instead of trying to avoid it. On the other hand, Nguyen, Yano, Yamada, Kuwano and Nguyen [7, 8], use a variation of the PFT to investigate people's attitudes and preferences regarding how they care for the environment and their lifestyle preferences; they discover a high influence of ambient noise on the appearance of frustration.

Other notable adaptations of the PFT are found in the works of Pervichko and Zinchenko [9], who use their version of the test for the evaluation of emotional regulation strategies in patients with stress-induced arterial hypertension. Gong, Mei, Xiang, Mei and Liu [10], contribute with a study on the frustration of students in university settings and conclude on the importance of detecting and treating the intolerance to frustration, since this negatively affects the motivation to comply with personal and institutional objectives. Finally, Yang and He [11] develop, following Rosenzweig's line, a specific scale to measure frustration tolerance in undergraduate students and highlight the need to be able to fight against setbacks; they insist on its importance to avoid distorting reality.

Of all these instruments, one of the most prominent is the scale of intolerance to frustration, Frustration Discomfort Scale, FDS [12], which determines four factors of intolerance. It is also known as a multidimensional scale of frustration and discomfort. This scale is relevant since, in addition, it suggests that frustration intolerance could be related to emotional problems and self-esteem.

2.1 Technology and Psychology: The Link for Virtual Reality

There is a marked tendency to create software programs to alleviate some tasks related to the tabulation and qualification of psychological tests. This, despite its usefulness, is nothing more than a minimal use of technology in Psychology. Mustaca [13], for example, refers to studies with educational objectives, which try to anticipate, through sensors connected to computers, the state of frustration of students when solving problems, and tries to build tutoring programs to avoid drop-out. Other researchers delve into the computerized generation of three-dimensional graphics, to produce environments and immersive experiences (VR as well); they include virtual scenarios to analyze professional work, such as Nylund and Landfors [14], who study frustration in the environment of video game developers, and find a distinction between a negative frustration, which can cause anger and affect the experience of the game. There are several research teams interested in using VR as support for psychological treatment, such as McEwen, Taillon-Hobson, Bilodeau, Sveistrup and Finestone [15], who find that when treating with VR people affected by cerebral infarction, there is a greater improvement, than for those who did not follow this treatment. Likewise, Morina, Ijntema, Meyerbröker and Emmelkamp [16] demonstrate that therapy through exposure to VR causes significant behavioral changes in real-life situations. Additionally, they observe that there is no significant variation between in vivo and VR exposures.

One of the fields, within Psychology, where VR has been used the most, is when treating phobias. Diemer, Alpers, Peperkorn, Shiban and Mühlberger [17] analyze the use of VR in studies of fear, phobia, and social anxiety, where using VR increases the feeling of presence and immersion. In the same style, North, North and Coble [18] use VR to treat fear of public speaking and find that it promotes significant improvements when compared to individuals from control groups where this is not used. Botella, Fernández-Álvarez, Guillén, García-Palacios and Baños [19], conduct a systematic study on the efficacy of psychotherapy with exposure to VR in phobias; they conclude that it is an effective help for the clinical psychologist, thanks to its flexibility and the control it allows. Carlbring [20] compares the use of VR with that of live therapy for the treatment of phobia to spiders; he asserts that while live therapy is more effective, VR is also a valid alternative.

Other related branches have also successfully ventured into the use of technology; such is the case of the studies by Pedroli et al., [21], who conclude that for the treatment of dyslexia in children, recovery exercises, in their traditional form with pencil and paper, can be boring and difficult; they use a video game to provide the idea that these types of current treatments can have a positive impact and have immediate effects. Regarding anxiety problems, Reyna et al., [22] determine that, to treat social anxiety disorder through cognitive behavioral therapy, the use of VR appears as a very promising form of therapy. Finally, it is worth mentioning the adaptation to VR of the Mini-Spin social anxiety test [3, 23], directly linked to the objectives of this project.

3 Methodology

The study was carried out with a mixed research methodology: qualitative and quantitative. The research design followed a twofold approach, using a phenomenological and descriptive logic, focused on frustration as a problem in university students, and using virtual reality as an improved tool in the diagnosis and treatment of the problem.

The sample was selected from three universities in Quito, considering students with an age range between 20 and 25 years old. The participants from two universities were psychology students, and from the third they were engineering students; this way, people with backgrounds from both, social and exact sciences, were considered. The sample was selected for convenience, considering factors such as: student accessibility, university attendance hours, age range, age group, and gender. To carry out the study, the process was first reviewed and counted with the approval of a University Ethics Committee on Research on Human Beings. Furthermore, all the participants signed an informed consent to participate in the research.

The research process first involved the application of two tests, Frustration Discomfort Scale (FDS) and Picture Frustration Test (PFT), both measuring frustration. Next, during test application, direct observation of the participants with note taking was used. Finally, using focus groups with experts, relevant elements from the PFT where selected as VR scenes.

At a qualitative level, the data from both the focus groups and the observations notebooks were systematized through the three coding stages: open, axial, and selective, working with unities, categories, and themes for the analysis. Quantitatively, the reliability of the test and the samples obtained were verified through the Pearson coefficient, as well as with the methodology of the exploratory and confirmatory factor analysis. Significant differences were sought through t-tests, using the statistical software R, version 3.15, and the stats package, version 3.5.1. Only significant differences were considered (95% confidence; $p < 0.05$).

As a first step, the sample size for the study was calculated using PowerTOST [24], considering the recommendations of minimum acceptable parameters detailed in [25, 26]. Specific details of the calculation can be seen in Fig. 1. A sample size N = 50 was determined but, considering that there will inevitably be a dropout percentage from the original group, the initial sample was increased, for security, by 50%, which gives us an expected sample size of 75 subjects, that were divided among the 3 participating universities (they will be called A, B and C in the paper). In practice, it was possible to initiate the study with a group of 88 subjects for the first test.

```
sampleN.TOST(theta0=0.05, theta1=-0.2,
        targetpower=0.9, CV=0.25,
        method="exact", robust=TRUE, logscale=FALSE, design = "paired")
```

Fig. 1. Sample size calculation.

The next step was to apply the Frustration Discomfort Scale (FDS), developed by Harrington [12]. This scale is based on factor analysis and determines, in a multidimensional way, intolerance to frustration. It is a psychological instrument based on the theoretical assumptions of Rational Emotive Behavior Therapy [27]. The FDS evaluates four emotional dimensions: intolerance to discomfort (F1), entitlement (F2), discomfort intolerance (F3) and achievement (F4). The test results present the levels of intolerance to frustration and when this intolerance appear in a subject. Moreover, these data were used to validate this study by comparing its equivalence with other similar studies.

After finishing the FDS, the subjects were asked to complete de Picture Frustration Test (PFT), better known as the Rosenzweig's test, in its traditional form (pen and paper). Two additional research questions, regarding this test, were defined to assess frustration in the subjects: do the answers from our sample can be considered the same as those from the normative population? Can it be expected that frustration will generate aggressiveness in some way, and if so, where is it aimed?

Finally, before proceeding to develop the VR prototype of the PFT, it was necessary to reduce the number of scenes, originally 24. Besides the practical reasons regarding the great amount of resources that would involve building that many VR scenes, there were three technical objectives: to reduce the time of application and processing of information, to streamline the creation and technical development of virtual scenarios and to reduce the possible fatigue of the subjects examined.

It was necessary then, a focus group with experts in the field of frustration. They discussed the required characteristics that the chosen scenes should have. It was concluded that it should be those producing the most frustration, to force the subject to react more spontaneously. Additionally, it was decided to reduce their number to 6 scenes, that will reach the VR stage; a survey was generated and applied to the subjects, to make the final choice.

The very last step for building the prototype of the VR tool, required the adaptation of formal software development methods related with agile lifecycles, linking them with other methods coming from the social sciences to collect the information from focus groups, interviews and tests; this produced a specific four stages methodology (presented on detail in [28]) that we resume in Fig. 2.

Fig. 2. Agile methodology for VR development

4 Results and Discussion

4.1 Frustration Discomfort Scale

Once applied the FDS, the data was compared with that of other international studies, similar in terms of objectives and population, to determine how alike the results are. Those studies were conducted in England [12], Italy [5, 29] and Ireland [30].

Table 1 shows the populations comparative graph. Although the size of our sample is rather towards the lower end, both mean and standard deviation are equivalent to the rest of the studies.

Table 2 presents the general information distributed by factors, where although our sample is located towards the upper end in terms of mean and standard deviation, the same trend presented by the other studies is maintained: values increase from factor 1 towards factor 4.

To determine whether the differences between the data can be considered statistically significant, the p-value was used, with a 95% confidence. Table 3 shows the comparison by total scores; the cells present the resulting p-value from the comparison between column and row; those values with significant differences are highlighted in italics ($p < 0.05$). No relevant dissimilarity pattern is found; differences exist with 2 of the

Table 1. General comparison between similar FDS studies

Study	Sample	Mean	Std. dev.	Place	Population description
Harrington (2005)	79	75,7	15,9	England	Undergraduate students, psychology
Tripaldi (2018)	117	75,61	19,39	Italy	General (less than 40 years)
Filipello (2014)	250	81,7	17,64	Italy	Undergraduate students
Stankovic (2011)	323	74,86	19,89	Ireland	Undergraduate students
This study	88	81,27	20	Ecuador	Undergraduate students, psychology, and engineering

Table 2. FDS results by factor

Study	Factor 1		Factor 2		Factor 3		Factor 4	
	$\bar{X}$	Ds	$\bar{X}$	Ds	$\bar{X}$	Ds	$\bar{X}$	Ds
Harrington (2005)	17,6	4,7	19,6	4,4	18,3	5,1	20,2	5,2
Tripaldi (2018)	16,85	4,28	19,23	4,76	18,59	5,15	20,94	4,98
Filipello (2014)	18,68	4,58	21,93	5,07	20,03	5,87	21,06	5,3
Stankovic (2011)	17,37	5,37	19,87	5,73	17,86	6,01	19,67	5,69
This study	18,83	5,37	19,7	5,58	20,57	6,41	22,14	6,25

Table 3. FDS p-values considering the totals. All studies compared.

	Tripaldi	Filipello	Stankovic	This study
Harrington	0,97	*0,005*	0,69	0,05
Tripaldi		*0,004*	0,72	*0,04*
Filipello			*1,59E−05*	0,86
Stankovic				*0,01*

4 studies, but all studies show a similar situation. In general terms, we believe that our data is consistent.

Finally, in Table 4, we compare, factor by factor, our study with the other four; the relationship is the same: certain factors show differences with other studies, but no conclusive pattern is shown.

The research that we are currently carrying out with the FDS is in general obtaining results that cannot be considered different from those in the other four studies. More in detail, the values obtained in factor 1 of the FDS for our study are consistent with those found by Harrington and Filipello; for factor 2, the values are even more uniform,

Table 4. FDS p-values by factor. This study compared with the others.

	Factor 1	Factor 2	Factor 3	Factor 4
Harrington	0,12	0,88	*0,01*	*0,03*
Tripaldi	*0,005*	0,51	*0,02*	0,14
Filipello	0,82	*0,001*	0,49	0,15
Stankovic	*0,03*	0,82	*0,0005*	*0,001*

since they coincide with almost all research groups, except those of Filipello; in factor 3, on the contrary, no similar results have been found except, with those of Filipello. Such dissimilarity is probably due to cultural influences or some characteristics of the investigated samples linked with emotional intolerance. This can be elucidated through future analyzes when additional data could be gathered. Finally, the p-values found in factor 4 indicate agreement between the results of our study and those from Tripaldi and Filipello.

4.2   Picture Frustration Test: Adaptation

When the PFT is applied, subjects can provide expected and unexpected responses. It is the frequency of these responses that will allow measuring the conformity of the answers with those of the population's arithmetic mean [1]. To establish whether an answer is expected or not, the test considers the origins of frustration, called "frustration factors". Each factor causes three ways to react. It was possible, then, to determine how many individuals give expected answers and how many do not, which translates into whether students are considered as adapted or not, regarding how they manage their frustrations. This sample had 73 subjects (32 men and 41 women).

In Table 5 it can be observed that, in general, the results report high percentages of "non-adaptation"; University C has the highest level and University A the lowest. In psychological terms, it should be clarified that the term "non-adaptation" indicates an ineffective management of frustration. The data analysis did not allow to clarify the origin or the consequence of this problem, although one could think of several hypotheses (cultural, psychological, educational, etc.). It is noteworthy that 61.6% of the subjects fall into the category of "not adapted", and that, if gender is considered, women would have greater difficulties in managing frustration.

4.3   Picture Frustration Test: Aggressiveness Direction

According to the PFT, aggressiveness can manifest itself in three directions: extrapunitive (directed towards the outside), impunitive (avoidance of aggression) and intrapunitive (directed towards oneself). Sometimes, it is not possible to determine a predominant trend because people do not always have it, or the data is insufficient to determine it. In these cases, it could be affirmed that these types of people do not show a stylistic predominance when it comes to directing their aggression. Likewise, it is possible that

Table 5. Adapted vs. Non-Adapted frustration handling by gender (AW = adapted women; AM = adapted men; NAW = Non-Adapted women; NAM = Non-Adapted-men)

	AW	AM	AT	NAW	NAM	NAT	Total
Univ-A	10	3	*13*	6	1	*7*	20
%	50%	15%	*65%*	30%	5%	*35%*	100%
Univ-B	0	13	*13*	4	13	*17*	30
%	0%	43,3%	*43,3%*	13,3%	43,3%	*56,6%*	100%
Univ-C	2	0	*2*	19	2	*21*	23
%	8,6%	0%	*8,6%*	82,6%	8,6%	*91,3%*	100%
TOTAL	12	16	*28*	29	16	*45*	73
%	16,4%	21,9%	*38,3%*	39,7%	21,9%	*61,6%*	100%

there are people that have two directions of aggression as a predominant trend. The following data were obtained regarding the direction of the aggression in the research sample (Table 6).

Table 6. Direction of aggressiveness; all students (E = extrapunitive; I = intrapunitive; M = Impunitive; Nt = No-Tendency)

	E	%	I	%	M	%	Nt	%
Univ-A	3	10,7	8	28,5	6	21,4	11	39,2
Univ-B	4	11,4	10	28,5	8	22,8	13	37,1
Univ-C	3	11,5	4	15,3	4	15,3	15	57,6
Total	10	11,1	22	24,4	18	20	39	43,3

Considering the frequencies, on Table 6, it could be said that the predominant trends in the total sample are those corresponding to the intrapunitive and impunitive directions, in that order. Table 7 indicates that there is no difference for men and women. It could be hypothesized that, once again, cultural influences, like prejudices would have much to do with this predominance; this could be backed up because the 3 universities are perceived in the social imaginary, as recipients of students of a certain type of socio-economic group.

4.4 Frustration and Virtual Reality: A Prototype

To build the VR prototype, it was first necessary to gather a panel of experts to discuss about characteristics that this product should have. It was then decided to implement six VR scenes, looking for those that could potentially produce the highest levels of frustration in the subjects. To find these scenes, a survey was designed and applied to the

Table 7. Direction of aggressiveness by gender (E = extrapunitive; I = intrapunitive; M = Impunitive; Nt = No-Tendency)

	E	%	I	%	M	%	Nt	%
M	4	10,2	11	28,2	9	23,0	5	38,4
W	6	12	11	22	9	18	4	48

participants, after they completed the PFT. They were asked to assess how much each sheet bothered them according to 5 levels of discomfort (it didn't bother, it bothered something, it bothered moderately, it bothered a lot and it bothered too much), with a score of 0 to 4 assigned to each level, respectively. The analysis of the surveys allowed to identify the sheets that caused the most frustration and/or anxiety, presented in Table 8.

Table 8. PFT sheets that cause more frustration/anxiety

Sheet #	Stimulus
2	It is unfortunate, the vase that just broke was the one my mother preferred
4	It is a pity that my car has broken down and that is why you missed the train
9	Even if you need your umbrella, you must wait until the afternoon, which is when the boss arrives
10	You are lying and you know it very well!
13	I cannot help you, although yesterday we agreed that we would do it today in the morning
24	Here is the diary you lent me. I am sorry my son broke it

Figure 3 shows some of the scenes in the chosen environment for its representation. The prototype is being developed for the Oculus hardware, but there is also a version for the Android system that can be used with a smartphone and a Google Cardboard viewer; this "light" version is being used for quick functionality tests. This version was submitted to the scrutiny of a test group, who were asked a series of questions related to the VR itself, the setting in the scene, the characters and the general feeling of comfort during the application. Next, a summary of the most outstanding elements.

Fig. 3. VR prototype scenes.

4.5 PFT Prototype Report

The first scene implemented and tested was number ten on the Rosenzweig's PFT, where the subject is accused, in front of a witness, of having failed to the truth. Participants mentioned feeling calm, in general, within the RV space, which they commented resembles "a judicial office"; they added that, while the test is more like a video game than to reality, it is convincing. Among the recommendations to make the experience more real, it was suggested that other parts of the person's body such as the legs could be added within the viewing space; in addition, the space is defined as "too perfect" so the participants suggest adding subtle defects for greater realism.

In relation to the characters, the features of the second individual entering the room stand out. The participants mentioned that he would appear to be upset and only for that reason they would feel accused. On the other hand, both the voice and the ages of the characters would correspond to authority figures.

The participants mention that the phrase said in the simulation, requires a context prior to the application, since the lack of it causes confusion that leads to monosyllabic responses. This request could be related to the cultural context, since culturally a strange person is not usually intrusive (excess of openness). For this reason, one would think that this picture would not evaluate frustration in an everyday situation but rather in an extraordinary one; likewise, the second character standing up passively produces more tension in the subjects, since they mention not knowing their function.

In general, the information collected is very encouraging about the capabilities of the tool; the results obtained agree with [13] regarding the importance of the gradual introduction of technology in the practice of Psychology. It should be remembered that as in [14], the interest is to contribute to the proper management of frustration. Although oriented towards treatment, in [15] the potential validity of the VR was already highlighted when compared with possible real scenarios; by following the line of [3, 23], we can validate these works and also highlight the possibilities of VR in combination with Psychology. Finally, it is possible to validate that the methodology initially proposed by [31], thanks to the adaptation conceived for this work, is effective.

5 Conclusions

This study has succeeded in taking another step for the integration of new technologies, in this case the VR, with the social and health sciences, particularly Psychology. This integration required adapting a methodology of organization and development for the project; the process followed has allowed us to adhere to what was planned and, as far as the fulfillment of objectives is concerned, the desired prototype has been achieved and user tests have been satisfactory.

The FDS would constitute a reasonably reliable and valid psychological instrument to conduct research on the issue of frustration. The significant correlations between the results achieved by the various authors already cited confirm this. Therefore, the FDS is a useful tool, among other things, to establish the validity criterion of other frustration assessment tools such as the Rosenzweig's PFT, which we used, like the FDS, to assess the levels of frustration and its management in a sample of university students, belonging to three universities in the city of Quito.

In addition to the technological development required to carry out this project, it was demonstrated the effectiveness of the new method, and its equivalence with the traditional method. At the same time, additional information was obtained regarding the frustration levels of young university students from Quito, which will be processed and will provide clues for possible prevention and intervention projects in this area.

References

1. Rosenzweig, S., Fleming, E.E., Clarke, H.J.: Revised scoring manual for the Rosenzweig picture-frustration study. J. Psychol. **24**, 165–208 (1947). https://doi.org/10.1080/00223980. 1947.9917347
2. Connor, K.M., Kobak, K.A., Churchill, L.E., Katzelnick, D., Davidson, J.R.T.: Mini-SPIN: a brief screening assessment for generalized social anxiety disorder. Depress. Anxiety **14**, 137–140 (2001). https://doi.org/10.1002/da.1055
3. Egas-Reyes, V., Hinojosa-Alcocer, R., Ordóñez-Camacho, D.: Mini-Spin y Mini-Spin-VR: equivalencia entre test de ansiedad virtuales y tradicionales. Enfoque UTE **9**, 43–52 (2018). https://doi.org/10.29019/enfoqueute.v9n1.230
4. Hornsveld, R.H.J., Nijman, H.L.I., Hollin, C.R., Kraaimaat, F.W.: An adapted version of the Rosenzweig Picture-Frustration Study (PFS-AV) for the measurement of hostility in violent forensic psychiatric patients. Crim. Behav. Ment. Health **17**, 45–56 (2007). https://doi.org/ 10.1002/cbm.638
5. Filippello, P., Harrington, N., Buzzai, C., Sorrenti, L., Costa, S.: The relationship between frustration intolerance, unhealthy emotions, and assertive behaviour in Italian students. J. Ration.-Emot. Cogn.-Behav. Ther. **32**(4), 257–278 (2014). https://doi.org/10.1007/s10942-014-0193-4
6. Keertish, N., Sharma, I.: Study of Frustration in Adolescents with Conversion Disorder (2015)
7. Nguyen, T., Yoshidome, R., Kuwano, S., Yamada, I.: Picture Frustration Test on environmental attitudes of the community living around Noi Bai International Airport. https://www.ing entaconnect.com/contentone/ince/incecp/2016/00000253/00000007/art00112. Accessed 07 Aug 2018

8. Nguyen, T.L., Yano, T., Yamada, I., Kuwano, S., Nguyen, H.Q.: Picture frustration study on attitudes towards life convenience and natural environment in Hanoi. In: INTER-NOISE and NOISE-CON Congress and Conference Proceedings, pp. 5222–5229. Institute of Noise Control Engineering (2015)
9. Pervichko, E., Zinchenko, Y.: Rosenzweig picture-frustration test modification for a study of emotion regulation strategies among the patients with stress-induced hypertension. Eur. Psychiatry **33**, S709–S710 (2016). https://doi.org/10.1016/j.eurpsy.2016.01.2115
10. Gong, P., Mei, Z., Xiang, Y., Mei, C., Liu, G.: Research on national defense students' frustration psychology and its management in pre-service training. In: Long, S., Dhillon, B.S. (eds.) MMESE 2017. LNEE, vol. 456, pp. 165–171. Springer, Singapore (2018). https://doi.org/10.1007/978-981-10-6232-2_20
11. Yang, X., He, H.: Developing a scale to measure undergraduates' antifrustration ability. Soc. Behav. Pers. **46**, 633–640 (2018). https://doi.org/10.2224/sbp.6555
12. Harrington, N.: The frustration discomfort scale: development and psychometric properties. Clin. Psychol. Psychother. **12**, 374–387 (2005). https://doi.org/10.1002/cpp.465
13. Mustaca, A.E.: Tratamiento psicológico eficaces y ciencia básica. Rev. Latinoam. Psicol. **36**, 11–20 (2004)
14. Nylund, A., Landfors, O.: Frustration and its effect on immersion in games: a developer viewpoint on the good and bad aspects of frustration (2015)
15. McEwen, D., Taillon-Hobson, A., Bilodeau, M., Sveistrup, H., Finestone, H.: Virtual reality exercise improves mobility after stroke: an inpatient randomized controlled trial. Stroke **45**, 1853–1855 (2014)
16. Morina, N., Ijntema, H., Meyerbröker, K., Emmelkamp, P.M.G.: Can virtual reality exposure therapy gains be generalized to real-life? A meta-analysis of studies applying behavioral assessments. Behav. Res. Ther. **74**, 18–24 (2015). https://doi.org/10.1016/j.brat.2015.08.010
17. Diemer, J., Alpers, G.W., Peperkorn, H.M., Shiban, Y., Mühlberger, A.: The impact of perception and presence on emotional reactions: a review of research in virtual reality. Front. Psychol. **6**, (2015). https://doi.org/10.3389/fpsyg.2015.00026
18. North, M.M., North, S.M., Coble, J.R.: Virtual reality therapy: an effective treatment for the fear of public speaking. Int. J. Virtual Real. IJVR **03**, 1–6 (2015)
19. Botella, C., Fernández-Álvarez, J., Guillén, V., García-Palacios, A., Baños, R.: Recent progress in virtual reality exposure therapy for phobias: a systematic review. Curr. Psychiatry Rep. **19**(7), 1–13 (2017). https://doi.org/10.1007/s11920-017-0788-4
20. Carlbring, P.: Single-session gamified virtual reality exposure therapy for spider phobia vs. traditional exposure therapy: a randomized-controlled non-inferiority trial with 12-month follow-up. In: DIVA (2017)
21. Pedroli, E., Padula, P., Guala, A., Meardi, M.T., Riva, G., Albani, G.: A psychometric tool for a virtual reality rehabilitation approach for dyslexia. Comput. Math. Methods Med. (2017). https://doi.org/10.1155/2017/7048676
22. Reyna, D., et al.: Virtual reality for social phobia treatment. In: Torres Guerrero, F., Lozoya-Santos, J., Gonzalez Mendivil, E., Neira-Tovar, L., Ramírez Flores, P.G., Martin-Gutierrez, J. (eds.) Smart Technology. LNICSSITE, vol. 213, pp. 165–177. Springer, Cham (2018). https://doi.org/10.1007/978-3-319-73323-4_16
23. Hinojosa-Alcocer, R., Ordóñez-Camacho, D., Egas-Reyes, V.: Virtual reality applied to psychological anxiety tests. In: 2017 International Conference on Information Systems and Computer Science (INCISCOS), pp. 329–333 (2017). https://doi.org/10.1109/INCISCOS.2017.13
24. Labes, D., Schuetz, H., Lang, B.: Power and Sample Size Based on Two One-Sided t-Tests (TOST) for (Bio)Equivalence Studies. CRAN (2018)

25. Martínez-Mesa, J., González-Chica, D.A., Bastos, J.L., Bonamigo, R.R., Duquia, R.P.: Sample size: how many participants do I need in my research? An. Bras. Dermatol. **89**, 609–615 (2014). https://doi.org/10.1590/abd1806-4841.20143705

26. Shieh, G.: Exact power and sample size calculations for the two one-sided tests of equivalence. PLoS One **11** (2016). https://doi.org/10.1371/journal.pone.0162093

27. Ellis, A.: Early theories and practices of rational emotive behavior therapy and how they have been augmented and revised during the last three decades. In: Bernard, M.E., Dryden, W. (eds.) Advances in REBT. LNICSSITE, pp. 1–21. Springer, Cham (2019). https://doi.org/10. 1007/978-3-319-93118-0_1

28. Ordóñez-Camacho, D., Paladines-Jaramillo, F., Egas-Reyes, V., Salazar, J.P., Realpe, V., Terceros, I.: Using virtual reality to assess the frustration level and its coping mechanisms in university students. In: 2019 International Conference on Information Systems and Computer Science (INCISCOS), pp. 290–295 (2019). https://doi.org/10.1109/inciscos49368. 2019.00053

29. Tripaldi, S., et al.: Frustration discomfort scale (FDS). A psychometric study of the Italian version. J. Ration.-Emot. Cogn.-Behav. Ther. **36**(3), 267–287 (2018). https://doi.org/10.1007/ s10942-018-0286-6

30. Stanković, S., Vukosavljević-Gvozden, T.: The relationship of a measure of frustration intolerance with emotional dysfunction in a student sample. J. Ration.-Emotive Cogn.-Behav. Ther. **29**, 17–34 (2011). https://doi.org/10.1007/s10942-011-0128-2

31. Mattioli, F., Caetano, D., Cardoso, A., Lamounier, E.: On the Agile Development of Virtual Reality Systems (2015)

Simulation of Vehicle Transit During an Eventual Eruption of the Cotopaxi Volcano in the Valle de los Chillos, Central Ecuador

Christian Sánchez Carrasco [ID], Oswaldo Padilla-Almeida [ID], and Theofilos Toulkeridis[(✉)] [ID]

Universidad de las Fuerzas Armadas ESPE, Sangolquí, Ecuador
ttoulkeridis@espe.edu.ec

Abstract. The short reaction times before the arrival of volcanic mud flows (lahars) after a sudden eruption of the Cotopaxi volcano, together with the increase of the population and the car park convert a vehicular agglomeration prior a sudden evacuation an eminent problem. This research proposes a simulation of vehicular traffic in the Chillos Valley in the Inter-Andean Valley of central Ecuador in the event of an eventual eruption through the application of free software geoinformatics tools. A vehicle capacity and classification around the study area has been conducted by selecting the period that presents a greater intensity of traffic as input for the simulation. Hereby two models of the road mesh have been generated, of which one presents the normal conditions of the roads while for the other, the nearby backflow. For the simulation, the traffic allocation zones were established and the Origin-Destination matrices have been elaborated. The optimal routes have been chosen for each case and the simulation time has been established based on the possible arrival times of the lahars. The results yield a critical scenario for the normal model, and a notable improvement over the counterflow model.

Keywords: Traffic simulation · Vehicular traffic · Cotopaxi volcano · Lahars · Forced evacuation

1   Introduction

The Cotopaxi is considered one of the most dangerous volcanoes in the world, showing in past eruptions catastrophic scenarios and thus preventing a possible eruption of equal magnitude in these times [1–4]. As the Cotopaxi volcano has shown recently in 2015 signs of unrest, and, knowing that its recurrence period of time is of about 117 years, while the last disaster has been in 1877, it is a matter of instances when the next stronger volcanic activity may be catastrophic [1, 5, 14, 15]. A fundamental part of the danger generated by a possible eruption of the volcano is in the formation of large flows of mud and debris (lahars) that would circulate through quite populated areas such as the Interandean Valley and the Valle de los Chillos, estimating some 300,000 inhabitants in the danger zones due to the lahars. Past eruptions have seriously affected areas near the volcano [6, 7]. Recent surveys have been conducted on the perception of risk associated

© Springer Nature Switzerland AG 2020
G. Rodriguez Morales et al. (Eds.): TICEC 2020, CCIS 1307, pp. 391–405, 2020.
https://doi.org/10.1007/978-3-030-62833-8_29

with the Cotopaxi volcano in the Valle de los Chillos evidencing a clear awareness of the risk that arises due to the reactivation of the volcano, but a great ignorance regarding the areas that would be most vulnerable [8–11].

New maps of lahar arrival times have been proposed illustrating the lahar flows on the Sangolquí-San Rafael sector [12, 13]. [12] proposed a model in which evacuation times are presented in the different zones and a model indicating the evacuation points horizontally (through the tracks) and vertically (towards buildings and infrastructure) in the areas where horizontal evacuation is difficult or almost inaccessible. However, even than [12] calculated only short evacuation times in view of the arrival of lahars in the study area. The current study proposes the generation of a model and simulation of vehicular traffic in the Valle de los Chillos that allows identifying the possible scenarios to occur on the roads when there is an eventuality on the part of the Cotopaxi volcano, which may serve as a supporting tool for decision making by the corresponding authorities and the public alike (Fig. 1).

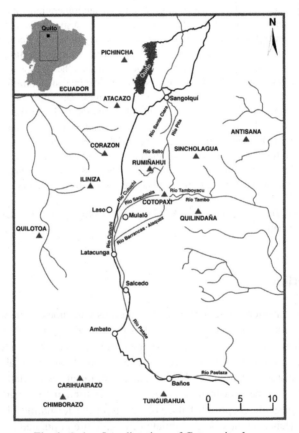

Fig. 1. Lahar flow directions of Cotopaxi volcano

2   Study Area and Theoretical Framework

2.1   Impact Area of Mud and Debris Flows (Lahars)

In the Andean Cordillera of Ecuador is situated the Cotopaxi volcano, which is known for its far-reaching and lethal lahars generated due glacial-ice melting during the last centuries [1–5]. These lahars have threatened in the past public and infrastructure alike to its northern, southern and eastern areas. In the northern zone lahars regularly transited through the Valle de los Chillos. The Valley of the Chillos, which belongs to the province of Pichincha, houses seven parishes belonging to two cantons, being Amaguaña, La Merced, Píntag, Conocoto, Alangasí and Guangopolo in the Quito canton and the city of Sangolquí in the Rumiñahui canton. The decision of who, how and when to evacuate potential hazard zones threatened by lahars may be fundamental for the survival and economic impact of villages and people living near the volcano [16, 17].

2.2   Evacuation Alternatives

Padilla and Bosque [12, 13], proposed a study in which both vertical (through infrastructure) and horizontal (through the road) evacuation points are determined, evacuation times are presented before the arrival of the mud flows and the areas where horizontal evacuation is compromised are determined, likewise, the it has been proposed a model in which the evacuation points and the optimal routes to be taken to speed up the horizontal evacuation process are identified. Figure 2 illustrates the arrival times of the lahars to the Valle de los Chillos presented, where the times vary from 15 to 21 min.

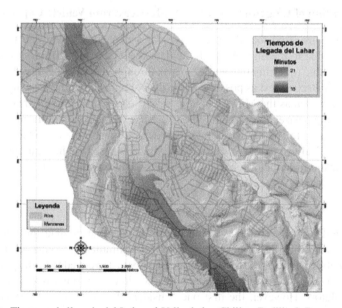

Fig. 2. Tiempos de llegada del Lahar al Valle de los Chillos. Padilla & Bosque, 2015

Furthermore, as a part of the results obtained by [13], also the evacuation points and for each of these, the safety points are presented (Fig. 3), which are located outside the lahar impact area. Additionally, the optimal routes for the effective displacement of people towards each of these safe points are presented.

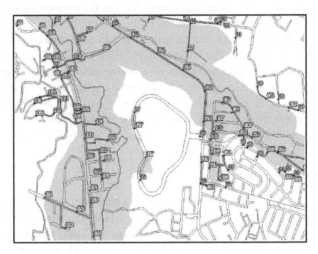

Fig. 3. Evacuation points, safe spots and optimal routes [13].

2.3   Generation of Origen-Destiny (O-D) Matrices from Vehicle Capacity

It should be considered that the routes present a dependency between them and an inconsistency due to the time at which the data was taken. [18–20] proposes heuristic models as suitable for estimating an OD matrix through vehicle gauging, which consists of adjust the matrix as best as possible to the data obtained after the capacity, following methodologies such as the MPME and the SPME (single and multiple path matrices). However, it emphasizes that these methods are used to update data from old gates or when it is needed to adapt measurements through a pivot. Due to a recent count, the "all or nothing" adjustment is recommended, which is based on the assumption that the route to be taken from the origin to the destination will be unique [21].

2.4   Vehicle Traffic Simulation

Transport modeling allows predicting the flow of vehicles that circulate through a specific transport network [22–24]. However, vehicle traffic simulation is generated through a computer platform that allows to perform a variety of tasks related to traffic planning and modeling [25–27]. There are two types of traffic simulators, microscopic and macroscopic simulators. However, the first one considers the individual movement of each vehicle and requires a high amount of data, using more complex models. Nonetheless, the more detailed results on the operation of the road network, the better and more useful it will be for analyzing concrete changes in vehicle flow. The second traffic simulator does not consider the individual movement of vehicles, as it considers their flow as continuous and in a group. It is usually used to model infrastructure projects in large cities [25–27].

2.5 Simulation of Urban Mobility (SUMO)

SUMO is an open source traffic simulation platform, which is purely microscopic and multimodal. It allows to simulate how a given traffic demand consisting of individual vehicles moves through a particular road network. The simulation allows addressing a large set of traffic management issues. It is purely microscopic as each vehicle is explicitly modeled and has its own route, moving individually through the network [28]. Hereby we considered the Extensible Markup Language (XML), which is considered a Meta - Language that allows the exchange of information in an orderly and hierarchical manner, as well as the communication between a large number of applications and programs, as is the case of the SUMO platform. We count also with the System Symbol (CMD), which is the command executor of Windows-based systems, allowing the execution of SUMO own commands. The symbol of the Windows 10 system from which the user communicates with the SUMO platform runs all kinds of applications of the platform, as well as those that run from Python, which are necessary for some simulations [28].

3 Methodology

3.1 Capacity and Vehicle Classification

In order to analyze the structure of vehicular traffic in the Chillos Valley, a manual vehicle count has been conducted on the main roads within the lahars area of influence. The arteries with the highest number of vehicles were identified and a total of 25 measuring points were established around them as well as a manual count has been performed following a previously proposed methodology by [29–32]. Traffic intensity is defined as the number of vehicles that circulate through a fixed section in a certain time range. For the current study the traffic intensity has been calculated in a period of one hour, for which the amount of vehicles that cross a fixed section in a 15 min span for each of the senses of the road has been measured. In this way the average equivalent traffic intensity was obtained and subsequently at this value it was multiplied by four in order to transfer it to one hour. Six measurement periods were taken for each point, being morning 1 (7 to 9 a.m.), morning 2 (9 to 11 a.m.), morning 3 (11 a.m. to 1 p.m.), afternoon 1 (2 to 4 p.m.), afternoon 2 (4 to 6 p.m.) and night 1 (6 to 8 p.m.). Figure 4 indicates the distribution of the measuring points along the area of influence of lahars and the periods of measurements thereof.

3.2 Models

The model (SUMO Network file) was generated by obtaining the information of the Open Street Map pathways and matching it to SUMO through the Windows command window (CMD) and extensible markup language (XML). Afterwards, an XML file was generated, which presents its configuration, indicating the input of the information, in this case obtained from OSM, it also presents the output of the network file compatible with SUMO and the projection in which the information is presented, defining the projection in UTM by default, specifically in the WGS84 zone 17S coordinate system, which is inherited from OSM. The types of tracks, priority, number of lanes per track, speed of movement and the types of vehicles that are allowed to travel on the different tracks, speeds, connections, track sizes, etc. are presented.

Subsequently, the NETEDIT program of SUMO was used, being a graphic network editor in which the existing aspects of the road network were edited, verified and corrected, such as traffic direction, traffic lights, connections and intersections, rounds and

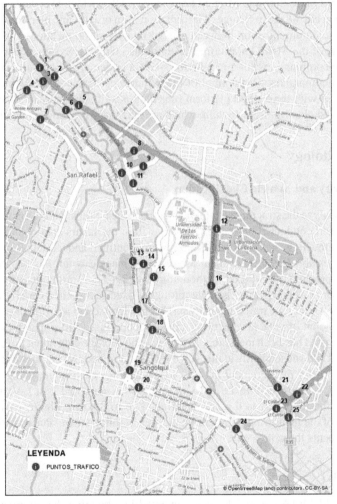

Fig. 4. Distribution of points for determining traffic intensity and measurement periods

the topology of the roads. Once the model is corrected, it is fundamental to perform a random simulation which allows identifying errors in the network. In order to add the route and trip parameters to the model it is necessary to start from a Python Script that is incorporated in the SUMO installation path with the name "randomTrips.py". SUMO will report errors that may exist in the SUMO GUI information section, errors that are best corrected before performing a real simulation.

3.3 Simulations

The structuring of the prediction model has been conducted in three stages, the first of which corresponds to the calibration stage, the second is the simulation stage and finally the validation stage, in which, we established its quality. The NETEDIT program of SUMO was used, which is a graphic network editor in which the existing aspects were edited, verified and corrected. Once the model was generated, the simulation was prepared in SUMO. In order to perform the simulation, the data of the carried out vehicle capacity will be used, the traffic allocation points (TAZ) will be assigned, the Origin-Destination matrix (OD) and the SUMO configuration file will be generated, so that they will be generated trips based on the model previously made. The TAZ file carries the points where the vehicle traffic is going to be assigned in the simulation. For the current investigation the origin points were matched with the 25 vehicle capacity points established, as well as the areas of the destinations of the vehicles, for which the safety points granted by [13] were used. Based on these parameters the XML file was generated. Based on what is established in the TAZ file, the Origin matrix was generated, where the Destination presents the starting point and arrival point of each vehicle, specifying the time in which the vehicles may leave the network and the amount of them. The trip generation file indicates the entry coverages (TAZ and OD) and gives the order to generate a new XML file in which all possible trips from the starting points to the destinations are specified. It should be noted that there are several options to get from one point to another and this file presents all these alternatives. This file is elaborated using the tool "OD2Trips" of SUMO. Once the travel file is generated, the route assignment file is created, for which it is necessary to consider the network file generated in the model and the new travel file as input and the output file is established as output routes. This file will present the optimal route for each of the vehicles in simulation. Finally, the configuration file is the one that allows the simulation to run within the SUMO visual platform (SUMO GUI), establishing the network file and the optimal routes as input and determines the simulation time. The simulation time was set to 25 min or 1500 s, being 4 min longer than the maximum lahar arrival time as previously specified. This has been necessary, as the simulation needs some 3 to 4 min to stabilize.

Two possible scenarios were established, one in which the evacuation of the vehicles is presented in the normal sense of the roads and another in which a counterflow is generated on the Rumiñahui Highway and on the General Enriquez Avenue. This occurs with the intention of favoring the flow of vehicles to the outside of the area of influence through the two main roads. Likewise, the entrance to the Chillos Valley was prohibited in the main roads for both cases, however, the cars that were already within the area need also to be evacuated (Fig. 5).

Fig. 5. Illustration of a section of the Rumiñahui highway in which it is shown on the left the model in normal conditions and on the right, the counterflow model. The arrows indicate the direction of the road

4   Results and Discussion

4.1   Vehicle Capacity and Classification

After the counts were made, traffic intensity values (vehicles/hour) were higher during the hours from 4:00 p.m. to 6:00 p.m. (afternoon II) for the direction of "going", while for the direction of "return". Higher values will appear in the schedule from 7:00 a.m. to 9:00 a.m. (morning I), values that are supported after what has been previously indicated. However, as listed in Tables 1 and 2, there is a large flow of vehicles for the sense of "return" both in the morning I and in the afternoon II hours, which is why we selected 4:00 p.m. to 6:00 p.m. (afternoon II) as the most conflictive in both directions of the way to carry out the simulations, in order to present the worst possible scenario.

4.2   Models

Two georeferenced models were generated, of which one presents the normal conditions of the roads while the other established a counterflow on the General Enriquez Avenue and the Rumiñahui Highway in order to accelerate the evacuation of vehicles and responding to a possible scenario that could arise in the road network before an eventual eruption of the Cotopaxi. It should be noted that the nodes were not altered between one model and another. Only the direction of the road and the connections with each of these were changed, so that the TAZ file will not be affected and may be useful for both models in the simulation. Subsequently, the correct functioning of the model was verified by means of a random simulation, thus checking that both the connections and nodes and directions of track are suitable for a subsequent simulation applied with satisfactory results. Figure 6 illustrates one of the models within the SUMO simulation environment.

4.3   Simulations

The simulation was performed following the normal conditions of the road for the aforementioned time. The points of origin were arranged starting from the 25 capacity points and the safety points based on the studies presented by [13]. Subsequently the

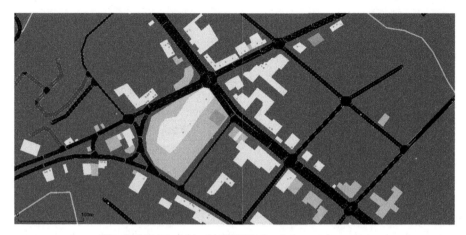

Fig. 6. Model within the SUMO simulation environment

closest evacuation points were established for each point of origin generating the optimal route for each of these and the simulation was run in SUMO GUI. Figure 7 illustrates a sector of the study area in which the flow of the vehicles in the simulation environment is SUMO.

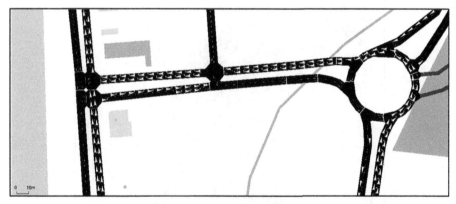

Fig. 7. SUMO simulation environment, round sector of the Universidad de las Fuerzas Armadas ESPE.

Table 1 presents a summary of the information obtained after the simulation under normal conditions.

The results obtained after the simulation demonstrate that of the 100% of vehicles that departed during this time, 55.76% arrived at their destination, while 44.24% remained in the road network, of which 82% remained detained due to the generated traffic jams. A map was generated using Kernel density for point entities [33–36], in which the traffic

Table 1. Simulation parameters at 25 min under normal (regular) conditions.

Simulation parameters		
Vehicles that departed	10098	100.00%
Vehicles in circulation	4468	44.24%
Vehicles that arrived at their destination	5630	55.76%
Collisions	2	
Detained	3703 (82%)	
Average speed (km/h)	3.2	
Relative average speed	0.2	

intensity for the different zones is displayed. Those where the intensity is lower and in red those where the intensity is greater are displayed in green (Fig. 8).

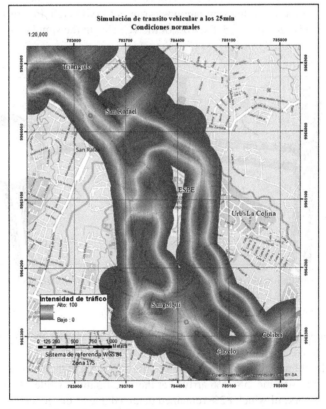

Fig. 8. Traffic intensity map after 25 min of simulation. (Color figure online)

On the other hand, and considering the amount of vehicles that do not manage to evacuate presented in Table 2 and the fact that each vehicle generally allows the transport of five persons, an approximate value of 40 855 people is obtained that would not be able to evacuate being trapped in their vehicles. The simulation was performed by establishing a counterflow on the Rumiñahui and Av. General Enriquez highway for a time of 25 min. Unlike the previous model, in this case most of the vehicles may evacuate through the backflow paths out of the Valle de los Chillos. However, Table 2 presents a summary of the information obtained after simulation under normal (regular) conditions.

Table 2. Simulation parameters at 25 min in counterflow.

Simulation parameters		
Vehicles that departed	6858	100,00%
Vehicles in circulation	1443	21.04%
Vehicles that arrived at their destination	5415	78.96%
Collisions	0	
Detained	670 (46.43%)	
Average speed (km/h)	13.752	
Relative average speed	0.8	

Like the previous simulation, a map was generated using Kerner density for point entities, in which the traffic intensity for the different zones is displayed, those where the intensity is lower and those where the intensity is higher (Fig. 9).

Considering the amount of vehicles that do not manage to evacuate (Table 2) and the fact that in each vehicle generally allows the transport of 5 people, an approximate value of 10 565 people is obtained who would not be able to evacuate through of their vehicles. When comparing both evacuation alternatives, there is a clear improvement in vehicular traffic for the second simulation in which the backflow is generated on the Rumiñahui Highway and Av. General Enriquez, showing a decrease of 25.01 for vehicles stopped by traffic jams %. In terms of vehicles that reach the safety sites, an improvement of 23.3% is noted between one simulation and another. To the previous fact the percentage of vehicles that are in free circulation and that could have the possibility of arriving at the safety sites is added if the arrival time of the lahars allows it, between one model and another there is an improvement 1.81% minimum, value due to the increase in vehicles that have already reached their destination and the decrease in vehicles stopped in the counterflow model. The increase of the existing speed in the flow of vehicles between one model and another, is given with 10.5 km/h (3.2 to 13.7), while the average relative speed shows an increase of 0.6 km/h, indicating a slight increase in the freedom of movement of vehicles at the time of evacuation.

As for the collisions, for the simulation under normal conditions, two were registered in the Colibri rounded sector, while for the counterflow simulation there were no collisions. The spatial analysis of the scenarios presented after the simulations at 25 min for each of the models indicated an evident reduction of conflict areas and a 40%

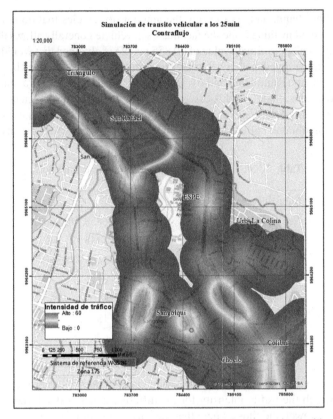

Fig. 9. Mapa de intensidad de tráfico a los 25 minutos de simulación.

decrease in the maximum value of vehicular traffic intensity, showing a considerable decrease in terms of to the amount of agglomerated vehicles in the streets. The analysis of the affected people, considering five occupants per vehicle for both cases, indicates a 25.89% decrease between the two models.

5 Conclusions

Manual gauging and classification methods, unlike automatic methods, represent an economical and efficient alternative for calculating traffic intensity.

The Open Street Map application for the generation of models in SUMO is especially useful when working with large areas, allowing to obtain basic information about the road network and giving us the alternative of working with georeferenced models.

The difference between microscopic and macroscopic type simulations was established, therefore, when applying the modeling of evacuation scenarios, the microscopic simulations are suitable, since they allow the individual study of each vehicle, granting the freedom to make decisions based on the conditions and requirements of the user and providing detailed information of the simulated scenarios.

The model alternative under regular conditions represents an impractical and impro-vised scenario, while counterflow models are a more suitable scenario for a proper evac-uation in the event of an eruption of the Cotopaxi volcano due to its great effectiveness presented in the simulation with respect to the other model.

Future researchers are recommended to expand the areas of vehicle capacity for further studies, since this would improve their distribution around the road network, allowing simulate scenarios even closer to reality.

Subsequently, it would be advisable for future research to conduct simulations of pedestrian evacuation towards safe sites. The SUMO platform also allows this type of simulations to be performed and it would be a great contribution to contrast the information presented in the current study together with that of a pedestrian evacuation.

References

1. Barberi, F., Coltelli, M., Frullani, A., Rosi, M., Almeida, E.: Chronology and dispersal char-acteristics of recently (last 5000 years) erupted tephra of Cotopaxi (Ecuador): implications for long-term eruptive forecasting. J. Volcanol. Geothermal Res. **69**(3–4), 217–239 (1995)
2. Pistolesi, M., Cioni, R., Rosi, M., Aguilera, E.: Lahar hazard assessment in the southern drainage system of Cotopaxi volcano, Ecuador: results from multiscale lahar simulations. Geomorphology **207**, 51–63 (2014)
3. Pistolesi, M., Rosi, M., Cioni, R., Cashman, K.V., Rossotti, A., Aguilera, E.: Physical vol-canology of the post–twelfth-century activity at Cotopaxi volcano, Ecuador: behavior of an andesitic central volcano. Bulletin **123**(5–6), 1193–1215 (2011)
4. Aguilera, E., Pareschi, M.T., Rosi, M., Zanchetta, G.: Risk from lahars in the northern valleys of Cotopaxi Volcano (Ecuador). Nat. Hazards **33**(2), 161–189 (2004). https://doi.org/10.1023/B:NHAZ.0000037037.03155.23
5. Aguilera, E., Toulkeridis, T.: El Volcán Cotopaxi, una amenaza que acecha, Sotavento edn. Quito, Ecuador (2005)
6. Rodriguez, F., Toulkeridis, T., Sandoval, W., Padilla, O., Mato, F.: Economic risk assessment of Cotopaxi volcano, Ecuador, in case of a future lahar emplacement. Nat. Hazards **85**, 605–618 (2016). https://doi.org/10.1007/s11069-016-2589-1
7. Echegaray-Aveiga, R.C., Rodríguez-Espinosa, F., Toulkeridis, T., Echegaray-Aveiga, R.D.: Possible effects of potential lahars from Cotopaxi volcano on housing market prices. J. Appl. Volcanol. **9**(1), 1–11 (2020). https://doi.org/10.1186/s13617-020-00093-1
8. Salazar, D., D'Ercole, R.: Percepción del riesgo asociado al volcán Cotopaxi y vulnerabilidad en el Valle de Los Chillos (Ecuador). Bulletin de l'Institut français d'études andines **38**(3), 849–871 (2009)
9. Toulkeridis, T., Jacome, A., Mato, F.: Ethics, policy, and risk assessment of the Cotopaxi volcanic crisis in Ecuador—Vulnerable society versus unprepared volcanic monitoring staff and authorities. In: Acevedo, R., Frías, J. (eds.) Geoethics In Latin America. TLASBS, pp. 153–170. Springer, Cham (2018). https://doi.org/10.1007/978-3-319-75373-7_11
10. Toulkeridis, T., Buchwaldt, R., Addison, A.: When volcanoes threaten, scientists warn. Geotimes **52**(11), 36 (2007)
11. Toulkeridis, T., Zach, I.: Wind directions of volcanic ash-charged clouds in Ecuador–implications for the public and flight safety. Geomat. Nat. Hazards Risk **8**(2), 242–256 (2017)

12. Padilla, O., Bosque, J.: Determinación de puntos de evacuación vertical y horizontal en caso de una erupción del volcán cotopaxi en el Valle de los Chillos, Sangolquí, Ecuador. Revista Geoespacial **11**, 67–79 (2014)
13. Padilla, O., Bosque, J.: Calculo, analisis y representacion de tiempos de evacuacion en el Valle de los Chillos frente a una eventual erupción del volcán Cotopaxi, p. 21 (2015)
14. Toulkeridis, T., et al.: Evaluation of the initial stage of the reactivated Cotopaxi volcano-analysis of the first ejected fine-grained material. Nat. Hazards Earth Syst. Sci. **3**(11), 6947–6976 (2015)
15. Vaca, A.V., et al.: Characterization of fine-grained material ejected by the Cotopaxi volcano employing X-ray diffraction and electron diffraction scattering techniques. Biol. Med. (Aligarh) **8**(280), 2 (2016)
16. Haynes, K., Barclay, J., Pidgeon, N.: The issue of trust and its influence on risk communication during a volcanic crisis. Bull. Volcanol. **70**(5), 605–621 (2008). https://doi.org/10.1007/s00 445-007-0156-z
17. Barclay, J., et al.: Framing volcanic risk communication within disaster risk reduction: finding ways for the social and physical sciences to work together. Geol. Soc. Lond. Spec. Publ. **305**(1), 163–177 (2008)
18. Bocanegra, H.L.: Estimación de una matriz origen-destino a partir de aforos vehiculares. Nuevo León: Tesis de Maestría en ciencias con especialidad en Ingeniería de Tránsito, Mexico (2005). 170 p.
19. Lundgren, J.T., Peterson, A.: A heuristic for the bilevel origin–destination-matrix estimation problem. Transp. Res. Part B: Methodol. **42**(4), 339–354 (2008)
20. Owais, M., Moussa, G.S., Hussain, K.F.: Sensor location model for O/D estimation: multi-criteria meta-heuristics approach. Oper. Res. Perspect. **6**, 100100 (2019)
21. FCEFyN: Modelos de predicción de la demanda. En D. d. Civiles. Córdoba (2014)
22. Valles, J.A.: Curso de TransCAD en Español (2019)
23. Hidas, P.: Modelling lane changing and merging in microscopic traffic simulation. Transp. Res. Part C: Emerg. Technol. **10**(5–6), 351–371 (2002)
24. Daganzo, C.F., Gayah, V.V., Gonzales, E.J.: Macroscopic relations of urban traffic variables: bifurcations, multivaluedness and instability. Transp. Res. Part B: Methodol. **45**(1), 278–288 (2011)
25. Krajzewicz, D., Erdmann, J., Behrisch, M., Bieker, L.: Recent development and applications of SUMO-Simulation of Urban MObility. Int. J. Adv. Syst. Meas. **5**(3&4), 128–138 (2012)
26. Barceló, J., Ferrer, J.L., García, D., Florian, M., Saux, E.L.: Parallelization of microscopic traffic simulation for ATT systems analysis. In: Marcotte, P., Nguyen, S. (eds.) Equilibrium and Advanced Transportation Modelling. CRT, pp. 1–26. Springer, Boston (1998). https://doi.org/10.1007/978-1-4615-5757-9_1
27. Rizzoli, A.E., Fornara, N., Gambardella, L.M.: A simulation tool for combined rail/road transport in intermodal terminals. Math. Comput. Simul. **59**(1–3), 57–71 (2002)
28. SUMO: Simulation of Urban MObility. Tutorials/Import from OpenStreetMap (2018). http://www.sumo.dlr.de/userdoc/Tutorials/Import_from_OpenStreetMap.html
29. Falcón, H.S., Tacoronte, D.V., Santana, A.G.: La movilidad urbana sostenible y su incidencia en el desarrollo turístico. Gestión y ambiente **19**(1), 48–62 (2016)
30. Martínez, J.M.D., López-Lambas, M.E.: Planes de Movilidad Urbana Sostenible en las Ciudades Españolas. CONAMA **2014**, 17 (2014)
31. Lindenau, M., Böhler-Baedeker, S.: Citizen and stakeholder involvement: a precondition for sustainable urban mobility. Transp. Res. Proc. **4**, 347–360 (2014)
32. Okraszewska, R., Romanowska, A., Wołek, M., Oskarbski, J., Birr, K., Jamroz, K.: Integration of a multilevel transport system model into sustainable urban mobility planning. Sustainability **10**(2), 479 (2018)

33. Gan, W.Y., Li, D.Y.: Hierarchical clustering based on kernel density estimation. Acta Simulata Systematica Sinica **2**, 302–307 (2004)
34. Zhang, P., Deng, M., Van de Weghe, N.: Clustering spatio-temporal trajectories based on kernel density estimation. In: Murgante, B., et al. (eds.) ICCSA 2014. LNCS, vol. 8579, pp. 298–311. Springer, Cham (2014). https://doi.org/10.1007/978-3-319-09144-0_21
35. Maurin, B., Masoud, O., Papanikolopoulos, N.P.: Tracking all traffic: computer vision algorithms for monitoring vehicles, individuals, and crowds. IEEE Robot. Autom. Mag. **12**(1), 29–36 (2005)
36. Echegaray-Aveiga, R.C., Rodríguez, F., Toulkeridis, T., Echegaray-Aveiga, R.D.: Effects of potential lahars of the Cotopaxi volcano on housing market prices. J. Appl. Volcanol. **9**, 1–11 (2020)

Generation of a Predictive Model of Urban Growth Through the Application of Cellular Automata in the Valley de los Chillos, Ecuador

Oswaldo Padilla-Almeida⬤, Paul León⬤, Eduardo Kirby⬤,
and Theofilos Toulkeridis(✉) ⬤

Universidad de las Fuerzas Armadas ESPE, Sangolquí, Ecuador
ttoulkeridis@espe.edu.ec

Abstract. The dynamism of the Quito Metropolitan Distract (QMD) in Ecuador has led to the creation of new living spaces in their surroundings, especially within the nearby Chillos Valley, which presented a marked increase on its land use and cover, allowing more space to human activities. However, this process lacked to be aligned with the plans established by local authorities. Nonetheless, the correct past, present and future analysis of this phenomenon may provide decision tools for the proper management of the territory and risks that the inadequate occupation may lead to. The purpose of the current study has been the structuring of a model to properly predict the phenomenon of urban growth, based on its historical trend, using the technique of cellular automata, along with considerations of probability of the spatial distribution provided by Markov chains and statistical analysis in order to determine the influence of physical and logistical variables. In order to accomplish such goal, initially, land coverage information layers for three different years have been generated, through satellite image classification. Once structured, the model has been validated using the kappa index, categorizing it as a model of well adjustment, certifying their use for the subsequent production of simulated land cover layers for the years 2020 and 2025. The analysis of the results identified the dynamic of growth, mainly characterized by the transformation of farmland into urban uses.

Keywords: Urban growth · Cellular automata · Predictive model · Land occupation · Stochastic model

1 Introduction

Since remote times humans mobilized and got associated looking for a territory that provides opportunities for a more comfortable life, thus forming consolidated urban areas with concentration of services. The existence of favorable conditions for the development of activities of all kinds, returns to the attractive territory for the arrival of new inhabitants [1]. As a consequence of these displacements, the cities begin to have an excessive growth complicating the fulfillment of the development plans [2].

Cellular Automata (CA) derived their name from the fact that they are cells, cells, or tesla and that their state are able to be changed in a simple transition according to certain

© Springer Nature Switzerland AG 2020
G. Rodriguez Morales et al. (Eds.): TICEC 2020, CCIS 1307, pp. 406–419, 2020.
https://doi.org/10.1007/978-3-030-62833-8_30

rules, changes that give them their status as automatons. The study of cellular automata dates back to the 1940s when the researcher Von Neumann gave birth to this field. After slow progress before the 60s and 70s the CA's were gradually gaining more attention in various fields and disciplines of scientific research particularly in Physics, Mathematics, Informatics and Biology (artificial life) currently having an area of application in the most varied fields.

CA's are a set of simple elements distributed in a space and locally connected. Thus, a transition function is defined which allows the change of state of each of the automata. The state of the automaton is produced as an output product of various inputs and of the various transition rules that have been created in a particular way for each case. The current state of the cell constantly changes in continuous iterations, which will give a total idea of the phenomenon represented and in a state of evolution after a certain time. However, the fundamental thing about this type of model is that it can represent phenomena in which the variables change discretely depending on their state and not continuously depending on a mathematical function.

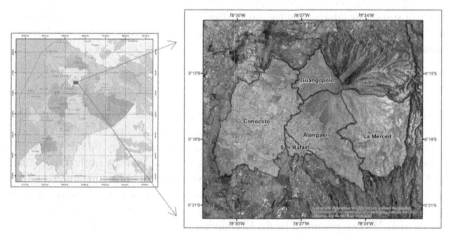

Fig. 1. Study area in the Valley de los Chillos. Courtesy Google Earth, Open Street Map

The area of Los Chillos Valley within the Inter-Andean Valley in Ecuador, began to be populated in an accelerated way when the inhabitants of Quito decided to look for domicile options far from the stifling center of the district, full of noise and pollution caused mainly by the vehicles that circulate abundantly in the arteries of the city [3]. The territory of this Valley has been previously dominated by the presence of large land for agricultural use due to the high productivity of its soil. However, when a great demand for habitable spaces was created, its use changed rapidly giving way to the advance of the urban sprawl [4, 5]. Thus, it was forming suburban areas due to the combined uses of the soil and making necessary the consideration of the densely populated rural areas as potential generating nuclei of new consolidated urban areas (Fig. 1).

2 Study Area

The study area is situated south of the QMD and its composed of the parishes of Conocoto, Guangopolo, Alangasí and La Merced, as well as the San Rafael parish, which belongs to the Rumiñahui Canton (Fig. 1). It is located in a valley that reaches the foothills of known elevations such as Cerro Ilaló, Pasochoa or Antisana, as well as the Lomas de Puengasí [6]. It has a warm climate throughout the year which ranges between 10° and 29°. The average height of this territory is 2500 m. According to data from the INEC Population and Housing Census conducted in 2010, by that time the five parishes together housed a population of 127,728 inhabitants. The total area of the study area is of about 121.43 km².

3 Methodology

The conducted process during the development of this study has been composed of five main stages, being obtaining geographic inputs, processing satellite images, generating layers of soil cover information for three different periods, generation of the predictive model and preparation of simulated products. These subprocesses are described in detail further below.

3.1 Stage 1: Obtaining Supplies

The necessary inputs included Landsat 7 images from the year 1999 and Landsat 8 from the year 2014, downloaded by use registration, through the Global Visualization Viewer utility (GLOVIS) and from the United States Geological Survey (USGS) page. The Aster images of the year 2007 have been facilitated by the Ministry of the Environment (MAE); In addition, the orthophotos of the cantons Quito and Rumiñahui and a DTM performed by SigTierras with a resolution of 5 m have also been used, as well as basic and thematic cartography of land use and coverage and of infrastructure and services, at a scale of 1: 25,000, generated by the Ecuadorian Space Institute (IEE).

3.2 Stage 2: Determination of Work Scale and Minimum Unit of Mapping

The work scale has been defined based on the resolution of the satellite images, from which the layers of land cover information have been generated. This has led to obtain a spatial resolution of 15 m., therefore the working scale has been established at 1: 50000. As for the minimum mapping unit (MMU), it has been calculated using Eq. (1), as described below:

$$MMU = MVU \times WS \tag{1}$$

Where:

MMU: minimum mapping unit
MVU: Minimum visible unit (measured in mm)
WS: Work scale

We considered a minimum visible unit of 4 mm × 4 mm, and that for the scale 1: 50,000, which leads to the fact that 1 mm on the map represents 50 m in the reality. The calculation yielded a result of 40,000 m^2, equivalent to 4 ha, as the value of the MMU for the present project.

3.3 Stage 3: Processing of Satellite Images

In order to obtain more processed images, a series of corrections and improvements have been applied, intervening in the geometrical, radiometric and spectral characteristics of them, seeking simultaneously that these are homogenized, in order to perform a more adequate comparison between the information obtained from such images, considering that each corresponds to a different sensor. The applied processing have been atmospheric correction, pan-sharpening, geometric and topographic correction.

3.4 Stage 4: Preparation of Land Cover Information

a) Definition of the thematic legend

Initially, the types of coverage present in the analysis area have been checked. Later, the legend elaborated by [7] has been chosen as a reference and adapted to the conditions of the area of interest. Due to the work scale and the purpose of the current project, we established that the classification of soil cover layers would be conducted based on the Level I categories of the aforementioned reference legend (Table 1).

Table 1. Thematic legend for classification. Modified of [7].

Code	Type of coverage
1	Forests
2	Shrub and herbaceous vegetation
3	Agricultural Land
4	Water reservoirs
5	Urban
6	Bare soil
7	Without information

b) Classification of satellite images

Initially, the soil cover information layer has been generated for the year 1999, using a hybrid classification method, in which the urban type covers, water reservoirs and areas without information have been obtained by means of visual interpretation. Furthermore, the types of natural cover (forests, shrub and herbaceous vegetation, pastures and crops and bare soil) have been extracted by means of automatic classification, applying a classification mask composed of the polygons obtained by interpretation. Once the entire image of that year has been classified, a consolidation of the classification file has been conducted to subsequently debug it, by eliminating the polygons with an area smaller than the minimum unit of mapping and the use of topological rules in order to avoid overlaps and hollow zones. The resulting file has been validated by calculating the kappa index from the confusion matrix, obtaining a value of 0.84, allowing cataloging the classified image as a quality product according to the criteria of [8].

Regarding the information layers of the remaining years (2007 and 2014), these have been elaborated through visual interpretation. This process has been performed in chronological order. In the case of the image of the year 2007, we started with the file generated for the year 1999 and the polygons were modified according to the notable changes in the corresponding image. For the year 2014, a homologous process was followed, based on the information of the year 2007. In the same way that for the classified image of the year 1999, both archives have been subjected to cartographic purification. The layers of information were named using the prefix "cob" and the last two digits of the year to which the information belonged. For example, the name of the land cover information layer for year 99 has been named "cob99".

3.5 Stage 5: Generation of the Predictive Model of Urban Growth

The structuring of the prediction model has been conducted in three stages, the first of which corresponds to the calibration stage, the second is the simulation stage and finally the validation stage, in which, we established its quality.

3.6 Calibration

This is the most important stage in the generation of the model, as in it we entered the variables and parameters that assign the characteristics and rules that allow to adapt the estimates to the reality of the area and the studied phenomenon. In order to achieve this, we performed the following three steps: a) Obtaining transition areas and images of the probability of changes through Markov chains; b) Analysis of urban growth, by comparison of land cover at different times; c) Study of the conditioning factors in the creation of new urban land.

The considered variables in this analysis have been determined based on previous studies [9–11], among others. The availability of information has also been considered, and the city model to which the analysis area is attached, corresponding to the polycentric type. In Table 2, the chosen variables are listed together with their description and obtained source.

Table 2. Determining variables for the creation of new urban land

Explanatory variable	Description	Source
Altitude (A)	Altitude in meters	DTM generated by SigTierras with 5 m pixel.
Visual basins (VB)	Areas with greater visibility to the surroundings	Own elaboration from the DTM
Distance to recreational areas (DRA)	Courts, parks, swimming pools	Own preparation based on coverage IEE 1:25000
Distance to educational centers (DEC)	Educational centers of all levels and types of administration	Own preparation based on coverage IEE 1:25000
Distance to Towns (DT)	Inhabited areas	Own preparation based on coverage IEE 1:25000
Distance to health centers (DHC)	Health infrastructure, both public and private	Own preparation based on coverage IEE 1:25000
Distance to main roads (DMR)	Highways	Own preparation based on coverage IEE 1:25000
Distance to secondary roads (DSR)	Perimeter roads or those that connect population centers	Own preparation based on coverage IEE 1:25000
Slope (S)	Slope in %	Own preparation based on coverage DTM

3.7   Statistical Analysis of the Process of Creating Urban Areas

Through this process we sought to establish which have been the variables that had a significant influence on the creation of new urban land and what has been the contribution of each of them. For this, initially, a correlation test has been performed using the Spearman method, in order to determine the existence of variables that provide redundant information on the probability of changing to urban land. In this regard, [9] indicated that a correlation value higher than 0.6 is needed to eliminate a variable. Hereby, only one case has been encountered that exceeded this value, corresponding to the pair included by the variables distance to villages and distance to educational centers, therefore, none has been removed.

Then a logistic regression of binomial type has been executed, in which the dependent variable has been constituted by the new urban land areas, assigning values of 1 to the pixels in which they have been found and 0 to the rest of the cells. [9], mentioned that the probability of the change occurring by chance ($Pr(>|z|)$) is one of the indicators that helps to establish this contribution, considering that the lower this probability, the higher the incidence of mentioned variable in the prediction of the change. For the present case, all the variables obtained a very low value in the field ($Pr(>|z|)$), which allowed to identify them as very significant.

Finally, the values of the variables have been normalized and the regression has been conducted again, in order to obtain the weighted coefficients that will be used in the elaboration of the image of probability of change from ground cover to urban type. Its result has been listed in Table 3, in which the conditioning variables have been presented coded.

Table 3. Summary of the binomial logistic regression with the normalized variables. *** Very significant Pr = 0 − 0.001, ** Not significant, Pr = 0.001 − 0.01, * Not significant, Pr = 0.01 − 0.1

	Estimate	Std. error	Z value	Pr(>|z|)
(Interception)	−8,651	0,073	−117,840	<2e−16***
A	7,391	0,086	86,140	<2e−16***
VB	1,431	0,020	72,040	<2e−16***
DRA	0,562	0,032	17,450	<2e−16***
DEC	0,529	0,034	15,710	<2e−16***
DT	−5,177	0,052	−99,860	<2e−16***
DHC	1,309	0,024	55,120	<2e−16***
DMR	−0,403	0,024	−16,520	<2e−16***
DSR	−0,787	0,034	−23,230	<2e−16***
S	−3,165	0,085	−37,160	<2e−16***

The variable height has a high positive impact on the explanation of the urbanization phenomenon. This is due to the fact that the lower and flat areas have been the first to inhabit within the analysis area, so the tendency has been to expand towards the higher areas. Likewise, the variables such as visual basin, distance to recreational areas, distance to educational centers and distance to health centers, have a positive impact, while distances to the center of the populated areas, to the main and secondary roads, and slopes, have a negative effect on the urbanization process. This dynamic allows to note that, in addition, the new urban areas have been mostly implemented in areas where the presence of service infrastructure is rudimentary or even non-existent.

3.8 Generation of the Image of Probability of Change of Coverage to Urban Type

The generation of the image of probability of change of coverage to urban type has been generated by means of the logistic function equation as shown below in Eq. (2), with the coefficients obtained in the logistic regression process [12].

$$P = \frac{e^{(b_0 + b_1 * x_1 + b_2 * x_2 + \cdots + b_k * x_k)}}{1 + e^{(b_0 + b_1 * x_1 + b_2 * x_2 + \cdots + b_k * x_k)}} \tag{2}$$

Figure 2 illustrates the image obtained from the described process. There, the areas with a more intense shade of red represent the places most prone to the creation of new buildings, and the closer the color converts to whitish yellow, the lower the likelihood of future urban-type belonging.

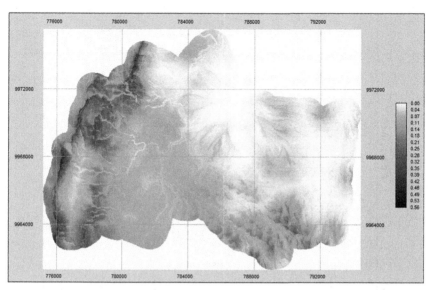

Fig. 2. Image of probability of belonging to urban type obtained by statistical methods (Color figure online)

3.9 Inclusion of the Probability Image Generated in the Set of Markov Probability Images

The image of probability of belonging to urban type generated by Markov Chains has been replaced by the previously obtained image. Hereby, we have the simulation stage and the validation itself. Once all the inputs have been prepared, the Markov Chains have been exercised, where the base year image has been used, corresponding to the year 2007. The previously generated Markov transition areas have also been used, as well as the previously adequate set of change probability images. The number of iterations has been set to seven for the steps to be given in one-year intervals. As a result of this process, we obtained the image of soil cover predicted for 2014, which is also the main input for the validation of the generated model.

Within the validation, we validated through the Kappa index, which determines the concordance of two categorical images. In our case it is the predicted image (image to be validated) and the previously classified image (reference image). For the evaluated model, kappa values of location have been of about 92%, of 90% and overall of 89%, allowing an excellent quality assessment to be assigned to the elaborated model.

The following is a summary of the process of structuring the predictive model, specifying the inputs and tools used during the calibration, simulation and validation stages (Fig. 3). The process has been developed using the information for the period 1999–2007 for the calibration and for the year 2014 for the validation.

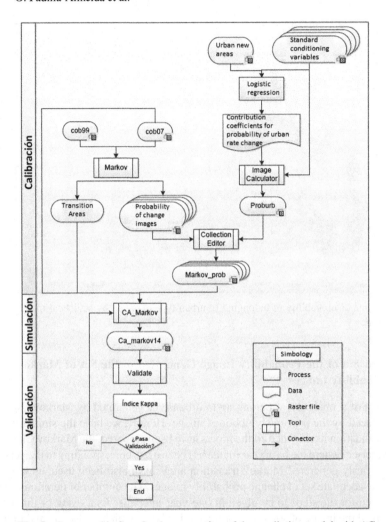

Fig. 3. Cartographic flow for the generation of the predictive model with AC

3.10   Development of Simulated Products

Finally, once the reliability of the model has been verified, the considerations, processes and variables that intervened in its generation have been accepted as valid, allowing its application for the simulation of the studied phenomenon in future years. With this background, images of land cover projected for the years 2020 and 2025 have been generated. The necessary steps during this process have been:

1. Generation of conditional probability images and transition areas with Markov chains: Such information has been obtained, according to the dynamics of the period 2007–2014.
2. Inclusion of the image of probability of change to urban type, generated by statistical analysis, in the model: In a similar way as described in the calibration stage, the image

of the probability of change to urban type obtained by means of statistical methods has been included within the sets of images of probability of change of both intervals of analysis (2014–2020 and 2014–2025).

3. Simulation: Using the Markov Chains, with the inputs and considerations mentioned in the previous points, the projected soil coverage images have been generated.

4   Results and Discussion

4.1   Historical Analysis of Urban Growth

By means of a comparison between the initial and final coverage of each analysis period, it has been possible to detect the changes that took place in these, allowing also to identify trends of change and the existence of more dynamic zones.

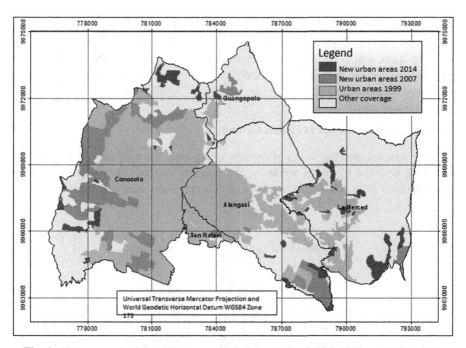

Fig. 4. Urban growth of the study area, within the periods of 1999–2007 and 2007—2014

In this regard, Table 4 lists the amount of area ceded by each type of coverage that has been affected by urban growth. Table 4 indicates that grass and crops is the coverage that has given more land for the creation of new urbanized land. In addition, the other types of coverage that changed in a lesser proportion to the urban type have been forests as well as shrub and herbaceous vegetation. During the first period more than 1000 hectares became part of the urban type, while for the second period, this amount became less than half, stating that the pace of urbanization was reduced. Figure 4 illustrates the

Table 4. Areas and percentages of contribution in the growth of the urban area, by type of coverage of origin.

Period	1999–2007		2007–2014	
Initial coverage	Area (ha)	%	Area (ha)	%
Forest	34,74	3,15%	63,47	14,14%
Shrub and herbaceous vegetation	79,67	7,23%	32,22	7,18%
Grass and crops	987,41	89,62%	353,32	78,69%
TOTAL	1101,83	100,00%	449,01	100,00%

urban areas existing in 1999, those created from that year until 2007, and the new areas established during the period 2007–2014.

When classifying the type of growth according to the categories proposed by [13], we obtained that for the period 1999–2007, 14.92% corresponded to fill growth, 7.68% has been dispersed and 77.40% margined. For the period 2007–2014, 18.08% corresponded to filling areas, while the dispersed growth gained notoriety, reaching 41.49% of the contribution, and the margined growth, decreased its occurrence, representing 40.42% of the new urban areas.

4.2 Prospective Analysis of Urban Growth

Figure 5 demonstrates the origin of the new urban areas for the years 2020 and 2025. Following with the historical tendency, the majority of these correspond to grazing and cultivation areas. The forest cover also yields important areas in each of the studied

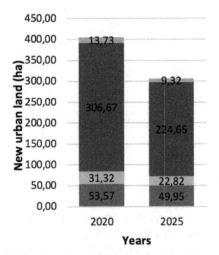

Fig. 5. Cumulative contribution in hectares by type of total coverage of new urban areas for the years 2020 and 2025. Bare soil in yellow; grass and cultivation areas in brown; shrub and herbaceous vegetation in light green; forest in dark green (Color figure online)

periods, similarly, the shrub and herbaceous vegetation is considerably reduced by urban growth.

It is also foreseen that areas of bare or eroded soil close to the current populated areas will be used for the construction of anthropic infrastructure. Accumulating the contributions of each of the dynamic coverage types of the study area, we obtained that during the 2014–2020 period, 405.28 ha would be increased to the category of urban coverage, while, for the period 2020–2025, the increase would be of about 306.73 ha. Below, the probable location of the new urban areas is able to be observed, both for the year 2020, and for the year 2025. There, it can be appreciated that most of the growth would occur at the edges of already established areas, and in a smaller proportion as the product of occupation of internal zones (Fig. 6).

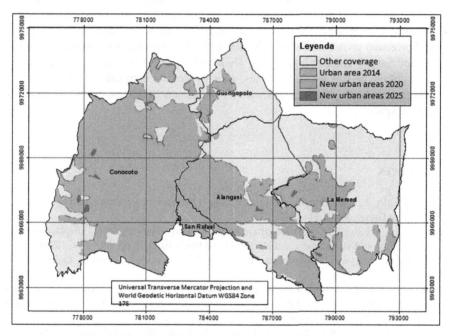

Fig. 6. Simulated urban growth for the years 2020 and 2025

5 Conclusions

- The obtained model demonstrates a good level of reliability, making it possible to ensure that the applied techniques and considerations to the present study have been adequate for modeling the evolution of urban land. In addition, throughout the calibration process, it has been possible to better understand the dynamics of small areas attached to large cities, providing bases for the analysis of similar areas in other parts of the country. Together, the generated information based on the nature of the expansion of the studied area may become a basis for decision-making that lead to a more appropriate and efficient occupation of the territory.

- After obtaining and analyzing the layers of land cover information at a scale of 1: 50000 for the years 1999, 2007 and 2014 of the study area, it was noted that urban land has been the predominant in all these periods, covering 37.03%, 46.06% and 49.80%, respectively, in each of the analyzed years. The coverage that more area has yielded has been that of grasses and crops being 762.97 ha in total, from 1999 to 2007. Also during this stage the resolution of the images and the consequent used work scale has been one of the biggest limitations for the consideration of a greater number of entities. These would have allowed the changes to be more detailed and observable, which in future studies thanks to the technological advances of the new sensors may counteract this limitation

- By means of the information that the projected images exhibit about the soil cover, urbanization problems of incompatible zones may be foreseen, or areas with difficulties for the coverage of basic services.

- The most developed parishes in the study area have practically exhausted their capacity for horizontal growth. However, the demand for residential and commercial infrastructure has remained at high levels. Therefore, it is expected that in the near future the typology of single-family homes, which currently dominates the territory, will change to make way for the construction of apartment buildings, that allow the use of vertical space.

References

1. Toulkeridis, T., et al.: Climate change according to Ecuadorian academics–perceptions versus facts. La Granja **31**(1), 21–46 (2020)
2. Lee, B.A., Hodge, D.C.: Social differentials in metropolitan residential displacement. In: Gentrification, Displacement and Neighborhood Revitalization, pp. 140–169 (1984)
3. Suasnavas Román, A.D.: Centro de protección para niños y adultos mayores. Quito, Ecuador (2012)
4. Rodriguez, F., Toulkeridis, T., Sandoval, W., Padilla, O., Mato, F.: Economic risk assessment of Cotopaxi volcano, Ecuador, in case of a future lahar emplacement. Nat. Hazards **85**(1), 605–618 (2017). https://doi.org/10.1007/s11069-016-2589-1
5. Echegaray-Aveiga, R.C., Rodríguez-Espinosa, F., Toulkeridis, T., Echegaray-Aveiga, R.D.: Possible effects of potential lahars from Cotopaxi volcano on housing market prices. J. Appl. Volcanol. **9**(1), 1–11 (2020). https://doi.org/10.1186/s13617-020-00093-1
6. Acosta, V.: Aspiracional de muchas familias. Revista Clave (2013). http://www.clave.com.ec/1125-Aspiracional_de_muchas_familias.html
7. MAE - Ministerio del Ambiente. Línea base de deforestación del ecuador continental. Quito, Ecuador (2012)
8. Landis, J., Koch, G.: The measurement of observer agreement for categorical data. Biometrics **33**, 159–174 (1977)
9. Garcia, A.M., Santé, I., Crecente, R.: Análisis de los factores que condicionan la evolución de los uso del suelo en los pequeños asentamientos urbanos de la costa norte de Galicia. Boletín de la Asociación de Geógrafos Españoles **54**, 57–79 (2010)
10. Aldana, A.T.: Cartografía de los cambios en las cubiertas artificiales de la Comunidad de Madrid-España. Revista forestal latinoamericana **35**, 59–86 (2005)

11. Plata, W., Gómez, M., Bosque, J., Aguilar, J.: Análisis de sensibilidad para un modelo de simulación de crecimiento urbano. Propuesta metodológica explícitamente especial. Geofocus **13**, 158–178 (2013)

12. Gómez Delgado, M., Bosque Sendra, J.: Validation of GIS-performed analysis. In: Joshi, P.K., Pani, P., Mohapatra, S.N., Singh, T.P. (eds.): Geoinformatics for Natural Resource Management, pp. 559–571. Nova Science Publishers (2009)

13. Xu, C., Liu, M., Zhang, C., An, S., Yu, W., Chen, J.M.: The spatiotemporal dynamics of rapid urban growth. Landscape Ecol. **22**, 925–937 (2007). https://doi.org/10.1007/s10980-007-9079-5

Application of Quality Tools for Evaluation of the Use of Geo-Information in Various Municipalities of Ecuador

Angélica Zapata[1,2], José Sandoval[1,2], Judith Zapata[1,2], Eduardo Ordoñez[1,2],
Verónica Suango[1,2], Julio Moreno[1,2], Christian Mullo[1,2], Edgar Tipán[1,2],
Karen Elizabeth Rodríguez[1,2], and Theofilos Toulkeridis[1,2(✉)] 📖

[1] Instituto Geográfico Militar, Quito, Ecuador
ttoulkeridis@espe.edu.ec
[2] Universidad de las Fuerzas Armadas ESPE, Sangolquí, Ecuador

Abstract. Thematic geoinformation, at a scale of 1: 25,000, related to studies of geopedology, production systems, climate, hydrology, infrastructure and socioeconomic, constitutes a relevant factor in the activities of administration, environmental planning and territorial planning. In Ecuador, the Military Geographical Institute (IGM), was in charge of generating multipurpose, reliable, georeferenced and integrated thematic geoinformation, at a semi-detailed level. This occurred for territorial planning and management, aimed at solving economic and social problems, through an investment project, which began at the level of fourteen cantons of the Guayas river basin (2009–2010). The same was later extrapolated at the national level (2011–2017) and the corresponding geoinformation was delivered to the Decentralized Autonomous Governments (GAD). Since 2012 it began to evaluate the use and level of application of said geospatial information to identify actions to improve the products and services generated within the framework of the project, hereby mainly to the cantons of the Guayas river basin project. The evaluation was performed in fourteen municipalities in the provinces of Guayas and Los Ríos, where it was found that 28% always used geoinformation, 38% used it sporadically and 34% did not use it. These results support the politicians and decision makers in the country, in the sense that they must carry out permanent evaluations on the use of geospatial information related to this type of project, otherwise the use of public resources would not be being used with objectivity and efficiency.

Keywords: Thematic geoinformation · Planning · Territorial ordering · Quality tools · Focus group

1 Introduction

The growth of towns and cities without planning leads to an appearance of activities unrelated to the environment and to a disorderly territorial occupation, which establishes jurisdictional imbalances and environmental degradation. Consequently, from the

G. Rodriguez Morales et al. (Eds.): TICEC 2020, CCIS 1307, pp. 420–433, 2020.
https://doi.org/10.1007/978-3-030-62833-8_31

experiences and conceptualizations that are known and derived from territorial planning in the world, carrying out planned processes of a political, technical and administrative nature, whose central objective is to organize, harmonize and manage the occupation and use of space, contributes to ecologically sustainable, spatially harmonious and socially just human development [1, 2]. Nowadays, terms such as remote sensing related to aerial photographs or multispectral images taken from satellites, satellite image processing, Geographic Information Systems (GIS), modeling or simplified representations of reality, cartography and maps are grouped together in a new concept called "Geoinformation". This is a process that allows different technologies to be combined in order to provide the spatial information required to better understand the problems that may arise in any branch of Earth Sciences, which is a relevant factor in administration activities, territorial ordering and planning, facilitating effective management of the resources currently available for sustainable development [3–9].

In Ecuador as of 2009, considering that the country was suffering the effects and impacts of the intensive and indiscriminate use of natural resources, leading to their depletion, destruction and degradation, creating imbalance and affecting the ecological integrity of the ecosystems, with an accelerated transformation of the territory, landscapes, erosion and soil degradation, related to the expansion of the agricultural frontier, logging and deforestation, inadequate agro-productive practices, expansion of urban borders, overgrazing and use of agrochemicals, among other sources of pressure forced the state institutions of the country that are generating cartographic-thematic information, particularly the Center for Integrated Surveys of Natural Resources by Remote Sensors (CLIRSEN). Since 2012 CLIRSEN was transformed into the Ecuadorian Space Institute (IEE), and whose Competencies were since 2019 assumed by the Instituto Geográfico Militar (IGM), in coordination with the National Secretariat for Planning and Development (SENPLADES) and other institutions. They conducted the investment project "Generation of geoinformation for the management of the territory and valuation of rural land in the Guayas river basin scale 1: 25,000", for the period 2009–2010, which involved fourteen cantons. Based on this experience and methodologies developed, for the period 2011–2017, the project was extrapolated at the national level, named "Generation of geoinformation for the management of the territory at the national level" [10–12].

Therefore, updated, reliable, georeferenced and integrated thematic geoinformation was generated, with a sufficient level of detail, aimed at improving the solution of problems and creating political, social, economic and environmental conditions. This occurred in order to recover the productive capacity of the population settled in the rural platform, in themes such geomorphology, soils, climate, hydrology, hydrometeorological hazards, land cover and use, natural cover, productive systems, infrastructure, spatialized socioeconomic aspects, among others. These may be viewed at the national level in the IGM geoportal (http://bit.ly/2qMvOPR), allowing the Decentralized Autonomous Governments (GAD) to generate projects that promote equity and social justice of the population in their charge, through the development and territorial planning plans, for a better use of the lands, increasing their productivity. Hereby, the main aim has been to raise the level of the quality of life of the population [13] (Moreno et al., 2018). The final, agreed and structured information was delivered to SENPLADES and directly to the GAD for their respective use. CLIRSEN was responsible, apart from generating thematic geo-information at a scale of 1: 25,000, to monitor and evaluate these products, supported by the governing institutions with which the agreements were signed, who endorsed the products generated, and the organizations responsible for the use of products such as the GAD at the cantonal or provincial level, planning zones of SENPLADES and other public entities.

In this sense, considering that the rapid advance of scientific and technological progress, especially visible in the processes of industrialization and the concomitant changes in our cultures and societies, experience teaches that the success of any development attempt depends on the goodness of knowledge of the economic, sociological and cultural factors of each country or region [14]. Whereas it is important to evaluate the products and services of the institutions dedicated to Research and Development (R&D), in order to demonstrate the effectiveness of the products developed and justify the given investments, especially since the technological generation, in particular the one that uses a proportion of public funds, has a high opportunity cost in the least developed countries [14]. It is precisely in this general framework where the present study is inserted, evaluating the use of information in the GAD, in order to propose guidelines for methodological analysis regarding the evaluation of the use of the generated geoinformation. CLIRSEN was responsible, apart from generating the thematic geo-information at a scale of 1: 25,000, to monitor and evaluate these products, supported by the governing institutions with which the agreements were signed, who endorsed the products generated, and the bodies in charge of using the products, such as the GAD at the cantonal or provincial level, SENPLADES planning zones and other public entities.

Considering that the quality of public management must be measured in terms of the ability to timely and adequately satisfy the needs and expectations of citizens, according to pre-established goals aligned with the higher purposes and purposes of public administration as well as according to quantifiable results that take into account the interest and needs of society [15, 16], CLIRSEN, in August 2012, as they were generating multipurpose geoinformation at the national level, and that the information generated in 2009–2010 in fourteen cantons of the project "Generation of geoinformation for the management of the territory and valuation of rural lands of the Guayas river basin, scale 1: 25,000 "was delivered to the respective municipalities, it carried out a cycle of evaluations in fourteen GADs of the provinces of Guayas and Los Ríos, which recently have been affected by natural disasters [17–20]. Hereby they applied quality tools, on the use and level of application of geoinformation, as well as to identify a variety of actions which improves the products and services generated within the framework of the project. Furthermore, this occurred in order to contribute to the progress of institutional management, aimed at good administration, planning and territorial ordering for sustainable development, with the participation of officials from the Subsecretary of Information from SENPLADES, from zones 5 and 8, and from the National Agriculture Information System (SINAGAP), who validated the study.

2 Study Area, Methods and Materials

The fourteen cantons involved in the study were those chosen within the research project "Generation of geoinformation for the management of the territory and valuation of rural land in the Guayas river basin, scale 1: 25,000", being Milagro, Naranjito, Simón Bolívar, Pueblo Viejo, Samborondón, Yaguachi, Babahoyo, Colimes, Daule, Jujan, Lomas De Sargentillo, Palestina, Salitre and Santa Lucía (Fig. 1).

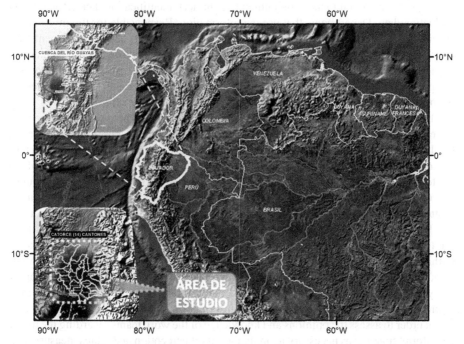

Fig. 1. The studied 14 cantons, located in the Guayas-Ecuador river basin.

In order to evaluate the use of geoinformation in the GAD, two quality management methods were applied being first the Focus group method, which is a qualitative research method that brings together interview participants, in which opinions about products or services are presented [21] and secondly the "4 M" (for the Spanish abbreviation) analysis method, which is a quality tool that helps to raise the root causes of a problem, analyzing all the factors that involve the execution of the process [22].

It is fundamental to highlight that the focus group methodology aims to identify improvement actions necessary to select projects that achieve impact results in products and services, that benefit the institution and citizens [21]. The 4M (methods, labor, machinery and raw material) are inherently part of the production processes, which, if not controlled from the roots, give rise to failures that subsequently significantly affect products and services, generating defects, reworks, accidents and/or incidents, wear and tear on machines, in-line stops, among others. That is, quality failures and therefore a waste of time and money [23]. In the used methodology, every problem has specific causes, and those causes need to be analyzed and tested, one by one, in order to check which one is really causing the effect (problem) that needs to be eliminated, as eliminating the causes, eliminates the problem.

For the evaluation of the use of geoinformation, in the GADs of the provinces of Guayas and Los Ríos, the customization of four parameters (4M) was considered (Fig. 2). The first being the workforce, which includes personnel, human talent, managers, headquarters, technicians from the involved areas, based on a variety of employment relationships (Free appointment, Appointment, Contract), identification data (Place, GAD evaluation date, Departments that use geoinformation, Responsible for the information provided, Technicians interviewed) and Analysis parameters (Type of employment relationship, Quantity, Education level (Postgraduate, third level, technology, technician, bachelor), Experience (Training, being Basic, intermediate and advanced GIS courses or specialized software course being Erdas, Geosig, Sprint, Envi), others related as Autocad, topographic surveys, etc., Personnel not related to the subject).

The second has been Methods, Processes, Regulations, where the existence of a variety of quality standards was analyzed such as Quality manual or quality standards, Quality certification (type, scope), Updated internal regulations and Use of national regulations. The third parameter has been Machinery, Technology and Infrastructure, where the technological capacity was fundamentally observed such as Computers (amount), Servers, Specialized software, Red wan, Internet access, Communications, Printers, Plotters, GPS navigation, GPS precision, Other specialized software, Work stations and Infrastructure (operating conditions). The last parameter has been the Raw Material (Geoinformation), where the following products were delivered to the 14 cantons: Orthophoto, Orthoimage, Planimetric mapping, scale 1: 25,000, Map of telecommunications and airport infrastructure, Geomorphology map, Geopedology map, Map of isohyets, isotherms, water quality sampling, hydrographic division, Land use map, Map of production systems and Socioeconomic information map.

In order to assess the opinions and knowledge of the work teams regarding the use of geoinformation, it was necessary to apply the Likert perception and scales measurement method, which is a very popular methodology, as it constitutes one of the most common ways reliable to measure opinions, perceptions and behaviors, discovering degrees of opinion that can help understand the feedback received, identifying aspects of the service or product that can be improved [23]. The parameters used in the questions posed in the use of the products were the frequency of use of geoinformation and the complexity of use in the application, where the used scale reached from 5 (maximum) to 1 (none) [24].

Considering that the actions and activities for the development of the competences must be approached from all areas, where the decisions of the work teams determine the importance of certain actions that affect the institutions as a whole and are not linked to the development of specific competences, it was fundamental to identify improvement actions in the fourteen municipalities, with the participation of officials from the SENPLADES zonal coordinators and MAGAP-SINAGAP, who validated the work on collecting the information. The parameters used to identify improvement actions were Product or service, Projects, Weakness, Improvement actions, Principal responsible and Description of activities.

3   Results and Discussion

Using the indicated methodologies, through work meetings, surveys were conducted with officials from the fourteen municipalities of which twelve where from the province of Guayas and two from the province of Los Ríos. Hereby, 90 surveys were conducted which participated in the same, evaluating the activity. This has been performed by CLIRSEN, technicians from the SENPLADES Subsecretary of Information, from zone 8 of Guayaquil and zone 5, as well as MAGAP-SINAGAP personnel.

3.1 Analysis of Parameters

a) Workforce, personnel and human talent: managers, headquarters, technicians

Of the fourteen municipalities surveyed, different labor relations, education levels and training received in the use of geoinformation (Table 1) were determined with respect to employees. From the results obtained, it can be indicated that 56% of the personnel are by appointment, 33% by contract and 11% by free appointment. Likewise, 60% have third level studies, 3% postgraduate, 15% technology, 3% technical and 17% baccalaureate. The average work experience of officials in the municipalities is of about 11 years. As detailed in Table 2, many officials trained in the use of geoinformation left their duties or were temporary staff or consultants sponsored by the municipalities.

Table 1. Personnel trained in the use of geoinformation

No.	Knowledge about the use of geoinformation	%
1	Experience in area	5
2	GIS-CLIRSEN courses (basic - intermediate - advanced)	31
3	GPS Course – CLIRSEN	7
4	*Specialized software (Erdas, Geosig, Sprint, Envi, others)*	8
5	Other related (Autocad, topographic surveys, etc.)	8
6	Personnel not related to the topic	39
Total		**100**

Table 2. Participation of GADs in courses related to the use of geoinformation

GAD GUAYAS	2010	2011	2012	Total
Milagro	30			30
Naranjito		4	3	7
Simón Bolívar	13			13
Pueblo Viejo		9	1	10
Samborondón	10	18	2	30
Yaguachi	8	6	1	15
Babahoyo	11	6		17
Colimes	5	6	1	12

(continued)

Table 2. (*continued*)

GAD GUAYAS	2010	2011	2012	Total
Daule	11	1	2	14
Jujan	2	6	2	10
Lomas De Sargentillo	4	3		7
Palestina	3		1	4
Salitre	9	6	4	19
Santa Lucía	6	2	3	11
Total	**112**	**67**	**20**	**199**

b) Methods, processes and regulations

Of the fourteen municipalities surveyed, 44% have institutional management documents, showing lack of knowledge on quality management issues, such as manuals, certifications, and indicator control systems (Table 3).

Table 3. Methods, processes and regulations

No.	Documents	Data			
		Si	%	No	%
1	Organic statute by processes/functional	11	78,6	3	21,4
2	Procedures manual (updated - year)	1	7,1	13	92,9
3	Quality manual or quality standards	2	14,3	12	85,7
4	Quality certification - type - scope	0	0,0	14	100,0
5	Updated internal regulations	10	71,4	4	28,6
6	Use national regulations	14	100,0	0	0,0
7	Results-based management – dashboards	5	35,7	9	64,3
Average			**43,9**		**56,1**

c) Machinery - technology - infrastructure

Some 71% do not have enough computers, 57% do not have specialized software and some 64% have plotters for the entire municipality. All municipalities have GPS navigation, while 36% use precision GPS (Table 4). In general, in 43% of the municipalities the working conditions are adequate.

Table 4. Components of the machinery, technology and infrastructure parameter

Component		Complete		Incomplete	
		Si	%	No	%
Technological capacity	Computers	4	28,57	10	71,43
	Servers	13	92,86	1	7,14
	Specialized Software	6	42,86	8	57,14
	Networks	13	92,86	1	7,14
	Internet access	10	71,43	4	28,57
	Communications	9	64,29	5	35,71
	Printers	14	100,00	0	0,00
	Plotters	9	64,29	5	35,71
	GPS navigation	14	100,00	0	0,00
	GPS precision	5	35,71	9	64,29
	Other specialized software	2	14,29	12	85,71
Infrastructure	Offices (state)	14	100,00	0	0,00
	Work stations	14	100,00	0	0,00
	Adequate operating conditions	6	42,86	8	57,14
	Meeting area	11	78,57	3	21,43

d) Raw material (geoinformation)

The effective percentage of use of the geoinformation delivered is 28%, while 38% of the municipalities use it sporadically (annual + semi-annual + quarterly + monthly) and 34% definitely do not use it (Table 5). The infrastructure, telecommunications and airport map is the least used, whereas the opposite happens with orthophotos, orthoimages and planimetric cartography. In most municipalities the geoinformation provided by

CLIRSEN considers it as a requirement for their land use plans, detecting that in several cases the technicians do not have the information but rather the consultants. The non-use of these products in many cases is due to the lack of technicians with adequate skills for the use of these products. Regarding the liker scale, a positive attitudinal direction was found regarding the use of geoinformation: 61% are between the medium, low and none complexity scale; while 39% consider it as maximum and high difficulty, since they do not have equipment, specialized software and personnel trained in the topics (Table 6).

Table 5. Frequency of use of geoinformation

No.	Product	Daily	Weekly	Monthly	Quarterly	Semiannual	Annual	No Use
		%						
1	Orthophoto	57	0	0	0	0	7	36
2	Orthoimage	50	0	7	0	0	7	36
3	Planimetric mapping, scale 1: 25,000	50	7	0	7	0	7	29
4	Telecommunications and airport infrastructure map	7	14	14	7	0	7	50
5	Geomorphology map	0	14	29	7	7	14	29
6	Geopedology map	0	7	29	0	7	21	36
7	Map of isohyets, isotherms, water quality sampling, hydrographic division	0	0	7	0	36	21	36
8	Land use map	7	29	7	7	0	14	36
9	Production systems map	7	21	21	7	0	14	29
10	Socioeconomic information map	0	7	21	29	0	14	29
Average		**18**	**10**	**14**	**6**	**5**	**13**	**34**

Table 6. Complexity of use of geoinformation

No.	Product	Maximum	High	Medium	Low	None
		%				
1	Orthophoto	36	7	14	36	7
2	Orthoimage	36	7	14	36	7

(continued)

Table 6. (*continued*)

No.	Product	Maximum	High	Medium	Low	None
		%				
3	Planimetric mapping, scale 1: 25,000	29	7	14	43	7
4	Telecommunications and airport infrastructure map	29	7	14	43	7
5	Geomorphology map	29	7	14	43	7
6	Geopedology map	36	7	7	43	7
7	Map of isohyets, isotherms, water quality sampling, hydrographic division	36	7	7	43	7
8	Land use map	29	7	14	43	7
9	Production systems map	29	7	14	43	7
10	Socioeconomic information map	29	14	14	36	7
Average		**31**	**8**	**13**	**41**	**7**

Some 70% consider the importance of the use of geoinformation delivered to the municipalities between maximum and high, and 30% consider it low or of no importance (Table 7).

Table 7. Importance of the use of geoinformation

No.	Product	Maximum	High	Medium	Low	None
		%				
1	Orthophoto	43	29	0	7	21
2	Orthoimage	43	29	0	7	21
3	Planimetric mapping, scale 1: 25,000	43	29	0	7	21
4	Telecommunications and airport infrastructure map	50	14	0	7	29
5	Geomorphology map	36	36	0	7	21
6	Geopedology map	43	29	0	7	21
7	Map of isohyets, isotherms, water quality sampling, hydrographic division	43	29	0	7	21

(*continued*)

Table 7. (*continued*)

No.	Product	Maximum	High	Medium	Low	None
		%				
8	Land use map	50	14	0	7	29
9	Production systems map	43	29	0	7	21
10	Socioeconomic information map	36	36	0	7	21
Average		**43**	**27**	**0**	**7**	**23**

Likewise, it was detected that 35% do not have access to the geoinformation generated, being of low level (14%) or none (21%), either due to the lack of trained personnel to use the information, or because they do not have geoinformation. This was delivered to the consultants and because their teams do not have sufficient capacity to install the software and the size of the information. Some 36% have high access and 29% medium level. Furthermore, from the listed information it was encountered that 79% of the inconsistencies found are with respect to the boundaries between cantons (planimetric mapping) and that orthophotos (36%), orthoimages (50%) and infrastructure map (43%) are not updated (Table 8).

Table 8. Inconsistency found in geoinformation

No.	Product	Limits	Outdated	No answer
		%		
1	Orthophoto	0	36	64
2	Orthoimage	0	50	50
3	Planimetric mapping, scale 1: 25,000	79	0	21
4	Telecommunications and airport infrastructure map	0	43	57
5	Geomorphology map	0	0	100
6	Geopedology map	0	0	100
7	Map of isohyets, isotherms, water quality sampling, hydrographic division	0	0	100
8	Land use map	0	0	100
9	Production systems map	0	0	100
10	Socioeconomic information map	0	0	100

From the information collected, it was found that the map of telecommunications and airport infrastructure is the only one that has been updated by some technicians from the municipalities (Table 9).

Table 9. Update of the geoinformation delivered

No.	Product	Permanent %	No
1	Orthophoto	0	0
2	Orthoimage	0	0
3	Planimetric mapping, scale 1: 25,000	0	0
4	Telecommunications and airport infrastructure map	43	57
5	Geomorphology map	0	100
6	Geopedology map	0	100
7	Map of isohyets, isotherms, water quality sampling, hydrographic division	0	100
8	Land use map	0	100
9	Production systems map	0	100
10	Socioeconomic information map	0	100

3.2 Identification of Actions to Improve Institutional Management

The recommendations identified by the participants were regarding training (65,38%), updating of geo-information (23,08%), advice (7,69%) and software-hardware (3,85%). However, the main improvement action is training on the use of geoinformation, for the aspects such as new technicians incorporated without experience in the use of geoinformation, the trained technicians are in other areas or left the municipality, the training was aimed at consultants sponsored by the municipality and having software as well as hardware that allow the use of geoinformation.

Due to budgetary restrictions, it is recommended that the training events carried out by the CLIRSEN-IEE be held in the facilities of a municipality where other nearby municipalities can participate, in order to avoid mobilization, lodging and food expenses, either due to the transfer to Guayaquil or Quito. Another point to highlight is the need to update the basic information of the municipalities, fundamentally their limits. Some technicians have updated information but do not have a procedure to consider it official. As an improvement action, it is also identified using free software to replace commercial software

4   Conclusions

The information is not used in the municipalities due to the high percentage of staff whose employment relationship is not permanent, with a high rate of staff turnover. There are no quality management issues, such as manuals, certifications and indicator control systems that are applied in these municipalities. Inferring that there are no responsible for continuous improvement processes or management innovation focused on customers and quality.

Maps of geomorphology, geopedology, isohyets, isotherms, water quality sampling, hydrographic division, land use map, production systems, and socioeconomic information are used as annexes in management plans and in several cases are delivered to consultants hired by the municipalities to prepare these plans. The non-use of these products, in many cases, is due to the lack of technicians with the appropriate skills to use them.

Evaluations of the use of geoinformation are needed, taking this study as a reference, to all the cantons involved in the project "Generation of geoinformation for the management of the territory at the national level", which is extrapolated to the national level of the Guayas river basin project, and other similar projects, which are beneficiaries of this type of information, in order to verify its applicability on the proper use of it, for the benefit of the country's development (land use plans), and therefore that of resources inverted publics that are oriented to satisfy the needs of interest groups.

References

1. Bocco, G., Mendoza, G., Priego, A., Burgos, A.: La cartografía de los sistemas naturales como base geográfica para la planeación territorial. México, D.F., SEMARNAT, INE-SEMARNAT, Centro de Investigaciones en Geografía Ambiental-UNAM (2009). https://bit.ly/2UXK3Mf
2. Gómez, D., Gómez, V.: Ordenación territorial. Mundi-Prensa, Madrid (2013)
3. Konecny, G.: Geoinformation: Remote Sensing, Photogrammetry and Geographical Information Systems. CRC Press, La Florida-Estados Unidos (2002)
4. Martínez, J.: Métodos para la planificación de espacios naturales protegidos. Editorial CSIC-CSIC Press, Madrid-España (2003)
5. Ratanopad, S., Kainz, W.: Land cover classification and monitoring in Northeast Thailand using Landsat 5 TM data. In: ISPRS Technical Commission II Symposium, Vienna, 12–14 July 2006 (2006). http://bit.ly/2ufnD0F
6. Almorox, J., López, F., Rafaelli, S.: La degradación de los suelos por erosión hídrica. Métodos de estimación, 1st edn. Universidad de Murcia, Murcia-España (2010)
7. Fuenzalida, M., Buzai, G., Moreno, A., García de León, A.: Geografía, geo-tecnología y análisis espacial: tendencias, métodos y aplicaciones. Santiago de Chile, Editorial Triángulo (2015). https://bit.ly/2UY3KDD
8. Buzai, G.: Geografía global y Neogeografía. La dimensión espacial en la ciencia y la sociedad. Polígonos 27, 49–60 (2015). http://dx.doi.org/10.18002/pol.v0i27.3246
9. Burrough, P., McDonnell, R., Lloyd, C.: Principles of Geographical Information Systems. Oxford University Press, Oxford (2015)
10. CLIRSEN, SENACYT, SENPLADES & MAGAP-SIGAGRO: Memoria técnica del cantón Naranjito. Módulo 2: "Suelos". Proyecto "Generación de geoinformación para la gestión del territorio y valoración de tierras rurales de la cuenca del río Guayas escala 1: 25 000" (2009). http://bit.ly/32arbOt
11. MIDENA, IEE, SENPLADES & MAGAP: Memoria Técnica del cantón El Triunfo. Geopedología. Proyecto "Generación de geoinformación para la gestión del territorio a nivel nacional escala 1: 25 000" (2013). http://bit.ly/32i870D
12. Espinosa, J., Moreno, J., Bernal, G. (eds.): The Soils of Ecuador. WSBS. Springer, Cham (2018). https://doi.org/10.1007/978-3-319-25319-0
13. Moreno, V., Lasso, L., Reyes, M., Haro, R., Cruz, G.: Aptitud agroecológica de tres cultivos estratégicos (maíz, arroz y caña de azúcar) en 14 cantones de la cuenca baja del río Guayas. Pro Sciences 2(13), 15–24 (2018). http://bit.ly/2VhpJZf

14. Cohen, E., Franco, R.: Evaluación de proyectos sociales. Instituto Latinoamericano y del Caribe de Planificación Económica y Social (ILPES/ONU). Centro Interamericano de Desarrollo Social (CIDES/OEA). Buenos Aires-Argentina: Grupo Editor Latinoamericano (1988). http://bit.ly/37LBv0p
15. Feinstein, O.: La institucionalización de la evaluación de políticas públicas en América Latina. Presupuesto y gasto público **68**, 41–52 (2012). http://bit.ly/39OwXI4
16. CLAD: Carta Iberoamericana de Calidad en la Gestión Pública. Aprobada por la X Conferencia Iberoamericana de Ministros de Administración Pública y Reforma del Estado. Adoptada por la XVIII Cumbre Ineroamericana de Jefes de Estado y de Gobierno. San Salvador, El Salvador (2008). http://bit.ly/2uSjKiL
17. Toulkeridis, T., et al.: The 7.8 mw Earthquake and Tsunami of the 16th april 2016 in Ecuador - seismic evaluation, geological field survey and economic implications. Sci. Tsunami Hazards **36**, 197–242 (2017a)
18. Toulkeridis, T., Mato, F., Toulkeridis-Estrella, K., Perez Salinas, J.C., Tapia, S., Fuertes, W.: Real-time radioactive precursor of the april 16, 2016 mw 7.8 Earthquake and Tsunami in Ecuador. Sci. Tsunami Hazards **37**, 34–48 (2018)
19. Chunga, K., Mulas, M., Alvarez, A., Galarza, J., Toulkeridis, T.: Characterization of seismogenetic crustal faults in the Gulf of Guayaquil, Ecuador. Andean Geol. **46**(1), 66–81 (2019)
20. Toulkeridis, T., et al.: Two independent real-time precursors of the 7.8 Mw earthquake in Ecuador based on radioactive and geodetic processes—Powerful tools for an early warning system. J. Geodyn. **126**, 12–22 (2019)
21. Humai-Sutton, A., Varela-Ruiz, M.: La técnica de grupos focales. Investigación en Educación Médica **2**(5), 55–60 (2013). http://bit.ly/2vRLp3a
22. Favia, C., Germanib, M., Marconib, M.: Un enfoque de 4M para un análisis integral y la mejora de líneas de montaje manual. Departamento de Ingeniería y Arquitectura, Università degli Studi di Parma, Parco Area delle Sáciense 181/A, Parma, Italia. Departamento de Ingeniería Industrial y Ciencias Matemáticas, Università Politécnica delle Marche, vía Brecce Bianche 12, Ancona, Italia (2017)
23. Padilla, G.: Proceso industrial sin fallas con las 4M's. Procesos del Tequila. Casa Sauza (2017). http://bit.ly/2Paiqyl
24. Llauradó, O.: La escala de Likert: qué es y cómo utilizarla (2014). http://bit.ly/32inpT5

Software Development

Design and Implementation of a Multi Agent Architecture to Communicate Reinforcement Learning Knowledge and Improve Agents' Behavior

David Alexander Cárdenas Guilcapi$^{(\boxtimes)}$ ⓘ, Henry Paz-Arias ⓘ, and Julián Galindo ⓘ

Escuela Politécnica Nacional, Quito, Ecuador
{david.cardenas,henry.paz,julian.galindo}@epn.edu.ec

Abstract. This research project presents a multi agent architecture which uses reinforcement learning. The goal is to design a system that able the agents to take advantage of its peers' knowledge. The knowledge of the environment is obtained from the reinforcement learning algorithm, Q-learning. While, the multi agent architecture sets a communication model among the agents of the system. To reach the goal, the present research project takes advantage of the Q-learning characteristic, off-policy, incorporating a condition before the use of ε-greedy. This condition allows the agents not to explore a state that has already been sent by another agent, or itself. In the proposed multi agent architecture the agents work in pairs. Each pair of agents have two different behaviors allowing them to communicate and work on relevant states of the environment. The conditions to send the states depend on the environment, specifically, it depends on the circumstances which the agent obtains a reward from the environment. The results evidences that the number of agent-environment interactions to improve agent's behavior is reduced by more than 90% through the proposed architecture.

Keywords: Multi agent system · Reinforcement learning · Q-learning · Epsilon-greedy

1 Introduction

A Multi Agent System is formed of a group of agents where these agents are computer systems with the capacity of taking actions in an autonomous way and interacting with other agents [1]. The proposed architecture combines a Multi Agent System with Reinforcement Learning, which refers to an Artificial Intelligence paradigm where the main goal is to optimize a numerical reward [2].

Fusté et al. work [3] presents an augmented reality app where agents aim to avoid obstacles as well as avoiding falling off a table. When an agent collides with an obstacle or falls off the table, a new agent is created, and a father and mother agents are assigned to it. The new agent learns when its mother or father collides with an obstacle or falls off the table. This behavior can be changed in a way that an agent does not need to wait for

© Springer Nature Switzerland AG 2020
G. Rodriguez Morales et al. (Eds.): TICEC 2020, CCIS 1307, pp. 437–452, 2020.
https://doi.org/10.1007/978-3-030-62833-8_32

its father or mother to make a mistake in the environment. In other words, to eliminate that sacrifice-like behavior.

To bring the behavior of the agents closer to one more like the human, reinforcement learning next to a multi agent approach is used. In this case, human behavior is related to the idea that humans can learn from its own experience as well as its peers.

Regarding reinforcement learning, the use of centralized planning and decentralized execution is considered. When an agent runs the learned policy, does not know about the actions and states of the other agents [4].

In the present work, agents cooperate looking for the same goal. Since it is a cooperation problem, a group of agents can reach a situation of stagnation. Stagnation can be caused because of the environment or social dilemmas between agents [5].

This works introduces a multi agent architecture where the agents work in pairs. The goal of this architecture is to show that an agent can change its behavior based on the influences of its similar. This way of acting is observed in humans, since people tends to do what those around are doing [6].

Agents learn about the environment through a Reinforcement Learning model, while the Multi Agent architecture permits the agents to interact with others. The integration of these two techniques will allow the agent to exchange messages with relevant information about the environment.

In order to test the agents, two environments were designed, these are called "Table" and "Steeplechase". Both, agents' objectives and rewards are different for each environment.

The purpose is to demonstrate that if the agents collaborate, an agent can learn faster about the environment, thus, reduce the number of mistakes made within the environment. The states perceived by the agents are positions and relative distances, as it is not necessary a big amount of processing.

In the second section, methodology is introduced. Results and discussion are found in the third section. Finally, the fourthsection contains conclusions and recommendations.

2   Methodology

2.1   Multi Agent Architecture Design

A paradigm is considered in the multi agent planning, which involves centralized planning, and decentralized execution [7, 8].

In the architecture introduced (see Fig. 1), agents work in pairs, each pair of agents is made up of an agent called "Explorer" and an agent called "Warehouse". There is one algorithm for the "Explorer" agents, and one algorithm for the "Warehouse" agents. These two types of agents differ in their functions. "Explorers" interact with the environment, obtain information from it in order to optimize its policy. On the other hand, "Warehouses" accumulate the information obtained by the "Explorers". An "Explorer" agent does not know about the info that their "Explorers" peers possess, and the same for the "Warehouse" agents.

At the beginning of an episode, "Explorers" requested the information accumulated by their respective "Warehouse" couple. The information accumulated is sent by all

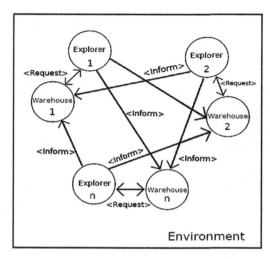

Fig. 1. Multi Agent architecture

the "Explorers" of the system when a reward from the environment is obtained. This means that "Explorers" contact all the "Warehouses" of the system but the "Warehouses" contact its couple only. Each couple it is identified by the number at the end of their name.

¿Would this architecture, with its work-in-pairs model, be able to communicate the knowledge necessary to make the agents learn faster about their environment?

2.2 Reinforcement Learning Models Design

Q-learning algorithm was chosen because of its off-policy characteristic, where the policy evaluated differs from the one that generates the data. ε − greedy was chosen as the behavior policy, since permits during exploration, to pick an action in a random way. Furthermore, exponential ε decay was implemented since tends to make the policy converge faster [2]. Once the agent obtains more information about the environment, the decay allows it to exploit more its knowledge.

Two environments were designed, "Table" and "Steeplechase". The objectives of the agents differ from one environment to the other, thus the rewards for each environment are also different.

Table Environment. This environment was inspired by Fusté et al. [3]. In the work introduced by Fusté, a group of agents have as goal avoiding objects placed on a table and avoiding falling off the table as well. When an agent fails at reaching its goal, a new agent is created and is assigned a mother agent and a father agent. These two agents are already in the environment, and the new agent will learn from them when they make a mistake. This means that for the new agent to learn, needs its mother and father to fail.

At designing the environment, the objective was established to be for the agent to leverage its own knowledge and its peers' as well. Furthermore, a non-hierarchy relationship was set, meaning that all the agents learn from all their peers. This environment is represented by a 21 × 21 matrix, the edges of the table are placed two spaces from the edges of the matrix, (see Fig. 2).

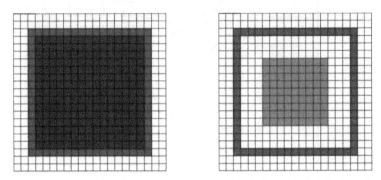

Fig. 2. Graphic representation of the environment "Table" during planning (left) and execution (right). (Color figure online)

During the planning, the starting position of the agent was any of those within the area represented in blue in Fig. 2. The size of this area is set this way in order to make the agents to explore as many states as possible. To test the policies, the area where the agents appeared was reduced (area in green in Fig. 2) with the purpose of observing a greater number of movements. Within the environment "Table" a state is represented by the x and y positions of the agent, considering a reference system which 0,0 point is placed at the top left corner of the matrix.

There are four actions available for the agent, in each of them the agent can move one space to the left, right, down or up.

The reward for a movement that did not exceed the edge had an initial value of 100. This reward is reduced depending on how close the agent to the edges is. That means the smaller the distance between the agent to one edge, the greater is the reward. For this, after each movement, the distance between the agent and each of the edges (Db) was computed, and the smaller of them was taken as described in Eqs. (1) and (2).

When this reward was constant, the agents remained in a central zone of the table because every movement had the same value. In contrast, by using Eqs. (1) and (2) the agents were motivated to move towards the edges of the table.

$$Db_i = (agent\ position - edge_i) \tag{1}$$

$$r = 100/(min(Db_i) + 1) \tag{2}$$

Agents received a negative reward when overpassing the edge. This "fall reward" (Fr) was given in terms of the maximum number of movements that the agent can take and the initial value of the reward movement by $-1, -100$, as shown in Eq. (3).

$$Fr = -100 * maximum\ number\ of\ movements. \tag{3}$$

This reward was obtained experimentally, since in this way the reward at the end of an episode in which the agent exceeded the edge, was negative.

Steeplechase Environment. This environment was not directly motivated by another research. The reason for developing this environment was based on empirical knowledge, specifically, that if a person sees another person fall, this person will be more alert not to fall too, an idea similar to the one exposed in [9]. This environment is a vector of size 12 and 3 obstacles were placed on it (See Fig. 3). The starting position of the agents was placed at the left end of the vector and the goal was place at the right end of the vector. The environment shows the starting position of the agent in color blue, the obstacles in red, and the goal in green. The objective of the agent was avoiding the obstacles and reaching the goal in the fewest movements.

Fig. 3. Graphic representation of the environment "Steeplechase" (Color figure online)

The state of the agent was represented by two distances:

- Distance between the agent and the nearest obstacle.
- Distance between the agent and the goal.

The actions available for the agent in this environment are:

- Jump action: move two places towards the goal.
- Step action: move one place towards the goal.

An episode finished when the agent "crashed" with an obstacle or "reached" the goal. That is, when the agent overlapped the position of the obstacle or goal, respectively.

Since the objective is reaching the goal in the fewest steps, the agent received a negative reward of -10 at each movement without crashing, because it was better for the agent obtaining a $x * (-10)$ reward instead of a $(x + 1) * (-10)$ reward.

Conversely, the reward for crashing with an obstacle (Cr) was defined in a different way and is seen in Eq. (4).

$$Cr = goal\ position - obstacle\ position_i \qquad (4)$$

This reward was designed in a way than as far the agent is from the goal, its reward would be worst. The reward for reaching the goal (Gr), Eq. 5, was 10 by the size of the environment, in this way, the agent would obtain a positive reward at the end of the episode.

$$Gr = 10 * size \qquad (5)$$

Integration of Reinforcement Learning Models in the Multi Agent Architecture.
Once the multi agent architecture and the reinforcement learning models were designed,

the next step was for the agents to communicate information obtained from the environment.

The communication process is based on the exchange and optimization of relevant states of the environment (see Fig. 4). At the beginning of an episode the "Explorer" requests more states to optimize, with that request, sends an LMS (List of Modified States). LMS is a list with relevant states that have been modified as a result of the exchange of information. The "Warehouse" agent responds with a list called LTMS (List of To Modify States). Therefore, there is another moment when information is exchanged. This moment is called IDM (Information Delivery Moment) and occurs when an "Explorer" obtains a reward from the environment.

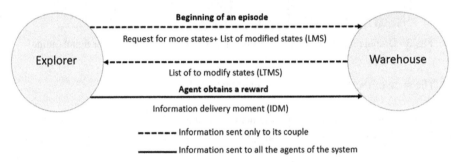

Fig. 4. Communication between "Explorers" and "Warehouses".

The relevant states are tuples, made up of the state where the agent obtained the reward, the action that took the agent to get the reward and the type of reward. These relevant states are sent from the "Explorer" to all the "Warehouses" of the system, whereas the LMS is sent only to its couple.

The "Warehouse" agent was designed to collect information from all the "Explorers", and to respond only to its couple. The information that receives is collected in a list called LRS (List of Received States), where repeated elements are not allowed.

When the "Warehouse" received the LMS and the request, a comparison between LMS and LRS was made to form LTMS. The relevant states that belonged to LRS but not to LMS were added to LRS (See Fig. 5). This process made possible that when the LTMS is sent as answer to its pair "Explorer", the "Explorer" would not check the states that were sent by its peers, more than once.

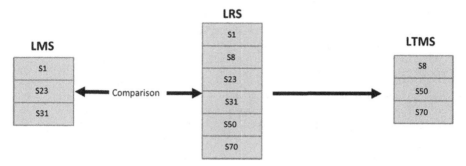

Fig. 5. Process of comparison between LMS and LRS to form LTMS.

Two types of rewards were set, a positive called "reward" and a negative called "penalty". When the "Explorer" obtained a positive reward, sent a [s, a, "reward"] tuple, but if a negative reward was received, the content of the tuple became: [s, a, "penalty "], making up a relevant state. Some lines were added to the Q-learning algorithm which are seen in the next piece of pseudocode:

```
Algorithm parameters: learning rate  α ϵ (0,1], ε small >0
Initialize Q(s,a), for all s ϵ S⁺, a ϵ A(s), arbitrarily
Loop for each episode:
Initialize S
   Loop for each episode step:
      Request info and send LMS
      Analyze LTMS
      Check LMS
      If S in LMS
           Take  arg maxₐ ∈ A(s)
      Otherwise
              Pick A from S using ε − greedy
              Take A, observe R, S'
              Q(S,A) ← Q(S,A) + α[R_{t+1} + γ maxₐ Q(S',A) − Q(S,A)]
              S ← S'
   Until S is terminal
```

Once the "Explorer" received the LTMS an analysis was made where the "Explorer" checks the type of reward of every relevant state. When the type of reward was "reward", it was verified whether the action in the tuple was the one with the greatest value. If it was, the tuple was straightly added to LMS. If not, this action was transformed in the greatest value action by adding a value of 100, and only after that, the tuple was added to LMS. When the type of reward was "penalty", it was a similar process. The difference relies in that the action was required to be the lowest value action, thus, the process to transform the action consisted of subtracting 100 instead of adding 100. This process is shown in the next piece of pseudocode:

```
Loop for each tuple (s-a-type of reward) of LTMS
If type of reward = "reward":
  If a = arg max_a ∈ A(s)
    Break
  Else
    a = arg max_a ∈ A(s) + 100
If type of reward = "penalty"
  If a = arg min_a ∈ A(s)
    Break
Else
    a = arg min_a ∈ A(s) - 100
Add tuple (s-a-type of reward) to LMS
```

The use of ε-greedy was restricted. This restriction is dependent of LMS, if the actual state of the agent is in a relevant state contained in LMS, ε-greedy was not used, but the highest value action for that state was taken. This process allowed the agent in an already optimized state, to directly exploit the best action. Consequently, the agent prevented the possibility of exploring a state again and take an action that could lead to a penalty.

In the environment "Table" the information was sent (IDM) when the agent exceeded the edge with "penalty" as type of reward. This allowed the "Explorer", after analyzing LTMS, to discard the lowest action value.

The "Steeplechase" environment had the two types of rewards meaning that the IDM occurred when the agent reached the goal or when hit an obstacle. In this environment the goal was not limited to reach the goal, but also, to get there in fewer steps. To achieve that objective a new list and an extra procedure were introduced. The new list is called the LORS (List of Optimal Route States). The fewer steps the agent made, the smaller LORS would be.

Once LTMS was analyzed and LMS was updated, a comparison was performed between LORS and LMS (see Fig. 6). After this comparison, the states that were a part of LMS but not of LORS, were deleted from LMS because were leading the agent to a longer route.

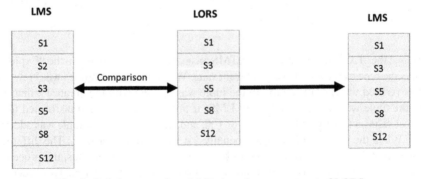

Fig. 6. Deleting states from LMS since they are not part of LORS.

It was established that a [s, a, "reward"] tuple would be stored for each state the agent stepped on through its way to the goal. These tuples are stored in a list called "Agent Route". If the goal was reached by the agent, the size of its route was compared to the size of the optimal route. If this new route found by the agent was smaller, it was set as the new optimal route. Once a new optimal route was found, the tuples of that route became part of LMS (see Fig. 7) and sent to the other agents, permitting the agent to follow the optimal route to the goal.

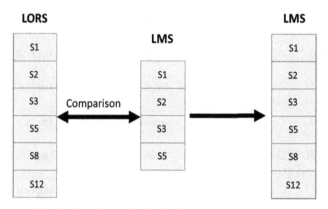

Fig. 7. Forming LMS after finding a new optimal route.

Finally, to quantify the difference between the number of interactions using the proposed architecture and not using it, the decrement percentage formula was used.

Since there is more than one autonomous agent and at least one of them uses Reinforcement Learning, it is a Multi Agent Reinforcement Learning problem [10]. Regarding the transfer of learning, this work is part of inter-agent transfer category. It is inter-agent because agents try to combine the information that was transferred with its own experience. Within this category, this work is part of a subcategory characterized by advising actions. Table 1 places this work next to other researches with the mentioned characteristic. It is a cooperative algorithm since agents have a common goal and it is assumed that the performance of one agent does not affect the performance of the others. Regarding the task of origin and the autonomy mapping, this work belongs to the implicit category as the reuse of learning happens only in the same domain.

There are differences between this work and the ones on Table 1. This work does not receive feedback from a human as in Griffith et al. work [11]. This work does not use the teacher-student framework either, as in [12–15]. This work does not include a method where the agents learn when or how to communicate as in [16, 17].

3 Results

3.1 Results for the Environment Table

The results of the agent without communication indicates that during learning the policy, the agent reached an approximately maximum reward after 45102 interactions, as shown

Table 1. Reinforcement learning models characteristics.

Reference	Learning algorithm	Selection of the task of origin	Autonomy mapping
Girffith et al. 2013 [11]	Greedy, adversary, cooperative	Implicit	Implicit
Torrey and Taylor 2013 [12]	Cooperative	Implicit	Implicit
Zhan, et al. 2016 [13]	Cooperative	Implicit	Implicit
Amir et al. 2016 [14]	Cooperative	Implicit	Implicit
Silva et al. 2017 [15]	Greedy, based on balance, collaborative	Implicit	Implicit
Fachantidis et al. 2018 [16]	Cooperative	Implicit	Implicit
Omidshafiei et al. 2018 [17]	Cooperative	Implicit	Implicit
Proposed paper	Cooperative	Implicit	Implicit

in Fig. 8a. The reward is called as approximately maximum due to Eq. (2). Regarding the errors, the agent stopped making mistakes by the 45102 interactions, as shown in Fig. 8b.

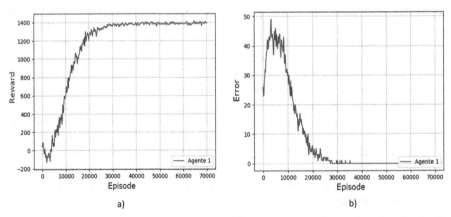

a)   b)

Fig. 8. a) Reward vs episodes for one agent with no communication during planning in the environment "Table". b) Error vs episodes for one agent with no communication during planning in the environment "Table".

At the time of testing the learned policy, the agent obtained a reward which ranged between 1470 and 1230, approximately, (see Fig. 9a), also as a result of Eq. (2). Instead, Fig. 9b shows that the agent learned an optimum policy as it made no mistakes.

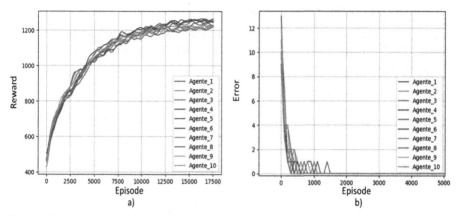

Fig. 9. a) Reward vs episode for 10 pairs of agents with communication during planning in the environment "Table". b) Error vs episodes for 10 pairs of agents with communication during planning in the environment "Table".

Figure 10a shows the best result for the environment "Table" which is obtained with 10 pairs of agents. It is observed that the agents reach a maximum margin reward, around 17,500 interactions, showing a 61,1% decrease. Figure 10b shows the incidence of errors, using the proposed multi agent architecture with 10 couples of agents. It is observed that the incidence of errors decreased to 0 before 2000 interactions for the entire system, showing a 98,31% decrease.

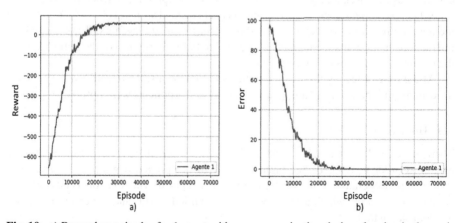

Fig. 10. a) Reward vs episodes for 1 agent with no communication during planning in the environment "Steeplechase". b) Error vs episodes for 1 agent with no communication during planning in the environment "Steeplechase".

At the time of testing the learned policies, the maximum reward obtained by 10 "Explorers" ranges between approximately 1180 and 930 because of Eq. (2). However, no mistakes were made, thus, the policies were optimal.

3.2 Results for the Environment Steeplechase

Figure 11a shows that one agent without communication received the highest reward around 51222 interactions. While Fig. 11b shows that the errors decreased to 0 after 51222 interactions.

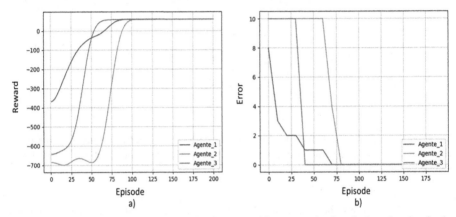

Fig. 11. a) Reward vs episodes for 3 pair of agents with communication during planning in the environment "Steeplechase". b) Error vs episodes for 3 pair of agents with communication during planning in the environment "Steeplechase".

Figure 12a shows the best result for this environment which was obtained with 3 couple of agents. Regarding the reward, one of the "Explorers" reached the maximum reward in 50 episodes approximately, and its peers needed around 100 episodes to reach the maximum reward too. Figure 12b shows that one of the agents did not exceed 40 interactions in reducing the incidence of errors to 0. Furthermore, for the entire system, the number of episodes did not exceed 100.

At the time of testing the learned policies with 3 agents, the reward was always the maximum, and the agents made no mistakes, thus, the policies were optimal.

3.3 Discussion

There are several approaches to multi agent systems where there is cooperation between agents in order to resolve the stagnation [8]. In the proposed multi agent architecture, agents cooperate by exchanging information. This information consisted of states, actions and rewards, which after an analysis, modified the Q function enabling agents to avoid stagnation.

Cooperation between agents is better observed in the environment "Table" where the agents modified states reported by their peers. This knowledge input prevented agents from make a mistake or stagnate in unexplored states.

The results in "Table" and "Steeplechase" environments show that there is a decrease in the number of interactions needed to improve the agents' behavior. This is, in part, because of the use of multiple agents since made possible to accelerate the exploration of the environment, similarly, to Majumdar's et al. [18].

A summary of the results for the environment "Table" is appreciated in Table 2. Regarding the number of episodes required to reduce the incidence of errors to 0, it is observed the best result was obtained with 10 couples of agents since it represents a decrease of 98.31%. It is also observed that the number of episodes to reach the maximum range of the value is the same. Because of agents communicate only when the edge is crossed, each agent learns by itself the fastest way to reach the edge and that number of episodes turn out to be 17500 approximately.

Table 2. Summary of results for environment Table (* Midrange).

With no communication		
No. agents	Episodes to achieve optimal reward	Episodes to reduce errors to 0
1	45 102	45 102
With communication (Using the proposed architecture)		
No. of pairs of agents	Episodes to reach optimal reward	Episodes to reduce errors to 0
1	17 500 approx.	4 283
3	17 500 approx.	1 030*
5	17 500 approx.	1 136*
10	17 500 approx.	760*

The range of the maximum reward is higher in a no communication environment. This is because of a so-called "rebound effect" where agents do not stay on the edge obtaining the maximum reward offered by the environment. Since after the LTMS analysis actions are encouraged or discarded, for this environment the action that takes the agent to fall off the table was discarded. From that moment, the agent will exploit its best action and that action could be or not the one that keeps the agent on the edge.

On the other hand, the agent with no communication continues exploring the environment until it finds that the best action is the one that keeps it on the edge. Eventually, the reward in a no communication environment is greater since is less discounted. However, is not considered a problem as the objective of the agent is not fall off the table.

A summary of the results for the environment "Steeplechase" can be found in Table 3. The best result is the one where 3 pairs of agents were used, since it represents a 99.89% decrease in the number of episodes required to reduce the incidence of errors to 0. The number of episodes required to reach the maximum reward represents a 99.88% decrease.

Table 3. Summary of results for environment Steeplechase (* Midrange).

With no communication

No. of agents	Episodes to reach optimal reward	Episodes to reduce errors to 0
1	51 222	51 222

With communication (Using the proposed architecture)

No. of pairs of agents	Episodes to reach optimal reward	Episodes to reduce errors to 0
1	108	107
3	59*	52 *
5	86 *	75*
10	100 *	58 *

4 Conclusions

This contribution shows a multi agent architecture by using reinforcement learning. The system was designed to reuse peers' knowledge by the agents through a work-in-pairs model. In this model, the number of "Explorers" and "Warehouses" must be the same. An "Explorer" with no "Warehouse" would wait for an answer and would not proceed to interact with the environment. On the other side, a "Warehouse" with no "Explorer" only collects information which cannot be used.

The Reinforcement Learning models allowed the agent to learn about the environment. The knowledge obtained is represented by states, actions and rewards, which form relevant states.

The sending of relevant states and the restricted use of epsilon-greedy allowed the agents to leverage their peers' knowledge and learned about the environment more rapidly.

Table 2 shows that the number of episodes decrease as the number of pair of agents increase, since there are more agents exploring more states in each episode. The maximum number of pair of agents during the experimentation was 10, due to processing limitations. This number of pair of agents obtains the best result with a 98.31% decrease in the number of episodes necessary to drops the errors to 0.

Table 3 shows the results for the environment "Steeplechase", the best result was obtained with 3 pairs of agents since all converge to the same route, this result shows a 99.88% decrease in the number of episodes necessary to drop the errors to 0.

The results of testing the multi agent architecture show the number of episodes required to drop the errors was reduced by more than 90%. This decrease in the number of agent-environment interactions indicates that the architecture was able to communicate the knowledge necessary for the agents to improve their behavior faster.

References

1. Wooldridge, M.: An Introduction to Multi Agent Systems. Wiley, Chichester (2009)
2. Sutton, R., Barto, A.: Reinforcement Learning: An Introduction. The MIT Press, Londres (2018)
3. Fusté, A., Amores, J., Ha, D., Jongejan, J., Pitaru, A.: Paper cubes: evolving 3D characters in augmented reality using recurrent neural networks. In: Workshop in Machine Learning for Creativity and Design, NIPS 2017 (2017). http://annafuste.com/portfolio/paper-cubes/
4. Kraemer, L., Banerjee, B.: Multi-agent reinforcement learning as a rehearsal for decentralized planning. Neurocomputing **190**, 82–94 (2016). https://www.sciencedirect.com/science/article/abs/pii/S0925231216000783?via%3Dihub
5. Hwang, K.S., Lin, J.L., Hsu, H.P.: A multi-agent cooperation system based on a layered cooperation model. In: 2014 IEEE International Conference on System Science and Engineering (ICSSE), pp. 149–153 (2014). https://ieeexplore.ieee.org/document/6887923
6. Dolan, P., Hallsworth, M., Halpern, D., King, D., Vlaev, I.: MINDSPACE: influencing behaviour through public policy (2010). https://www.instituteforgovernment.org.uk/sites/def ault/files/publications/MINDSPACE.pdf
7. Kim, D., et al.: Learning to Schedule Communication in Multi-agent Reinforcement Learning (2019). https://arxiv.org/abs/1902.01554
8. Foerster, J.N., Yannis, M.A., de Freitas, N., Whiteson, S.: Learning to Communicate with Deep Multi-Agent Reinforcement Learning (2016). https://papers.nips.cc/paper/6042-learning-to-communicate-with-deep-multi-agent-reinforcement-learning.pdf
9. Bonghez, S.: Wise people learn by other people's mistakes, fools by their own… In: PMI® Global Congress (2009). https://www.pmi.org/learning/library/wise-people-learn-mistakes-knowledge-management-6862
10. Silva, F., Costa, A.: A survey on transfer learning for multiagent reinforcement learning systems. J. Artif. Intell. Res. **64**, 645–703 (2019). https://jair.org/index.php/jair/article/view/11396
11. Griffith, S., Subramanian, K., Scholz, J., Isbell, C.L., Thomaz, A.L.: Policy shaping: integrating human feedback with reinforcement learning. In: Advances in Neural Information Processing Systems (NIPS), pp. 2625–2633. https://smartech.gatech.edu/handle/1853/53270
12. Torrey, L., Taylor, M.E.: Teaching on a budget: agents advising agents in reinforcement learning. In: Proceedings of 12th the International Conference on Autonomous Agents and MultiAgent Systems (AAMAS), pp. 1053–1060 (2013). https://papers.nips.cc/paper/5187-policy-shaping-integrating-human-feedback-with-reinforcement-learning
13. Zhan, Y., Bou-Ammar, H., Taylor, M.E.: Theoretically-grounded policy advice from multiple teachers in reinforcement learning settings with applications to negative transfer. In: Proceedings of the 25th International Joint Conference on Artificial Intelligence (IJCAI), pp. 2315–2321 (2016). doi:https://dl.acm.org/doi/10.5555/3060832.3060945
14. Amir, O., Kamar, E., Kolobov, A., Grosz, B.: Interactive teaching strategies for agent training. In: Proceedings of the 25th International Joint Conference on Artificial Intelligence (IJCAI), pp. 804–811 (2016). https://dl.acm.org/doi/10.5555/3060621.3060733
15. Silva, F., Glatt, R., Costa, A.: Simultaneously learning and advising in multiagent reinforcement learning. In: Proceedings of the 16th International Conference on Autonomous Agents and Multiagent Systems (AAMAS), pp. 1100–1108 (2017). https://dl.acm.org/doi/10.5555/3091125.3091280
16. Fachantidis, A., Taylor, M., Vlahavas, I.: Learning to teach reinforcement learning agents. In: Machine Learning and Knowledge Extraction, pp. 21–42 (2019). https://www.mdpi.com/2504-4990/1/1/2

17. Omidshafiei, S., et al.: Learning to teach in cooperative multiagent reinforcement learning. In: Workshop on Lifelong Learning: A Reinforcement Learning Approach (2018). https://arxiv.org/abs/1805.07830
18. Majumdar, A., Benavidez, P., Jamshidi, M.: Multi-agent exploration for faster and reliable deep q-learning convergence in reinforcement learning. In: 2018 World Automation Congress (WAC), pp. 1–6 (2018). https://ieeexplore.ieee.org/document/8430409

Evaluation of Utility Function Algorithm for Congestion Control in Computer Networks

Jimmy Carrión[1] , Patricia Ludeña-González[1,2](✉) , Francisco Sandoval[1] ,
and Rommel Torres[1]

[1] Departamento de Ciencias de la Computación y Electrónica, Universidad Técnica
Particular de Loja, San Cayetano Alto s/n, 11-01-608 Loja, Ecuador
{jrcarrion3,pjludena,fasandoval,rovitor}@utpl.edu.ec
[2] Universidad Politécnica de Madrid, Nikola Tesla s/n, 28031 Madrid, Spain
http://www.utpl.edu.ec, http://www.upm.es

Abstract. In computer networks, the huge amount of heterogeneous
transmitted data causes the performance of the networks to decrease.
Congestion is a problem that causes network underutilization and packet
loss. Two approaches have been identified in the literature to treat congestion: mitigation, mainly with the management of window size; and,
avoidance, with an explicit assignment of transmission rates. In this
paper, congestion control using avoidance is proposed with the implementation of a Utility Function Algorithm (UFA). UFA is a variation of
the centralized B-Neck algorithm that uses the max-min fair criterion,
UFA integrates the quality of service (QoS) approach. UFA assigns each
session the bandwidth it needs according to its type of traffic and considers the traffic of all sessions to distribute the available bandwidth so that
all sessions can have a better level of QoS. In the experimentation, three
test scenarios with variations of mixed traffic and different link capacities
are specified. B-Neck and UFA were implemented in Matlab to measure
their performance using metrics: the transmission rate allocation, utility
of each session, and the Gini coefficient to measure fairness in allocation.
The results show that UFA achieves better performance in all scenarios
because it allocates only the bandwidth that each session needs.

Keywords: Congestion control · Utility function · QoS · Real-time
applications · Elastic applications · Computer networks

1 Introduction

The massive use of the Internet for activities such as teleworking, online education, electronic commerce, leisure, among others, is impacted by the congestion
problem causing issues in the performance of these applications and degrades
the user experience [1–3].

The congestion problem occurs when the sender transmits packets too fast
and the buffer queue at any intermediate node reaches its maximum storage

G. Rodriguez Morales et al. (Eds.): TICEC 2020, CCIS 1307, pp. 453–467, 2020.
https://doi.org/10.1007/978-3-030-62833-8_33

capacity [4,5]. Also, the fluctuations that cause users to connect and disconnect to the network are another trigger for congestion [6].

A congested node produces serious consequences to the network such as packet loss, re-transmissions [5], and delay, degrading network performance [7], and in the worst-case scenario, total network collapse. For these reasons, it is important to have mechanisms that control congestion with strategies for the allocation of network resources.

There are many criteria in order to managed the congestion. For example; Express Pass [8] is a point-to-point credit-based control algorithm for congestion control on data centers, in addition to using the principle of fairness, uses the credit package to increase network flow without worrying about data loss. Improves the convergence at optimal rates reducing the flow competition time (FCT) drastically and ensures high network utilization using small amounts of buffers. Ashour, Wang, Aybat, Lagoa, and Che [9] propose an almost optimal allocation for traffic generated by real-time applications, optimizing the network utility functions expressed as the individual utility sum for each user, uses the non-concave utility function as a practical model of user experience quality (QoE).

Another approach proposes an online dynamic distributed algorithm, which takes advantage of Lyapunov's optimization techniques to maximize network utility, applies a trade-off between the performance and fairness of multiple network flows in the service chain and the network virtualization function (NFV). To achieve compensation relies on a utility function with an inequality bias [10].

Iiduka [11] proposes two distributed algorithms to solve the network utility maximization problem (NUM), under the condition that each source has its own convex-concave utility function and each link has its own capacity restriction.

In addition, an interesting criterion is fairness allocation. For instance, in [12] CHOKeH is proposed. It uses partial state information per flow, in order to distribute the bandwidth equitably. It manages the active queue through dividing into two dynamic regions, thus the bandwidth is limited for flows least affected by congestion. In another hand, COALA [13] is hybrid algorithm to avoid the congestion through routing. It is used in wireless sensors network and routes the traffic to less congested paths proactively. Then, in its reactive phase, the algorithm uses congestion status notification signals in order to reduce the traffic carried.

The approach of this work for congestion control is the allocation of resources based on the principle of max-min fairness. Some works exist in this area, Mozo, López and Fernández [14] propose the centralized and distributed B-Neck algorithm, which calculates the max-min fair transmission rate for each session. B-Neck is a proactive algorithm that does not depend on congestion signals, once it has converged to its optimal rates it stops creating additional traffic until new changes are presented in the network, this algorithm static property, can be applied to low consumption energy systems.

PERC [15] is a distributed control algorithm based on the principle of max-min fair allocation for flow transmission rates, it has a proactive behavior since it does not depend on the congestion signals or the data transfer volume, it uses the message passing strategy to communicate the shared rates throughout the network, designed for the use in high-speed network systems, where the convergence time is necessarily low.

In this context, this work proposes a centralized algorithm for congestion control using utility functions. The main contributions of this paper can be summarized as follows:

- It gives a literature review about congestion control and utility functions in the quality of service (QoS) context and discusses the benefit of utility functions to improve the network performance.
- It proposes a variation of centralized B-Neck algorithm with incorporating of utility functions, named UFA, in order to allocate the available bandwidth between all sessions.
- It implements and compares both algorithms: centralized B-Neck and UFA. Results show that UFA improves performance and fairness in terms of individual sessions and the whole network.

The rest of this paper is organized as follows: Section 2 presents the background used in this work. An algorithm based on utility function, UFA, is described in Sect. 3. The methodology used in the evaluation is presented in Sect. 4. The Sect. 5 presents the simulations results for the B-Neck and UFA. Finally, conclusions are summarized in Sect. 6.

2   Background

2.1   Utility Functions

Different definitions exist in the literature regarding the utility function of an application concept, for instance, Jin, Wang, Palaniswami, Li, Zhang, Wang and Sun [16,17] defined it like a measurement of performance application based on provided network services, for example, the transmission delay, the loss ratio, and the bandwidth. Meanwhile, Chen et al. [18] described the utility function as a user satisfaction strategy, within the framework of resource allocation with the measurement of application performance.

In this work, we consider the utility as a function of the allocated bandwidth only, which is a common assumption in the related literature. Hence, it is important to classify the types of applications according to the traffic generated by the users. A common classification in the literature [17,19], presents three types of applications, namely: real-time applications, elastic applications, and linear applications.

Elastic applications are not sensitive to transmission delay and rather tolerant throughput [16], for example, within this group are the traditional data applications such as web browsing, file transfer, electronic mail, and remote terminal access. The utility function for this class of applications is described by a convex bandwidth function, where the utility performance increases as bandwidth increases, however, there is a decrease in marginal improvement, too. So, the elastic service e has a concave utility function $U_e(y)$ given by [17]

$$U_e(y) = \omega(\log(ay + b) + d),\tag{1}$$

where a, b, d, and ω are parameters of service e: a and b are the elasticity and the inelasticity of service e and service r respectively; d is slack variable to shift the curve; and, ω is the willingness-to-pay of the session which requests service e. Finally, y is the assigned service rate.

In contrast, real-time applications, that are so common today such as audio and video delivery, are generally delay-sensitive and may have hard QoS requirements. For these types of applications, performance can be severely degraded by bandwidth degradation. A widely used model in the literature for this class of applications is a convex but not concave at the lower bandwidths function like a sigmoidal or discontinuous function. Therefore, the sigmoidal utility function, $U_r(y)$, of real-time or inelastic service r, with service rate y, can be describe by [17]:

$$U_r(y) = \omega\left(\frac{1}{1 + e^{-a(y-b)}} + d\right),\tag{2}$$

where a, b, d, and ω are parameters of service r.

Meanwhile, applications, where there is a linear relationship between utility and bandwidth, can be characterized by expression $U_l(y) = my$ when considering that the line through the origin of the Cartesian plane. In this case, m represents the slope of the line.

2.2   Centralized B-Neck Algorithm

One strategy used to solve the congestion problem is to apply the principle of max-min fairness to the assignment of network resources. But a question arises when making an equitable allocation, how effective and fair can an equitable assignment be?

Therefore, to solve this question, it is important to understand what an equitable allocation of resources means: for example, if a network formed by nodes $R1$, $R2$, $R3$, $R4$, $R5$, $R6$, $R7$ and $R8$; sessions A, B, C, D and E; sessions cross-links as show Fig. 5(a), then, when making an equitable assignment for links, each session receives $1/1$, $1/2$ and $1/3$ of C_e capacity of link. Therefore, the sessions A, B, and D are limited by the lowest $1/3$ assignment in the link e_4, nodes $R3$ to $R5$; note that sessions A, B and C cannot allocate more resources $1/1$ or $1/2$ in other links, because of its bottleneck rate $1/3$.

In [14] a centralized max-min fair algorithm, named centralized B-Neck, is presented. Figure 1 shows a flow diagram of the centralized B-Neck algorithm, which allocates max-min by discovering the bottlenecks one after the other, starting with the most restrictive bottlenecks and after, finding bottlenecks of the next highest level.

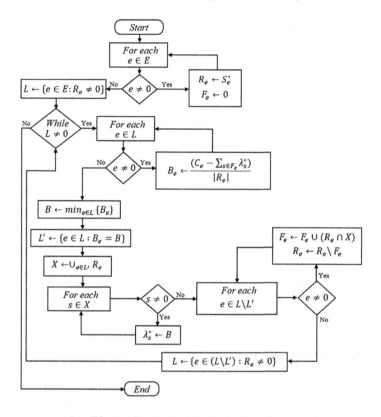

Fig. 1. Centralized B-Neck algorithm

In Table 1 we have the variables to be able to follow the process of assigning B-Neck as found in the flowchart of Fig. 1: at the beginning of the algorithm, the set of sessions S_e^* is in the unrestricted session set R_e and the set F_e starts empty. Then the links e that belong to the set of links E are assigned to the set L. Now with the links of the set L, it calculates the bottleneck bandwidth with the formula 3.

$$B_e = \frac{(C_e - \Sigma_{s \in F_e} \lambda_s^*)}{|R_e|} \tag{3}$$

Once the bottleneck rate B_e of all the links has been calculated, B is found as the smallest bottleneck rate. Then the subset L' is formed with the links corresponding to $B_e = B$, and the subset X is formed with the links that belong to L' that is found in the set of restricted sessions R_e.

The next step is to assign the max-min fair rate to the sessions that are in X, $\lambda_s^* = B$ and changing them to the set of sessions without restrictions F_e. Finally, the sets F_e, R_e and L are updated to continue a new iteration looking for the highest bottleneck rate.

Table 1. Main notation B-Neck centralized algorithm

Variables	Descriptions
e	Directed link
E	Set of directed links
S^*	Set of active session
S_e^*	Set of sessions in S^* that cross e
R_e	Set of all sessions which are restricted at link e
F_e^*	Set of all the sessions in S_e^* that are unrestricted at link e
L	Initially $L = E$
L'	System bottlenecks
B_e	Estimated bottleneck rate of a link e
C_e	Bandwidth allocated of e
s	Session
λ_s^*	Max-min fair rate of session s
B	Minimum among the estimated bottleneck rates
X	Subset of S^*

3   Proposed Algorithm

In Sect. 2.2 it introduced max-min fair criterion, using the network in Fig. 5(a) with link capacity of 10 Mbps, the fairness allocation is 3.33 Mbps for each session in the most restrictive bottleneck. But, if the network could have information about the type of traffic that each session carries, would the allocation still be fair?. Let be two sessions, the first one is a real-time sessions streaming audio and video, for example applications like Netflix and Youtube, it needs a minimum of 4 Mbps to have a good QoS. The second one is an elastic application, for example download a file data.pdf that only needs 1 Mbps. Applying the B-Neck algorithm the fair distribution is not achieved, because more data rate is assigned to the session that only requires 1 Mbps, this bandwidth is not used, and if it is assigned to another session that it needs it would surely contribute to improving network performance. Therefore, it is necessary to include, in the congestion control protocols, the information provided by the utility functions, in order to determine an appropriate utility for each session and to improve the network experience for all sessions in general.

This paper modifies the centralized B-Neck algorithm to make a max-min fair allocation of available bandwidth, with respect to the maximum utility of each session in the link, this new algorithm is named Utility function algorithm (UFA). Figure 2 shows the UFA algorithm. Each source has a predefined kind of traffics and a utility function assigned. The process starts in the same way as the centralized B-Neck, until the assignment of the links e to the set L. Then for each link e of L, the utility value $U(y)$ for each session s is estimated based on the link capacity. $U(y)$ is in a range from 0 to 1; where 0 is the lowest utility and

1 is the highest utility of the session. The link capacity is the maximun utility 1, so it is distributed evenly among all the sessions that go through that link.

According to the value of the utility, it calculates the estimated bottleneck rate B_s, using the inverse function of the utility function. In each iteration, the available capacity of the link C^* is the difference between the capacity of the link C_e and the sum of the rates of the restricted sessions in the set F_e. After we assign the estimated bottleneck rates B_s to the set of bottleneck rates of the link B_e. Then, it finds the minimum bottleneck rate B, and the sets L' and X are formed, where for each session $s \in X$ the max-min fair rate $\lambda_s^* = B$ is assigned. This process is repeated until the algorithm finds data rates for all sessions.

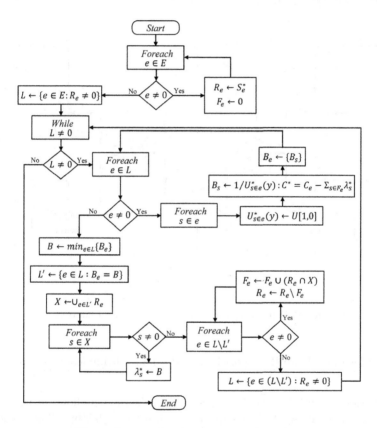

Fig. 2. Proposed utility function algorithm

4   Methods

In this section, the methodology used to evaluate the performance of the centralized B-Neck algorithm and utility function algorithm is described. The algorithms are deployed in Matlab. The B-Neck algorithm is validated using the scenarios proposed in [14], in each case with our implementation the response max-min fair is obtained. Three metrics are used to compare the algorithms.

4.1 Scenarios

In this work the network is considered as a directed graph $G = (V, E)$, where the nodes (hosts and routers) are V and the links are E.

In the Fig. 3 we can show a typical network scenario. It has eighteen nodes: eight routers interconnected, five sources where the flows are generated; and five destinations where the flows of the session will arrive. The maximum capacity of the links is 20 Mbps. The traffic used in the performance evaluation is mixed, thus the flows of the session can belong to best effort, linear or real-time applications. Table 2 gives a summary of the main characteristics. Figure 4 depicted the utility functions used in the simulations.

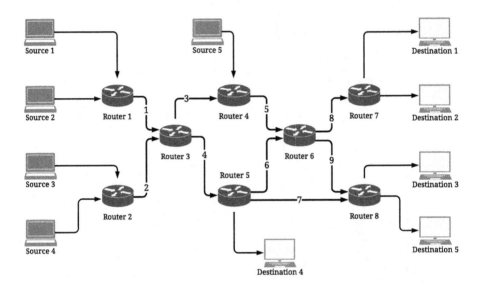

Fig. 3. Typical network topology in Internet context

In order to evaluate the algorithms performance it implements three scenarios:

- Scenario 1: The Fig. 5(a) shows the paths taken by the flows of the sessions present in the network. The capacity of all links is 20 Mbps. The sessions A, B and D share the link from router R3 to router R5, and therefore represent a bottleneck. In addition, all real-time application has as initial requirement $b = 5$.
- Scenario 2: The topology showed in Fig. 5(a) is used in this scenario. So, the route for the flows of the sessions, the capacity of the links, and the parameters of the utility functions are similar; however, $b = 6$ for session A, and $b = 2$ for session E.
- Scenario 3: In this case, the same session paths and utility function parameters are considered as in scenario 1, but the capacity of the links that carry the

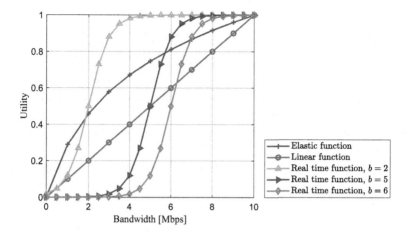

Fig. 4. Utility functions: elastic function applications (i.e. FTP, DNS, SMTP); real time applications (i.e. audio, video); and linear model

sessions is modified to values of 10 Mbps and 20 Mbps to verify the operation, in Fig. 5(b) is can see the assigned links capacity.

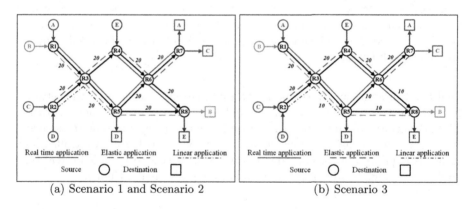

(a) Scenario 1 and Scenario 2   (b) Scenario 3

Fig. 5. Directed graph $G = (V, E)$ for each scenario

4.2 Metrics

The metrics used to evaluate the performance of the proposed algorithm are: the assigned transmission rate which is the bandwidth that the session can use based on its utility function, the utility achieved according to the assigned transmission rate and the Gini coefficient to measure the fairness achieved with respect to the utility.

Table 2. Simulation scenarios

Scenario	Links capacity	Flows	Utility function*
Scenario 1	20 Mbps	A real-time	$a = 2,\, b = 5,\, \omega = 1$
		B elastic	$a = 1,\, b = 1,\, \omega = 1/\log(C_e + 1)$
		C elastic	$a = 1,\, b = 1,\, \omega = 1/\log(C_e + 1)$
		D linear	$m = 1/C_e$
		E real-time	$a = 2,\, b = 5,\, \omega = 1$
Scenario 2	20 Mbps	A real-time	$a = 2,\, b = 6,\, \omega = 1$
		B elastic	$a = 1,\, b = 1,\, \omega = 1/\log(C_e + 1)$
		C elastic	$a = 1,\, b = 1,\, \omega = 1/\log(C_e + 1)$
		D linear	$m = 1/C_e$
		E real-time	$a = 2,\, b = 2,\, \omega = 1$
Scenario 3	10 Mbps to 20 Mbps	A real-time	$a = 2,\, b = 6,\, \omega = 1$
		B elastic	$a = 1,\, b = 1,\, \omega = 1/\log(C_e + 1)$
		C elastic	$a = 1,\, b = 1,\, \omega = 1/\log(C_e + 1)$
		D linear	$m = 1/C_e$
		E real-time	$a = 2,\, b = 2,\, \omega = 1$

*$d = 0$ for all flows in all scenarios.

Transmission Rate: It is the bandwidth that the session can use to transmit the data. Bandwidth is calculated based on the type of traffic required by the application used. The assigned transmission rate is a function of the link capacity and bottleneck levels.

Utility: It is a measure of the performance achieved by sessions on the network. It is calculated according to the amount of bandwidth assigned by each algorithm. Thus, the utility is a function of the transmission rate assigned to each session and is computed using the equations defined in the Sect. 2.1. For elastic traffic, high transmission rates are not needed to obtain utilities close to 1, while for real-time applications, high bandwidths are required, generally greater than b.

Gini Coefficient: It is an index that allows measuring the fairness level, its value is in the range between 0 and 1, where 0 represents a totally fair distribution, while 1 represents a totally unfair allocation [20]. The Gini coefficient is the area between the diagonal and the Lorentz curve. The Lorentz curve is a graphic representation of the accumulated concentration of resources, in this case, assigned transmission rates, in relation to the distribution curve of the frequencies of the sessions. The Gini coefficient is applied to the utility achieved by each session according to its assigned transmission rate; so, the algorithm that presents values closest to 0 is the one that makes a fairer distribution of bandwidth [21].

5   Results

The results for scenario 1 are presented in Fig. 6. Figure 6(a) shows the assigned transmission rate for each session. The most restrictive link is going through three sessions A, B, and D sharing 20 Mbps, it causes that B-Neck centralized algorithm assigns 6.67 Mbps for each one. Instead, UFA allocates 5.08, 4.02, and 10.8 Mbps for sessions A, B and D, respectively.

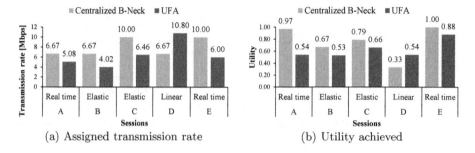

(a) Assigned transmission rate   (b) Utility achieved

Fig. 6. Scenario 1 results with link capacity 20 Mbps.

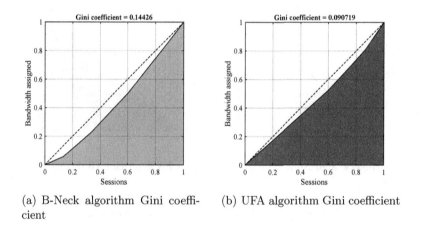

(a) B-Neck algorithm Gini coeffi-   (b) UFA algorithm Gini coefficient
cient

Fig. 7. Gini coefficient comparison for scenario 1

Figure 6(b) depicts the reached utility for both algorithms. Sessions A, B, C, D and E obtain 0.97, 0.67, 0.79, 0.33 and 1.00, respectively. With this utility allocation the Gini coefficient is 0.14426 (See Fig. 7(a)). On the other hand, UFA achieves utilities of 0.54, 0.53, 0.66, 0.54 and 0.88, respectively, in the Fig. 7(b) it can see the Gini coefficient of 0.090719. Thus the first algorithm is less fair than the second, the last one decreases the utility level of the sessions with a greater allocation to increase the utility of session D, which in the first algorithm has 0.33 of utility. Also, the utility affectation depends on the type of traffic, for example, for the session E B-Neck assigned 10 Mbps and achieved a utility of 1, but with the new algorithm a utility of 0.88 is obtained by assigning a resource of 6 Mbps; therefore, the utility function algorithm optimizes network resources by assigning to each session what it needs.

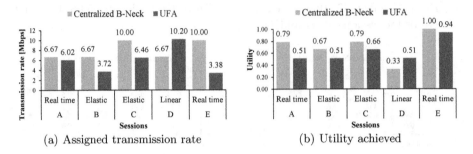

(a) Assigned transmission rate (b) Utility achieved

Fig. 8. Scenario 2 results with link capacity 20 Mbps and different b for real-time sessions

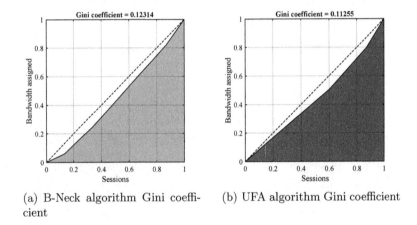

(a) B-Neck algorithm Gini coefficient (b) UFA algorithm Gini coefficient

Fig. 9. Gini coefficient comparison for scenario 2

The results obtained for scenario 2 are shown in the Fig. 8. In this scenario the required transmission rate b is different for the real-time sessions, A and E with 6 Mbps and 2 Mbps, respectively. Centralized B-Neck algorithm allocates the transmission in the same form as in scenario 1, instead, UFA considers the specific utility function in each session (see Fig. 8(a)), which in order are 6.02, 3.72, 6.46, 10.2 and 3.38 Mbps. Figure 8(b) shows the achieved utility for sessions with both algorithms. The most substantial change is found in the allocation of the session E, with the algorithm based on the utility its transmission rate is 3.38 Mbps, achieving a utility of 0.94 since its initial requirement has decreased $b = 2$. On the contrary for session A the initial requirement increases to 6, causing the B-Neck utility to decrease to 0.79. While UFA results show the sessions A, B and C reached 0.51.

The Gini coefficient for both algorithms is shown in Fig. 9. UFA achieves 0.11255 and the centralized B-Neck reaches 0.12314, although the values are similar, it is maintained that the first algorithm is more equitable than the second. The adaptation of the transmission rate assignment to the type of traffic of each session is evident, which improves the fair performance of the network.

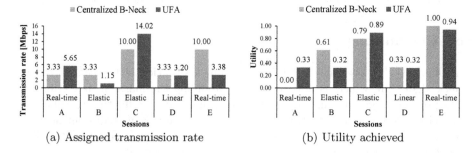

(a) Assigned transmission rate   (b) Utility achieved

Fig. 10. Scenario 3 results with variable link capacity and different b for realtime sessions

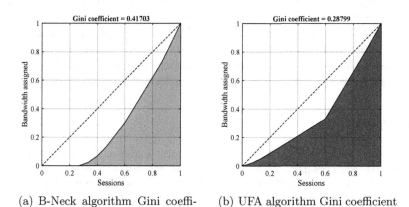

(a) B-Neck algorithm Gini coeffi-   (b) UFA algorithm Gini coefficient
cient

Fig. 11. Gini coefficient comparison for scenario 3

The Fig. 10 depicts the results for scenario 3 with links capacity between 10 to 20 Mbps. The bottleneck has 10 Mbps of capacity sharing for the sessions A, B and D. For this reason, B-Neck allocates 3.33 Mbps for each session in this link. On the other hand, UFA achieves 5.65, 1.15 and 3.2 Mbps, respectively (see Fig. 10(a)). By forcing a more restrictive bottleneck, the utility of the sessions decreases considerably as can be seen in Fig. 10(b). The sessions A, B and D have utilities of 0, 0.61 and 0.33, which implies that, in practice, session A would not transmit data. For the same sessions, UFA achieves 0.33, 0.32 and 0.32 as their utility, respectively. Therefore, it observes that when the type of traffic is not considered in the allocation of bandwidth, real-time applications are the most affected, especially when network resources decrease and their initial requirement b is high.

The Gini coefficient for scenario 3 is calculated for both algorithms in Fig. 11, and it is observed that in this situation the UFA utilities are more equitable with a value of 0.28799 compared to the B-Neck with a value of 0.41703.

6 Conclusions

In this work, we present the UFA algorithm, a variation of the centralized B-Neck algorithm, which assigns bandwidth applying the max-min fair criterion. The proposed algorithm uses the utility functions that describe the type of traffic in each section to assign the transmission rate according to its requirement. UFA benefits applications in real-time since the allocation is made based on its utility function; thus, the QoS level is improved for all applications.

B-Neck and UFA were implemented in Matlab and the fairness was measured using the Gini coefficient. The results show that UFA achieves optimization of resources in cases where the session has achieved high utility and therefore resources remain that can be assigned to other sessions with low utility. In addition, UFA achieves greater fairness in all simulated scenarios.

For our future work we propose a distributed UFA algorithm for the assignment of resources in the network. In addition, we suggest evaluating the performance of this protocol in dynamic scenarios, which will allow to consider additional elements present in real congestion scenarios in the analysis.

References

1. Huang, S., Dong, D., Bai, W.: Congestion control in high-speed lossless data center networks: a survey. Fut. Gener. Comput. Syst. **89**, 360–374 (2018)
2. Huang, J., Li, S., Han, R., Wang, J.: Receiver-driven fair congestion control for TCP outcast in data center networks. J. Netw. Comput. Appl. **131**, 75–88 (2019)
3. Zhang, T., Huang, J., Wang, J., Chen, J., Pan, Y., Min, G.: Designing fast and friendly TCP to fit high speed data center networks. In: Proceedings of the International Conference on Distributed Computing Systems, July 2018, vol. 2018, pp. 43–53 (2018)
4. Turkovic, B., Kuipers, F.A., Uhlig, S.: Fifty shades of congestion control: A performance and interactions evaluation. CoRR, abs/1903.03852 (2019)
5. Millán, G., Fuertes, G., Alfaro, M., Carrasco, R., Vargas, M.: A Simple and fast algorithm for traffic flow control in high-speed computer networks. In: 2018 IEEE International Conference on Automation/XXIII Congress of the Chilean Association of Automatic Control (ICA-ACCA), pp. 1–4 (2018)
6. Welzl, M.: Network Congestion Control: Managing Internet Traffic. Wiley, Hoboken (2006)

7. Zhao, L., Qu, S., Huang, X., Luo, J.: Congestion control of wireless sensor networks using discrete sliding mode control. In: Proceedings of the 31st Chinese Control and Decision Conference, CCDC 2019, pp. 2462–2466 (2019)
8. Cho, I., Han, D., Jang, K.: ExpressPass: End-to-end credit-based congestion control for datacenters. CoRR (October 2016)
9. Ashour, M., Wang, J., Aybat, N.S., Lagoa, C., Che, H.: End-to-end distributed flow control for networks with nonconcave utilities. IEEE Trans. Netw. Sci. Eng. **6**(3), 303–313 (2019)
10. Gu, L., et al.: Fairness-aware dynamic rate control and flow scheduling for network utility maximization in network service chain. IEEE J. Sel. Areas Commun. **37**(5), 1059–1071 (2019)
11. Iiduka, H.: Distributed optimization for network resource allocation with nonsmooth utility functions. IEEE Trans. Control Netw. Syst. **6**(4), 1354–1365 (2019)
12. Abbas, G., Manzoor, S., Hussain, M.: A stateless fairness-driven active queue management scheme for efficient and fair bandwidth allocation in congested internet routers. Telecommun. Syst. **67**(1), 3–20 (2018)
13. Kandris, D., Tselikis, G., Anastasiadis, E., Panaousis, E., Dagiuklas, T.: COALA: a protocol for the avoidance and alleviation of congestion in wireless sensor networks. Sensors **17**(11), 2502 (2017)
14. Mozo, A., López-Presa, J.L., Anta, A.F.: A distributed and quiescent max-min fair algorithm for network congestion control. Exp. Syst. Appl. **91**, 492–512 (2018)
15. Jose, L., Yan, L., Alizadeh, M., Varghese, G., McKeown, N., Katti, S.: High speed networks need proactive congestion control. In: Proceedings of the 14th ACM Workshop on Hot Topics in Networks, HotNets-XIV, New York, NY, USA. Association for Computing Machinery (2015)
16. Jin, J., Wang, W.-H., Palaniswami, M.: Utility max-min fair flow control for multipath communication networks. Networks **11**, 12 (2007)
17. Li, S., Zhang, Y., Wang, Y., Sun, W.: Utility optimization-based bandwidth allocation for elastic and inelastic services in peer-to-peer networks. Int. J. Appl. Math. Comput. Sci. **29**(1), 111–123 (2019)
18. Chen, L., Wang, B., Chen, X., Zhang, X., Yang, D.: Utility-based resource allocation for mixed traffic in wireless networks. In: 2011 IEEE Conference on Computer Communications Workshops (INFOCOM WKSHPS), pp. 91–96 (2011)
19. Zhang, T., Jin, J., Zheng, X., Yang, Y.: Rate-adaptive fog service platform for heterogeneous IoT applications. IEEE IoT J. **7**(1), 176–188 (2020)
20. Sitthiyot, T., Holasut, K.: A simple method for measuring inequality. Palgrave Commun. **6**(1) (2020)
21. Genčev, M.: A note on a property of the Gini coefficient. Commun. Math. **27**(2), 81–88 (2020)

Performance Analysis of the Migration of a 400 Gb/S-NRZ Optical Ring to a 1.6 Tb/S-PAM4 Ring

Andrés Veloz Domínguez[1]([✉]) and Germán V. Arévalo[2]

[1] Facultad de Ingeniería, Pontificia Universidad Católica del Ecuador, Quito, Ecuador
waveloz@puce.edu.ec
[2] Carrera de Ingeniería en Telecomunicaciones, Universidad Politécnica Salesiana,
Cuenca, Ecuador
garevalo@ups.edu.ec

Abstract. In this paper, we aim to demonstrate the feasibility of upgrading the CELEC EP 40 channel, 400 Gb/s, NRZ, DWDM ring, using PAM-4 modulation with the same 40 channels transmitting each at 40 Gb/s, for achieving a total capacity of 1.6 Tb/s. To overcome the problem related to the dispersion sensitivity of PAM-4 in long-distance links, we employed a dual technique of compensation, in the optical and electrical domain, based on dispersion-compensating fibers and in electrical pre-distortion of the PAM-4 signal. Simulation results show that the upgrade to 1.6 Tb/s is feasible using low-complexity changes in the current infrastructure. In the shorter links of the ring, it is enough the use of optical dispersion compensation, and a BER = 10-9 is achievable with an optical received power of about −19 dBm, whilst in the longest links, the electronic pre-distortion is mandatory for avoiding a penalization of about 3 dB for getting the same goal BER if the pre-distortion is not used. We validated the simulations with a comparison with experimental results for the longest link, 165 km, of the ring. Experimental and simulations results show nearly de same values of non-pre-distortion penalty and receiver sensitivity, for achieving the same goal BER.

Keywords: PAM-4 · Dispersion compensation · Pre-distortion · DWDM · Gray coding · Optical ring

1 Introduction

The exponential increase of the traffic generated by the streaming services based in ultra-high-definition video, the social networks, and the emerging technologies of the Internet of Things (IoT), has substantially risen the users' bitrate demands. This new era of the information and communication technologies (ICT) requires the use of next-generation telecommunications technologies [1]. Among other, the four-level pulse amplitude modulation (PAM-4) is one of the most popularly employed technique in next-generation

Funded by the Telecommunications Research Group (GIETEC) of Universidad Politécnica Salesiana and supported by the Engineering Faculty of Pontificia Universidad Católica del Ecuador.

high-speed metro and regional networks' optical transceivers, due to its potential to twice the bitrate capacity keeping the simplicity of the intensity-modulation (ID) with direct-detection (DD) techniques, i.e. there is no need of using costly coherent detection systems [2–5].

On the other hand, in metropolitan and regional optical rings, dense wavelength multiplexing (DWDM), in combination with reconfigurable optical add-drop multiplexers, is often used for increasing the capacity and the total amount of traffic transported in the network [6].

Currently, the Ecuadorian Company of Electric-Energy Transportation (CELEC-EP) owns a large optical network infrastructure, based mainly on optical grown-wire (OPGW) cables widely spread around the Ecuadorian territory, as shown in Fig. 1 [7]. It includes an 863 km DWDM backbone ring that covers a big region in the center of the country [7, 8]. This backbone ring was deployed more than 10 years ago and uses 40 wavelengths, separated 100 GHz among them, each one of them transmitting data at 10 Gb/s, using on-off keying non-return-to-zero optical modulation (OOK-NRZ). Therefore, the total capacity of this DWDM NRZ optical ring is 400 Gb/s. Nonetheless, recent years' increase in the traffic-demands has taken this network infrastructure to operate close to its current limits.

Fig. 1. CELEC-EP national network of optical fiber [7].

Thus, in the short term, it will be necessary to upgrade the CELCEL-EP ring, preferably with low cost of investments and avoiding a significant increase in the system's complexity. A feasible option for increasing the capacity, with a low increase of complexity, is the use of PAM-4 because it improves the channel bandwidth efficiency, allowing the use of simple photodiodes for directly detecting the intensity of the received signal. Particularly, the use of Gray coding in PAM-4 signals presents a good performance of the transmitted signal in noisy channels [9].

A problem related to the use of PAM-4 in long links is the distortion caused by the optical fiber dispersion. Given that the type of fiber employed in the CELEC-EP optical ring is mostly G652.D, the dispersion introduced in the signal by the optical fiber is significant, especially in links with more than 100 km of distance. In combination with the use of dispersion-compensation fibers, the use of electronic pre-distortion of the signal is a good and cheap option for compensating the dispersion when using PAM-4 modulation [2, 10, 11].

In this paper, we demonstrate de feasibility of upgrading the current CELEC-EP optical backbone ring, from 400 Gb/s up to 1.6 Tb/s, using low-complexity improvements in the network infrastructure. The remaining of this paper is organized as follows: Sect. 2 describes the upgraded network, Sect. 3 presents the details of the simulation, Sect. 4 indication the simulation results, Sect. 5 explain the experimental setup, Sect. 6 demonstration experimental vs simulations results, and the most relevant results of this research are presented, and, Sect. 7 concludes the paper.

2 Scenario and Network-Upgrade Parameters

The main goal of the network upgrade is to increase its capacity using the same optical distribution network (ODN). A good trade-off between the increase of bandwidth capacity and design's validity-time is 10 years. Based on the forecasts for global and regional data network traffic [12], we selected as the basis for this upgrade planning, an increment of four times the current capacity of the network. Besides, a greater increment of the capacity could result in non-affordable investments.

We focus only in the backbone optical ring that interconnects Quito, Totoras, Riobamba, Molino, Zhoray, Milagro, Pascuales, Quevedo, and Santo Domingo cities, with a total distance of about 863 km of optical fiber.

For the increment of four times of the current capacity, i.e. to 1.6 Tb/s, keeping IM-DD as the transmission technique, there are mainly three options: i) incrementing four times the number of channels, from 40 to 160, but this option is very unpractical from the economic and technical point of view; ii) upgrading the 10 Gb/s-NRZ transceivers to 40 Gbs-NRZ transceivers, which mean that adjacent channels would have a small spectral separation between them when placed in the 100 GHz channel-spacing DWDM grid; besides, this would mean changing the current transmitters of 10 GHz of bandwidth for transmitters with four times greater bandwidth (i.e. 40 GHz), which could imply a significant increase in costs; iii) the use of PAM-4 modulation instead of NRZ so that the 40 Gb/s per channel could be reachable by a 20 GBd/s transmission, which would demand lower bandwidth in the transmitters and more free bandwidth spacing between adjacent DWDM channels. On the other hand, using PAM-4 combined with an increment of twice the number of DWDM channels (later in the future), from 40 to 80 channels, will permit an increment of the capacity to 3.2 Tb/s. Therefore, this last option has been the one we chose for this network-upgrade simulation.

3 Simulation Setup

The simulation covers the 863 km of the optical ring which is composed of the links between nine Ecuadorian cities, as detailed in Table 1. Notice that there are four links longer than 100 km, two of them are even longer than 150 km. Figure 2 details the whole simulation setup of the optical ring, including the optical rings and ROADMs.

Table 1. Length of the CELEC-EP ring links

Starting-ending node	Distance [km]
Quito – Totoras	115
Totoras – Riobamba	44.4
Riobamba – Molino	165
Molino – Zhoray	55.3
Zhoray – Milagro	126
Milagro – Pascuales	56.5
Pascuales – Quevedo	150.3
Quevedo – Sto. Domingo	108
Sto. Domingo – Quito	84.2

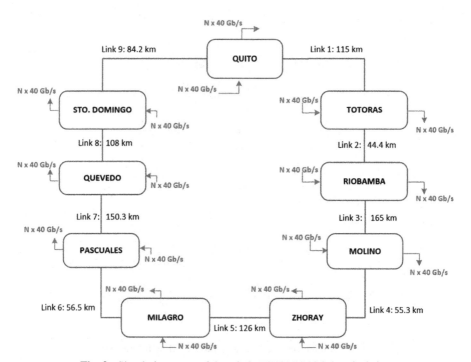

Fig. 2. Simulation setup of the whole DWDM PAM-4 optical ring

For the setup of a 40-channel 1.6 Tb/s ring, we included 40 transmitters multiplexed in the same link. And, given that the equalization in the Add-drop multiplexers is mandatory, all channels that continue the transmission in a given link have the same optical power. Therefore, the interaction among them is the same, i.e. no high power channels are interacting with low power channels, which could generate a nonlinearities-related problem. But it is not the case.

For simulating the upgraded optical ring, we employed Optsim® optical systems simulation software in co-simulation with Matlab®. A 40-wavelengths ROADM inserting and extracting 20 GBd/s (40 Gb/s) PAM-4 channels, simulated with Matlab-Optsim, is shown in Fig. 3.

Notice that the PAM-4 signals, including the pre-distortion setup in the electric domain, are simulated in a Matlab module embedded in Optsim, on the transmitter side. In each Matlab module, it is first generated a pseudo-random binary sequence (PRBS), with

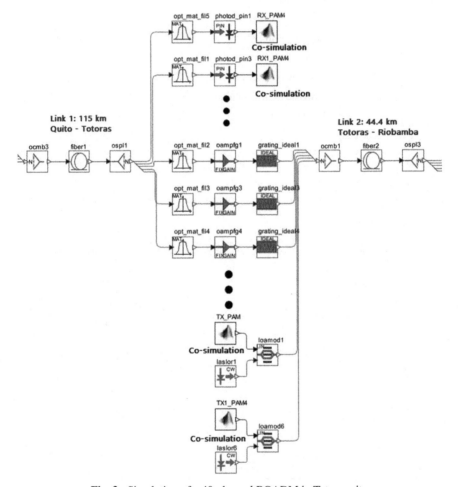

Fig. 3. Simulation of a 40-channel ROADM in Totoras city.

106496 bits of length, for simulating the users' data. The optical sources are Lorentian continuous wave (CW) lasers with 8 dBm of optical power tuned to the correspondent channel's wavelength in the C-band of wavelength transmission. We employed external Mach-Zehnder (MZ) linear intensity modulators, with 6 dB of internallosses, for the optical data modulation. The optical fiber was parametrized for simulating a G562D fiber with attenuation: 0.2 dB/km, chromatic dispersion (CD): 16 ps/nm*km, and polarization-mode dispersion (PMD): 0.2 ps/√km. The dispersion compensation was simulated with dispersion compensation units (DCU), as it is performed in the real ring, configured for compensating the total of the accumulated dispersion, due to CD, using the expressions described in (1) and (2). Moreover, with this setup, it could be used the same DCU that are currently employed in the network.

$$Dispersion\left[\frac{ps}{nm}\right] = CD\left[\frac{ps}{nm \cdot km}\right] * Link\_length[km] \tag{1}$$

$$Dispersion\_compensation = -Dispersion\left[\frac{ps}{nm}\right] \tag{2}$$

The amplification of the optical signals was performed by optical amplifiers with similar amplification values as those employed in the current optical ring. The use of a variable optical attenuator (VOA) allowed us to simulate the increase in the channel attenuation, for testing purposes. In the receivers, we employed PIN photoreceivers whit responsivity R = 0.8. The post-processing was configured in a Matlab module for de signal filtering, PAM-4 decoding, and BER estimation. Due to its better BER performance, we employed Gray coding instead of Duobinary coding in the PAM-4 signal generation [9].

As is illustrated in Fig. 4, an undesired effect of the dispersion is the differential distortion of the PAM-4 signal. In consequence, in reception, the lower levels of the signal have greater amplitude than the upper levels, as seen in the eye diagram of the non-pre-distorted received signal shown in the figure. In the longest links of the CELEC-EP ring, we included a pre-distortion technique, which, is basically a differential modification of the levels in the PAM-4 transmitted signal. Therefore, the signal arrives at the receiver with symmetric amplitudes, as seen in the eye diagram of the pre-distorted received signal of Fig. 4.

4   Simulation Results

The simulation included each one of the optical ring links detailed in Table 1 and Fig. 4, nevertheless, we focus the presentation of the results to the shortest, the longest, and one of the medium-length links. The performance of a given link was analyzed based on the BER in the link vs the received optical power. We stressed each link through the insertion of a differential optical attenuation from a variable optical attenuator (VOA). In order to keep a real-life scenario, we configured all the devices of the simulation setup with parameters of real commercial devices.

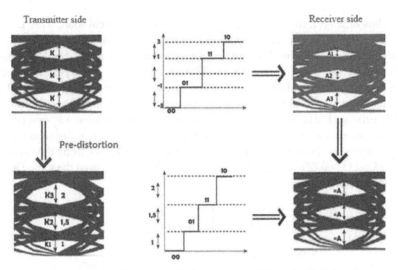

Fig. 4. Illustration of the pre-distortion technique employed in the PAM-4 signals generation.

The pre-distortion technique significantly improved the BER when employed in long links, especially in Pascuales-Quevedo (150.3 km) and Riobamba-Molino (165 km) links. This is due to the received eye diagram becomes almost symmetrical when applied a proper pre-distortion in the transmitted signal, as can be seen in Fig. 5. In shorter links the effect of the pre-distortion is marginal, and in the shortest links, like Molino–Zhoray (55.3 km) and Milagro-Pascuales (56.5 km) there is no need of using the pre-distortion technique.

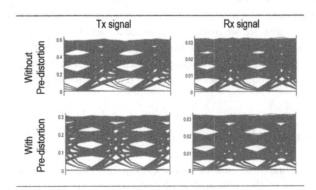

Fig. 5. Eye diagrams of transmitted and received signals with and without pre-distortion

The BER performance of the Milagro-Pascuales link (56.5 km) and Quito-Totoras (115 km) link is presented in Fig. 6. Notice that the optical received power demanded to achieve a BER of 10-9 is −18 dBm for the Milagro-Pascuales link. This constitutes a a very good performance for a 40 Gb/s signal. In the eye diagram shown in the inset (a) of the figure, it is evident that there is no need of a pre-distortion of the transmitted signal because the received eye-diagram is very symmetrical. In Milagro-Pascuales link even with very low signal-levels, like −25 dBm, the BER is still good: 5•10-7. For the larger Quito-Totoras optical fiber link (more than two times larger) it is evident the presence of 3 dB penalty for reaching the same 10-9 BER (i.e. in this link it is required an optical power of −15 dBm for reaching such BER). In this case, it is noticeable an eye-asymmetry effect due to the fiber dispersion (inset b). Nonetheless, the use of pre-distortion does not significantly improve the BER. As well, in this case, a low power signal like −24 dBm is still enough for getting a fairly good BER: 2•10-5.

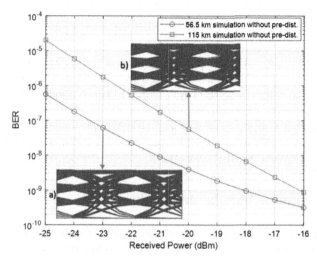

Fig. 6. BER performance of the Quito-Totoras (115 km) and Milagro-Pascuales (56.5 km) links.

5 Experimental Setup

In order to validate the simulation results we experimentally deployed a single-channel link with the same length of the longest link of the CELEC-EP ring, i.e. the 165 km Molino-Riobamba link.

The experimental setup shown in Fig. 7 details the set of equipment we employed for the experimentation. The optical source was a DFB laser tuned in the 1550 nm wavelength with an optical power of 6 dBm. The signal generation was performed using a 25 GHz – 65 GSa/s arbitrary waveform generator (AWG). Here we generated 106496 bits coded, using the Grey's code [10], as a pre-distorted PAM4 signal. The optical source was externally modulated by a 20 GHz MZ modulator, driven by the electrical-PAM4 signal injected by the AWG at 20 GBd/s, i.e. at 40 Gb/s.

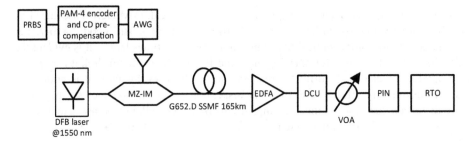

Fig. 7. Diagram of the experimental setup

The PAM4 signal was transmitted in a 165 km link deployed with standard single-mode fiber (SSMF) - G652.D. The optical amplification was performed by an EDFA with 20 dB of gain, and the DCU was deployed by a spool of dispersion compensating fiber (DCF) designed to compensate 160 km of G652.D fiber. A variable optical attenuator (VOA) was employed for testing purposes.

In the receiver's side, we employed a 25 GHz PIN photodetector and a 20 GHz – 80 GSa/s real time oscilloscope (RTO) for performing the off-line post-processing (i.e. the PAM4 decoding and the BER estimation).

6 Experimental vs Simulation Results

In Fig. 8 it is depicted the simulated and experimental performance of the longest link, i.e. the Riobamba-Molino (165 km). Notice that in this link it was mandatory the use of the pre-distortion technique to get a BER of 10-9 with a reasonably achievable received power: −5 dBm. The effect of the dispersion in this long link is evident when watching the received eye diagrams of the non-pre-distorted signal (inset a) and the pre-distorted signal (inset b). Without the use of pre-distortion, a BER of 10-9 is actually non-achievable, because it would demand too much amplification, or transmitted power, for having a received power equal or even greater than 0 dBm (which would be the power for having a BER of 10-9 when the signal is not pre-distorted). In general, in this link, not using the pre-distortion technique implies a penalty of about 2.5 dB in comparison to a transmission with pre-distortion. Evidently, this link has a huge penalty even when using pre-distortion. However, if the goal BER would be not an errorless one (i.e. 10-9) but an FEC-limit goal BER (i.e. approximately 10-3), then the optical received power can be lowered to −14 or −15 dBm, which are very much achievable received powers using a lower (and less-costly) amount of amplification in the optical link. The simulated results are validated by the experimental results which present similar curves of BER, especially for the pre-distorted PAM4 signal results.

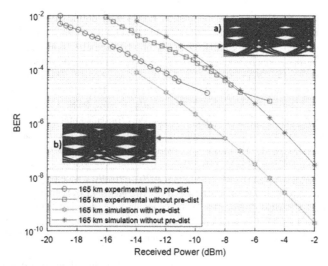

Fig. 8. BER performance of the Riobamba-Molino link (165 km).

7 Conclusion

A design and simulation, including an experimental validation of results, of the upgrade-performance of the CECEL-EP optical ring, from 400 Gb/s NRZ to 1.6 Tb/s PAM-4, has been presented in this paper. Results show that making low-cost low-complexity changes in the current network infrastructure, is technically feasible for achieving the desired performance. It is remarkable that with the proposed design, the same optical links, optical amplifiers and dispersion compensating units can be employed in the new 1.6 Tb/s network. Moreover, shorter links would demand only the change to a PAM-4 modulation for increasing each of the 40 channels from 10 Gb/s to 40 Gb/s, keeping the same intensity modulators or, at most, replacing them with 20 GHz transmitters, instead of needing devices with 40 GHz of bandwidth. Only the longest links of the ring would require a low-complexity pre-distortion technique in the electric domain, as a complement to the dispersion compensation in the optical domain. A BER of 10-9 was obtained with a received power of −19 dBm in the shorter links and, in the longest links, the electronic pre-distortion avoided a penalization of 3 dB for getting the same goal BER if the pre-distortion is not used.

Acknowledgment. A. Veloz and G. Arévalo thank the funding for making this research given by the Telecommunications Research Group (GIETEC) of Universidad Politécnica Salesiana.

References

1. Kim, D.: A 2020 perspective on 'a dynamic model for the evolution of the next generation internet – implications for network policies': towards a balanced perspective on the internet's role in the 5G and industry 4.0 era. Electron. Commer. Res. Appl. **41**, 100966 (2020)

2. Feng, N., Sun, X.: Hierarchical modulation PAM4 with digital Nyquist pulse-shaped for flexible multi-ONU provisioning in NG-TDM PON. Opt. Fiber Technol. **53**, 102063 (2019)
3. Xu, J., Du, J., Ren, R., Ruan, Z., He, Z.: Optical interferometric synthesis of PAM4 signals based on dual-drive Mach-Zehnder modulation. Opt. Commun. **402**(March), 73–79 (2017)
4. Li, L., Bi, M., Fu, Y., Miao, X., Zhu, Q., Hu, W.: Power budget enhancement in NG-EPON system employing novel twisted-PAM4. Opt. Commun. **410**, 627–631 (2018)
5. Nagarajan, R., Bhoja, S., Issenhuth, T.: 100Gbit/s, 120km, PAM 4 based switch to switch, layer 2 silicon photonics based optical interconnects for datacenters. IEEE - Inphy (2018)
6. Sarmiento, S., Altabas, J.A., Izquierdo, D., Garces, I., Spadaro, S., Lazaro, J.A.: Cost-effective DWDM ROADM design for flexible sustainable optical metro-access networks. J. Opt. Commun. Netw. **9**(12), 1116 (2017)
7. CELEC-EP: Mapa Nacional de Fibra Óptica (2020). https://www.celec.gob.ec/transelectric_p ruebas/index.php?option=com_content&view=article&id=124&Itemid=289&lang=es
8. Betancourt, P., Cevallos, A., Aguilar, D.: Evaluacion tecnica de la red de fibra optica de CELEC EP - TRANSELECTRIC a traves de la cual la empresa TRANSNEXA S.A. E.M.A. presta sus servicios de telecomunicaciones a nivel nacional e internacional. Escuela Politécnica del Ejército (2013)
9. Arévalo, G.: Effectiveness of Grey coding in an AWGN digital channel data transmission. Ingenius **14**(12), 30–34 (2015)
10. Arévalo, G.V., Villavicencio, M., Flores, G.: Experimental demonstration of a PAM-4 based 20 Gb/s PON using dispersion pre-compensation. In: 2019 XVIII Workshop on Information Processing and Control (RPIC), pp. 2019–2021 (2019)
11. Zhang, Q., et al.: Demonstration of CD pre-compensated direct detection PAM4 40 km transmission in C-band using DDMZM. Opt. InfoBase Conf. Pap. **3**, 3–5 (2014)
12. Cisco Annual Internet Report (2018–2023) (2020). https://www.cisco.com/c/en/us/soluti ons/collateral/executive-perspectives/annual-internet-report/white-paper-c11-741490.html. Accessed 17 Jun 2020

RAPL: A Domain Specific Language for Resource Allocation of Indivisible Goods

Israel Pineda[1]([⊠]) [iD], Cristopher Zhunio[1] [iD], Franklin Camacho[1] [iD],
and Rigoberto Fonseca-Delgado[2] [iD]

[1] Yachay Tech University, Urcuquí, Ecuador
{ipineda,cristopher.zhunio,fcamacho}@yachaytech.edu.ec
[2] National Institute of Astrophysics, Optics and Electronics, Sta. Ma. Tonantzintla,
San Andrés Cholula, Mexico
rfonseca@inaoep.mx

Abstract. We propose a new Domain Specific Language (DSL) to represent and solve resource allocation problems of indivisible goods. Resource allocation problems can be represented using matrices; this representation is flexible and has interesting mathematical properties that the solution can exploit. However, the programming of such a problem using a general-purpose programming language might include an unnecessary level of complexity. This new DSL allows the user to declare the agents and their preferences of resources. Also, the language can manipulate those elements with the proper operations involved in the resource allocation problem. The proposed DSL can measure efficiency criteria such as Pareto optimality, measure fairness criteria such as Envy-free, and represent results using matrices. This work shows the structure of the interpreter of this language and provides details about the scanner, parser, and interpreter for this language. This DSL will be called Resource Allocation Programming Language (RAPL). We hope that the easiness of use of this DSL can motivate further research on this topic.

Keywords: Domain Specific Language · Language grammar · Interpreted language · Resource allocation · Indivisible goods

1 Introduction

A Domain Specific Language (DSL) is a programming language intended to solve a particular problem or reduced set of problems within a given domain. The domain of the problem has to be well-defined to ensure its proper implementation and operation. This kind of language emphasizes on providing the proper techniques to represent and solve the problems within that domain. The particular domain that we study in this work is the resource allocation of indivisible goods. Some examples of DSL, in different domains, are SQL (for queries), R (for statistics), HTML (for web pages). Many more DSL exists but are only know in small niches due to the nature of the language. These languages are intended to be used by a particular group of users. In contrast, general-purpose

© Springer Nature Switzerland AG 2020
G. Rodriguez Morales et al. (Eds.): TICEC 2020, CCIS 1307, pp. 479–492, 2020.
https://doi.org/10.1007/978-3-030-62833-8_35

languages are designed to solve any problem that is representable by a computation model. Thus, general-purpose languages are more popular. Most popular general-purpose languages are Python, C/C++, Java, JavaScript, among others.

As its name suggests, a resource allocation consists in assigning to a group of agents all available goods. However, this task, which apparently is simple, becomes complicated as the allocations try to fulfill specific criteria. The allocations should be fair to ensure that every agent has a minimal level of satisfaction. Another alternative is that the allocations should be efficient in the sense of not improving individual welfare by making others worse.

In this work, we proposed a new DSL to represent and solve the resource allocation of indivisible goods. The name of our proposed Domain Specific Language is RAPL, which stands for Resource Allocation Programming Language. The language is an interpreted one. This work provides details of several elements of the interpretation process and shows examples of how to use this new language.

This paper is organized as follows: Section 2 briefly reviews recent related works. Section 3 explains the components of the resource allocation problem. Section 4 presents the proposed programming language. Section 5 shows the results using the language. Section 7 shows the future work and finally, Sect. 8 has the conclusions.

2   Related Work

Resource allocation of indivisible goods is an actively researched topic both within mathematics and computer science with many applications across the board. Several results have been presented over the years about mathematical proofs, algorithms, and variations of the problem and its solutions [2,3,5–7]. To the best of our knowledge, there is no special programming technique or language to work with these kinds of problems. Thus, researchers use general-purpose programming languages.

On the other hand, research on the design and implementation of programming languages is a classic field of study in computer science [8,9] that continues to generate new ideas and developments [13]. New languages and design principles [1,12] are developed continuously to fulfill new needs and to adapt to modern challenges of computing and to tackle new applications. Also, DSLs have received a fair amount of attention [10] because they are a powerful tool to solve and express problems more succinctly. However, the literature shows that there is no active project trying to bridge these communities.

In our literature review, we have found two somehow related projects. They are aimed to manipulate matrices and arrays with some special functions. First, there is a DSL that can interpret matrix and array operations such as summation, +, subtraction, −, and multiplication, ∗. This language is available in the following link: https://github.com/mattp94/vector-matrix-dsl; it was developed in Clojure, a functional general-purpose language. This language does not support actual matrix multiplication because the '∗' operator only multiplies element-wise. It is a basic project that does not seem to be maintained anymore; it can work well with matrices but this language does not really work with the problem of resource allocation.

Second, Red [11] is a multi-paradigm language. The documentation of the language describes it as a full-stack language. There is a DSL which we will call Little Matrix (https://github.com/toomasv/matrix) due to the description provided in the repository. This DSL can process matrices and is adapted to work with Red. This language is more sophisticated than the previously introduced language. Little Matrix supports a set of binary operations, which includes +, −, ∗, /, %, ∗∗, >>, <<, >>>, *and*, *or*, *xor*, *div*, and ×. It supports unitary matrix operations like *transpose*, *rotate n*, *swap rows*, *determinant*, among others. Besides, it supports the use of parenthesis to change the priority. Little Matrix also lacks specific tools to tackle the resource allocation problem.

To the best of our knowledge, there is no DSL specially created to represent and solve resource allocation problems. This shows that there is a need for a language that it is easy to use and that aids to the creation and resolution of resource allocation.

3   Components of the Resource Allocation Problem

In this section, we break down the components that are involved in the resource allocation problem. Let us now define a precise naming convention that will be used throughout the rest of the document.

Let N and M be finite sets, which we will call the agents set and the resources set, respectively. Agents are the entities interested in receiving the resources. It is important to mention that the resources are divided into two main groups: divisible resources and indivisible resources. As its name implies, divisible resources refer to the resources that can be distributed among several agents, that is, several agents can obtain a fraction of this resource. While the indivisible resources have to be distributed entirely to a single agent; this means, each resource should be assigned only to one agent. Our proposed DSL deals only with indivisible resources.

One of the problems studied in the resource allocation area is how to distribute, fairly and efficiently, all resources among the agents. Fairness and efficiency depend on the preference that each agent defines over resources. In general, these preferences are measured through utility functions, that is, each agent, $i \in N$, has an utility function over all the subsets of M, $u_i : 2^M \to \mathbb{R}^*$, where $\mathbb{R}^*$ are the positive reals including zero. Furthermore, we will assume that each agent has the same budget to distribute its utility among the resources, and the utility functions are additives.

To give the notions of efficiency and fairness, we will present a matrix approach to some basic definitions. For a detailed review see [4].

3.1 Matrix Approach

All the information on the problem is encoded as matrices. Here, we provide a brief description of the several matrices that have to be considered. In this approach, we will start by giving the definition of an allocation; remember that $|N| = n$ and $|M| = m$.

Definition 1. *A matrix A, of size $n \times m$, is an allocation from the resources M in the agents N if for each column $r \in M$, there is only one $i \in N$ such that $A[i, r] = 1$ and for all $j \in N$, with $j \neq i$, $A[j, r] = 0$.*

The preferences of the agents are established in a matrix with non-negative inputs.

Definition 2. *A matrix V, of size $n \times m$, is called a valuation matrix if $V[i, r] = v_i(r)$ for all utility functions v_i, with $i \in N$ and $r \in M$.*

For each allocation, we can calculate the utility matrix.

Definition 3. *Let A be an allocation. The utility matrix of A, denoted by V_A, is a matrix defined by*

$$V_A[i, j] = V[i, *] \cdot A^\top[*, j]$$

for all $i, j \in N$. I.e. $V_A[i, j]$ is the inner product between the i-th row of V, $V[i, *]$, and the j-th column of $A^\top$, $A^\top[*, j]$.

From this matrix, we can see that $V_A[i, j]$ determines the valuation that the agent i gives to the assigned, through A, to the agent j. This allows us to identify the envy among agents; for example, if $V_A[i, j] > V_A[i, i]$ means that the agent i values more the allocation that received the agent j than its own allocation. The classic notion to measure fairness is envy free. The utility matrix allows us to see the envy explicitly, this is one advantage of matrix approach.

Definition 4. *A allocation A is envy free if for all $i, j \in N$,*

$$V_A[i, i] \geq V_A[i, j]$$

The efficiency property, or Pareto Optimal, in an allocation, determines a type of social fairness. That is, there is no other allocation that can improve the satisfaction of one agent without making another one worse.

Definition 5. *An allocation A is Pareto Optimal if, for all allocation A'*

$$[\exists i \in N, V_{A'}[i, i] > V_A[i, i]] \Rightarrow [\exists j \in N, V_{A'}[j, j] < V_A[j, j]]$$

One way to find optimal Pareto allocations is through social welfare functions. Particularly, through utilitarian social welfare and Nash social welfare.

Definition 6. *Let A be an allocation.*
The utilitarian social welfare of A, denoted by $SW_u(A)$, is defined as

$$SW_u(A) = tr(V_A) \tag{1}$$

The Nash social welfare of A, denoted by $SW_{Nash}(A)$, is defined as

$$SW_{Nash}(A) = prod(V_A) \tag{2}$$

where V_A is the utility matrix of A,

$$tr(V_A) = \sum_{i \in N} V_A[i, i]$$

and

$$prod(V_A) = \prod_{i \in N} V_A[i, i].$$

Let N^M be the set of all feasible allocations of M resources among N agents. The maximum social welfare will be the set of all allocations that maximizes a social welfare SW, this is

Definition 7. *The maximum social welfare, denoted by MSW, is defined as*

$$MSW = \{A \in N^M : SW(A) \geq SW(B), \forall B \in N^M\}, \tag{3}$$

we will denote MSW_u to the SW_u, and MSW_{Nash} to the SW_{Nash}.

On the following theorem, we say that all allocations in MSW_u or in MSW_{Nash} are Pareto Optimal, the proofs can be seen at [4,5].

Theorem 1. *Suppose that all utility functions are additive and non negative. If $A \in MSW_u$ or $A \in MSW_{Nash}$, then A is Pareto Optimal.*

Another advantage of the matrix approach is to explicitly obtain all allocations in MSW_u. For this, it is necessary to know which agent maximizes the utility of each resource. This information is represented in a matrix.

Definition 8. *A matrix T, of size $m \times n$, is called transition matrix if, for all $i \in N$ and all $r \in M$, $T[i, r] = 1$ when $V[i, r] \in \max\{V[k, r] : k \in N\}$, otherwise $T[i, r] = 0$.*

An allocation is transitory if each resource is assigned to a utility-maximizing agent.

Definition 9. *Let T the transition matrix and A an allocation. We said that A is a transitory allocation if,*

$$\forall r \in M, \exists i \in N, \ such \ that \ (A[i, r] = 1 \Rightarrow T[i, r] = 1) \tag{4}$$

The theorem of characterization is:

Theorem 2. *An allocation A is transitory if, and only if, $A \in MSW_u$.*

An immediate result is

Corollary 1. *All transitory allocation is Pareto Optimal.*

In this section, we defined all the information of the resource allocation problem that will be used in the programming language.

4 RAPL Programming Language

The name RAPL stands for Resource Allocation Programming Language. RAPL is an interpreted, high-level, domain-specific programming language developed in Python. RAPL is an interpreted language, which means that instructions are executed directly without a previous compilation of the program into machine-language instructions. The advantage of this feature is that the programs written in RAPL will be easier to execute. RAPL is also dynamically typed and includes type inference, which means that the programmer does not have to specify object types within the code. The programming paradigm supported by RAPL is declarative. This paradigm was chosen in the design because most of the code for this DSL is expected to be logical-mathematical operations.

RAPL needs to perform several steps to be able to execute the program; these are standard processing steps of a interpreter. Figure 1 shows the overall flow of the process that takes the program written in RAPL, from the character stream to its execution. Next, we describe the most relevant aspects of the interpretation of a RAPL program.

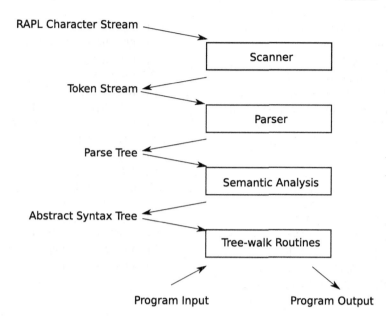

Fig. 1. RAPL interpretation process

4.1   Scanner

A RAPL program has to be typed in a Command-Line Interface (CLI). This means that the code to be interpreted by the RAPL interpreter is introduced in a shell line by line. The scanner takes a line of code as a sequence of characters and converts them into tokens. A token object consists of the type of the token, a value, a start position, and an end position. The scanner ignores empty spaces and tabs. Then, depending on the character found in the introduced line of code, a type of token is created. The full list of token types can be found in the Listing 1.1. There are three groups of constants that the scanner uses to classify the tokens *DIGITS, LETTERS* and *LETTERS_DIGITS*. If the current character is a digit, a number kind of token type is returned. If the current character is a letter, the scanner checks if it is a keyword or an identifier, and creates the respective token type. The complete list of supported keywords is presented in Listing 1.2. An illegal-character error is returned by the interpreter if it finds an error during this step.

Listing 1.1. Tokens of the RAPL Programming Language

```
TT_INT = 'TT_INT'
TT_FLOAT = 'FLOAT'
TT_IDENTIFIER = 'IDENTIFIER'
TT_KEYWORD = 'KEYWORD'
TT_PLUS  = 'PLUS'
TT_MINUS = 'MINUS'
TT_MUL = 'MUL'
TT_DIV = 'DIV'
TT_POW = 'POW'
TT_EQ = 'EQ'
TT_AT = 'AT'
TT_PER = 'PER'
TT_UTIL = 'UTIL'
TT_NASH = 'NASH'
TT_EVAL = 'EVAL'
```

```
TT_PO = 'PO'
TT_LPAREN = 'LPAREN'
TT_RPAREN = 'RPAREN'
TT_LSQUARE = 'LSQUARE'
TT_RSQUARE = 'RSQUARE'
TT_LCURLY = 'LCURLY'
TT_RCURLY = 'RCURLY'
TT_EE = 'EE'
TT_NE = 'NE'
TT_LT = 'LT'
TT_GT = 'GT'
TT_LTE = 'LTE'
TT_GTE = 'GTE'
TT_COMMA = 'COMMA'
TT_ARROW = 'ARROW'
TT_EOF = 'EOF'
```

Listing 1.2. Keywords of the RAPL Programming Language

```
'VAR'
'AND'
'OR'
'NOT'
'IF'
```

```
'THEN'
'ELIF'
'ELSE'
'FOR'
'TO'
'STEP'
```

4.2 Parser and Semantic Analysis

Once the scanner returns the list of tokens, the parser tries to build the abstract syntax tree (AST) out of that list. Depending on the encountered tokens, the parser creates a type of node which determines the correct sequence of token types. If there is an error, a syntax error or an expected character error is returned. Here, the preference of interpretation within nodes is determined based on the grammar used in the design of the language. The grammar of the language is presented next and shows the complete grammar of RAPL using the Extended Backus–Naur Form (EBNF). RAPL has four object types so far: *Value, Number, List, Matrix*. A number can be an integer or a float. A list is a sequence of Numbers, separated by commas ',' and enclosed by brackets. A matrix is a sequence of Lists, separated by commas ',' and enclosed by curly brackets.

⟨*expr*⟩   ::= ⟨*KEYWORD:VAR*⟩ ⟨*IDENTIFIER*⟩ ⟨*EQ*⟩ ⟨*expr*⟩
                    | ⟨*comp-expr*⟩ ((⟨*KEYWORD:AND*⟩|⟨*KEYWORD:OR*⟩)
                        ⟨*comp-expr*⟩)*

⟨*comp-expr*⟩   ::= ⟨*NOT*⟩ ⟨*comp-expr*⟩
                    | ⟨*arith-expr*⟩ ((⟨*EE*⟩|⟨*LT*⟩|⟨*GT*⟩|⟨*LTE*⟩|⟨*GTE*⟩)
                        ⟨*arith-expr*⟩)*

⟨*arith-exprr*⟩   ::= ⟨*term*⟩ ((⟨*PLUS*⟩|⟨*MINUS*⟩) ⟨*term*⟩)*

⟨*term*⟩   ::= ⟨*factor*⟩ ((⟨*MUL*⟩|⟨*DIV*⟩) ⟨*factor*⟩)*

⟨*factor*⟩   ::= ⟨*INT*⟩|⟨*FLOAT*⟩
                    | ⟨*power*⟩

⟨*power*⟩   ::= ⟨*atom*⟩(⟨*POW*⟩ ⟨*factor*⟩)

⟨*atom*⟩   ::= (⟨*PLUS*⟩|⟨*MINUS*⟩) ⟨*factor*⟩
                    | ⟨*LPAREN*⟩ ⟨*expr*⟩ ⟨*RPAREN*⟩
                    | ⟨*trans-expr*⟩
                    | ⟨*matrix-expr*⟩
                    | ⟨*list-expr*⟩
                    | ⟨*if-expr*⟩
                    | ⟨*for-expr*⟩
                    | ⟨*while-expr*⟩

⟨*list-expr*⟩   ::= ⟨*LSQUARE*⟩ (⟨*expr*⟩ (⟨*COMMA*⟩ ⟨*expr*⟩)*)?
                        ⟨*RSQUARE*⟩

⟨*matrix-expr*⟩   ::= ⟨*LSQUARE*⟩ (⟨*list-expr*⟩)+ ⟨*RSQUARE*⟩

⟨*if-expr*⟩   ::= ⟨*KEYWORD:IF*⟩ ⟨*expr*⟩ ⟨*KEYWORD:THEN*⟩
                        ⟨*expr*⟩ (⟨*KEYWORD:ELIF*⟩ ⟨*expr*⟩ ⟨*KEYWORD:THEN*⟩
                        ⟨*expr*⟩)* (⟨*KEYWORD:ELSE*⟩ ⟨*expr*⟩)?

⟨*for-expr*⟩   ::= ⟨*KEYWORD:FOR*⟩ ⟨*IDENTIFIER*⟩ ⟨*EQ*⟩ ⟨*expr*⟩
                        ⟨*KEYWORD:TO*⟩ ⟨*expr*⟩ (⟨*KEYWORD:STEP*⟩ ⟨*expr*⟩)?
                        ⟨*KEYWORD:THEN*⟩ ⟨*expr*⟩

⟨*while-expr*⟩   ::= ⟨*KEYWORD:WHILE*⟩ ⟨*expr*⟩ ⟨*KEYWORD:THEN*⟩
                        ⟨*expr*⟩

4.3 Operators

RAPL supports basic mathematical binary operations like summation, subtraction, division, multiplication, and exponentiation. The binary operators for two NUMBERS are: $+$, $-$, $/$, $*$, $\hat{}$. Parentheses are also supported and can be used to change the priority on calculations.

Unary operators are also supported by RAPL. Thanks to this, expressions like *-5* make sense. Other unary operators are also available for matrices and are explained below.

RAPL also supports variable declaration. The reserved keyword to declare a variable is *VAR*, followed by a LETTER_DIGIT identifier. This means that a variable name cannot start with a number in RAPL. A variable can store a number or a matrix and can be use to construct complex expressions.

RAPL also recognize logical operators such as $>$, $<$, $>=$, $<=$, $==$, AND, OR, IF, NOT, THEN, ELIF, ELSE. And also support *for* and *while* loops.

For resource allocation problems purpose, in RAPL, all the problem information is represented in the valuation matrix (see Definition 2). Where every agent's preference on every resource will be presented in each corresponding cell.

A feasible allocation for a resource allocation problem will be presented as a binary matrix. Since RAPL is intended to solve problems using indivisible resources, there will be only one number '1' per column.

The matrix operations that the language supports are:

- $*$ for standard matrix multiplication,
- $+$ for standard matrix addition,
- $-$ for standard matrix subtraction,
- $/$ for matrix index value,
- @ for matrix transpose,
- % to get transition matrix from a valuation matrix,
- : to get utility matrix from a valuation matrix and a feasible allocation,
- # to get utilitarian social welfare from utility matrix,
- $\sim$ to get Nash social welfare from utility matrix.

4.4 Interpreter

If the parser returns the AST with no errors, the interpreter is called to execute operations and show results. The AST is a map of nodes that the interpreter has to visit in a specific order. The interpreter then visits a node and tries to return the desired result from every node. The interpreter returns a run-time error if there is an error during this stage. The type of nodes can be *NumberNode, MatrixNode, ListNode, BinaryOpNode, etc.*. For example, if the interpreter visits a binary operation node, it is expected to have a left node, an operator node, and a right node. Once the entire AST has been visited by the interpreter with no errors, the result is showed on the screen.

Figure 2 shows examples of the possible errors that are detected by RAPL through the overall flow.

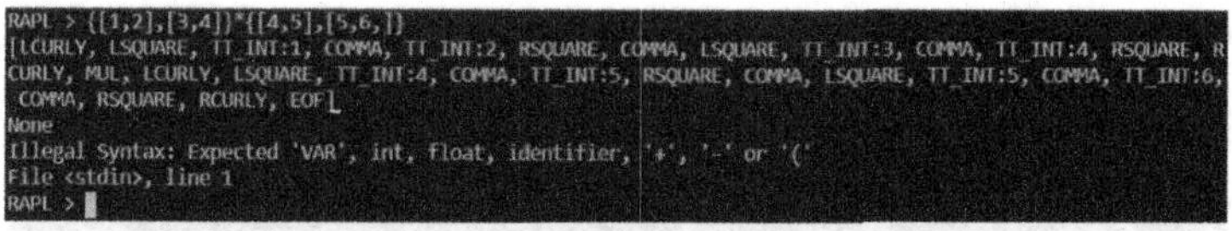

(a) Parser error

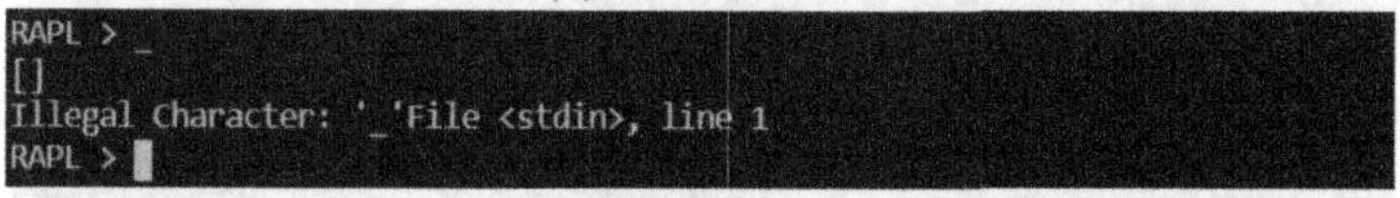

(b) Scanner error

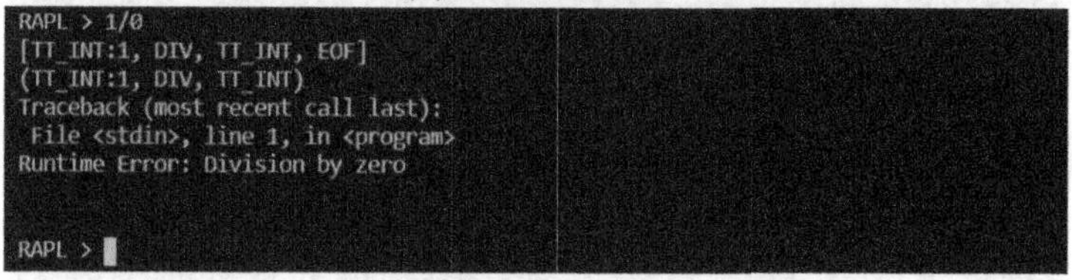

(c) Interpreter error

Fig. 2. Errors detected in the interpretation process by RAPL.

5   Results

The main result of this work is an easy-to-use domain-specific language, which includes operators designed to represent and solve resource allocation problems. Also, this DSL can perform conventional matrix operations. For example, obtaining a Pareto Optimal allocation from a resource allocation problem, using the transition matrix, can be done with two lines of code in RAPL. Another example, calculating the Nash social welfare or the Utilitarian social welfare, from a utility matrix, can be done in 1 line of code in RAPL.

Example 1. Figure 3 shows an example of how to solve a resource allocation problem using the proposed language. First block defines a valuation matrix called 'a', which represents a resource allocation problem involving 3 agents and 4 resources. The second block defines 'b' that is the allocation to be analyzed. Then, 'b' is replaced with its transposed matrix, using the unary operator '@'. Later, the product of matrices 'a' and 'b' is stored in 'c', which represents the utility matrix. Finally, the SW_u and the SW_{Nash} are computed using the unary operators '#' and '∼'.

As shown in Sect. 3, the multiplication between the valuation matrix and the transposed allocation matrix results in the utility matrix. The utility matrix is useful for seeing the envy between agents and calculating the Utilitarian Social Welfare (SW_u) and Nash Social Welfare (SW_{Nash}). Also, using the transition matrix, it is easy to obtain a Pareto Optimal allocation. The RAPL code in Example 1 shows a complete summary of a resource allocation problem, returning

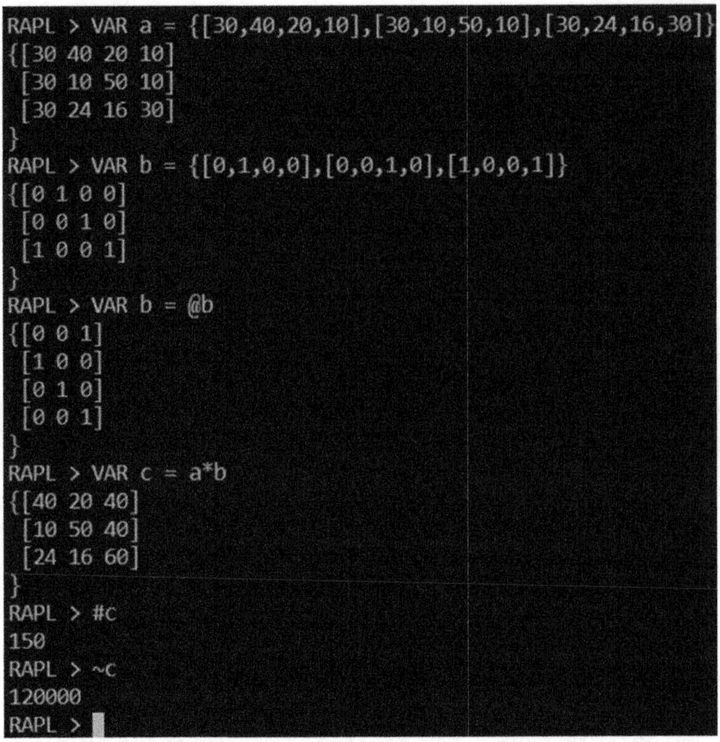

```
RAPL > VAR a = {[30,40,20,10],[30,10,50,10],[30,24,16,30]}
{[30 40 20 10]
 [30 10 50 10]
 [30 24 16 30]
}
RAPL > VAR b = {[0,1,0,0],[0,0,1,0],[1,0,0,1]}
{[0 1 0 0]
 [0 0 1 0]
 [1 0 0 1]
}
RAPL > VAR b = @b
{[0 0 1]
 [1 0 0]
 [0 1 0]
 [0 0 1]
}
RAPL > VAR c = a*b
{[40 20 40]
 [10 50 40]
 [24 16 60]
}
RAPL > #c
150
RAPL > ~c
120000
RAPL >
```

Fig. 3. Execution example of a program using RAPL, with some operators. "RAPL >" is the prompt of the interpreter.

the utility matrix, the transition matrix, the SW_u, and the SW_{Nash} of a feasible allocation in 7 lines of code.

Example 2. Figure 4 shows how to select a Pareto Optimal allocation, and visualize the envy among agents. Given a valuation matrix 'a' in the first block, we calculate the transition matrix with operator '%', and assign it to 'T'. Then, two allocations 'b' and 'd' were considered, where 'b' is transitory by Definition 9 and Pareto Optimal for the Corollary 1. Later, the utility matrices of each allocation 'b' and 'd' are calculated in 'c' and 'e', respectively, with the operator ':'. In 'c', we can see that only agent 3 envies agent 1; while in 'e', the agent 3 has no envy, but the other two agents shows envy.

In the previous example, few lines of code allowed us to study the envy among agents of two different allocations.

Our results show that RAPL is able to describe the allocation problem very succinctly with a clean syntax and that the calculation of the allocations is done with few lines of code. This syntax avoids the clutter that general-purpose programming languages produce when trying to represent and solve this sort of problems.

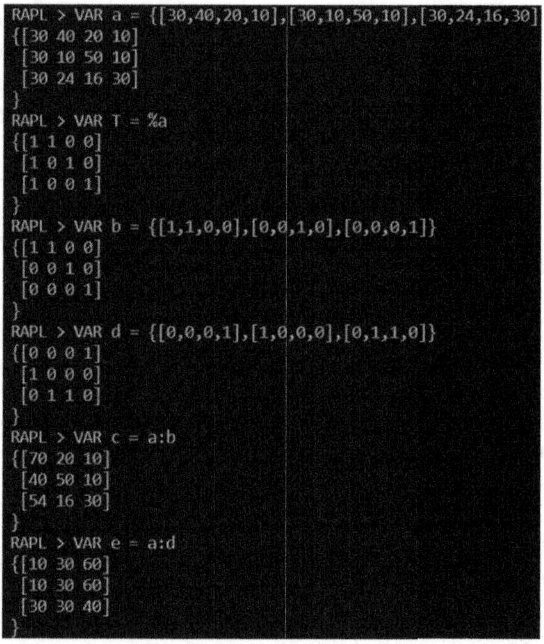

```
RAPL > VAR a = {[30,40,20,10],[30,10,50,10],[30,24,16,30]
{[30 40 20 10]
 [30 10 50 10]
 [30 24 16 30]
}
RAPL > VAR T = %a
{[1 1 0 0]
 [1 0 1 0]
 [1 0 0 1]
}
RAPL > VAR b = {[1,1,0,0],[0,0,1,0],[0,0,0,1]}
{[1 1 0 0]
 [0 0 1 0]
 [0 0 0 1]
}
RAPL > VAR d = {[0,0,0,1],[1,0,0,0],[0,1,1,0]}
{[0 0 0 1]
 [1 0 0 0]
 [0 1 1 0]
}
RAPL > VAR c = a:b
{[70 20 10]
 [40 50 10]
 [54 16 30]
}
RAPL > VAR e = a:d
{[10 30 60]
 [10 30 60]
 [30 30 40]
}
```

Fig. 4. How to use the operators '%' and ':' to get the transition matrix and the utility matrix.

6   Future Work

Other operations can be implemented using the current ones in RAPL to build upon them. In the future, we can add an operator to identify whether an allocation is transitory or not. Furthermore, an operator that returns every possible transitory allocation can be implemented to improve the user experience when working with our proposed language. Another operator planned to be implemented in the future is to compare the Nash social welfare among transitory allocations, and return the allocation that maximizes this value. That operator would then return the fairest allocation among the most efficient ones.

The inclusion of additional objects could help detect errors in the early stages of the program interpretation. Another significant improvement in the future could be to add multi-line statements support. Although the interactive shell is an useful tool to experiment with, we would like to create and interpret scripts in the future to facilitate experimentation with more significant scenarios.

7   Conclusions

Domain Specific Languages have several advantages when it comes to representing a particular kind of problem. The implementation of RAPL showcases that the resource allocation problem, that is mathematically and computationally challenging, can be model and solved using a few lines of code. RAPL has basic operators, easy to use, focused on obtaining the utility matrix of an allocation; from this point, complex properties as fairness and efficiency can be easily identified.

In this work, we have described several elements of the design and implementation of a DSL. We provided information about the scanner, parser, and interpreter, and showed examples about how this kind of language facilitates the manipulation of matrices of a resource allocation problem.

References

1. Brooks Webber, A.: Modern Programming Languages: A Practical Introduction, 2nd edn. Franklin, Beedle & Associates Inc., USA (2010)
2. Camacho, F., Chacón, G., Pino Pérez, R.: Resource allocation under uncertainty: an algebraic and qualitative treatment. CoRR http://arxiv.org/abs/1805.06864 (2018)
3. Camacho, F., Chacón, G., Pino Pérez, R.: A qualitative framework for resource allocation. RISTI, Revista Ibérica de Sistemas e Tecnologias de Informação, pp. 121–132 (2019). http://www.risti.xyz/issues/ristie19.pdf
4. Camacho, F., Zhunio, C., Fonseca, R., Castillo, Z.: Asignación de recursos con eficiencia y justicia débil en el bienestar social utilitario. To be published in RISTI, Revista Ibérica de Sistemas e Tecnologias de Informação (2020)
5. Caragiannis, I., Kurokawa, D., Moulin, H., Procaccia, A.D., Shah, N., Wang, J.: The unreasonable fairness of maximum Nash welfare. ACM Trans. Econ. Comput. (TEAC) 7(3), 1–32 (2019)
6. Chevaleyre, Y., Endriss, U., Maudet, N.: Distributed fair allocation of indivisible goods. Artif. Intell. 242, 1–22 (2017). https://doi.org/10.1016/j.artint.2016.09.005
7. Endriss, U., Maudet, N., Sadri, F., Toni, F.: Negotiating socially optimal allocations of resources. J. Artif. Intell. Res. 25, 315–348 (2006). https://doi.org/10.1613/jair.1870
8. Hughes, J.: The design and implementation of programming languages. Technical report PRG40, Oxford University (July 1983)
9. Knudsen, J., Thomsen, K.: A conceptual framework for programming languages. DAIMI Report Series, vol. 14, no. 192 (April 1985). https://doi.org/10.7146/dpb.v14i192.7464
10. Kosar, T., Mernik, M., Carver, J.C.: Program comprehension of domain-specific and general-purpose languages: comparison using a family of experiments. Empir. Softw. Eng. 17(3), 276–304 (2011). https://doi.org/10.1007/s10664-011-9172-x
11. Rakocevic, N.: Red Programming Language (2020). https://red.github.io/. Accessed 22 Jun 2020
12. van Rossum, G., Drake, F.L.: The Python Language Reference Manual. Network Theory Ltd. (2011)
13. Scott, M.L.: Programming Language Pragmatics. Morgan Kaufmann, Burlington (2000)

E-Move: Domain Specific Language for People with Movement Disorders

Rafael Valencia-Ramos[1]([⊠]) [iD], Luis Zhinin-Vera[1,2] [iD], Oscar Chang[1] [iD], and Israel Pineda[1] [iD]

[1] School of Mathematical and Computational Sciences, Yachay Tech University, Urcuqui 100650, Ecuador
rafael.valencia@yachaytech.edu.ec
[2] MIND Research Group - Model Intelligent Networks Development, Urcuquí, Ecuador
http://www.mind-researchgroup.com

Abstract. Programmers with movement disorders do not currently have a language that aids them to write code. This work proposes the creation of E-Move, a friendly Domain-Specific Language (DSL) that tolerates involuntary typing errors. E-Move targets programmers who suffer from involuntary movements in their upper extremities related to movement disorders caused by neurodegenerative conditions such as Parkin-son, myoclonus, chorea, tics, dystonia, and tremor. This work describes the three essential elements that allow the proposed programming language to work effectively: the grammar, the back-end, and the front-end. Additionally, several illustrative examples showcase the usage of E-Move. E-Move was developed using Python, textX, and Pure Python Compiler Infrastructure (PPCI). The result is a programming language that tolerates involuntary typing. Therefore, more people can access coding, which is an important skill.

Keywords: Domain-Specific-Language · Movement Disorders · textX · PPCI

1 Introduction

A Domain-Specific Language (DSL) is a programming language that is highly specialized to solve problems within a particular domain [6, 8]. The syntax of the language provides an enhanced expressiveness that is useful within a given domain. This syntax increases the productivity of the programmer when using the language [4].

Although programming is an essential skill for most professions, not everyone can use programming languages. Neurodegenerative disorders can cause physical limitations that debilitate the upper extremities and are incurable in some cases. Therefore, it is important to provide new tools that allow people suffering from these diseases to use technological tools such as programming languages. An example of such disease is Parkinson, which affects more than 10 million people around the world. The probability of having Parkinson's disease increases with age, approximately four out of a hundred people are diagnosed before the age of 50 [7]. Parkinson's disease is not the only one; there are many other diseases related to involuntary movements, including myoclonus, chorea, tics, dystonia, and tremors [1].

G. Rodriguez Morales et al. (Eds.): TICEC 2020, CCIS 1307, pp. 493–500, 2020.
https://doi.org/10.1007/978-3-030-62833-8_36

This work proposes the E-Move programming language as an alternative for people who struggle in their interaction with programming languages due to their mobility problems. E-Move targets programmers who present involuntary movements in their upper extremities, providing a friendly and forgiving language that is flexible with typing errors. E-Move DSL proposes a flexible grammar that tolerates alphabetical typing errors and a back-end capable of solving numerical typing errors.

2 Related Work

Several programming languages try to facilitate a coding process that has accessibility as a goal. Some examples of this kind of language are Quorum, Boostrap, and Myna.

Quorum [10] is a relatively new programming language designed for blind people and people with reduced vision. The programming language includes support for 3D gaming, music, and other activities. Quorum is the first evidence-oriented programming language to be proposed. It uses evidence from field data and randomized controlled trials in its design. This approach provides, to the research community, an organized way to influence the design of the language over time.

Schanzer et al. [9] proposed Bootstrap; it is a computing curriculum and after-school program for students with a broad range of disabilities, including visual and sensory-motor impairments. The block programming editor has accessibility-enabled features, to read code based on meaning instead of syntax. It also provides a hands-free configuration. Bootstrap uses video game programming to reinforce algebra and geometry concepts to improve the student experience with mathematics. The game structure connects specific mathematical concepts with the game behaviors.

Wagner et al. [11] described Myna as a Java application driven by voice and parallel executed to Scratch. Myna processes and interpret voice commands from the user, according to a pre-defined grammar, then simulate the mouse and keyboard actions within Scratch. Myna helps people with motor disability, especially young children, to learn to program. On the other hand, Scratch (https://scratch.mit.edu/) is a project of the Lifelong Kindergarten Group at the MIT Media Lab developed to help young people learn programming through collaborative work, while promoting creative thinking. Scratch is a programming language based on blocks, these blocks have a puzzle-like shape, and the objective of the programmer is to join the pieces to achieve a certain action or behavior.

3 Preliminaries

In this section, we provide a brief overview of the tools used to design and implement the E-Move programming language. These tools are textX and PPCI, a suitable combination that aids the development of a new programming language.

3.1 TextX Library

TextX [4] is an open-source meta-language created to design and develop a Domain-Specific Languages using Python. The goals of textX are to be simple, have a readable grammar, and have a simple work ow. The Arpeggio PEG (Parsing Expression Grammars) parser [3] was used as the basis for textX to remove the burden of translating parsing trees to abstract representations. Arpeggio is a PEG grammar interpreter, implemented as recursive descent parser with memoization. PEG is an alternative to context-free grammar that allows creating a new syntax [5].

TextX executes the following steps:

1. Construct an Arpeggio parser and a meta-model at run-time.
2. Create a meta-model with the entire information about the language and generate a set of Python classes based on the grammar rules.
3. Parse the program or model written in the new language and constructs a graph of Python objects [4].

3.2 PPCI Library

Pure Python Compiler Infrastructure (PPCI) contains different interfaces for various programming languages and the capability to translate the intermediate code into machine code. PPCI is written entirely in Python [2]. The PPCI project includes:

- A compiler, an assembler, a linker, and a build system,
- Language front-ends: Brainfuck, C, c3, WebAssembly,
- CPU back-ends: 6500, arm, avr, m68k, microblaze, msp430, openrisc, risc-v, stm8, x86 64, xtensa.

4 E-Move Programming Language

4.1 Grammar Definition

E-Move implements a grammar that is exible with alphabetical typing errors. This grammar uses textX for its design and implementation. The full grammar definition of E-Move DSL is shown below.

$$\langle program \rangle \models \langle statement^* \rangle$$
$$\langle statement \rangle \models \langle expression \rangle \mid \langle assignment\_statement \rangle$$
$$\langle assignment\_statement \rangle \models \langle ID\ /(a,r,m,o) \rangle \langle /ID^* \rangle\ '=' \langle digits \rangle$$
$$\langle expression \rangle \models \langle operation\ /ID^* \rangle (\langle digits \rangle \langle variable^* \rangle)^+\ '-'\ \mid\ \langle digits \rangle$$
$$\langle operation \rangle \models 'a'\ \mid\ 'r'\ \mid\ 'm'\ \mid\ 'o'$$
$$\langle digits \rangle \models \langle digit \rangle (\langle union \rangle \langle digit \rangle)^*$$
$$\langle variable \rangle \models \langle ID \rangle$$
$$\langle digit \rangle \models '0\text{-}9'$$
$$\langle union \rangle \models '+'$$
$$\langle ID \rangle \models 'A\text{-}Z'\ \mid\ 'a\text{-}z'$$
$$\langle comment \rangle \models //non\text{-}newline^*newline$$

Grammar 1: E-Move DSL.

The language considers the first character of each token as a command and ignores the rest of the string. The production rule that allows that is /ID*. The production rule /ID* shows up twice in the grammar to eliminate all possible alphabet typing errors.

The grammar rede nes the concept of numbers and basic operations. It de nes a number with two or more digits as a set of digits joined by a concatenation character. The operation rule de nes which operations are accepted. It contains four attributes represented by the letters a, r, m, o. Each of these attributes will be interpreted as the arithmetic operations addition, subtraction, multiplication, and division. These letters are separated from each other on the keyboard. Thus, they are a safe way to represent the basic arithmetic operations so that it minimizes typing commands incorrectly. Also, the grammar speci es that the operations have at least two elements to operate with them.

Each line of code of our proposed language must end with the character \-". Any alphanumeric string that begins with the characters \/", is considered a comment.

4.2 Front-End Design

E-Move DSL has the following production rules de ned in the grammar: program, statement, expression, assignment statement, variable, operation, digits, union, digit, and comment. Each of these rules is transformed into Python classes using textX. This process is the creation of the metamodel. The metamodel is used to create instances of objects in a model created based on grammatical rules. Listing 1.3 shows a complete E-Move model. Basically, a model is the program written in the new programming language that follows the rules established in the grammar.

Figure 1 shows that textX creates a Python class for each rule of the language description. Additionally, a BASETYPE node is created and integrated automatically.

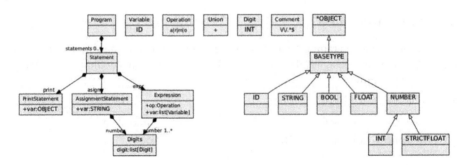

Fig. 1. Meta-model of the grammar

Listing 1.1 shows an example of E-Move DSL that explains the operation of the language.

```
1  asd    33  23 -   //  3+2
2  ref    54      36- //  5-3
3  mnk    72  62 -   //  7*6
4  opl    41  20 -   //  4/2
```

Listing 1.1: E-Move program with arithmetic operations

For example, if the user of E-Move DSL writes asd or aws, the grammar will only consider the rst letter as a command. Therefore, any of the previous commands are interpreted just as a; this example generalizes to all operations. Listing 1.1 presents the implementation of the four operations that are currently supported by the grammar. Figure 2 shows the parse tree created by textX following the model presented in Listing 1.1.

4.3 Back-End Development

The E-Move DSL back-end is developed with Python using the PPCI library. The Python classes created by textX are translated into an intermediate representation (IR) code using PPCI. The IR aims to generate a set of abstract instructions where we can perform machine-independent code optimization. Then, this optimized IR is translated into machine code.

The textX context processor system creates a compilation function that takes a model as an input and outputs an IR module. This translation process resolves numerical typing errors. The numerical characters accepted by the language must be written correctly, maintaining the tolerance of typing errors.

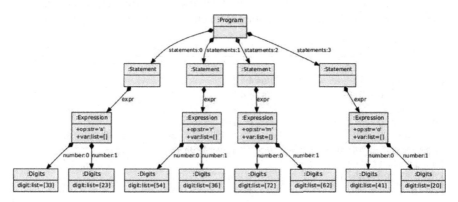

Fig. 2. Model representation using the meta-model of the grammar.

Numbers have a special treatment during the execution of the back-end. The modules that process the IR only take the rst digit of the number following a similar criteria as the one used to identify the commands during the front-end.

Arithmetic operations use the IR related functions from PPCI to connect with the letters a, r, m and o that represent each one of them. Similarly, the behavior of the rule assignment statement is also de ned to use the \= " sym-bol. Also, the back-end implements the logic needed to work with multiple-digit numbers. The \+ " operator is used to concatenate di erent digits to create big-ger numbers. In this case, the \+ " operator does not represent addition. Listing 1.2 shows an example that contains assignments with multiple-digit numbers.

```
1  dgh  =    29+45+6     // d=  246
2  gh   = 4+87+6321      // g=  486
3  wt   = 21+36          // w=  23
```

Listing 1.2: E-Move program with multiple-digit operations

A special PPCI function called ir to object is used to translate from IR-code into an object for the architecture x86 64. Finally, a Linux executable from the object code is created using the function api.objcopy from PPCI.

5 Results

This section presents a complete example of a program written with the proposed E-Move programming language. Listing 1.3 shows a model that contains the four basic arithmetic operations, assignments, handling of multiple-digit numbers, and comments.

Listing 1.4 shows the result of executing the program from Listing 1.3. For example, the rst line indicates the result of the rst addition, the operation is 4 plus 3 plus g, g was previously assigned to 4 thus the result is 11. This showcases the execution of the different rules implemented in the front-end and back-end.

Here, we can also check that the language tolerates typing errors and that it can handle negative numbers similar to the behavior and functionality of any existing programming language.

```
1  // Assignments
2  gf  =  44                       //g=4
3  srta     = 56+45+89             //s =548
4  // Addition
5  add  4  3  g-                   //   4+3+4
6  afd   45  32    gtr -           //   4+3+4: Both    ad di ti on s  are  the  same .
7  ase  sdf    67+45 gt 96+85 -    //   548+64+4+98
8  // Substraction
9  rty   67  989+45+8 -            //   6 -948
10 ry   5  2 -                     //   5 -2
11 // Multiplication
12 mmn  5  4-       // 5*4
13 mmm  54  45 -    // 5*4: Both   multiplications   are  equal .
14 mkj  48  6 -     // 4*6
15 // Division
16 ors   10+00    20 -   //     10/2
17 os  13+00 21-         //     10/2
```

Listing 1.3: E-Move program showing assignment, single-digit operations, multiple-digit operations, and comments.

a1	:0011	m1	:0020
a2	:0011	m2	:0020
a3	:0714	m3	:0024
r1	: -0942	o1	:0005
r2	:0003	o2	:0005

Listing 1.4: Model Execution Output

6 Conclusions

In this work, we describe E-Move, a DSL that targets programmers who suffer from involuntary movements in their upper extremities. E-Move uses Python, textX, and PPCI for its design and implementation.

This newly proposed programming language has components that include accessibility in its core. Thus, it is friendly and tolerant of involuntary typing errors. The grammar and the front-end of E-Move resolve all alphabetical typing errors while the back-end resolves the numerical typing error. Our new language includes support for arithmetic operations with single-digit and multiple-digit numbers, for assignments, and comments.

As future work, we propose to develop a study about the interaction between E-move and programmers that suffer movement disorders. In this way, E-move could increase the number of features that it offers, including more arithmetic operations or a transpiler to a general purpose programming language.

References

1. Abdo, W., Warrenburg, B., Burn, D., Quinn, N., Bloem, B.: The clinical approach to movement disorders. Nat. Rev. Neurol. **6**, 29–37 (2010). https://doi.org/10.1038/nrneurol.2009.196
2. Bouwman, W.: ppci: A compiler for arm, x86, msp430, xtensa and more implemented in pure Python (2020). https://pypi.org/project/ppci/
3. Dejanovic, I., Milosavljevic, G., Vaderna, R.: Arpeggio: a exible peg parser for python. Knowl.-Based Syst. **95**, 71–74 (2016). https://doi.org/10.1016/j.knosys.2015.12.004
4. Dejanovic, I., Vaderna, R., Milosavljevic, G., Vukovic.: Textx: a python tool for domain-specific languages implementation. Knowl.-Based Syst. **115**, 1–4 (2017). https://doi.org/10.1016/j.knosys.2016.10.023
5. Ford, B.: Parsing expression grammars: a recognition-based syntactic foundation. In: Proceedings of the 31st ACM SIGPLAN-SIGACT Symposium on Principles of Programming Languages, POPL 2004, pp. 111–122. Association for Computing Machinery, New York (2004). https://doi.org/10.1145/964001.964011
6. Klemes, J.J., Varbanov, P.S., Liew, P.Y.: Novel domain-specific language framework for controllability analysis **33**, 559–564 (2014). https://doi.org/10.1016/B978-0-444-63456-6.50094-6
7. Marras, C., et al.: Prevalence of parkin-son's disease across North America. NPJ Parkinson's Disease **4** (2018). https://doi.org/10.1038/s41531-018-0058-0
8. Parsons, M.F.R.: Using Domain-Specific Languages. Addison Wesley, Boston (2010)
9. Schanzer, E., Fisler, K., Krishnamurthi, S.: Bootstrap: Going beyond programming in after-school computer science. http://citeseerx.ist.psu.edu/viewdoc/summary?doi=10.1.1.398.8507

10. Ste k, A., Ladner, R.: The quorum programming language (abstract only). In: Proceedings of the 2017 ACM SIGCSE Technical Symposium on Computer Science Education, SIGCSE 2017, p. 641. Association for Computing Machinery, New York (2017). https://doi.org/10.1145/3017680.3022377
11. Wagner, A., Rudraraju, R., Datla, S., Banerjee, A., Sudame, M., Gray, J.: Programming by voice: a hands-free approach for motorically challenged children (2012). https://doi.org/10.1145/2212776.2223757

A Software Architecture Proposal for a Data Platform on Active Mobility and Urban Environment

Christian Quinde[1], David Guillermo[1], Lorena Siguenza-Guzman[2] (ID),
Daniel Orellana[3,4] (ID), and Paola Pesántez-Cabrera[2(✉)] (ID)

[1] Faculty of Engineering, Universidad de Cuenca, Cuenca, Ecuador
{christian.quindet,david.guillermof}@ucuenca.edu.ec
[2] Department of Computer Science, Faculty of Engineering,
Universidad de Cuenca, Cuenca, Ecuador
lorena.siguenza@ucuenca.edu.ec, paola.pesantezc@gmail.com
[3] LlactaLAB - Sustainable Cities Research Group, Department of Space and Population,
Universidad de Cuenca, Cuenca, Ecuador
daniel.orellana@ucuenca.edu.ec
[4] Faculty of Agricultural Sciences, Universidad de Cuenca, Cuenca, Ecuador

Abstract. Over time Geographic Information Systems (GIS) have evolved from monolithic software to dynamic platforms interacting with other systems. Consequently, characteristics such as availability, scalability, interoperability, and failure handling have become essential. Due to the vast diversity of applications and user levels, and the growing complexity of data types and models handling geospatial data, information management has developed into a complex, often overlooked task, leading to delayed results and/or disorganization of information. The goal of this paper is to propose a software architecture design to support mobility data collection, analysis, and visualization. The proposal is based on the process for software architectures stated by Bredemeyer Consulting, comprising five stages: commit, requirements, design, validation, and deployment. Likewise, the Attribute Driven Design (ADD) method has been used for the design stage where the selected architectural pattern was Service Oriented Architecture (SOA) since it provides the scalability and interoperability attributes required for this study. The Architecture Tradeoff Analysis Method (ATAM) has been chosen to identify the risks of the proposal and to evaluate the architecture to ensure that all requirements have been satisfactorily met. The model was validated using the data and projects of the LlactaLAB research group.

Keywords: Software architecture · Geospatial information · Geographic Information System · Attribute Driven Design · Architecture balance analysis method

1 Introduction

Currently, the efficient and effective management of data and processes is a critical factor in all kinds of domains such as education, health, economy, transportation, among

© Springer Nature Switzerland AG 2020
G. Rodriguez Morales et al. (Eds.): TICEC 2020, CCIS 1307, pp. 501–515, 2020.
https://doi.org/10.1007/978-3-030-62833-8_37

others. Within the context of *mobility*, the classic concept involved only traffic and transportation engineering, solving the problems that arose using basic measurements like the width of the street, the number of vehicles that circulate, and others. Nowadays, the paradigm has changed towards an approach where mobility is being studied as a phenomenon of human behavior [1]. This implies the necessity of a multidisciplinary analytical framework, involving disciplines such as architecture, urban planning, sociology, psychology, geography, among others [2]. Likewise, this new vision implies that vast amount of heterogeneous data must be integrated, analyzed, and modelled using different algorithms and methods [3] to produce useful knowledge for decision-makers to leverage available resources, improve urban planning, and enhance the sustainability of cities [4].

Geographic Information Systems (GIS) is an organized integration of hardware, software, data, people and processes to capture, store, manipulate, analyze, and display geographically referenced information [5]. *Geoprocessing* is a key concept in GIS; its goal is to provide tools and frameworks for performing analysis and managing geographic data, e.g., calculating optimal routes through a transportation network, analyzing and searching for patterns at crime locations, predicting which areas are prone to landslides or forecasting the effects of a flood [6, 7]. The most widely used systems for geoprocessing are QGIS (open source software) and ArcGIS (private software) [7]. The integration of GIS with the Web has made it accessible to a wider public, leveraging data sharing and integration in real-time, as well as accessing to platform-independent GIS analysis tools. Whereas in 2000, Refractions Research released PostGIS, open-source support for spatial objects in PostgreSQL [8]. In the last decade, the pervasive use of GPS (Global Positioning System)-enabled smartphones and location-aware social media has produced an incommensurable amount of spatial-enriched data, which has been further harnessed by Volunteered Geographic Information (VGI) approaches, such as OpenStreetMap [9]. Geographic Information Science research has focused on taking advantage of these novel massive datasets and producing the best possible scientific evidence to support decision-making for facing the mobility and sustainability challenges of the 21st century [10].

In this context, the development of a reliable and scalable software system (platform) would be an essential tool for several geoprocessing tasks for mobility studies: a) pre-processing (automatic or semi-automatic import of the collected data from different sources and their preparation for storage and integration into a standard structure), b) analysis (methods based on data mining, geospatial analysis, and statistical analysis), and c) post-processing (display and publication of the results in a friendly and interactive manner). This platform requires and must be based on the design of a robust software architecture that will help developers to identify and prevent any unforeseen events that may arise during the development process [11]. Software architecture is a bridge between the business goals and the resulting end-system [12, 13]. It defines and describes the structure and relationships of each system, subsystem, or software component that is modeled to form a cohesive whole [14] (i.e., represents the elements of the system, what each part does, their behavior over time, and their interaction with each other) [12, 13]. However, there is not an ultimate software architecture capable of managing mobility data suitably for all possible cases and needs. Therefore, this work aims to propose a software architecture oriented to achieve the abovementioned geoprocessing tasks for the analysis of mobility and urban environments, allowing the different researchers and users to access and interact with all the generated information on a single platform, enhancing their potential for analysis, models and assisting evidence-based discussions and decision-making.

The design of the software architecture is based on the process of software architectures stated by Bredemeyer Consulting, which comprises five stages (i.e., commit, requirements, design, validation, and deployment) [15]. It is worth mentioning that these stages are similar to those of design thinking [16] and other similar methods and techniques, especially when user experience is taken into consideration. Likewise, the Attribute Driven Design (ADD) method has been used for the design stage, where the selected architectural pattern was Service Oriented Architecture (SOA) [17] since it provides the scalability and interoperability attributes required for this study. Finally, the Architecture Tradeoff Analysis Method (ATAM) has been chosen to identify the risks of the proposal and to evaluate the architecture to ensure that all requirements have been satisfactorily met [18]. To validate the software architecture, the data and projects of the LlactaLAB – Sustainable Cities Research Group[1] were used. This group is part of the Interdisciplinary Department of Space and Population of the Universidad de Cuenca (Ecuador). Until now, LlactaLAB has managed and stored their data separately and manually (e.g., geospatial files, surveys, records in spreadsheets, etc.), which has generated difficulties and problems for data maintenance and updating. These challenges are highly connected with knowledge management as discussed in [19]. Nevertheless, some standards commonly used and supported at LlactaLAB include Web Map Service (WMS), Web Feature Service (WFS), Catalog Service for the Web (CSW), among others, all supported by the Open Geospatial Consortium OGC [20].

The remaining structure of this paper is as follows. Section 2 discusses the related work. Section 3 describes the development of the proposed architecture, its requirement analysis, design, and validation. Finally, Sect. 4 presents conclusions and future work.

2 Related Work

In some studies, related to geographic data management, the architecture pattern that predominates for geospatial information is SOA. The Service-Oriented Architecture has several benefits over the client-server architectures since it provides an open and interoperable environment. It promotes the exchange of geospatial data [21]. According to Friis-Christensen et al., SOA is more efficient than standard GIS applications and provides real-time information more easily [22].

For instance, Krämer and Senner propose a software architecture that allows the processing of large geospatial data sets in the cloud [23]. This process is executed using big data techniques or algorithms such as Map-Reduce, allowing distributed execution among several servers on the cloud, offering a user interface on the web. The implementation of jobs is proposed through a job manager; this is considered as the orchestrator of the processes. The communication among servers is carried out through a distributed

---

[1] https://llactalab.ucuenca.edu.ec/.

file, processing, and storing large amounts of data on the cloud [23]. Considering that mobility collected by sensors and Voluntary Geographic Information (VGI) could be integrated into mobility, Castanhari et al. propose a solution to the challenge of integrating multiple heterogeneous data sources with differences in their structures and content using a service-oriented data architecture [24]. This architecture is based on a model of architectural components and their relationships, in which each element is intended to integrate a different data source and communicate them in an automated mode using algorithms. This solution provides useful information serves to make decisions regarding floods [24]. In the same line, Olivera and Holanda propose a service-oriented architecture for environmental data management in which the interoperability, integration, and exchange of related data on land use rely on the concept of ontology to support the problem of semantic heterogeneity in different databases [25]. Likewise, Melis et al. propose an architecture based on micro-services to discover urban barriers that prevent people with physical limitations from moving easily, exposing each part of the process as a microservice and managing its execution through orchestration of components [26]. In addition, Malek considers that many systems focused on geospatial data management are complex and distributed. Still, most advances in this domain do not have an explicit architectural approach to software [27]. According to Ramsey, there is no appropriate architectural methodology for the design or construction of geographic platforms or geographic web information systems [28]. In this work, the strengths and advantages of three proposed architectural approaches were evaluated: client-server, SOA, and cloud computing, of which, an architectural style will be applied depending on the application context, resources, and needs of the entity. All in all, it can be concluded that the use of services in software architecture with a mobility approach offers advantages such as scalability, interoperability, and integration of heterogeneous data sources and that the application of various architectural styles is possible if necessary.

Moreover, having very few works related to the subject of study, it is important to consider some operative platforms that are already deployed on the web and that were a guide and basis for the proposed architecture at the level of graphic interface design and also in certain functional aspects. Table 1 details the identified platforms which have several characteristics in common with the one expected to achieve.

3   Software Architecture Proposal

This section details all the processes and characteristics necessary for the development of the proposed software architecture, which is divided into three parts: analysis of requirements, design of the software architecture, and architecture validation. It also specifies the data model, sequence diagrams, and architectural views that allow the developer or development team to understand how the system should be implemented. In this work, LlactaLAB is used as a case study because they focused on sustainable cities and active mobility. This group was looking for a technological solution that will allow them to automate, integrate, and manage their diverse information sources, processes, and applications, aiming to make them available to the community.

The system for management, analysis, and visualization should allow the collection and storage of data in various formats (shapefiles, gpx, files, videos, images, tables). In

Table 1. Identified platforms used as a baseline for the proposed architecture

Platform	Country	Description
Hexaba[a]	Argentina	It is an experimental module of data science and urbanism, written in the software R. It has various functionalities such as visualization by layers, urban scoring for the generation of indices using variables, regression analysis by selecting variables to explore, clustering with the possibility of determining the number of clusters to generate, and a variable laboratory where previously-stored variables can be combined for later use
Autotraffic[b]	Mexico	It provides a simple interface for quick access to the different layers or services offered by the community that manages the mobility information of the city exposed on the web
Cidade Plena[c]	Brazil	It is made up of six areas that provide data on compactness, land use, social cohesion, habitability, environmental support, and infrastructure of the Brazilian municipality of Lajeado in the state of Rio Grande do Sul in Brazil

[a] https://nahuelpatino.shinyapps.io/hexaBA/.
[b] https://autotraffic.com.mx/.
[c] http://cidadeplena.com.br/.

addition, it must allow data to be collected from mobile devices such as smartphones or GPS, it should allow to perform geospatial analysis, statistical analysis, and data mining analysis of the stored information, as well as viewing and downloading the data both processed/analyzed as originals.

3.1 Mapping Requirements to Software Architecture

For the development of the proposal, the architecture is built iteratively through a preliminary analysis of the architectural drivers, that is, the foremost functional, quality and business requirements, and a project feasibility study. To determine the architectural drivers, it is necessary to identify the highest priority business objectives. These objectives become quality scenarios or use cases. From this list, those that will have the most significant impact on architecture should be chosen. Architectural design can begin once the architectural conductors are defined. The requirements analysis process will then be influenced by the questions generated during the architectural design.

For the initial development of architecture, an object-oriented technique called Responsibility Based Design (RBD) can be used to help to define the critical components of the architecture. The software requirements specifications (SRS) defined by LlactaLAB were analyzed, which were transformed into functional requirements, specified based on the template proposed by IEEE 830 for the specification of software requirements. The objective of this process is to clarify where to go and what the software architecture must achieve. Several techniques were used to collect requirements, such as document review, group discussion, evaluation of personal experiences and interaction, and introspection with the LlactaLAB team. This whole process was accomplished through mostly biweekly meetings with the presence of directors or representatives, project leaders, and researchers in charge of the architecture design.

This phase allowed defining some main characteristics of the project, such as having files that represent geographic information in different formats (e.g., .shp, .kml, .geojson). These files were analyzed and served to establish what types of formats the architecture must support for data management. In this stage, the priority of information and requirements collected together with the interested parties were also analyzed and established, as well as the architectural drivers; the tables or graphs were made according to the established needs (e.g., use cases, context diagrams, and component diagrams). User needs were broken down into functional, non-functional requirements, and system constraints. In this phase, multiple use cases that can occur in the system were also detailed, system dependencies and relationships, as well as the actors related to the use cases (i.e., administrator, member, and user).

Based on the SRS, the system requires compliance with the following functionalities and processes. It should offer the possibility of managing geospatial and mobility-related data in the best manner for later use; this also implies uploading and downloading of original data. The system should allow pre-processing, which includes a function for automatic or semi-automatic import of the collected data and their preparation for storage and integration in a common structure. It should provide the ability to perform an analysis process, which includes methods based on data mining, geospatial analysis, and statistical analysis. It needs to bring the possibility of post-processing, which contains functions for displaying and publishing the results in a friendly and interactive fashion. The system needs to offer the opportunity of collecting primary data using global positioning devices such as GPS. It should allow expanding the development of a smartphone application to record the movement of people and perceptions of the journey. Finally, it also requires exploring the use of mobile video logging to study specific behavior at the individual and drone scale for aggregate behavior in defined spaces.

Figure 1 presents the work environment of the system, showing each external entity that interacts with the central system and the activities carried out between the network and these entities. This diagram portrays the system without details of its internal structure because it seeks to focus attention on external actors and events that should be considered in developing a complete set of system requirements and constraints. For instance, the client system sends geospatial files, tables, documents, images, and videos from the client to the server. It also allows requests for analysis (geospatial, statistical, data mining, etc.) of the available metadata and presents them on screen. The external geospatial data collection devices collect and send GPS data either in real-time or asynchronous to the central system for later use. The mobile devices allow loading forms with information that is collected in the field. The file storage system (Drive) is the unit that has the function of storing all types of data gathered either for backup, for later use, or to make it available to users. The management, analysis, and visualization system of data on mobility patterns is the core system of the platform. It performs the role of server, service provider, executor of analysis functions, among others. In addition, this system has the purpose of serving as a tool for the validation and verification of geospatial data stored in the file storage system, as well as to facilitate mechanisms to store these processed files in a database. Additionally, the user or interested public will be in charge of publishing the geographical layers.

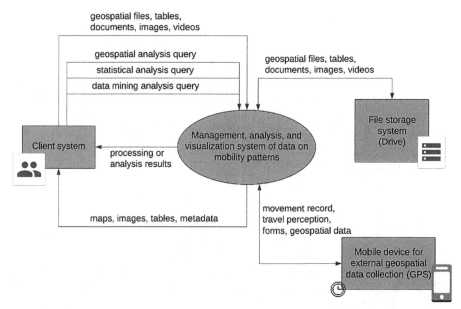

Fig. 1. Context diagram of the system for management, analysis, and visualization of data on mobility patterns.

Figure 2 presents the methodology that solved the management (collection, storage, analysis, and visualization) of data on mobility patterns. The process consists of four stages: 1) the collection stage that focuses on the gathering of data from multiple sources and different formats (shapefile, gpx, tables, videos, and files); this data is stored in a directory structure for future filtering; 2) the storage stage, where the filtered and validated data is deposited in a specific repository and, also, the geospatial information is registered in a geospatial database to reuse it more efficiently; 3) the analysis stage that focuses on performing geospatial, statistical or data mining analysis; and, 4) the visualization stage that represents the step after performing some analysis, i.e., the visualization on a dashboard presenting the results for decision-making.

3.2 Software Architecture Design

This phase designs the system at a high level and specifies architectural guidelines for designers. The components involved in the system, their interactions, and their assigned responsibilities are described in detail, to satisfy the requirements identified in the previous stage. All this using architectural patterns (i.e., n-level and SOA) to provide attributes such as robustness, availability, portability, and usability to the system.

Architecture Overview. Being a geographic information system, its architecture is composed of two main parts, the client and the component and geoprocessing servers as illustrated in Fig. 3. Each component must adequately fulfill its responsibility; thus, the system works synergistically, efficiently, and effectively to meet the needs of Llacta-LAB. The client (consumer of services) primarily consists of the web application and the mobile devices that will consume web services. In this context, the mobile app allows

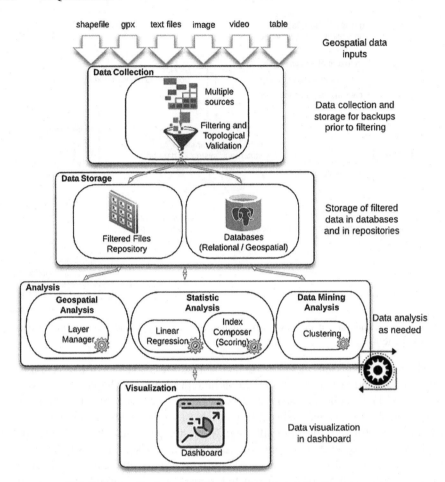

shapefile   gpx   text files   image   video   table

Geospatial data inputs

Data Collection

Multiple sources

Filtering and Topological Validation

Data collection and storage for backups prior to filtering

Data Storage

Filtered Files Repository

Databases (Relational / Geospatial)

Storage of filtered data in databases and in repositories

Analysis

Geospatial Analysis

Layer Manager

Statistic Analysis

Linear Regression

Index Composer (Scoring)

Data Mining Analysis

Clustering

Data analysis as needed

Visualization

Dashboard

Data visualization in dashboard

Fig. 2. Data collection, storage, analysis, and visualization process.

the consumption of file storage services (forms, images, videos, etc.). The mobile framework provides a set of tools to facilitate the development of mobile applications, such as methods to consume web services and to create friendly graphical interfaces for mobile devices.

The client web application represents the client-side web interface, which allows all requests for web services to execute analysis or data management operations. The Web Framework provides a set of tools to facilitate the development of client-side web applications, such as methods for consuming web services, creating a pleasant graphical web interface adaptable to screen resolutions, among others. JavaScript libraries allow presenting geographic layers and interactive maps in web browsers.

The proposed architecture, depicted in Fig. 3, also includes a Broker (intermediary/orchestator), in charge of connecting the client with the server separating dependencies such as the programming language. The broker plays a key role in load balancing and the prevention of bottlenecks during the consumption of services. The last main

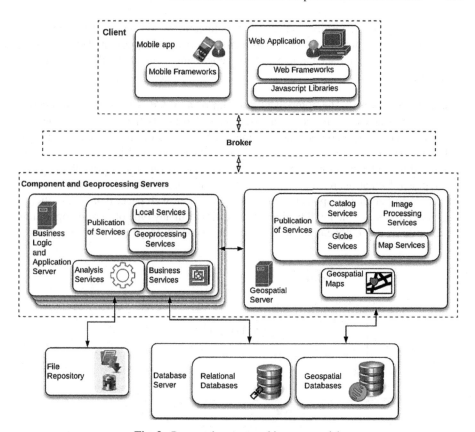

Fig. 3. Proposed system architecture model.

part is the component and geoprocessing servers (service provider), in charge of performing the necessary operations to meet business objectives, as well as providing or making available the required services to clients for both analysis and geographic layers. The business logic and application server is responsible for making geospatial analysis and management services available. The analysis services make some services available such as union, intersection, linear regression, scoring, sum, arithmetic mean, and others. The business services provide data management services such as uploading files of different types; "CRUD" operations (i.e., create, read, update and delete) on/from projects, members, roles, related entities, the publication of services, etc. The geospatial server provides consultation services of WFS, WMS layers, etc., to the central server and the public. This server also provides an API (Application Programming Interface) that allows performing actions such as publishing layers, retrieving layers, and more. The map services are basically, and mainly the layers published abroad in the different supported standards. The file repository represents the place where files such as tables, images, videos, forms, among others, are stored and organized in folders or directories.

An additional part of the architecture is the database server, composed of both geospatial and relational databases. The relational databases are in charge of storing the data that will allow the system to relate each project with its members, members with roles, projects with analysis results, analysis with publications, and other relationships that assess the proper control of the system as a whole. Finally, the geospatial databases are in charge of saving the data and metadata of geographic layers that will be used by the geospatial server.

System Components. The component diagram of a system allows the identification of the dependencies among components. Figure 4 presents the components defined for this system. These components are intended to cover the needs or requirements of LlactaLAB; they represent the entities and services involved in the context of the system. Mobile Device allows the integration and interaction of the device that collects geographic information, forms generated in the field, images and videos captured by the camera. Web Server is responsible for storing the main web page, that is, the client's graphical interface, which will be the means to carry out any type of existing operation. Presentation is a component of the Web Server, primarily responsible for presentation

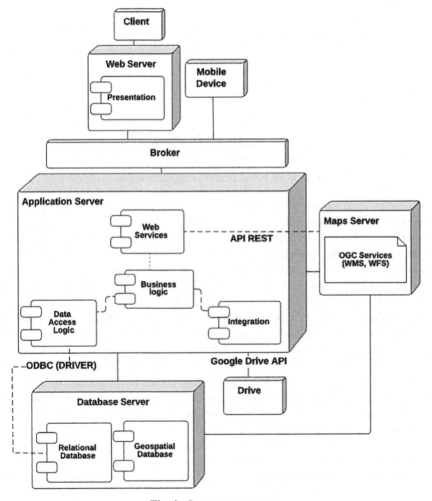

Fig. 4. System components.

logic as well as the proper display of data. The broker is an intermediary component in charge of connecting the client (Mobile Device, Web Server) with the central server (Application Server). This element allows storing the services that the primary server provides as if it were a catalog. Application Server makes available the services of layer analysis, file management, and other business services such as CRUD operations. This server includes web service, business logic, data access logic, and integration. Web Service is responsible for creating and publishing the services that the client will use through the broker. Business Logic is in charge of storage coordination, data validation, integrity verification, and even carrying out analysis operations. Data Access Logic contains activities that mainly allow access to the database, queries to it, data insertion, and other necessary procedures in the database. Integration performs the file connection and storage operations in the repository.

Maps Server exposes the services of geographic layers through different well-known protocols such as SOAP (Simple Object Access Protocol) or REST (REpresentational State Transfer). Each protocol has its advantages and challenges of use, describing the services it provides through a WSDL (Web Services Description Language), thus, a client can consume them. Database Server stores the databases of the entire system and is composed of the relational and geospatial databases.

The geospatial database establishes a connection with the Maps Server to manage information related to space, such as points, lines, polygons, and, in general, maps. To this end, the use of the PostGIS plugin on a PostgreSQL database is proposed. The Drive is an external element of the system where the files will be stored in directories organized by file type. Each specific component assumes a particular role that must be fulfilled to achieve the objectives of the system.

In addition, some recommendations for the system implementation were also established to ensure that sufficient data is available about the different drivers associated with the system and that these are appropriately prioritized to continue with the next steps. Appendix A shows the main recommendations established.

3.3 Validating the Software Architecture

The evaluation of software architectures allows the detection of risks and defaults that might cause delays or severe problems in the projects. This assessment examines the system or subsystem to see if it meets the quality criteria or if it deviates so much from the architectural requirements. It is considered as one of the best practices.

Thus, the proposed architecture was evaluated using the Architecture Tradeoff Analysis Method (ATAM). This method takes as input any artifact that has been produced by the design and evaluates the consequences of architectural decisions regarding the requirements of system drivers. Finally, the result of the evaluation consists of a list of found risks. There are five phases to perform ATAM evaluations: preparation of the assessment, familiarization of the evaluation, pre-assessment adjustments, evaluation, and development of the final report. After an evaluation with this method, project plans should incorporate actions that implement risk mitigation strategies [13].

The evaluation superficially verifies that the architecture effectively meets some attributes such as interoperability, usability, scalability, etc. However, this does not guarantee compliance with the characteristics described. In addition, it identifies certain risks

(R) that must be considered when implementing this architecture to monitor and try to mitigate them, as well as the non-risks (NR) or strengths of the platform (as detailed in Table 2). For the mitigation of possible risks, it is necessary to consider specific protocols or periodic actions, as well as a contingency plan to try to control these incidents as much as possible. For example, it is crucial 1) to back up the information periodically using manual or automatic mechanisms at moments that do not affect the use of the services, 2) to have an alternate processing center to guarantee the continuous delivery of services in the event of the central servers falling/failing, 3) to consider the use of a load balancer to avoid saturating the server, and 4) to evenly distribute the load to the others thus avoiding server overload, among others. The planning, analysis, and execution of these actions will depend on the policies, norms, or standards of the entity.

Table 2. Risks and non-risks identified to be considered when implementing the architecture.

#	Risks	#	Non-risks
R1	The exact availability of external services cannot be known since they are not reached by internal personnel	NR1	Scalability, given the separation of nodes (n-levels)
R2	The number of queries and requests grows uncontrollably, overloading the server	NR2	Maintainability, given the separation of layers
R3	The broker server could tend to become a bottleneck	NR3	Usability, since the client interface is separated from the central server
R4	Possibility of increasing the response time	NR4	Security, since the execution of processes is controlled
R5	Temporary fall of the layer server	NR5	Performance, since the servers are dedicated exclusively to specific tasks
		NR6	Maintainability, given the global instance that is provided to the classes

4   Conclusions

Mobility is a complex system that requires a multidisciplinary approach. It is considered part of the "right to the city" and determines the access of people to other fundamental rights such as education, basic services, and jobs, and ultimately shapes the possibilities for a sustainable and equitable urban life. Most specialized institutions and research groups including LlactaLAB, argue that active mobility together with affordable, high-quality public transit systems are the cornerstones for sustainable mobility. Such conclusion is sustained on several long-term multidisciplinary studies that must incorporate both global research results and local particularities of cities and require the conflation of heterogenous information from a variety of sources and kinds. In this study, a software architecture for a mobility data analysis platform has been proposed. This proposed architecture is feasible, viable, and scalable according to the current resources available to LlactaLAB and can be effectively implemented in the short term.

Based on the literature review and the analysis of requirements, it was concluded that a service-oriented architecture is the most appropriate for a platform focused on mobility, due to the inherent principles that its use implies. At the level of web platform design, of the three Websites that manage geographic information mentioned in Sect. 2, the best model or platform used as a guide is Hexaba. This platform is considered as the most suitable and important to the requirements of LlactaLAB, serving as a guide for the design of graphical user interfaces in the current proposal.

Regarding the design development methodology, the process of software architectures proposed by Bredemeyer Consulting was selected, since it generates straightforward results. As for the Software Requirements Specification (SRS), it followed the IEEE 830 standard. Likewise, for the design of the architecture, ADD was identified as the ideal design methodology. Finally, ATAM methodology was used for highlighting the resulting risks and not risks when implementing the architecture. Furthermore, architectural patterns have been identified that support the user requirements and restrictions for the correct operation of the system, as well as considering the use of the n-level pattern for structuring the system components. This will allow easy replacement and/or maintenance of any element located at the n-level. At the communication level, it was decided to use the service-oriented architectural pattern, since it allows generating loosely coupled components with high scalability.

This proposal can be improved and adapted to specific requirements, regardless of the technologies used, due to its interoperability and scalability. Moreover, it will allow an easy and straightforward migration of components to Cloud Computing when required. A couple of important contributions are the database design (omitted due to space, but accessible at Appendix B) and the proposed processes for data collection, analysis, and visualization. The proposed approach will reduce costs, time, and effort for implementing the final mobility and urban environment analysis platform.

Recommendations for implementation were also established, such as programming languages, hardware capacity for adequate performance, architectural patterns that provide benefits to architecture, design patterns that, to some degree, provide elegant and organized development or development frameworks. That makes life easier for the developer. In addition, the emphasis is made on possible risks that may emerge over time, and that must be considered not only by the developers but also by all those interested in the system.

The software architecture proposed in this study is considered an important contribution for the work of LlactaLAB and other similar research groups on urban studies, since it serves as a model for future work, research, and implementation. Finally, a study on usability will be performed as future work. This is, how users deal with the proposed architecture and how it would perform in the real environment.

Acknowledgments. This study is part of the research project "Patrones de movilidad activa y entorno urbano: Pies y Pedales 2", supported by the Research Department of the University of Cuenca (DIUC).

Appendix A – Recommendations for the System Implementation

The recommendations for the system implementation can be found online at https://drive.google.com/file/d/1IRjbUG5Hpl2X9hTvZkpbbCDHNs3pl6TB.

Appendix B – Database Design for the Proposed Architecture

The database design for the proposed architecture can be found online at https://drive.google.com/file/d/1YaOUNl-dM3DKHWMllda-_Mp2jdkpxN0F.

References

1. Düh, J., Hufnagl, H., Juritsch, E., Pfliegl, R., Schimany, H.-K., Schönegger, H.: Data and Mobility: Transforming Information into Intelligent Traffic and Transportation Services. Proceedings of the Lakeside Conference 2010. AISC. Springer, Heidelberg (2010). https://doi.org/10.1007/978-3-642-15503-1
2. Orellana, D., Hermida, C., Osorio, P.: A multidisciplinary analytical framework for studying active mobility patterns. Int. Arch. Photogramm. Remote Sens. Spatial Inf. Sci. **XLI-B2**, 527–534 (2016). https://doi.org/10.5194/isprs-archives-XLI-B2-527-2016
3. Antoniou, C., Dimitriou, L., Pereira, F.: Mobility Patterns, Big Data and Transport Analytics: Tools and Applications for Modeling. Elsevier, Amsterdam (2018)
4. Shiftan, Y.: Transition Towards Sustainable Mobility: The Role of Instruments, Individuals and Institutions. Routledge, Abingdon (2016)
5. Santovenia Díaz, J., Tarragó Montalvo, C., Cañedo Andalia, R.: Sistemas de información geográfica para la gestión de la información. ACIMED **20**, 72–75 (2009)
6. Environmental Systems Research Institute, Inc.: Analysis in ArcGIS for Desktop. https://desktop.arcgis.com/en/arcmap/10.3/main/analyze/what-is-geoprocessing.htm
7. Büehler, K., McKee, L.: The OpenGIS Guide: Introduction to Interoperable Geoprocessing; Part 1 of the Open Geodata Interoperability Specification (OGIS). Open GIS Consortium, Incorporated (1996)
8. Refractions: Refractions Research : PostGIS History, http://refractions.net/products/postgis/history/
9. Senaratne, H., Mobasheri, A., Ali, A.L., Capineri, C., Haklay, M.: (Muki): a review of volunteered geographic information quality assessment methods. Int. J. Geogr. Inf. Sci. **31**, 139–167 (2017). https://doi.org/10.1080/13658816.2016.1189556
10. Lizárraga Mollinedo, C.: Movilidad urbana sostenible: Un reto para las ciudades del siglo XXI. Economía, sociedad y territorio. **6**, 283–321 (2006)
11. Sommerville, I.: Software Engineering. Addison-Wesley, Boston (2007)
12. Keeling, M.: Design It!: From Programmer to Software Architect. Pragmatic Bookshelf, Raleigh (2017)
13. Bass, L., Clements, P., Kazman, R.: Software Architecture in Practice. Addison-Wesley Professional, Boston (2012)
14. Pressman, R.S.: Software Engineering: A Practitioner's Approach. Palgrave Macmillan, London (2005)
15. Bredemeyer Consulting: Resources for Software Architects and Enterprise Architects. http://www.bredemeyer.com/
16. Kostrzewski, Mariusz: One design issue – many solutions. different perspectives of design thinking – case study. In: Uden, L., Hadzima, B., Ting, I.-H. (eds.) KMO 2018. CCIS, vol. 877, pp. 179–190. Springer, Cham (2018). https://doi.org/10.1007/978-3-319-95204-8_16

17. Mcheick, H.: Applying ADD model to enhance quality of SOA applications. Int. J. Bus. Data Commun. Netw. (IJBDCN) **8**, 17 (2012). https://doi.org/10.4018/jbdcn.2012100105
18. Blokdyk, G.: Architecture Tradeoff Analysis Method: A Clear and Concise Reference. CreateSpace Independent Publishing Platform, Scotts Valley (2018)
19. Marczewska, M.: Knowledge as a key resource contributing to the development of eco-innovations by companies-suppliers of environmentally sound technologies. In: CBU International Conference Proceedings, vol. 4, pp. 240–247 (2016). https://doi.org/10.12955/cbup.v4.806
20. Open Geospatial Consortium: OGC Standards | OGC. http://www.ogc.org/docs/is
21. Zhang, C., Li, W., Zhao, T.: Geospatial data sharing based on geospatial semantic web technologies. J. Spat. Sci. **52**, 35–49 (2007). https://doi.org/10.1080/14498596.2007.9635121
22. Friis-Christensen, A., Ostländer, N., Lutz, M., Bernard, L.: Designing service architectures for distributed geoprocessing: challenges and future directions. Trans. GIS **11**, 799–818 (2007). https://doi.org/10.1111/j.1467-9671.2007.01075.x
23. Krämer, M., Senner, I.: A modular software architecture for processing of big geospatial data in the cloud. Comput. Graph. **49**, 69–81 (2015). https://doi.org/10.1016/j.cag.2015.02.005
24. Castanhari, R.E.S., dos Santos Rocha, R., Camargo de Andrade, S., Porto de Albuquerque, J.: A software architecture to integrate sensor data and volunteered geographic information for flood risk management. In: Proceedings of the ISCRAM 2016 Conference, p. 12, Rio de Janeiro, Brazil (2016)
25. Vera Olivera, H., Holanda, M.: A GIS web with integration of sheet and soil databases of the Brazilian Cerrado. In: 7th Iberian Conference on Information Systems and Technologies (CISTI 2012), pp. 1–6. IEEE, Madrid (2012)
26. Melis, A., Mirri, S., Prandi, C., Prandini, M., Salomoni, P.: A microservice-based architecture for the development of accessible, crowdsensing-based mobility platforms. In: 2016 International Conference on Collaboration Technologies and Systems (CTS), pp. 498–505 (2016)
27. Malek, S., et al.: An architecture-driven software mobility framework. J. Syst. Softw. **83**, 972–989 (2010). https://doi.org/10.1016/j.jss.2009.11.003
28. Ramsey, P.: The State of Open Source GIS, pp. 1–49. Refractions Research Inc. Victoria (2007)

Technology and Environment

Multitemporal Evaluation of the Recent Land Use Change in Santa Cruz Island, Galapagos, Ecuador

Deniz Estefanía Barreto-Álvarez[1,2], Marco Gerardo Heredia-Rengifo[1],
Oswaldo Padilla-Almeida[2], and Theofilos Toulkeridis[2(✉)]

[1] Universidad Estatal Amazónica, Puyo, Ecuador
[2] Universidad de las Fuerzas Armadas – ESPE, Sangolquí, Ecuador
ttoulkeridis@espe.edu.ec

Abstract. We have been able to conduct a multitemporal analysis of land use change, in Santa Cruz Island, Galapagos, for the period from 2016 to 2019. This has allowed to detect changes, deducing the evolution of the natural environment or the repercussions of human action over the environment. The tools used have been with satellite images, in order to determine the state of fragmentation of the landscape. The changes in land use were derived from the cross tabulation of Landsat 8 images, with a spatial resolution of 30 m taken in October 2016, March 2019, using the PCI, IDRISI and ArcGIS programs. The defined categories were clouds, agricultural/forest mosaic, growing vegetation, infrastructure and soil. The main results demonstrated that changes in land use are determined by anthropic degradation, mainly in the conversion of native vegetation to agricultural spaces and the expansion of livestock. Demographic growth and monocultures are putting pressure on the forest, transforming areas of forest vocation into agricultural crops. The changes in coverage have meant a fragmented landscape with different degrees of disturbance, which lead to a decrease in the surface of natural habitats, reduction of the size of the fragments and their isolation.

Keywords: Galapagos · Ecological restoration · Forest · Landsat · Remote sensing

1 Introduction

When a certain visible or a molesting degree of environmental alteration with sometimes losses of habitat and biological resources has occurred due to human activities such as degradation, often an ecological restoration project may help to regain previous conditions [1, 2]. Such enhancement of these altered ecosystems has occurred in a variety of occasions in diverse environments [3–6].

After the Ecuadorian government declared the Galapagos Islands a National Park in 1959, some two decades later the UNESCO declared Galapagos a World Heritage Site for its scientific prestige and support for the National Park's conservation efforts

© Springer Nature Switzerland AG 2020
G. Rodriguez Morales et al. (Eds.): TICEC 2020, CCIS 1307, pp. 519–534, 2020.
https://doi.org/10.1007/978-3-030-62833-8_38

in 1978 [7–9]. Due to the presence of unique ecological sites and species in a prestigious environment, the Galápagos archipelago became with up to 300 thousand visitors annually a highly frequented tourist destination with its associated consequences of an economic growth such as unsustainable population expansion, socio-economic stratification, social unrest, public services and infrastructure under pressure, increase in the number of invasive species and numerous conflicts with conservation goals and authorities [10–12]. Also associated with such alterations, increase occurred with the prices of land, houses and local products, rising up also public expenses for services, education, health, water and infrastructure in the four populated islands [13, 14].

Santa Cruz Island, being with some thirty thousand citizens the most populated of the Galápagos, extends to an area of approximately 55,800 ha. There are important changes in the agricultural area, where 49% of the 14,841.3 ha of total area, have changed to other types of plant cover due to invasive species in 1998, in addition a process of change in the growth and occupation of the territory.

In the Political Constitution of Ecuador, it is established that the province of Galapagos will have a special regime and according to Article 238 for the protection of the areas subject to this regime, the rights of internal migration, labor or any other may be limited within them. activity that may affect the environment, as well as the residents of the respective area, affected by the limitations of constitutional rights, will be compensated through preferential access to the benefit of available natural resources and the formation of associations that ensure family wealth and welfare.

However, due to the human activities, invasive flora and fauna and the morphological, geological and climatological characteristics of Santa Cruz Island, the loss of surface of native vegetation is evident and is in decline, therefore, national and international institutions have opted for create the project called "Green Galapagos 2050" that seeks to recover the native vegetation of the island through the use of "Ecological Restoration" techniques [15]. Therefore, the main aim of the current study has been to establish an evaluation of such changes within a most recent period of time with the performance of a multitemporal analysis of the potential land use changes by using satellite images.

2 Study Area and Used Data

The most central island of the Galapagos is a 1.3 Ma old large shield volcano with a high abundance of parasitic cones, large lava tubes and pit craters and is subdivided into two main units [16, 17]. The older unit is the platform unit, while the younger unit is represented by lavas of the Shield series. The lavas of the platform series include faulted and uplifted parts which appear today as independent islands such as Baltra, Seymour and Las Plazas of which the latter one was formed evidently below the sea surface [18]. These old and therefore lower units show intercalations with marine carbonates with a precipitation depth of <100 m. Based on their morphology and the lack of vegetation, the younger overlying lavas of the Shield series appear to be as young as a few thousand years old [16, 18]. These lavas, which mainly flowed from the summit but also from the flank of the volcano, are composed of a range of different volcanic materials, all similar to the other volcanoes of the archipelago [17, 19–22].

On Santa Cruz Island, temperature ranges from 20 °C to 31 °C and the altitudinal range varies from 0 to 864 m above sea level. The annual precipitation of 0 to 300 mm per year for the coastal part, while on the high lands is between 300 and 1,700 mm (Fig. 1).

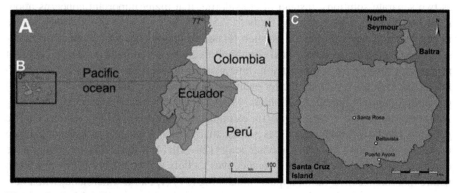

Fig. 1. Study area for the multitemporal evaluation of land use change in Santa Cruz Island, Galapagos, west of Ecuador

Unlike the majority of protected areas (PA's) in the world, where PA's are surrounded by urban and or rural areas, in Galapagos occurs the opposite, where PA's completely surround urban and rural areas of the four inhabited islands (Fig. 2). PA's are units of conservation conflicts, which focus on studying the interactions between human and other species (mainly wildlife) and or ecosystems. However, these interactions encompass many interrelated forms and aspects between human activities and natural systems [23].

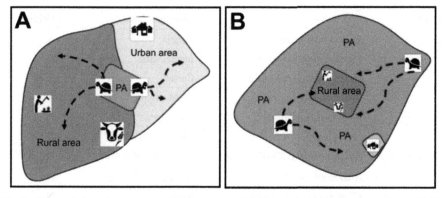

Fig. 2. The turtle icon demonstrates different interactive directions (dashed arrows) where wildlife moves outward from protected to rural and urban areas (a) and inward from PAs to rural and urban areas (b). The comparison illustrates the landscape geography of the establishment of protected areas (PA). a) Typical case that establishment of an PA (red) surrounded by urban (orange) and rural (green) areas. b) The particular case of Galapagos in which the PA completely surrounds rural (green) and urban (orange) areas [33] (Color figure online).

There are four main causes that underlie conservation conflicts [24]: (1) The different understanding of the relational values of human nature, which gives rise to conflicts when the intrinsic and instrumental values of nature they are confronted and disputed as two separate solutions, instead of considering that many important concerns about nature could be a shared element for both [25]; (2) the exclusion of interested parties in conservation planning, which is often related to the presence, imposition or extension of protected areas, where local communities are removed from their lands without proper consultation or compensation, thus generating growing conflicts between different stakeholders involved, like for example, park managers and farmers [26, 27]; (3) power asymmetries among stakeholders, which are related to particular actors, generally within organizations or institutions (for example, governments, NGOs), which exercise greater control over certain resources and use that 'power' to control and take advantage of the control of other resources of other actors [28–30]; (4) historical factors that, on the one hand, are related to historical perspectives, beliefs and practices related to human nature that make conservation appear threatening [31] or, on the other hand, when new conservation perspectives they assume that historical perspectives and human nature related to practices are threatening [32].

Table 1 lists the species that are used for the ecological restoration of Santa Cruz Island in the Proyecto Galápagos Verdes (Green Galapagos Project; GPV - 2050), which is an initiative of several institutions that seeks the sustainability of the province of Galapagos through ecological restoration and sustainable agriculture. The GPV is a model of applied science based on a socio-ecological system altered towards a functional system [34, 35].

Table 1. Geographical distribution of species in the study area. N: native; E: endemic; C: cultivated

Island	Species	Common name	Origin
Baltra	*Acacia macracantha Humb*	Acacia	N
	Bursera malacophylla	Incense tree	E
	Castela galapageia Hook	Castela	E
	Opuntia echios var	Giant cactus	E
	Parkinsonia aculeata L	Parkinsonia	N
	Scalesia crockeri Howell	Crocker's scalesia	E
Santa Cruz	*Alternanthera echinocephala*	Headed chaff flower	N
	Alternanthera filifolia	Leafed chaff flower	N
	Clerodendrum molle Kunth	Kunth	N
	Conocarpus erectus L	Button mangrove	N
	Gossypium darwinii G. Watt	Darwin's cotton	E
	Ipomoea pes-caprae	Beach morning glory	N
	Maytenus octogona	Leatherleaf	N

(*continued*)

Table 1. (*continued*)

Island	Species	Common name	Origin
	Miconia robinsoniana Cogn	Miconia	E
	Piscidia carthagenensis Jacq.	Piscidia	N
	Psychotria rufipes	White wild coffee	N
	Scalesia affinis	Radiate-headed scalesia	E
	Scalesia pedunculata Hook.	Tree scalesia	E
	Cucumis sativus L	Cucumber	C
	Solanum lycopersicum L	Wild tomato	C
	Theobroma cacao L	Cocoa tree	C

3   Methodology

We have used and georeferenced two LANDSAT 8 images of the years 2016 (27 of April) and 2019 (25 of May), with a medium high degree of cloudiness for the year 2019 and a minimal for 2016. The bands B1, B2, B3, B4, B5, B6, B7 have been added to match the original bands and form a Santa Cruz raster file. Then, the change in land use has been analyzed by comparing landsat8 images using geoinformatics tools with the techniques *cross tabulation* and the process of obtaining the normalized vegetation index and the multitemporary normalized vegetation index as processing verification tools. The programs used for the processing of the images and their corresponding analysis have been *ARCMAP 10.3*, *PCI* (trial mode) and *IDRISI* [36].

For the beginning of the processing, the band 1 of the year 2016 (B1_2016) has been used, which was imported into the PCI program, obtaining as a result a layer in PCIDSK format. Of the 12 bands obtained, the bands B2, B3, B4 were used, of which the B5, B6, B7 have been applied to perform a Transfer Layer whose result was a RASTER format image called 2016B1B7. With the Raster obtained 2016B1B7 an unsupervised classification was conducted, generating five classes being 1) Clouds, 2) Forest, 3) Growing vegetation, 4) Infrastructure and 5) soil. Using the *Run Classification* command and using the *Maximum LikeHood method*, the Raster Classified named 2016B1B7_CLASS has been obtained. From the 2016B1B7_CLASS raster using the *EXTRACT BY MASK* tool and the raster called SC_CLASES16 has been obtained, where the classification of the Santa Cruz Island classes is visualized. With the use of the *RECLASSIFY* tool the raster called SANTACRUZ16 is obtained. Using the *IDRISI* program, the SANTACRUZ16 raster using the *GEOTIFF/TIFF* command produces a raster in the *GEOTIFF/TIFF* format called SANTACRUZ16 (Fig. 3).

The mentioned process was repeated for all bands (B1 - B7) of the year 2019, of which the resulting raster has been SANTACRUZ19. The rasters SANTACRUZ16 and SANTACRUZ19 were analyzed using the technique called *CROSSTAB* (cross tabulation). The *CROSS TABULATION* is a fairly basic but effective technique, which is used

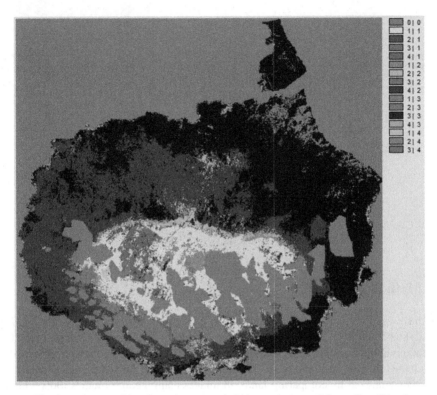

Fig. 3. Raster resulting from the cross tabulation technique of Santa Cruz Island

to find the relationship between two categorical variables. For this study the *CROSSTAB* tool that has the *IDRISI* program was used. For the analysis to be consistent and the results to be real, the images had to be classified in the same number of categories that were 0: Clouds; 1: Forest; 2: Growing vegetation; 3: Infrastructure and 4: Soil (Fig. 3).

The process of the Normalized Difference Vegetation Index (NDVI) has been performed with two bands 2016B1B7 - 2019B1B7 using the *TRANSFER LAYER* tool to perform a multitemporal combination of the RGB obtaining a 201619_B1B14 raster where the seven bands of 2016 and the seven bands of 2019 are obtained and a RGB multitemporary combination is performed [37]. For the realization of the two models, the following process has been applied; Model 1, use of the infrared (IR) band of the year 2019, IR2016 and red (R) 2016, obtaining the infrared band raster. Model 2) NDVI of 2016, NDVI2019 and AZUL2016 where the resulting raster of the NDVI has been obtained. It should be clarified that each of these bands was placed in each canyon, that is, IR2019 was in the red canyon IR2016 in the green canyon and Red2016 in the blue canyon. From this two RASTERs were obtained that we placed as NDV_TOTAL where two different models were obtained in order to conduct comparisons, as used also in previous studies [73, 74].

The Multitemporal Normalized Vegetation Index has been used for a third check, the bands B5_2016 and B4_2016 were used separately. With the Raster Calculator tool

(NDVI formula: IR-R/IR + R) and NDVI16 was obtained that reflects the growing vegetation for 2016 and a similar procedure has been performed for the year 2019.

4 Results and Discussion

We analyzed the change in land use by comparing lansat8 images using geoinformatics tools, as listed in Table 2 from the given four classes defined on Santa Cruz Island in two different periods of time being March 2016 and April 2019.

4.1 Agricultural and Forest Mosaic Class

This category has been established based on agricultural and forestry aptitude, which are formed by the grouping of the edaphic, geomorphological and climatic characteristics of the rural area. The items with the highest production volume are coffee (*Coffea arabica*), corn (*Zea mais L*), cucurbits, vegetables, citrus, fattening and small-scale dairy production [38]. Due to the conditions of continuous humidity, plant productivity remains high throughout the year [39–41], the expansion of the agricultural frontier could increase the loss of biodiversity, jeopardizing the long-term supply of the ecosystem services on which human well-being depends [42, 43]. There has been a migration trend to cities, which has led to the accelerated expansion of invasive species [44]. Invasive species are considered one of the main threats that may be able to break the fragile ecological balance [45]. The overall productivity of the local agricultural and livestock sector is relatively low and lacks to meet the local demand [46]. The forest is dominated by the endemic tree *Scalesia pedunculata* and constitutes the habitat of many endemic and native species. Historically, the Scalesia forest has been widely cut down, so that only 1% of this type of habitat remains on Santa Cruz Island [47]. The Scalesia forest is dominated by the short-lived tree *Scalesia pedunculata* and some species of scattered shrubs, suggesting that there are vacant niches [48]. In addition, *S. pedunculata* experiences a massive periodic death as a regeneration mechanism [49].

Table 2. Comparative values resulting from the processing of satellite images of the years 2016–2019

Category	Classes	2016 Hectars	%	2019 Hectars	%	Differ. 2016–19
0	Empty	86.398,11	50,26%	86398,11	50,26%	0,00%
1	Agricult. and forest mosaic	12.481,20	7,26%	12747,15	7,42%	0,15%
2	Growing vegetation	5.756,85	3,35%	31127,49	18,11%	14,76%
3	Infrastructure	657,99	0,38%	425,25	0,25%	−0,14%
4	Bare soil/rock	66.603,51	38,75%	41199,66	23,97%	−14,78%
	Total	171.897,66	100,00%	171.897,66	100,00%	

4.2 Growing Vegetation Class

For the year 2019 the Growing Vegetation Class had an area of 31,127.49 ha (18.11%) while in 2016 it had an area of 5,756.85 ha (3.35%). This yielded an increase of 25,370.64 ha, which proves the effectiveness of the Galápagos Verde 2050 project, as being a multi-institutional and interdisciplinary initiative that, on the one hand, seeks to contribute to the sustainability of the archipelago through restoration actions ecological and sustainable agriculture, and on the other, become an example for the world by demonstrating that it is possible to achieve sustainable development [35] (Fig. 4).

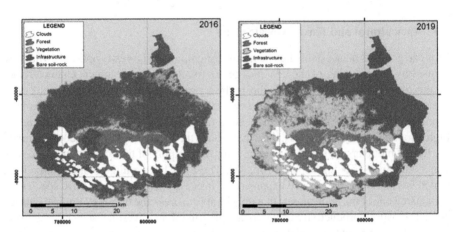

Fig. 4. Multitemporal evaluation of land use on Santa Cruz Island, Galapagos.

Hereby, the main objectives of the project have been fivefold such as: 1) to contribute to the restoration of degraded ecosystems with the purpose of recovering and or maintaining their capacity to generate services for the human being; 2) to control and or eradicate invasive introduced species in areas of high ecological value; 3) to accelerate the recovery process of native and endemic flora species of the archipelago of very slow natural growth; 4) to reduce the risk of entry of exotic species through sustainable agricultural production, by contributing to local self-supply; and 5) to contribute to energize the economy through sustainable agricultural production and at any time of the year. The three phases of Project 2050 have been firstly Phase 1 (January 2014 to December 2016), which included ecological restoration actions in the Baltra, Santa Cruz, South Plaza and Floreana islands. Secondly, Phase 2 (January 2017 to December 2018), where ecological restoration actions were implemented in degraded ecosystems of Floreana and defined as priorities by the Directorate of the Galapagos National Park (DPNG) and finally Phase 3 (January 2019 to December 2050), where the benefits of using the Groasis (TG), Cocoon and Hidrogel Technology technologies are planned to restore the ecosystems and species defined by the DPNG [35].

4.3 Infrastructure Class

As an infrastructure class, the populated centers have been geo-referenced as urban (Puerto Ayora) and rural (Bellavista and Santa Rosa). For the year 2016, the surface area of the infrastructure identified has been 657.99 ha, being equivalent to 3.34% of the evaluated supervision. Urbanization is commonly considered as a positive process linked to economic and social development, where rural areas are transformed into urban centers [50]. However, there is some concern about the impact modus vivendi has on large urban settlements in populated centers in Santa Cruz due to the tendency to expand [51]. For the year 2019 the infrastructure occupied an area of less than 425.25 ha (0.25%).

The landscape transformation has a great impact on biodiversity, water cycles, local and regional climate, and a range of ecosystem services. This is particularly important in nearby urban areas or within protected areas, and that are growing in area and population, as in Santa Cruz and other islands, where urban settlements arose before the establishment of the Galapagos National Park [52]. The resulting value for 2019 is influenced by the percentage of clouds (greater than 30%) in the satellite image of the Landsat 8 sensor, since there has been an expansion of the infrastructure (Fig. 5), corroborating a potential increase of the impermeable surface with a deep implication for the human-ecological systems of Santa Cruz [53]. Specifically, the growth of urban areas in the Galapagos are related to a deterioration of wildlife health [54] and endemic vegetation [55] human health and infrastructure [56, 57] and in the relationship between wildlife and humans [58].

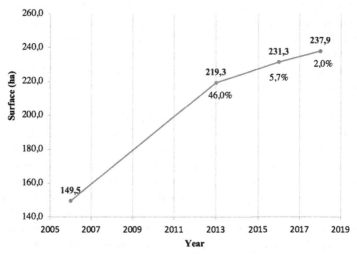

Fig. 5. Infrastructure dynamics in Santa Cruz for the time period of 2006 to 2018. Data represent hectares, in red increase in percentages. (Color figure online)

Although there are new efforts to understand how population growth affects public services in the Galapagos Islands [57, 59] and the contribution to the invasion of exotic species [60], there is a lack of research to assess the impact of urban infrastructure growth on endemic species and how urban ecology programs may be built to improve potential impacts. Urban growth is usually accompanied by an increase in the impermeable surface [61], which is defined as a type of surface material that does not allow water infiltration directly into the ground and is mainly associated with asphalt infrastructures and concrete in urban areas, including streets, parking lots, homes and roofs [62, 63]. The amount of impermeable surface in a landscape is an important indicator of its environmental quality [64]. The most obvious direct driver of the land change in Galapagos is related to the development of the tourism industry on the islands [13, 56]. However, there are many underlying causes, beyond number of people who come to Galapagos to live or visit, which contributes to the increase of impervious surfaces on the islands. The reasons for this may have to do with cultural expectations or the belief that pavement is a sign of progress or development in a border environment, which is also related to the lack of environmental awareness of the immense social and ecological value of Green spaces for locals [65–67].

4.4 Bare Soil-Rock Class

Bare soils and rocks are a basic component for the Galapagos ecosystems. Remote sensing technologies have been one of the main methods to provide detailed information on land use and cover [68]. The regular soils in Santa Cruz are composed of bare rock, while in the arid zone (up to 120 m above sea level) there is a thin layer of lithosols. From this area up to 450 m above sea level (within the agricultural zone), there are soils with thicknesses of up to 1 m, with a clayey texture and in some cases silty loam to fine sand [69]. In 2016 there has been a floor area of 66,603.51 ha equivalent to 38.75% of the simulated area. Hereby, the given soils are formed after the decomposition of lava flow surfaces caused by weathering. The modern landscape is covered with poorly developed black soils. The oldest soils are brown Andisols, and the oldest surfaces exhibit eroded and highly cohesive Red soils. The average soil pH is 6.37 to 6.52 in the humid highlands of Santa Cruz Island. For the year 2019 the ground cover is of about 41,199.66 ha (Table 3).

The soils of Santa Cruz store around 706 Gg of Organic Soil Carbon (COS) in the top 10 cm. COS is a small part of the global carbon cycle, which involves the carbon cycle through the soil, vegetation, the ocean and the atmosphere [70]. The accumulation of COS is mainly due to climatic factors that are influenced by the altitude and direction of the winds. An increase in rainfall, as predicted by climate change scenarios, will result in a general increase in COS populations and will probably modify the composition of vegetation species within the different bioclimatic strata of the islands [71]. COS is important for its contributions to food production, mitigation and adaptation to climate change, and the achievement of the Sustainable Development Goals (SDGs). Soil biodiversity (including organisms such as bacteria, fungi, proto zoos, insects, worms, other invertebrates and mammals) combined with COS, shapes the metabolic capacity of soils and is believed to play a crucial role in increasing food production and resistance to climate change. Climate change is one of the main threats to ecosystems in Santa Cruz [72].

4.5 Cross-Tabulation Procedure

The results of the cross-tabulation procedure obtained from the IDRISI program are displayed in Table 3. The 0 is not taken into account because they are black pixels outside the study area. Some 8507.79 ha have been maintained between 2016 and 2019,

Table 3. Cross tabulation results

Hectars (Ha)	Legend of 2016	Legend of 2019	Elements of 2016	Element changes in 2019
86398,11	0	0	Empty	Empty, unconsidered
8507,79	1	1	Agricultural and Forest	Agricultural and Forest
492,48	2	1	Vegetation	Agricultural and Forest
119,7	3	1	Infrastructure	Agricultural and Forest
3627,18	4	1	Bare soil-rock	Agricultural and Forest
3313,44	1	2	Agricultural and Forest	Vegetation
1906,65	2	2	Vegetation	Vegetation
107,55	3	2	Infrastructure	Vegetation
25799,85	4	2	Bare soil-rock	Vegetation
3,87	1	3	Agricultural and Forest	Infrastructure
3,15	2	3	Vegetation	Infrastructure
299,61	3	3	Infrastructure	Infrastructure
118,62	4	3	Bare soil-rock	Infrastructure
656,1	1	4	Agricultural and Forest	Bare soil-rock
3354,57	2	4	Vegetation	Bare soil-rock
131,13	3	4	Infrastructure	Bare soil-rock
37057,86	4	4	Bare soil-rock	Bare soil-rock

492.48 ha ceased to be growing vegetation and became an agricultural and forest mosaic, while some 119.7 and some 3627.18 ha has gone from being infrastructure and bare soil respectively to growing vegetation between the same time period. Furthermore, some 3313.44 ha has changed from being agricultural mosaic and forest to growing vegetation, as well as some 107.55 ha of infrastructure and some 25799.85 ha of bare soil-rock. This is the most significant change. The changes towards infrastructure has been of 3.87 ha of previously agricultural and forest mosaic, 3.15 ha of growing vegetation and 118.62 ha of bare soil-rock. Finally, the change into bare soil-rock has been of some 656.1 ha of agricultural and forest mosaic, 3354.57 ha of vegetation and some 131.13 ha from infrastructure, while 37057.86 ha remained as bare soil-rock.

According to the general table of the years 2016 to 2019, it is obtained that the agricultural and forest mosaic has increased by 0.15% compared to the year 2016. The growing vegetation is 14.76% more abundant than the one found in 2016 which is the most significant change found. Infrastructure has decreased by 0.14% compared to 2016. Bare soil has decreased by 14.78% due to the increase in vegetation and agricultural mosaic and forest, as previously mentioned.

We analyzed the change in land use by comparing landsat8 images using geoinformatics tools, where we performed the Multitemporal Normalized Vegetation Index and the NDVI. The comparisons with NDVI show that there were changes for the year 2019 with a multitemporal combination with infrared and red bands in RGB (8_4_3), where the magenta color is the change of vegetation. It has been verified that the vegetation has not undergone changes. The blue color and variation in the same contrast does not change from the land use coverage and the yellow and green color exits a slight variation, but without obvious changes. We performed the multitemporal combination of NDVI in RGB (11_10_1), where the magenta color presents a change of vegetation, again verifying that the vegetation has not undergone changes. The blue color and variation in the same contrast does not change the coverage of use ground. The yellow and green color equal slight variation, but without obvious changes.

Therefore, a change detection is intended to identify the variation of given cell between two images, in this case, the study takes into account two images of 2016 and 2019 in similar periods, which are georeferenced so that the cell of one image is the same as the other. Therefore, the detection identified whether or not there has been any change. This may be verified where the bare soil-rock in 2016 and in 2019 has been covered by vegetation, as the change detection highlighted this area (Fig. 6).

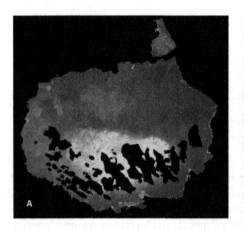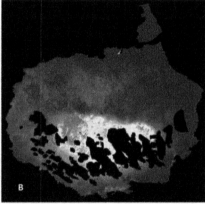

Fig. 6. A) Raster resulting infrared band of 2016 B) Raster resulting from the NDVI of 2019.

5   Conclusions

The visual comparison between the methodologies used of NDVI demonstrated a variation in the land use of Santa Cruz Island, both in the part of growing vegetation and the variation of soil and forest.

The application of remote sensing techniques in threatened ecosystems such as the Galapagos Islands has proven to be a powerful tool for decision making. Specifically in the case of Santa Cruz Island, it will allow precise mapping and modeling techniques at relatively low costs to combat invasive species such as guava and wax apple.

The prevalence of the fragile island ecosystem now depends on the urban metabolism present in the villages of the archipelago.

References

1. Peterson, C.H., Lipcius, R.N.: Conceptual progress towards predicting quantitative ecosystem benefits of ecological restorations. Mar. Ecol. Prog. Ser. **264**, 297–307 (2003)
2. Palmer, M.A., Ambrose, R.F., Poff, N.L.: Ecological theory and community restoration ecology. Restor. Ecol. **5**(4), 291–300 (1997)
3. Allen, C.D., et al.: Ecological restoration of southwestern ponderosa pine ecosystems: a broad perspective. Ecol. Appl. **12**(5), 1418–1433 (2002)
4. Palmer, M.A., et al.: Standards for ecologically successful river restoration. J. Appl. Ecol. **42**(2), 208–217 (2005)
5. Zedler, J.B.: Progress in wetland restoration ecology. Trends Ecol. Evol. **15**(10), 402–407 (2000)
6. Kondolf, G.M., Micheli, E.R.: Evaluating stream restoration projects. Environ. Manag. **19**(1), 1–15 (1995)
7. Simmonds, J.: UNESCO world heritage convention. Art Antiquity L. **2**, 251 (1997)
8. Stovel, H.: The evaluation of cultural properties for the World Heritage List. Ekistics, 255–260 (1994)
9. Makoto, F.E., Castillo, M.: The challenges in Galapagos: a view from UNESCO. Galapagos Res. **65**, 37–39 (2008)
10. Kenchington, R.A.: Tourism in the Galapagos islands: the dilemma of conservation. Environ. Conserv. **16**(3), 227–232 (1989)
11. Padilla, L.R., Gottdenker, N., Deem, S.L., Cruz, M.: Domestic and peridomestic animals in Galapagos: health policies and practices. In: Parker, P. (ed.) Disease Ecology, pp. 269–291. Springer, Cham (2018). https://doi.org/10.1007/978-3-319-65909-1_10
12. Mestanza, C., Botero, C.M., Anfuso, G., Chica-Ruiz, J.A., Pranzini, E., Mooser, A.: Beach litter in Ecuador and the Galapagos islands: A baseline to enhance environmental conservation and sustainable beach tourism. Mar. Pollut. Bull. **140**, 573–578 (2019)
13. Pizzitutti, F., et al.: Scenario planning for tourism management: a participatory and system dynamics model applied to the Galapagos islands of Ecuador. J. Sustain. Tour. **25**, 1117–1137 (2017)
14. Pazmiño, A., Serrao-Neumann, S., Low Choy, D.: Towards comprehensive policy integration for the sustainability of small islands: a landscape-scale planning approach for the Galápagos islands. Sustainability **10**(4), 1228 (2018)
15. Jaramillo, P., Cueva, P., Jiménez, E., Ortiz, J.: Galápagos Verde 2050. Puerto Ayora, Isla Santa Cruz: Fundación Charles Darwin (2014). http://www.darwinfoundation.org/en/scienceresea rch/galapagos-verde-2050/
16. Reynolds, R.W., Geist, D.J.: Petrology of lavas from sierra negra volcano, isabela island, galápagos archipelago. J. Geophys. Res.: Solid Earth **100**(B12), 24537–24553 (1995)
17. Toulkeridis, T.: The volcanoes of the Galapagos. Quito, Ecuador, 322 p. (2019)
18. White, W.M., McBirney, A.R., Duncan, R.A.: Petrology and geochemistry of the Galápagos Islands: Portrait of a pathological mantle plume. Journal of Geophysical Research: Solid Earth **98**(B11), 19533–19563 (1993)

19. Snell, H.M., Stone, P.A., Snell, H.L.: A summary of geographical characteristics of the Galapagos Islands. J. Biogeogr. **23**(5), 619–624 (1996)
20. Jorda-Bordehore, L., Toulkeridis, T., Romero-Crespo, P.L., Jordá-Bordehore, R., García-Garizabal, I.: Stability assessment of volcanic lava tubes in the Galápagos using engineering rock mass classifications and an empirical approach. Int. J. Rock Mech. Min. Sci. **89**, 55–67 (2016)
21. Jordá-Bordehore, L., Toulkeridis, T.: Stability assessment of volcanic natural caves – Lava tunnels – Using both empirical and numerical approach, case studies of galapagos islands (Ecuador) and lanzarote Island (Canary – Spain). Rock Mechanics and Rock Engineering: From the Past to the Future. In: International Symposium on International Society for Rock Mechanics, ISRM 2016; Cappadocia, Turkey, vol. 2, pp. 835–840 (2016)
22. Padrón, E., et al.: Fumarole/plume and diffuse CO_2 emission from Sierra Negra volcano, Galapagos archipelago. Bull. Volcanol. **74**, 1509–1519 (2012)
23. Peterson, I., Harder, R., Robinson, I.K.: Probe-diverse ptychography. Ultramicroscopy **171**, 77–81 (2016)
24. Redpath, S.M., et al.: Understanding and managing conservation conflicts. Trends Ecol. Evol. **28**, 100–109 (2013)
25. Chan, K.M.A., et al.: Opinion: why protect nature? Rethinking values and the environment. Proc. Natl. Acad. Sci. U.S.A. **113**, 1462–1465 (2016)
26. Andrade, G.S.M., Rhodes, J.R.: Protected areas and local communities: an inevitable partnership toward successful conservation strategies? Ecol. Soc. **17**, 14 (2012)
27. Benjaminsen, T.A., Svarstad, H.: The Death of an Elephant: Conservation Discourses Versus Practices in Africa. In Forum for Development Studies, pp. 385–408. Taylor & Francis, London (2010)
28. Armitage, D.R., et al.: Cogestión adaptativa para la complejidad socioecológica. Frente. Ecol. Reinar. **7**, 95–102 (2009)
29. García-Frapolli, E., Ramos-Fernández, G., Galicia, E., Serrano, A.: The complex reality of biodiversity conservation through natural protected area policy: Three cases from the Yucatan peninsula. Mexico. Land Use Policy **26**, 715–722 (2009)
30. Raik, D.B., Wilson, A.L., Decker, D.J.: Power en la gestión de recursos naturales: una aplicación de la teoría. Soc. Nat. Recursos **21**, 729–739 (2008)
31. Niemelä, J., et al.: Identifying, managing and monitoring conflicts between forest biodiversity conservation and other human interests in Europe. For. Policy Econ. **7**, 877–890 (2005)
32. Campbell, L.M.: Práctica de conservación local y discurso global: una ecología política de la conservación de las tortugas marinas. Ana. Asoc. A.m. Geogr. **97**, 313–334 (2007)
33. Benitez-Capistros, F., Couenberg, P., Nieto, A., Cabrera, F., Blake, S.: Identifying shared strategies and solutions to the human-giant tortoise interactions in Santa Cruz, Galapagos: a nominal group technique application. Sustainability **11**(10), 2937 (2019)
34. Jaramillo, P.: Galápagos Verde 2050: Una oportunidad para la restauración de ecosistemas degradados y el fomento de una agricultura sostenible en el archipiélago. In: Informe Galápagos 2013–2014. DPNG, CGREG, FCD y GC. Puerto Ayora, Galápagos, Ecuador, pp. 133–143 (2015)
35. Jaramillo, P., Cueva, P., Jiménez, E., Ortiz, J.: CDF. 2014. Green Galapagos 2050. Puerto Ayora, Galapagos, Ecuador, 54 p. (2014)
36. Irwansyah, E.: Geographic Information System (GIS) Using IDRISI Software: Application in Coastal Management. Geoinforma (2012)
37. Reyes, D.: Use of multitemporal indexes in the identification of forest fires - a case study of Southern Chile. In: 2019 Sixth International Conference on eDemocracy & eGovernment (ICEDEG), Quito, Ecuador (2019), pp. 203–210. https://doi.org/10.1109/icedeg.2019.873 4443

38. MAG: Informe de Gestión: Periodo 1 de enero al 31 de diciembre de 2018. Dirección Distrital de Galápagos – Ministerio de Agricultura y Ganadería, 26 p. Galápagos, Ecuador (2019)
39. Blake, S., Guézou, A., Deem, S.L., Yackulic, C.B., Cabrera, F.: The dominance of introduced plant species in the diets of migratory Galapagos tortoises increases with elevation on a human-occupied island. Biotropica 47, 246–258 (2015)
40. Blake, S., et al.: Seed dispersal by Galápagos tortoises. J. Biogeogr. 39, 1961–1972 (2012)
41. Blake, S., et al.: Vegetation dynamics drive segregation by body size in Galapagos tortoises migrating across altitudinal gradients. J. Anim. Ecol. 82, 310–321 (2013)
42. Kier, G., et al.: A global assessment of endemism and species richness across island and mainland regions. Proc. Natl. Acad. Sci. U.S.A. 106, 9322–9327 (2009)
43. Kreft, H., Jetz, W., Mutke, J., Kier, G., Barthlott, W.: Global diversity of island floras from a macroecological perspective. Ecol. Lett. (2007)
44. Galapagos National Park Service: One Area in Need of Renovation. Research Priorities of the Directorate of the Galapagos National Park (2009)
45. Bush, M.B., Restrepo, A., Collins, A.F.: Galápagos history, restoration, and a shifted baseline. Restor. Ecol. 22(3), 296–298 (2014)
46. Puente-Rodríguez, D., Bos, A.B., Koerkamp, P.W.G.: Rethinking livestock production systems on the Galápagos islands: organizing knowledge-practice interfaces through reflexive interactive design. Environ. Sci. Policy 101, 166–174 (2019)
47. Mauchamp, A., Atkinson, R.: Pérdida de hábitat rápida, reciente e irreversible: Los bosques de Scalesia en las islas Galápagos. In: Informe Galápagos 2009–2010. Puerto Ayora, Galápagos, Ecuador (2010)
48. Itow, S.: Zonation pattern, succession process and invasion by aliens in species poor insular vegetation of the Galápagos islands. Glob. Environ. Res. 7, 39–58 (2003)
49. Jäger, H., Tye, A., Kowarik, I.: Tree invasion in naturally treeless environments: impacts of quinine (Cinchona pubescens) trees on native vegetation in Galapagos. Biol. Cons. 140, 297–307 (2007)
50. Poumanyvong, P., Kaneko, S.: Does urbanization lead to less energy use and lower CO2 emissions? A cross-country analysis. Ecol. Econ. 70, 434–444 (2010)
51. López, J., Dunn, J.: Título del artículo. In: Informe Galápagos 2015–2016. DPNG, CGREG, FCD, pp. 57–61 (2017)
52. ME (Ministerio de Economía): Primer Censo de Población del Ecuador 1950; Dirección General de Estadísticas y Censos: Quito, Ecuador (1960)
53. Walsh, S.J., Mena, C.F.: Coupled human-natural systems: interactions of social, terrestrial & marine sub-systems in the Galapagos islands. Proc. Natl. Acad. Sci. U.S.A. 113, 14536–14543 (2016)
54. Zylberberg, M., Lee, K.A., Klasing, K.C., Wikelski, M.: Variation with land use of immune function and prevalence of avian pox in Galapagos finches. Conserv. Biol. 27, 103–112 (2013)
55. De la Torre, S.: Research in agricultural and urban areas in Galapagos: a biological perspective. In: Walsh, S.J., Mena, C.F. (eds.) Science and Conservation in the Galapagos Islands, pp. 185–198. Springer, New York (2013). https://doi.org/10.1007/978-1-4614-5794-7_11
56. Walsh, S.J., McCleary, A.L., Heumann, B.W., Brewington, L., Raczkowski, E.J., Mena, C.F.: Community expansion and infrastructure development: implications for human health and environmental quality in the Galapagos Islands of Ecuador. J. Lat. Am. Geogr. 9, 137–159 (2010)
57. Ragazzi, M., Catellani, R., Rada, E.C., Torretta, V., Salazar-Valenzuela, X.: Management of urban wastewater on one of the Galapagos islands. Sustainability 8, 208 (2016)
58. Denkinger, J., Quiroga, D., Murillo, J.C.: Assessing human–wildlife conflicts and benefits of Galápagos sea lions on San Cristobal Island, Galápagos. In: Denkinger, J., Vinueza, L. (eds.) The Galapagos Marine Reserve: A Dynamic Social-Ecological System, pp. 285–305. Springer, New York (2014). https://doi.org/10.1007/978-3-319-02769-2_13

59. Reyes, M.F., Trifunović, N., Sharma, S., Kennedy, M.: Data assessment for water demand and supply balance on the island of Santa Cruz (Galápagos islands). Desalin. Water Treat. **57**, 21335–21349 (2016)
60. Toral-Granda, M.V., et al.: Alien species pathways to the Galapagos Islands, Ecuador. PLoS ONE **12**, e0184379 (2017)
61. Dams, J., Dujardin, J., Reggers, R., Bashir, I., Canters, F., Batelaan, O.: Mapping impervious surface change from remote sensing for hydrological modeling. J. Hydrol. **485**, 84–95 (2013)
62. Wang, J., Huang, B., Fu, D., Atkinson, P.M.: Spatiotemporal variation in surface urban heat island intensity and associated determinants across major Chinese cities. Remote Sens. **7**, 3670–3689 (2015)
63. Yang, J., He, Y.: Automated mapping of impervious surfaces in urban and suburban areas: linear spectral unmixing of high spatial resolution imagery. Int. J. Appl. Earth Obs. Geoinf. **54**, 53–64 (2017)
64. El Garouani, A., Mulla, D.J., El Garouani, S., Knight, J.: Analysis of urban growth and sprawl from remote sensing data: case of Fez, Morocco. Int. J. Sustain. Built Environ. **6**, 160–169 (2017)
65. Zhang, B., Xie, G., Zhang, C., Zhang, J.: The economic benefits of rainwater-runoff reduction by urban green spaces: a case study in Beijing. China. J. Environ. Manag **100**, 65–71 (2012)
66. Jenerette, G.D., Harlan, S.L., Stefanov, W.L., Martin, C.A.: Ecosystem services and urban heat riskscape moderation: water, green spaces, and social inequality in Phoenix. USA. Ecol. Appl. **21**, 2637–2651 (2011)
67. Young, R.F.: Managing municipal green space for ecosystem services. Urban For. Urban Green. **9**, 313–321 (2010)
68. Benítez, F., Mena, C., Zurita-Arthos, L.: Urban land cover change in ecologically fragile environments: the case of the Galapagos islands. Land **7**(1), 21 (2018)
69. Ministerio de Agricultura, Ganadería, Acuacultura y Pesca (MAGAP): Proyecto: Almacenamiento de agua para uso agropecuario a través de micro-reservorios en la provincia de Galápagos. Santa Cruz – Puerto Ayora (2014)
70. FAO: Carbono Orgánico del Suelo: el potencial oculto. Organización de las Naciones Unidas para la Alimentación y Agricultura Roma, Italia (2017)
71. Rial, M., Cortizas, A.M., Taboada, T., Rodríguez-Lado, L.: Soil organic carbon stocks in Santa Cruz island, Galapagos, under different climate change scenarios. CATENA **156**, 74–81 (2017)
72. Larrea, I., Di Carlo, G.: Climate change vulnerability assessment of the Galapagos Islands. World Wildlife Fund/Conservation International, Quito, Ecuador (2009)
73. Villacís, M.G.M., Ruiz, D.A.C., Powney, E.P.K., Guzmán, J.A.M.,& Toulkeridis, T.: Index relationship of vegetation with the development of a Quinoa Crop (Chenopodium quinoa) in its first phenological stages in central Ecuador based on GIS techniques. In: 2020 Seventh International Conference on eDemocracy & eGovernment (ICEDEG), pp. 191–200. IEEE (2020)
74. Ruiz, D.A.C., Villacís, M.G.M., Kirby, E., Guzmán, J.A.M., Toulkeridis, T.: Correlation of NDVI obtained by different methodologies of spectral data collection in a commercial crop of Quinoa (Chenopodium Quinoa) in central Ecuador. In: 2020 Seventh International Conference on eDemocracy & eGovernment (ICEDEG), pp. 208–215. IEEE (2020)

Uncertainty Reduction in the Neural Network's Weather Forecast for the Andean City of Quito Through the Adjustment of the Posterior Predictive Distribution Based on Estimators

Ricardo Llugsi[1,3]([✉]) [ID], Allyx Fontaine[2], Pablo Lupera[1] [ID], Jessica Bechet[2] [ID],
and Samira El Yacoubi[3] [ID]

[1] National Polytechnic School, Quito, Ecuador
{ricardo.llugsi,pablo.lupera}@epn.edu.ec
[2] Université de Guyane, Cayenne, French Guiana
{allyx.fontaine,jessica.bechet}@univ-guyane.fr
[3] Université de Perpignan via Domitia, Perpignan, France
yacoubi@univ-perp.fr

Abstract. The weather forecast in cities as Quito is highly complicated due to its proximity to Latitude 0° and because it is located in the Andes mountains range. A statistical post-processing is compulsory in order to improve the output from the physical model and to improve the weather forecast in the city. A neural network can be applied in order to carry out this task but it is necessary first to reduce its uncertainty. The Bayesian Neural Networks (BNN) have been studied deeply thanks to its probability analysis, the uncertainty can be approximated. In this paper an analysis founded on the adjustment of the posterior predictive distribution based on estimators is carried out in order to reduce the prediction error variation (implicitly the uncertainty) in a Short-Term Weather Forecast for the Andean city of Quito. From the analysis it is obtained a maximum error forecast of 12% and it is proven that for Long Short Term Memory (LSTM) structures, the variation of the error reduces almost to the half with weight-decays of 2.04×10^{-7} and 2.23×10^{-7}.

Keywords: Neural network · Uncertainty · Bayesian · Weight decay · Walk forward validation · Dropout regularization

1 Introduction

In Meteorology it is well known that obtaining the weather forecast becomes difficult getting closer to the Equator. This happens because of any variation in the meteorological system at the Intertropical Convergence Zone significantly alters the output of the physical model of any forecast system. If additionally, it is brought to an end that the Andes mountain range crosses latitude 0°, the weather forecast for a city located in this place will become very difficult. The city of Quito is located at a height of 2800 m

© Springer Nature Switzerland AG 2020
G. Rodriguez Morales et al. (Eds.): TICEC 2020, CCIS 1307, pp. 535–548, 2020.
https://doi.org/10.1007/978-3-030-62833-8_39

above the sea level in the Andean Region of Ecuador and it is crossed by the equatorial line. The geographical shape of the city influences the meteorology of the place, mainly creating microclimates. And even the convective process caused by the altitude difference between the city and the Guagua Pichincha Volcano deeply affects any classical methodology applied for weather forecast too. The core of a Weather Forecast System is the physical model, but a statistical post-processing is necessary too in order to correct erroneous outputs. For the physical model, the establishment of initial conditions is crucial and in order to do so information from ground stations are required. A Weather Forecast System regularly uses the data from Conventional Weather Stations (CWS), Automatic Weather Stations (AWS) and Satellite Imagery with the aiming of predict weather [1]. In developing countries, the satellite imagery has become the main source to generate weather forecast because of implementing CWS and AWS is costly. In general, in Ecuador the data from CWS is taken 3 times per day what implies a high probability of erroneous weather forecast. In the light of the above it has to be said that the physical model needs adequate initial conditions to start its processing and its weather forecast always needs to be corrected for any imprecision that can occurs in real time. The main problem in a Weather Forecast systems that relies a lot on satellite imagery is that the system does not show the on surface convective systems that are generated for the presence of clouds. This becomes a big problem because of the geography of the Andean Region and, especially in Quito, does not have enough surface information for the lack of AWS transmitting data in real time [2]. This problem can be solved through the implementation of AWS with internet transmission capabilities to send data (i.e. temperature, humidity, pressure, etc.). Bearing in mind the geography of the Andean Region, and specially the city of Quito, this alternative is costly and hard to maintain. One alternative is the acquisition of data through low cost small single-board computers and machine learning. Namely, the data acquired comes from sensors connected to the single board computer and entered into a neural network to implement a prediction of a certain parameter (i.e. temperature). In this point how to determine the uncertainty of the predicted data is crucial to know if the neural network is performing properly as the statistical post-processing needed to correct the data from the physical model. Bayesian Neural Networks (BNN) uses the concept of probability distributions over their weights, mainly because it allows to capture the uncertainty within the learning model. In [3] it has been proved that any neural network using dropout regularization becomes a Bayesian Network and additionally the author derivate some concepts from the Bayesian analysis (more precisely the adjustment of the posterior predictive distribution based on estimators during the use of the dropout regularization technique) that possibly can be applied to decrease (in a certain way) the uncertainty in the model's forecast. It is necessary to consider that in [3] the author focuses its efforts in the treatment of images nevertheless its guidelines could be applied in treatment of Time Series as is proposed in this work. In this paper several trials to prove the above have been conducted and the findings discovered using this approach together with the walk-forward validation are presented.

The paper is organized as follows: Sect. 2 describes the problem that originate the present analysis and the actual situation of the city of Quito. Section 3 is committed to describes the preliminaries related to the proposed method, related works, uncertainty in Bayesian modelling as well as in Neural Networks, the Walk Forward validation technique, the AWS network implementation, the description of the neural network used and how the experimentation was conducted. The results of the trials and a discussion of the outcomes are presented in Sect. 4, while Sect. 5 concludes this work and gives some perspectives for future works.

2   Problem Statement

Quito is an Andean city located at 2850 m above mean sea level. in the north of the Sierra region in Ecuador. Its approximate dimensions are 50 km long in a south-north direction and 4 km wide from east to west. It is located at the foot of the active volcano Guagua Pichincha and is populated with approximately 2.7 million inhabitants, thus becoming the most populous city in Ecuador. The city is divided in its central part by the hill of El Panecillo (3035 m above the sea level) and to the east by the hills of Puengasí, Guanguiltagua and Itchimbía. This geography creates several microclimates that makes very difficult to get a proper forecast of the weather for the city. In order to show the magnitude of this problem the topographic map of Quito [4], courtesy NASA/JPL-Caltech, is presented in Fig. 1.

Fig. 1. Topographic Map of Quito.

Bearing in mind that the output of the physical model in a Forecasting system should be corrected, a statistical post-processing based on Neural Networks could be applied to improve the weather forecast in the city. The first step to use the neural network is the environmental data acquisition that, in this case, comes from AWS installed in the city.

Since its creation (1961) the National Institute of Meteorology and Hydrology (INAMHI) is responsible of the establishment, operation and maintenance of the Hydro-meteorological Stations Network of the country. With the purpose of carrying out a proper measurement of climate parameters INAMHI has installed 3 conventional stations [4] in Quito: Iñaquito, Izobamba and La Tola. These stations are kilometers apart from each other and in consequence do not allow the acquisition of proper data. Bearing in mind that INAMHI just has 3 AWS in Quito five new AWS for data acquisition were installed in February of 2020, see Fig. 1 and Table 1. The temperature data between the period March 18th 2020 to May 31st 2020 from this new AWS networks were considered to be entered to the Neural Network.

Table 1. Geographic Coordinates of the AWS

AWS	Latitude	Longitude	Altitude
1	0°19′34.40″S	78°32′59.88″W	3014.5
3	0° 8′25.32″S	78°30′20.32″W	2917.6
4	0° 0′14.42″N	78°26′35.60″W	2408.4
5	0°1′34.89″S	78°33′18.17″W	2909.9
6	0°12′50.66″S	78°31′18.38″W	2976.1

3   Materials and Methods

3.1   Related Work

The Bayesian modelling has become more popular during recent years, principally because it uses the variation of the weight distribution of a neural network to induct a Bayesian behavior in a certain model. This allows the determination of certain parameters such as uncertainty, without the necessity of a deep change in the structure of the neural network. In [5] a framework that allows to estimate the probabilistic robustness for a BNN with statistical guarantees (i.e., with a priori error and confidence bounds) was developed in order to obtain a reliable image recognition system. This work focuses mainly in the development of BNNs that takes into account model and data uncertainty to capture the probability of the existence of adversarial examples in an image. The use of Bayesian Modelling has aroused so much curiosity that even analysis at "unit level" [5] and other kind of Bayesian neural networks [6] (i.e. functional variational Bayesian Neural Networks (fBNNs)) have been developed. In the 1st case the aim was to characterize the marginal prior distribution of the units in Deep Learning and in the 2nd case was to carry out tasks such as extrapolation in large datasets over various structures with reliable uncertainties. Despite the apparent advantages offered by the Bayesian Modelling, some authors state that approximate Bayesian inference methods struggle to capture true posteriors probabilities [7]. So it is important to evaluate properly and carefully a method based on Bayesian modeling when it is implemented together with new approaches, as in this case where the Walk Forward validation is used. In order to do that different error metrics such as RMSE (Root Mean Squared Error), MSE (Mean Squared Error), MAE (Mean Absolute Error) and MAPE (Mean Absolute Percentage Error)) are adopted to guarantee an adequate analysis of the proposed method.

3.2 Uncertainty in Bayesian Modelling

The Bayesian modelling is commonly used because it gives a standard approach to model uncertainty through probability. The Bayes' theorem [9] describes a relationship between conditional probabilities. In Bayesian regression the aim is to obtain the parameters .. of a function $y = f^\omega(x)$ that are likely to have generated the outputs $Y = \{y_1, \ldots, y_N\}$ given the training inputs $X = \{x_1, \ldots, x_N\}$. If a dataset X, and Y is given, then the posterior distribution of the function can be described as follows in Eq. (1) [3]:

$$P(\omega|X, Y) = \frac{P(Y|X, \omega)P(\omega)}{P(Y|X)} \tag{1}$$

Where:

$P(\omega)$:   Prior distribution of the degree of belief about the parameter ω before the measurements in the dataset are taken.

$P(Y|X, \omega)$:   Likelihood function, which indicates the probability of obtaining measurement results in the dataset, with that value of parameter ω.

$P(\omega|X, Y)$:   Posterior distribution representing the state of knowledge about parameter ω, after new information has been gained from the measurements

Assuming that the probability distributions follow a continuous function, the Eq. (1) can be rewritten as in the Eq. (2) [3, 9]:

$$P(\omega|X, Y) = \frac{P(Y|X, \omega)}{\int P(Y|X, \omega)P(\omega)d\omega}P(\omega) \tag{2}$$

When the integral, presented in Eq. (2), is evaluated it can be said that the likelihood is marginalizing over ω (marginal likelihood). Now, bearing in mind that the value of the integral of the denominator could be considered as a normalizing factor, called *model evidence*, the last equation is written in the following way, see Eq. (3) [3]:

$$P(\omega|X, Y) \propto P(Y|X, \omega)P(\omega) \tag{3}$$

Finally, if new dataset x^* is entered in the model, a prediction of the outputs could be obtained through integration as it is showed in Eq. (4) [3].

$$P(y^*|x^*, X, Y) = \int P(y^*|x^*, \omega)P(\omega|X, Y)d\omega \tag{4}$$

This process is known as Inference. It can be seen that the Bayesian probability theory offers a good method to define the model's uncertainty. Nevertheless, it is associated with high computational cost. For the sake of the argument it needs to be said that $P(\omega|X, Y)$ cannot be evaluated analytically but it can be approximated. In [3] a variational distribution $q_\theta(\omega)$, parametrised by θ, is proposed to evaluate the posterior probability for the Bayesian process in an easiest way. In order to approximate the variational distribution as close as possible to the one from the original model, the Kullback–Leibler (KL) divergence [10] is applied to measure the similarity between two distributions. When

KL divergence is minimized the predictive distribution is approximated to the following relation, see Eq. (5) [3]:

$$P(y^*|x^*, X, Y) \approx \int P(y^*|x^*, \omega)q_\theta^*(\omega)d\omega =: q_\theta^*(y^*|x^*) \tag{5}$$

In Eq. (6), the expected log likelihood (first term) and the prior KL (second term) can be joint to establish the Cost function for the inference, this procedure is known as Variational Inference (VI) [3]. The concept of VI is nowadays broadly applied as a method from machine learning that approximates probability densities through optimization.

$$\hat{\mathcal{L}}_{VI}(\theta) = -\frac{N}{M}\sum_{i\in S}\int q_\theta(\omega)\log p(y_i|f^\omega(x_i))d\omega + KL(q_\theta(\omega)||p(\omega)) \tag{6}$$

Here S is a randomly sampled set of M indices from $\{1, \ldots, N\}$. Then using a Monte Carlo estimator [3] and [7] Eq. 6 can be rewritten as follows, see Eq. 7:

$$\hat{\mathcal{L}}_{MC}(\theta) = -\frac{N}{M}\sum_{i\in S}\log p(y_i|f^\omega(x_i))d\omega + KL(q_\theta(\omega)||p(\omega)) \tag{7}$$

The Monte Carlo (MC) estimation is used in VI to estimate the expected log likelihood (namely the integral in Eq. (6)).

Finally optimizing $\hat{\mathcal{L}}_{MC}(\theta)$ to find the optima the following can be written, see Eq. 8 [3]:

$$\widehat{\Delta\theta} \leftarrow -\frac{N}{M}\sum_{i\in S}\frac{\partial}{\partial\theta}\log p(y_i|f^\omega(x_i)) + \frac{\partial}{\partial\theta}KL(q_\theta(\omega)||p(\omega)) \tag{8}$$

With the last relation the divergence between $q_\theta(\omega)$ and $P(\omega|X, Y)$ is minimized.

3.3 Uncertainty in Neural Networks

In the case of Bayesian Multilayer Perceptron [8], the uncertainty could be determined analyzing the stochasticity of the parameters of the model. This is because stochastic regularization techniques are extensively used to improve the learning of the neurons in the network thanks to the injection of stochastic noise in the model. One of the most popular stochastic techniques implemented in neural networks is dropout. Dropout is used in neural networks as a way to avoid over-fitting. In [3] a Feed-forward neural network (with a single hidden layer) is analyzed and it is shown that dropout approximately integrates over the models' weights. Bearing in mind the above, the dropout's stochastic noise can be transformed from the feature space to the parameter space as follows, see Eq. (9) [3]:

$$\hat{y} = \sigma\left(x\left(diag\left(\hat{\epsilon_1}\right)M_1\right) + b\right)\left(diag\left(\hat{\epsilon_2}\right)M_2\right) \tag{9}$$

Where:

$\hat{\epsilon_1}, \hat{\epsilon_2}$:   Binary vectors to represent the dropout process (layer 1 and 2 [3]).

M_1, M_2 :   Weight matrix for the outputs of the layers 1 and 2.
b :   Bias vector.
$\sigma(.)$:   Sigmoid function

Considering that: $\widehat{W_1} := diag(\widehat{\epsilon_1})M_1$ and $\widehat{W_2} := diag(\widehat{\epsilon_2})M_2$ the Eq. (9) can be rewritten in the following way, see Eq. (10) [3]:

$$\hat{y} = \sigma\left(x\widehat{W_1} + b\right)\widehat{W_2} =: f^{\widehat{W_1}, \widehat{W_2}, b}(x) \tag{10}$$

Bearing in mind the Eq. (10), the cost function for dropout can be written as follows, see Eqs. (11) and (12) [3]:

$$\widehat{\mathcal{L}}_{drop}(M_1, M_2, b) := -\frac{1}{M} \sum_{i \in S} E^{\widehat{W_1^i}, \widehat{W_2^i}, b}(x_i, y_i) + \lambda_1 ||M_1||^2 + \lambda_2 ||M_2||^2 + \lambda_3 ||b||^2 \tag{11}$$

Where:

$$E^{\widehat{W_1}, \widehat{W_2}, b}(x, y) = \frac{1}{2}\left\| y - f^{\widehat{W_1}, \widehat{W_2}, b}(x) \right\|^2 \tag{12}$$

Note: The parameters λ_i are related to the method used in [3] to enter the weight decay in the weights matrices and the bias vector in a Feed-forward neural network (with a single hidden layer).

Finally, the cost function can be optimized in the following way, see Eq. (13) [3]:

$$\widehat{\Delta\theta} \leftarrow -\frac{1}{M\tau} \sum_{i \in S} \frac{\partial}{\partial\theta} \log p\left(y_i | f^{\omega}(x)\right) + \frac{\partial}{\partial\theta}\left(\lambda_1 ||M_1||^2 + \lambda_2 ||M_2||^2 + \lambda_3 ||b||^2\right) \tag{13}$$

Where:

τ :   Precision of the model.
λ_i :   Weight-decay to minimize validation error

3.4   Adjustment of the Posterior Predictive Distribution Based on Estimators

Inspecting Eqs. (8) and (13), it can be said that the both follow a similar optimization procedure. So, the key of the proposed procedure presented in [3] is that, through the comparison between the optimization procedures for Bayesian modelling and for the Dropout regularization technique, it could be concluded that a neural network already trained with dropout behaves as a Bayesian network. Based on the above, the author uses the dropout during test time in order to obtain approximate samples from the posterior function. Namely, the outcome from the neural network are considered as the approximate samples from the posterior predictive distribution. In order to adjust these samples unbiased estimators should be calculated for the mean and the var(y) of the posterior predictive distribution as is described in Eqs. (14) and (15) [11]:

$$\widehat{\mathbb{E}}(y) = \frac{1}{T} \sum_{t=1}^{T} f^{\widehat{\omega}_t}(x) \tag{14}$$

$$\widehat{\mathbb{E}}\left(y^T y\right) = \tau^{-1} I + \frac{1}{T} \sum_{t=1}^{T} f^{\widehat{\omega}_t}(x)^T f^{\widehat{\omega}_t}(x) - \widehat{\mathbb{E}}(y)^T \widehat{\mathbb{E}}(y) \tag{15}$$

Where:

$f^{\widehat{\omega}_t}(x):$ Output of the Bayesian neural network.
$t = 1, \ldots, T:$ Samples from the posterior predictive distribution

The mean of the posterior predictive samples can be assumed as the unbiased estimator of the mean of the approximate distribution $q_\theta(\omega)$. The sample variance plus a term $\tau^{-1} I$ is also an unbiased estimator of the variance of $q_\theta(\omega)$. Bearing in mind the above the adjustment of the term τ allows to obtain the best outcome of the network. Now this adjustment can be done in a way that can allows to obtain the term λ as is described in the Eq. (16) [11]:

$$\lambda_i = \frac{(1 - P_i) l_i^2}{2N\tau} \tag{16}$$

Where:

$l_i^2:$ Prior length-scale.
$P_i:$ Dropout probability of the elements in vector $\widehat{\epsilon}_i$, $0 \le P_i \le 1$ for i $= 1, 2$

3.5   Walk Forward Validation

Adopting the classical approach of dividing the available data into training, validation and testing, in order to validate the model, implicitly biased the data validation towards the most recent period under analysis. This schema is not valid for the environmental data because of it faces non-stationary Time Series. For the sake of the example, it can be said for instance, that maybe the last day is a good approximation for next day, but maybe it's not. And on the other hand, maybe the first week of the month would hold some important patterns to evaluate, but these would be lost in the approach mentioned above. Walk Forward Analysis does optimization on a subset of the training set that change its size every iteration during the process. Namely, the goal of this technique is to minimize the curve fitting on the out-of-sample data by shifting a moving window. The train set is expanding each time step (tWL samples) and the test set is fixed at one time step ahead [12], see Eq. (17). As a consequence, there are multiple out of sample periods and the process is looking at these results combined at the end of every iteration [13].

$$TW = \sum_{i}^{n} tWL_i \tag{17}$$

Where:

TW : Testing Window.
tWL_i : Window length for test per iteration

The main advantage is that the model is updated each time step with new data received. It implies that a robust estimation is provided. The main disadvantage of this schema is the additional computational cost generated for all the subset predictions. It has to be said that a period of 24 h has been adopted to carry out a proper data analysis.

3.6 AWS Implementation

The AWS are implemented with low cost small single-board computers, in this case the Raspberry Pi platform. The AWS collect information of temperature, humidity and pressure. This Information is acquired every 20 s and is averaged every minute as is recommended by the WMO in [14] and then saved in the internal memory of the device. After that, the information is transmitted to a FTP server located at the cloud through the use of the WIFI (Wireless Fidelity) card of the Raspberry. With the aim of a proper data acquisition the parameters have been calibrated with the PEAKMETER MS6508 Digital Temperature Humidity Meter as secondary standard method of calibration. The data has been analyzed and corrected in a stage before the ingress to the Neural Network. The tasks performed at this stage were polynomial interpolation and correction of abnormal measurements. The interpolation was applied to complete data (hours in some cases) lost because of energy cuts. And the second one was performed in order to correct abnormal weather values (peaks) produced at the moment of the storage.

3.7 Neural Network and Scenarios

Neural networks are computer programs that try to emulate the brain behavior thanks to the use of mathematical functions called neurons. This structures have the capabilities for detecting relationships and patterns that can be used to predict the next likely scenario for different types of data (i.e. images, time series).

In the other hand a Recurrent Neural Network (RNN) is a type of artificial neural network capable to work with previous outputs to be used as inputs while having hidden states. The main disadvantage of this kind of structure is the exploding and vanishing gradient of the loss function with respect to the weights of the network [15].

LSTM is a type of Recurrent Neural Network (RNN) with memory stages called "cells". This type of neural network implements an architecture that adds memory capabilities, that makes this structure suitable for time-series analysis. The internal information of this network can be updated or deleted by the use of special structures called gates. The neural network structure used in this work were stacked LSTM with 2 layers. This neural network has been already implemented successfully obtaining Short and Long-Term Predictions [16–18]. Depending of the amount of data entered in the network typically low error values are achieved, RMSE: 4.75, MSE: 2.78 and RMSE: 0.086 respectively.

The testing scenarios are presented bearing in mind the data acquired for the AWS shown in Fig. 1. The 1st scenario (Case 1) to be evaluated is the Temperature prediction for the AWS under analysis based on past Temperature values of the same Station. In the 2nd scenario (Case 2) the Temperature prediction is based on past Temperature value of all the Station in the network.

3.8 Description of Parameters

The Keras library was used to build and compile the model on a CPU device, with 8 cores, 2.10 GHz Core Clock and 16 GB of memory size. During the Neural Network computing it was seen that usually, the 70% of the CPU and the 45% of the Memory resources were engaged with the simulation tasks. The Adam optimization algorithm was working with the following parameters: learning rate $= 0.001$, beta_1 $= 0.9$, beta_2 $= 0.999$, epsilon $=$ 1e-08. The backpropagation algorithm requires a specified number of epochs or exposures to the training dataset to be trained. For the data splitting, well tested distribution is 70%, 15%, 15% respectively [18]. The number of epochs used to fit the models 70. Each epoch is partitioned into groups of input-output pattern pairs called batches. This defines the number of patterns that the network is exposed to before the weights are updated within an epoch. Considering that it also implies hardware optimization, because not too many input patterns should be loaded into memory at a time, the adopted size of the batch was 16. The Rectified Linear Unit (ReLu) function activation was implemented. And finally, in the light of that the Walk Forward technique is assumed for data validation a down sampling stage has been added to resample the data to 1-h step instead of 1-min.

3.9 Experiments

In the light of that Bayesian neural network strongly relying in the determination of the inference, the selection of an adequate dropout percentage is going to be crucial to determine the proper weight decay of the network to decrease the uncertainty in the forecast. The Eq. (16) was used to enter the λ_i values in the Dense layer placed after every dropout operation and accomplish with the above. For the trials a length scale of 0.01 was assumed and percentages of 0.18, 0.2, 0.25 and 0.15, 0.21 were defined for the dropout regularization technique and the precision of the model respectively. As established in [1] the L2 regularization was defined for the Dense layers in order to induce priors on the weights (following a Gaussian distribution) and the MSE (mean squared error) is adopted as loss function. Additionally, after several trials it was determined that 1500 iterations were adequate as limit in the Monte Carlo method to estimate the output of the neural network. The temperature predictions for AWS 1 are going to be analyzed for the different trials and the outcomes of the experiments (taking into account the two possible scenarios presented in Sect. 3.2) are discussed bearing in mind the metrics of error: RMSE, MSE, MAE and MAPE. Finally, the number of iterations described for the trials in Sect. 4.2 obeys to the observed prediction from the same network at different times.

4   Results and Discussion

4.1   Results from the Experiments

The number of units per layer adopted for the LSTM neural network was L1: 200, L2: 100. This number of units per layer were selected aiming at reduce as much as possible the processing time of the model without lose the precision. In [19] a proposed value of $\lambda = 8 \times 10^{-5}$ was applied in a feed forward neural network to improve the learning. This value was analyzed initially and was modified experimentally to values around 10^{-7}. For the trials a maximum of 10 trials in different times (so as not to enlarge the image) has been made in order to show the reduction of the uncertainty in the prediction of the network. In the Tables 2 and 3, a comparison between the maximum values (variations) of RMSE, MSE, MAE and MAPE for all the iteration is presented to try to establish a base of comparison of the prediction's uncertainty.

Table 2. Parameters and forecast information for LSTM (without Bayesian Modelling)

Scenario	P_i	RMSE (°C)	MSE (°C)	MAE (°C)	MAPE (%)
Case 1	0.18	1.3	5.9	1.4	6.8
Case 2	0.25	2.3	12	2.4	10.6

Table 3. Parameters and forecast information for LSTM (with Bayesian Modelling)

Scenario	P_i	τ	RMSE (°C)	MSE (°C)	MAE (°C)	MAPE (%)
Case 1	0.18	0.15	2.23	1.0	3.4	0.9	4.3
Case 2	0.25	0.15	2.04	1.3	5.9	1.5	6.4

In order to present a more in deep perspective of the work carried out in this paper, shown below, Figs. 2 and 3, the MAPE variation analysis for the LSTM network.

4.2   Discussion

It can be seen that in the case of Bayesian modelling applied to the LSTM neural network, the variation of the error has been reduced for the both scenarios under analysis, see Table 2 and 3. The error in the forecast information for LSTM for the Case 1 is reduced from 1.3 °C to 1.0 °C for RMSE, from 5.9 °C to 3.4 °C for MSE, from 1.4 °C to 0.9 °C for MAE and from 6.8% to 4.3% for MAPE; when $P_i = 0.18$, $\tau = 0.15$, $\lambda = 2.23 \times 10^{-7}$. In the other hand the maximum error in the forecast information for LSTM for the Case 2 is reduced from 2.3 °C to 2.04 °C for RMSE, from 12 °C to 5.9 °C for MSE, from 2.4 °C to 1.5 °C for MAE and from 10.6% to 6.4% for MAPE; when $P_i = 0.25$, $\tau =$

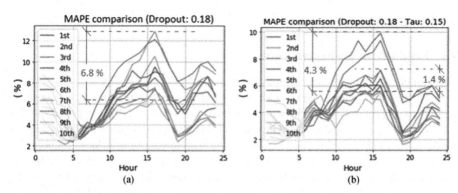

Fig. 2. MAPE comparison for the neural network with LSTM structure (Scenario 1). (a) Without Bayesian Modelling, (b) With Bayesian Modelling.

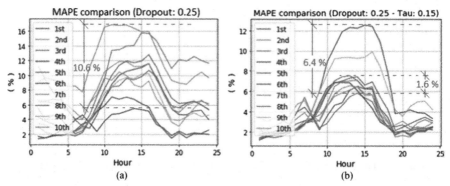

Fig. 3. MAPE comparison for the neural network with LSTM structure (Scenario 2). (a) Without Bayesian Modelling, (b) With Bayesian Modelling.

0.15, $\lambda = 2.04 \times 10^{-7}$. The MSE value is quite particular because it has been reduced almost to the half.

Additional information can be obtained from the graphic analysis of the Figs. 2 and 3, where the MAPE error using the walk forward validation with steps of 24 h is shown. Among all the errors metrics the MAPE error was selected because the percentage analysis can show clearly the variation of the neural network's output, namely the uncertainty in the prediction of the Temperature of an AWS. In Figs. 2 and 3 it can be seen the network's output for 10 different trials (in different times). In these figures it can be said that the 80% of times, the predictions can be grouped in values that are closer to the real value expected for the prediction. The boundaries for these curves can be determined in order to appreciate the decrease in the error prediction. Bearing in mind the above, a sharply decrease in percentages of the MAPE can be observed (from 1.4%, and 1.6% respectively).

5   Conclusions

An analysis of the error variation to describe the behavior of the uncertainty in a neural network using metrics such as RMSE, MSE, MAE and MAPE has been successfully carried out.

In this work it has been proof that the uncertainty in the predictions of a neural network (applied for a Short-Term Weather Forecast) can be reduced through a proper adjustment of the posterior predictive distribution based on estimators during the use of the dropout regularization technique.

From the analysis it is obtained a maximum error forecast of 12% and it is proven that for LSTM structures, the variation of the error reduces almost to the half with weight-decays of 2.04×10^{-7} and 2.23×10^{-7}.

One of the key tools to conduct this analysis was the walk forward validation since it facilitated the analysis of the prediction error over 24 h what is an acceptable time range covered by a Short-Term weather forecast for the city of Quito.

The use of stochastic regularization techniques can be exploited to improve the learning of the neurons in the network thanks to the injection of stochastic noise in the models [20].

Acknowledgment. The authors would like to thank the French Ministry for Europe and Foreign Affairs, and the French Embassy in Ecuador for the support in the present work through the Solidarity Fund for Innovative Projects (FSPI).

References

1. Rasp, S.: Statistical Methods and Machine Learning in Weather and Climate Modelling. Ludwig Maximilians Universität München (2018)
2. Serrano, S., Ruiz, J., Bersosa, F.: Heavy rainfall and temperature proyections in a climate change scenario over Quito. Ecuador La Granja Revista de Ciencias de la Vida (Universidad Politécnica Salesiana) **25**, 16–32 (2017)
3. Gal, Y., Ghahramani, Z.: Dropout as a Bayesian Approximation: Representing Model Uncertainty in Deep Learning. University of Cambridge (2016)
4. SRTM data, National Geospatial-Intelligence Agency (NGA) and the National Aeronautics and Space Administration (NASA), USA (2010). https://www2.jpl.nasa.gov/srtm/
5. Luca Cardelli L., Kwiatkowska M., Laurenti L., Paoletti N., Patane A., Wicker M.: Statistical guarantees for the robustness of bayesian neural networks. In : Proceedings of the Twenty-Eighth International Joint Conference on Artificial Intelligence (2019)
6. Vladimirova, M., Verbeek, J., Mesejo,, P., Arbel, J.: Understanding priors in bayesian neural networks at the unit level. In: ICML 2019 - 36th International Conference on Machine Learning (2019)
7. Sun, S., Zhang, G., Shi, J., Grossey, R.: Functional variational bayesian neural networks. In: International Conference on Learning Representations (2019)
8. Yao, J., Pan, W., Ghosh, S., Velez, D.: Quality of uncertainty quantification for bayesian neural network inference. In: ICML Workshop on Uncertainty and Robustness in Deep Learning (2019)
9. Neal, R.: Bayesian Learning for Neural Networks. Lecture Notes in Statistics. Springer (1996)

10. Willink, R., White, R.: Disentangling Classical and Bayesian Approaches to Uncertainty Analysis. Technical Report No. CCT/12-08. BIPM: Sevres. France (2012)
11. Jordan, M., Ghahramani, Z., Jaakkola, T., Saul, L.: An introduction to variational methods for graphical models. Mach. Learn. **37**(2), 183–233 (1999)
12. Dotlic, D., Ipekci, B., Dulin, J.: Uncertainty in Profit Scoring (Bayesian Deep Learning). Seminar Information Systems (WS18/19). Humboldt-Universität zu Berlin (2019)
13. Ladyzynski, P., Zbikowski, Z., Grzegorzewski, P.: Stock Trading with Random Forests, Trend Detection Tests and Force Index Volume Indicators. Artificial Intelligence and Soft Computing. In: International Conference on Artificial Intelligence and Soft Computing ICAISC, pp. 441–452 (2013)
14. Narayanaa, F., Turhan, L.: Preserving Order of Data When Validating Defect Prediction Models. California Polytechnic State University (2018)
15. Guide to Meteorological Instruments and Methods of Observation, WMO, vol. 8 (2008)
16. Kamal, I., Bae, H., Sunghyun, S., Yun, H.: DERN: Deep ensemble learning model for short and long-term prediction of baltic dry index. Appl. Sci. **10**(4), 1504 (2020)
17. Hewage, Pradeep., Behera, Ardhendu., Trovati, Marcello, Pereira, Ella: Long-short term memory for an effective short-term weather forecasting model using surface weather data. In: MacIntyre, John, Maglogiannis, Ilias, Iliadis, Lazaros, Pimenidis, Elias (eds.) AIAI 2019. IAICT, vol. 559, pp. 382–390. Springer, Cham (2019). https://doi.org/10.1007/978-3-030-19823-7_32
18. Alzahrani, A., Shamsia, P., Daglib, C., Ferdowsi, M.: Solar Irradiance Forecasting Using Deep Neural Networks. Complex Adaptive Systems Conference with Theme: Engineering Cyber Physical Systems. Elsevier (2017)
19. El Yacoubi, S., Fargette, M., Faye, A., de Carvalho, W., Libourel, T., Loireau, T.: A multilayer perceptron model for the correlation between satellite data and soil vulnerability in the Ferlo, Senegal. Int. J. Parallel. Emergent and Distrib. Syst. **34**(1) (2018)
20. Krogh, A., Herts, J.: A simple Weight Decay Can Improve Generalization. Advances in Neural Information Processing Systems 4 (1991)

Territorial, Population and Economic Analysis of a Potential Volcanic Disaster in the City of Latacunga, Central Ecuador Based on GIS Techniques – Implications and Potential Solutions

Alexander Robayo N.[1] ⓘ, Jaime Llorca[2] ⓘ, and Theofilos Toulkeridis[1](✉) ⓘ

[1] Universidad de las Fuerzas Armadas ESPE, Sangolquí, Ecuador
ttoulkeridis@espe.edu.ec
[2] Universidad de Barcelona, Barcelona, Spain

Abstract. The current economic study has been performed about a territorial analysis in the area of potential lahars flows from the Cotopaxi volcano within the city of Latacunga, central Ecuador. We have used as inputs the plan of development and land-use planning 2016–2028, studies concerning this topic and field data obtained from surveys to the affected properties, consulting on variables of typology of the construction, use of the land and economic through a property study. The use of geographic information systems over such information allowed to obtain results in order to determine the human losses by lahar risks, to quantify the surface and estimate the affected population and probable death toll. Furthermore, it determines the economic losses by lahars in Latacunga, and quantify the total value of losses in the event of an eruption of Cotopaxi, and finally, it proposes the relocation in safe areas of the inhabitants at high and medium risk, estimating the cost of relocation versus the application of mitigation measures, specifically engineering works.

Keywords: Lahars · Human involvement · Economic impact · Risks · Relocation zones · Mitigation measures · GIS

1 Introduction

Land use studies have the purpose of leading authorities and population alike to deal with a great proportion of information, which may be used on a better oriented planning of existing and future development of urban constructions and strategic infrastructure. Such studies may lead also to either to an expansion of already habituated areas or on contrary to the relocation of such potentially vulnerable zones by the recurrence of natural hazards [1–3].

Ecuador is situated within the Pacific Ring of Fire, where around 60% of the world's active continental volcanoes are concentrated [4]. The active Quaternary volcanism of the Ecuadorian Andes is a product of the subduction of the oceanic Nazca plate below the

© Springer Nature Switzerland AG 2020
G. Rodriguez Morales et al. (Eds.): TICEC 2020, CCIS 1307, pp. 549–563, 2020.
https://doi.org/10.1007/978-3-030-62833-8_40

continental Caribbean and South American plates [5, 26–28]. There are 255 volcanoes in the country of which 19 are considered potentially active, of these eight (Cotopaxi, Tungurahua, Guagua Pichincha, Antisana, Cayambe, Quilotoa, Reventador and Sangay) have presented eruptive activity in the last 500 years, making Ecuador extremely vulnerable to volcanic events and corresponding hazards [6]. With a Volcanic Explosivity Index (VEI) of up to 5, the Cotopaxi volcano is one of the most dangerous in Ecuador [7–10, 25]. The major volcanic hazard has been lahars, which result usually by the emplacement of pyroclastic flows generating a partial melting of the surface area of the glacial cover at its peak. Such lahars have historically devastated natural drainage areas in the northern, eastern and southern surrounding of the volcano, claiming lives and infrastructure [11–14].

The city of Latacunga, which is located some 33 km of the southern flank the Cotopaxi Volcano, has been the most affected by lahars in previous eruptions. Since the last devastation in 1877, this sector has become agricultural areas, industrial zones and even worse, residential areas. The population in this city has increased by 6.9 times since 1950 (10389 inhabitants) up to the year 2012 (63800 inhabitants) [15]. Currently, the lack of urban space forces the population to occupy high risk areas. The authorized as well as the illegal urban growth, the non-existence of territorial planning together with the ignorance of hazard information as well as the need to have a home of their own, forces the population to settle in a disorderly manner, exposing themselves to the occurrence of an eruptive event of Cotopaxi. Therefore, it is necessary to study the spatial incidence of these processes and their impact on urban settlements in the area.

The main aim of the current study has been to analyze the impact in the city of Latacunga, in the area of lahars within a potential eruption of Cotopaxi and to determine the human and economic affectation, by means of the use of geographic information systems, in order to relocate the involved population in suitable areas and with a corresponding planning of the territory.

2 Study Area and Past Volcanic History

The Canton Latacunga belonging to the Province of Cotopaxi, had in 2014 a population of 183446 inhabitants [15] distributed in an area of 138630.60 ha (ha), with a population density of 13.23 inhabitants/ha. The Province of Cotopaxi has taken advantage of its geographical location for its development, since it has been benefited with road works, railways, airport and others that have allowed its development, as well as the mobilization of agricultural production which is what prevails in the Province. It is a territory with great natural, heritage and cultural variety of high tourist attraction for its historical, architectural and cultural value, which has marked its identity and social memory, considered as National Cultural Heritage since 1982 [16]. Latacunga is also considered one of the most important cities of the Interandean region for its growth and development. At the same time this city is the essential economic engine of the mountain range, being the cantonal capital and the capital of the province of Cotopaxi. In the Canton there are around 90 industries among the main branches are: metallurgical, tanneries, mills, assembly workshops, agglomerates, beverages, meat processing, flower growers, plastics and sausages, in addition to the production of aluminum, steel products, paper, flour, cement, agro industry and dairy products. These industries have boosted the economy by converting it into the currency generator of the central Highlands.

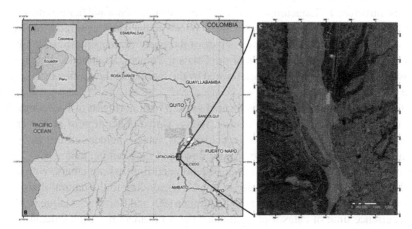

Fig. 1. Location of the Cotopaxi volcano and its lahar flows and their transit through the city Latacunga [23].

The landscape of the Canton Latacunga, has been formed by an intense volcanic activity, along different geological episodes and erosive processes that acted in pre-existing reliefs, determining a dominant landscape of structural terraces including mostly glacial and volcanic deposits within mountainous reliefs [17]. Being a distinctly volcanic zone, the central zone of the Canton known as the Inter-Andean Valley, is formed by fillings of mainly pyroclastics, sediments and lahars, being predominantly from the Cotopaxi Volcano.

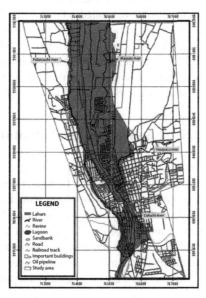

Fig. 2. Map of Latacunga and the potential zones affected by the emplacement of lahars [12].

Located to the South-East of the Province of Cotopaxi, The City of Latacunga, is geologically settled on cangahuas (sediments of volcanic origin), deposits of lahars, colluvial and lacustrine deposits, ash, volcano-sedimentary tuffs and conglomerates of pumices. Structurally, Latacunga is controlled by a system of normal faults with a general NE-SW orientation in the northern part and NW-NW to the south, covered by quaternary deposits [17]. The Canton Latacunga is part of the upper drainage basin of the Pastaza River and particularly the sub-basin of the Patatan, Cutuchi, Saquimala, Alaquez, Barrancas and Tolugchi rivers, which are formed by the melting of the south western ice-cap of the Cotopaxi volcano [18, 19].

The volcano Cotopaxi, which is located some 33 km northeast of Latacunga, has a vast and detailed studied eruptive history, with a varied generation of strong eruptive phases with VEI´s of up to 5 and volcanic hazards, which include fall-out and precipitations of pyroclastic material, pyroclastic flows and far-reaching lahars [19–23]. The main hazards with a high potential of destruction and life-loss are lahars, with an estimated total volume of up to 360 million m^3, corresponding to the natural drainages of the rivers Cutuchi (180 millions of m^3), Saquimala (90) and Barracas-Aláquez (90) [13]. The recurrence time of catastrophic emplacements of lahars has been calculated to be every 117 ± 70 years, of which last event dated in 1877 [11, 12].

There are 226 towns located within the canton that are in a zone of volcanic hazards, of which 47 correspond to the area of very high hazard zone (lahars), 79 are in the high hazard zone (fall of pyroclastic flows and lava), 100 in the zone of Lower hazard zone (fall of pyroclastic materials). The urban area of Latacunga is affected in 9390.16 Ha by the emplacement of lahars, [17], putting in serious risk the population in addition to the urban infrastructure, roads, bridges, health equipment, education, potable water network, sewerage and public as well as private constructions.

The Territorial planning and the Development Proposal of 2016–2028 foresees a tendential scenario towards the possible eruptive event, with the propositions for the relocation of residential areas and collective use sites [17]. Such proposals, indicate that 13676 properties will be affected by being located in the transit of lahars in urban parishes, of which 8257 are on construction properties and 5419 on unconstructed land. The largest property damage would be in the parish Eloy Alfaro with 3365 housing units, the San Buenaventura parish with 1525 properties, Juan Montalvo with 66 affected properties, La Matriz with 2320 properties, and 981 properties of the Ignacio Flores Parish. Similarly, in the rural parishes the affectation will be in a total of 2754 affected lands.

3   Constructive Typology and Economic Valuation

The Canton Latacunga presents similar characteristics to the cities of the Ecuadorian Highlands as regards the access of the population to housing, with a similar settlement pattern. There is an index of more than 10% of dwellings with deficient structures located in areas of population dispersion where a typology of traditional housing in the functional and formal predominates, high number of dwellings present lack of comfort. Another considerable group are dwellings that do not have an adequate system of wastewater. The demand for housing is satisfied by limited real estate speculation the urban area of Latacunga, while in the urban centers of the parishes it is not profitable for them to offer housing due to the low purchasing power of the population, accompanied by a deficit in the infrastructure of services and roads. It is estimated that in the year 2026 9473 homes will be required in the area of rural parishes [17].

To estimate the demand for new housing, the growth of new homes that will be formed during the Plan period is taken as a basis. The number of members of each household is projected based on the census information, which is why the number of dwellings required is the result of dividing the population by the number of new households that will be formed. However, this relationship is not real, since the potential demand is not considered. This is the relative number of people who demand tenure and are not going to lease, whether or not they have the acquisition possibilities, while the effective demand corresponds to the new families that can afford to finance a home. For this the central government has strengthened a system of economic incentives for both the construction and purchase of houses already built.

According to the Census [15], in the urban area of the city of Latacunga there are 29,988 homes. For the year 2017 it requires 4,191 homes and by the year 2026, 59,107 homes, therefore the demand with respect to 2010 is 29,119 units of housing in the area of urban parishes and the periphery. For this a policy of consolidation of vacant areas and planning of urban land is required, either by individual units, housing developments and housing programs under the type of horizontal property.

On the other hand there are levels of overcrowding that manifests when the number of bedrooms does not fit the number of family members. It is considered normal when it is less than three people per bedroom, therefore many homes require an increase in surface area. Nonetheless, it is not always possible since housing may be a department, in addition to the cost that may be able to affect the popular economy. For the advancement of housing coverage, it is a priority to have a law that regulates and controls the land market, so that municipal policies have a specific territorial management in housing programs and projects located in areas that do not have risks. In addition to another policy of incorporating more area within the city limits with all the requirements that this entails such as urban services and road connectivity. But meanwhile the processes of settlement increase beyond municipal control with disjointed occupation models of the consolidation of the social fabric and yet still located in areas vulnerable to risks, especially of volcanic origin.

According to studies carried out by the Municipality [17], they indicate that the land currently available is enough to accommodate the projected population by the end of 2017. Therefore, in order to fit the demand for future housing, land should be increased or strategies to be applied. urban densification and territory management, considering a population growth trend. It is estimated that by the year 2026 an additional area of 563 ha will be required. The limit of the urban area of Latacunga was established by municipal ordinance on January 25, 1995, progressively the municipal administrations have incorporated territory, unjustifiably because there has been no demographic pressure [17].

Based on the Municipal Cadastre updated to April 2015, the current urban limit has an area of 3415.26 ha, the area of registered properties is 26769 housing units corresponding to 2542.93 ha (74.45%), of which 1311.44 ha correspond to buildings built and 1231.00 ha to unbuilt land, in addition to 463.33 ha (13.55%) corresponding to public space. The territorial units have been classified according to economic activity, location, behavior in the integration or disaggregation of the territory and urban space, thus determining a variety of economic activities for urban parishes by the year 2015 [17].

In riverbanks there are incompatibilities of use between residential and agricultural-industrial areas, in addition to the location in risk areas. Within the city of Latacunga a consolidated area is recognized that corresponds to the part enabled by a road and potable water services, sewerage, collection of solid waste and public facilities, with land and buildings with different economic activities and compatible urban uses, corresponds to urbanized land. On the other hand, the consolidation area, which does not have road infrastructure and services, its integration and qualification is scheduled subject to compliance by the owners, the regulations and capacity to provide public services, usually located at the limit of consolidated area, corresponds to the developable land.

The main conflict of use of urban land is based on the consolidation of the territory, since of the 26769 properties registered, 13820 properties (51.63%) have a level of consolidation between 5.77% and 68.89%. More than half of the territory is not built, ratifying an average density of 22.75 inhab./ha. The territorial units (TU) contemplate orographic, topographic, water resources, types of soil, climate and natural environment that have conditioned the linear occupation of plains framed by the course and basins of the rivers that cross the city. Therefore, the municipality has divided into ten territorial units contained between the causes of the 6 rivers (Pumacuchi, Cutuchi, Aláquez, Yanayacu, Cunuyacu and Illuchi) and the current urban limit.

4 Methodology

The scheme of the methodology used for the development of this project is based on five phases. These are composed of a) Analysis of the development plan (DP) and land management (LM) 2016-2028, in relation to the affectation by natural hazards and the settlements of the population in zones of risk of lahars; b) Characterization of Census areas and criteria used for field work; c) Characterization of land use and construction typologies in the risk area; d) Determination of the economic impact on the real estate sector by the route of lahars, through the use of GIS and field data; e) Determination of relocation areas, through the use of GIS, for areas affected by lahars risks.

5 Results and Discussion

5.1 Use of Urban Land and Construction Typologies in Areas of Lahars

The economic sector of the affected area is considered to be that some 9% have a high economic level of the area, while the majority with 74% are of average and 17% are of the low range. Usually the high economic level is located in more remote areas of the city, while the average corresponds to the new urbanizations that are developing just in the risk area and the low mainly to the downtown area of the city. At the farm level, the variables analyzed yielded the following results: in terms of land use, 67% corresponds to residential or housing area, 2% industrial, 16% commercial use, 3% corresponds to public use and 12% without use or properties that are empty. For this reason, in the case of relocation, a reduction of 15% was considered, which corresponds to public use and vacant lots. Priority relocation would correspond to residential, commercial and industrial use. The type of construction corresponds with 60% to concrete, so the impact on the infrastructure could support the impact by lahars, 7% is adobe that would practically not resist the affectation or destruction, and 33% corresponds to mixed constructions, block or other material, which like the previous ones because they do not have an adequate structure would therefore not support the affectation by lahars.

Regarding the age of construction, the results indicate that 11% correspond to new constructions between 2 to 5 years, 40% have an age between 5 and 10 years, 33% between 10 and 20 years, 15% more 20 years and only 1% are in poor condition. The finishes of the construction only applies to the properties that have buildings, the results indicate that 9% corresponds to excellent finishes, which ratifies the 9% obtained in high economic level that corresponds to block areas, 56% has normal finishes, 26% few finishes and 9% without finishes meaning they are unused works.

5.2 Risk of Lahars in the City of Latacunga and Impact on the Population

Considering that the lahars is a phenomenon of dispersion, which decreases with distance, the Euclidean distance from the axis of the drainages has been considered. In addition the slope that ascends as it moves away from the drainages is analyzed since Latacunga is located in a valley. In this way the danger that the study area has, has been determined. Similarly, the affected population in each class is quantified. The results indicate an estimated of 5472 inhabitants who are at high risk, 19097 inhabitants at medium risk and 282 inhabitants at low risk. The total of estimated inhabitants who are in the risk area is of about 24851 inhabitants. From the data extracted from the surveys an estimate of the total affected population has been performed. This is based on the number of housing units, which in total correspond to 5070 housing units, estimating an average of five persons per housing unit resulting to a population of 25350 inhabitants. We also estimated the number of rooms or dormitories, with leads to a total of 13288 rooms. Considering an average of two persons per room, a total of 26576 inhabitants is estimated. Finally the population is calculated by the number of bathrooms per unit of housing, determining that there are 8014 bathrooms, considering an average of three persons per bathroom, leading to an estimated population of 24042 inhabitants (Table 1).

Table 1. Calculation of the population estimate

Number of housing units						
Individual	2 units	3 units	4 units	5 units	More than 5 units	Total
2527	725	243	36	16	14	
2527	1450	729	144	80	140	5070
Amount of rooms						
1 room	2 rooms	3 rooms	4 rooms	5 rooms	Above 5 rooms	
207	871	1405	746	268	280	
207	1742	4215	2984	1340	2800	13288

(*continued*)

Table 1. (*continued*)

Number of housing units

Amount of bathrooms

1 bathroom	2 bathr.	3 bathr.	4 bathr.	5 bathr.	Above 5 bathr.	
1348	1595	608	218	56	50	
1348	3190	1824	872	280	500	8014
By number of units **Average 5 persons**		**By amount of rooms** **Average 2 persons**		**By amount of bathrooms** **Average 3 persons**		
25350		26576		24042		

The average of the three calculations corresponding to 25323 inhabitants is determined and compared with the data obtained from the map. It corresponds to 24851 inhabitants, confirming that the estimate is well determined. In general it has been possible to be estimated that there is a total population at risk of affecting lahars of around 25,000 inhabitants. The map of human affectation by lahars risks (Fig. 3), presents three levels of risk, where the description of high risk corresponds to the area with the highest confluence of lahar, which could cover or destroy the property and the construction, considering records of heights of up to 10 m above the level of the channel. In this area the population is highly vulnerable due to the proximity to the danger of the path of the lahar, having an estimated time of 50 min to be evacuated to safe areas. This area has a surface of 33.22 ha and it is estimated that there are 5492 inhabitants who would have to evacuate. The description of the average risk corresponds to the zone of median confluence of lahars, reaching heights of up to 1 m above the level of the street. In this zone the population is vulnerable to the danger of the path of the lahar, having a time estimated of 1 h and 40 min to evacuate (Figs. 1 and 2).

Vertical evacuation could be carried out, meaning to go up to higher floors of buildings considered as safe. That comply with that their construction is of concrete, the deck is of terrace, exceeds the three floors of construction and have accessibility directly from the street or through a frontal retreat. This area has an area of some 265.24 ha and it is estimated that there are 19097 inhabitants that would have to evacuate, despite having a larger area than the high risk area. The population concentration is not that high, because there are many empty areas or with agricultural dedication. The description of the low risk corresponds to the zone with low affectation of the lahar. It is in the limits of reach of the lahars, which reach heights of up to 0.20 m above the level of the street. In this zone the population is not vulnerable to the danger of the route del lahar, and may be evacuated for security to meeting areas or perform vertical evacuation, or stay in their homes. This area covers some 24.78 ha and it is estimated that there are 282 inhabitants.

According to data of the Municipal Cadastre of April 2015, the urban limit of the city of Latacunga has an area of some 3415.26 ha, with 26769 housing units distributed in 2542.93 ha (74.45%), where the total area affected by risk of lahars determined is of about 323.24 ha. corresponding to 12.71% of housing units. The estimated total affected population based on the map is of 24871 inhabitants.

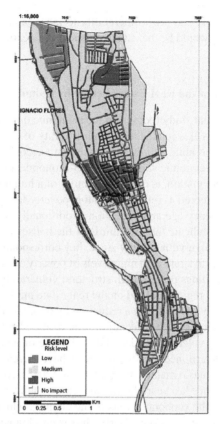

Fig. 3. Map of impact of lahars on human life in the city of Latacunga.

Some 18% of the urban buildings of the Canton have low vulnerability indexes, 58% are medium and 25% high. Buildings with low vulnerability are located preferentially in the central area of the canton, those with medium vulnerability are scattered throughout the canton and those with high vulnerability are located west of Loma Alcoceres. It has been also determined that the most dangerous areas that border the river channel, is largely constituted by buildings of medium vulnerability, very low vulnerability and there are no buildings of high vulnerability [17].

The most widely used variables for all constructions and with greater importance in the study area are: number of floors, type of floor, material of the walls, topography and type of roof, followed by other customized variables, which may increase or reduce vulnerability such as: form of construction, state of conservation, year of construction, mezzanines and structural system.

These variables allowed to determine the vulnerability of buildings. In the case of flooding of lahars of the Cutuchi River, the entire part of the sewage network's discharges lines would be directly affected, leaving the sewage of the city of Latacunga without possibility of evacuation, in the same way it would be affected. Furthermore, some 90% of the drinking water network in the western section would be destroyed, while the road network presents moderate and low vulnerability to lahars and ash fall. The elements without danger of lahars would be the catchments and the treatment plant of the city of Latacunga [17].

5.3 Economic Impact of the Real Estate Sector by Lahars

Considering that the current study focuses on the economic quantification of infrastructures and that this value is also related to the vulnerability of construction, many of the variables used in the vulnerability study were taken into account, as well as others that will allow determine the economic value. The socio-economic and demographic vulnerability of the exposed population, is the susceptibility of a human group to suffer some damage or loss. We considered as related indicators poverty for unsatisfied basic needs, type of housing, dependency age and education. Additionally, we checked the type of housing, where the data indicate that two thirds of the houses of the canton Latacunga are in the lower limit of high vulnerability since they correspond to the category where families generally belong to strata with high levels of poverty and dissatisfaction of basic needs and where the buildings present high structural vulnerability [17].

The development of a region is based on the real estate market. In Ecuador in recent years, this sector has been affected with a reduction by 60% (APIVE, 2017). Latacunga has not been the exception of this affectation, due to the alert issued in 2015 of the eruption of the Cotopaxi volcano, the demand in the sale of houses has been reduced. However in the areas, determined as safe, the prices have increased.

The real estate sector has remained so far that year (2018), two factors have affected the construction sector since last year: the announcement of the projects of surplus value and inheritance law and the economic crisis in the country, which translates into a fall in demand. The data of the real estate market has been obtained through field work. We searched the real estate market for those properties for sale, located in the risk area, where 30 properties were determined. The same survey has been applied to each property in order to quantify the value of the property. In addition the commercial value, coordinates (UTM-WGS84) have been determined, in order to have a spatial distribution within the study area. Base cartography 1: 5000 of the Military Geographical IGM & INEC has been used and the data have been normalized applying 30% for the scores of the blocks and 70% for the scores of the properties, obtaining the property value, which was divided by the area of the property in order to obtain the value per square meter. By means of a statistical analysis of the value per square meter of each property, a filtering of the data has been conducted, filtering them with the criterion of finding values that are within ± 2 standard deviations with respect to the mean, that is 95% of the data. Once the statistical analysis and the filtering of the data were performed, four values, a maximum, a minimum and two intermediate values were identified. For the assignment of the economic value, 4 values corresponding to the maximum, minimum and two intermediate values were determined, in order to subsequently to decide which one to work with. The following equation has been used:

$$\text{Economic value} = \frac{\text{property weight} \times \text{property value.}_1}{\text{property weight.}_1} \quad (1)$$

The property weight$_1$ corresponds to the maximum, minimum and intermediate values of the statistical analysis of the values per square meter. The property weight are the values corresponding to the properties of the entire study area. The values obtained are: maximum value of 575 USD/m^2, minimum value of 83 and intermediate values of 213 USD/m^2 and 312 USD/m^2. Using the least squares criterion, it has been determined that the value of 312 USD/m^2 is the most suitable to be used. This property corresponds to a weight of 0.8725.

The economic value of all the properties surveyed has been determined by the following equation:

$$\text{Economic value} = \frac{\text{property weighting} \times (312\text{USD})}{(0,8725)} \tag{2}$$

The total sum of the properties has been performed according to the block sector. In this way the economic value at the block level has been yielded. Thus, the map of economic impact on the real estate sector has been developed by the lahars in the Canton Latacunga. Three classes with the same intervals criterion were identified. Additionally, two classes were added, of which one was to represent zones without information and the other was for higher values than very high ones.

Of the map of economic impact by lahars (Fig. 4), which illustrates the value that each of the blocks represents according to the studied variables, has been categorized into three intervals: a) blocks whose cost ranges from USD 6,000 to USD 900,000, whose surface total corresponds to 52.53 ha; b) blocks whose cost range from USD 900,000 to USD 2'000,000, whose total area corresponds to 59.72 ha; and c) blocks whose cost range from USD 2'000.000 to USD 10'000.000, whose total area corresponds to 117.10 ha. In addition, two classes have been added, with no information corresponding to 53.71 ha and blocks whose cost is higher than USD 10,000,000, whose total area corresponds to 124.71 ha. The cost per block corresponds to the value of the land, physical infrastructure and basic services.

Once the map of economic impact has been performed, the blocks are assigned a value, as indicated before, in the database related to the map, a summation is conducted of each of the blocks and their assigned cost, obtaining as a result the total values in each of the indicated intervals. Thus, for the interval of 6,000 to 900,000 USD, the total cost is of about 34,093,119 USD, for the range of 900,000 to 2,000,000 USD, the total cost is of about 99,837,071 USD, for the interval of 2,000,000 up to 10,000,000 USD, the total cost is of about 251,190,258 USD. Finally for the greater interval of 10,000,000 USD, the total cost is of about 245,039,876 USD and the total value of all the intervals has been calculated to be of about 630,196,324 USD, which would correspond to a total loss of the entire affected area [29].

If the maps of human impact by risks of lahars and the map of economic impact by lahars are contrasted, we may indicate that the range of 6,000 to 900,000 USD, 100% of it correspond to medium risk, the interval of 900,000 up to 2,000,000 USD, 95% corresponds to medium risk and 5% to high risk, the interval 2,000.000 up to 10,000.000 USD, 85% corresponds to medium risk and 15% to high risk and for the greater interval of 10,000.000 USD, 75% corresponds to medium risk and 25% to low risk. With these indicated considerations, the cost of total losses in the areas corresponding to medium and high risk would correspond to approximately 568,936.355 USD.

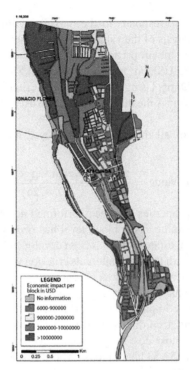

Fig. 4. Economic impact to the real estate sector based on lahars in the city of latacunga

5.4 Relocation Areas for Areas Affected by the Risk of Lahars

Based on the orthophoto scale 1: 30000 of Latacunga, the zones that would not be affected have been determined, while the area and number of affected blocks has been determined in order to determine the area to be relocated. The affected area may be reduced by 15%. This value corresponds to public areas and roads, further available spaces for relocation considering the proximity to the urban part and smooth or flat slope (less than 10°). The area that fits the conditions corresponds to 373.79 ha.

The area determined in the study that may be used as a relocation site for the properties, distributes the zones that are in high and medium risk (Fig. 5), considering the variables close to the city and slope less than 10%, covering a total of 373.79 ha, requires a relocation of some 298.46 ha, which correspond to the area that is in medium risk (265.24 ha) and high risk (33.22 ha). Out of them, the 15% correspond to public areas and without use (determined from the results of the survey), an area of some 253.69 ha is required. Of the costs per square meter determined in the study, the mean low value corresponding to 213 USD c/m^2 is taken, determining a total value USD 540,359,700, which includes the cost of land, construction and basic services, ratifying the value obtained in the previous point of about 568,936.355 USD.

The mitigation activities may include vulnerability studies, territorial order plans, relocation programs of human settlements, strengthening of buildings and vulnerable infrastructure, monitoring and control of deforestation and human settlements in risk

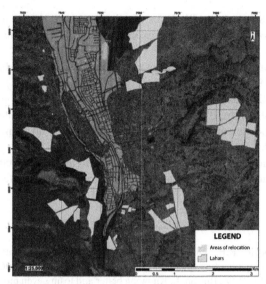

Fig. 5. Relocation sites (in yellow) for the public based on the potential impacts of lahars in the city of Latacunga (Color figure online)

areas, and construction of dikes and dams in strategic areas of the bed of rivers and streams. This study only considers the last mitigation techniques for comparison, since these structural measures refer to engineering works that store, reduce force, channel the trajectory, divert, disperse flows to forested areas.

Mitigation often requires the combination of different strategies, since a single technique may not be sufficient. The study taken as a reference, is based on the construction of hydraulic dams and structures and complementary facilities to perform its operation safely. It is determined that the main streams that form the Cotopaxi unravel in the southwestern part are feeders of the Saquimala River, the constructions will be implanted in the Saquimala and San Lorenzo ravines since they capture the largest volume of lahars, being far from the population and it is aimed at obtaining greater height of the mitigation work [19].

As a result of the study, the referential budget for the Quebrada Saquimala Dam is of about 55,314,251 USD and for the Dam in the San Lorenzo Stream is of about 31,090,082 USD, therefore, the total cost of the two dams will be USD 86'404,333. The considerations for the dams is that each ravine covers 25% of the glacier, with a filling time of 15 min, meaning that 50% of the glacier would evacuate by other drainages or exceed the dams [24].

6 Conclusions

Affected areas by lahars in previous eruptions are currently agricultural, industrial and residential areas, the latter located to the north and around the Cutuchi and Aláquez Rivers, occupying risk areas, based on illegal and disordered growth.

The 2016-2028 Latacunga PD lacks of a land management plan, regulations and regulations that control settlements, missing also a clear risk management policy or contingency plans.

We determined three risk levels, high risk (33.22 Ha with 5492 hab.); medium risk (265.24 Ha. and 19097 hab.) and low risk (24.78 Ha and 282 hab.), of which a value of USD 630'196,324 has been estimated in case of total loss in the impact zone corresponding to infrastructure. It is required to relocate 298.46 Ha. That correspond to the surface that is in medium and high risk, which would require an estimated total value of USD 540,359,700.

The State and local authorities need to invest in engineering structures that, together with other mitigation measures, would lead to not losing a single life.

References

1. Burby, R.J., Deyle, R.E., Godschalk, D.R., Olshansky, R.B.: Creating hazard resilient communities through land-use planning. Nat. Hazards Rev. **1**(2), 99–106 (2000)
2. White, G.F., Kates, R.W., Burton, I.: Knowing better and losing even more: the use of knowledge in hazards management. Glob. Environ. Change Part B: Environ. Hazards **3**(3), 81–92 (2001)
3. Du, S., Van Rompaey, A., Shi, P., Wang, J.: A dual effect of urban expansion on flood risk in the Pearl River Delta (China) revealed by land-use scenarios and direct runoff simulation. Nat. Hazards **77**(1), 111–128 (2015). https://doi.org/10.1007/s11069-014-1583-8
4. Small, C., Naumann, T.: The global distribution of human population and recent volcanism. Glob. Environ. Change Part B: Environ. Hazards **3**(3), 93–109 (2001)
5. Kellogg, J.N., Bonini, W.E.: Subduction of the Caribbean plate and basement uplifts in the overriding South American plate. Tectonics **1**(3), 251–276 (1982)
6. Tobin, G.A., Whiteford, L.M.: Community resilience and volcano hazard: the eruption of Tungurahua and evacuation of the faldas in Ecuador. Disasters **26**(1), 28–48 (2002)
7. Aguilera, E., Toulkeridis, T.: El Volcán Cotopaxi, una amenaza que acecha. Sotavento Ed, Quito, Ecuador (2005)
8. Toulkeridis, T., Arroyo, C.R., D'Howitt, M.C., Debut, A., Vaca, A.V., Cumbal, L., et al.: Evaluation of the initial stage of the reactivated Cotopaxi volcano-analysis of the first ejected fine-grained material. Nat. Hazards Earth Syst. Sci. Discuss. **3**(2015), 6947–6976 (2015)
9. Rodríguez, R.: Avalúos: Tipologías constructivas y concepto de depreciación, Universidad Autónoma de Centro América, Ingeniería Topográfica y Catastral, Peritajes y Avalúos, Costa Rica (2015)
10. Toulkeridis, T., Zach, I.: Wind directions of volcanic ash-charged clouds in Ecuador–implications for the public and flight safety. Geomatics Nat. Hazards Risk **8**(2), 242–256 (2017)
11. Barberi, F., Coltelli, M., Frullani, A., Rosi, M., Almeida, E.: Chronology and dispersal characteristics of recently (last 5000 years) erupted tephra of Cotopaxi (Ecuador): implications for long-term eruptive forecasting. J. Volcanol. Geoth. Res. **69**(3–4), 217–239 (1995)
12. Aguilera, E., Pareschi, M.T., Rosi, M., Zanchetta, G.: Risk from lahars in the northern valleys of Cotopaxi volcano (Ecuador). Nat. Hazards **33**(2), 161–189 (2004). epaguilera1@espe.edu.ec
13. Pistolesi, M., Cioni, R., Rosi, M., Cashman, K.V., Rossotti, A., Aguilera, E.: Evidence for lahar-triggering mechanisms in complex stratigraphic sequences: the post-twelfth century eruptive activity of Cotopaxi Volcano, Ecuador. Bull. Volcanol. **75**(3), 698 (2013)

14. Pistolesi, M., Cioni, R., Rosi, M., Aguilera, E.: Lahar hazard assessment in the southern drainage system of cotopaxi volcano, Ecuador: results from multiscale lahar simulations. Geomorphology **207**, 51–63 (2014)
15. INEC (2010) http://www.ecuadorencifras.gob.ec. Obtenido de fascículo provincial Cotopaxi: http://www.ecuadorencifras.gob.ec/wp-content/descargas/Manu-lateral/Resultados-provin ciales/cotopaxi.pdf
16. Hernández-Ramírez, J.: Los caminos del patrimonio. Rutas turísticas e itinerarios culturales. Pasos. Revista de turismo y patrimonio cultural **9**(2), 225–236 (2011)
17. GADML, Gobierno Autónomo Descentralizado Latacunga. Plan de Desarrollo y Ordenamiento Territorial 2016–2028 Latacunga (2015)
18. Bernal, C., Christophoul, F., Darrozes, J., Soula, J.C., Baby, P., Burgos, J.: Late Glacial and Holocene avulsions of the Rio Pastaza Megafan (Ecuador–Peru): frequency and controlling factors. Int. J. Earth Sci. **100**(7), 1759–1782 (2011)
19. Fichamba S, Ñacata S.: Diseño de obras de protección, regulación y control de lahares en el Río Saquimala en la zona Sur Occidental del Volcán Cotopaxi, Tesis de Pregrado, Carrera de Ingeniería Civil, ESPE, Repositorio (2016)
20. Barberi, F.: INECEL. Proyecto Hidroeléctrico San Francisco. Estudio Complementario de Vulcanología (1992)
21. Biass, S., Bonadonna, C.: A quantitative uncertainty assessment of eruptive parameters derived from tephra deposits: the example of two large eruptions of Cotopaxi volcano, Ecuador. Bull. Volcanol. **73**(1), 73–90 (2011)
22. Pistolesi, M., Cioni, R., Rosi, M., Aguilera, E.: Lahar hazard assessment in the southern drainage system of Cotopaxi volcano, Ecuador. Results from multiscale lahar simulation. Geomorphology **207**, 51–63 (2014)
23. Toulkeridis, T., Jacome, A., Mato, F.: Ethics, policy, and risk assessment of the Cotopaxi volcanic crisis in Ecuador—vulnerable society versus unprepared volcanic monitoring staff and authorities. In: Acevedo, R.D., Frías, J.M. (eds.) Geoethics in Latin America. TLASBS, pp. 153–170. Springer, Cham (2018). https://doi.org/10.1007/978-3-319-75373-7_11
24. Rodriguez, F., Toulkeridis, T., Sandoval, W., Padilla, O., Mato, F.: Economic risk assessment of Cotopaxi volcano, Ecuador, in case of a future lahar emplacement. Nat. Hazards **85**(1), 1–14 (2016). https://doi.org/10.1007/s11069-016-2589-1
25. Vaca, A.V., Arroyo, C.R., Debut, A., Toulkeridis, T., Cumbal, L., Mato, F., et al.: Characterization of fine-grained material ejected by the Cotopaxi volcano employing x-ray diffraction and electron diffraction scattering techniques. Biol. Med. (Aligarh) **8**(280), 2 (2016)
26. Toulkeridis, T., Chunga, K., Rentería, W., Rodriguez, F., Mato, F., Nikolaou, S., et al.: The 7.8 M_W Earthquake and Tsunami of the 16th April 2016 in Ecuador - Seismic evaluation, geological field survey and economic implications. Sci. Tsunami Hazards **36**, 197–242 (2017)
27. Toulkeridis, T., Mato, F., Toulkeridis-Estrella, K., Perez Salinas, J.C., Tapia, S., Fuertes, W.: Real-time radioactive precursor of the april 16, 2016 Mw 7.8 earthquake and tsunami in Ecuador. Sci. Tsunami Hazards **37**, 34–48 (2018)
28. Toulkeridis, T., Porras, L., Tierra, A., Toulkeridis-Estrella, K., Cisneros, D., Luna, M., et al.: Two independent real-time precursors of the 7.8 Mw earthquake in Ecuador based on radioactive and geodetic processes—powerful tools for an early warning system. J. Geodyn. **126**, 12–22 (2019)
29. Echegaray-Aveiga, R.C., Rodríguez, F., Toulkeridis, T., Echegaray-Aveiga, R.D.: Effects of potential lahars of the Cotopaxi volcano on housing market prices. J. Appl. Volcanol. **9**, 1–11 (2020)

Prototype of a Low Cost Turbine
for the Generation of Clean Energy
in the Ecuadorian Amazon

Bryan Guáitara[1], Jorge Buele[1,2(✉)] ⓘ, Franklin W. Salazar[1] ⓘ,
and José Varela-Aldás[2] ⓘ

[1] Universidad Técnica de Ambato, Ambato 180103, Ecuador
{bguaitara2617,fw.salazar}@uta.edu.ec
[2] SISAu Research Group, Universidad Tecnológica Indoamérica, Ambato 180212, Ecuador
{jorgebuele,josevarela}@uti.edu.ec

Abstract. Access to electricity supply in remote areas is limited, despite having wealth of other natural resources such as water. This document presents the design and construction of a scale electric generation system, taking advantage of the hydraulic energy produced by a constant flow of water flow. For this, the turbine design is described, which is based on the principles of Francis and Kaplan. In addition, the structural design made in CAD/CAM software and the actual implementation of the system are shown. To determine the generated electric potential, the electromagnetic analysis is performed based on the Maxwell-Faraday equation and the respective calculations. The validation of this proposal is determined by conducting experimental tests with balanced, unbalanced, series and parallel coils and with their implementation in a home.

Keywords: Hydraulic turbines · Renewable energy · Power generation · Mechanical design · 3D print

1 Introduction

The generation of energy using fossil fuels such as coal, oil, natural gas and radioactive fuels has caused damage to the atmosphere and as a consequence they are part of current global warming [1, 2]. It is estimated that the environmental impact generated is 31 times higher than the so-called "clean or renewable energies", since they reduce the number of pollutants and their territorial distribution is less concentrated [3]. Among the options to reduce dependence on oil as the main energy, currently solar, wind, hydraulic and various forms of biomass are used; wind energy being the friendliest with the environment [4]. Increasing the participation of renewable energies ensures long-term sustainable electricity generation at a better cost. If applied in a socially responsible way, they can offer employment opportunities in rural and urban settings and thus promote zonal and local technological development [5].

One of the oldest clean energy sources with the greatest capacity for generating global electricity supply is hydroelectric energy (moving water). Formerly this system

© Springer Nature Switzerland AG 2020
G. Rodriguez Morales et al. (Eds.): TICEC 2020, CCIS 1307, pp. 564–571, 2020.
https://doi.org/10.1007/978-3-030-62833-8_41

included a small dam, from which a tributary of water ran to a wheel with blades that when moving generated kinetic and potential energies [6]. In the 19th century, this process was technified and the appearance of hydroelectric power plants began, with little profitability given the strong economic investment. Despite this, in the 20th century it presented a resurgence with the development of the electric generator and the improvement of the hydraulic turbine and the demand for electricity increased [7]. The environmental impact it generates is positive, since in its process it does not emit polluting products, although its construction can flood large areas of land and modify the flow of rivers [8].

Its high implementation costs have motivated several investigations, in which smaller designs are made, as shown below. In [9] 3D design of a Pelton turbine is shown using the SOLIDWORKS working environment and its subsequent construction. The design is done using aluminum and cubes manufactured on a 3D printer, using PLA plastic. For the simulation of the water head, the water pump is used. Similarly, in [10] the design of a Pelton and Darrieus type mini turbine is described. This research takes advantage of rainwater and turns it into drinking water, using a 6-stage filtration and treatment of water. Finally, in [11] the design and construction of mini Pelton-type hydraulic turbines is presented, which can generate electrical energy and are used domestically to power electrical appliances. The results show the feasibility of to implement this type of smaller system, without problems.

Most scale turbines are developed using the Pelton model, for this application it has chosen to use the Francis and Kaplan principles. Using mechanical design software, each of the parts that make up the structure have been designed for subsequent 3D printing. The material used is PLA and aluminum, which guarantees a low-cost proposal. During the design, the corresponding electromagnetic analysis of the design is carried out, to ensure the necessary voltage production at a frequency of 60 Hz. Experimental tests demonstrate the preliminary results of the voltage production, for subsequent testing in a real house [9–11].

This document is organized in 5 sections. Section 1 describes the introduction and related works. In Sect. 2 the turbine design is presented and in Sect. 3 the structural design. The calculations developed and the experimental results are in Sects. 4 and 5 respectively. Finally, the conclusions are shown in Sect. 6.

2   Turbine Design

2.1   Electric Generator

An axial flow electric generator is designed, which allows obtaining three-phase voltage signals sinusoidal. This generator is composed of a system of permanent magnets that establish a constant magnetic field B and a system of windings on which a variable magnetic flux occurs in the time ϕt. This flux varies as a function of time, thanks to the relative movement that occurs between the coils and the permanent magnets when the rotor rotates. This type of generator allows modifying the frequency of the voltage signal, increasing or decreasing the number of magnetic poles in the system; reason why high rotational speeds are not required to achieve high frequencies in the voltage signal. As stated, the prototype presents 16 permanent magnets and 12 induction coils.

2.2 Coupling and Turbine

Pelton turbines are regularly used in systems with closed channels (pipes). To generate the pressure that moves the turbine, it is necessary to direct the flow from a considerable height by a fall through pipes, which complicates its design and installation. Given the geographical area where this prototype is to be installed, the characteristics of other types of turbines have been analyzed. The Francis type works horizontally, using the flow with a system that directs the flow by moving the propellers. The blades are positioned vertically obtaining an almost perpendicular contact, taking advantage of the circular flow generated by the spiral box in which the propeller is placed. On the other hand, the Kaplan type, have blades with a calibrated inclination angle to work with a flow parallel to the axis. Placing the propeller with the shaft vertically takes advantage of the weight of the fluid, but loses much of the force of the horizontal flow. By analyzing the feature of each turbine, the propeller is designed so that the drive is initially tangential and continues axially, taking advantage of the initial flow and potential energy due to the weight of the fluid. This, thanks to the variation in the angle of incidence along the propeller blades, this helps to take advantage of more efficiently the flow and the gravity, reducing the complexity of the system.

3 Structural Design

To ensure that the design can be reproduced in masse, automatically, flexibly and at low cost, the structural design has been carried out using CAD/CAM software. For this application, using AUTOCAD software, the structure shown in Fig. 1 is elaborated; where a 6 mm core can be seen, with a separation of 3 mm at a circumference of 3 mm and joined by its tangents.

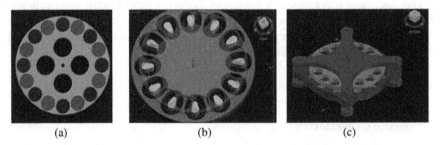

(a)   (b)   (c)

Fig. 1. Design of: (a) Rotor of permanent magnets with its distribution. (b) Distribution of the coils in the stator. (c) Final coupling of the generator parts.

Open water channel systems are typically rectangular in cross-sectional area and average 40 cm wide with a height of 30 cm; for reasons of theoretical study, this prototype is built in a 3:1 scale. The parameters of the turbine wheel are limited by the dimensions of the water entrainment tank. The coil that connects to the flow is made up of four curves with radii 18 cm, 16 cm, 14 cm and 12 cm and has a perforation in the center where the propeller is placed, which has an 8 mm radius on its axis and generally a height of 7 cm.

The number of blades is one of the most relevant design parameters. If this number is too high, the displacement effect on the turbine is severe and this will cause the increase in hydraulic loss. Whereas, if the leaf number is too low, the loss of the diffuser will increase with the growth of the diffuse extension of the flow path. Given this, it has been determined to place 6 blades, which provides stability to the structure and a better dynamic performance of the fluid. For the design, a free flow speed of 5 m/s is determined, which is chosen according to the structural conditions of the water channels in the region, where the optimal rotation speed will be chosen based on the generation of maximum power. The final design of the entire prototype is presented in Fig. 2.

 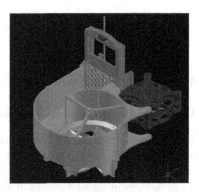

Fig. 2. Final design of the Francis and Kaplan type turbine.

3.1 Prototype Construction

For the prototype implementation, the AutoCAD generated file (.stl and .dwg) must be sent to the Repetier-Host Mac program to generate the (gcode) file. This file is necessary for 3D printing, at this time it is loaded onto the micro SD card which is read by the Prusa I3 3D printer. By printing the document from the rotor the following product is obtained, in this step, the 16 neodymium magnets are placed in it. As shown in Fig. 3. Before this step, the enameled wire is weighed to facilitate winding and thus not count each turn, with a total weight of 77 g with the mold and 62 g only the enameled copper wire. Mean implementation costs are briefly described below: external structure $70; propeller $90; Alternator (molds structure $32, magnets $50 and coils $8) $90, with a total of $250.

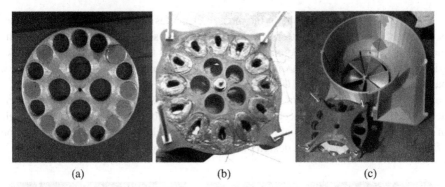

(a)   (b)   (c)

Fig. 3. (a) Placement of each coil in the stator. (b) Portable three-phase electric generator: bottom view. (c) Prototype implemented.

4 Calculations Developed

4.1 Obtaining the Electric Potential

The generator is designed based on materials that can be found commercially in Ecuador, in this case the magnets that are made with cylindrical neodymium are 25 mm in diameter, 10 mm high and a magnetic field of 0.8635 [T]. In addition, the design is focused on the use of movement, using 4 groups of 3 coils and 16 magnets in each stage. The frequency is 60 Hz, the one used in this continent.

To obtain the generator potential, in this case the Maxwell-Faraday equation is used in its integral form, as shown in (1).

$$\oint \vec{E} * d\vec{l} = -\int \frac{d\vec{B}}{dt} d\vec{S} \tag{1}$$

Solving the integral of the first member of the equation results in the electric potential and in the second member is replaced by the electric flow, is obtained (2).

$$\varepsilon = -\frac{d\phi}{dt} \tag{2}$$

Faraday also established that the magnetic flux in a wire loop is the same product of the area enclosed by the loop, the magnetic field on the same surface and the cosine of the angle of the loop with respect to the magnetic field. Since the magnetic field is changing over time, in this case it is rotating, the magnetic field is established as a function of an angular velocity, as shown in (3).

$$\phi = B * S * \cos(\omega * t) \tag{3}$$

After replacing the equations, the expression is obtained based on known variables (4).

$$\varepsilon = -\frac{d(B * S * \cos(\omega * t))}{dt} \tag{4}$$

Since it is working with coils, i.e., a set of turns, the previous expression is multiplied by N turns, as expressed in (5).

$$\varepsilon = 2\pi fNBA * \sin\left(\frac{\pi}{2}\right) \tag{5}$$

$$\varepsilon = 2\pi(26)(1000)(0.2158)\left(185.59 * 10^{-6}\right) * \sin\left(\frac{\pi}{2}\right) = 5.837\,[V]$$

Therefore, the electric potential through the 4 coils is:

$$\varepsilon = 23.35\,[V]$$

5 Experimental Results

To extract energy from the water, a thrust force T directed upstream must be generated. In this axial marine current turbine, thrust is obtained by turning the blades, which creates a pressure drop across the turbine. The ideal power drawn, which is not what would actually be recovered on the shaft, is the product of the flow of water through the turbine and the pressure drop across the turbine. Table 1 shows the results obtained in the experimental tests. The current value achieved is 1.6 [A] and with a voltage of 85.7 [V] it allows an approximate power consumption of 137 [W].

Table 1. Voltages and frequencies obtained with different coil configurations.

Sample	Frequency [Hz]	Balanced coils [V]	Unbalanced coils [V]	Serial coils [V]	Parallel coils [V]
1	10	18,4	18	35,6	7,72
2	20	35,2	30,2	50,8	17,7
3	30	52,8	44,6	95,6	28,5
4	40	65,6	31,2	77,7	38,5
5	50	50.4	75,2	95,7	44,83
6	60	61.4	91,6	112,7	53,45
7	70	71,13	104	133.2	65,7
8	80	81,2	120	151	66,88
9	90	87,25	137	166,17	85,7

This prototype is tested in a small house that does not have a light supply, it is located next to a river in the Ecuadorian Amazon. Variations of the power drawn in a free stream of water with various hydrodynamic flow conditions produces enough power to light two lights and provide light to the home. To extract the maximum possible power, the water turbine must operate at a suitable speed of rotation. For a specific rotation condition, power depends on the speed of the water flow, for example, it increases with the speed of the water flow that occurs when it rains and the river increases its flow. After these experiments it has been determined that if the phases of the two generator stages are connected in parallel, the output current can be increased without reaching temperatures that may affect the operation of the system.

The resistance and wear of the propeller is improved by covering it with catalyzed resin, this increase its resistance and stability, extending its useful life. The resistance analyzes performed are shown in Fig. 4.

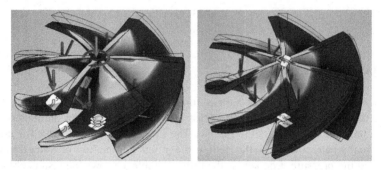

Fig. 4. Resistance analysis: At the starting point (left) and with the propeller in motion (right).

When reviewing the bibliography described, it can be seen that Pelton type turbines are the most used, but as already explained in Sect. 2, the design characteristics are not the most suitable for the currents of the rivers of the Ecuadorian Amazon. This is why the combination of the Francis and Kaplan designs works well in this application. Although they are similar prototypes, including in terms of the manufacturing material (PLA), this proposal presents a catalyzed resin coating, which allows for greater durability and resistance for better usability.

6   Conclusions and Future Work

A Francis and Kaplan type turbine has been developed, as a variant to Pelton's designs, which as seen in the literature are the most widely used. This hybrid design consists of a propeller that produces a spiral incidence flow to a vertical incidence flow (Francis), moving a propeller (Kaplan) that takes advantage of the flow. Despite having developed a prototype to scale and with low-cost materials (3D printing PLA), the efficiency of the system could be demonstrated. Although the extracted power increases with the rotation speed, until obtaining maximum power, the water turbine maintains a constant voltage production. The experimental results with different coil configurations make it possible to establish that the coils placed in series have greater stability at the time of a real application. These results are still preliminary, and it is necessary to increase the number of experiments, so the percentages of real power generation performance and turbine power cannot be established yet.

This document is part of a larger investigation and as future work it is proposed to improve this initial version and to use more resistant materials while preserving the design made. This system could offer the possibility of providing the electric light service for those homes that live in remote places and their living conditions are precarious.

References

1. Burke, M.J., Stephens, J.C.: Political power and renewable energy futures: a critical review. Energy Res. Soc. Sci. **35**, 78–93 (2018). https://doi.org/10.1016/j.erss.2017.10.018
2. Ho, L.W.: Wind energy in Malaysia: past, present and future. Renew. Sustain. Energy Rev. **53**, 279–295 (2016). https://doi.org/10.1016/j.rser.2015.08.054
3. Gielen, D., Boshell, F., Saygin, D., Bazilian, M.D., Wagner, N., Gorini, R.: The role of renewable energy in the global energy transformation. Energy Strateg. Rev. **24**, 38–50 (2019). https://doi.org/10.1016/j.esr.2019.01.006
4. Oree, V., Sayed Hassen, S.Z., Fleming, P.J.: Generation expansion planning optimisation with renewable energy integration: a review. Renew. Sustain. Energy Rev. **69**, 790–803 (2017). https://doi.org/10.1016/j.rser.2016.11.120
5. Good, N., Ellis, K.A., Mancarella, P.: Review and classification of barriers and enablers of demand response in the smart grid. Renew. Sustain. Energy Rev. **72**, 57–72 (2017). https://doi.org/10.1016/j.rser.2017.01.043
6. Singh, V.K., Singal, S.K.: Operation of hydro power plants-a review. Renew. Sustain. Energy Rev. **69**, 610–619 (2017). https://doi.org/10.1016/j.rser.2016.11.169
7. Zeng, S., Liu, Y., Liu, C., Nan, X.: A review of renewable energy investment in the BRICS countries: history, models, problems and solutions. Renew. Sustain. Energy Rev. **74**, 860–872 (2017). https://doi.org/10.1016/j.rser.2017.03.016
8. Barbour, E., Wilson, I.A.G., Radcliffe, J., Ding, Y., Li, Y.: A review of pumped hydro energy storage development in significant international electricity markets. Renew. Sustain. Energy Rev. **61**, 421–432 (2016). https://doi.org/10.1016/j.rser.2016.04.019
9. Tomović, R., Tomović, A., Mumović, M., Vujošević, V.: Development of construction of mini hydro power plant model based on Pelton turbine. In: Karabegović, I. (ed.) NT 2018. LNNS, vol. 42, pp. 405–412. Springer, Cham (2019). https://doi.org/10.1007/978-3-319-90893-9_48
10. Gagarin, J.O., Lunas, A.K., Orticio, W.P., Torres, L.F., Magwili, G.V., Pacis, M.C.: Wind energy and hydroelectricity generation using mini turbine installed in downspout with rainwater treatment. In: HNICEM 2017 - 9th International Conference on Humanoid, Nanotechnology, Information Technology, Communication and Control, Environment and Management. pp. 1–5 (2017)
11. Ighodalo Okhueleigbe, E.: Mini-hydro turbine: solution to power challenges in an emerging society with abundance of water. Am. J. Eng. Technol. Manag. **2**, 7 (2017). https://doi.org/10.11648/j.ajetm.20170202.11

Evaluation of the Surface Temperature Applied in Aquaculture Based on Satellite Images in Coastal Ecuador

Karol Arellano Pérez[1] , Pablo Padilla Lascano[1] , Iñigo Molina Sánchez[2] ,
Oswaldo Padilla-Almeida[1] , and Theofilos Toulkeridis[1(✉)]

[1] Universidad de las Fuerzas Armadas – ESPE, Sangolquí, Ecuador
ttoulkeridis@espe.edu.ec
[2] Universidad Politécnica de Madrid, Madrid, Spain

Abstract. The surface temperature is the radiant temperature of the earth's surface. It is also a fundamental variable when determining the climatic variability on a coverage of interest. We evaluated the surface temperature in shrimp ponds present in the Puná Island located in southwestern Ecuador, for the years 2014 to 2017, from Landsat 8 OLI/TIRS images and ASTER-GED emissivity data, as the biophysical characteristics that this island presents have become one of the main reasons for a large number of shrimp companies to base operations in this territory. An example of this is the presence of several pools that meet specific temperature parameters for the cultivation of the species *Litopenaeus vannamei*, better known as the Pacific white shrimp. There are a variety of algorithms to calculate the surface temperature. We applied four different algorithms, of which the first two are split-window, based on the differential absorption of two thermal bands to correct the atmospheric effects. There residual two algorithms are two mono-channels, which use the radiance of a thermal band and perform the residual atmospheric correction through of atmospheric parameters. Hereby, the split-window algorithm stands out, which indicated an average surface temperature for the four years in the range of 26.38 °C to 30.59 °C. It is also within the optimum range (22 °C to 30 °C) for the cultivation of this species. Therefore, our study most likely represents as a possible alternative to other methods, the use of remote sensing for the estimation of the surface temperature in large areas of shrimp ponds.

Keywords: Shrimp farms · Surface temperature · Split-widow

1 Introduction

The observation of the Earth's surface has become a mandatory task of land planners and other interested groups in the optimization of land use or evaluation of any surface changes [13, 26, 36, 43, 44]. Since 1972, the first civil satellite ERTS-1 called Landsat 1 has been launched into space, which has been followed by several more up to 2013 providing daily global observation data [20]. Later, the ASTER sensor, similar to Landsat,

© Springer Nature Switzerland AG 2020
G. Rodriguez Morales et al. (Eds.): TICEC 2020, CCIS 1307, pp. 572–586, 2020.
https://doi.org/10.1007/978-3-030-62833-8_42

provided high spatial resolution data in 14 bands, ranging from visible wavelengths to thermal infrared. However, one of the capabilities of ASTER data is that they are used by other spatial instruments for subsequent validation and calibration. Both, the Landsat 8 sensor and the ASTER sensor detect thermal infrared and emissivity data, respectively, which are essential for the calculation of the temperature at the earth's surface [21, 22].

The calculation of the surface temperature may be understood as a relationship between the energy emitted by the surface and the energy received at the sensor [23]. However, the atmosphere produces distortions in the radiance values that reach the sensor from the earth's surface, generating temperature results at the top of the atmosphere and not at the level of the Earth's surface, which explains the need to eliminate the intrusive component of the atmosphere through a calculation of surface temperature based on mathematical algorithms [29]. For the control of the temperature in the water of shrimp ponds, usually measurements are performed in situ by means of a common thermometer or through probes incorporated to oxygen, pH and similar parameters [9, 27]. This technique, in addition to presenting high operating costs, has the drawback of providing a point measure, which, although it may be sufficiently precise, lacks to be representative for large areas [33]. For the aforementioned reasons, there has been a need to obtain a more representative form to cover a larger scale, which may be provided by the use of sensors or artificial satellites applied in the Earth's surface observation.

Therefore, the main aim for the current study has been to search the ideal application of a variety of algorithms for the subsequent calculation of surface temperature, in order to obtain representative data on surface temperature in shrimp ponds that generally cover large extensions of territory, using the thermal bands of the Landsat 8 OLI-TIRS sensor as well as the ASTER-GED emissivity data.

2   Study Area and Used Data

The study area is located in the Puná Island, which is situated the opening of the Gulf of Guayaquil, in southwestern Ecuador, ($\varphi = 2° \ 51' \ 50''$S, $\lambda = 80° \ 07' \ 26''$W; see Fig. 1). The island has an approximate extension of 919 km², of which a large part of Ecuador's shrimp companies are located [2]. Shrimp is currently the second largest non-oil product in the country and therefore of great importance for its economy [24]. The species *Litopenaeus vannamei*, which is better known as Pacific white shrimp is the one with the highest production on the Island. Its optimal development requires in the pools intended for cultivation a specific temperature being between 20 °C and 32 °C, of which the optimum ranges between 22 °C and 30 °C [30, 41]. The shrimps industry in the Island of Puná has been relatively slightly affected by Ecuador's strong earthquake in 2016, although situated in the range of damages of the seismic event [8, 39, 40].

The used images have been four multi-time scenes recorded by Landsat 8 satellite obtained from NASA's EARTHDATA portal on March 11, 2014, May 17, 2015, May 19, 2016 and October 13, 2017, all with a Path 11 and Row 62 regarding the Landsat world grid. For the current study, we handled the thermal bands 10 (TIRS-1) and 11 (TIRS-2) whose spatial resolution is 100 m with image resuscitated at 30 m. In addition, bands 13 (TIR-4) and 14 (TIR-5) of images from the ASTER GED (Advanced Spaceborne Thermal Emission and Reflection Radiometer Global Emissivity Database) mission were

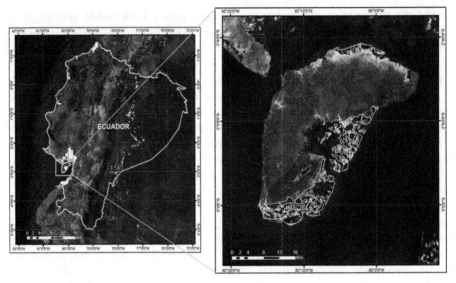

Fig. 1. Study area in the Puna Island, Southwestern Ecuador

selected to obtain global emissivity data from scenes acquired between 2000–2008, with a spatial resolution of 100 m covering the study area. All images have been georeferenced to the WGS84 system with UTM coordinates (Zone 17 South) in Ecuador, a country of severe hazards [8].

3   Methodology

The methodology was structured in two main sections. In the first place the handling and obtaining of the emissivity data is exposed, and in the second place the calculation of surface temperature.

3.1   Emissivity

The ratio between the ability of a real body to emit radiation (surface emission) and that of the black body (ideal radiator emission) at the same temperature is called spectral emissivity expressed as $\varepsilon(\lambda)$ [19]. In the study the emissivity data were not calculated directly with the bands TIRS-1 (10.6–11.19 μm), TIRS-2 (11.5–12.51 μm) of the Landsat 8 sensor, as is commonly done. Instead we proceeded to use the data of the bands TIR-4 (10.25–10.95 μm) and TIR-5 (10.95–11.65 μm) of the ASTER GED sensor, which as listed in Table 1, present wavelengths with similar ranges. Therefore, they may be able to be considered as valid emissivity data for each thermal band, hereby replacing their required emissivity's in the algorithms.

Table 1. Correspondence between LANDSAT 8 thermal bands and ASTER-GED emissivity data

	Sensors	
	Landsat 8 OLI/TIRS	ASTER-GED
Band	TIRS-1 (Band 10)	TIRS-4 (Band 13)
Wavelength	10.6–11.19 μm	10.25–10.95 μm
Band	TIRS-2 (Band 11)	TIRS-5 (Band 14)
Wavelength	11.5–12.51 μm	10.95–11.65 μm

3.2 Surface Temperature

We applied two different methods in order to determine the surface temperature based on the two-channel or split-window method and the mono-channel or single-channel method. Two calculation algorithms have been exposed in each one of the used methods.

a) Two Channel/Split-Window (SW)

The Split-Window method corrects atmospheric effects based on differential absorption in two adjacent spectral bands, located in the atmospheric window between 10.5 μm and 12.5 μm [33]. According to [5], several modifications have been performed to the algorithm initially proposed by [42] in his study to estimate the sea surface temperature.

Becker & Li Algorithm. According to [5], the split-window algorithm equation is given by:

$$T_s = A_0 + P\frac{(T_i + T_j)}{2} + M\frac{(T_i - T_j)}{2} \tag{1}$$

$$A_0 = 1.274 \tag{2}$$

$$P = 1 + 0.15616\frac{(1 - \varepsilon)}{\varepsilon} - 0.482\frac{\Delta\varepsilon}{\varepsilon^2} \tag{3}$$

$$M = 6.26 + 3.98\frac{(1 - \varepsilon)}{\varepsilon} + 38.33\frac{\Delta\varepsilon}{\varepsilon^2} \tag{4}$$

$$\varepsilon = \frac{\varepsilon_i + \varepsilon_j}{2}; \Delta\varepsilon = \varepsilon_i - \varepsilon_j T_j \tag{5}$$

Where:

T_s represents the surface temperature, T_i y T_j represent the brightness temperature for Landsat 8 bands 10 and 11 respectively, A_0, P and M are the coefficients for thermal spectral radiance and its transmission in bands 10 and 11, ε represents the average emissivity, $\Delta\varepsilon$ the difference in emissivity, while ε_i and ε_j represent the emissivity of bands 13 and 14 of ASTER-GED respectively [10–12].

Sobrino Algorithm.
According to the equation of [35], the split-window algorithm is given by:

$$T_s = T_i + C_1(T_i - T_j) + C_2(T_i - T_j)^2 + C_0 + (C_3 + C_4 W)(1 - \varepsilon) + (C_5 + C_6 W)\Delta\varepsilon \tag{6}$$

Where:
  $C_0 - C_6$ are the values of the algorithm coefficients obtained by simulation [17] and W is the vapor content in the atmosphere [16, 18, 31].

b) Mono/Single-Channel (SC)
The Single-Channel method uses the radiance measured by the satellite sensor in a single thermal band and in turn performs the residual atmospheric correction through the estimation of atmospheric parameters obtained from the Atmospheric Correction Parameter Calculator proposed by [4]. Finally the surface temperature is obtained through the inverse function of Planck [28, 36].

Barsi Algorithm. According to [3], the equation of the mono-channel algorithm is given by:

$$L_S = \tau\varepsilon L_T + L_{\lambda\uparrow} + \tau(1 - \varepsilon)L_{\lambda\downarrow} \tag{7}$$

$$L_T = \frac{L_S - L_{\lambda\uparrow} - \tau(1 - \varepsilon)L_{\lambda\downarrow}}{\tau\varepsilon} \tag{8}$$

$$T_S = \frac{K_2}{\ln\left[\frac{K_1}{L_T} + 1\right]} \tag{9}$$

Where:
  L_S represents the radiance of the band 10 (TIRS-1) of the Landsat 8 sensor, L_T is the corrected radiance, ε represents the average emissivity of the bands 13 and 14 of ASTER GED, τ is the transmittance, $L_{\lambda\uparrow}$ and $L_{\lambda\downarrow}$ the ascending and descending atmospheric radiance respectively, K_1 and K_2 the constants of the thermal bands obtained from the image metadata.

Jiménez Muñoz Algorithm. According to [15], the equation of the single-channel algorithm is given by:

$$T_S = \gamma\left[\frac{1}{\varepsilon}(\psi_1 L_T + \psi_2) + \psi_3\right] + \delta \tag{10}$$

$$\gamma \approx \frac{T_b^2}{b_\gamma L_T}; \quad \delta \approx T_b - \frac{T_b^2}{b_\gamma} \tag{11}$$

$$\psi_1 = \frac{1}{\tau}; \quad \psi_2 = -L_{\lambda\downarrow} - \frac{L_{\lambda\uparrow}}{\tau}; \quad \psi_3 = L_{\lambda\downarrow} \tag{12}$$

Where:

  L_T represents the radiance of band 10 (TIRS-1) of the Landsat 8 sensor, T_b is the brightness temperature of the band 10, $b_\gamma = c_2/\lambda = 1324$ for TIRS-1 [17, 32].

4 Results

The results obtained by the single-channel and two-channel method are summarized in the histograms of Figs. 2, 3, 4 and 5, and are detailed in Tables 2 and 3, where the minimum, maximum and average value of the surface temperature for each year is indicated, in addition to the differences between the algorithms.

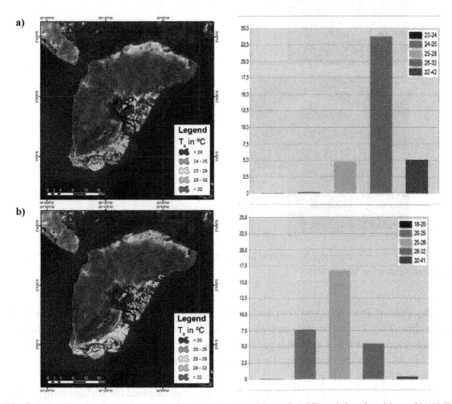

Fig. 2. Year 2014, temperatures obtained by the algorithm of a) [5] and the algorithm of b) [35] and their respective histograms

4.1 Two Channel/Split-Window (SW)

For the year 2014, the histograms (Fig. 2) demonstrate that the surface temperature data exhibits a greater accumulation of pixels, being in the range of 28 °C to 32 °C for the case of the algorithm of [5] and in the range of 25 °C to 28 °C for the algorithm of [34, 35]. For the year 2015, the histograms show that surface temperature data documents a greater accumulation of pixels, being in the range of 32 °C to 34 °C for the case of the first algorithm and in the range of 28 °C to 30 °C for the second algorithm (Fig. 3).

For the following year 2016, the histograms demonstrate that the surface temperature data exhibit a greater accumulation of pixels, being in the range of 33 °C to 35 °C

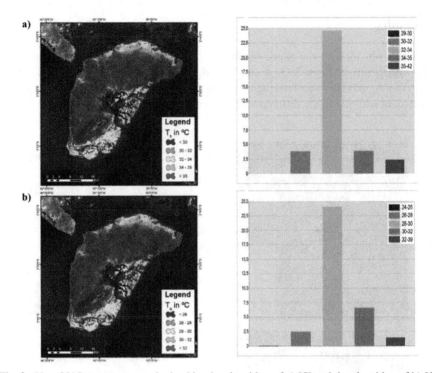

Fig. 3. Year 2015, temperatures obtained by the algorithm of a) [5] and the algorithm of b) [35] and their respective histograms

for the case of the first algorithm and in the range of 28° C to 30 °C for the second algorithm (Fig. 4). In the last studied year in 2017, the histograms illustrate that the surface temperature data exhibit a greater accumulation of pixels, being in the range of 30 °C to 33 °C for the case of the first algorithm and in the range of 26 °C to 29 °C for the second algorithm (Fig. 5).

In the last studied year in 2017, the histograms illustrate that the surface temperature data exhibit a greater accumulation of pixels, being in the range of 30 °C to 33 °C for the case of the first algorithm and in the range of 26 °C to 29 °C for the second algorithm (Fig. 5).

4.2 Mono/Single Channel (SC)

Histograms of 2014 (Fig. 6) document, that the surface temperature data exhibit a greater accumulation of pixels, being in the range of 20 °C to 25 °C for the case of the algorithm of [3] as well as for the algorithm of [17]. In the year 2015, the histograms indicate (Fig. 7), that the surface temperature data exhibit a greater accumulation of pixels, lying in the range of 33 °C to 36 °C for the case of the algorithm of [3] and in the range of 34 °C to 37 °C for the algorithm of [17]. For the year 2016, the histograms show that the surface temperature data indicate an accumulation of pixels, which remains in the range of 34 °C to 36 °C for both algorithms (Fig. 8). For the year 2017, the histograms show

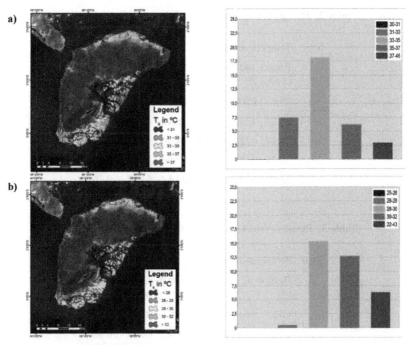

Fig. 4. Year 2016, temperatures obtained by the algorithm of a) [5] and the algorithm of b) [35] and their respective histograms

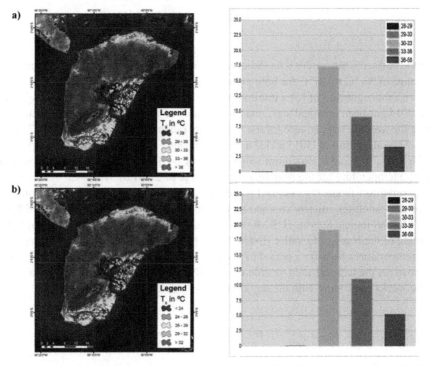

Fig. 5. Year 2016, temperatures obtained by the algorithm of a) [5] and the algorithm of b) [35] and their respective histograms

Table 2. Results of the temperature obtained by Split-Window

Year	Temperature in °C					
	Becker and Li (1990) [5]			Sobrino et al. (1996) [35]		
	min	max	avg	min	max	avg
2014	23.23	42.87	30.05	18.45	40.98	26.38
2015	29.44	42.02	33.15	24.36	38.83	29.41
2016	30.28	45.93	34.33	25.94	42.97	30.59
2017	28.02	55.82	33.17	23.51	54.67	29.46

Table 3. Results of the temperature obtained by Single-Channel

Year	Temperature in °C					
	Barsi et al. (2005) [3]			Jimenez Muñoz et al. (2009) [17]		
	min	max	avg	min	max	avg
2014	23.23	42.87	30.05	18.45	40.98	26.38
2015	29.44	42.02	33.15	24.36	38.83	29.41
2016	30.28	45.93	34.33	25.94	42.97	30.59
2017	28.02	55.82	33.17	23.51	54.67	29.46

that the surface temperature data indicate an accumulation of pixels, which remains in the range of 33 °C to 36 °C for both algorithms (Fig. 9).

With the algorithm of [3] a minimum value of T_S of 13.50 °C corresponding to the year 2014 has been obtained and a maximum value of T_S of 61.22° C for the year 2017, while the average temperature for the four years ranged between 22.80 to 36.27 °C. In case of the algorithm of [17] yielded a minimum value of T_S of 13.51 °C corresponding to the year 2014 and a maximum value of T_S of 64.36 °C for the year 2017, with an average temperature for the four years in the range of 23.01 to 37.25 °C.

In order to validate the obtained results, data have been generated by a combination of infrared satellites, microwaves and in-situ data, which were used by the United Kingdom Meteorological Service (UKMO), which are post-processed by the Oceanographic Institute of the Navy of Ecuador (INOCAR). The final products have been average surface temperature charts for a period of seven days and with a resolution of 4 km. Table 4 summarizes the temperatures recorded by the INOCAR near the study area (Isla Puná), in the weeks coinciding with the day of image capture.

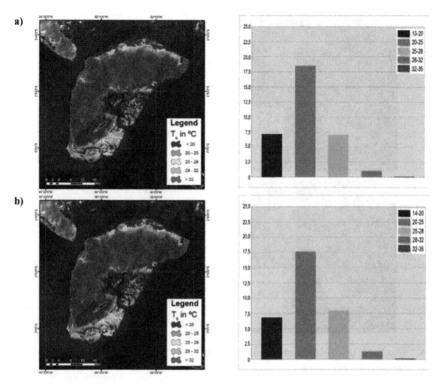

Fig. 6. Year 2014, temperatures obtained by the algorithm of c) [3] and the algorithm of d) [17] and their respective histograms

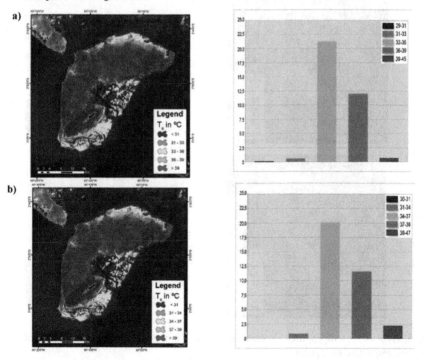

Fig. 7. Year 2015, temperatures obtained by the algorithm of c) [3] and the algorithm of d) [17] and their respective histograms

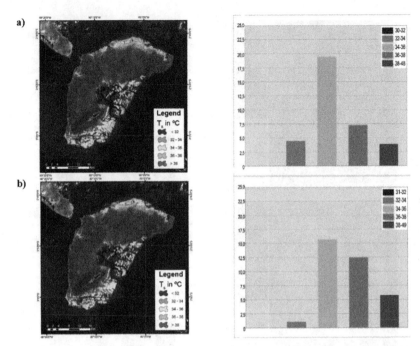

Fig. 8. Year 2016, temperatures obtained by the algorithm of c) [3] and the algorithm of d) [17] and their respective histograms

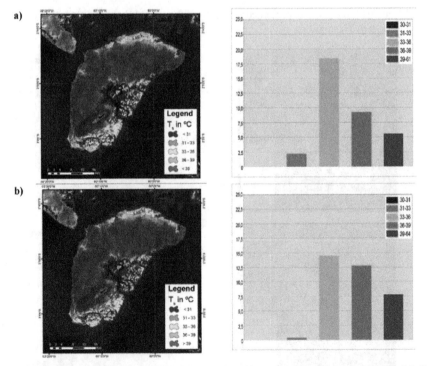

Fig. 9. Year 2017, temperatures obtained by the algorithm of c) [3] and the algorithm of d) [17] and their respective histograms

Table 4. Registered temperature by INOCAR [14]

Week (INOCAR)	Image capture date (LANDSAT 8 OLI/TIRS)	Surface temperature (INOCAR)
10–16 March 2014	11 of March	26 °C–27 °C
11–17 May 2015	17 of May	28 °C–29 °C
16–22 May 2016	19 of May	27 °C–28 °C
9–15 October 2017	13 of October	24 °C–25 °C

5 Discussion

In the current study we have used thermal data recorded by bands 10 and 11 of the Landsat 8 OLI-TIRS sensor and ASTER emissivity data. In the same way, two algorithms for the single-channel method and two for the split-window have been evaluated, being focused on the calculation of surface temperature in shrimp pools present on Puná Island for the time period between 2014 to 2017. In the case of the split-window (two-channel) method proposed by [5] and [35], the average surface temperature range for the four years has been 30.05 °C to 34.33 °C and 26.38 °C to 30.59 °C respectively.

The later has greater similarity with respect to the intervals recorded by INOCAR in the studied years yielding temperature ranges of 26 °C to 27 °C, 28 °C to 29 °C, 27 °C to 28 °C and 24 °C to 25 °C respectively. Such data agree with the temperature ranges that present a greater accumulation of pixels in the histograms (Figs. 2, 3, 4 and 5) generated from the algorithm of [35].

All these data comply with the optimum temperature (22 °C to 30 °C), which according to [41] need to be present within the pools intended for shrimp farming. With regard to the single-channel methodology formulated by [3] and [17], the average surface temperature range in the four years, has been 22.97 to 36.90 °C and 23.19 to 37.92 °C, respectively. In conjunction with their histogram intervals (Figs. 6, 7, 8 and 9) they differ significantly from the range recorded by INOCAR and that proposed by [41]. This may not be valid in unusual years such as those when the ENSO phenomenon appears [45].

It is worth mentioning that when applying the different methodologies, extremely high values have been presented in all algorithms, which is due to the fact that around the shrimp pools different soil coverings have been present, which generates in results outside the common surface temperature ranges of the area.

Finally, the split-window and single-channel methodologies for the calculation of surface temperature have been implemented, by combining data acquired by the Landsat 8 OLI-TIRS and ASTER sensor, of which the latter provided specific data on the emissivity variable as an alternative to those commonly generated through methods based on the Normalized Vegetation Index (NDVI), which, while measuring the intensity of radiation that the vegetation emits, does not reflect precisely what the water radiates [1, 6, 7, 25, 37, 38].

6 Conclusions

The split-window (two-channel) algorithms, in contrast to the single-channel algorithms, proved to be the most appropriate for surface temperature calculation. Among which (split-window) stands out the one proposed by [35], which presented values within the surface temperature range considered optimal in pools intended for shrimp farming. It would also represent a significant reduction in resources in terms of those invested in on-site techniques for temperature measurement in large areas of shrimp pools.

It is fundamental to highlight the proposed methodology, since, in most of the studies related to the subject, data from a single sensors are used, which may generate certain inconsistencies in the values of variables related to the object of study, in this case the water in the shrimp pools.

References

1. Alatorre, L.C., et al.: Temporal changes of NDVI for qualitative environmental assessment of mangroves: shrimp farming impact on the health decline of the arid mangroves in the Gulf of California (1990–2010). J. Arid Environ. **125**, 98–109 (2016)
2. Armas, W., Izquierdo, L.: Caracterización y propuesta técnica de la acuicultura en la parroquia rural de Puná del cantón Guayaquil. Tesis de Grado, Escuela Superior Politécnica del Litoral, Facultad de Ingeniería Marítima y Ciencias del Mar, Guayaquil, Ecuador, 110 p. (2010)
3. Barsi, J.A., Schott, J.R., Palluconi, F.D., Hook, S.J.: Validation of a web-based atmospheric correction tool for single thermal band instruments. In: Earth Observing Systems X, vol. 5882, p. 58820E. International Society for Optics and Photonics, August 2005
4. Barsi, J., Barker, J., Schott, J.: An atmospheric correction parameter calculator for a single thermal band earth-sensing instrument. In: IGARSS 2003. 2003 IEEE International Geoscience and Remote Sensing Symposium, Proceedings (IEEE Cat. No. 03CH37477), vol. 5, pp. 3014–3016 (2003)
5. Becker, F., Li, Z.-L.: Towards a local split window method over land surfaces. Int. J. Remote Sens. **11**(3), 369–393 (1990)
6. Carlson, T.N., Ripley, D.A.: On the relation between NDVI, fractional vegetation cover, and leaf area index. Remote Sens. Environ. **62**(3), 241–252 (1997)
7. Cevallos, L.N.M., et al.: A NDVI analysis contrasting different spectrum data methodologies applied in pasture crops previous grazing–a case study from Ecuador. In: 2018 International Conference on eDemocracy & eGovernment (ICEDEG), pp. 126–135. IEEE, April 2018
8. Chunga, K., Mulas, M., Alvarez, A., Galarza, J., Toulkeridis, T.: Characterization of seismogenetic crustal faults in the Gulf of Guayaquil, Ecuador. Andean Geol. **46**(1), 66–81 (2019)
9. Cuéllar-Anjel, J., Lara, C., Morales, V., De Gracia, A., García Suárez, O.: Manual de buenas prácticas de manejo para el cultivo del camarón blanco Penaeus vannamei. OIRSA-OSPESCA, C.A. Panamá: New Concept Publications (2010)
10. Dwivedi, A., Khire, M.: Application of split- window algorithm to study Urban Heat Island effect in Mumbai through land surface temperature approach. Sustain. Cities Soc. **41**, 865–877 (2018)
11. Galvis, S., Prada, R.: Uso de Imágenes Satelitales Landsat 8 para la estimación de temperatura superficial de la tierra, caso de estudio: Ibagué-Tolima. Trabajo de Grado, Universidad de Manizales, Facultad de Ciencias e Ingeniería: Especialización en Sistemas de Información Geográfica, Manizales, Colombia, 53 p. (2017)

12. Hassaballa, A.A., Matori, A.B.: The use and evaluation of split-window techniques for NOAA/AVHRR surface temperature extraction over different surface covers: case study (Perak Tengah & Manjong) area, Malaysia. Int. J. Civil Environ. Eng. IJCEE-IJENS **11**(05), 22–27 (2011)

13. Howard, R.A., Michels, D.J., Sheeley Jr., N.R., Koomen, M.J.: The observation of a coronal transient directed at Earth. Astrophys. J. **263**, L101–L104 (1982)

14. INOCAR: Instituto Oceanográfico de la Armada del Ecuador (2018). Temperatura Superficial del Mar: https://www.inocar.mil.ec/web/index.php/productos/temperatura-superficial-del-mar

15. Jiménez Muñoz, J., Cristóbal, J., Sobrino, J., Sòria, G., Ninyerola, M., Pons, X.: Revision of the single-channel algorithm for land surface temperature retrieval from landsat thermal-infrared data. IEEE Trans. Geosci. Remote Sens. **47**(1), 339–349 (2009)

16. Jiménez-Muñoz, J., Sobrino, J.: Split-window coefficients for land surface temperature retrieval from low-resolution thermal infrared sensors. IEEE Geosci. Remote Sens. Lett. **5**(4), 806–809 (2008)

17. Jiménez-Muñoz, J., Sobrino, J., Skokovic, D., Mattar, C., Cristóbal, J.: Land surface temperature retrieval methods from landsat-8 thermal infrared sensor data. IEEE Geosci. Remote Sens. Lett. **11**(10), 1840–1843 (2014)

18. Li, S., Geng-Ming, J.: Land surface temperature retrieval from landsat-8 data with the generalized split-window algorithm. IEEE Access **6**, 18149–18162 (2018)

19. Mira, M., Gordillo, J., González-Guerrero, O., Pons, X.: Análisis comparativo de métodos para la estimación de la emisividad en la banda térmica del sensor TM de Landsat-5. GeoFocus **19**(Artículos), 55–80 (2017)

20. NASA, & USDOI: Landsat Missions Timeline I Landsat Missions (2018). https://landsat.usgs.gov/landsat-missions-timeline

21. NASA: ASTER overview (2014). https://lpdaac.usgs.gov/dataset_discovery/aster?fbclid=IwAR1HAAjx-X7Dm1xmcx_opcQ8thDR-JC4Cte5aG4mHJOBQCnhZ6RjMHd7Xbs

22. NASA: Aster Mission (2018). https://asterweb.jpl.nasa.gov/mission.asp?fbclid=IwAR0B0A6t0Dc6m0EEBaiv84eZH8By06B_DXgG-jobu63_uoPdcuXpjsNlI-o

23. Pasapera, J.: Validación de la emisividad y temperatura de la superficie del suelo usando datos del satélite Landsat 8. Tesis de Grado, Universidad Nacional de Córdoba, Facultad de Matemática, Astronomía y Física, Córdoba, Argentine, 110 p. (2014)

24. Peña, L.: El Sector Camaronero del Ecuador y las Políticas Sectoriales: 2007–2016. Tesis de Grado, Pontificia Universidad Católica del Ecuador (PUCE), Facultad de Economía, Quito, Ecuador, 97 p. (2017)

25. Pettorelli, N., Vik, J.O., Mysterud, A., Gaillard, J.M., Tucker, C.J., Stenseth, N.C.: Using the satellite-derived NDVI to assess ecological responses to environmental change. Trends Ecol. Evol. **20**(9), 503–510 (2005)

26. Plag, H.P., Rothacher, M., Pearlman, M., Neilan, R., Ma, C.: The global geodetic observing system. In: Advances in Geosciences: Solid Earth (SE), vol. 13, pp. 105–127 (2009)

27. Rojas, A.A., Haws, M.C., Cabanillas, J.A.: Buenas Prácticas de Manejo para el Cultivo de Camarón. United States Agency for International Development (Cooperative Agreement No. PCE-A-00-95-0030-05). The David and Lucile Packard Foundation, 51 p. (2005)

28. Rosenbluth, M.N., MacDonald, W.M., Judd, D.L.: Fokker-Planck equation for an inverse-square force. Phys. Rev. **107**(1), 1 (1957)

29. Sarría, A.: Cálculo de temperatura de superficie a partir de imágenes Landsat, NOAA y Sentinel-3. Universidad Politécnica de Valencia, Escuela Técnica Superior de Ingeniería Geodésica, Cartográfica y Topográfica, Valencia, Spain, 10 p. (2018)

30. SEMARNAT: Construccion, operación y mantenimiento de la granja para el cultivo semi-intensivo de camarón blanco (litopenaeus vannamei) con ubicación en la sindicatura de el Dorado, municipio de Culiacan, estado de Sinaloa. Secretaría de Medio Ambiente y Recursos Naturales, México, 66 p. (2018)

31. Shahid, M.: Land surface temperature retrieval of landsat-8 data using split window algorithm-a case study of Ranchi district. Int. J. Eng. Dev. Res. (IJEDR) 2(4), 3840–3849 (2014)

32. Simon, R., Tormos, T., Danis, P.-A.: Retrieving water surface temperature from archive LANDSAT thermal infrared data: application of the mono-channel atmospheric correction algorithm over two freshwater reservoirs. Int. J. Appl. Earth Obs. Geoinf. 30, 247–250 (2014)

33. Sobrino, J., et al.: Teledetección (J.A. Sobrino (ed.)). Servicio de Publicaciones, Valencia, España (2000)

34. Sobrino, J.A., et al.: WATERMED-WATer use Efficiency in natural vegetation and agricultural areas by remote sensing in the MEDiterranean basin. In: IGARSS 2001. Scanning the Present and Resolving the Future, Proceedings. IEEE 2001 International Geoscience and Remote Sensing Symposium (Cat. No. 01CH37217), vol. 7, pp. 3158–3160. IEEE (2001)

35. Sobrino, J., Li, Z.-L., Stoll, M., Becker, F.: Multi-channel and multi-angle algorithms for estimating sea and land surface temperature with ATSR data. Int. J. Remote Sens. 17(11), 2089–2114 (1996)

36. Tang, H., Li, Z.L.: Quantitative Remote Sensing in Thermal Infrared: Theory and Applications, 279 p. Springer Science & Business Media, Heidelberg (2013)

37. Tatem, A.J., Goetz, S.J., Hay, S.I.: Fifty years of earth observation satellites: views from above have lead to countless advances on the ground in both scientific knowledge and daily life. Am. Sci. 96(5), 390 (2008)

38. Tong, P.H.S., Auda, Y., Populus, J., Aizpuru, M., Habshi, A.A., Blasco, F.: Assessment from space of mangroves evolution in the Mekong Delta, in relation to extensive shrimp farming. Int. J. Remote Sens. 25(21), 4795–4812 (2004)

39. Toulkeridis, T., et al.: The 7.8 M_w earthquake and tsunami of the 16th April 2016 in Ecuador - Seismic evaluation, geological field survey and economic implications. Sci. Tsunami Hazards 36, 197–242 (2017)

40. Toulkeridis, T., Mato, F., Toulkeridis-Estrella, K., Perez Salinas, J.C., Tapia, S., Fuertes, W.: Real-time radioactive precursor of the April 16, 2016 Mw 7.8 earthquake and tsunami in Ecuador. Sci. Tsunami Hazards 37, 34–48 (2018)

41. Young, F., Reinoso, B.: Cultivo del camarón marino (Penaeus) en Ecuador. Metodología y técnicas utilizadas. Recomendaciones. Inst. Nac. Pesca Bol. Cient. Tec. Guayaquil 5, 1–43 (1982)

42. McMillin, L.M.: Estimation of sea surface temperatures from two infrared window measurements with different absorption. J. Geophys. Res. 80(36), 5113–5117 (1975)

43. Cepeda, M., Palacios, I., Tierra, A., Kirby, E.: Multiresolution analysis in the visible spectrum of Landsat - TM images through Wavelet Transform. Geographia Technica 13(1), 20–29 (2018)

44. Palacios, I., Castro, S., Rodríguez, F.: Carbon storage as environmental service in three natural reserves of Ecuador. Revista Geoespacial 16(1), 1–14 (2019)

45. Mato, F., Toulkeridis, T.: The missing Link in El Niño's phenomenon generation. Sci. Tsunami Hazards 36, 128–144 (2017)

E-waste Management: A Case Study of Municipalities of Santa Elena Province - Ecuador

Maria Gabriela Campuzano[1]([✉]) [iD] and Tania Crisanto[2] [iD]

[1] Universidad Estatal Península de Santa Elena – UPSE, La Libertad, Ecuador
mcampuzano@upse.edu.ec
[2] Universidad de las Fuerzas Armadas – ESPE, Sangolquí, Ecuador
ttcrisanto@espe.edu.ec

Abstract. Waste of electrical and electronic equipment (WEEE or e-waste) is constantly growing worldwide as information and communications technologies (ICT) and electronics penetrate the market to satisfy society current needs. Development requires reducing the technological gap with the undesired consequent increment of e-waste. Inadequate handling and disposal of these residues poses a threat to environment and health, specially in developing countries. E-waste has been thoroughly studied worldwide; however, there is limited research about this topic in Ecuador and its municipalities. This case study focused on the current e- waste management system of the three municipalities of Santa Elena Province of Ecuador in order to propose improvements. Total WEEE generation and generation rates were estimated. Qualitative research methods were used to map the main stakeholders and to analyze the current waste management scheme. Literature review was performed, and field work included observation, interviews and surveys. Most of the stakeholders were approached during this study. The awareness and willingness of citizens to participate in campaigns and initiatives was evaluated. A comparison with other Ecuadorian cities is presented to tailor recommendations for municipalities. Two stages are suggested to improve the current scheme as the province faces many challenges closing open dump sites and including e-waste management in the current agenda.

Keywords: Electronic waste · Waste management · Municipality · Santa Elena

1 Introduction

Waste of electrical and electronic equipment (WEEE) or e-waste refers to any electrical and electronic equipment (EEE) or piece of it that has reached the end of its life or end of use. E-waste can be described as anything powered by electricity or batteries discarded by its user and is related to a wide range of devices including computers, mobile phones, refrigerators, lamps, stoves, printers, vacuum cleaners, toasters, blenders [1, 2]. Information and communications technologies (ICT) and electronics have evolved to reach each member of the society; consequently, e-waste generation has increased rapidly

© Springer Nature Switzerland AG 2020
G. Rodriguez Morales et al. (Eds.): TICEC 2020, CCIS 1307, pp. 587–598, 2020.
https://doi.org/10.1007/978-3-030-62833-8_43

to meet the current needs [3]. Constant innovation of EEE reduces replacement times generating more discarded equipment. In many cases it is cheaper and more convenient to buy new equipment rather than repair or improve the old one; therefore, a cycle called "trash and buy" has been established [4]. It was estimated that 53.6 Mt (7.3 kg/inh) of e-waste were generated in 2019 and it is expected to reach 74.7 Mt (9 kg/inh) in 2030. Asia produced 24.9 Mt (46.5%), Europe 12 Mt (22.4%), the Americas 13.1 Mt (24.4%), Africa 2.9 Mt (5.4%) and Oceania 0.7 Mt (1.3%) [2].

E-waste is composed of valuable materials as metals and plastics; however, when it is managed improperly, it poses a threat to environment and human health as toxic materials can reach water bodies and the atmosphere. In a circular economy, e-waste recycling is necessary to supply minerals for electronic manufacturing industry which demands more and more supplies [5]. When properly handled, urban mining of e-waste has a great potential, as in some cases it has proven to be more cost effective than virgin mining [6]. In some developing countries, WEEE recycling is performed by an informal sector which lacks environmental and health protection and, in some cases, open burning takes place. Around areas where this polluting practice takes place, pollutants are present in soil, air, water and humans [7].

Every country has different waste management systems and waste generation rates. By 2016, e-waste generation in America continent represented 11.3 Mt (11.6 kg/inh). The country with the highest value was Brazil with 1 500 kt (7.4 kg/inh) and Ecuador accounted for 90 kt (5.5 kg/inh) [1]. In 2019, e-waste generation in America increased to 13.1 Mt (13.3 kg/inh). Brazil maintained as the country with the biggest production with 2 143 kt (10.2 kg/inh) and Ecuador registered 99 kt (5.7 kg/inh) [2]. It is clear, that e-waste generation has increased and will keep growing in the region and in Ecuador. The data presented is consistent to the fact that Ecuador, like other developing countries, is increasing its consumption of EEE and generating more waste as efforts are made to reduce the technology gap.

Ecuadorian government has created incentives to increase e waste exportations, so entities can promote this practice and generate additional revenues [8]. Despite that, most of the e-waste generated is landfilled or placed in emerging cells or open dumps. The amount of WEEE recycled is limited because few companies perform this kind of recycling due to difficult procedures and limited technology [9]. There is a research for the current situation and perspectives for Ecuador which studied WEEE management system in the county according to stakeholder's role and political, socio-cultural and technical view [10]; however, e-waste management has not been studied thoroughly in Ecuador yet. There are not studies available for e-waste management from a municipal approach. Municipalities are in charge of waste management; consequently, it is essential to include them in the research. This study analyzed the WEEE management system of the three municipalities of Santa Elena Province, evaluating the current model and suggesting improvements towards a circular economy and sustainability.

2   Ecuadorian E-Waste Legal Framework

In this section, an analysis of the legal framework applicable to waste of electrical and electronic equipment management is presented. Figure 1 represents regulation related to e-waste at a national level. In 1993, Ecuador adopted Basel Convention which regulates transboundary hazardous waste movements and restricts it commerce to accomplish an adequate environmental management. Ecuadorian Constitution of 2008 assigns rights to nature which is called "Pacha Mama" and prohibits the entrance of hazardous waste into the country [11]. Since 1999, the Environmental Management Law regulates hazardous waste generation for production and services sectors [12]. The Ministry of Environment published agreements as part of regulation. Agreements 161 and 142, published in 2012, introduces the principles of cradle to grave, polluter pays and extended producer responsibility for hazardous substances, hazardous and special waste to control pollution of these substances and categorizes e-waste as a special waste [13, 14]. Used electric and electronic equipment national policy was published as ministry agreement 190 in 2013 providing guidelines for and adequate e-waste management including the extended producer responsibility principle for importers and national producers [15]. In Ministry agreement 191, the extended producer responsibility principle is applied to used mobile phones [16]; however, there is not regulation to apply this principle for other type of e-waste. The Environmental Organic Code, in force since 2017, acknowledges the extended producer responsibility in the entire life cycle for no hazardous waste, hazardous and special waste [17].

Fig. 1. Legal framework for e-waste management in Ecuador.

Despite that the mentioned legal framework has been created, there is regulation missing to accomplish an adequate e-waste management. From all the types of e-waste, only mobile phones have targets and regulation in order to accomplish the extended producer responsibility principle. The Ministry Agreements mentioned before motivated an incentive which related importation quota increase to used mobile phones collection [18]. However, this policy stopped in 2016 and collection rates were reduced from

14.01% in 2014 to 3.81% in 2016 because importers had no longer this benefit [19]. The government has not established other incentives or penalties for improving e-waste collection in the country. Despite that, some municipalities and private companies have implemented collecting and recycling initiatives.

3 Methods

This study included qualitative and quantitative research methods for the different components as it is shown in Fig. 2. This methodology has been established after a literature review that revealed that e-waste management had been evaluated using diverse approaches and different methodologies by several authors and that in many cases this topic is studied using qualitative research methods [20–22]. The study area is Santa Elena Province which is divided in three municipalities: Santa Elena, Libertad and Salinas. This research assessed e-waste management for these three municipalities and made recommendations for improving the current situation. The qualitative methodology for this study included field visits, observation, interviews and surveys.

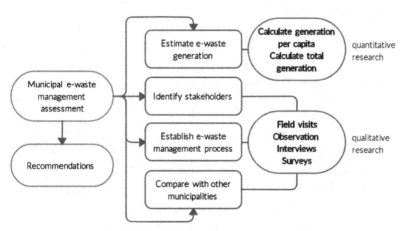

Fig. 2. Methodology used for each component.

E-waste generation was estimated from 2015 to 2018 considering that Ecuadorian databases offered information for this period. Total generation was estimated multiplying generation rate per number of inhabitants.

The average amount of WEEE produced per inhabitant for each municipality was estimated using national e-waste rates, municipal waste rates and population. E-waste generation values for Ecuador were obtained from the Global E-waste Statistics Partnership statics published as the renowned Global E-waste Monitor [1, 2]. Waste generation per inhabitant records for municipalities were retrieved from the environmental economic databases of the National Institute of Statistics and Census (INEC) [23]. The number of inhabitants was obtained from population projections made by INEC [24].

Considering that Santa Elana province's e-waste management system had not been studied before, first, it was necessary to analyze the role of organizations and people related to this sector. The main stake holders were listed during literature reviewed; however, during field visits and interviews other institutions were identified. A list of the stakeholders interviewed in this study is presented in Table 1.

Table 1. List of stakeholders interviewed

Category	Stakeholders
Municipalities, national government	Municipalities of Salinas and La Libertad Waste Management Departments
	EMASA, Municipal Cleaning Enterprise of Santa Elena
	Ministry of Environment
Recyclers	Informal recyclers
	Presidents of recyclers associations in each municipality
	Scrap dealers
	Second hand EEE retailers
	Owners and technicians of EEE repair shops
	E-waste recycling companies of Guayaquil
EEE consumers and WEEE generators	Public in general

Literature review and field work aided to establish the current e-waste management process. Each municipal government was visited and officials in charge of waste management participated in semi-structured interviews. Personnel from the Ministry of Environment were approached to gather information related to national regulation and its implementation in the province. Formal recyclers are gathered in associations; therefore, each president was contacted and replied to semi structured interviews. Scrap dealers, second hand EEE retailers, owners and technicians of EEE repair shops and informal recyclers were approached with unstructured interviews so they can freely communicate details of their activity. Phone interviews were carried out to personnel of recycling companies in Guayaquil city since the e-waste collected in the province is sold there.

To gather information related to WEEE management process and the willingness of people to participate in related campaigns, this study performed 400 face to face and online valid surveys. The survey sample size was calculated using Santa Elena Province population and a confidence level of 95%. Public in general was interviewed with structured questionnaires. In order to recommend improvements to the current e-waste system, a comparison was made with three other cities which showed advances in this field. First, literature review was carried out and then face to face and phones interviews were applied to officers related to waste management in each municipality.

4 Results and Discussion

The following section presents and discusses the most relevant results obtained during the research.

The amount of e-waste generated estimation is shown in Fig. 3 for the three municipalities of Santa Elena province from 2015 to 2018. Table 2 displays generation rate, population and total generation for 2018 so a comparison can be carried out. Municipal generation increases through time which is consistent to worldwide trend. Sana Elena municipality has the highest total generation despite of presenting the least generation per capita as it is highly populated. These figures are expected to grow in the near future because more EEE is consumed as the current technological gap is reduced and development goals are accomplished.

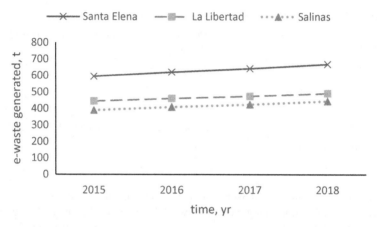

Fig. 3. Estimation of e-waste generation for each municipality

Table 2. Comparison of e-waste generated estimations for different municipalities for 2018

	Population	E-waste generated per inhabitant (kg/in)	Total e-waste generated (t)
Santa Elena	180.494	3,7	670
La Libertad	114.123	4,3	492
Salinas	89.485	5	445

The most important stakeholders involved in WEEE management are included in Table 3. Regulation is essential for waste management as it is the main driver for developing and adequate system. Waste management is regulated by national legal framework and municipal ordinances. National e-waste legal framework could be strengthened to promote improvement in WEEE management and creation of ordinances. The main government entity is the Ministry of the Environment which has an office in the province.

During the research, it was evident that e-waste management is not in the agenda for the province. There are not planned or executed programs for WEEE in the local scenery. Used mobile phones have been collected in cities like Quito and Guayaquil by mobile phone companies as a response to Ministry of Environment regulations; however, this initiative has not taken place in this province. The only program reported is collection of used televisions by a private company.

Table 3. Stakeholders in e-waste management related to Santa Elena province

Stakeholders		Responsibilities/roles
Authorities	National Government and National Assembly	Approving environmental law
	Ministry of Environment	Environmental law, regulation for e-waste management at national level
	Ministry of Foreign Affairs Commerce	Regulation and taxes for importing EEE
	Municipal Decentralized Autonomous Government	Waste management regulation with a local approach. Collection and disposal of e-waste
Governmental organizations, private organizations and non-governmental organizations		Campaigns for improving e-waste management
Production and sales	Manufacturers, distributors, retailers	Manufacture, import, distribute and sell EEE
Consumption and generation	Households	Buy EEE and generate WEEE
	Private sector	
	Public sector	
Refurbishing and repair		Obtain spare parts form WEEE, repair EEE, refurbish EEE
Collection and disposal	Formal recyclers	Collect, disassemble and sell WEEE
	Informal recyclers	
	Scrap dealers	
	Municipal Decentralized Autonomous Government	Collect and dispose WEEE

Only Santa Elena has created a public municipal company to manage waste called EMASA EP, the other two municipalities have a department in charge of this function. Regulation is in place for waste management; however, e-waste collection does not have an important role in it. Figure 4 shows the current process of waste management from generation to final disposal including storage, reusing and recycling. Interviewees mentioned that they store obsolete EEE since there is not a point of collection. Mainly computers and mobile phones undergo the path of reutilization and are available in the secondhand market. Big electric appliances as washing machines, refrigerators and television are sold to scrap dealers or to repair shops at low prices. Technicians get spare parts of these appliances and in some cases remanufacture them.

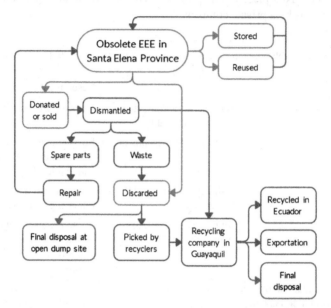

Fig. 4. Current e-waste management process for municipalities of Santa Elena Province

Santa Elena's residues correspond to 30% for organic, 28% paper and cardboard, 8% plastic, 10% glass, 6% scrap metal and 18% others, while the other cities have not reported characterization. Residues are not classified at the source in none of the three municipalities. There are few so called "clean points" for discarding paper and plastic in some parks and shopping centers. In Salinas, two points for depositing used batteries were found, one in the municipality government building and the other in a shopping center. Since there is not a differentiated collection, e-waste arrives to open dumps or is picked by scrap dealers, base recyclers and informal recyclers called "chamberos". Base recyclers are organized in associations in each municipality. Interviews performed to recyclers revealed that the main products collected are paper, cardboard and plastic and the quantity of e-waste that they get is small. After collection, the recovered materials are sold to recycling companies in Guayaquil. Some e-waste is donated or sold to repair workshops where EEE are disassembled in order to get spare parts.

Residues have their final disposal in four controlled open dumps in the province and only one municipality have hospital waste in an exclusive cell. Municipal workers interviewed revealed that municipal governments are aware of the need to build a landfill and that studies and commitments have been made for that. The three municipalities have signed an agreement and established a "mancomunidad" which is kind of an association to build a unique landfill instead of three in separate sites. A study for the mancomunidad landfill was carried out in 2013, however, it has not yet been implemented. In 2019, another agreement was signed in order to start this initiative again. During visits and interviews, no plans for e-waste were found in the municipalities; however, interviewees said they would support initiatives and campaigns.

Literature review showed that some countries have the problem that scavengers burn e-waste to recover precious metals polluting the environment and harming their health. During the research, there was no evidence that suggests that this inadequate practice happens in Ecuador neither in the province of Santa Elena.

Surveys applied to citizens results are tabulated in Table 4. This stage of the research was established to determine the awareness of public of WEEE affectation and the willingness to participate in e-waste related initiatives. A high percentage of interviewees are related to the concept of e-waste and its implications to environment. A significant portion of citizens answered that they would support campaigns to collect e-waste as some interviews demonstrated that it is a common practice to store used EEE because people consider that at some point it would worth something. Refurbished equipment acceptance is around 50% because respondents are not sure of warranties and reliability as in some cases it is sold in the informal market.

Table 4. Results of surveys applied to public in general

	No	Yes
Do you know what e-waste refers to?	22%	78%
Are you aware that e-waste pollutes the environment?	33%	67%
Would you support an e-waste collection campaign?	2%	98%
Would you buy a refurbished electrical or electronic equipment	53%	47%

An adequate waste management is not consolidated in the province since no landfills are in place and differentiate collection has not been yet implemented for households. Consequently, WEEE management improvements are expected to face many challenges. In certain way, part of waste hierarchy is present in the current system as reutilization and recycling takes place. Secondhand market should be more formal and be reinforced. Differentiated collection has been delegated to scrapdealers, formal recyclers and informal recyclers despite that waste management is part of municipal governments competences. When recycling companies in Guayaquil were approached, they mentioned that they do not have offices or representatives in the province; however, they showed interest in buying e-waste if formal collection would take place.

Some municipalities have implemented e-waste collection across the country; however, most municipalities have not created or promoted this kind of programs. A comparison between municipalities which have executed initiatives related to waste of electrical and electronic equipment management and Santa Elena is presented in Table 5. This will aid to establish recommendations at the end of the study.

In most cases, e-waste differentiation is not compulsory, only Cuenca has established fines when e-waste is not classified. Some cities such as Quito and Cuenca have built

Table 5. Comparison of different Ecuadorian e-waste management schemes

	Santa Elena	Cuenca	Loja	Quito
Differentiated collection of e-waste	No	Yes	Yes	Yes
Points for e-waste collection	No	Yes	No	Yes
Collection of e-waste from generation site	No	Yes	Yes	No
Fines for unproper disposal in place	No	yes	No	No
Private companies for e-waste recycling	No	No	No	Yes
Collection of e-waste by recyclers	Yes	Yes	Yes	Yes

collection points for these and other special waste. Loja and Cuenca have made arrangements so trucks can pick periodically e-waste from households. Mainly in Guayaquil and Quito, private companies as Vertmonde, Intercia, Recynter and Reciclametal recycle and dispose e-waste.

When Santa Elena's municipalities are compared with other ones which have landfills and have undergone a stream of differentiated collection of waste, it is revealed that there are many aspects to consider to improve general and e-waste management. Despite that current waste management has many deficiencies, there is the opportunity to change this reality and implement a pioneer and sustainable scheme as some cities have done. It is suggested, in order to comply with national regulation, to build a landfill instead of an open dump for each municipality. It could be considered recycling sorting even electricity generation by landfill gas at that site, as it happens in Cuenca and Quito. The first stage of collecting e-waste should include collection points. The willingness surveys demonstrated that a significant part of the population is interested in handling WEEE for recycling or an adequate disposal. At a second stage, differentiated collection should be implemented for recyclable residues including WEEE. Cuenca has a mature system; therefore, it is feasible to implement fines for unproper disposal. Since, Santa Elena province faces many challenges to improve its current system, this practice it is not recommended in this study. Every initiative also needs to include recyclers in order to succeed and avoid obstacles in its execution.

5 Conclusion

This case study assesses the current e-waste management scheme for the three municipalities of Santa Elena province. It was estimated that the province's WEEE generation reached 1.607 t and that the average rate is 4,3 kg per capita for 2018. The three municipalities have similar urban solid waste management. In general, WEEE management improvements plans or campaigns are not under consideration by municipal authorities since waste management is not a priority. The waste hierarchy principles of reuse and recycling are in place, however, there are not incentives to increase their use. Differentiated collection from households has not been implemented and this activity is carried out by recyclers and scrap dealers. E-waste gather by recyclers is transported to Guayaquil and sold to recycling companies. Unsorted e-waste ends in open dump sites.

The results of this research showed that citizens are aware of the menace of unproper e-waste management and its threats to environment and human health. There is a significant willingness to participate in initiatives and campaigns to collect these residues. Municipal authorities should reinforce reduction, reutilization and recycling activities to increase the quantities that undergo these streams and reduce at minimum the amount open dumped or landfilled. It is imperative, to stop the current inadequate practice of open dumping residues and build landfills in the three municipalities. This study recommends for a first stage e-waste collection points and for a second stage differentiated collection at a household level as it is performed in other cities of the country. It is important to include current recyclers in campaigns and incentives. An adequate WEEE management can only be accomplished when it is part of an integral solid waste management system implemented by municipalities.

Acknowledgements. The authors acknowledge Universidad Estatal Peninsula de Santa Elena for its financial support through the research project "E-waste management in Santa Elena province".

References

1. Baldé, C., Forti V., Gray, V., Kuehr, R., Stegmann, P.: The global e-waste monitor – 2017. United Nations University (UNU), International Telecommunication Union (ITU) & International Solid Waste Association (ISWA), Bonn/Geneva/Rotterdam (2017)
2. Forti, V., Baldé, C., Kuehr, R., Bel, G.: The global e-waste monitor – 2020. United Nations University (UNU), International Telecommunication Union (ITU) & International Solid Waste Association (ISWA), Bonn/Geneva/Rotterdam (2020)
3. Adeola, F.: WEEE generation and the consequences of its improper disposal. In: Vegliò, F., Birloaga, I. (eds.) Electronic and Optical Materials, Waste Electrical and Electronic Equipment Recycling, pp. 13–31. Woodhead Publishing (2018). https://doi.org/10.1016/b978-0-08-102057-9.00002-0
4. Avvannavar, S.M., Mutnuru, R.K., Shrihari, S.: E-waste management. In: Gökçekus, H., Türker, U., LaMoreaux, J. (eds.) Survival and Sustainability. Environmental Earth Sciences, pp. 1433–1438. Springer, Berlin, Heidelberg (2010). https://doi.org/10.1007/978-3-540-95991-5_134
5. Zeng, X., Yang, C., Chiang, J.F., Li, J.: Innovating e-waste management: from macroscopic to microscopic scales. Sci. Total Environ. **575**, 1–5 (2017). https://doi.org/10.1016/j.scitotenv.2016.09.078
6. Zeng, X., Mathews, J.A., Li, J.: Urban mining of e-waste is becoming more cost-effective than virgin mining. Environ. Sci. Technol. **52**(8), 4835–4841 (2018). https://doi.org/10.1021/acs.est.7b04909
7. Vaccari, M., et al.: WEEE treatment in developing countries: Environmental pollution and health consequences—an overview. Int. J. Environ. Res. Public Health **16**(9), 1595–1616 (2019). https://doi.org/10.3390/ijerph16091595
8. Noroña, C., Noroña, J., Paladines, J.: Análisis de la exportación de los desechos electrónicos y su incidencia en el comercio exterior del ecuador. Espirales Revista Multidisciplinaria de Investigación **3**(26), 40–49 (2019)
9. Bermeo, J., Rea, V., López, R., Pico, M.: El reciclaje la industria del futuro en Ecuador. Universidad Ciencia y Tecnología **22**(87), 29–36 (2018)

10. Vanegas, P., et al.: E-waste management in Ecuador, current situation and perspectives. In: Handbook of Electronic Waste Management, Butterworth-Heinemann, pp. 479–515 (2020). https://doi.org/10.1016/b978-0-12-817030-4.00013-9
11. Asamblea Nacional Constituyente. Constitución Política del Ecuador. Quito (2008)
12. Ministerio del Ambiente. Texto Unificado De Legislación Secundaria De Medio Ambiente (TULSMA), Quito (1999)
13. Ministerio del Ambiente: Acuerdo Ministerial 142: Listados Nacionales de Sustancias Químicas Peligrosas. Desechos Peligrosos y Especiales, Quito (2012)
14. Ministerio del Ambiente.nisterio del Ambiente: Acuerdo Ministerial 161: Reglamento para la Prevención y Control de la Contaminación por Sustancias Químicas Peligrosas. Desechos Peligrosos y Especiales, Quito (2012)
15. Ministerio del Ambiente. Acuerdo Ministerial 190: Política Nacional de Postconsumo de Equipos Eléctricos y Electrónicos en Desuso, Quito (2013)
16. Ministerio del Ambiente. Acuerdo Ministerial 191: Instructivo de aplicación del principio de responsabilidad extendida del productor establecido en el Reglamento para la prevención y control de la contaminación por sustancias químicas peligrosas, desechos peligrosos y especiales, Quito (2013)
17. Ministerio del Ambiente. Código Orgánico, Quito (2017)
18. Comité de Comercio Exterior. Resolución 67: Restricción cuantitativa anual para la importación de teléfonos celulares, Quito (2012)
19. Ministerio del Ambiente. Fortalecimiento de Iniciativas Nacionales y Mejora de la Cooperación Regional para el Manejo Ambientalmente Racional de los COPs en Residuos de Aparatos Eléctricos y Electrónicos (RAEE) en los Países de América Latina, Quito (2018)
20. Dias, P., Bernardes, A.M., Huda, N.: Waste electrical and electronic equipment (WEEE) management: an analysis on the Australian e-waste recycling scheme. J. Clean. Prod. **197**, 750–764 (2018). https://doi.org/10.1016/j.jclepro.2018.06.161
21. Ismail, H., Hanafiah, M.M.: A review of sustainable e-waste generation and management: present and future perspectives. J. Environ. Manage. **264**, 110495 (2020). https://doi.org/10.1016/j.jenvman.2020.110495
22. Xavier, L.H., Xavier, V.A.: Modelling e-waste management towards the circular economy concept: a South America case study. In: Bungartz, H.-J., Kranzlmüller, D., Weinberg, V., Weismüller, J., Wohlgemuth, V. (eds.) Advances and New Trends in Environmental Informatics. PI, pp. 81–87. Springer, Cham (2018). https://doi.org/10.1007/978-3-319-99654-7_6
23. Instituto Nacional de Estadística y Censos. Estadística de información ambiental económica en gobiernos autónomos descentralizados municipales: residuos sólidos. INEC, Quito. https://www.ecuadorencifras.gob.ec/gad-municipales/
24. Instituto Nacional de Estadística y Censos. Estadística. Proyección de la población ecuatoriana, Quito INEC. https://www.ecuadorencifras.gob.ec/proyecciones-poblacionales/

Author Index

Printed in the United States
By Bookmasters